ISBN 978-1-5279-2935-7
PIBN 10941149

JOURNAL OF JURISPRUDENCE,

1866.

VOL. X.

EDINBURGH:
T. & T. CLARK, LAW BOOKSELLERS, GEORGE STREET.
GLASGOW: SMITH AND SON. ABERDEEN: WYLLIE AND SON.
LONDON: STEVENS AND SONS.

MDCCCLXVI.

TURNBULL AND SPEARS, PRINTERS, GEORGE STREET, EDINBURGH.

CONTENTS.

THE

JOURNAL OF JURISPRUDENCE.

BANKRUPTCY REFORM.

MR MOFFATT, the chairman in 1864 and 1865 of the Select Committee of the House of Commons on Bankruptcy Law, has shown so much earnestness in his desire to amend the English Bankrupt Law, that whatever falls from him will justly receive from the public much consideration. We therefore feel that no apology is required for reverting to one of the proposals contained in a paper by him, read in October to the meeting of the Social Science Association, and reproduced in the *Law Magazine*. It will be recollected that, in 1864, Mr Moffatt wished the Committee to report to the House that 'while the evidence has proved the English Bankrupt Law to be a costly failure, it has shown that the Scotch system is a practical success.' The Committee did not then report in these terms; but suggested the propriety of a further investigation, the result of which, however, was, that they last year recommended the adoption of a considerable portion of the Scotch system, which Mr Moffatt tells us will include 'the appointment of trustee or curator to be chosen by the creditors, to be paid by them according to agreement; . . . to have power to reject or admit claims of creditors, subject to appeal to the Judge; to be subject to the revision of one or more of the creditors, who should be appointed by the others. . . . Accounts to be rendered in full to the Accountant-General in Bankruptcy, who shall certify to their accuracy before the trustee is entitled to payment for his services.—Trustee to report as to the conduct of bankrupt.—Trustee to be subject to the supervision of a Judge, and liable to dismissal in case of misconduct.' Were this all that is proposed; although we might have pointed out that it is impossible for one accountant in bankruptcy, or for fifty to audit the accounts of all the bankruptcies in England, and that in Scotland it is a committee of creditors, not the accountant, who audits the trustees' accounts; yet we should, on the whole, have congratulated our English friends on the probability that they will soon have a good Bankrupt Law. But much more than this is proposed; and in this further proposal we cannot but feel that we ourselves have a most material interest. Even commercially related as Scotland and England are, it may be quite possible, or in the meantime necessary, however inconvenient, to maintain minor differences between the laws of the two countries. But such sweeping changes in the law as will be effected by the abolition of imprisonment for debt, and by enacting the continuing liability of the bankrupt for his debts, can hardly be introduced on one side of the Tweed without affecting those who live on the other.

The Committee of the House of Commons have already recommended that imprisonment for debt should be abolished; and Mr Moffatt and Lord Westbury unite in a desire to make the future profits of a bankrupt liable for his present debts, and to make his discharge entirely dependent on the goodwill of his creditors.

Mr Moffatt refers to Lord Lyndhurst's Report in 1844 to the House of Lords, and admits that, in that report, the 'question of liability to pay debts out of after acquired property' 'is argued *in extenso;*' and further, says that that report 'suggests that the existence of such liability, though rarely productive to creditors, would tend to paralyze the future exertions of debtors.' He also tells us, that the Commission 'which investigated the subject in 1840, reported strongly against the proposal to retain the liability for unsatisfied debts upon after acquired property.' Still he dwells upon all the arguments which were disregarded, as he admits, in these reports, and tells us, that although 'adduced twenty years since, they have lost none of their force by age.' He further says, 'A law which may afford to creditors the means of prompt possession and equable distribution of assets of insolvent estates, with further right of recovery upon the after acquired property of insolvents, is undoubtedly the desideratum from the creditor's point of view. On the other hand, the debtor should be freed from all personal coercion by the abolition of arrest and of imprisonment for debt, or the interference of previous creditors in his after pursuits, *until such time* as he may have acquired property to discharge the old liabilities.' In support of the position which he takes up, Mr Moffatt quotes from a letter written to himself by Lord Westbury, who says, '*Let this be the law.* On a man becoming bankrupt, grant him, on his surrender, protection from imprisonment for debt (so long as that absurdity continues), but let his future estate remain liable to his debts until he gets a voluntary discharge from his creditors.'

The suggestions of Mr Moffatt and of Lord Westbury are made, as the former says, from a creditor's point of view; but we think that the point cannot have been very elevated, and that if Mr Moffatt will look a little more deeply into the matter, he will see that the suggestions made will operate less for the benefit of the body of creditors generally, than for that of the great capitalist. These suggestions, if carried out, will, in our opinion, do more to injure the commercial prosperity of this country than any of the other jejune experiments in bankruptcy legislation which have lately been made in England. We are at a loss to conceive how it can be expected that any man can start a new concern with success, if he have the debts of the old concern still hanging about his neck. Does Mr Moffatt think that the mercantile world will give credit? Can he suggest any workable plan by which the creditors of the new concern can be kept safe, the *credit* of the bankrupt (for bankrupt he still is) maintained, and yet the creditors of the old concern receive the surplus profit of the new? The scheme is extravagant. A very different picture presents itself to our minds. Abolish the discharge, and you convert the energetic, hopeful man, striving to retrieve his position, into a man without energy or hope, and therefore incapable of effort,—the man who might yet give employment to thousands, into one who is an object of disgust to himself, and who almost inevitably will become a burden on society—one, in fact, who for all the good he will henceforth do, might as well be sold *trans Tiberim* at once. Not one in a hundred will ever afterwards prove himself a useful member of society. Misfortune will be punished as a crime. The man who has once failed will be practically shut out for the future from trade; and consequently, all business will become centred in a few hands, to the profit of the large capitalist alone, and to the great injury of our commerce, and loss of our working classes.

But Mr Moffatt is a purist. He says, 'There can be no question that the whole principle of law should be to maintain the inviolability of contracts; but this is practically reversed in every instance in which a creditor is compelled to give other than a voluntary acquittal to the debtor for the unsatisfied portion of the debt.' Surely it must have occurred to Mr Moffatt in his capacity of a legislator, if not otherwise, that abstract propositions, which might be printed in letters of gold in the laws of Utopia, must be somewhat modified to meet the exigencies of everyday life. Nothing, for instance, ought to be more inviolable than the right of property; and yet we question whether Mr Moffatt himself maintains that it is tyrannical in the public interest to invest railway companies with compulsory powers of purchase.

We cannot go the length of those who say, 'If a man embarked in trade accepts a bill to pay six months hence, there is as clearly as possible a tacit understanding that he only promises to pay, if, when the period arrives, he have the wherewithal to pay. Every merchant takes the bill of another on this footing, and if innocent bankruptcy intervene, there is not, morally speaking, any breach of contract.' Still a practical legislator must have regard to the risks, uncertainties, and necessities of trade, which, indeed, lie at the foundation of the Bankrupt Laws, and in consequence of which the enforcement of mercantile claims is withdrawn from the operation of the ordinary machinery of the law. Lord Westbury says, 'Is it not a mistake to attempt, in a system of rules for the collection and distribution of the assets of a bankrupt, to create a code for enforcing commercial morality? . . . . This attempt to combine the punishment of the dishonest or reckless debtor with the collection and distribution of his remaining property is, in my judgment, a very great mistake. . . . . I would abolish it altogether. If a man has committed a fraud, let him be punished by the . . . . criminal law, ... but do not attempt to administer criminal law or a *quasi* criminal law in bankruptcy.' But does not Lord Westbury see that the withdrawal of the discharge from a bankrupt is one of the most penal measures which can be passed; and does he not propose to administer this very measure in bankruptcy, inasmuch as the adjudication of bankruptcy will declare to the bankrupt that he shall not be discharged until he has paid the uttermost farthing?

We agree with Lord Westbury in this, that bankruptcy law should be entirely of a civil character; but we cannot agree with him in thinking that the Court of Bankruptcy 'has but one function—the collection and distribution of the debtor's assets.' We admit that, indeed, to be its first function, and one quite separable from all the rest. But we hold to it, that in this country, where we have not, and cannot have, tribunals of commerce, the Bankruptcy Court is the only court in which any check can be given to such commercial immorality, as is greatly to be blamed, but yet does not amount to fraud.

In a former number,[1] we stated that the object of all bankruptcy law was twofold, and ought to embrace: 1. The cheap and quick realization and distribution of the assets of the bankrupt; and 2. The general advantage of society, and the protection of the trading community; objects which include the restoration of the innocent bankrupt to society, and the suspension or absolute refusal of discharge to the bankrupt who, by a criminal court, has been found guilty of fraud, or who, by reason of his reckless folly and imprudence, is, in the eyes of the bankruptcy Judge, dangerous to the trading community. We still hold that the latter, no less than the former, must form an important part of any sound legislation. The Bankruptcy Court is, as we have said, the only court in which cognizance can be taken of an offence not amounting to fraud, and it is the only appropriate court. No other can deal with such cases without involving either the country or the creditors, who have already lost their money, in the most difficult and expensive investigations. The Bankruptcy Court, on the other hand, has necessarily, in the course of investigating into the affairs of the bankrupt, been placed in possession of all the information attainable on the subject, and it can dispose of these questions without involving any one in expense.

Lord Westbury and Mr Moffatt would constitute the creditors in each bankruptcy a tribunal to determine as to the discharge of the bankrupt. But it cannot be doubted that in the hands of creditors there would be a miscarriage of justice. In some cases, prejudiced by their feelings of loss, the creditors would be too severe; and in other cases, worked on by the bribe of a contribution from the bankrupt's friends, they would grant discharge to one who ought never again to have been let loose on society as a person entitled to credit. We would take all power as to the discharge away from the creditors and confer it on the Bankruptcy Court alone, who, after hearing the trustee and the creditors, would, without doubt, apply the general principles of justice to each case.

In regard to the question of imprisonment for debt, various conflicting opinions were expressed before the committee; and we do

[1] See No. for *January* 1865.

not well understand how Mr Moffatt, as an upholder of the inviolability of contract, comes to be an advocate for the abolition of that penalty. For ourselves, we do not see how the system which prevails of granting credit for small purchases could be maintained for a day, unless the shopkeeper were protected by this safeguard. Failure to pay, we admit, affords a *prima facie* case of breach of contract, and we would accordingly put the failed person in prison at the instance of any creditor; but if the creditor were unable to show a probable case of fraud, the debtor should obtain immediate liberation under the bankruptcy laws.

In fine, if it were permitted to us to express ourselves sententiously, we would say, *Let this be the law.* Let imprisonment for debt continue, but let the Judge in bankruptcy have power to grant liberation, unless there be suspicion of fraud, when he ought to be bound to hand the case over to a public prosecutor.

If a man has been guilty of fraud, let the criminal court punish him criminally, and let the Bankruptcy Court say that the man found guilty of fraud is incapable of trust, and of obtaining discharge.

Let all minor offences, such as gambling, reckless extravagance, wild speculation, improvidence, and undue delay in declaring insolvency, be dealt with in the Bankruptcy Court and punished, not by imprisonment, but by the delay or absolute refusal of discharge.

Let creditors be heard; but let the discharge or non-discharge rest with the Court alone.

We are aware that the Committee of the House of Commons has suggested that the dividend should, to a certain extent, regulate the discharge of the bankrupt; and we observe that a writer in the *Economist* recently suggested the following scale:—The debtor who pays 15s. per £ to be entitled to his discharge at once.

10s. per £, ...	after 3 years.
6s. 8d. per £, ...	" 6 "
under 6s. 8d. per £, ...	" 10 "

Any such scale is of course purely arbitrary. It is no doubt worthy of consideration, whether the effect of some such rule would not be to check reckless speculation, and lead to declarations of insolvency before the ruin of creditors is involved in that of their debtor, as so often occurs under the present law; and so far the scheme seems to be greatly preferable to that of Mr Moffatt and Lord Westbury. But where the Court has the means of disposing of each case on its own merits, which it has in Scotland, and which it ought to have in England, we question the prudence of adopting any mere arbitrary criterion.

THE YELVERTON DAMAGES CASE.

We will not be suspected of writing with any bias in favour of the side which prevailed in the recent trial. Throughout the progress of the Yelverton controversy we have pleaded the cause of the unfortunate lady, who has again sustained defeat on an issue collateral to that, the prosecution of which she seems to have made the settled purpose of her life. When the question was a personal one between her and the man whom she claimed as her husband, we did not hesitate, in presence of the prevailing diversity of opinion, to express our conviction that both the law and the justice of the case were upon her side; that in all her relations with Major Yelverton marriage and marriage only was in her mind,—and in his mind also, and that his assumption of a different position was an after thought which occurred to him after the performance of acts which had brought him within the pale of legal obligation. These views the opinions of the majority of the Judges in the House of Lords have refused to entertain; and we cannot but regret that through an unwise pertinacity in prosecuting such collateral issues as that with the *Saturday Review*, Miss Longworth has been doing her best to convert her best friends into little more than lukewarm supporters.

But the case with the *Saturday Review* presents another, and, in all its public aspects, a much more important issue than any which this remarkable history has yet suggested; and in making it the subject of a few remarks at the present time, we will endeavour, as far as possible, to consider its bearings as a legal question, and to separate it from the disturbing elements with which it has been so largely intermingled.

From all that is known or reported of the manner in which the verdict was reached, it is not probable that the case will go far to convert sceptics in the efficacy of jury trial. The result is likely to be the other way. For, as a popular question, that is, with the public generally, and even among those in the profession who have not taken the pains to refer the grounds of action to the rules of law by which they are controlled, there is no doubt a general impression that there was a miscarriage of justice on the occasion. The opinion of the English press has been almost universally expressed to the effect that the verdict of the jury was wrong; and if that view prevails in England, where, upon the marriage question, the judgment was more decidedly unfavourable to Miss Longworth than it was in this country, it is not to be wondered at that the same view should be adopted in Scotland. The objection that has been most generally urged is, that the verdict was contrary to evidence; and we understand that a new trial has been moved for on precisely the same ground.

That, apart from the question, whether the article complained of is a libel, and as such infers legal liability, much of the popular feeling is referable to the terms in which the article is couched, we think is very probable. And there is much in it with which we cannot and do not sympathize. The reference to the Lord Chancellor, for instance, is in the highest degree unbecoming, and unworthy of the position which the *Saturday Review* enjoys as an exponent of high and educated thought. As to the remaining passages which bear upon Miss Longworth, we do not hesitate, as matter of taste, to express the same opinion; just as we think from the point of view from which we have looked at the Yelverton case, that they are utterly mistaken and misjudged. But we hesitate to affirm that, according to the law of libel as it obtains in this country, and in general principle, they are identical—they ground a legal claim for slander. In commenting on the case of Miss Longworth, the reviewer had before him an almost incalculable mass of materials: the history of her life and character, so far as it was shadowed forth in her correspondence,—the history of her connection with Major Yelverton, so far as it fell under the observation of witnesses, —his story of that connection, as he publicly unfolded it at the Irish trial,—the whole proceedings at the trial,—the damaging interlocutor of Lord Ardmillan,—the favourable judgment of the Inner House,—the variety of opinion as that was manifested in the public press,—the final proceedings in the Court of Appeal,—their result, and the renewed expression of public feeling. By means and out of these materials, the Saturday Reviewer undertook to say what in his opinion the character of Miss Longworth was; and it is not disputed that these materials having become public property, he was entitled to put them to any legitimate use he could. Whether he did put them to a legitimate use, is the question which we have afterwards to consider. At present we refer to them only for the purpose of showing upon what widely dissimilar grounds the reviewer brought two parties into the same condemnation; for we venture to think that in the article the Lord Chancellor fares as badly as Miss Longworth. But in pronouncing judgment on the opinion which the Lord Chancellor delivered in Miss Longworth's case, the only consideration with which it was relevant for him to deal, was the sufficiency or insufficiency of the reasoning by which his conclusion was deduced. He was entitled to say that it was a weak judgment, careless of the facts, defective in argument, defective in law. But none of these things is said. The reviewer goes entirely out of the province in which he is entitled to pass judgment on the Chancellor, when he makes insinuations against his private character, under pretence of impeaching his judicial opinion. A distinction which the law recognises in this kind of libel is, as we will afterwards see, fitly illustrated by a comparison of these two cases.

We have said enough in the preceding paragraph for the purposes of this discussion, in reference to the victory upon which the reviewer was commenting; and anything we have omitted is sufficiently in the knowledge of our readers. The general principles of the law of libel, notwithstanding all that has been said and is supposed to the contrary, are clear and explicit enough, at any rate in the law of Scotland. The difficulty that is felt in any case is not one of principle, but of application of principle to varying facts and circumstances, and arises from the fact that the question of feeling which is generally in issue, is not one that can be disposed of by any fixed and determinate rules. It is easy enough to understand the law of libel as a legal proposition, when it says that no man shall be held up to private ridicule, contempt, and scorn; but how difficult is it to say when that result has been established: how much more difficult to pronounce to what extent it has been established in one case more than in another. And while the general principle of law is clear, there is one thing having reference to the well-known doctrine of privilege which is clear also,—that a public newspaper is in the eye of the law amenable to the same laws as a private individual. A private individual is not entitled to cast imputations on the moral character of another. Neither is a newspaper; and accordingly, in the case of *Davis* v. *Miller*, when, under pretence of reviewing a work of missionary travels, the pursuer was held up to public reprobation as being hostile to the doctrines of Christianity, and as rejoicing, from personal inclination, in certain immoral scenes which he described as having personally witnessed, it was held, and most justly, that a libel had been uttered for which reparation was due. The *ratio* of that case, and of every case of the same kind, is quite obvious, that an individual is not to be held, by coming forward—with whatever object—before the public as an author, thereby to surrender his right to have his private character safe from the attacks of calumny and slander. In the case of Miller, no plea was stated in defence to the *veritas* of the libel, and for the most substantial reason, that it could not possibly be substantiated. It could, at least, only have been proved by pointing out passages in the work in which the author said—or said in effect—'I disbelieve the doctrines of Christianity;' 'I attended the heathen rites I mention out of personal sympathy with them;' and such passages the pursuer who complained of the libel was of course satisfied could not be found. Merely to say that a person must be of immoral character because he attends scenes of an immoral nature, would, we hope, never be accounted such proof of immorality *de facto* as to justify a public journalist in advancing the charge with impunity. And accordingly, the case of *Miller* v. *Davis* went to the jury upon the only issue that it could go, namely, whether the libel complained of was fair criticism in the interests of the public, and the defender was justified in making it; and the jury, believing that it was not, but an attack on private character, awarded damages.

Newspaper slander therefore has no privilege. It is just the slander of a private individual. But the important question is, What is newspaper slander? It was clear what it consisted of in the case of Miller, because the jury held the article complained of to be an attack on private character—and private character is not before the reviewer of a work. The question cannot easily be answered in a direct way, or in such a way as to indicate a general rule. But some light may be thrown on the subject by considering certain things which a newspaper is entitled to do. It may review the conduct of public men without imputing motives, with a greater latitude, as the subject under discussion falls within the pale of historical and political opinion. It would not be libel, for example, as we understand the law, if a newspaper should say of Mr Bright that he entertains revolutionary ideas, and is therefore a dangerous man; but it would be libel to say that his political conduct is guided by a private hatred of the present occupant of the throne. Again, a newspaper is entitled to report proceedings of a public nature, and to comment on them; but the report must be fair, and the comment must be upon what is properly before it by reason of the liberty of the press. It is not libel, for example, for a newspaper to report a public trial in which the subject under investigation affects private character; but it would be libel to separate the part bearing injuriously on private character, and to publish it by itself, and to publish in that way, what but for its privilege would be libellous, such as a speech of counsel. It would not be libel for a newspaper to comment on the facts ascertained at a public trial,—a trial, for example, for murder,—to the extent of saying that the verdict of the jury acquitting the prisoner was bad, and he ought to have been convicted; but it would be libel if, going beyond these facts, and proceeding on what was not evidence, it should, in the face of acquittal by the jury, affirm the prisoner guilty. It is difficult to state these propositions in precise language. The latter is the one to which it appears to us that the case of the *Saturday Review* will be best assimilated; and we take an illustration of it. Suppose that at the recent trial of Dr Pritchard in the High Court of Justiciary, the Crown had only insisted in the charge of murder of the wife, and that in consequence no evidence had been led as to the murder of the mother, and that the jury had acquitted the prisoner. A public journalist commenting on these facts would have been entitled to impeach the verdict as contrary to evidence, and to say that it *proved* the prisoner to be the murderer of his wife; but he would not be justified in holding up the jury to reprobation, and stating that they had acquitted a man that was known in every household in Glasgow to be the murderer of his mother-in-law. And this brings us to the question—and it is really a very simple one—between the *Saturday Review* and Miss Longworth. Had the reviewer, in his damaging remarks, the evidence in the case before him, and that only? Did the evidence admit of the construction he put upon it? We must confess to have some difficulty in answering these questions in the negative. Our own opinion of the judgment of the case has been made, we hope, sufficiently clear. We think that the view taken by the *Saturday Review* is not the sound one. But the question that must be answered is, whether it is excluded by the evidence,—in other words, is not a view that could be taken by a fair and reasonable mind writing for public instruction and in the interest of the public morals, and not being so, must be taken to be a libel on private character, and not a critique upon the evidence. Here, again, we are compelled to negative the question, because to do otherwise, would be to set up the opinion of an individual as the test of a fair and reasonable mind. The judgment pronounced by the *Saturday Review* is not, in the direction which it takes, an isolated one. Omitting certain expressions which involve these matters of taste, it is conceded that, in effect, as much and more had previously been said against Miss Longworth. No doubt it is trite law that repetition of a slander is no justification, but, on the contrary, an aggravation of the offence complained of. And it is upon this principle that a newspaper writer would not be exempt from liability in repeating a slander, which, but for the privilege in him who first uttered it, would be libellous. But we have not yet heard that a journalist has been held liable for adopting the same view that was contained in the judicial exposition of a case; and we assume it is not in dispute that the *Saturday Review* was not more damaging to Miss Longworth than Lord Ardmillan. We admit that that is not conclusive of the question, whether the article complained of is justifiable criticism, or an attack on private character. It is not conclusive, because, for example, it might be shown that Lord Ardmillan had travelled beyond the record, and the evidence falling properly within it. But who, in regard to a case which has provoked such a diversity of opinion, would seriously think of going beyond the fact that similar views had been expressed before, in determining the question whether these views were lawful criticism or a libel? In a case like Miss Longworth's, which has been made the foundation of indiscriminate public treatment, public opinion is the only standard to which any question as to whether a criticism does or does not constitute a libel can be referred; and in presence of a divided public opinion, it is impossible to answer the question either way. Miss Longworth may feel it is very hard for her that that should be so, but her case has become, by her own surrender, a discussion upon evidence; and no person has better reason to know what diversity of opinion that evidence has given rise to. To attempt, in such circumstances, to pronounce the view of any particular period to be the only fair and reasonable one, to the exclusion of all others, so as to say that one exceeds fair criticism, while another does not, is a practical absurdity. The whole story has become public property, and one section of the public, by no means unimportant, has already pronounced upon it as unfavourable a judgment as any that a jury will be called upon to reprove. We do not doubt that Miss Longworth was deeply injured in her feelings by the article in the *Saturday Review.* But the law is changed since Lord Ellenborough in the case of Cobbett announced that consideration as the test of libel. The liberty of the press has effectually silenced every such restriction.

At the trial, and in the discussion that followed after it, a good deal was said about the plea of *veritas.* No exception was taken on the point to the charge of the presiding Judge, and it will therefore raise no question on the motion for a new trial. And it is difficult to see that the pursuer's skilful management of her case could have been bettered by any such objection. Since the case of *Mackellar* v. *The Duke of Sutherland*, it is very clear that the *veritas* of a libel constitutes absolute exemption from legal consequences; but it is also very clear what the plea means. To set it up, a defender must establish a logical contradictory. It will not avail him if he merely produce facts that are contrary to the pursuer's case. For example, if one man charges another with being a thief, he must condescend and prove specific acts of theft,—nothing short of that will save him. It goes no length at all in a question of liability for a published slander to prove, as against the presumption of innocence, that the object of it was transacting in a suspicious manner, or has had the repute of the character, or even has committed acts to which morally, and according to every consideration but that of proof, the obnoxious stigma attaches. The proposition involved in a pursuer's case, who brings an action for libel upon such a ground, is that he has been unjustly slandered, because he never stole; and the defender cannot prove the slander to be true, and thereby excuse himself, unless he establishes an absolute contradictory of that proposition by proving the time, place, and manner in which a specific act of theft was committed. And if that be the meaning of the plea of *veritas*, it can be matter for no surprise that it formed no part of the defence of the *Saturday Review* to Miss Longworth's action against it. For what a surrender of the strength of the defender's case would it have been to introduce it! If we are right in the principles of law we have enunciated, it was sufficient justification of the *Saturday Review* to establish that its view was not excluded by the evidence in the case. For that purpose no special defence was required: the foundation of it was necessarily contained in the pursuer's own case. But a plea of *veritas* would have required the defender to hold out not only that his view was not excluded, but that it was the true one. He might do so either through the evidence in the cause, or apart from it; but whatever was his mode of proof, that burden was by reason of his defence, not imposed upon him.

New Books.

Digest of the Law of Scotland for Justices of the Peace. By HUGH BARCLAY, LL.D. Third Edition. Edinburgh: T. and T. Clark. 1865.

IT is not often we find a book take its place as a standard work of reference so rapidly as Sheriff Barclay's *Digest of the Law of Scotland for Justices of the Peace.* The fact is, although professing a limited object, the learned Sheriff has constructed a book of far wider utility than he had in view. There is hardly a subject which can be named upon which information is not to be obtained, with references to the more recent authorities. The second edition appeared in 1855; so it was high time that a new one should appear, embracing the numerous Acts of Parliament which have since then been added to our statute book. It is sufficient to name the Bankruptcy (Scotland) Act 1856, the Nuisance Removal Act, the Mercantile Law Amendment Act, and the Joint-stock Companies Act. Then there are the Prisons (Scotland) Act, the Mines Inspection and Regulation Acts. Then there is the Act amending the Public Houses Acts, the Merchandise Mark Act, the Poor Removal Act, and the Police and Improvement Acts; while still later there come the Alkali Works Act, the Factory Act Extension, the Summary Procedure Act, and the Trespass Act. These are all noted, and of many of them all the principal provisions are enumerated. Any day a justice may be called upon to act under the provisions of any of these statutes; and whether we regard those who have to administer them, or those who have to advise or conduct proceedings under them, we know of no work which can be compared with this in usefulness as a handbook and a guide.

A Manual of Civil Law; containing a Translation of and Commentary on the Fragments of the Twelve Tables, and the Institutes of Justinian; the Text of the Institutes of Gaius and Justinian arranged in parallel Columns; and the Text of the Fragments of Ulpian, and of Selections from Paul's *Receptæ Sententiæ.* By PATRICK CUMIN, M.A., Balliol College, Oxford, Barrister-at-law. Second Edition, Enlarged. London: Stevens and Sons. 1865.

THIS handsome volume is creditable to the printer, publisher, and papermaker. How far it does honour to the gentleman who claims the title of its author, our readers may be better able to judge when we have laid before them a sketch of the history of the book, and a statement of what it contains. The first edition appeared in 1854, and, making an appeal to the memory rather than to the intellect, was not unfrequently purchased by that class of students who attend lectures on the Roman law as a task which they must go through. It was, in short, a 'crib,' not of the best kind. This earlier Manual was less pretentious in its appearance and price; in fact, it was rather a shabby little post octavo, and cost 10s. 6d. It consisted of an introduction, giving a very meagre history of the Roman law till Justinian, and of a catechism upon the *Institutes*, professing to be, between questions and answers, a complete translation of that work. It was said in the preface, that, to supply the defect of elementary works on Civil Law in the English language, the author had had recourse to the *Manual of Civil Law* by Lagrange, which had already gone through six editions in France. 'Perhaps,' it is said, 'the author might have contented himself with a mere translation; but as he proceeded with his task, he seemed to find occasional defects and obscurities which he hoped to remedy. Using, therefore, the manual in question as a foundation, and retaining the form of question and answer, he has diligently consulted the original Institutes of Justinian and Gaius, the Digest and Code, and particularly the Commentaries of Ortolan and Ducaurroy. . . . . .' 'Out of these materials,' he continues, 'he has constructed the following work, which is intended as a Translation of and Commentary on the Institutes of Justinian.'

The preface of the second edition now before us, states that the first has been for some time out of print, and that in this edition 'the English portion has been cast into a new form, and somewhat enlarged. The object has been to furnish a complete Manual of Civil Law for the use of students, containing both the original texts of the elementary works on Roman law which survive, and an explanation in English.' The reference to Lagrange and the other recondite authorities named in the preface of 1854, is quietly dropped; and the reader is left to account for the extraordinary similarity in arrangement and in the turn and order of every sentence, on the theory of some wonderfully pre-established harmony between the minds of the French 'docteur en droit' and the English barrister from Balliol. For, so far as we have read, text and notes are substantially a translation of Lagrange, with variations too unimportant to entitle the translator to dub himself author. It omits a number of references, and it adds a passage from Grote's *History of Greece*, on the distinction between *nexum* and *addictio*, the reference to which was in Mr Sandars' edition of the *Institutes* published in 1853. In form, the new edition differs from the earlier one, as well as from Lagrange, mainly in omitting the questions, and supplying the necessary words in the answers, so as to make the Manual a treatise or commentary instead of a catechism. Were it worth while, we might notice instances of the manner in which the 'conveyance' has been performed, such as the translation of 'colégataires' and 'commodataire,' not once, but repeatedly, by the barbarous words *collegetarii* and *commoditarius*. On the whole, however, it is only fair to say, that the meaning of the French original has in most cases been caught with sufficient accuracy. Where Mr Cumin wanders from his original, he is not generally happy. Lagrange, for instance, does throw some little light upon the Roman trichotomy of *jus naturæ*, *jus gentium*, and *jus civile*, at the commencement of the *Institutes*; but Mr Cumin so abridges his explanations as to darken the whole matter, and, translating *jus gentium* by 'Law of Nations,' altogether omits to show, as a conscientious instructor would do, how it differs from the system which now bears that name. M. Lagrange has at least told us categorically that they are not the same.

An equally striking case of appropriation is presented by the second part of this new edition, which contains the 'original texts' above mentioned. These texts were not, as the preface leaves us to imagine, part of the former edition. In fact, they are the only 'enlargement' which we can discover,[1] and they are in reality an exact reprint of the useful work known as 'Gneist's *Syntagma*.' The only difference consists in the omission of the title-page, the preface, some of the annotations on the Twelve Tables, and a portion of Dr Gneist's notes. By what principle of selection, if any, Mr Cumin has been guided in making these omissions, we are not informed, and have been unable to detect. The whole of Gneist's notes to the first 107 pages of his text are omitted. Then suddenly the notes are resumed, and from p. 464 to 779 of Mr Cumin's edition text and notes are given, so far as we have observed, entire, except that the printer has omitted to reproduce on the first page of each sheet the 'signature' '*Gneist Institutiones*.'—It is true that, in a way, Mr Cumin acknowledges his obligations to the German editor; but he does not do so on the title-page, as decency required. Mr Cumin writes: 'The Latin text is the same as Rudolph Gneist's, from whose preface I extract the following explanations:—In my edition of Gaius, I have retained Gœschen's divisions;' and so on for two pages and a half out of the three which he calls his preface, without marks of quotation, or any difference of type. The first person is used throughout, and a cursory reader of the preface may, and probably will, fail to notice the allusion to Dr Gneist. One glancing over the preface, as prefaces are usually read, will naturally imagine that the glib mention of Bœcking, Mommsen, and the Breviary of Alaric, are all proofs of Mr Cumin's own erudition, and of his right to use such phrases as 'I edit;' 'my edition;' 'I have supplied *lacunas;*' 'I have explained the comments of the text by comments of my own,' etc., etc. We do not recollect to have seen anything so like a mere reprint which professed to have any other character; and except that Gneist's print of the Twelve Tables, *minus* some of his notes, and *plus* a translation by an Oxford friend, is prefixed to Mr Cumin's adaptation of Lagrange instead of to the *Syntagma*, it is difficult to see why the student should not use the originals. We do not think it necessary further to characterize the performance of Mr Cumin. It need only be added, that

[1] It would be unfair to Mr Cumin not to acknowledge an addition of ten lines in English on the title-page of Ulpian, and of four lines on the first page of *Pauli Sententiæ*.

his book is published at the price of 25s., and that the *Manuel* and *Syntagma* may be got for 4s. 6d. each.

Even if Mr Cumin had attained the object indicated in his preface in a legitimate manner, it is doubtful whether the plan adopted is the best. In the first place, it is a great mistake to bind together Gneist's *Syntagma* and the *Manual of Civil Law*. Those who want the 'crib' are either unable or unwilling to read the texts; while those who wish to read or consult the texts will prefer the cheaper and more complete Leipsic edition. But beyond this, the multiplication of mere abridgments of the Roman law, and paraphrases of the *Institutes*, is not, to our thinking, a healthy symptom as regards the study of the ancient jurisprudence. Nothing can equal the sterility of a handbook such as this to one who really wishes to study Justinian; it disgusts the genuine and intelligent student, though it may serve the purpose of one who merely seeks to pass an examination. Its real mission, whatever its editor may profess, is to supersede the original texts, not to elucidate them. Mr Cumin, who has availed himself so freely of the labours of Gneist, including his scholarly and businesslike preface, has naturally avoided all allusion to the passage in that preface in which he lauds the abundance of illustration in Bœcking's edition of Gaius: 'ut ex hoc veluti centro in fontes et adminicula studiorum excurrere tirones possent.' Yet he (Gneist) laments in language, alas! too applicable to ourselves, that students do not avail themselves of the aids offered them: 'Neque tamen excurrunt;' and 'one doubts whether a new age of Roman jurisprudence has really arisen, when you see what are the studies of those who are entering or have entered on forensic practice. I am almost tempted to say, that the more abundant and more convenient the aids to study, the more slight and imperfect do their studies become.' He ascribes this failure in a great measure to the neglect of exegesis in the schools, and mourns that while 'we begin to neglect and abandon Tribonian, we do not see Gaius take his place. Our forefathers so diligently studied the *Digesta* and the *Code* that they remembered the Fragments by their initial words. Then followed a period when we used to learn and commit to memory, as the foundation of our learning at least, the Institutes of Justinian. But now the old foundations are removed, and the new system has but an uncertain and tottering basis. Our youth are not brought up on those simple elements of Gaius and Ulpian which would imbue their minds with the principles of Roman law, attract them, nourish them, win their minds to a love of the science. But now we quote the jurists, weaving passages into our prelections and our books as mere ornaments and superfluities. Then you would scarcely believe how slender is the utility of handbooks (Denique Chrestomathiarum quam exigua utilitas sit, vix credideris). Thus young men descend into the forum with but a slight and weakly hold upon science, and the many and various propositions which they had learned easily vanish from their minds.'

The mistake of those who write and read such books as this, and of the teachers who recommend their use, consists in a misapprehension of the true value of the Roman law. That lies mainly in the method of the great jurists of the second and third centuries, not in the arrangement of their fragments made in an age of intellectual decrepitude and moral corruption, not even in the material contents of the *corpus juris*. No jurists ever had so firm a grasp of leading principles as Papinian, Paulus, Gaius, Ulpian, and their fellows. 'The principles and maxims of their science,' says their greatest modern expositor, 'appear to them not as creatures of their own arbitrary will, but as real existences whose nature and genealogy have become known to them by long and intimate intercourse. Thus their whole method has a certainty found nowhere else but in mathematics; and it may be said, without exaggeration, that they calculate with their ideas. . . . For them law has no separate existence; its essence is rather human life itself viewed in a particular aspect. If jurisprudence is detached from this its object, legal science or theory may proceed on its solitary way unaccompanied by the normal apprehension of the legal relations (concrete cases); the science may then attain a high degree of formal development and yet want all reality, all practical application. Just in this respect is the method of the Roman jurists most excellent. If they have to decide a case, they start with the most lively apprehension of the facts and their connection; and we see the whole relation arise before our eyes, step by step, and assume a new form. It seems as if the particular case were the starting-point of the whole system of jurisprudence, which is developed out of it. Thus their theory and practice do not stand apart: their theory is formed and adapted for the readiest and most immediate application, and their practice is always ennobled by scientific treatment. In every principle they see at the same time a case in which it is applicable: in every case they see the principle by which it is determined; and in the ease with which they pass from the general to the particular, and from the particular to the general, their perfect mastery is evidenced. And in this method of discovering and demonstrating the law is their peculiar and distinctive merit, unlike the German Schöffen in this respect, that their art reaches scientific perfection in regard of its cognitions and its language, yet without suffering in the perspicuity and vivacity which are usually peculiar to more primitive ages.' (*Savigny, Das Beruf unseres Zeitalters für Gesetzg. und Rechtswiss.*, pp. 30, 31.)

THE MONTH.

Inner House Practice.—Reform in the Court of Session has so long been a subject fruitful of controversy, and barren in result, that the recent Act of Sederunt might have been expected—and we are glad to say that the expectation has not been disappointed—to be hailed with satisfaction and with thankfulness. But the tide of reform which has once set in, is not to be lightly kept back. And accordingly it is matter for no surprise, that grievances that have long been endured in patience, are now loud in complaint, and clamorous for redress. One of these—and not the least considerable—is the present practice according to which the same case is liable to be called day after day within half an hour of the adjournment of the Court. No doubt the evil is to a certain extent unavoidable. But surely some remedy may be devised to obviate the necessity, or at least to mitigate the rigour of a practice which has a most material influence in determining the unpopularity of the Court of Session both with the country and the profession. These remarks are immediately suggested to us by a case which recently depended in the First Division (*The Magistrates of Aberdeen* v. *Irvine*), about which we mention the following facts: It was first put out for hearing on the 9th of November during the extended sittings. It was three times called after 3 o'clock; for three days after it had been partly heard it was not called at all; and it was not taken to *avizandum* till the 7th of December, after it had been partly heard on each of eight different days. This case does not equal the celebrated case of *Gordon* v. *Grant*, in the time of Lord Justice-Clerk Hope, where the interlocutor runs, 'having heard parties' procurators at great length on nineteen different days.' Still it is difficult not to see that several days' discussion might have been saved. The objection which most readily occurs is, of course, the expense which is thereby entailed on litigants, so long as the rule of the profession is maintained that counsel in the Inner House are entitled to refreshers for every day that a case is called; and no consideration could be held more relevant to determine the Court to instant action in the matter. But the practice involves, at the same time, a very obvious obstacle in the way of succinct and effective pleading. Recapitulation which cannot be avoided lengthens the debate, and the argument is presented piece-meal and in fragments. Another evil—and it is one which the dignity of the Court may reasonably be expected to hold in view—is, that agents who come from the country to attend the debates, must either do so at an enormous outlay of time and money, or cease to attend them altogether. A remedy which suggests itself at once—and it would be difficult to devise a simpler one—is, that certain days should be set aside for the hearing of causes in the Summar Roll, and others for those in the Short Roll. Some difficulty is, of course, to be looked for in arranging the details of this scheme. Cases on the Summar Roll do not preserve the same regularity of condition that cases do in the Short Roll. And it might occasionally result from the plan we suggest that the Summar Roll of the day would be exhausted before the hour for the adjournment of the Court; but taking advantage of the half-day on Saturday, we are satisfied that the plan could be put into operation with tolerable security both to the time and the convenience of the judges. Another remedy is, that no case in the Summar Roll should be called in preference to a case in the Short Roll which has been partly heard. To this it may be objected that there is a certain amount of summary procedure in the Court requiring instant despatch; but as Saturday is set apart for the Summar Roll, nothing could be delayed beyond a week; and the class of cases does not occur that would be injured by such delay. And even if these proposals were found impracticable, why, it may be asked, should the Court not so adjust the rolls, or call the cases, as to prevent the hardship and expense which, in many cases, it is quite obvious will be the result of pursuing a strict undeviating order? Surely that is within the power of the Court, and its machinery elastic enough to admit the exercise of such discretion.

Legal Education.—We should be glad to hear that this subject, which we understand is at present under consideration of the Faculty of Advocates, in connection with the recently instituted degree of Bachelor of Laws, and has also been before one at least of the Universities, was followed by some action. Our readers are aware that the degree was established by an ordinance of the Commissioners acting under the last Universities Act, and requires candidates, being also Masters of Arts, to undergo an examination in the six following branches: Constitutional History; Public Law, including both public and private international law; Civil Law; Conveyancing; the Law of Scotland; and Medical Jurisprudence,—special regard being had to the subject of public law. The applications for the honour have not as yet been very numerous; but if a high standard of examination is maintained—by which we mean something more than merely formidable-looking questions—we have no doubt it will become an object of considerable solicitation; and a great deal might be done to make it so, by conferring upon it the privilege or recognition that attaches to other degrees. It is some time ago since the Faculty of Advocates, with, we think, a wise discrimination, resolved that the degree of Master of Arts should be held to be sufficient evidence of the general literary instruction which is required of every candidate for admission to the Bar. We think that a similar resolution might now be beneficially passed as to the degree of Bachelor of Law, with reference to the professional qualifications which intrants are now called upon to evidence by examination. We look upon this as a reasonable tribute to the degree itself, which contemplates, if it has not already assumed, a high standard. In Scotland, the interdependence between the Universities and the professions is so great, that a degree of this sort, necessarily the aim of a limited number, has no chance to establish itself unless it is fostered in every possible way. It is of very little use—in this country it is found so practically—to found a chair in a University, such, for example, as the chair of Public Law, unless the higher walks of the profession come to an understanding that the new branch shall form a subject of examination of those who seek admission to their ranks. We do not by any means commend the doctrine that knowledge should be declared the possession of any particular spot, by the restriction of students to appointed seats of learning. If a candidate for the Bar has learned his civil law under Professor Rudorff of Berlin, why should he not be taken on trial as readily as one who has learned his under Professor Muirhead at

Edinburgh? and he is so received by the Faculty of Advocates. Neither Professor Muirhead nor any other teacher, guided by a high sense of duty and enthusiasm for his subject, would regard it as unfair to allow his contemporaries to compete with him. But he would have good ground for complaint if the various legal corporations of the country should resolve that henceforth civil law should be excluded from their list of pass qualifications. The practical result of that would be, that thereafter civil law should be no longer taught in Scotland. A degree such as that of Bachelor of Law is on precisely the same footing. As a general rule, it will not be sought in Scotland, except by those who look forward to the practical pursuits of a profession; and even with them it will very soon cease to be an object of aspiration, unless it is invested with some mercantile and tangible value. But not only on the ground of justice to the degree itself, but on a higher ground still, we plead that a professional sanction should be set upon it. It is no doubt true, and it is a possible objection we do not fail to notice, that the subject which the Commissioners desire shall have special regard, is not the law of Scotland; and it may be said with some plausibility and a *prima facie* colour, that the degree can be no evidence of qualification in that branch. But who does not know the difference, both in the standard and in the mode of examination, between a competition for University honours and a struggle to pass into a profession? These are directed in the one case to test general proficiency, and it is just general proficiency in law that an intrant should be expected to possess; and they are so directed in the other, that the direst lack of cultivation, and that of a professional kind too, fails to be detected. And accordingly, we do not hesitate to believe that the University test, notwithstanding the limitation that attaches to it, is at one and the same time more stringent and more effective than the professional one. If that be so, it is quite clear that the recognition of the new degree by the professions would serve a double purpose, and have a doubly beneficial result,—would, in the first place, tend to promote the interests of the higher legal education generally, and would introduce better informed, more cultivated men into the ranks of professional life. We are glad to observe that the degree is recognised by the Procurators Act as a sufficient test of professional qualification; but we fear that the other requirements of that Act are such as practically to neutralize that recognition, by making it almost impossible for those who desire to become members of the different bodies of procurators to give the University attendance in the Faculty of Law which is required for the degree. But even this faint formal recognition is not given by the Faculty of Advocates or the other societies forming part of the College of Justice, nor do they even require evidence that intrants should, either in this country or elsewhere, have studied the subjects embraced by the lectures of the Professors of Public Law, and of Constitutional Law and History. Strange that the first recognition of the new scientific culture of law should have come from those bodies who are popularly supposed to represent the least advanced branch of the legal profession!

The late Sheriff of Linlithgowshire.—Mr John Cay, who died in Edinburgh on the 13th of December, was called to the Bar in 1812, and was appointed Sheriff of Linlithgowshire on the elevation of Mr J. H. Mackenzie to the bench as Lord Mackenzie in 1822. He had thus occupied that honourable position for forty-three years; and he was at his death, with the single exception of Sheriff Rutherfurd of Roxburghshire, the oldest sheriff in Scotland. His death was the consequence of an accidental fall last August, by which his thigh-bone was fractured. Mr Cay was a man of sound judgment and good parts; well read in law, and not without a taste for letters, as might be expected of the early friend of J. G. Lockhart, who was four years his junior at the bar. He was highly respected in his own county, both for his zeal and ability in the county business, and for the manner in which he performed his judicial duties. His decisions were well considered, and were regarded with such confidence that they were rarely advocated.

His interest in everything connected with his county, and his zeal for the monuments of Scottish history, led him to make strenuous efforts for the conversion of the ancient palace of Linlithgow into a court-house. Although in this he was unsuccessful, many will sympathize with his desire to secure the preservation of a building of such associations by adapting it to a useful and not unworthy purpose. Among his brethren of the bar he will long be gratefully remembered in connection with their Widows' Fund, of which he was one of the originators, and the first collector. In that office, as in everything, he was distinguished for diligent and careful accuracy; and to his enthusiasm the great prosperity of the Fund is in no small degree attributable. As chairman of the

Sheriffs' Committee, Mr Cay had an opportunity of making many valuable suggestions in regard to current legislation, and he is understood to have done much useful work in that capacity. Previous to the Act of 1861 he was one of the Sheriffs Commissaries for taking proofs in consistorial causes. He was author of an *Analysis of the Scottish Reform Act, with Decisions in the Courts of Appeal*, of which the first part was published in 1837,—a work of great care and considerable authority. He also wrote two pamphlets; one entitled an *Analysis of the Burgh Registration Act;* and the other, published only last summer, *Outlines of the Procedure at Elections for Members of Parliament.* The death of Mr Cay will lead to no changes at the Bar, as, under the Act 16 and 17 Vict. c. 92, he is succeeded by Mr Tait, the Sheriff of Clackmannan and Kinross, these counties and Linlithgowshire being now united under the same Sheriff and Commissary.

Law of Agent and Client.—In the law of agent and client several points have been under discussion during the past year, which are of considerable interest, and some of them we should have hardly thought were now open.

(1.) For instance, it sounds a very elementary proposition, that an agent having, as such, got possession of his client's title-deeds, is not entitled to use them for other than his client's purposes. Yet twice has this point been *sub judice* during the judicial year just closed;—as might be expected, in both cases raised by country writers. The question first came to the Court of Session from Airdrie, that hot-bed of petty litigation, in the case of *Marshall* v. *Molison*, Dec. 7, 1864, *ante*, vol. ix. p. 5 (3 Macph. p. 191), in which the principle was curiously mixed up with its equitable correction, that the agent has a right of hypothec over his client's titles, in security of his own business account.

In an action against Marshall, in which he was represented by an agent of the name of Morrison, a former agent named Molison was examined as a haver, and produced certain titles belonging to Marshall, over which he (Molison) claimed a right of hypothec. This was set forth in Marshall's own record, and so was known to Morrison, who, as Marshall's agent, borrowed the same, and, Marshall having died, was alleged to be proceeding to use them *against* his representatives, when they applied to the Court to have him ordained to deliver them up. It was clear that it was only as Marshall's agent that he had obtained possession of them; and as Molison no longer demanded them to enable him to make good his hypothec, the Court ordered them to be delivered up. That was a favourable case for modifying the rule, for there were distinct allegations that Marshall had no right to the document specially wanted, and that in fact it belonged to another party whose agent Morrison had by this time become; but the First Division held unanimously that such a question was beyond the scope of the inquiry, whether Morrison was entitled to retain the document against Marshall, and ordered it to be delivered up.

Notwithstanding that the point had thus been so recently ruled, it was again raised in Aberdeenshire, and was again determined in the Bill Chamber during the autumn vacation, and effect, as might have been expected, was given to the principle recognised in the case of *Marshall* v. *Molison*.

(2.) A somewhat kindred discussion, at least as involving the measure of the agent's right over his client's papers, arose in the case of *Skinner* v. *Henderson*, June 2, 1865 (3 Macph. 867), which may be noticed, not as having established any new doctrine, but as setting in a clear light what was already settled in the old cases of *Johnstone* v. *Bell*, 1821, 1 S. 90, and *Paul* v. *Mathie*, 4 S. 424. The trustee in a sequestration applied to the Sheriff for an order for delivery of a back letter or agreement, qualifying certain *ex facie* absolute dispositions of heritable subjects by the bankrupt. The disponees, who were in possession of this deed, were interpelled from giving it up by the agent who had prepared it, and who claimed a right to retain it on the ground that it was hypothecated to him for his account in connection with it, both as against the bankrupt and the other parties to the deed. The Court held the law-agent, who had lodged defences, bound to deliver up deeds in his possession affecting the bankrupt's estate, but only under reservation of his full right of lien, if such right exists.

(3.) In *Scotland* v. *Henry*, July 19, 1865, *ante*, vol. ix. p. 163 (3 Macph. p. 1125), another point was mooted, which we may presume to be now settled. In *Knox* v. *M'Caul*, Lord Rutherfurd's judgment in *Taylor* v. *Forbes* was not before the Court, but the argument in *Scotland* v. *Henry* turned in a great degree upon its soundness, and the Second Division have unanimously, while reserving it, practically overruled it. The kind of case before the Court was this: An agent was employed by the trustee in a sequestration, on the condition, as the trustee said, that the estate alone, and not himself, the trustee, should be liable. The estate was insufficient to meet the account, whereupon the agent sued the trustee, who set up in defence his special bargain. This not being admitted, the question arose, whether the trustee was entitled to prove the alleged bargain *prout de jure*, or was limited to writ or oath of the agent, as the latter contended, founding upon Taylor's case, where the bargain alleged was that the solicitor undertook business gratuitously, except as regarded outlay, reserving his right to recover costs from the opposite party in the event of the business being conducted to a successful issue? The business having terminated unsuccessfully, an action was raised for the whole accounts; and the defender sought to prove the arrangement *prout de jure.*

(4.) The remaining point which formed the subject of decision was one raised by the Court, for no one appeared to resist the demand made in the case of *Walls* v. *Speirs*, Feb. 17, 1865, *ante*, vol. ix. (3 Macph. 536), namely, for interest on a business account from a year after the date of the last item. Decree was ultimately given for interest as craved.

Calls to the Bar.—Mr William Frederick Hunter and Mr William Macintosh were called to the Bar on the 5th of December.

Correspondence.

PROOFS BY COMMISSION.

(*To the Editor of the Journal of Jurisprudence.*)

SIR,—It may by some be accounted treason in the camp to suggest the slightest doubt of the propriety of an institution which all who are engaged in the practice of the law cherish as the very apple of their eye. But I feel it a duty to direct attention, and with my best approval, to the frequency with which the Court, and particularly the Second Division, have recently called in question the expediency of the ascertainment of the facts of a case by commission. The Lord Justice-Clerk is known to be favourably inclined towards the promotion of jury trial, and some may be disposed to think that his views on this matter are tinged more or less with the bias resulting from a theory. But apart altogether from the question of the extension of jury trial, and leaving out of view the fact that the discontinuance of one practice will lead of necessity to the institution of another, it is quite obvious to any unprejudiced observer that the greatest possible injury is being done to the profession by the present tendency to appeal to a commissioner rather than a jury. So long as jury trials are conducted with the expense that now attaches to them, and continue to be magnified into the same ludicrous proportions which the paltriest case may not despair of reaching, I fear that argument against proofs by commission, by reason of their costliness, will not be received with much favour, and can be directed but with little point. But there is abundance of other considerations to demonstrate the evil of the practice. There is, in the first place, no greater ally of the law's proverbial delay than a commissioner. Owing his appointment, for the most part, to the good wishes and the friendly feelings of the agents—and it is notorious that a nominee of the Court is in no better case—he is ready to lend himself to any arrangement that may suit the convenience of parties; and has no eye, and is not expected to have an eye for anything beyond it. The same objection, though not to the same extent, applies to jury trials, in regard to which it has always seemed to me that the practice of the Court has been too lax in admitting postponement and delay; but it seems to me quite obvious, that if this mode of determining facts is to preserve its popularity, it will become absolutely necessary that the powers and duties of commissioners be more clearly defined, and more peremptorily enforced. I add no more to what is said every day—and said with justice too—of the cumbrousness of the machinery. The most glaring defect of the system is the obligation which it imposes on the judges of pronouncing on the facts of a case as jurymen. And this is not in any respect a light matter. In the first place, it is not justice to the Court. To listen to comments upon evidence day after day, with the attention that is necessary to be able to embody all the leading facts in an opinion, and to prepare findings, is an intolerable burden that should not be laid upon the supreme tribunal of the country, except when it cannot absolutely be avoided. It is not justice to the parties. The judges are called upon to act as jurymen, without the assistance which jurymen have—and no one who has had any experience in the weighing of evidence but knows what a valuable aid it is—of seeing the witnesses, and personally observing their manner and deportment. And everybody feels how much easier it is to arrive at a quick and satisfactory result upon facts heard than upon facts laboriously acquired by reading, and intermingled with argument. But I am fast drifting on to the vexed question of the efficacy of jury trial, upon which I have no intention and no desire now to enter. My object has simply been to point out some of the evils of a practice which are universally felt, and are, I regret to say, on the increase.—I am,

JURIDICUS.

THE

JOURNAL OF JURISPRUDENCE.

SHERIFF-COURT REFORM.

NUMBER AND EMOLUMENTS OF SHERIFF-SUBSTITUTES.

AMONG the Acts of Parliament which the last session produced was one which possessed considerable interest for the mercantile and legal community of England, but which, as was perhaps natural, has received little attention in Scotland. We allude to the Act by which a limited jurisdiction in equity was conferred upon the English county court judges, and, simultaneously, an addition of £300 per annum was made to their salaries. Our sheriff courts have, from time immemorial, exercised an equitable jurisdiction in certain classes of cases to an unlimited extent. This jurisdiction is one of which suitors very largely avail themselves, and we feel convinced that, in England, the recent act will be attended with the very best results, and that it will soon be found there, as elsewhere, that the administration of equity and law together will prove in the highest degree satisfactory to litigants. The other portion of the act, namely, that which authorises an increase of salary upon the increase of jurisdiction is one which recognises an important principle, viz., that the public in making any largely increased demands on the time and labour of its servants is bound to increase their emoluments. This principle has been too often lost sight of in Scotch legislation. Almost every year adds to the duties performed in our sheriff-courts. These new duties, practically speaking, in the great majority of cases, are laid upon the sheriff-substitutes.* If

* The number of Acts throwing new duties on the Sheriff-Courts since the last increase of salaries in 1853, amounts to upwards of seventy. We may mention those for Registration of Births, Deaths, and Marriages, for the Valuation of Lands and Heritages, the Friendly Societies Act, the Burial Grounds Act, the Reformatory

we consider the amount of additional work which has thus been thrown upon them since the time when the last general increase in their salaries took place, and the change in the expense of living, we begin to think that their demand for a revision of their scale of remuneration is not without reason. The liberality of parliament has already authorised the Lords of the Treasury to increase the maximum salary of certain sheriff-substitutes to £1400 per annum, although we never could understand how that act came to be passed, as the increase was not made dependent on the amount of work done, for those whose salaries are increased have colleagues doing precisely the same amount of work; nor upon length of service, because, though, in point of fact, it took effect in the case of men who had served long, the increase might fall to one who had held the office for one year only; nor upon superior position, for their colleagues exercised exactly the same jurisdiction as they did. Still the act recognised the principle that readjustment of the scale of remuneration was required.

This has been also partially acknowledged by the Treasury, who, under their discretionary power to raise the salaries of sheriff-substitutes to any point within £1000, have, in Aberdeen, Dundee, and Perth, recently increased the fixed salaries payable out of the consolidated fund to an extent which makes the whole remuneration amount to about £1000 a-year.

But after all, the amount of work done is not a fair criterion to go upon. A judge of certain qualification is required, and his whole time is demanded by the public. He is restrained from the power, if his work be light, of spending his vacant hours remuneratively in his district; a power which, before 1852, all sheriff-substitutes possessed, and which was even recognised by Government, in such cases as that of the late sheriff-substitute of Elginshire, who held also the Government office of Distributor of Stamps. We by no means disapprove of the restriction—nay would perhaps extend it. The administration of justice would not be more endangered by a sheriff being a factor, than by a procurator-fiscal being the law-agent of a party against whom, or

School Act, Dwelling-houses for Working Classes Act, the Passenger Act, Factories Act, Joint Stock Company's Act, Bankruptcy Acts, Nuisance Acts, Boundaries of Burghs Acts, Acts for Regulation of Lunatics and Asylums, General Police Act, Protection of Fresh Water Fish Acts, Prison Acts, Regulation of Unions Act, Registration of County Voters Act, Schoolmasters and Parochial Buildings Act, Vaccination Act, Paupers Removal Act.

those for whom he is responsible, a criminal charge founded on negligence may be brought. In both cases, in such a country as this, the actual administration would probably be pure, but in both alike it ought to be above the shadow of suspicion. One effect of the present regulations is that the emoluments of the resident magistrate are sometimes greatly inferior to those of the officials of his court.

The great practical obstacle in the way of increasing the salaries of sheriff-substitutes throughout the country has always been the very great number of these officials, coupled with the somewhat notorious fact that, if the salary be tested by the work actually performed, many are greatly overpaid. England has sixty county court judges; Scotland has fifty-five sheriff-substitutes. It is no doubt true that the jurisdiction of the Scotch judges is much more extensive, and the duties much more multifarious than fall to the lot of the English official. In addition to being the county court judge (and with a vastly larger jurisdiction, both in law and equity) the sheriff-substitute performs duties analogous to those of bankruptcy commissioner, of lunacy commissioner and (assisted by the procurator-fiscal) of coroner, and when we add his criminal jurisdiction, both as a judge and magistrate—for he performs a great part of the work done by the English magistrates, both at petty and at quarter sessions—it is evident that the fair comparison between the numbers of the Scotch and English officials is not simply setting the fifty-five sheriff-substitutes against the sixty county court judges, but against an array of bankruptcy and lunacy commissioners, of coroners, of recorders, of magistrates, whose name is legion. Nevertheless, allowing full weight to these considerations, it must be admitted that the number of sheriff-substitutes is much too great. This has gradually been forcing itself upon public attention. Some two or three years ago Mr Grahame, the sheriff-substitute of Dunblane, published a letter to Lord Kinnaird, suggesting the amalgamation of a number of the jurisdictions. In April 1864, a series of letters appeared in the *Edinburgh Courant*, in which the same idea was wrought out in greater detail, and a scheme of abolition and fusion was propounded, whereby full employment would be given to nearly all the sheriff-substitutes who were retained, while it was proposed to distribute the salaries of the suppressed offices, so as to raise the minimum drawn by those who were left.

Parliament having now authorised an increase in the maximum salary, is it too much to think that the Lords of the Treasury would be fully warranted in making such small grants within the discretion already confided to them, as would in combination with a systematic suppression of superfluous offices, raise the minimum to something approaching one-half of what the English County Court Judges receive? Such a sum would be by no means too large, even in the more remote districts, for the position of a Sheriff-Substitute, who is now in general, a member of the bar, in all cases is a man of a liberal and expensive education, and expected to associate on terms of equality with the county families, besides maintaining the dignity of the resident representative of the law in the district.

The practical difficulty in determining which Sheriff-Substitutes shall be retained, and which abolished, arose very much from the impossibility of obtaining accurate statistics of the amount of business transacted in each court. This, however, is now in the way of being remedied. An elaborate series of returns was moved for by Mr Baxter, the details, it is understood, having been prepared by a Sheriff-Substitute. Another series of returns was also moved for by the Lord Advocate; and the Sheriff-Clerks of the various counties are at present engaged in the preparation of both sets. These are of the most voluminous and minute character, and will provide ample material as a basis for any discussion that may take place in the ensuing Session of Parliament. We understand that a considerable instalment of the returns will be ready to be laid upon the tables of the two houses, immediately upon their assembling. When this shall have been done we may probably return to the subject of Sheriff-Court Reform, and consider some of the details that ought to claim the careful attention of the legislature. For that its attention must early be directed to the subject we think cannot be doubted.

Meanwhile no one can deny the importance in giving increased weight and influence to the position of the local judges, of placing their emoluments on such a footing as shall make this office an object of ambition to men of high legal attainments and experience, for there is no reason why an increase of salary should not be accompanied by a stipulation for increased professional standing. Three years standing we cannot but think quite insufficient, as a general rule, to afford a guarantee for that experience required for the discharge of the multifarious duties thrown on the Sheriff-Substitutes,—much longer standing is required for the County Court judgeships in England. We are very far, indeed, from saying that the ranks of the Sheriff-Substitutes do not already contain many men who are all that can be desired. Many of those who took office while the emoluments were miserably inadequate, were so, and of late years the appointments have been accepted by many able and rising men at the bar. The whole body are, nearly without exception, valuable public servants both as magistrates and judges. Among the later appointments many have accepted office under the belief that they would participate in that amelioration of their position which they thought they saw slowly, but steadily approaching. This is, we think, the best answer to the complaints that are sometimes heard, that men who have recently been appointed, knew what they were taking, and should not agitate for an increase of salary,—a complaint, not perhaps so entirely without justification, or so easily answered, when directed against those who seek for this increase by the abolition of the office of the Principal Sheriffs, from whom they have received their appointments. We should not wonder if the recent promotion of one of the Sheriff-Substitutes of Edinburgh to the office of Sheriff-Depute of Aberdeenshire, had a material effect in checking that branch of the agitation.

We have, however, somewhat digressed from what we had proposed to ourselves as the peculiar object of this paper, viz., the desirability of a reduction in the numbers of Sheriff-Substitutes, and a reconstruction of the districts under their charge. The principle upon which the distribution of these officials throughout Scotland was based, was that all the lieges might have cheap and speedy access to a judge at their own doors, and that the benefit of a stipendiary magistrate might be available in the administration of criminal justice throughout the land, whether in the preparation of cases to be tried before the Court of Justiciary in Edinburgh or on Circuit, or in the trial of offenders by the Sheriff-Substitute himself, or by the Sheriff, if he thought proper to attend, summarily, or with the assistance of a jury. It is evident, however, that a distribution of officials over the country, made at a time when the facilities of locomotion were so vastly inferior to what they now are, must stand in need of a thorough revision. Vicinity is now measured not by distance but by time, and a judge is much nearer the doors of a litigant if separated by twenty miles of railway than by ten of road. The Act of 16 & 17

Vic., cap. 92, which amalgamated certain of the Sheriff depute-ships has now by the lapse of time come nearly into full operation, and while effecting a considerable saving to the public purse has not diminished in the slightest degree the benefit which the amalgamated counties were in use to receive from their non-resident sheriffs, while each county had one of these officials to themselves. Facilities of railway communication have even since the date of that act increased so much that we can easily see how the number of these officials might be still farther diminished without in the least impairing the principle of the double Sheriff-ship.

But our present concern is with Sheriff-Substitutes, whose number might easily be diminished by at least a dozen. A glance at the railway map of Scotland will, even without the statistics which we have been promised, suggest those which ought to be abolished. Those of Tain and Nairn in the North, Dunblane or Clackmannan and Kinross in the midland counties, Selkirk and Peebles in the south, imperatively demand such treatment. It is little short of an absurdity to say that it is necessary to maintain well paid judges in these distrcts. Now that the Highland rail-way is open, Fort-William is not farther from Inverness than Kingussie used to be, and surely our island population of 100,000 is not so unruly as to require five and a-half Sheriff-Substitutes to look after them, although we admit that from the peculiarity of their position they require exceptional treatment. Nor when we see Sheriff-Substitutes of the highest reputation discharging the whole duties of districts with populations varying from 100,000 to 150,000, can we imagine a good reason for Stirling-shire with its 91,000 remaining divided into two districts now that the county is intersected with railways.

We would not propose that in the towns where a Sheriff-Substitute should cease to reside, the ordinary Sheriff Courts should cease to be held. On the contrary, not only would we retain a small debt court in each town, but we should propose that it be made imperative on the Sheriff-Substitute to hold an ordinary court in each once a week, or oftener if required. We have heard a difficulty suggested as to the mode to be adopted in conducting the criminal and especially the magisterial business in such amalgamated jurisdictions. Probably the simplest plan would be that one procurator fiscal and Sheriff-Clerk depute should be appointed for the amalgamated district, and that all persons should be brought to the town when the Sheriff-Substitute should reside, and declarations there taken from them, and then recommitted to the jail of the town, or district, where they had been arrested. The expence of travelling by railway is so very moderate, that it would cost less probably now to bring a criminal from Falkirk by rail to Stirling, or from Nairn to Elgin, than before the days of railways, to convey him to the county town by gig or carriage. If it be thought desirable that there shall be no diminution in the number of procurators-fiscal, all that would be necessary would be that these officials should also go by railway to the town where the Sheriff-Substitute should reside, if it was necessary to take a declaration from a prisoner on a day when the Sheriff-Substitute was not to visit the town where the fiscal's office was. But as we have already said, we should propose that at least one visit per week should be made by the Sheriff-Substitute to each town which had formerly the benefit of his continued residence. By a little arrangement all trifling criminal cases could be taken upon these days, and it would only be the more serious cases where instant apprehension was necessary, that would require the conveyance of the criminal to the residence of the Sheriff-Substitute, and the attendance there of the Procurator-Fiscal, and perhaps of an Inspector of Police. The cost to the country, and the inconvenience to the officials, would, we believe, be of the most trifling character, and not for one moment to be weighed in the balance with the great benefit which the public would derive from the elevation of the position of Sheriff-Substitute, and infiuitessimally small if compared with the inconvenience even now existing in large counties, such as Ross, Aberdeen, and Perth.

Let us glance hurriedly at pecuniary results. We throw out of view Edinburgh and Glasgow, the counties of Aberdeen, with a population of 221,569 inhabitants, Ayr with 198,971, and Forfar with 204,425, because these figures only require to be stated to satisfy any one that if there be any great inequality of districts, there should be a re-adjustment, and such as would entitle both the Sheriff-Substitutes in these counties to be put on an equal scale, and that the highest, except in such towns as Edinburgh and Glasgow. Although the population of Renfrewshire had not reached 180,000 in 1861, we have little doubt that with Glasgow extending into it, and Greenock daily developing, the Sheriff-Substitutes both of Paisley and Greenock, having regard alike to the population they have charge of, to the importance of the duties they have to discharge, and to the expense of living ought also to be placed on the highest scale; but from this rough glance we shall not exclude them as we do those of Aberdeenshire, Ayrshire, and Forfarshire. There remain forty-two Sheriff-Substitutes, with average salaries of £577 per annum. It does not require much arithmetic to see that the abolition of ten, and the re-distribution of their salaries among those who would in future do their work, would raise the minimum salary from £500 a-year to upwards of £750, and that the abolition of twelve of them would raise it to upwards of £800.

The proposed changes could not, we fear, be carried out without legislative interference, as although Sheriffs have power, with consent of the heads of the Court of Session, to increase the numbers of Sheriff-Substitutes, they have no power, so far as we are aware, to diminish them. A very short Act, of three or four clauses, however, would be sufficient, as all details as to the offices to be abolished, and the number of courts to be held in the towns where these have hitherto existed, might be left for settlement, either to an Act of Sederunt, or to regulation of the Sheriffs, with consent of the heads of the Court of Session, and the Lord-Advocate, with concurrence of the Treasury, if need be.

New Books.

Trial by Jury in Europe and America: its Advantages, its Defects, and their Remedies. (*Erfahrungen über die Wirksamkeit der Schwurgerichte in Europa und Amerika, über ihre Vorzüge, Mängel und Abhülfe.* Von Dr. K. J. MITTERMAIER. Erlangen: 1865).

THIS work is from the pen of the well-known criminal jurist, Professor Mittermaier of Heidelberg, author of "The Criminal Law of England, Scotland, and North America viewed in connexion with their moral, political, and social condition," and of a treatise on Capital Punishment recently translated into English. To Dr. Mittermaier chiefly is due the credit of the introduction into Germany of trial by jury in criminal cases.

But he candidly admits that, as administered in that country, it labours under serious defects. To remedy these is his aim; and he thinks that this may best be done by investigating the working of the institution in other countries, viewing it in connexion with national characteristics, and the differences of national legal systems, and thence determining what to avoid and what is worthy of imitation. The book before us is the result. Its information, collected from the most trustworthy sources—from Ministers of State, Judges, Crown Officers, and Advocates—is accompanied throughout by valuable criticisms and suggestions of improvement, which the varied experience of the writer enables him to offer.

Dr. Mittermaier lays down as one great fundamental principle not sufficiently attended to by law reformers, that trial by jury is intimately connected with the moral, social, and political condition of a people. Juries lose their proper character in countries where the political party-spirit runs so high that one half of the people strives by all the means in its power to further the ends of the Government, while the other half does its best to thwart them. In such a case the Government would naturally endeavour to have no one selected to act on a jury but those of whose support it was assured. And the natural result would be, that the verdict of a jury would come to depend, especially in the trial of political offenders, merely on the preponderance in the jury of one party or of the other. If the party feeling, instead of being political is religious, the danger is almost greater. In countries where a low standard of education and of moral feeling prevails, where the people do not reverence the law or its administrators, where they do not hold inviolate the sanctity of an oath, there a reliable verdict from a jury is not to be expected. If the judges do not occupy a professionally independent position, or the Crown Prosecutor, instead of being the servant is the tool of the Government, the highest legal offices will be conferred, not on men fitted for them by their talents, uprightness, or professional skill, but on those who will most unscrupulously carry out the designs of their superiors. The consequence of this will be groundless and tyrannical prosecutions. Proceedings on both sides will inevitably be carried on with a degree of rancour and ill-feeling wholly destructive of anything like impartiality and sound judgment. And as to the juries themselves, one of two things will happen—either they will be intimidated into a servile obedience, or they will be roused into mistrust and bitter opposition. In either case justice will suffer.

These views, which the Professor brings forward in an introductory chapter, he subsequently illustrates when treating of the various countries in their order. We may give an example or two to show the way in which our author works out his idea.

In England, he tells us, trial by jury, which has developed itself but gradually in the course of centuries, enjoys safeguards such as no other land can boast. There, opposition between judge and jury is unknown. An Englishman looks upon the office of juryman neither as a political right, nor, like the Germans, as an honour. He simply regards it as he would any other duty which, as a citizen, he is called upon to discharge. He has perfect confidence in the judge, and views him in the light of a disinterested party, whose instructions are entitled to weight in aiding him to arrive at a final decision. In England, from the circumstance that jury trial is extended also to civil cases, juries have never been invested with the political character they have acquired in other countries. Political party spirit does not constitute an element in the administration of the law. It has done so at one or two periods of popular agitation, but these are exceptional cases, which we need not take into account. The only control to which judges and juries are alike subject, is that of public opinion, as expounded by a free press.

If we turn to Ireland we cannot but be struck with the close degree in which the administration of justice is dependent on the social condition of the people. Though the Irish legal system is the same as that of England, it has been modified by influences to which the other has not been subjected. The chief of these are, according to Dr Mittermaier, the religious intolerance of the two leading sects, the neglect of education, the famine which has at various times visited the country, the formation of secret societies, and, not the least powerful, jealousy towards the English. How prejudicially these worked on the trial of criminals appears from the statistics quoted by our author. The acquittals were at one time out of all proportion to the convictions. In 1849, out of 170 trials for murder, 138 resulted in an acquittal; and of 21,202 criminals tried for various crimes in that year, 20,700 escaped punishment! Of late years, however, as the condition of the country has improved, criminal justice has made corresponding progress. And in the very latest instances, in the

Fenian trials now going on in Ireland, we have seen no unwillingness on the part of the juries to aid in the vindication of the law.

The American criminal system, formed originally on the English model, has in course of time sustained many important modifications. From the democratic nature of the Government, and the consequent equality of all ranks, the constitution of their juries rests on a different basis from the English. The lists of jurymen are framed in quite another way. For the people are too jealous of their privileges to entrust this to any single individual corresponding to the English Sheriff. It is in the essence of democracy to distrust men in authority, even when of their own appointing, and to invest them with as little power as possible. Hence crime is not nearly so promptly discovered nor so energetically followed up in America as with us. The judges, who are often elected by the people, are so much controlled by popular opinion as to lose their independence. "There is no country," says Dr Mittermaier, "in which prejudice and particular opinions are so dangerously powerful as in America." Whether opinions on national politics, or on general subjects, such as slavery, are in question, a jury will almost always return a verdict corresponding to the number of its members who are of the same way of thinking as the prisoner. Especially is this the case where religious tenets are involved; for America is quite a nursery-garden of religious sects.

The influence of national character on criminal procedure is nowhere more felt than in the United States. That country has been colonised at various times by settlers from almost all the countries of Europe; and their descendants still retain certain traces of their original variety of parentage. In Massachusetts, Connecticut, and other New England States, where, as Dr Mittermaier expresses it, "the Anglo-Norman element prevails in the population, and the good old English spirit of fidelity and deference to the law is still maintained by the English colonists," the restraining power of justice is greater, and the working of Jury Trial is much more efficient. Where the population is more mixed, for example in the Western States, whose inhabitants are chiefly of Irish extraction, a jury is much more pliable and capable of intimidation, This is due to the all-prevalent spirit of party, "and to the absence of those good qualities which characterise the English portion of the population." In the States peopled mostly by Germans, juries have retained their national sterling qualities ("*den guten Geist der Deutschen*"). But the Germans complain, that in trials where they are the parties, and jurymen of a different nationality are to decide, an unjust spirit of partisanship comes into operation.

Following up the general principle that the Jury Court is influenced by national idiosyncrasies, the professor points out the error of those writers who attempt to prescribe a model Jury to serve as a pattern for all nations equally. The disposition of the people, the state of society and civilization, and the course of politics, are all to be given effect to, when the establishment or improvement of the Jury Court in a country is in question. At the same time it cannot be denied that the leading idea in all countries is the same. But this does not consist, the Author warns us, merely in communicating to the people a share in the administration of justice. This was equally the basis of the Roman institution of *judices*, and of the Sheriff Courts of feudal times.

The professor urges that in importing into a country the institution of a Jury Court, regard must be had, not only to the different conditions referred to above, but also to the existing criminal system of that country. They must be reciprocally modified, so as to produce one harmonious whole. If the legal code outstep the limits of the popular comprehension, by drawing fine distinctions, or indulging in legal subtilities, or if the severity of the punishments are out of all proportion to the offences, a Jury Court will be of very little use. It will be found also that the soundness of the verdicts will depend most vitally on the simplicity of process. Everything which has a tendency to mislead the Jury must be carefully avoided. Measures must be taken, to secure a fair and exhaustive statement of the arguments on either side, perfect freedom in the defence, and impartiality in the Court. As an instance of the folly of not observing this general principle, Dr. Mittermaier cites the case of some of the German States, who, when in 1848 adopting Trial by Jury, retained their old system of secret written procedure in criminal causes, and merely superadded a "patchwork of Jury Court regulations."

Reviewing in detail the criminal procedure of those countries where trial by Jury is established, Professor Mittermaier takes as the two great representative systems which serve more or less as a model for all the others, the French, and the English or

Scotch. The former, though it has been followed by all the European continental nations, deservedly incurs the severe censure of our author. He quotes with approbation the words of M. Laboulaye a recent French writer, when referring to the criminal laws of France: "L'esprit de ces lois est encore le vieil esprit d' inquisition, elles cherchent des coupables plus que des innocents." To account for this inquisitorial character of criminal procedure in France, we must keep in view the early history of Jury Trial in that country. It was introduced during the storms of the Great Revolution, and at once assumed in the eyes of both rulers and people, a political character quite at variance with its true nature. It was used chiefly in the trial of political offenders, to obtain convictions against whom, the government, for its own security, was constrained to use every means in its power. To this cause we must attribute many features of the French Jury Court, to which Dr. Mittermaier takes exception. There is no doubt that it gave rise to the *pouvoir discrétionnaire* conferred on the Judge, of using whatever means he deems serviceable to the discovery of the truth; and the Code charges "his honour and conscience" to that effect. The *président* abuses this right by examining the prisoner in court, and in the course of a long seriesof artfully conceived questions, eliciting proofs of his guilt from his confused and often contradictory answers, or even from his very looks and gestures.* To show that we are not exaggerating, we may quote a single sentence taken from the Report of the Commissioners appointed in 1808 to frame the French Criminal Code, and given by Dr. Mittermaier in a foot-note. The Commission expatiating on the advantages of this cross-questioning of the prisoner by the Judge, does not hesitate to say: "Rien n'est muet, rien n'est inutile dans le débat; la contenance, le sang froid, ou le trouble, les variations, l'altération des traits, les impressions diverses forment un corps d'indices qui soulèvent plus ou moins le voile dont la vérité est enveloppée."

But there soon arose on the part of juries a spirit of opposition to the excessive anxiety of the Crown officers to obtain convic-

* What would the German Professor say to Governor Eyre's method of judging of the state of Jamaica and the reports of *discontented looking* men riding about the country? We suspect if the annals of our arrests were enquired into, it would be found that looks and gestures had often been what first directed the attention of the police to the prisoner.

tions. They declined to be used as a mere political tool, and to be intimidated into a passive submission to the commands of a corrupt government. They claimed the right of thinking for themselves, and of freely exercising the powers with which the law had invested them. Hence arose that want of confidence in the persons composing the jury, which, as Dr Mittermaier points out, is a fundamental characteristic of French criminal procedure. This feeling of mistrust lies at the root of the various provisions of the Code which tend to limit the powers of the jury, and render them more dependent on the court. It is the key to the meaning of the French rule by which the jury, instead of returning a general verdict on the whole evidence, must confine itself to answering certain questions on matters of fact put to them by the judge, who, in accordance with these, himself pronounces the verdict. At the same time, in order to guide the jury in their replies, there is prescribed in the Code (Art. 342) a set of instructions, to be read over to the jury in every case before they retire, and of which a copy in large type is to be affixed to the wall of their retiring room. From this directory we learn that the law does not require the jury to hold a fact as proved because attested by a certain number of witnesses, or to regard a proof as insufficient if not established by so many witnesses, documents, or corroborative circumstances. No—the law simply asks them the question, "*Avez-vous une intime conviction?*" and by this question are prescribed the limits of their duties. It is on inward conviction, and not by maturely weighing and considering every fact in the evidence, that a French jury is to arrive at a decision. It is an affair of the feelings, not of the understanding. Hence, from the commencement of the case, the aim of the Prosecutor is to excite in the minds of the jury a conviction of the prisoner's guilt, while the counsel of the accused uses all his powers of persuasion to enlist their feelings on the side of his client. We can thus account for the passionate vehemence and melo-dramatic declamation which form so conspicuous a part of the proceedings at a French criminal trial.

Our author condemns in strong terms the French system of the judge putting to the jury questions on the mere facts, and not allowing them to return a general verdict. The supporters of this system appeal to the example of England, where they say it is a maxim that the jury is judge of the facts only, not of the law. Dr Mittermaier contends, that however applicable this may have been to juries in their embryo state, when they partook more of the nature of witnesses summoned to give from their private knowledge information of some crime which had been committed, yet it no longer holds good in England. The very circumstance that a jury may by their verdict find the prisoner not guilty of the crime charged, but guilty of some other modified one (*e.g.*, not guilty of murder, but guilty of manslaughter), proves according to onr author, that the jury are not only entitled, but bound, in a certain measure to consider the law of the case as well as the facts. The judge, no doubt, is supposed to furnish in his charge to the jury information as to what facts are sufficient to constitute in law the crime libelled; but the jury may return a verdict at variance with the directions so given. Such a verdict, in Scotland at least, could not be set aside.

In several other points besides those referred to above, our author takes exception to the French system. He strongly reprobates the mixing up of the results of the preliminary proceedings with those of the trial itself. In France this occurs, owing to the custom of the Crown Prosecutor, when a witness answers a question at the trial otherwise than he did at his precognition, to read out the latter in court, if it is more prejudicial to the prisoner than the other; and if a witness is prevented from appearing in court to give his evidence, or if he is dead, his precognition taken before the magistrate is read to the jury. This of course is of advantage to the side of the prosecution, as it precludes the cross-examination for the defender. Still more unfavourable to the prisoner is the power conferred on the judge (Code, Art. 269) of calling, in the course of the trial, for the production of any witnesses whom he may think able to throw light on the case. This right is the more dangerous, since it is enacted that "witnesses thus called shall not be put upon oath, and their declarations shall be regarded merely as information."

But as if the enactments of the Code were not sufficient to attain the ends of justice, there exists a rule in the Jury Court unauthorised save by the usage of practice. The Court, if not satisfied with the finding, may order the jury back to reconsider their verdict. They are supposed to do so on the ground that the verdict is incomplete, ambiguous, or contrary to evidence. Since, however, they are not required to specify on which of these grounds they object to the finding of the jury, it is evident to what abuses such a proceeding may lead, and how juries, by repeated remits, may be overawed into giving a decision such as is desired by the Court. Results show us that juries have not unfrequently been sent back to reconsider a perfectly regular verdict. In such a case, there always arises a contention as to how much the second finding can alter the first, or prejudice the rights already acquired by the prisoner under the first verdict.

In no country has Jury Trial had to struggle with so many difficulties as in Germany. It was introduced, as in France, at an unfortunate time—when the country was disturbed by the revolutions of 1848. It thus acquired the character of a political institution, which, as we have seen, proved so destructive of its efficiency in France. This notion was unfortunately assisted by its being confined, in some of the German States, to trials for political and press offences. In the then excited state of political parties, it was to be expected that the convictions would depend more on the politics of the jurymen than on the guilt of the prisoner. But the institution of a Jury Court was unpopular on other grounds. Dr. Mittermaier tells us that statesmen and rulers opposed it, because it was a democratic institution, and would tend to undermine the principle of monarchy. Scientific men discouraged it because they thought the interests of science would suffer, from giving to unlearned citizens a share in the administration of the law. Lastly, among practical jurists, there were many enemies to the establishment of a Jury Court. They esteemed it an insult to the dignity of the judges, and an encroachment on the part of the citizens, who wished to take the deciding of the most important questions out of the hands of men who, by a long course of legal study and practice, were much better fit to deal with them.

Dr. Mittermaier in tracing the history of Jury Courts in Germany since 1848, divides it into three periods—which will be found to correspond a good deal with the course of politics in that country. The first period, extending from 1848 to 1852, was one of great national excitement. Owing to the state of the country in the latter half of 1849, numerous political trials took place. In these many persons who had been prominent leaders in the revolutions of 1848, played the part of denouncers and informers, wishing to atone for their past offences by increased zeal for the cause of their new masters. The worthy citizens, who acted as jurymen, either from the small amount of confidence they placed in the testimony of these witnesses, or from finding an apology for the prisoners in the excited state of the times, were easily moved to return favourable verdicts. It was these acquittals which swelled the ranks of the opponents of the Jury Court. Statesmen and jurists pointed to them as proof of the dangerous tendency of such an institution. And, among the people, there were many who, calling to mind the terrors of the Revolution of 1848, and the often expressed necessity for greater stringency in punishing sedition, bitterly condemned a procedure which could permit the escape of such agitators.

The second period in the history of the German Jury Court, extends from 1853 to 1858. It is marked by a fierce onslaught on juries. In several States, as in Austria and Saxony, they were abolished altogether. Where they were permitted to remain, their powers were limited as much as possible. On the part of the Government vigorous efforts were made to exercise a control in the appointment of the jurymen, and to give more extended powers to the judges. But the greatest curtailment of the prerogative of the Jury Court, was that borrowed from the new French Code, the withdrawal of political offences from their jurisdiction. At the same time, it cannot be denied that the sympathy of the people for the new institution had become more general. It had taken root among them, they began to understand its true nature, and to desire to take a part in its important functions.

The third and last period fixed by our author, includes the years from 1859 to the present time. It is characterised by an ever-increasing recognition of the utility and true functions of the Jury Court. The number daily waxes greater of both theoretical and practical jurists, who admit that trial by jury, when properly regulated, secures the political freedom of the people no less than the energetic operation of the penal laws. As a sign of the reaction of feeling, it may be mentioned that the Austrian Government are at the present moment framing a measure, having for its object the re-introduction of the Jury Court into the Austrian Empire.

It is unnecessary to examine in detail the procedure in the German Jury Corut. Though based upon that of France, it has avoided, Professor Mittermaier informs us, many of its defects. Still there is great room for improvement, and the Professor points to our system as that from which improvements are to be borrowed. He says:—"The fact deserves attention, that both in France and Germany the conviction is daily gaining ground, that an immense improvement might be effected in our present mode of conducting jury trials, by a proper application of the principles on which the English, *and more especially the Scotch*, criminal procedure is based; but at the same time we must recollect that the English system is marred by great blemishes which it is our bounden duty to avoid."

It is always instructive to learn the opinion of intelligent observers in other countries on the subject of our institutions, even those as to which we have reasonable ground to expect the opinion to be in our favour. Certainly in the present instance we have no cause to be disappointed. Professor Mittermaier always speaks of the Scotch Criminal System in the highest terms, contrasting it throughout with that of England, by no means always to the advantage of the latter. He does not go over the subject at as great length as we might expect, having already treated it elaborately in his former work on the English, Scotch, and American Criminal Systems, to which he constantly refers us. But he gives us a general view of the two systems, displaying a most extensive acquaintance both with the history and literature of our law. The knowledge of our legal institutions he has not acquired from books alone. He has visited our country, he has been in our law courts, and can speak with all the authority of a practical lawyer.

Dr Mittermaier tries to account in the outset for the striking differences to be met with in the systems of two countries so long and intimately connected as Scotland and England. On this point he observes:—"Although the Scotch Criminal Process rests on essentially the same basis as the English, it yet possesses so many characteristics peculiar to itself, that, without a knowledge of these, it would be impossible to gain a proper insight into the working of Jury Trial in Scotland. As circumstances which it is important to take into account, it may be mentioned that Roman Law forms part of the Common Law of Scotland, that it is systematically studied at her Universities, and gives a character of profoundness to her Jurisprudence which is wanting in that of England. The subtility and shrewdness of the Scotch nation exercises a powerful influence on the administration of the law. The members of the Faculty of Advocates, joined together by a common bond of union (*innerlich verbrüdert*), and in the possession of a most valuable library, occupy a worthy position in society, and enjoy the high esteem both of the judges and of the public."

Our author then proceeds to observe, that much of the efficiency of a criminal system depends on the manner in which the investigation preliminary to a trial is conducted. The system ought to be such, that while providing that no criminal shall escape justice, its organisation shall be calculated to protect the innocent. In this respect, remarks the Professor, the Scotch precognition, under the superintendence of a public prosecutor, has many advantages over the English proceedings before a coroner. And the provision of our law, by which, in case of the Crown officer declining to prosecute, the injured party may himself pursue, is a safeguard against the arbitrary use of the authority with which he is invested.* But Dr Mittermaier recognizes other influences as tending in the same direction, and quotes, apparently with approbation, the "remarkable utterance" of the Lord Advocate, in his address at the Social Science Congress of 1860, "that the institution of a Public Prosecutor, under the influence of public opinion and parliamentary responsibility is, as far as the practical working of it is concerned, the best mode in which the criminal affairs of a country can be conducted." As a good instance of the way in which this control by public opinion and Parliament is expressed, the Professor refers, in a foot-note, to the M'Lachlan case. Our author states, as an objection to the Scotch system, that the Procurators-fiscal being paid, not by salary, but according to the number of causes, have a strong inducement to bring vexatious prosecutions. This used formerly to be the law, but we had ourselves discovered the blot and it is now almost universally remedied. Another and more serious objection which Dr Mittermaier takes to the proceedings preliminary to trial is the emitting of a declaration by the prisoner before the magistrate. He thinks that this "*inquisitorial proceeding*" is dangerous towards the innocent, and apt to lead the jury into error. He quotes from a speech by Sheriff Barclay, at the meeting of the Social Science Meeting of 1860, who stated that, "as to prisoners' declarations, he was strongly of opinion that they were nothing more than a continuance of the old system of torture." "The caution," adds Dr Mittermaier, "always given to the prisoner, that he is not bound to answer questions, is no protection. No doubt, the accused, if he is a sharp fellow or an experienced hand, gives either no answer at all, or else tells a craftily-contrived story. But

* There cannot be a higher testimony to the efficiency of the prosecutions by the Crown than the desuetude into which private prosecution has fallen.

a nervous man may be so frightened and confused by the course of ingenious questioning to which he is subjected, as to give equivocal or vague replies, which, when read out at the trial, will have a strong tendency to mislead the jury."

Dr Mittermaier discusses in turn the leading features of a Jury Trial in Scotland. He thinks it an important advantage that in the High Court of Justiciary three Judges preside, who can consult together in deciding questions of law. The formation of the iists of jurymen, and their classification into common and special jurors meets with his special commendation. "In this way," he observes, "the Scotch jury consists of a happy admixture, securing an interchange of views between men of a higher walk in life, and those belonging to a less-favoured circle of society."

The Scotch indictment our author thinks preferable to the English in some respects. It is fuller in its information, shows the accused at whose instance he is prosecuted, and indicates to what points he will have to direct his defence. On the other hand, Dr Mittermaier thinks that the syllogistic form of the indictment renders the style cumbersome. He also disapproves of including several prisoners and several dates, and separate acts in the same libel, even where all refer to the same offence. It tends he says, to confuse the jury. Perhaps it might do so, but for the judges charge, to which he entertains, as it seems to us, an unreasonable objection. In practice we do not remember to have seen any mischief arise from the combination of prisoners and charges in one indictment. If the court anticipates any evil results they have the power to separate the trials. On the other hand the present system saves a great deal of useless repetition, and, therefore, of weariness to juries and all others engaged in conducting the trial.

There is one principle which our author most strongly contends for, and that is, fair play for the prisoner; or, as he expresses it, "equality between the two parties in the encounter of wits" (*im geistigen Kampfe*). In this respect he gives his preference to the Scotch system rather than the English. He eulogises the rule of our law by which the Court is bound to provide counsel for the prisoner. And, on the same principle, he shows a decided predilection for our order of procedure, which gives to the prisoner's counsel the last word with the jury. He also admires the plan of a preliminary interlocutor on the relevancy, which not only saves the trouble of perhaps going through a long case, only to have the verdict set aside, but also better enables the prisoner to make up his mind whether to plead guilty or not.

With regard to the laws of evidence—though, as Dr Mittermaier observes, they are in their essential points much the same in the two countries—he thinks that England has the advantage of us in two respects. In the sister country the prisoner's declaration is much more seldom used against him at his trial. And the English law is more stringent with regard to the admission as evidence of the depositions of dying witnesses. The Professor also prefers the English rule that requires unanimity on the part of the jury, and is of opinion that it increases public confidence in their verdicts. He alludes to the greater choice of verdicts which the jury has in Scotland. But while recapitulating the arguments both for and against the third verdict of "Not Proven," he carefully abstains from expressing his own opinion on the subject.

Strange to say, the Professor censures in our criminal procedure what is usually regarded as one of its chief excellences, viz., the judge's charge. It is apt, he says, to mislead the jury, especially in cases of circumstantial evidence; and all the more, from the judge being in the position of a neutral party, whose opinion is therefore entitled to greater weight. In support of his views the Professor cites the case of Smethurst, where the judge analysed the evidence of several scientific experts, but displayed, according to our author, a profound ignorance of all science; the case of Townley, in which on the question of insanity the judge showed himself unacquainted with the progress of medical psychology; and the recent cases of Jessie M'Lachlan and Franz Müller, where, as the author affirms, the unfavourable verdicts were due entirely to the one-sided charges of the judges. Much as we esteem Dr. Mittermaier's criticisms generally, we think that, in regard to Müller's case, his national feeling has got the better of his sound judgment, and it is not necessary to approve of the judge's charge in the Maclachlan case in order to think that the verdict of the jury was thoroughly justified by the evidence.

Our space does not permit us to follow Professor Mittermaier in his researches through all the countries of Europe. For these we must refer to the book itself. But one word as to Italy. When Napoleon, in 1806, conferred a penal code on the kingdom of Italy, he asserted that the Italians did not possess the qualities fitting them for the privilege of trial by jury. He refused to accord, even to his own countrymen, the Corsicans, the institution of a jury court, though in other respects extending to them the French Code. The present Criminal Code, introduced in 1859 after the changes made by the Treaty of Villafranca, is unfortunately based on the French law. Dr Mittermaier deplores that the Italian Government did not rather adopt as their model the Maltese Criminal Code of 1856, which is founded on the Scotch system, and has been found to work so well. The Italian Government itself recognises the necessity of an amendment of the Criminal Law; and first, in 1861, some improvements were made. And in 1863 and 1864 several reforms were projected, though they have not yet been carried into effect.

In establishing the Italian Jury Court on a firm basis, many serious difficulties have to be encountered. "Every one," says Dr Mittermaier, "who has any acquaintance with the Italian people, is aware of what a strange sympathy exists among them for persons accused of crime. An offender whose apprehension is sought, knows that he may reckon pretty well on receiving from the people every assistance to escape; while the citizens do their best to evade the duty of acting as witnesses, and when brought into Court, give their evidence, as a general rule, in favour of the accused." This he attributes to the way in which prosecutions for political offences were carried on under former Governments;—to the use of spies, and even bribery, being resorted to, in consequence of which the people came to regard as martyrs those pursued by Government;—to the want of proper means of education, the baneful influence of the clergy, teaching that the most heinous sin, even the breaking of an oath, may be atoned for by pious exercises, and the want of desire among the citizens for participation in public affairs. Notwithstanding this gloomy picture, Dr Mittermaier does not endorse the unfavourable judgment of the first Napoleon, founding his hopes on "the wonderful natural endowments of the Italians, their intellectual ability, their quickness of apprehension, and capacity for profiting by instruction." But we must remember that it is the solid, and not the showy qualities of mind, which contribute to the successful discharge of the functions of a jury. We cannot conclude without expressing to the author our admiration for the zeal and ability displayed in the production of this most valuable contribution to legal literature—the most complete repertory of information on the subject of jury trial which we possess.

* The scheme of the code was, we understand, submitted for revision to Mr. Jameson, now Sheriff of Aberdeenshire, and materially altered in consequence of suggestions made by him.

JURY TRIAL IN THE DAYS OF EDWARD I.

We have, in another article, given a German view of the advantages and defects of our present system of trial by jury. It may amuse our readers to compare with our modern feelings, the earliest strictures on that "palladium of our liberties" with which we happen to be acquainted. These are contained in an Anglo-Norman ballad, of the reign of Edward I., the author of which seems to have had excellent opportunities of judging of the capacity of the jurymen of his day. It seems to us to be a singularly striking and picturesque expression of individual feeling, and probably of popular feeling also. We extract a translation from the "Janus," a long-forgotten Edinburgh Miscellany, in which the writers are anonymous. But it is known that Wilson and Lockhart were the principal contributors; and it is impossible not to recognise in the ease and fluency, the simplicity and vigour of the following lines, the accomplished hand of the translator of the Spanish ballads:—

TRANSLATION.

'Tis forty pennies that they ask, a ransome fine for me;
And twenty more, 'tis but a score, for my lord sheriff's fee:
Else of his deepest dungeon the darkness I must dree;
Is this of justice, masters?—Behold my case and see.

For this I'll to the greenwood,—to the pleasant shade away;
There evil none of law doth wonne, nor harmful perjury.
I'll to the wood, the pleasant wood, where freely flies the jay;
And, without fail, the nightingale is chaunting of her lay.

But for that cursed *dozen*, God show them small pitie;
Among their lying voices they have indicted me,
Of wicked robberies and other felonie,
That I dare no more, as heretofore, among my friends to be.

In peace and war my service my Lord the King hath ta'en,
In Flanders and in Scotland, and Gascoyne his domain;
But now I'll never, well I wiss, be mounted man again,
To pleasure such a man as this I've spent much time in vain.

But if these cursed *jurors* do not amend them so,
That I to my own country may freely ride and go,

The head that I can come at shall jump when I've my blow,
Their menacings, and all such things, then to the winds I'll throw.

All ye who are indicted, I pray you come to me,
To the green wood, the pleasant wood, where's neither suit nor plea;
But only the wild creatures, and many a spreading tree;
For there's little in the common law but doubt and misery.

If meeting a companion, I show my archery,
My neighbour will be saying, "he's of some company—
He goes to cage him in the wood, and worke his old foleye";
For men will hunt me like the boar, and life's no life for me.

If I should seem more cunning about the law than they,
"Ha! ha! some old conspirator, well train'd in tricks," they'll say;
O wheresoe'er doth ride the Eyre, I must keep well away:—
Such neighbourhood I hold not good, shame fall on such I pray.

I pray you all, good people, to say for me a prayer;
That I in peace may once again to my own land repair:
I never was a homicide, not with my will I swear,
Nor robber, Christian folk to spoil, that on their way did fare.

This rhyme was made within the wood, beneath a broad bay-tree;
There singeth merle and nightingale, and falcon soareth free.
I wrote the skin, because within was much sore memory,
And here I fling it by the wood, that found my rhyme may be

Correspondence.

ACCOMMODATION OF JURORS.

(To the Editor of the Journal of Jurisprudence.)

Sir,—I fear the subject of this letter can hardly be interesting to Students of Jurisprudence, at the same time, if a practical inconvenience to parties engaged gratuitously in the administration of Justice be capable of remedy, I trust you may think it worth while to call public attention to it.

I refer to the accommodation which is provided for Jurymen who are cited to attend the Criminal, and particularly the Circuit Courts of the country. The existing arrangements in civil causes do not seem to afford occasion for remark, and may safely be left under charge of the interests which the parties on both sides have to see to the comfort and convenience of those with whose deliberations they have so much concern. But there is no doubt that the practice in criminal trials is very much in need of amendment. In Edinburgh the evils complained of do not bulk sufficiently to be appreciated, because trials in the High Court of Justiciary seldom extend beyond a single day, and it is comparatively easy to determine when and to what extent the services of Jurymen will be required. But the case is different in large Circuit Towns, where the proceedings continue for several days, and it is impossible for the Court to exercise much indulgence without incurring the serious risk of retarding business, and even of greater evils. That the Judges who attend on Circuit do everything in their power to provide facilities for the convenience of Jurymen is acknowledged. According to the present practice, and we have immediately in view the practice in Glasgow, the one hundred Jurymen who are cited to the Circuit are kept moving from one Court to another, much to their own personal discomfort, and to the interruption of the proceedings, sometimes for as long a period as a week, and not unfrequently for as many as twelve hours in a day. Now for the remedies, 1. Might not one set of Jurymen be cited to serve in one Court, and a different set in the other? A great deal of unnecessary noise and confusion would thereby be avoided. 2. Might not the Jury have a room to themselves besides that in which they are sent to deliberate when empanelled to try a cause? They are the only class of persons connected with the proceedings of the Court who are subjected to the indignity of having no retiring room. The Judges have one—so have the counsel—so have the witnesses. Why should this be so? In a large mercantile community like that of Glasgow the evil assumes a grave aspect. If ampler accommodation than exists at present were provided Jurymen might attend to the more urgent calls of their business in the intervals when they are relieved from attendance in Court; and we have reason to know that this indulgence, which meanwhile is impracticable, would be hailed as a great privilege. Surely those whose valuable time is given gratuitously to the public are deserving of all consideration.—I am, &c., B. A. W.

THE MONTH.

The late Professor A. Montgomerie Bell.—The Legal Profession and the University of Edinburgh have sustained a serious loss in the death of Alexander Montgomerie Bell, Esq., W.S., Professor of Conveyancing, which took place on the 19th of January. The chair which he filled had, when occupied by such men as Macvey Napier, and Allan Menzies, come to be recognised as of high importance in training the legal practitioners of Scotland. To these accomplished lawyers Mr Bell proved no unworthy successor. He was a distinguished student at the University of Glasgow, and retained through life his relish for literary pursuits. Recommended by his well-known ardour in legal study, his skill in conveyancing, matured by long experience, as a partner of one of the leading business firms of Edinburgh, and by his sound judgment, and high sense of honour, he was elected in 1856 by his brethren of the Society of Writers to the Signet, to the vacant Professorship. Having thus obtained, as he used to express it, "the prize of his life," he set himself with the greatest zeal to make his class the means of usefulness he considered it fitted to be—and in his Lectures the principles of the Law of Scotland as applicable to the transfer of property, were expounded with the utmost clearness, and the most anxious care that his students should, in every step of practical business, trace up to the fountain-head of principle the rules on which they were taught to proceed. His lectures, however, were but a part of the teaching afforded to his class; the periodical examinations, in the conduct of which no labour was spared, were considered by his students as a most valuable part of their training.

Hence, too, it was that when in 1861, he was attacked by that disease of the chest, under the effects of which he ultimately succumbed, he was able, though his Lectures were read for him for several Sessions by friends, to keep the command of the class, by adjusting the questions, and revising the examination papers. More recently, his health had been so far regained that he was able, besides attending to business in his chambers, to preside in the class-room, and he continued to do so until within a week before his death. Although, except in the business of his Chair, he avoided coming before the public; he took a lively interest in, and held decided opinions on all public questions. He was, through life, a consistent member of the Liberal party in politics, and was for many years an active and earnest elder of the Free High Church. His premature removal, at the age of 56, will be mourned by a large circle of private friends, to whom he was endeared by the charm of amiable and winning manners, tempering an almost sternsense of the right and just, and by a quiet humour enlivening the sagacious counsels of the man of business.

The Fore-Shore.—We direct the attention of our readers to an interlocutor pronounced by Lord Jerviswoode on the meeting of the Court after the Christmas recess, in the case of the Lord Advocate against Colonel Maclean of Ardgour. The action involves the claim which has recently been advanced by the Crown to a right of property, *jure coronæ*, and as part of its hereditary revenues in the Fore-shore round Scotland, to the extent of what lies between high and low water mark of ordinary spring-tides. The question is an important one, both as regards its public and its private aspects. This has been recognised in its latter bearing by the formation of an association composed of proprietors whose lands are bounded by the sea, who have leagued themselves with the view of resisting and opposing the pretensions of the Crown. Its importance as a public question lies in the fact that a patrimonial right of property is asserted by the Crown, without any reservation of the rights and servitudes which the common law and immemorial usage have given to the public. We do not suppose that any denial is intended by the Crown of the general principle of public trust, applicable to many kinds of Crown property, but it is quite obvious that claims, such as are maintained in this action, may be enforced in such a way as to render the principle quite inoperative, and there is no guarantee that that will not be done. The present case is a good illustration of the danger that may be thus incurred. The claim to the fore-shore, in the case of Colonel Maclean, was asserted by the Crown, on occasion of his proceeding with certain operations with a view to the improvement of his estate. Corran Ferry, a part of the estate of Ardgour, being suitable for the erection of a pier or jetty, Colonel Maclean had obtained leave to make the erection from the Lords Commissioners of the Admiralty. The sanction thus obtained having been communicated to the Crown, the Commissioners of Woods and Forests required Colonel Maclean to take from them a conveyance of the site of the shore requisite for the purpose, and also to pay the expenses of making a survey and a valuation of it. These pretensions having been resisted, the action followed, which Lord Jerviswoode has just decided in favour of Colonel Maclean. As the action is laid, it is quite clear that what the Crown proposes to convey is an absolute right of property. The manner and extent in which the right may be exercised are of course liable to difference, according to the character of the subject. Perhaps as full and extensive a possession as the shore admits of was made out by Colonel Maclean of Ardgour. The Lord Ordinary held that he had proved to have used it along with his predecessors, by the carrying away of stones for the erection and repair of houses and offices, of gravel for the maintenance of the public and private roads on the estate, by the manufacture of kelp, and by the pasturing of his sheep and cattle on the sea ware and the meadows that are frequently found on the west coast between high and low water. Under a Crown conveyance, we presume that Colonel Maclean would be entitled, upon the theory according to which the claim is advanced, to maintain such possession, to the exclusion of the use of every other. But might he so exercise his right of property as to interfere with the uses, through time immemorial, of the public? Could he, for example, make erections on the shore, or take away gravel and stones to such an extent as to prevent or obstruct the public right of passage? We observe that, in Colonel Maclean's pleadings, the uses of the public are expressly reserved, and we repeat that we do not suppose it is contemplated by the Crown to call these in question; yet any breach of them would be seen to be protected by the terms of the proposed conveyance. Whatever is intended, we think it is matter for regret that any uncertainty should prevail in regard to such an important public question.

It is not our practice to comment upon proceedings that are still *sub judice*, and from that practice we do not intend to deviate in the present case. But the claims of the Crown in this direction have recently been pushed to such an extent, and have elicited so much remonstrance, that we consider ourselves quite justified in indicating what is likely to be the public view of the question. The case of Colonel Maclean decides none of the principles of law which are in controversy, and therefore possesses little beyond a personal interest. He holds the estate of Ardgour under a barony title, and the Lord Ordinary has decided that his possession of the shore is to be looked to, to determine the boundaries of the estate, so far as they are in dispute in the present action. His Lordship in short interprets the title by the character and the extent of the possession, and does nothing more. Next to no light is thrown upon what is the precise legal significance of a title of barony.

Considered from the public view, a patrimonial right of property in the shore, vested in the Crown, capable of transmission to a subject with corresponding title of course in the purchaser to make subsequent alienations, certainly appears a somewhat alarming proposition. There is of course no difficulty in understanding this in reference to other kinds of Crown property which are claimed on the same footing as the fore-shore, namely, that it is a *jus regale*. The right to fish for salmon, for example, round the shores, and in the bays and estuaries of Scotland, may be made the subject of a conveyance in a Crown charter, and it is no longer a doubtful question that the Crown is entitled to assert the right just as there is no longer any doubt that it may be exercised without injury to the right of the public to use the sea. But it is quite obvious that no question as to public right can arise in such a case, because the patrimonial right of property and the right of common use do not come into competition, they can be exercised together, and to their full extent. But it is difficult to conceive an alienable right of property in the fore-shore existing side by side of an inalienable right of use in the public. So far at least as the superficial area of the shore is concerned, there is no room for both, or if there is, the patrimonial right must be so inappreciable as not to be worth protection. One of the most important acts of possession proved in the case of Colonel Maclean was the pasturing of sheep and cattle upon the ware, and on sea meadows lying on the shore. But to make that right available, it is necessary that fences should be brought down from the adjoining lands across the shore, and that could not be done without encroaching on the public right of free uninterrupted passage. We do not pronounce on the legal import of the claims thus advanced by the Crown, but it strikingly suggest the proverb, *le jeu ne vaut pas la chandelle.* The common notion in regard to the sea-shore has hitherto been that it belongs to the owner of the adjoining land as part and pertinent of his estate, not so much as an absolute right of property, but as an incidence of natural position, which gives him, in preference to others, an opportunity of operating upon it; and it is difficult to see why so innocent a notion should be disturbed at great cost, while next to nothing is to be gained by it.

The Dunbog Case.—We hope that, in the trial of Elizabeth Edmiston, who was sentenced last month in the High Court of Justiciary to penal servitude for five years, we had, so far at least as the authorities are concerned, the last act enacted in this extremely painful case. Not the least interesting part of the proceedings in the High Court was the simple common-sense way in which the case of the Crown, depending mainly on the self-accusation of the prisoner in open court, was tendered and received without challenge from the bench or bar of its perfect competency and fairness. The supposed severity of the sentence has called forth a considerable expression of public opinion, but we hesitate to say that the complaints are well founded. No doubt allowance is to be made for the excitement that prevailed in the parish, and how far religious excitement will lead people astray, whose conduct is otherwise sober and respectable, does not require to be pointed out in Scotland. And it has always been held a circumstance relevant to infer mitigation of punishment, that an accused party voluntarily takes upon himself the burden of his own crime; and that is specially extenuating in the present case, because suspicion for long attached to other people, and the same charge had already been preferred against another. But it is difficult either to think of or deal lightly with the language of the letters, indicating a ferocity of natural disposition, and an abandonment of human feeling perfectly terrible in the case of a young woman of no ordinary intelligence; and it must not be forgotten that the case was very properly taken in connection with the proceedings at Dunbog, which have been, at one and the same time, a scandal to the country, and the cause of much individual suffering and annoyance.

Proofs by Commission.—We are glad that in at least one influential quarter, this practice is not to be allowed to continue without protest. Attention was again called to the subject by the Lord Justice-Clerk, in a recent case in his division, and though it is probable enough that his Lordship's views are tinged with some bias, born of his proclivities, towards jury trial, there is no doubt that the evils which are growing out of the system involve a serious risk to the interests of the profession. Such a fact as one that has recently transpired, that a proof allowed, in 1861, was not reported till December 1865, is surely too discreditable to admit of the possibility of its repetition. And yet there is no guarantee that such may not be the case if, proofs by commission being continued, the peremptoriness of diets is not to be insisted on, and Commissioners are to be left, without any power of control, in the hands of the parties, and only amenable to their wishes and convenience. Why the practice should be continued at all, we do not understand, and we have repeatedly pointed out a remedy, which, we have no doubt, would be as efficient as it is accessible. Every judge in the Outer House has a blank day; why should this leisure not be utilized, and the Lords Ordinary appointed to take proofs in cases that are not the subject of jury trial,—if not in their own hand, at least under their superintendence. There is not a more common complaint, and it is never heard louder than from the lips of judges themselves, that they are placed at a disadvantage in disposing of a case on evidence by not seeing the witnesses. In their blank days they might have this indulgence. But whether it is regarded as indulgence or not, we are quite satisfied that it ought to be imposed upon them as a duty. For the delays arising out of proofs, not the Court but counsel and agents are responsible. But litigants know little beyond the fact that their cause has been so many years in court, which, accordingly, they regard with some of that asperity of feeling which is vividly expressed (see p. 51) towards a jury in the old days, when they practically combined the functions of witnesses and jury. Alas that there is now no pleasant green wood "where's neither suit nor plea." Somewhat of the strict rules of the Act of Sederunt, which is working such a reform in the Outer House, if applied to proofs, would do much to remedy the evil.

The Sheriff-Substituteship of Aberdeen.—After a long and laborious service, Mr Watson has resigned his office of Sheriff-Substitute of Aberdeen, followed into his retirement by the respect and good wishes of the community whose social improvement he had so unweariedly at heart. No notice of Mr Watson could be esteemed complete or satisfactory that did not acknowledge, in the first place, the untiring industry with which he prosecuted his professional work, and at the same time attended to the multifarious interests which are naturally incidental to so extensive and populous a jurisdiction as the County of Aberdeen. He acquired, early, a very enviable reputation as a social reformer. His name has been identified more particularly with the progress of Ragged Schools, and although differences of opinion exist, and will continue to exist as to the soundness of the principle upon which these schools are based, there is no doubt that to Mr Watson belongs the honour of the idea which led to their original institution. It is not, perhaps, always an advantage that the judge ordinary of so extensive a jurisdiction as Aberdeen should have the social tendencies for which Mr Watson is so honourably known, but it would be unfair to withhold the acknowledgment that few men could have indulged and reconciled them more compatibly than he did with the obligations of his public office. Mr Watson's successor is Mr John Comrie Thomson, advocate, who was called to the bar in 1861. Mr Thomson does not enter upon his new office without familiarity with its duties, having had considerable practice at the bar, and having acted on two occasions in a similar capacity in Edinburgh. These facts obviate the objections that might have been urged to his appointment to so a responsible office, on the ground of his want of standing.

Court of Inquiry into Casualties at Sea.—We are glad to see that this subject, which has been before the public, more or less for the last ten years, has again been made the subject of discussion at a recent meeting, attended chiefly by shipowners and masters of ships, held in London, under the presidency of Mr Crauford, M.P. The subject has interest for the kingdom generally, as the same law is applicable to the three countries. The meeting appears to have been immediately suggested by the proceedings of the Board of Trade, in regard to the loss of the "Duncan Dunbar," and a resolution, preliminary to the business of the meeting, was passed to the effect that the owner of that vessel, having been honourably acquitted, after a lengthened investigation, by a Court of Competent Jurisdiction, of having contributed in any way to the loss of his ship, any subsequent attempt on the part of a public department to reflect on the finding of that Court, or on the evidence on which its conclusions were based, or on the reputation of the accused, is repugnant alike to the principles of natural justice, and the maxims of English law. The meeting was called with the view of expressing dissatisfaction with the manner in which such inquiries are conducted at present, under the assessors of the Board of Trade, who are not skilled to pronounce upon the evidence submitted to them; and it is proposed to substitute in their place a trial by jury, composed of nautical men, who are to return their verdict in the usual way. The resolutions passed at the meeting had special reference to the case of the "Duncan Dunbar," and one expresses the opinion "that the nautical assessors who assist at these Courts of Inquiry should in no case be salaried officials of any department, but that they should be selected by rotation from a list of shipmasters, who have passed examination for competency prescribed by the Board of Trade; and that an appeal should be allowed from the finding of the Court of Inquiry to the High Court of Admiralty, whose decision should be final."

THE

JOURNAL OF JURISPRUDENCE.

CAPITAL PUNISHMENT.

In a previous number of this Journal (September 1865) we took occasion to deal with this subject, in connexion with the trial of Dr. Pritchard; but our remarks extended little further than a notice of a clever *brochure* by M. Alphonse Karr, who combated the views advanced on the other side of the question by M. Jourdain of the *Siècle*. Since then, the subject has been invested with additional interest by the publication of the report of the Commissioners appointed to inquire into the operation of the laws as to capital punishment. That the question is one of vital importance to the interests of the state there can be no doubt. And from whatever point of view it may be looked at, whether as admitting of or requiring much argument, or as placed, as many think, beyond the scope of it, it is equally clear that it would be unsafe to deal with it in any other way than as raising an important, if not a difficult problem, in the science of social economy. We are ourselves inclined to the opinion, that the discredit which, in recent years, has come to attach to the extreme penalty of the law, as a punishment of crime, is due in great measure to that spirit of bastard speculation which is so much in vogue at present, and one of the leading characteristics of which is the exclusion of the facts and the experience of the world. It is impossible to say what mischief has not been brought, by the prevalence of this spirit, to the interests of our country, both at home and abroad. In Jamaica it claims for ruffians of insatiable ferocity, who thirst for blood for its own sake,—who have no other sense but one for the gratification of their own bodily lusts, the same standard of law and privilege that determines the policy of a government ruling over a refined and educated people. At home it shows us the worst villains, who have systematically and with deliberation repressed every trace of human feeling, selfishly indulging their evil passions, and adding the guilt of cowardice to the guilt of crime, the objects of sympathy and commiseration, and, what is worse, guiding the administration of the state towards costly schemes for their reformation or improvement. But hollow as this spirit may be—and it could not be more hollow than it is repulsive—it would be both unsafe and unwise to deny it recognition. It may be that only rank and noxious weeds are born of it; but these may serve to retard the ripening of, if they do not altogether choke the fruits of truth and knowledge.

The report of the Commissioners, we are sorry to say, is anything but satisfactory. In the first place, it appears to us that it is not warranted by the evidence. On the leading question, for example, as to the expediency of maintaining capital punishment as a rule, as a punishment for the crime of murder, it gives forth anything but a certain sound. No doubt for this there is some pretext, in the fact that a number of witnesses were examined before the Commissioners who very unequivocally expressed their opinion that capital punishment should be at once abolished. But no proper sense of the duty that lay upon the Commissioners can rear up this pretext into justification. For it is not the number of witnesses, but the weight of the evidence, that should determine the result, and dictate the terms of the report. It is true that the primary object of the Commission is to collect evidence, and that that is furnished in an appendix in the precise form in which it was taken; but it is also true that the Commissioners were selected from their assumed fitness to guide the evidence, and to pronounce a distinct opinion upon it; and the country and Parliament have reason to complain if that is not done. Now it appears to us that the report does not fairly express the import of the evidence on this question, as showing the state of feeling prevailing in the country, among those who are best qualified to form an opinion, and entitled to be heard upon the subject. For what weight does a sermon by the Rev. Lord Sydney Godolphin Osborne, breathing the air of Exeter Hall, or the observations made by a score of prison chaplains, carry against the deliberate opinion of such men as Lord Cranworth, Lord Wensleydale, the Home Secretary, and the

Solicitor-General of Scotland? We think it admits of no doubt that the evidence given by these witnesses, when fairly read, is favourable—and that in no undecided way—to the continuance of capital punishment upon its present footing. There is certainly evidence on the other side, and evidence which is entitled to weight. But the Commissioners do not appear to have attempted to strike a balance between the opposing arguments; and from that it is not difficult to infer strong predisposition on the part of several of their number.

But the report is still more liable to objection, by reason of the surrender which has been voluntarily made by the Commissioners of the functions which were delegated to them, and from the discharge of which alone could be expected any practical issue to their labours. We are informed that they "forbear to enter into the abstract question of the expediency of abolishing or maintaining capital punishment, on which subjèct differences of opinion exist among them;" and for such forbearance we feel extremely grateful. A disquisition on the principles of eternal justice, by a Parliamentary Commission, might prove edifying, but could scarcely be expected to contain much lively reading. Nobody, however, ever dreamt of entrusting the Commissioners with any such useless duty. It would have been as much to the purpose to ask them to pronounce on the merits of original sin. What was remitted to them was, "to inquire into the provisions and operation of the laws now in force under and by virtue of which the punishment of death may be inflicted upon persons convicted of certain crimes; and also into the manner in which capital sentences are carried into execution." By the terms of their appointment, accordingly, the Commissioners were called upon to deal with capital punishment as a fact, as part of the administration of the law rested upon principle, and sanctioned by practice; and they were asked to say whether, as appeared from the evidence, the people of this country had come to look upon it with disfavour, and it was necessary, in view of the change in public opinion, to change the law; not whether the law itself is in accordance with abstract principles of right and wrong, and with the rules and practice of either the Mosaic or Christian economy. Here, again, in the interpretation of their office, we observe a bias on the part of the Commissioners, and a very marked disinclination to grapple with the practical aspects of the question.

The main features of the report relate to the punishment of murder, and to the form which that punishment should take. The Commissioners are of opinion that it is expedient to alter the present law of murder, and leaving the definition of murder, and the distinction between murder and manslaughter untouched, they propose, in accordance with the plan which is acted upon in several of the United States of America, to divide the crime of murder into two classes or degrees, with the view of confining the punishment of death to the first or higher degree. Their views are embodied in the following propositions and recommendations. (1.) That the punishment of death be retained for all murders deliberately committed with express malice aforethought, such malice to be found as a fact by the jury. (2.) That the punishment of death be also retained for all murders committed in or with a view to the perpetration, or escape after the perpetration, or attempt at perpetration, of any of the following felonies:—murder, arson, rape, burglary, robbery, or piracy. (3) That in all other cases of murder, the punishment be penal servitude for life, or for any period not less than seven years, at the discretion of the court. The punishment of murder so retained, the Commissioners recommend should be carried out by private executions within the precincts of the prison.

Although professing themselves not called upon to deal, by the terms of their appointment, with the subject of infanticide, the Commissioners recommend that an Act should be passed, making it an offence, punishable with penal servitude or imprisonment, at the discretion of the Court, unlawfully and maliciously to inflict grievous bodily harm, or serious injury upon a child during its birth, or within seven days afterwards, in case such child has subsequently died, and that no proof that the child was completely born alive should be required. With respect to the offence of concealment of pregnancy, they are of opinion that no person should be liable to be convicted of said offence upon an indictment for murder, but should be tried upon a separate indictment. The Commissioners also recommend that a practice formerly prevailing in England, but having no application to Scotland, the power on the part of the Judge of recording sentence of death, should be revived. This is a provision intended to meet the case of a Judge who considers that the punishment of death should not be awarded, although the jury have found a verdict of guilty, and will exert himself to see that it is not carried out. It is thought, and seemingly with great justice, that in dealing with the important issues of life and death, such a useless formality as pronouncing a sentence which is not to be executed, would be well dispensed with. Prefixed to the report of the Commissioners is a summary of the evidence, under different heads, which will be found useful for reference, and is carefully and skilfully prepared.

The most important subject, undoubtedly, for both countries, with which the commission deals, is the relation of capital punishment to the crime of murder. The proposed changes, however, would have a greater effect on the state of the law in Scotland than in England. For the distinction which is proposed by the Commissioners between murder with and murder without premeditation, has, in recent years been gaining ground, with our neighbours across the Tweed. It has, of course, always existed among ourselves, and any system of law would be barbarous without it. But our recognition of it is placed upon a different footing from that which has latterly prevailed in England, and is now proposed by the Commissioners. With us it has always been a question of fact with the jury, not a rule of law to be laid down by the judge. The underlying principle from which the law starts is of course the same in both countries—that is, that no person shall be found guilty of the crime of murder unless there is malice proved against him, or an intention to kill, or to do that which results in death. The difference lies in the manner in which the fact is ascertained. In Scotland, the definition of murder is general, and the malice express or implied,—a necessary element in the crime of murder,—arises upon the facts that are laid before the jury. According to the scheme of the Commissioners, the definition is to be particular, and the jury are to be limited in their consideration of the facts to the effect of arriving at a finding that accords with the strictness and the exclusiveness of a legal principle. We must confess to a very decided preference for our own system. For it admits within the scope of the law the infinite variety of fact that lies on the debateable ground betwen murder properly so called, about which no person has any doubt, and those cases which, in England, fall under the category of manslaughter, and in Scotland, of culpable homicide. To determine by the application of an unbending principle of law, when homicide shall be visited by the punishment of death, and when the punishment shall be only arbitrary, is a practical impossibility, or if practicable, is only so at the risk of introducing inequality of punishments, and therefore operating injustice. In the scheme of the Commissioners, malice aforethought constitutes an essential element of the crime of murder, and is to be ascertained as a fact by the jury. But it is quite obvious that malice may be in a culprit's mind, and yet there is no way in which it can be legally evidenced, or evidenced in any other way than as surmise. In that case the jury could not find the fact, or if they did, they would be applying to it a standard by which they did not judge of the other facts of the case. And yet, is there any doubt that, in a great number of cases, where malice cannot be directly proved, it is there, notwithstanding, in all its force and virulence, and that the common mind has no difficulty in inferring it? By resorting to a positive and unbending definition—and if any change is to be introduced, it must be made so—the Commissioners incur the risk of withdrawing from its operation many cases that, according to their own view of the principle, clearly fall within the scope of it. For if malice aforethought is to be found as a fact necessarily precedent to a conviction for the crime of murder, is it not certain that juries will require proof of it by facts antecedent to the *res gestæ* of the crime under investigation, or if they infer it, as we assume is consistent with the Commissioners' scheme, they will only do so when it stares them in the face and is unavoidable? The Commissioners do not deny that every murder dictated by malice should be punished by death, but the manner in which they propose to ascertain malice is so narrow and ineffective that we do not hesitate to say that, in nine out of ten cases it would not be detected, and in the tenth case it might exist in the least degree of all.

We do not, of course, as we have already said, suppose that the commissioners intend to limit the proof of malice aforethought to facts and circumstances antecedent to the act which grounds the charge of murder. Our object simply is to show that by adopting a peremptory definition they run the risk of including a number of cases which *ex concessis* are to be esteemed as murder, and which, as appears from the report, they are anxious to distinguish from another branch of crime. But to their proposal to suppress the distinction between express and implied malice—and the latter term is here used in a different sense from that in which we have just considered it—we cannot assent, and we have no doubt whatever that it will be generally pronounced o be at variance with at least the genius of the law of Scotland. Direct proof of malice, of course, is always the most satisfactory, and it is always, and most properly, anxiously looked for; but the law admits at the same time of malice being inferred from the character of the act done and from the circumstances which attend it. Accordingly, a prisoner who has voluntarily debauched and debased his moral character to such an extent that he is incapable of self-control, and, yielding to his evil passions, assaults another with such ferocity that death ensues, is, in the eye of the law worthy of capital punishment just as much as the man who has deliberately planned and compassed the life of his victim. That is undoubtedly the law of Scotland, and we have reason to believe that it has worked well and to the satisfaction of the people; and moreover, that a very general impression prevails that in the presence of other predispositions towards fierce and unruly passions it is not desirable to abate the rigour of the law. And according to abstract principle, of which the commissioners are so shy, we think there is no room for the distinction, because it is a very narrow view indeed of the doctrine of punishment to suppose that it is upon the act itself, or on its immediate accessories alone, that the vials of the law's wrath are poured. No doubt the shock to the public mind is greater—the elements of crime that are cognisable by the law bulk more largely in view in the case of a deliberate poisoner than of a besotted brutal ruffian. But is the law not to take account of the voluntary surrender which the latter has made of the hold which he once had upon his moral purpose? We see little difference in the cases beyond what might be produced by the lapse of time operating upon different degrees of coarseness and depravity. We are very far indeed from saying that there is not in many cases an appreciable difference between the two classes or gradations of crime that are now before us. But we believe that its recognition would be more safely left to the touchstone of facts operating on the minds of jurymen, who are naturally disposed towards merciful views where these are possible, and by whom the popular distinction between deliberate and involuntary crime is anything but ignored.

That the scheme of the commissioners wears a certain logical aspect may be conceded, and it may be conceded also that wherever the exposition of the law under fixed and determinate rules is practicable, logical methods should be resorted to; but the practical operation of our own system has proved so beneficial that we should regret to see any change in the present law of murder, so far at least as Scotland is concerned. Experience has amply shewn that juries will take into their own hands to say, even against the ruling of judges, what degrees of murder shall receive the punishment of death; and we have more confidence in the common sense, and in the sense of justice of a jury, than in the sufficiency of any definition or rule of law to determine a safe and consistent practice.

It does not seem necessary, in dealing with the report of the commissioners, to consider the arguments that are in common use for or against on the question of the expediency of retaining capital punishment. It is impossible to read the evidence annexed to the report without seeing that several members of the commission would very gladly have availed themselves of any pretext for recommending its total abolition. And one is surprised and must lament to see such names as Sir Fitzroy Kelly, Mr Justice Shee, and Mr Lawson, the Attorney-General of Ireland, cited in favour of this view. But the commissioners have not seen their way to ground any recommendation upon these exceptional opinions; and agreeing as we do with Mr Baron Bramwell that the question is withdrawn from argument, we shall not now pause over its discussion. The bulk of the evidence is clear to the effect that punishment by death is a greater deterrent to crime than any other, and in view of these materials for arriving at a safe and satisfactory judgment, it is useless to indulge in social theories or abstract considerations of the principles of right and wrong. Murder is the greatest crime that can be committed against society, and if it be the fact that the law has already ascertained the best means for its prevention or repression, it is needless to go a step further in the controversy. Nothing will permanently continue to promote the interests of the state that is not in itself morally and socially right; and accordingly, when we are told by Lord Cranworth, Mr. Baron Martin, Sir George Grey, and all the Justiciary Judges of Scotland, that so far as their experience and observation go, punishment by death has more influence than any other in exciting a dread of crime, it is quite vain to talk platitudes about the inviolability and sacredness of human life. In the state of the evidence, as we have already said, we feel that there is no call upon us to argue the question. But it is clear that there is one great fallacy underlying the views of those who preach the doctrine of abolition, and that is the erection of the measure or extent of punishment as the criterion which determines the criminal population towards crime, or its avoidance. A man commits theft, or robbery, or murder because his nature is depraved, and the transgression of the law is the natural result of his corruptness; and considerations of future punishment have very little weight except in the earlier stages of vice and crime. And accordingly, the true remedy for crime is to be found, not in the substitution of one form of punishment for another, but in the education and the enlightenment of the people.

It seems to have been desired by some of the commissioners that the opinion of some of the lower orders, of such classes as are generally found haunting the places of public execution should have been obtained in order to decide whether the deterring influence of capital punishment is appreciated by those to whose condition it is generally applied. We must confess ourselves somewhat amused by this fastidiousness. We are not Utopian enough to anticipate any form of human society where people shall not exist that are only moved by considerations of physical restraint, and we require no assurance that the gibbet and its hideous accessories is a solemn fact, teaching far more instructive lessons than any other example that civil policy has yet devised.

It does not appear that the report is liable to the same objections which we have stated against other parts of it, in so far as it recommends that executions should hereafter be carried out in private. There seems to be a considerable amount of evidence justifying this proposal. We are glad to see that in the opinion returned by the seven criminal judges of Scotland a very decided view is expressed in favour of the present system; and we observe, appended to the report of the commissioners, a declaration, moved by the Lord Advocate, and signed by four other members, refusing assent to the views of the commissioners. The simple question in dispute here is, whether more harm is caused by the degrading influences of a public execution, than good is done by the terror which it inspires in those who witness it. And we fear that the question does not admit of any other appeal than to one's own consciousness and conviction. It certainly never can be reduced into a simple question of evidence. The case presents a mere balance of probabilities, in deciding between which we must be guided by our knowledge of human nature and our experience of life, and of the world. According to our thinking it is perfectly idle to talk of corrupting influences as applicable to classes and conditions of society that have already reached the lowest stage of degradation, who are at open war with all law and order, and must be taught submission to it in a manner which they can understand. And it seems to us equally clear that the mere reading or hearing from others that the vengeance of the law was satisfied would have little weight in comparison with the personal witnessing of the ghastly method of its execution. The former implies a certain amount of imagination, and a power of conception which it would be very unsafe for the law to give the British ruffian credit for.

It is to be regretted that the commissioners have not felt it to be their duty to deal with the subject of infanticide more comprehensively than they have done. In pointing and objecting to the requirement of the law, that there shall be positive proof that the child has been completely born alive before the crime can be held to be established, they shew that they have reached the very heart of the question.

Our law has of late exhibited a very marked and wholesome tendency to abate the stringency of this very hazardous, if somewhat logical theory; but it is quite obvious that unless the law is immediately and expressly placed upon a different footing, but little will be gained in the way of mitigating an evil which is beginning to wear a very grave social aspect. So far as the recommendations of the commissioners go, they appear to us to be entitled to approbation. No doubt it will always be a difficult problem to determine in the period of the progress of birth when injuries have been wilfully caused, and when they are due to natural causes; but that is an evil incident to the situation, and is unavoidable. It would be a great matter to get rid of the theory that the law shall regard nothing as crime until the child has acquired the character of *persona*, by reason of its complete separation from the mother. Every person who is acquainted with the practice of our criminal courts is well aware that that is the great obstacle in the way of conviction for the crime of child-murder; and it is an obstacle which is felt in nine out of ten cases to operate to the scandal of justice, and to the peril of the best interests of society. But our regret that the commissioners have not more fully investigated the subject does not arise from the feeling that much can be done in the way of finding remedies within the compass of the law itself. For the check to be devised for the growing prevalence of infanticide appears to us to be fully as much of a social as of a legal problem. The law has been administered, at different stages of its history, with stringency, and with laxness; and statistics have never at any time exhibited any appreciable decrease in the extent of the crime. The evil has struck its roots deep into the hollowness which surrounds many of our social and domestic relations, and much will require to be done in the way of clearing and paving the way by diffusing sound moral instruction before satisfactory results, or results of any other kind than we have already, can be expected.

THE LAW OF HYPOTHEC.

THE Report of the Royal Commission on the Law relating to the Landlord's Right of Hypothec has now been before the public for some months, and the Lord Advocate has announced in his place in parliament that a bill will be introduced for the amendment of the law, in conformity with the recommendations of the Commissioners. It may not be improper to lay before our readers at this time a few observations on a subject of considerable public importance and interest, without prejudice to our returning to it, should it seem necessary, when the bill has been introduced.

The history of the objections to the present law is not without interest. Lord Kames (Elucidations, Art. 10) finds fault with the principle according to which the hypothec on the crop "is sustained for the rent only of that precise year of which it is the product." In the case of rents payable beforehand (by which he seems to mean rents payable six months before the legal terms, and not merely before a crop has been reaped), he complains that the landlord cannot use his hypothec for a year after his rent becomes due. The tenant however suffered in his view a far more serious inconvenience where the terms of payment were late. At Candlemas 1760, for instance, he must have as much of the crop on hand as to satisfy a year's rent, viz., the rent of 1759; and as much even at Lammas 1760, as to satisfy half a year's rent.

"A hardship more intolerable," he proceeds, "cannot well be figured: it is by the sale of corn that the tenant procures money for paying his rent;

and yet the hypothec so interpreted, instead of promoting payment, is the very thing that retards it. Consider the thing in a different view. Late terms of payment are intended to favour the tenant, that he may have full time to procure money for paying his rent; and yet, according to the effect given to the hypothec, he gets not a moment's delay; or, which comes to the same, he has no benefit by the delay. I would not, however, be understood to plead for a hypothec on corn, equally permanent with that on cattle. . . . . With respect to any single crop, it is sufficient that it be hypothecated for the rent of a single year; a new crop will succeed, to be a security for the next year's rent. And if corn is to be hypothecated for a single year's rent only, it ought to be the half-year's rent that is current when the corns are reaped, and the half-year's rent immediately preceding. By that plan, the hypothec is as little oppressive as possible to the tenant; and no less beneficial to the landlord, than if any other year's rent were secured by it.

"The hypothec under consideration, whether affecting corn or cattle, is, in its nature, so singular, as to create a doubt, whether such a legal conception of it can be formed, as to account for all its avowed consequences. It is admitted, that a hypothec upon the cattle, bars not the tenant from aliening any particular horse, ox, or sheep, or even quantities of them; provided sufficiency be left for the hypothec. It follows clearly, that no individual is hypothecated; and yet, upon that supposition, it is difficult to conceive that the whole stock or herd can be hypothecated. To avoid that difficulty, one is led to think, that there is no hypothec here in a proper sense; but only a preference given to the landlord before the tenant's other creditors, not as having any real right, but upon equitable considerations; a preference *inter chirographarios*, as termed in the Roman law. But in avoiding *Scylla*, we are driven upon *Charibdis*. If the hypothec be reduced to a preference *inter chirographarios*, it cannot affect *bona fide* purchasers for a valuable consideration; which however it does by established practice. In short, this hypothec seems not easily reducible to just principles."

The subject seems to have attracted little attention after this, until the case of *Dalhousie* v. *Dunlop & Co.* in 1828 and 1830 (6 S. 626, and 4 W. & S. 420), in which it was decided that a *bona fide* purchaser of grain, which has been delivered and paid for, is liable to the landlord in second payment of the price where the rent of that crop has not been paid, and that even when the purchase has been made in public market by sample. We have never been able to see that the Courts were tied down by previous decisions or authorities to this distinction between a sale by sample in public market, and a sale by bulk in public market. The old cases do not make such a distinction, and the only grounds for it seem to be that at the time when the privilege of public market was established in favour of commerce, all sales were in bulk; and that the English rule of market overt in respect to stolen goods applies only to sale by bulk. The law, however, was so fixed in favour of the landlord's right to follow (droit de suite); and a considerable desire for a change of the law in this respect seems to have been felt by certain parties for some years after. That desire, however, was not so strong as to produce any effect. Lord Brougham, who was at first disposed to reverse the judgment of the Court of Session, and expressed himself in his opinion very strongly as to the inexpediency of a doctrine "so greatly tending to fetter commerce,"—prepared a bill with the view of protecting the interests of *bona fide* purchasers, which was withdrawn because it did not receive adequate support in Scotland. This was the case with a bill brought into the House of Lords by Lord Belhaven in 1834; with one proposed shortly after in the House of Commons by Mr. Gillon, M.P. for Linlithgowshire, and also with one introduced in 1836 by Mr. Chalmers, M.P. for Montrose. Again, in 1850, Lord Brougham introduced a bill "for the removal of obstructions in the corn trade" in Scotland. This bill called forth an adverse report from the Society of Writers to the Signet, and it was withdrawn. The same fate befell a subsequent bill introduced by the same indefatigable reformer. These efforts seem to have been directed merely to remedy the inconveniences and injustice arising from the landlord's right to recover in the hands of a *bona fide* purchaser the crop of a year for which the rent is unpaid, or its price. Yet it cannot be said that they proved altogether fruitless; for, in the recent inquiry, the opinions of all classes of witnesses in favour of abolishing this part of the law were almost unanimous.*

The case of *Barns* v. *Allan* (June 1, 1864, 2 Macph. 1119), in which it was held that grain could be followed even when converted into meal, and that a sale in a meal-dealer's shop is not a sale in open market, inaugurated (as our readers are aware), the latest movement against the landlord's hypothec. This movement resulted in the report and evidence now before us. The recent controversy involves far larger issues than those which preceded it, for questions are raised not merely as to the obstruction to the corn trade occasioned by the right to follow grain, but also as to the justice and expediency of the landlord's privilege in general. As there are no longer (with the exceptions we have indicated) any who oppose the abrogation of the rule estab-

* Only Mr. Hare, Mr. Melville, W.S., Colonel Graham, and Colonel M'Inroy, expressed opinions in favour of retaining it.

lished by *Dalhousie* v. *Dunlop*, and *Barns* v. *Allan*, we propose to confine our remarks to the more general aspects of the question. And we must premise, that the inquiry has been conducted, upon the whole, in a satisfactory manner, and that the report itself is distinguished for terseness and perspicuity beyond most other productions of the same kind. On the whole, the Commissioners are justified in their opinion, that "the information laid before them has been very complete, and is exhaustive of the subject."

It may be said, that those who seek the removal or modification of an existing institution such as the landlords' hypothec, must take the burden of proving that it is either unjust or inexpedient. We doubt whether this rule is in all cases correct. May it not be said with equal truth, that this preference is opposed, *prima facie*, to the principles of commercial law and the tendency of all recent legislation, that such privileges have of late been giving way before new principles of political economy, and that the presumption which is now established in favour of the freedom of commercial contracts, and against all class privileges, lays the onus on the defenders of the hypothec? On the question of free-trade this is not perhaps the place to speak; but we may be allowed to examine the landlord's right of hypothec as it stands in connection with the general policy of the law.

The Commissioners say, "there can be no doubt that the law of Scotland on this subject is derived from the law of Rome," (Rep. p. vii). It is right to inquire a little more narrowly than they have done how this portion of the law of Rome was transferred into our system. The doctrine of the civil law relating to tacit or legal hypothecs has not been regarded as the happiest of its bequests to modern jurisprudence. In most European countries, even in those where that system has been most reverently cherished, modern legislation has left little of the Roman law of *Hypothecæ* except the name. The older law of Germany, and other continental laws, tended in this direction, by excluding conventional hypothecs over corporeal moveables, and allowing such securities to be constituted, as in our law, only by actual tradition (*Faustpfand, Pignus* *); while the feudal notions of

* "Pignus appellatum est a pugno, quia res quae pignori dantur, manu traduntur." Gaius in Dig. 50, 16, 238, s. 2 (*de verb sig.*) Of course we do not adopt the etymology of Gaius, though that of the German equivalent of *Pignus* might seem to lend it some countenance.

land tenure have necessarily altered the conception and details of the system of mortgages (*Hypotheken*). A German would now define *Hypothek* as that right of pledge which a creditor obtains in an immoveable thing belonging to his debtor by an entry in a public register, thus altogether dissociating the word from its original connection with chattels. Our law very early exhibited a repugnance to conventional hypothecation of moveables (Balfour's Practicks, p. 194); and Lord Stair, after referring to the numerous tacit hypothecs of the Roman law, says—"But our custom hath taken away express hypothecations of the debtor's goods, without delivery, and of the tacit legal hypothecations hath only allowed a few, allowing ordinarily parties to be preferred according to the priority of their legal diligence, that commerce may be the more sure, and every one may more easily know his condition with whom he contracts." (Stair i. 13, 14; comp. iv. 25, 1). A comparison of our tacit hypothecs with the list of real and spurious tacit hypothecs given in writers on Roman law, sufficiently shows the tendency to discourage such preferences, except in a few cases which the law has considered as peculiarly entitled to favour. Reference may be made to the cases of *Hamilton* v. *Wood*, 1788, M. 6269, Hailes 1039, aff. 3 Pat. 148; *Wood & Co.* v. *Weir's Crs.*, 1 Bell's Com. 527, n. 3, as to hypothec on ships for repairs in home ports; *Maxwell* v. *Wardroper*, 1726, Mor. 6266, as to hypothecs on ships for cost of building; *Cushney* v. *Christie*, 1676. Mor. 6237, and *Muirhead* v. *Drummond*, 1792, 2 Bell's Com. 28, as to the hypothec for the price over goods sold; *Maclellan's Crs.* v. *Burns*, 1735, Mor. 6240, *Johnston* v. *Warden*, 1778, 5 B. S. 478, as to hypothec of workmen over a house for repairs executed on it, &c.

There is a considerable analogy between the landlord's hypothec and the maritime hypothecs, both tacit and conventional —these are derived from the general law-merchant, and exist only in favour of those without whose aid the ship could not have accomplished its voyage, or even been in a condition to put to sea and earn freight. The landlord's hypothec is in favour of him without whose consent the crop could never have been sown, the fruits of which it is sought by the opponents of the law to make available for the general creditors of the farmer. The term writer's hypothec, is a mere misnomer as regards the claim found on the possession of title-deeds, which is a mere right of retention. The law-agent's hypothec, meaning thereby the security which he has over the expenses found due to his client in a litigation which he has himself conducted, is a peculiar and anomalous right over a fund called into existence by the agent's own exertions. This can afford no illustration on either side of the present argument.* The landlord's right of hypothec seems to have been first firmly established on its present footing by judicial decisions in the early part of the seventeenth century, as a surrogate for that absolute property of "the master of the ground" in the fruits, which was then gradually becoming a mere theory. Nothing in the history of Scotland is more worthy of attention than the very slow process by which tenants were emancipated first from actual bondage, and then from entire subserviency to the landlord, and dependence on his favour. For the history of the first stages of this process few materials remain; but its various steps are sketched with sufficient probability by Lord Kames, both in his *Law Tracts* (Tr. iv. p. 162, foll., 4th edit.) and *Elucidations* (Art. 10., p. 70, edit. 1800). At first, and even after the system of cultivation by bondsmen had ceased, the landlord seems to have had every right of a proprietor in the fruits of the ground. Each successive step in the progress of improvement lessened this right, and to a corresponding extent conferred a right of property or quasi property on the cultivator. Yet, even after the statutes of 1449 and 1469, which, by making his right real, constituted the tenant's charter, his property in the fruits was far from being exclusive or absolute. Even Erskine, on the principle of the Roman law, says, that all growing fruits belong truly to the proprietor of the ground, and become the tenant's only by reaping; and for many years, as in England to this day, the law of distress was the natural consequence of the landlord's property in the fruits to the extent of his tack-duty. It was probably growing partiality for the civil law, and the endeavour after what was considered a more learned, or a

* Mr Dalziel's argument in favour of the landlord's hypothec from the analogy of mercantile *liens*, or *rights* of *retention* (Evid. p. 228) is altogether irrelevant. There seems to be no such analogy. The policy of the law is summed up in the maxim, that possession infers property in moveables (Bell's Com. ii. 22, &c.) Hypothecs are exceptions to that principle, or limitations or infringements of it; while lien is an extension of it. Retention is a right in security over a moveable which "depends on possession, and expires with the loss of it." (Ibid.) Hypothec is a right in security over a movable which, contrary to principle, is permitted without possession. The one is just the reverse of the other. The one is introduced for the convenience of commerce; the other is, in the ordinary case, proscribed as unfavourable to com-

more philosophical expression of the legal institution, which caused the development of the old law of distress into the landlord's hypothec and sequestration.

Various causes have been assigned for the retension in our early law of the landlord's claim upon the fruits beyond what is easily reconcilable with the exercise of the rights which even then an occupier was held to possess. But the necessity of providing the landlord with a stringent and effectual security for his rent, is plainly seen in an institution, of which the name at least survives in our books, and which, we cannot but think, was one of the most powerful motives to the judicial construction of the hypothec to which we have referred. For centuries after tenants became freemen, their condition was so depressed, the capital at their command was so scanty, that few could supply the seed, cattle, and implements necessary for the cultivation of the ground. This the landlord did by way of steelbow; a contract which put tenants in a position similar to that of *métayers*, but with this difference, that a fixed rent was often paid for the use of the steelbow goods, instead of a fixed proportion of the produce. It was not only natural, but most just and expedient in the state of society in which this custom prevailed, that very ample security should be provided in favour of the "master;" and indeed we cannot but consider its existence a very sufficient warrant for the introduction or continuance of the landlord's hypothec. The contract of steelbow was somewhat peculiar, and lawyers used to have difficulty in deciding whether it was a species of *mutuum* (*Ersk.* iii. 1, 18) or a location. Neither was it fixed without hesitation that the steelbow goods became the tenant's property during the lease, nor could it have been so settled but for the hypothec by which the owner was secured (*Ersk. l.v., Bankt.* i. 12, 2, *Mor. Dict. voce* Steilbow). Indeed, the property of the tenant was subject to limitations other than the hypothec; for it was found very early that steelbow goods fell under the master's single escheat (*Boyd* v. *Russel*, 1609, Mor. 5386) and went to the donatar, and not to the executors of the heritor, though he died before the ish of the tack (*Lawson* v. *L. Boghall*, 1628, Mor. 14778). So late as 1764 it was held, though with much division of opinion,* that steelbow could not be affected by the

* Lord Kames, contending that it was let in assedation as much as the lands, and could not but be the landlord's property, and others thinking that it was the property of the tenant, who had the free use and power of disposing of it.

diligence of the tenant's creditors in prejudice of the master (*Macvicar* v. *Butler*, 5 B.S. 897. Mor. 6208). This decision shows the intimate connection in principle between steelbow and hypothec; for although it appears that the landlord claimed no hypothec in the ordinary sense, it seems to have been thought that in the last year of the tack, when steelbow fell to be restored, "it was to be considered as rent for which the master had an hypothec over all the goods on the farm." (Comp. Bell's Princ. 1264).

We have entered thus fully on the subject of steelbow, because it illustrates the state of society in which the landlord's hypothec took its shape, and because we cannot but hold it to have been itself one of the considerations which fixed the nature of that privilege. It must be granted by the most violent opponents of the existing law, that in times past hypothec was eminently beneficial, indeed indispensable to the well-being of the country. But it by no means follows of course that it is so now, when the governing principle of contracts relating to agriculture has within a few generations been entirely changed. Mr. Mill points out, that in early states of society "all transactions and engagements are under the influence of fixed customs. . . . . Rights thus originating (*i. e.* in custom), and not competition in any shape, determine, in a rude state of society, the share of the produce enjoyed by those who produce it. The relations, more especially, between the landowner and the cultivator, and the payments made by the latter to the former, are, in all states of society but the most modern, determined by the custom of the country. Never, until late times, have the conditions of the occupancy of land been (as a general rule) an affair of competition" (*Mill's Political Economy*, B. II., ch. iv., vol. i. p. 293). The question which has to be decided on the evidence laid before the late Royal Commission is, whether circumstances are so changed by this alteration of the governing principle of contracts for occupancy of land, or, in other words, by the increase of capital and civilization, as to require the abolition or modification of the law of landlord's hypothec, which was admittedly beneficial in a ruder age?

It would serve no good purpose to analyse minutely evidence which has been so fully before the public, much of which on both sides is unavoidably mere reiteration of the same arguments and opinions, and which has already been so ably, and upon the whole, so fairly summed up in the report of the Commissioners. The result of its perusal is to confirm the opinion expressed in this journal (*ante* vol. viii. p. 395), before the commencement of the inquiry, that the law of landlord's hypothec, as it now exists, is decidedly injurious in its working. At the same time, however, we concur with the Commissioners in thinking that its repeal "would certainly be followed by alterations in the tenancy of land in Scotland," which would seriously affect the condition of the poorer tenantry in many parts of the country. How far any permanent injury would arise to the valuable class of small farmers, may be doubted; indeed it may be argued that they would in the long run reap as great benefit from a modification of the law as any. We think that the apprehension of danger on this side is exaggerated, just as the expectation of advantage to the larger farmers is exaggerated on the other side. We cannot help thinking that if the law were injurious to the tenant with capital to the extent alleged, we should have found back-hand rent more rare in practice, and the hypothec and its evils lessened in range. Upon the whole, the powerful opposition which the proposal of a larger change would necessarily excite, and the darkness in which its consequences are involved, lead us to the conclusion that we should not for the present aim at more than the improvements suggested by the Commissioners. These are—1. Protection of all *bona-fide* sales of grain delivered and paid for. 2. The limitation of the landlord's right to sequestrate to a period of three months after each half-yearly portion of rent becomes due. 3. The registration of all sequestrations. They also propose to declare, that stock belonging to another, and taken in to be grazed or fed, shall only be liable to the amount of the consideration agreed to be paid to the tenant; and that no sequestration for the rent of an agricultural subject shall extend to household furniture or agricultural implements; or to imported manure, lime, tiles, or feeding-stuffs brought upon the ground, but not incorporated with the soil, consumed, or otherwise applied to the purposes for which they have been procured.

LAW STUDIES.

No. I.—The Moral Sciences' Tripos Examination at Cambridge.

Probably the greatest defect in the education of the higher classes in this country, hitherto, has consisted in the absence of any proper connecting links between studies which are merely learned and abstract, and those which have reference to the business of life. Both have been conducted with energy and zeal. There has been no sparing of time, labour, or money on either. Both have been conducted successfully, too, in so far as success was possible whilst they were prosecuted apart. We have made good scholars, and mathematicians, and occasionally even metaphysicians; and we have made hard-headed practising lawyers, and hard-working committee-men, and secretaries of state. Nor has it been rare for the two characters to be combined in the same individual. We have had scholars and philosophers who were lawyers and statesmen; and we have had statesmen and lawyers who were philosophers and scholars. Those who have attained to the highest eminence in either department have frequently excelled in both; and as regarded them, that the strength which they derived from the vigorous exercises in which they had engaged in the one sphere, served to guide and sustain their labours in the other, was no secret either to themselves or to the rest of the world. Every judgment which Lord Stowell pronounced in the Court of Admiralty, bore the plainest traces not of the knowledge only which he acquired, but of the habits of thought which he formed, during the days when he was a college tutor at Oxford. Had Lord Stair not been a professor of philosophy, it is scarcely probable that he would have been the author of the only really philosophical treatise on the municipal law of Scotland that adorns our legal literature. Burke and Pitt were statesmen and scholars. Sir George Lewis was a scholar and a statesman. Lord Macaulay and Mr. Gladstone alternately exhibit the one character and the other in more prominent relief; yet both are indissolubly entwined in all that either of them has written or said. Such instances as these might be greatly multiplied; but however numerous, they are still exceptional, and they have depended on personal characteristics which developed themselves in later life, far more than on educational training.

In the case of the normal Englishman, his learned and practical life have been wholly apart; and in the vast majority of instances the one has terminated when the other began. Once a Bachelor or Master of Arts of a reputable University (unless he embraced a college life), the prestige of belonging to the class of persons who have received the highest instruction has satisfied his ambition; and he has applied himself to his professional studies, or to the practical duties which his position as a member of society imposed on him, as if his degree, and the academical studies which led to it, had no more bearing on the occupations of his life than his coat of arms. If the learned tastes which he has acquired should prove too strong to be separated from his personal character, he indulges them in his leisure hours, and keeps up his scholarly acquirements as mere accomplishments. In the discharge of his duties as a professional man, a citizen, or a man of the world, they afford him no more direct or conscious aid than the habit of sketching which he may have acquired during an autumn residence in Switzerland, or the taste for the sonatas of Beethoven and the symphonies of Mozart, which his wife's piano may have engendered. Nor is this by any means entirely the result of a trivial and commonplace mind. That those whose speculative faculties are of a high order will find their own way from the abstract dogmas of science to the concrete maxims by which practice is governed, from the experience of the past to the rules which are to guide the present, is unquestionable. We have mentioned instances of men who have done so; and such instances, more or less conspicuous, we may hope will recur. But such is not the common case. To the vast majority, even of those who are capable of performing the journey, the way must be shown. If the seed so laboriously implanted during the first twenty years of their lives is really to sustain and enrich them with its fruits, the reaper's art must be taught them. The scattered and conflicting lessons of history must be gathered, harmonised, and built up for them into the sciences of politics and political economy; ethics must be exhibited as the basis of jurisprudence; even the abstracter processes of thought, through which they have been dragged as students of logic and metaphysics, must be exhibited in their bearings on the problems, possible and impossible, of human life and destiny.

The defect which we have here indicated appears at last to have been discovered; and, what is more to the purpose, very effectual means adopted for supplying it, in one at least of the great English universities. We refer to the regulations for the moral sciences tripos, adopted by the Senate of the University of Cambridge in 1860. According to these regulations all students who shall pass with credit the examination in the subjects which we are about to enumerate, are entitled to admission to the degree of Bachelor of Arts; but it is provided, that with the exception of candidates for degrees *jure natalium*, no student be admitted to this examination who has not passed the examination in additional mathematical subjects of the previous examination. This condition being satisfied, all students, without farther reference to what have hitherto been regarded as the special studies of the university, may proceed to an examination, which is thus characterised—"The subjects for examination shall be considered to form two groups, the one embracing (1) Moral philosophy; (2) Mental philosophy; (3) Logic;—the other group, (4) History, and political philosophy; (5) Political economy; (6) Jurisprudence. Eleven out of the twelve papers shall contain an equal number of questions from either group, and the twelfth paper shall contain questions in the history of philosophy. The questions shall be in part of a special kind, having reference to *books* on the subjects; and in part of a general kind, having reference to the subjects themselves. These latter questions may take the form of theses for essays. It shall be the duty of the Board to mark out lines of study in the several subjects before mentioned, and to publish a list of books in relation to which questions shall be set; modifying the same from time to time as occasion may require. *If a candidate wish to confine his attention to two subjects, he shall not be thereby precluded from obtaining a place in the first class.* Candidates who may be thought worthy of honours are to be arranged in each class in the order of merit."

This very extensive and complete examination extends over no less than six days, the hours of attendance being from 9 to 12 in the morning, and from 1 to 4 in the afternoon. Lists of authors and books are prescribed "for the purpose of marking the general course which the examination is to take in the several subjects." But though the Board recommends that in the examinations questions be proposed having reference to the books in these lists, it is provided that opportunity shall be given to the candidates to show a knowledge of other works, both ancient and recent, in which the same subjects have been treated with the same or different views.

Were it not for the very sensible provision we have already mentioned, that a candidate, if he choose, may confine his attention to two subjects, these lists would shake our faith in the examination altogether. *They are far too complete.* It can be no very difficult matter for a party of educated gentlemen in middle life, after they have done ample justice to a breakfast such as the board of a hospitable Cambridge Don alone can exhibit, to resolve themselves into a board of a somewhat less genial description, and write down the names of all the men who are world-famous in mental, moral, and political science. It is an effort of which a corresponding board of Kirkaldy penny-newspaper-men would probably prove equally capable when they had cleared their porridge-plates. Whether the lists which they prepared would exhibit the same impartiality with reference to creed and sect, religious and philosophical, that so honourably distinguishes the lists of the Cambridge magnates, is another matter. If the intention of these lists is simply to direct students to the best writers on the various subjects, we are so far from questioning their utility that we should feel much disposed to suggest the propriety of their being adopted, with some slight modification perhaps, into our own university calendar. But we confess that they have awakened our suspicion that a spirit of "cram" may not impossibly pervade the examination to a greater extent than we should consider desirable, and that what looks so magnificent on paper may end, after all, only in smattering on a grand scale. On one point, at all events, we are clear, viz., that if any unhappy candidate should attempt to burden his luckless brains with the amount of mental nourishment which is here set before him, the effect would be to encumber, overload, benumb, and finally deaden his speculative and meditative powers, rather than to stimulate and sustain them.

We doubt, moreover, if the teaching at present supplied by the University of Cambridge be *a cause* at all adequate to produce the examination *as an effect.* The programme of professors' lectures is so meagre as scarcely to enable us to judge of their character; but from the scanty provision which is made for the professorial element at Cambridge in point of emolument, and from the professors—men unquestionably of the highest personal eminence—

being mostly non-resident, we fear that the bulk of the teaching is tutorial, and consists simply in "getting up" the books, or portions, we shall hope, of a few of the books enumerated in the lists.

In Scotland we manage these studies quite differently. That we are not altogether unsuccessful in our management of them may perhaps be inferred from a fact which appears on the face of the very lists of which we are here speaking. Against the "*eleven* of all England," who are singled out as acknowledged celebrities, there are no less than *nine* Scotchmen. If we were to assert our claims to Brougham on the ground of a Scottish education, and to Stuart Mill and Kant on the ground of Scottish descent, we should have a positive majority; whereas our population has never much exceeded a seventh of that of England, and our universities are leafless and poverty-stricken to an extent that it would bewilder the imagination of a Cambridge board to conceive. In Scotland we certainly never had anything half as complete on paper as this moral sciences tripos examination. We have improved in this respect of late, as we hope to shew in a future article, but that we are still *apparently* very far in the rear must be frankly acknowledged. The Cambridge moral sciences examination has not been long in operation. It is possible that our English friends, by its help, may now shoot ahead of us; but hitherto we have more than kept our relative position in these studies, and taking into account the adverse circumstances against which we have contended, it is perhaps even now not unimportant, in estimating future possibilities, that we should inquire into the differences of the systems which we have respectively pursued.

The moral sciences have always been regarded, amongst us, pre-eminently as subjects for professorial teaching; and, notwithstanding the outcry that has been made against lecturing, (which, when a language is in question, has much of our sympathy) we lean to the belief that lecturing here is thoroughly in place, The main distinction between lecturing, in the Scotch sense of professorial prelection, and lecturing in the English sense of tutorial exposition (for the word is not unknown in the South), we take to be, that the professorial lecturer is expected to propound a system of his own, whereas the tutorial lecturer has done his duty if he inculcates the system of another with accuracy and precision. Now the difference in the effect of these two exercises, both upon pupil and teacher, we believe to be very great. The professorial lecture is not so much a lesson as an example. It may, and generally we believe does communicate even positive knowledge with greater life and freshness. But the main advantage is, that, in following it, the student actually beholds the independent efforts in which he is expected ultimately to engage. He sees them performed by another before his very eyes. He is not simply told the results of discussions, or even dragged through the stages by which they appear to have been reached, but he assists at every step of the process, and accepts the final result as if it were his own success, or repudiates it as if it were his own failure. He has all the advantages for study over the recipient of mere tutorial instruction, which a botanic garden affords as contrasted with a *hortus siccus,* or a living fencing master, with a series of engravings of *tierce* and *quart.* When we say that it is the duty of a professor to teach a system of his own, we do not of course mean that the system must necessarily be, in substance, new or original. If it is wholly new, it will not be true; because there is no department either of thought or learning which does not rest on the activity of the past. In order to do justice either to his subject or himself, a professor is not only entitled, but bound to avail himself of what has been done by others. If he is in a condition to advance his subject, so much the better for the progress of his pupils, as well as for his own reputation. There is nothing that gives such spirit to all parties as the feeling that they are discovering new truth, that they are really making way and cutting fresh paths for themselves and others through the primeval jungle of ignorance and error. But whether discovery be within the reach of his abilities or not, the system which a professor teaches must be his, in the sense of being thought through, and worked out, by him; so as to have become the embodiment of his own belief and the expression of his own opinions. To this extent the subjective character we have indicated, forms an element inseparable from all creditable professorial teaching; and this just as much when the subject is practical and concrete, as when it is theoretical and abstract. The positive law of nations, for example, belongs to the former category. It is not a speculative subject at all; on the contrary it is a system, if not of ascertained truth, at least of received doctrine. But a professor of this subject would not discharge his duty were he simply to teach what has been said to be the law of nations by any one text writer, or by any number of text writers. He must teach the law of nations itself, as he himself understands it to exist, for the time being; and he must derive his knowledge from historical examples which are not obsolete, from usages which are in green observance, and from the statements and counter statements of diplomatists, as they appear in the latest state documents within his reach. There is no reason why he should not call in the aid of those who have written systematically on the subject. He may read the *de jure belli et pacis* from end to end once a week; and sleep with it under his pillow, if that be a comfort to him, as it was to Gustavus Adolphus. But he cannot shift to the shoulders even of Hugo Grotius, the responsibility of interpreting the law of nations to the generation which he himself is appointed to instruct. Hugo Grotius is dead, and he is living; and it is he, and not Hugo Grotius, who is bound to discover and interpret, to the best of his abilities, the law which governs the international relations of the civilised world in the nineteenth century.

But though for these reasons we prefer the professorial to the tutorial method, and believe it to be more conducive to the formation of those self-helping habits of mind, without which no real intellectual work can ever be performed, we regard the moral sciences tripos examination as now organised at Cambridge as a great institution, and one highly deserving of our own study, and, in many of its features, of our imitation. Beyond any other academical arrangement in this country, it has solved the problem of bringing the abstract sciences of logic, metaphysics and ethics, in contact with the concrete sciences of political philosophy, political economy and jurisprudence; and it was this problem, the solution of which we indicated at the outset of our article as the great educational desideratum of the day. In a subsequent article we shall have something to say of the degree of Bachelor of Laws, as conferred by the two great universities of England, and as recently so successfully revived in the University of Edinburgh. J. L.

THE MONTH.

Proofs by Commission.—Even at the risk of wearying our readers with a thrice-told tale, we are glad to recur to this subject as often as we are in a position to point out indications that the term of its long dominion is approaching. We have had more than once occasion to quote the opinion of the Lord Justice-Clerk, and that which is rarely if ever unequivocal is on this point in the highest degree explicit and distinct. His Lordship's testimony is all the more important in corroboration of our views, that while agreeing in the condemnation of "Proofs by Commission" as about the worst and most cumbrous part of our legal machinery that ever was devised, he is desirous of substituting jury trial in its place, whereas we have always steadily advocated the opinion that the duty of advocating the facts in a case should devolve upon the Lord Ordinary, before whom it depends, and should be overtaken by him in blank days. In the case of Murray's Executors *v.* Forbes, recently disposed of in the Second Division, on a motion for a new trial, the Lord Justice-Clerk observed, "The Sheriff-Substitute of Banffshire allowed a proof on 9th January 1862, which he thought right to quash as incompetently taken. This proof was taken by commission. Forty-seven witnesses were examined; their evidence occupies 100 printed pages; and the proof was advised by the Sheriff-Substitute on 25th May 1864, more than two years after it was allowed. On the other hand, when it was resolved to send the case to a jury, issues were adjusted on the 5th December 1865, and the trial took place on the 28th of the same month. It occupied only one day. Six witnesses were examined for the pursuer, eight for the defender, and my notes of their evidence fill only seventeen pages. These facts, I think, require no comment." There may be more of the glitter of antitheses than the force of real argument in this appeal in favour of jury trial, but it must be conceded that his Lordship's remarks are pointed by at least a palpable and clamant case.

The effect of the new system of calling upon parties immediately to make up their minds to go to proof on disputed facts, or renounce probation whenever they have closed a record, has been to create a temporary disturbance in the state of the Outer House debate rolls. In so many cases issues have been adjusted, or orders for proof taken, that the debates in cases where there is no dispute as to facts have been nearly exhausted, while, until the proofs ordered are reported, or verdicts returned on the issues sent to juries, the debates in the remainder cannot take place. Much of this delay would be saved to litigants, and full occupation found for the Lord Ordinary by the very simple improvement of empowering their lordships to take proofs—or rather by preventing their granting commissions to take proofs in Edinburgh—coupling this with power to take them on their blank days. The working of this system under the conjugal rights act, with the aid of an interpreter, has proved an entire success. So the Lord Advocate could not, in introducing a short Bill to effect this object, be charged with proposing speculative changes, of which the effect is uncertain; and he could calculate on support from all branches of the profession, for we know of none who are satisfied with the present mode of taking proofs. His lordship himself showed that he was not satisfied with the existing state of matters, for he himself proposed a change in his procedure acts. We, therefore, call upon his lordship not to withhold an improvement which all desire merely because it is simple and convenient of ascertained efficiency.

Poor Law.—In another part of our columns we publish the report of a case recently disposed of in the House of Lords, which raises a very important point in the practical administration of this branch of law. The House of Lords, affirming a judgment of the Court of Session, obtained only by a majority of one—the judges being seven to six—have found that a parochial board is not entitled to apply its poors' fund in relief of able-bodied persons who are, from want of employment or other causes, temporarily in distress, but are not in the sense of the statute proper objects of parochial relief. The arguments in the Court above, as in the Court here, turned mainly on the construction of the section of the Poor Law Amendment Act, and, keeping in view the stringency of its provisions, with the literal and technical tendencies of the House of Lords, the result was to be anticipated. Yet we think there is cause for regret that the more equitable and practical views of the minority of the Court of Session have not prevailed. No doubt a great many evils are to be apprehended from any diversion of parochial funds from their appointed object, and there are few local economics in which a greater number and variety of interests are involved. But that is the very reason why the discretion which was proposed to be extended to the inspector of poor is not likely to be abused. Beyond this risk there was nothing against the views upon which the appellants relied except the peremptoriness of the Act of Parliament; and we must confess, although quite aware that we are not advancing a legal argument, that the opinion of the Lord President, the framer of the Poor Law Amendment Act, to the effect that he considered, and he had intended so to frame it, that the clause in question did not exclude the class of persons which were sought to be brought under its operation, does not seem to us to have been treated with the respect and consideration which, we think, it ought to have been received. There never, perhaps, was a case more strongly justifying a departure from the traditions of the Court of Appeal, looking to the practical benefits that might be looked for from the views of the minority in the Court below. Because the history of our country in recent years has made it quite evident that occasions of derangement and disturbance, such as was proposed to be relieved by the Parochial Board of Dundee, are likely from time to time to arise. These must be met, of course, in some way or other, and as the interference of Boards has been declared illegal, it is difficult to see where any other remedy is to be found except in direct and general legislation.

Lord Lyon King-at-Arms.—By the death of the Earl of Kinnoull, the high post of Lord Lyon King-at-Arms in Scotland, equivalent to the office of Earl Marshall in England, has become vacant. The late Earl's commission was dated as far back as 1796, and was issued in favour of his father and himself conjointly. However the vacancy may be filled up, we hope the opportunity will not be lost of sweeping away the many cobwebs that have gathered round and somewhat obscured the practical utility of the office, and that the light of day will be allowed to enter into the administration generally. We recommend the regulations that prevail in regard to fees to serious consideration.

It was but the other day that we called attention to the importance of this department in the Register House, both in regard to heraldry and genealogies, and as regulating and controlling the whole body of messengers-at-arms. The days are past when the mysteries of this last office were such as to require regulation by a separate department. The baton, or "rod of peace," is nearly as much devoid of terror as the "horn," and the advantages of the office, generally, instead of being so great as to make it necessary to limit the number of messengers by statute, are so reduced that the difficulty is, except in larger towns, to find men to undertake its duties and responsibilities; of which the natural consequence and the evidence is, that there are constant applications to the Court of Session to grant authority to sheriff-officers to serve writs which, without such warrant, could be served only by messengers.

The general inference is, that between the transfer of business to sheriff-courts, and the simplification of forms generally, the functions of the messenger-at-arms are nearly at an end.

The impression to be gathered from the report of "The Commissioners on the Courts of Justice," of which we give an extract below, is that the control exercised by the Lyon office over messengers was not on a satisfactory footing when the Commission sat (1822), it is not likely that the diminished importance of the messenger's office has led to increased efficiency; we would suggest, as matter for enquiry, whether the remaining functions of messengers might not be transferred to sheriff-officers. This might require some little adjustment of the qualications of the latter body, but we are satisfied that, with the aid of the sheriffs, the regulations as to their admission might easily be made such as to satisfy the requirements of the public safety.

From the remarkable length of time during which Lord Kinnoull held office—no less than seventy years—the report of the Commissioners has not been dealt with, and nearly half a century has elapsed since it was given in, which necessarily detracts from its value. One or two extracts may, however, not be without interest at the present time:—

"With respect to the jurisdiction of the Lord Lyon in the granting and matriculating of arms, we think it enough to state, that the rules to be observed by him in the exercise ot these powers, do not appear to be fixed with precision; and that in so far as it shall be considered material to have the same ascertained, a new revision of these rules by competent authority seems to be required."

. . . .

"We do not presume, in a question of this nature, to offer any opinion as to the particular regulations which it would be expedient to adopt. If the extent of the Lord Lyon's right in the grant of arms and armoural distinctions shall be defined, the proper allowance for each admits of being ascertained and limited by the same authority."

Having explained the control which the Lyon Office is *supposed* to exercise over messengers, they say, "We have already alluded to the obstacles in the way of the Lord Lyon's control over Messengers-at-Arms, occasioned by the want of any adequate fund for defraying the prosecutions against them, which are competent by the statutes and injunctions."

. . . .

"We humbly recommend, therefore, that as the duties of the Lyon Depute are of a judicial nature, it should be provided, that the peason to be appointed by the Lord Lyon as his Deputy, should be a member of the Faculty of Advocates, of not less than three years standing at the bar; that provision should be made for preventing the union of that office with the office of Lyon Clerk, and that the appointment to the latter office, namely, that the Lyon Clerk, should hereafter be reserved to His Majesty.

"We humbly recommend that a new regulation of the whole fees should take place, calculated to produce not less than £1800; that the whole amount of these fees should be made payable to Exchequer," and that instead of the variable receipts "from fees, the Lord Lyon and other officials should be remunerated by salaries, reserving a surplus from the fees which shall be establishlished, of £100 as a fund in Exchequer towards defraying expenses of prosecutions to be carried on by the Procurator Fiscal."

What arrangements have been made for carrying out these recommendations we are really not aware; the lapse of time since they were made, of itself, suggests the propriety of reconsideration. Effect has been given to the recommendation that the Lyon-Depute should, as being a judicial officer, be a member of the bar, and whoever knows anything of the state of the Lyon office knows that the result has been to impart a life, and a method, and an efficiency to its operations which have long been unknown.

Legal Intelligence.—The office or Attorney-General at the Cape of Good Hope has been conferred upon an English barrister. We are not aware that any of the legal officials at the Cape are now members of the Scotch bar. It used to be otherwise there, and also in our West India colonies, where the civil law prevailed, and in Ceylon. If ever there were a time when we should have expected the interests of the Scotch bar to be maintained, we should have expected it to be when the Dean of Faculty—the man most interested in the Scotch bar—holds the office of Lord Advocate, that which gives him most power to enforce the claims of the bar. We are glad that he has at least secured a firm hold in the Mauritius, where the offices of Chief-Justice and Procureur-General are both held by members of the bar, and we rather think one of the Puisne Judges also, though a native of the Mauritius, studied in Scotland and passed advocate.

English Juries.—We notice that a bill has just been brought into Parliament by Sir C. O'Loghlan with the view of relaxing the rigour of the present system of jury trial in England, so far at least as its practical details are concerned. The measure has been suggested by the proceedings that have recently occurred in connection with the case of Charlotte Winsor, whose sentence of death has twice been respited. The bill proposes to give the judges the power of discharging the jury whenever they consider that step necessary, and of ordering refreshments for the jury, which is at present incompetent by the law of England, and of receiving their verdict on a Sunday, which we suppose to be now illegal, Sunday being *dies non juridicus.*

Confederate Cruisers.—We discussed the *Alabama* claims last summer at such considerable length that we cannot allow ourselves to resume the subject in consequence of the publication of the correspondence relating to the *Shenandoah*, in regard to which the position of our Government was still stronger than as to the *Alabama*. We are pleased to hear from the speech of the Attorney-General the other night in his place in Parliament, that before any of the discussion arose, our Government, conscious that our Foreign Enlistment Act was a most imperfect piece of legislation, proposed to the American Government a joint revision of their act and the British. Even those who have hitherto doubted the good faith of Great Britain must, we should think, now be satisfied; and were anything wanted to complete the true picture of the relative positions of America and Britain, it is to be found in farther statement of Sir Roundell Palmer, that since the close of the struggle the Americans have again refused to enter upon any joint reconsideration of our Foreign Enlistment Acts!! Though this country and America are the two in which the provisions of such acts are most likely to have important bearing on the peace of the world, and although they truly relate to the municipal law, we are inclined to think that other maritime States also might take part in any such discussion as that proposed.

English Law of Sale.—Though fictitious biddings at sales by auction in order to kee pthe price up have been repudiated in the Courts of Law in England, yet, strange to say, the Courts of Equity have interposed in their favour. For some time back the expediency of so doing has been much doubted, and Lord Cranworth, in giving judgment in the case of *Mortimer* v. *Bell* in November last, half promised, should the question arise purely, to upset the rule. We are glad to observe that that energetic law reformer, Lord St. Leonards, has interposed to remove the blot by introducing a bill which will have material effect in correcting the present state of the law.

THE

JOURNAL OF JURISPRUDENCE.

HISTORICAL SKETCHES IN THE LAW OF SCOTLAND.

No. III.—The Laws of David I.—(*Continued.*)

Before taking leave of the criminal code under King David, it may be worth while to note one or two provisions, which, in their quaint and humorous conception of justice, seem to retain an impress of the personal character of their author. That character, of which the lineaments are thus strangely recalled to us, I believe to have belonged to no other than the monarch himself. One of such quaint laws is the following among the Burgh laws:—"*De querela blaa et blodi.* Si quis verberando fecerit aliquem blaa et blodi ipse qui fuerit blaa et blodi prius debet exaudiri sive prius venerit aut non ad querimoniam faciendam. Et si uterque fuerit blaa et blodi qui prius accusaverit prius exaudietur."—Ll. B. 82. Still more humorously conceived is the method of expiation proposed by the following law:—"*De eo qui interfecit alienum canem domesticum.* Item statuit dominus rex si aliquis injuste et contra legem alterius canem interfecerit vigilabit et custodiet ejus fimarium per annum et diem (He shall wak upon that mannis myddin for a 12 month and a day), aut omnia damna infra dictum tempus per eum sustentata pro defectu canis sui restaurabit sine ulla contradictione."—(Ass. R. David 33.) What authority but that of royalty would venture to place on the statute-book a penalty so apt and yet so ludicrous as the first of the above alternatives? And does not the alternative which follows look like the commonplace interpretation of the royal Nemesis by some matter-of-fact councillor?

The criminal statutes of King David's reign are not the only ones from which it is possible to collect some personal traits of that monarch's character, and it is interesting to find that the traits to be gathered from such sources entirely harmonise with the character for gentleness, humanity, and piety uniformly ascribed by contemporaneous chroniclers to a monarch who has been called the Justinian of our Scottish jurisprudence, but whose true place is that of a more primitive legislator. Among such characteristic laws may be cited the following:— "*Quilibet debet uti propriis terris suis,*" a rubric to the principle of which it were scarcely possible to demur, but the practice of which, as the law proceeds to show, had not been much in fashion. "Item definivit rex quod qui terras possident eisdem propriis terris suis utantur atque in iis se et suos pascant nec iis liceat quod hucusque solebant agere scilicet propriis terris parcere et terras alienas devastare et sicut possessionibus suis propriis uti. Hanc scilicet pravam consuetudinem rex modis omnibus prohibet ne diucius sub sua potestate aliquis sic precise agere presumat sub sua plenaria forisfactura."—(Ass. R. David 26.) To a similar purport is the following law:—"*De transitu per terras alienas.* Item decrevit et deliberavit rex quod si quis major vel minor curiam regis adierit vel alia racionabili causa compellente cum tot hominibus pergat ut sibi convenit ne superflua multitudine secum ducta terras regis episcoporum seu aliorum eundo et redeundo devastet. Item cum in itinere suo ad cujuscunque domini domum vespere venerit ab eo hospitium roget et postquam cum concessione vel jussione ejusdem secundum morem patrie homines partiti domos intraverint ab iis a quibus recepti sunt per violenciam cibos supra vires eorum non exigant sed secundum possa eorum. Et si dominus terre dederit aut preceperit quid detur iis accipiant. Quod si aliquis ex eis ad quos ordinati sunt hospitem quem dominus suus juste preceperit sibi suscipere ejiceat et foris esse jejunantem facit propter hoc dabit domino suo unam vaccam."—(Ass. R. David 27.) Still more illustrative of a desire to preserve throughout the country habits of mutual hospitality and civility is the following:— "*De transitu per terram alicujus domini sine licencia.* Preterea decrevit rex quod si quis decretum suum predictum transgrediendo terram alicujus domini sine licencia vel concessione ejus intraverit et per violenciam cibos ab hominibus sumserit pro hac injuria domino illius terre octo vaccas emendet et deinceps ab ejusmodi iniquitate abstineat. Precipit eciam rex quod causa charitatis sub sua potestate conveniens et legalis hospitalitas custodiatur et omnis vastacio hostilis et violencia penitus extinguatur nec ulterius ab aliquo fieri presumatur."—(Ass. R. David 28.)

The following laws are even yet more plain in their evidence of the personal character and authority of King David himself as their source; and indeed, without questioning their genuineness so far as to impute an intentional fiction to their authorship and substance, it would be impossible to resist the force of that evidence. To convey an adequate impression of the evidence given by these laws corroborative of the traditional character of this sovereign as gathered from other sources, it will be necessary to cite entire the few laws now particularly referred to. They are as follows:—"*De pace regis data peregrinis et mercatoribus.* Item precipit Dominus Rex ut omnes homines in regno in officiis fideliter vivant et propria negocia fideliter agant. Qui vero peregrini sunt et loca sanctorum pro remedio anime sue visitare volunt firmam pacem eundo et redeundo habeant ut nemo iis injuriam faciat. Caveant et ipsi ut legaliter se contineant. Mercatores autem sive per terram sive per aquam venientes rectitudinem regis regi per ministros suos plenarie reddant sicut in diebus regis patris sui constitutum erat. Omnes autem ministri qui in mansionibus ecclesiarum vel alibi in regno commorantur in suis ministeriis fideliter agant et sua lege juste utantur et regi fideles sint. Quorum eciam nomina et numerum per aliquem fidelem rex scire vult. Prefatam autem constitucionem ideo constituit ut inter peregrinos mercatores et ministros suos in regno commorantes distanciam non cognoscat et unusquisque in officio suo fideliter vivat."—(Ass. R. David 29.) Again—"*De proteccione regis concessa pauperibus et debilibus.* De pauperibus et debilibus constitutum est ut omnes qui cunctorum auxilio destituti sunt sint sub procuracione et proteccione domini regis in regno suo ubi sunt vel assidue esse debent. Et ideo jure concedit quod si aliquid ab eis furatur et postea probator aliquis reperiatur qui furtum vult probare is furem nominabit coram testibus idoneis super sanctum altare eo modo quo mos est in Scocia et jurabit verum esse quod affirmat de prefato fure et restauretur quod furatum est ac si proprium regis esset. Et si concedendo veraciter confirmaverit quod ab eis sine lege et judicio per vim aliquid abstulit reddat quod abstulit et regi octo vaccas pro transgressione emendet."—(Ass. R. David 30.) Again—"*De ponderibus in emendo et vendendo.* Statutum est a rege David ut commune et equale pondus (quod dicitur pondus Cathanie) in emendo et vendendo omnes homines in tota Scocia custodiant. Divina namque lex precipit dicens non habebis in sacculo tuo diversa pondera majus et minus nec erit in domo tua modius major et minor sed pondus habebis justum. Si quis contra decretum divine legis aliquod inequale pondus sibi usurpaverit regie justicie octo vaccas emendet pro transgressione."—(Ass. R. David 31.)

After the laws which indicate the personal character of King David fall to be noted certain others which relate to constitutional matters. The principle, valued as an ancient maxim of the law of England, namely, that a man must be tried by his peers, is no less distinctly enunciated as an institution in the ancient laws of Scotland. No one was obliged to receive sentence, or to be judged by a person of inferior rank to himself, so that an earl should suffer judgment from none less than an earl (comes per comitem), baro per baronem, vavasor per vavasorem; but the person of less degree might be tried by the greater (Ass. R. David, l. 5). The principle is older than the separate functions of a jury, to which constituent of a court of justice it has come to be in modern times applied. Another familiar principle meets us in the prohibition against provosts or bailies of a town to meddle with *the pleas pertaining to the Crown*, unless by special commission from the Justiciar. *Quoniam talis appellacio et responsio ad judicium coram justiciario vel ejus certo actornato debet fieri* (Ass. R. David, 12). This law indicates a fact of which we should otherwise be well assured, namely, that the expression *pleas pertaining to the Crown*, referred to in Magna Charta, is one whose meaning had been well understood and fixed at a date much earlier than that great monument of the liberties of England. The provision of the great charter on this head is more comprehensive. It is that "No sheriff, constable, coroner, or other our bailiffs, shall hold pleas of the Crown." I am not aware whether at this early date in Scotland sheriffs or barons were prohibited from holding pleas of the crown. Neither is it very easy to gather what crimes at this early period came within this category. If it be true, as English writers assert (Reeves' Hist. of Eng. Law, vol. I., p. 281), that at the time of Magna Charta the crimes of theft, forgery, coining, as well as treason, murder, manslaughter, robbery, and other graver crimes were considered to be among the pleas of the crown, it is clear that the jurisdiction of inferior judges in Scotland in criminal matters was never restricted within the bounds assigned to it by the "ancient liberties" of England.

It seems probable that the category of "pleas of the crown" in our early laws was borrowed from the language of some of the ancient charters of the English kings; but it may be doubted whether in our early practice the distinction really obtained any very extensive recognition. Indeed, there is one provision among these laws which expressly extends the jurisdiction of the barons in an important criminal matter, namely, by enacting that those barons who had the power of *furca and fossa* in the case of theft, given by their charters, should also have the power of a capital sentence in cases of homicide. And it was provided that after open accusation and defence made in their courts the case should not be compromised without leave of the king (Ass. R. David, 13).

If little care was taken to limit the authority of inferior judges within the local bounds of their jurisdiction, these local bounds were, on the other hand, strictly defined, and there was an express prohibition made against a practice whereby under pretence of acting on the king's service it seems that sheriffs used sometimes to execute warrants without the bounds of their commission (Ass. R. David, 10). A person living within one sheriffdom wishing to poind the goods of a person living in another sheriffdom must first obtain the leave of the sheriff of that shire, and proceed to execute his diligence with the assistance of that sheriff or his bailiff (Ass. R. David, 22). And no one could poind the goods of another within the lands of any one without the leave of the lord or baron of those lands (Ass. R. David, 23). There appears reason to believe that the original course of every plaint of personal wrong, whether criminal or civil, with the exception of some grave matters, called, as before-mentioned, pleas pertaining to the crown, lay, in the first place, within the jurisdiction of the barons, from whence they might be appealed to the sheriff, from whom, in the last place, lay the appeal to the *aula regis*, or supreme court of the king himself. It is certain that under the legislation of King David all persons were prohibited from bringing their causes (with the exceptions already mentioned) into the king's court unless they had, in the first place, been brought before the sheriff's or baron's court (Ass. R. David, 24). That the sheriff's jurisdiction was in certain cases appellate from, or supplementary to that of the baron's may be inferred from passages in Glanville and the Regiam Magistatem; and it is very probable that in the time of David their jurisdiction was called into requisition in those cases only where the barons were proved or presumed to have failed in doing justice.

There is one duty of the sheriff which has frequently in the present day been rigorously enforced by his judicial superiors, and in which it has been held that the sheriff-substitute cannot represent him. To the hard worked sheriff-depute, prematurely recalled by the etiquette of the circuit court from the pleasant Venafrian fields whither he has betaken himself after the "*clientum longa negotia*," it may be some consolation to reflect that the like duty was, under the heaviest penalties, required from his predecessors in office, when by a Royal Decree in the time of David I., a sitting of the king's court was ordered within a stated time to be held in each county. But then he had the company of the rest of the county dignitaries, the bishop, the earl, and the barons or lords of each territorial district or township within the county, all of whom, under the king's *plenaria forisfactura*, were summoned to attend his court when it should assemble under that royal ordinance (Ass. R. David, 25).

It is note-worthy to glance at the ancient sanctions by which the King's Peace or Gyrth was formerly surrounded, of which is preserved a curious specimen among these Assize Regis David (C. 14). The word Gyrth is connected with the Anglo-Saxon *Grith peace* (German *Friede*), and the word Gyrthol originally signifies the *seat of peace* (Friede-Stuhl). The kindred word girth, signifying enclosure, appears to be connected with the original idea through the circle of stones environing the ancient places of judgment. If so, it is a striking instance of concrete meaning, becoming through symbolism engrafted upon an earlier abstract one, a process perhaps worthy of attention from philologists, who delight in investigating the inverse process. The law of King David in question takes up the subject at a time when the Gyrthol is already to some extent fixed in position; but its intimate connection with the king's peace in this passage, and the evidence of the Scandinavian words, cited by Jamieson under this head, leave no doubt that the original idea implied in the word was an ambulatory protection, or peace depending upon the monarch's personal presence, or on his proclamation, or on the proclamation of any one having authority to invoke it in his name. The Sanctuary which has superseded this gyrth or gyrthol in the later law of Scotland is an idea obviously borrowed from a Hebrew source, become familiar ʻh the popular use and adoption among ourselves of their

Sacred Scriptures. The passage of the law now referred to, may, from its antiquarian interest, be worth quoting entire. It is as follows:—"Si quis in aliquo loco videlicet in gyrthol vel alibi ubi aliquis postulet pacem domini regis et domini tenementi malo zelo levat pugnum suum ad percutiendum alium et hoc per duos homines fideles possit probari dabit domino regi quatuor vaccas et ei quem percutere voluit unam vaccam. Et si percutiat eum pugno non abstrahendo sanguinem dabit domino regi sex vaccas et ei quem percussit duas vaccas. Et si sanguinem traxerit dabit regi ix. vaccas et ei quem percusserit tres vaccas. Et si interficiat eum cum pugno dabit regi xxix. vaccas et unam juvencam. Et satisfaciet parentele interfecti secundum assisam terre." The idea of the pax nuntiarum, adverted to in a previous paper, was evidently borrowed from this ancient idea of the *pax regis*, and was happily adapted by David, as before mentioned, for the purpose of encouraging the commerce of the burgh fairs.

A similar law, of less antique form, is entitled "*De violencia facta in curia regis*," and runs thus:—"Si quis traxerit cultellum ad alium in curia domini regis percutiatur per medium manus ejus. Et si traxerit sanguinem abscindatur manus ejus. Et si interfecerit aliquem dabit regi xx vaccas et unam juvencam et pacem faciet cum parentibus interfecti et cum rege secundum assisam regni scocie."

It may be worth while, in concluding the present paper, to note a provision affording some insight into the economical condition of the servile class. "Quilibet liber homo potest relinquere suam libertatem si voluerit in curia domini regis sed illam libertatem nunquam iterum in vita sua recuperabit." Such passages are historically valuable, if not in affording a clue to the nature of the servile *status* in this country, at least in recording the fact of its existence. The disappearance of such a status in this country, as well as in England, has been effected by steps so unobserved by contemporaries as almost to elude the notice of the historian; and so imperceptible has been the process that it has been gravely denied that the status ever existed in either country. It may be admitted, indeed, that the status of slavery, or serfdom (the distinction between the words is grounded in no essential difference), was never in this country precisely identical with the corresponding status in the Roman law. Still less was it ever similar to the caricature of that status which lately existed in certain of the American States. But it cannot be doubted that however modified by the laws and customs peculiar to each country, the *status* of servitude in all was essentially the same thing. The Roman lawyers were right when they placed slavery among the institutions of the *jus gentium*. They wrote as they observed the fact in their own day, and in their own world, and their maxims were those of positive law, and not of morals. The disappearance of servitude from Europe (completed within the present generation), and the growth of the sentiment which has relegated it for ever from these shores, is one of the most curious chapters in the history of civilization, and one which still remains to be written. I speak not now of the American States, where the institution is an anomaly in its rise as well as in its fall. It is not the place here to enter on so large a subject, nor to claim or disclaim for our country the origin and source of the idea which makes slavery impossible. Rather let us congratulate ourselves that we are not alone in giving a home and a reality to the idea, and let us give all credit to others who claim to share it and defend it as the permanent mark of our common European and Christian civilization.

CONVEYANCE OF HERITAGE AND HERITABLE SUCCESSION.

The laws of the period now under review relating to heritable succession and to the conveyance of heritage are particularly interesting, not only as presenting the earliest distinct phase of heritable rights in Scotland, but also as throwing considerable light upon certain principles of the law of real property in England. Modelled (as already observed) upon English customs, the Leges IV. Burgorum of David I. stand alone not only as an authentic code of Scotch law of the 12th century, but also as a genuine record of customs prevailing in England at the same period. There is no other contemporaneous record of such customs now extant which approaches that code in completeness or comprehensiveness, and it is not until Glanville's treatise in the following century that the historian or the lawyer is furnished with any systematic account of the law of England.

In the early law of heritable succession the line is not always distinctly marked by which the rights of the heir-at-law on the one hand and the power of devise or bequest on the other are defined and recognised. The two principles are in natural antagonism, and it is not within the sphere of the present sketch to determine the controversy as to which of them, if either, has the better right to be considered the primary or original one. It is assumed both by Stair and Erskine that the primary rule of inheritance pointed out by the law of nature is to give effect to the disposition of the owner, and they both regard the rights of the legal heirs, in the absence of such a disposition, as flowing from the presumption that the proprietor would have named them had he made a destination. The view, however, more in favour with those who have examined the actual facts presented by a study of ancient law is that legal succession is an older institution than that by destination, and was already matured in periods when the power of the owner to modify it by an expression of his will is yet in a rudimentary form. It is ingeniously and powerfully argued by Mr. Maine in his "Ancient Law," that the power of bequest exercised by will, or any similar instrument in modern law, is due to the invention and gradual improvement of the "Testamentum" of the Roman jurisprudence. Be this as it may, it is a fact recorded by Tacitus, that at a period when the *testament* of the Roman law had attained its full proportions and capacities for giving effect to the will of the testator, the *Germans* had "Nullum testamentum." Such is the terse expression of the Roman historian to describe an institution, barbarous, no doubt, to his conception of jurisprudence, whereby the rights of the heir-at-law are held inviolate. If it be assumed as a correct description of the customs of those Teutonic races from whom, apart from our large debt to the Roman jurisprudence, our own legal institutions are derived, the assumption will be found in exact accordance with the facts that meet us in the laws of the period now under review, for in these laws may be clearly seen the antagonism between the testament of the Roman law and the "nullum testamentum" of the German preserved in a system, of which the barbarian element forms the groundwork, but where the more civilised forms of the Roman jurisprudence have taken root and are destined to flourish and fructify.

The spirit of that part of our law commonly called feudal was opposed to alienation of landed property, not only by devise in contemplation of death, but by any act even *inter vivos.* It was in the customs of the burghs that this principle of inalienability was first relaxed. The burgess who had acquired lands by *con-*

quest, or by the fruits of his own industry and mercantile success, is deemed to have a larger right to dispose of them than he who had acquired by inheritance from an ancestor. "Quilibet burgensis potest terram suam de conquestu dare aut vendere et ire quocumque voluerit libere et quiete nisi sit in calumpnia" (Ll. B. 21 and 42.) And the rules of succession in case of his not having so disposed of them in his lifetime are laid down with great precision—"Si burgensis terram vel terras adquisiverit in burgo et puerum heredem habuerit et eas non assignaverit alicui aute mortem suam filius ejus vel filia ejus heres cedat in hereditatem tocius terre sue quam pater suus habuit die quo fuit vivus et mortuus. Salvo hoc quod uxor ejus desponsata in tota vita sua quamdiu erit vidua interiorem partem domus que dicitur *le flet* tenebit. Heres autem ejus habebit ulteriorem partem domus capitalis si in ea habitare voluerit. Si autem aliam dotem habuerit ipsa sua dote, et heres capitali domo gaudebit" (l. 23.) If a burgess had two wives, and had children by each, all his heritage, as well as the conquest which he had acquired during the life of the first wife, and which he had not assigned to any one (non assignaverit alicui) before his death, went to his son and heir by the first wife, and the conquest acquired during the lifetime of the second wife, and not assigned to any one before his death, went to the son and heir of the second wife. And the second wife had a right to remain in the house of the first heir only for forty days after the death of her husband (l. 24.) It will be remarked that in these laws there is no appearance of any single *vox signata* to express the conveyance of heritage. "Dare," "Vendere," "assignare" are all used as equivalents to the expression of a complete conveyance.

In the *leges burgorum* occurs the earliest statement in our laws of a principle which has enjoyed singular vitality both in our own and in the sister country. From the modern interest which thus attaches to it the entire passage may be worth quoting. It is as follows:—"*De burgagio collato in liberum maritagium* Si aliquis acceperit burgagium cum aliqua in liberum maritagium et cum ea genuerit masculum vel feminam et casu contingente moriatur uxor viri illius et post mortem matris si filius vel filia vivat vel moriatur vir illo burgagio omnibus diebus vite sue gaudebit sed illud ultra nec vendere nec impignorare potest. Et si illa nocte qua nascitur filius vel filia simul moriatur mater et filius vel filia adhuc vir gaudebit bonis illius terre in vita sua ita tamen quod vir ille habeat testimonium duorum legalium virorum vel mulierum vicinarum qui audierunt infantem clamantem vel plorantem vel braiantem. Et sic si plures terras acceperit in maritagium cum uxore sua. Si vero prolem non genuerit dicta terra revertetur ad proximos heredes uxoris sue" (l. 41.) The principle here enunciated is accurately preserved in the laws both of England and Scotland to the present day with regard to estates of inheritance of land in which the wife is seised unless the right has been renounced or waived (as it usually is) by a marriage settlement. In both systems it is known by the name of the curtesy or courtesy, and is one of the most valuable witnesses to the common origin of our systems of customary law.

Besides the liberty of disposition given to burgesses of their conquest, another principle whereby the inalienable nature of landed property is relaxed, is the power under certain conditions of disposing of heritage "in necessitate," or by a person burdened with debt which he has no other means of paying. He who voluntarily disposed of his inherited lands to meet his exigencies was obliged in the first place to make the offer of sale to the nearest heirs, (I presume at a moderate price, though we are not told how it is estimated), and they took the property under the burden of maintaining the vendor; and if they could not or would not accept it within the time allowed them for the option, the owner could sell to anybody at the best advantage (Ll. 41, 114.) A like power of sale was given to the creditor who had executed diligence against either the person or lands of the debtor; and he could, after allowing a similar option of purchase to the nearest relations and friends, sell the lands to the best advantage, and, after retaining the amount of his debt, pay the balance to the heir (Ll. 89, 90.) It appears that even after a sale the relations could redeem the lands if they offered to do so *bona fide*, and not by fraudulently borrowing money for the purpose with the view of obtaining the advantage of an increased value of the lands (l. 91.) If a feuar at a certain reserved rent were thus obliged to sell his feu, the granter of the feu was, with regard to the right of preemption, held as the nearest relation (l. 95.) Mortgage (*terra in vadimoniis posita*) was also at this time in use, and this, no doubt, formed another means whereby lands might be aliened to the prejudice of the heir (l. 79.)

It is clear that under the laws of the period now in contemplation lands, whether of heritage or conquest, might be granted, sold, or demised either gratuitously or onerously to the next lawful heir, for it does not appear that any other than the heir had ever the right to challenge a deed of any kind disposing of heritable property. But if a father gave away lands either of heritage or conquest to a son in *legitima potestate* for no other consideration than love and favour, the son was obliged to maintain and succour him should he afterwards fall into poverty even by his own fault, and, should he refuse to do so, the father might resume possession and sell to any one (l. 107.) In *legitima potestate* also, it appears that a father having several landed properties might give away one to each of several sons, and the heir could not challenge the deed (l. 108.)

The phrase *legitima potestate* in the laws of this period is opposed to the expression *in lecto egritudinis sue de qua moritur.* The two expressions are more familiarly known in the later law of Scotland as *liege poustie*, and *on deathbed*, and the principle to which they relate as the *law of deathbed.* The *law of deathbed* is another of those principles of Teutonic custom which is clearly enunciated in the Leges Burgorum, and which has stood firm to the present day against all the assaults of innovation and all the importations of Roman law. It is thus enunciated—"Consuetudo burgorum est quod nullus burgensis in lecto egritudinis sue de qua moritur aliquas terras quas hereditarie possedit in burgo nec alias quas acquisierit in sanitate sua a vero herede possit alienare vel alicui dare ab herede aut vendere nisi forte ere alieno esset oneratus quia de necessitate oportet ipsum terras vendere vel alienare cum necessitas legem non habet. Et nisi heres ejus nec posset nec vellet eum de omni debito suo deliberare" (l. 101.) Apart from the law of deathbed, I am not aware that there was at this period any authority for the theory which established itself at a later period that a will or testament is not a *habilis modus* of conveying heritable property. There appears nothing in the spirit of these laws to combat the position that a devise by last will, if *executed* in liege poustie, and otherwise consistent with the conditions restricting alienation, would be equally efficacious with any other mode of conveyance. At all events, it would create a good title if suffered through pious respect or otherwise to pass unchallenged by the heir-at-law, and there are passages in some of the old cartularies which would be difficult to reconcile with a contrary hypothesis. One other quotation will complete the list of restrictions in the power to alienate heritage.

It can scarcely be doubted that the above restrictions on the alienation of heritable property contained in the Leges Burgorum were not confined in their operation to lands of burgesses, but were part of the law of heritage obtaining throughout the country in general. It is clear from the whole scope of the Leges Burgorum that their tendency, in so far as they regarded the property of burgesses alone, was rather in favour of relaxation of the laws against alienation, and the general existence of the law of deathbed at the present day is a proof that the law just cited was the expression of a universal principle as applied to the alienation of heritable property. As to the main position above maintained, that land which had been obtained by the owner through inheritance could not be aliened to the prejudice of the heir, the evidence is chiefly of a negative character, but the conclusion is inevitable from the manner in which the exceptions are stated. There was one point on which the rights of the heir were still more jealously guarded, namely, his right to the principal messuage or house of the ancestor—"Nullus potest alienare messuagium suum capitale ab herede suo nec inde dotare uxorem suam si terram aliquam aliam vel terras habuerit ad uxorem suam dotandam vel pro necessitate vendendam" (l. 106.)

The principle of our law of succession in moveables, whereby a portion is reserved as the right of the children is enunciated in the Leges Burgorum in a law which, so far as it goes, accurately describes the right known as *legitim* in the present day. The law, which is remarkable for its statement of the antiquity already assigned to the custom, is as follows:—"Consuetudo est in omnibus burgis Scocie a tempore de quo non extat memoria in contrarium quod si aliquis burgensis liberos procreaverit de uxore sua legitima et ipse decedat tercia pars omnium bonorum debetur filiis et filiabus ipsorum. Legitimus autem filius primogenitus et heres ejusdem viri et uxoris habebit eandem porcionem bonorum quam et filii alii videlicet equalem cum aliis liberis nisi ipse primogenitus fuerit forisfamiliatus" (l. 115.) The law does not say what becomes of the other thirds, but it may be presumed the disposal of them was similar to that obtaining in the present day, though it may not be so clear what was the course adopted when the father died leaving children but no widow.

The law of guardianship enunciated in the Leges Burgorum is similar to that prevailing in our law at the present day. The person and moveables are committed to the charge of the relations by the mother's side, and the heritage to that of the relations on the father's side (l. 98.)

The form of giving seizin in burgage subjects was as follows:— The vendor stood within the house, and came out, and the purchaser stood without and came in. The seller gave the provost one penny upon his exit, and the buyer the same sum for his entrance and sasine. Upon an excambion each gave the provost twopence upon the ceremony. The proceeding required no legal formalities or appearance in court, but was sufficient if done in presence of the neighbours (Ll. 52, 111.) The prescription in burgage subjects was short, requiring only a year and day possession to fortify a title to subjects purchased *bona fide*, and without notice, unless the claimant were a minor (l. 10.)

R. C.

THE LIABILITY OF SHIPOWNERS FOR LOSS OR DAMAGE OF GOODS FROM FAULTS IN NAVIGATION.

As this question is at present attracting much attention among commercial men, and occasioning considerable discussion, it may not be inopportune to devote a portion of our space to its investigation. On every such subject it is highly expedient that both men of business and men of law should be heard; for by this co-operation a satisfactory solution of the question is the more likely to be obtained.

The liability of shipowners for loss or damage to goods occasioned by faults in navigation takes its origin in the Edict of the Roman Prætor "Nautæ, Caupones, Stabularii quod cujusque salvum fore receperint, nisi restituent, in eos judicium dabo." Although this edict has not been formally incorporated into Scotch law, its principle operates in our jurisprudence as it does in every other system of Europe. Its extreme harshness, which required shipowners, innkeepers and stablers to answer at all hazards for the safety of the goods placed under their charge, has undergone, however, considerable modification. The principles of equity have everywhere rendered the acts of God and the king's enemies a sufficient excuse for inability to restore the goods.

The favour shown in Britain to the shipping interest has led to several statutory limitations in addition to those equitable modifications. The first legislative enactment on this subject (7 Geo. ii., c. 15) passed in 1733 through both Houses of Parliament without a division. It was introduced in consequence of a petition from the London shipowners, who had become alarmed at the opinion expressed in the case of Boucher *v.* Lawson, to the effect that shipowners were responsible for bullion, jewels, &c., embezzled by the shipmaster. The Act proceeds on the preamble, "That it is of the greatest consequence and importance to this kingdom to promote the increase of the number of ships and vessels, and to prevent any discouragement to merchants and others from being interested and concerned therein;" and it enacts that the owners shall not be liable for the embezzlement of the master (without their knowledge), beyond the value of the ship, its appurtenances, and the freight. In 1786 the London shipowners, in consequence of another case, again took alarm and applied to Parliament. Their petition was listened to and an Act (26 Geo. iii., c. 86) was passed applying the same limits to their liability for loss occasioned by robbery in which the master and mariners were noway concerned. Similar protection was, by 53 Geo. iii., c. 159, granted to the shipowners from any loss or damage occasioned by any act, neglect, matter or thing done, omitted or occasioned without their fault or privity, to any goods shipped after 1st September 1813. The Merchant Shipping Act, 1854, modified and consolidated these various enactments, and it in its turn has on this point been altered by the Merchant Shipping Act, 1862, which in Sec. 54 declares that the owners of any British or Foreign ship shall not be answerable where the untoward event occurs without their actual fault and "privity in damages for loss of life or personal injury, either alone or together with loss or damage to ships, boats, goods, merchandise, or other things, to an aggregate amount exceeding fifteen pounds for each ton of their ship's tonnage; nor in respect of loss or damage to ships, goods, merchandise or other things, whether there be in addition loss of life or personal injury or not, to an aggregate amount exceeding eight pounds for each ton of the ship's tonnage."

These statutes have greatly limited the responsibility of Shipowners, and altered very much the application of the Edict Nautæ Caupones Stabularii. While carriers by land are still subjected to much of the severity of the edict, carriers by sea, from the dangers to which they are naturally exposed and the partiality of British legislation towards naval interests, have had the burden considerably lightened.

In addition, however, to those limitations introduced, 1st, by the principles of equity, and 2d, by express legislative enactment, shipowners have also protected themselves by inserting express exceptions in their contracts. There cannot be the slightest doubt of their right so to limit their responsibility; and the question as it arises now is not so much on the bearings of the general principle as on the meaning of the particular stipulation. The respective rights and obligations of shipowners and shippers are now determined by the terms of the charter-party or bill of lading, which is the instrument of their contracts. Formerly the sole exception contained in these instruments—beyond that always implied, whether inserted or not, "the Act of God and the King's enemies"—was "the Perils of Sea." This was regarded for many a day as quite sufficient, until the decision in the English case, Smith *v.* Shepherd,* in which, however, it is said, there was neither charter-party nor bill of lading, so that the case must have been decided on the principles of common law. The facts of this case were briefly these:—before the time of the accident which occasioned the action at law, there was at the entrance to the harbour of Hull a bank on which vessels used to lie in safety, but part of it had been swept away by a great flood, so that it became perfectly steep instead of shelving towards the river. A few days after the flood a vessel was wrecked on this bank, and her mast attached to a part of the wreck was allowed to float about the river. This waif striking against defendant's vessel forced her on the sand bank where she stuck, but where she would have been in no danger had the bank been in its former situation. On the ebb of the tide, however, the ship sunk in the water and much of the cargo was spoiled. The defendant offered to show that there had been *no actual negligence;* but this defence was rejected, and a verdict for the plaintiff was given. Several shipowners alarmed at this decision had recourse to Parliament. They failed, however, in obtaining from the Legislature the desired protection; and accordingly additional exceptions were inserted in their charter-parties and bills of lading: viz., those still in use, "The Act of God, the Queen's enemies, Fire, (from these they are protected by common law or statute), and all and

* *Vide*, Shee's Abbot, 10th Edition, (1856) pp. 285 & 287.

every other dangers and accidents of the seas, rivers, and navigation of whatever nature and kind soever."

For seventy years shipowners have lain in what they fancied absolute security under the broad shield of these universal terms. On scarcely a single occasion have they been required by shippers to pay for loss or damage to goods. The explanation of this long immunity is to be found not so much in the invulnerability of their defence, as in the almost perfect protection which the shippers derived from marine insurance. It would be beside our present purpose to enter upon this collateral subject, further than is necessary in the way of explanation. The more that shipowners excluded from their liability, the more did shippers require to cover in their policies of insurance. Hence the laboured attempt to embrace all possible risks in the policy; "Touching the adventures and perils which the said Company are contented to bear, and to take upon them in this voyage: they are of the seas, men-of-war, fire, enemies, pirates, rovers, thieves, jettisons, letters of mart and counter-mart, surprisals, takings at sea, arrests, restraints, and detainments of all kings, princes, and people of what nation, condition, or quality soever, barratry of the master and mariners, and of all other perils, losses, and misfortunes that have, or shall, come to the hurt, detriment, or damage of the said goods or merchandises and ship, &c., or any part thereof."

The great dangers to which goods at sea are inevitably exposed,—against which the shipowners' responsibility is no protection,—and the almost absolute security afforded for a small premium by insurance companies, have necessitated the universal practice of underwriting. By this means, the merchant may not only protect himself against the loss of his goods, but may even secure his estimated profit upon them, in the event of their being lost. The confidence with which this system of insurance has inspired the mercantile world has reduced the number of those who do not avail themselves of it to the lowest figure. When the assured meet with any loss, recourse is at once had to the insurance company or the underwriters, and the claim is seldom refused, or even objected to. When, on the other hand, the goods of those merchants who, saving their premiums, act as "their own underwriters," are lost or damaged, they have themselves to bear it. Such is a brief and somewhat meagre outline of our shipping system, which has wrought satisfactorily for so long a time, and which, it is boasted, has cost so little in the expense of litigation.

Quite recently, however, shipowners have been roused from their fancied security, by discovering that their broad shield of exceptions is not so impervious to legal darts as they fondly imagined. Within the last year or two, it has been held in the three cases noted below,* that they are liable to the shippers of goods for loss or damage caused by the negligence or faults in navigation of the master and seamen. In the first case, the loss was occasioned through a collision with another vessel, which the plaintiffs declared, "arose, and was wholly caused by and through the gross carelessness, negligence, mismanagement, and improper conduct of defendants, by their servants and mariners in that behalf, and not otherwise." The defendants pleaded that the goods were damaged "by the excepted perils." The question was therefore directly raised; and the Court of Exchequer unanimously held the shipowners liable for the consequences of their servants' gross negligence, which, though not "the *causa proxima,* was the immediate and real cause." As Baron Bramwell puts it, "The question is, what is the contract? The defendants' vessel running foul of another vessel by the gross negligence and carelessness of those who were managing it is certainly not an accident within the meaning of the exceptions in the bill of lading. Looking at the word "accident" in connection with the other terms used, it is clear to my mind that the defendants are not protected by it." The second is a still stronger case in point, in as far as the loss or damage is connected to the shipowners by a longer and more circuitous route. The master of the "Norway" voluntarily—*i.e.*, when under no statutory obligation to do so—employed a pilot to take his vessel down the Irrawaddy. The pilot negligently let her go aground on a shoal, from which she was got off in a few hours without apparently sustaining any damage. Shortly afterwards she sprung a leak, and part of the cargo, rice, was thrown overboard before they could reach Mauritius. Here the ship was repaired and the damaged part of the cargo sold, the remainder

* (1.) *Lloyd* v. *The General Iron Screw Collier Company.* Court of Exchequer, 30th May 1864.

(2.) *The Norway.* Admiralty Court, 22d Nov. 1864.

(3.) *Denholm* v. *The London and Edinburgh Shipping Company.* Before Lord Kinloch and a Jury, 17th February 1865.

being brought safely to Liverpool. The plaintiff urged that the shipowner was responsible for the loss occasioned, "because it was the ulterior consequence of the negligence of himself or his agents;" to which the defendants replied, that "these damages were the results of the perils of the seas; but if of the pilot's negligence, the defendants are not responsible." The Right Honourable Dr Lushington held, that though the jettison might have been necessary to avoid perils of the sea, still both it and the sacrifice of the damaged rice at Mauritius were occasioned by the grounding of the vessel on the shoal, which occurred through the negligence of the pilot, for which he held the shipowners responsible. The remaining case was the well-known Scotch one tried before Lord Kinloch and a jury, 17th February 1865. Eight tons of potatoes were lost by the wreck of the London and Edinburgh Shipping Company's steamer 'Prince Alfred,' which struck on a rock off Flamborough Head in a sudden fog, when the master reckoned the vessel to be ten miles to seaward. The issue sent to the jury was, "Whether through the fault of the defenders, or of those in their employment and for whom they are responsible, the said screw steamship was lost, and the said potatoes were not delivered to the loss, injury, and damage of the pursuers?" The jury unanimously found for the pursuer.

It is difficult for one not personally or intimately connected with the shipping interest to understand and appreciate the effect which these cases have had on the minds of shipowners. To us they seem to have been clearly, naturally, and correctly decided; to them they seem to violate the principles of eternal justice. Perhaps a little obtuseness of vision and incoherency of speech are to be expected from those who have been rudely roused from a seventy years' slumber. How otherwise are we to explain the manner in which the result of these cases is spoken of by no less intelligent a gentleman, and (on these subjects) high authority, than the chairman of the Leith Chamber of Commerce. In a pamphlet on this subject,* lately published by that gentleman, he says, speaking more particularly of the 'Norway' case, "The result, then, of this judgment appears to be, that the general principle of the common law, according to which a master is re-

* An Examination of the Question of the Liability of Shipowners, for loss or damage of Goods from Faults in Navigation. With Appendix containing reports of cases and references to authorities. By John Warrack, Chairman of the Leith Chamber of Commerce. Edin., A. & C. Black. 1866.

sponsible for the acts of his servants, overrides and obliterates such express stipulations on the subject of accidents, as those contained in bills of lading. This is directly opposed to the view that has commonly been held, that express stipulations on any matter must always be regarded as qualifying or limiting the application of the general rule to that matter," p. 12. It would be doing injustice to Mr Warrack's intelligence, which is abundantly displayed in other parts of his pamphlet, not to suppose that he perceives the hollowness of this sophism. No violence has been done to the principle of law, that express stipulations limit the general rule. It has only been declared that the express stipulations in the particular contract in question were not sufficient to prevent the general rule of the master's responsibility applying in the special circumstances of these cases. These decisions have not been on any point of principle, but merely on the interpretation of terms; and it has been found that the exceptions contained in bills of lading do not cover accidents occasioned through the negligence or fault of shipmasters and mariners.

Mr. Warrack, perfectly understanding this, passes from the region of sophistry, and contends with much ingenuity and force that the interpretation put upon the terms is inaccurate. One strong argument employed is the usual understanding among merchants and shipowners that the latter are not responsible for accidents at sea, though attributable to default. We are not quite sure that this understanding was quite so usual and unquestionable as is here taken for granted; and we suspect that the prevalent practice among merchants of insuring contributed more to the security of shipowners than any definite notion of their liability: for a merchant who was assured against all risks never would incur the expense and trouble of a hazardous litigation to make good a claim against the shipowners for damages, which he could at once obtain from the underwriters. The uninsured, who had not this reason for saving the shipowners, may have been chiefly deterred from bringing an action against them by the consideration that at least four-fifths of the accidents were really excepted by the terms of the bill of lading, and that in the remaining fifth—caused by default for which the owners might be liable—it would be almost impossible to prove sufficient fault or negligence. In nearly every case the only evidence regarding the accident would be that of the master and mariners, whose negligence was said to have caused it, and whose characters and means of living depended to a great extent on the action resulting in favour of the shipowners. Carriers by land are not so favourably circumstanced; for generally other witnesses than the servants of the company can be obtained to testify regarding the circumstances or nature of the place in which the accident occurred. Would a coach proprietor not think himself mightily secure, if his responsibility for loss or damage were limited to the cases of accident occasioned by the fault or negligence of the driver; and that fault or negligence required to be proved by the testimony of the driver alone?

Against the usual understanding of these terms said to be held by merchants and shipowners, may be placed the general opinion of them expressed by the leading legal authorities. The subject is perhaps nowhere treated more fully and minutely than in Addison on the Law of Contracts, and although the passage is rather a lengthy one, we give it entire.

"From losses occasioned by the Act of God, by the Queen's enemies, and the dangers and perils of the sea, and of navigation, the carrier by water is, and has always been, exempt by the common law; but he is not exempt, nor does the exception in the bill of lading or other contract of affreightment exempt him from accidents occasioned by his own negligence and misconduct, or want of skill, or the negligence, misconduct, or want of skill of the persons whom he has trusted with the navigation of the vessel. The expression, 'Act of God,' denotes natural accidents, such as lightning, earthquake, and tempest, and not accidents arising from the negligence of man. And the term, 'dangers and accidents of the sea and navigation,' denotes the dangers and accidents peculiar to the ocean and to navigation from port to port, which no human care or skill can guard against or surmount, such as accidents resulting from the irresistible violence of the winds and waves and tides and currents; the destruction of a perishable cargo or of living animals from the rolling of a ship in a storm; jettison of goods from irresistible necessity to lighten the ship and save her from foundering; the grounding of a vessel on the hard and uneven bottom of a dry harbour in which she had been obliged to take refuge; or on a sunken rock or sandbank not generally known and not marked on the ordinary charts or maps; irresistible attacks of pirates; the accidental breaking of tackle by which a vessel is moored in port, and accidental collisions in fogs or storms, where no blame is imputable to either of the vessels striking together: and not losses, which, though caused immediately by the violence of the winds and waves, or the rising of the tide, are imputable to the ignorance or supineness, or the negligence or want of skill of the master or commander and mariners, whatever may be the effect given to the term 'perils of the sea,' as between the underwriter and insurer in certain policies of insurance."*

* Addison on the Law of Contracts, 4th edition, (1856), p. 477.

This exhaustive and emphatic statement renders it almost unnecessary to refer to further authority on the subject. We may allude, however, to our highest and almost our only authority on Commercial Law, Professor Bell.* Mention is there made of the extension of the exceptions in the bill of lading to which we have already referred, and it is said, "This is only an express enumeration of the inevitable perils which, by law, would excuse the owners from responsibility. Formerly the exception was expressed in terms more brief, 'the dangers of the sea excepted.' . . . . . But it does not appear that the alteration changes much the rule of responsibility which would have been applied under the old form. . . . . It is essential that it shall be a peril unavoidable. If due skill, vigilance, and care could have avoided or repaired the misfortune, the owners will be liable." And, in his latest work, 'Principles,' when speaking of the responsibility of the owners under their contract, he says, § 435—"When the loss, directly or indirectly, arises from want of skill or faulty navigation (as deviation from the right course) the owners will be liable."

After these explicit statements upon the very point given by Addison and Bell—the highest English and Scotch authorities—it may be subject of regret, but it is still more subject of astonishment, that the usual understanding among merchants and shipowners is (if indeed it really be), that the latter are exempted by that clause in their bill of lading from the injurious consequences of the ignorance or negligence of their servants.

It appears that the alarmed shipowners are meditating a petition to Parliament, after the manner of their predecessors in 1733 and 1786. Mr. Warrack strongly urges the expediency of this course. We doubt very much, however, whether it would succeed; and we should not greatly regret its failure, for we deem such procedure quite unnecessary. The shipowners have the remedy in their own hands. There is no need of a *deus ex machina*—no necessity for Queen, Lords, and Commons helping them to strike a bargain as to the carriage of hides or herrings. What is it they desire? Exemption from all responsibility for the want of skill and diligence on the part of their servants? If that be their object, why don't they say so? They find by these recent decisions that in their previous contracts they have not so said. Let them do it henceforth—they are quite entitled, what-

* Bell's Commentaries, (5th edition), vol. i., p. 559.

ever may be its effect—and they will be perfectly secure. The clause of exception might run, "All and every the dangers and accidents of the seas, rivers, and navigation of whatever nature and kind, whether caused by the act of God, the Queen's enemies, or by the grossest negligence and culpability of the master and seamen, excepted." That is the protection they desire. To that point they wish Parliament to limit their liability. Why, then, do they not openly and explicitly insert these terms in the instruments of their contracts? Because the extravagance of the demand, when stated in plain English, would startle the most highly assured shipper. While it might, indeed, benefit the shipping interest by additional protection, it would entail corresponding disadvantage in scaring commerce. The only ground on which shipowners can base their plea to be more leniently dealt with than other common carriers, is the natural dangers inherent to the element on which they traffic. This consideration, together with the favour always shown to the shipping interest, has led to the many exemptions from liability enjoyed by shipowners. There are, however, other interests to be considered and protected. Shipping is only the servant, and must not be made the lord, of commerce. The very dangers to which our foreign trade is exposed afford a strong argument against extending further the irresponsibility of shipowners; for it is necessary to shield international trade by every means in our power, and not to increase these very dangers by weakening or destroying the strongest and only barrier against them—the vigilance and skill of our mercantile marine.

In addition to the legal aspect, in which alone we have hitherto regarded this subject, there is a monetary or economic one, which also claims our attention, although the other be the more appropriate to this journal. The monetary side of the subject is discussed at considerable length, and with much skill by Mr. Warrack; and it is with less confidence that on one or two points we differ from one who is so worthy of a deferential hearing. From this point of view the question thus presents itself—Will it be for the advantage of shippers that the responsibility for loss or damage of goods through default be laid on the shipowners? It is said that instead of a benefit this will prove a decided pecuniary disadvantage. The shippers, it is argued, cannot, in reliance on this responsibility, cease insuring with underwriters, because the majority of sea perils do not occur through negligence, for which alone the shipowners are responsible. But if they do insure with underwriters, their protection is perfect, and they do not require to come upon the owners for reparation in case of loss or damage; while the owners, on the other hand, to secure themselves against the risk of being so held liable for loss or damage through default, will exact from shippers in the form of additional freight a sum sufficient to pay the increased insurance. The result, then, of the change of law by these decisions will be, it is alleged, that the shippers, for whose benefit the decisions were intended, will be required doubly to insure their goods—once with the underwriter, and once with the shipowner—while the protection thereby secured will be noway increased, for although the goods be totally lost, and that through default, the merchant can be entitled to no more than "once and single payment."

With all deference to Mr. Warrack, we somewhat doubt the apparent strength of this argument. He acknowledges that the existing state of the relation of parties was determined by an understanding of the law, which has been by these decisions shown to be erroneous. We imagine, therefore, that when the law of the case is correctly understood, a re-adjustment of relations will take place. When parties clearly know their legal situation, their mutual charges will soon proportionate themselves to the trouble, expense, and risk which each party has to bear. As it appears by the statistics quoted by Mr. Warrack from the "Wreck Register," 1863, (published by the Board of Trade, March 1865,) that no less than 25·80 per cent. of the whole losses of the year are attributable to default, for which the shipowners are now held liable—they share the risk with the underwriters in the proportion of about one to four. If, therefore, a fourth, or—leaving a margin for doubtful cases—a fifth of the risk be thus transferred from the underwriter to the shipowner, is it not consistent with the simplest principles of trade that the underwriter transfer to the shipowner a proportionate share of his premium, or, in other words, charge less for this decreased risk from the shipper, who then pays proportionally more to the shipowner for the increased risk borne by him?

Altogether irrespective of this, however, we entertain the firm conviction that it would be for the shipper's ultimate advantage that the responsibility for loss or damage of goods through default be laid upon the shipowners, although the immediate result of this should be to increase the shipper's freight without greatly or at all lessening his premium. There is a growing belief in many quarters that the almost total irresponsibility heretofore enjoyed by shipowners is not for the advantage of the general mercantile community. The only safeguard against the "perils of the sea" lies in the skill, vigilance, and efficiency of the master and mariners. But these are chosen and controlled entirely by the shipowners, who through insurance are freed from the risk of any loss occasioned by their carelessness or insufficiency. It is matter of pecuniary indifference to the fully insured owner whether his ship be skilfully or negligently navigated. If it arrive in safety, he gets his legitimate reward; if it go to the bottom, he loses nothing. Nay more, it may occur, and cases do frequently arise, when the insured owner would be a greater gainer by the loss than by the safety of the vessel, when the commander and seamen would more truly consult their employer's pecuniary interest by wrecking the vessel than by saving it. This ought not so to be. Those who have the sole control of any class of servants ought not to be entirely freed from liability for the consequences of their conduct. The baneful result upon our mercantile marine of such freedom from responsibility is more startling than could have been expected. Within the last fifty years the annual per centage of loss on British shipping has nearly quadrupled. In 1816-17-18—before the introduction of steam in the propulsion, or of iron in the construction of vessels, when the science of meteorology was unknown, when seamen were more illiterate and less aided by scientific instruments, accurate charts, and all other sources of safety—the average general loss, as stated by Mr. Lanco of Lloyds, was only 1·57 per cent. In 1850 it was 2·8 per cent., while in 1854 it had risen to nearly 4 per cent., and now by the last wreck returns (1863) it stands almost at 6 per cent. A large proportion of these—at least one fourth—is occasioned by default in some form or other. Thus 176 casualties are attributed by the Board of Trade to "inattention, carelessness, and neglect," and 171 collisions to "bad look-out," "neglecting to show proper light," "neglect or misapplication of rule of road at sea," "want of seamanship," and "general negligence and want of caution."*

* Since the above was written the wreck returns for 1864 have been published, and they place the matter in a still stronger light; for while the total number of losses has decreased from 1664 to 1390, the number ascribed to carelessness, negligence, fault, &c., has increased from 347 to 446.

All these and the like accidents are preventable. That they would also to a great extent be prevented if that were made the interest of those who alone can prevent them, viz., the shipowners, is manifest by comparing the per centage of casualties falling on the mercantile navy with the per centage falling on the Royal navy, or on those large self-insured companies, as the Cunard line, or the Peninsular and Oriental Company. While the losses in the former have gone on increasing, in the latter they have been decreasing.*

The bearing of all this on the interests of shippers of goods is very direct and manifest. Their cargoes are at present exposed to many dangers, additional to the natural "perils of the sea;" and against all these dangers they have to protect themselves by large insurances. Decrease the risks, and the premiums will be proportionally reduced. One-fourth at least of all the casualties which occur are preventable, because they are occasioned by default which might be avoided. The only way of accomplishing this is by placing the liability for these casualties on those who alone can prevent them. If by any means the shipowners can be made to feel that it is for their interest that these avoidable accidents cease, they will prevent them; and then the merchant will have to insure himself not against one hundred casualties as at present, but only against seventy-five.

T. F.

* This phase of the subject was brought by Mr. Chadwick under the attention of the Social Science Association at its meeting in October last at Sheffield. A *resumé* of his address will be found in the November number of this journal, p. 372. After pointing out the injurious consequences of shipowners' irresponsibility, he expresses the hope that Chambers of Commerce and the general public may join in an application "to Her Majesty's Government for a commission of inquiry to revise the past course of legislation, and to prepare efficient measures of prevention as well as of repression." This expression of hope finds an odd comment in Mr. Warrack's pamphlet, wherein the chairman of the Leith Chamber of Commerce exhorts the same parties to petition Her Majesty's Government to extend this irresponsibility of shipowners to its utmost limit.

New Books.

Notes on Scotch Bankruptcy Law and Practice, with reference to the Proposed Amendment of the Bankruptcy Law of England. By GEORGE A. ESSON, Accountant in Bankruptcy in Scotland. Edinburgh: Edmonston & Douglas. 1866.

THIS pamphlet, from the pen of the accountant in bankruptcy, is intended as a contribution to an object which has always been strenuously advocated in this journal,—an assimilation of the Bankruptcy Laws of the United Kingdom. The Select Committee of the House of Commons having, after an anxious inquiry into the working of the Bankruptcy Laws, both in England and Scotland, reported in favour of the introduction into England of a modification of the Scotch system of bankruptcy, Mr Esson, in the pamphlet before us, has explained, for the benefit of the legal and commercial community in England, the nature and working of that system. Nor are we aware of any treatise in which our system is so shortly, and at the same time so clearly stated, and its operation so distinctly brought out. The work is divested as much as possible of all Scotch technicalities, and when the introduction of these was inevitable, they are explained by their English synonymes or analogues. The result of the working of the Scotch Bankruptcy Act of 1856 has, according to Mr Esson (than whom no man is better entitled to speak with authority), been upon the whole most satisfactory. A few imperfections in details are pointed out; in particular, it appears that some additional powers might now with advantage be bestowed upon the accountant in bankruptcy in controlling the accounts of trustees. Mr Esson is also of opinion, that the commissioners (or "inspectors," as the Select Committee propose they shall be called in England) should receive remuneration according to a rate to be fixed by the accountant in bankruptcy, with reference to the circumstances of each case. The giving of remuneration is supported, on the ground that it is usually done in all cases where the time of business men is occupied; we believe Mr Esson might have added, that it ought to be given, in order to secure more attention by commissioners to the affairs of the bankruptcy, and make them more efficient aids to, as well as checks on, the trustee. Upon the modifications which the Select Committee propose to introduce into the Scotch system, while transplanting it into England, Mr Esson makes some valuable remarks. The most sweeping change which is proposed by the Committee is the entire abolition of imprisonment for debt. In discussing this subject in January 1865, we stated our opinion that the public were not yet ripe for such a revolution, and the facts brought forward by Mr Esson confirm us in that opinion. We observe that at a meeting of representatives of the various chambers of commerce of the United Kingdom, which was held on 27th February, the following resolution was adopted:—"That this meeting does not approve of the abolition of imprisonment for debt under any judgment, decree, or order of any Court." The Appendix to the pamphlet contains a table of the number of civil prisoners in Scotland from 1840 to 1863, from which it appears that the daily average in the whole prisons of Scotland is only 72. This shews that the engine of imprisonment in Scotland is not used oppressively; but that the power of adopting this *ultima ratio* is a powerful instrument for the recovery of just debt can scarcely be doubted, and is amply established by the evidence which Mr Esson adduces. The introduction into England of something analogous to the Scotch process of *cessio bonorum*, to be administered by the same courts as are in future to exercise bankruptcy jurisdiction, is recommended by Mr Esson, as enabling the law of imprisonment of debt to be maintained, while its rigour is tempered, without applying "the great engine of adjudication of bankruptcy to the very small, but very necessary, purpose of releasing from prison insolvent debtors who have no estates."

Another modification of the Scotch law which the Select Committee suggest, and which also meets with disapproval from Mr Esson, is the proposal to establish a distinct Supreme Court of Bankruptcy in London. His suggestion is "to combine the benefits of the two systems, by appointing a chief judge for the ordinary jurisdiction of the Court, and uniting with him certain judges of the superior courts for the appellate jurisdiction." The feasibility of this suggestion, borrowed to some extent apparently from the constitution of the Divorce Court, depends so much upon the amount of work at present performed by the English judges, that we are unable to express an opinion, whether it would be found in practice that sufficient time was available for the discharge of the new duties to be imposed on them. It is more in accordance with the English system to subdivide jurisdiction, and limit the labours of the judge to a special department. We confess to a prejudice in favour of our system of having the whole law administered by every judge; and if we lose something in uniformity, we cannot but think that the law gains at last by the evolving of sound principles out of the conflict of views occasionally manifested. The vice-Chancellors, with the existing right of appeal, seem to supply all that is wanted when taken in connexion with the Committee's recommendation of the entire abolition of the district Bankruptcy Courts, and the transfer of their jurisdiction to the County Courts,—a course amply justified by the successful working of the bankruptcy jurisdiction of the Sheriff Courts, conferred on them in 1856.

Various other of the recommendations of the Select Committee are examined by Mr Esson; and in the Appendix will be found some valuable tables shewing the practical working of the Scotch Act of 1856. On one point, upon which great difficulty has been felt in England, we are glad to have some information, namely, prosecutions for fraudulent bankruptcy; even in the imperfect state of our law, it seems two or three such prosecutions take place annually, in circumstances which result either in the conviction of the bankrupt, or in his absconding from justice. This shows our law to be no dead letter, and that probably but slight alteration is required to make it fully meet the wants of the case. The great difficulty is to give a definition of what is fraudulent bankruptcy, and for the solution of this difficulty Mr. Esson offers some contributions in his chapter on the subject.

THE MONTH.

Court of Session.—The last month has been distinguished by the magnitude and importance of some of the cases decided in the Court of Session. There was, in the first place, the Cluny case, in which the Court, by a majority of their number—the case having been argued before the whole Court—repeated the judgment in the Dalswinton case, that a destination to an individual, and his 'heirs whatsoever,' cannot be made the foundation of a good entail. But the importance of the decision lies in the summary fashion in which the Court set aside the directions of the trust-deed, on the ground that these were not framed in accordance with the provisions of entail law, and were therefore inoperative. Colonel Gordon, it will be remembered, left a trust-deed, in which he directed his trustees to invest the residue of his estate, amounting to upwards of £200,000, in the purchase of lands, to be entailed upon his son, according to the destination above mentioned. Mr Gordon raised an action against his father's trustees, in which he concluded that they should be made to pay to him the residue in their hands, seeing that they could not execute a valid entail. The Court have given decree to that effect. But five of the Judges were of opinion that such interference with the expressed wishes of a truster was unwarrantable.

A case of perhaps greater magnitude, as regards the stake involved, and one raising points of considerable difficulty and delicacy, was the Duntocher Succession case. Last summer, the Court, in a question between the heir-at-law and the beneficiaries under the testament, decided that a declaration, by which certain parties were called as substitutes to the heir instituted, truly formed part of, and was a continuation of the dispositive clause of the deed, although locally disconnected from it; and the view then taken was made the foundation of the judgment to which we are at present referring. It has now been decided that one of the parties called as substitutes in the declaratory clause is an heir of provision entitled to challenge a deed to his prejudice, executed upon deathbed by the heir instituted, and that an heir who is only invested by the deed under which he takes, with the ordinary rights which the law attaches to the fee of property, cannot upon deathbed alter to the prejudice of an heir of provision.

In Clements *v.* Macaulay, the Court pronounced a judgment of considerable interest and importance in itself, and the grounds upon which it was rested indicate that the future discussions in the case will be of the same nature. In the year 1862, in the middle of the civil controversy in America, certain parties entered into a joint adventure in the Southern state of Texas, the object of which was to export cotton from the South to the West Indies, and by running the blockade to import a cargo of munitions of war for the service of the Confederate Government. A steamer was chartered for that purpose, but was destroyed by the Federal cruisers upon her second voyage. The partners afterwards disagreed as to the proceeds of the adventure, and an action was instituted in the Court of Session at the instance of one partner against another, who was the manager of the undertaking, and the holder of the funds. Jurisdiction was founded by the arrestment of the defender's property in this country. There was, therefore, no doubt as to the competency of the *forum*. But the defender objected, that although the Court of Session was a competent, it was not a convenient forum, because questions, and particularly a question, as to the legality of the contract, would arise, involving consideration of the municipal law of a foreign country, and it was, in view of that, desirable that the rights of parties should be ascertained in the foreign tribunal. The Court have decided that this is both the competent and the convenient *forum*. Texas, the place of entering into the contract, was the tribunal indicated by the defender as the proper one to try the question, but the Court have held that the Texan courts would have no jurisdiction in the matter. The question as to the legality of the contract is, in the opinion of the Court, one of international, and not of municipal law, the point raised being, whether the Confederate States were to be regarded as constituting a belligerent power, or a mere gang of rebels. In whatever way the question was answered considerations of public law must be the ground of judgment, and accordingly, the Supreme Court of Scotland was as convenient a *forum* in which to ascertain the rights of parties, as the Supreme Court of any other country. In delivering his opinion, the Lord Justice-Clerk remarked that the Court had never sustained the plea of *forum non competens*, except when a defender objecting to the jurisdiction of the Court of Session was in a position to point out another competent *forum*.

Two other cases occurring during the month raise questions of a cognate character. In the case of the North British Railway Company against the Inspector of Poor of the City Parish of Edinburgh, the Court have held that the refreshment rooms belonging to the company fall to be valued separately and are liable to be assessed for poor rates upon that footing. The rooms are let to tenants, and the majority of the Court hold that, therefore, they do not fall to be considered and dealt with under the general undertaking of the company. The cab stands and book stalls which the Inspector also proposed to assess separately, are held to be included in the general undertaking, and to fall under the valuation of the Assessor of Railways and Canals. The case was argued before seven judges, there having been a division of opinion in the Second Division, and the judgment was reached by a majority of one. The case of Bailie *v.* Hay is perhaps a still more important one in point of principle. The Police Commissioners of the burgh of Inverness, acting under the Inverness Burgh Act, to which the Valuation Act, so far as necessary, is made applicable, propose to assess the pier at Kessock ferry for the purposes of the Act. A part of the pier—the part on which the assessment is sought to be laid—lies within the parliamentary bounds, and the liability is sought to be imposed upon that footing. The pier was built by Colonel Baillie, whose lands are situated on the other side, and who has under a Crown Charter a right of ferry between the two coasts. The pier has been held by the Court to be merely an adjunct of the ferry, and the ferry is held not to be assessable on the principle that it is a highway, as much so as a turnpike road which is exempt from liability. The Lord Justice Clerk illustrated his position by supposing that instead of a ferry, the water were bridged over. In that case there would be a road which would clearly not be liable, and he did not see that a mere alteration in the mode of transit made any difference in the principle of the assessment.

The late Act of Sederunt.—We cannot find ourselves at the close of another Session without adverting to the beneficial operation of the late Act of Sederunt. Work has been done, and not, as in former times, the mere appearance of it. In truth, matters are proceeding so expeditiously that the fear has been expressed that the remedy which was devised to reform the Court of Session is going to reform it out of existence. If speedy justice is to make an end of the Court of Session, let the result be known as soon as possible; the country cannot afford to keep up an expensive institution merely for the benefit of a profession, however numerous its members may be, and whatever its historical or national traditions. But he must be very blind and ignorant, and careless of all experience, who fails to perceive that the Court of Session can be rehabilitated only by such measures as that which has recently been in operation. The great aim must always be to determine the preference of litigation in favour of the supreme rather than the inferior Courts of the country; and there is a strong predisposition in the country which only requires to be encouraged in favour of the former. There is no longer any doubt that the machinery of the Court of Session is capable of being worked with as great and more certain expedition than that of the Sheriff Court, and litigants may be trusted, by a sense of their own interests, to prefer the one tribunal to the other. We are not aware that any statistics have yet been obtained as to the operation of the Act of Sederunt, but the rapid manner in which cases now disappear from the roll is the best evidence that it is working well.

Bills in Parliament.—This Session of Parliament has opened with good prospects for the compass of useful Scotch legislation. We have in the first place a Trusts (Scotland) Bill to provide greater facilities for the administration of trusts estates, and to make certain powers and provisions which are now usually inserted in trust deeds incident to the office of trustee. This bill, the general features of which we cordially approve of, is in the main a repetition of the bill of last year, which we discussed when laid before Parliament. We also printed the observations upon it by a committee of the Faculty of Advocates. The bill of this year no longer provides, as its predecessor did, *per incuriam*, that all marriage contracts should be revocable.

There is also an Entail Amendment Bill, by which it is proposed to enact

> "That it shall be lawful for any heir of entail, being of full age and in possession of an entailed estate in Scotland, holden by virtue of any tailzie dated on or after the *first day of August one thousand eight hundred and forty-eight*, to acquire such estate in whole or in part in fee simple, or to sell, alienate, dispone, charge with debts or incumbrances, lease, feu, and excamb such estate in whole or in part, with such and the like consents, and in such way and manner as by the Act Eleven and Twelve Victoria, chapter thirty-six, intituled, 'An Act for the Amendment of the law of Entail in Scotland,' would enable him to disentail, sell, alienate, dispone, charge with debts or incumbrances, lease, feu, and excamb such estate in whole or in part, if holder under a tailzie dated prior to the said first day of August one thousand eight hundred and forty-eight."

Last year a committee appointed to inquire into the subject reported their opinion "that the poors' rates on the one hand, and the other local rates on the other, ought not to be assessed on two different valuations of rental, the one the gross and the other the nett, but that they should alike be assessed on one and the same valuation," and "that the just principle for estimating the rent or yearly value of lands and heritages for the purpose of local taxation, is that provided in Scotland (in accordance with the principle adopted in England and Ireland) for the poors' rate, by the Act of Eighth and Ninth Victoria," and the committee further recommended certain alterations in the Valuation Act, in order to ascertain in a uniform manner the amount of deductions authorised by the Poor Law Act, and also suggested certain other amendments which it would be, in their opinion, advisable to make in the said Valuation Act. With a view to giving effect to these suggestions, we have a bill relating to the subject of valuation of lands and heritages, under which it is proposed that the assessors are to ascertain and state the rates, taxes, and public charges affecting lands, including the amount of assessment for building and repairing churches and manses, spreading the expense of these over the whole period over which the burden may be intended by 25 and 26 Vict., c. 58; also the amount of average annual cost of repairs, insurance, and other expense necessary to keeping the subjects in order; and the assessors are to deduct the sum of these from the gross rental, and thenceforth all poors' rates and other local rates leviable according to the Valuation Roll, are to be levied according to the rentals so ascertained, and the Parochial Boards are not in future themselves to make such deductions, but to take the nett rental as is ascertained. The other provisions it is unnecessary to detail here.

Then there is a Poor Law Officers Superannuation (Scotland) Bill to provide retiring allowances to officers employed in parishes in Scotland in the relief of the poor. The allowance is not in any case to exceed two thirds of the salary, whether computed according to a fixed sum or to a poundage, and, like the salary, is to be paid out of the ordinary assessment. Twenty years' service at least in administering the law relating to the management of the poor in Scotland is required, and no officer shall be entitled to such an allowance who is not sixty years of age.

Of the Writs Registration (Scotland) Bill it is unnecessary to say anything further in the columns of this journal, as it was discussed at considerable length last year. Holding it to be a thoroughly sound well-considered measure, which promises to be of great advantage to the country, we can but trust that no opposition will induce the Lord Advocate to abandon it.

About the most important measure of all is the proposed amendment of the Summary Procedure Act of 1864. The leading provision in the new bill is the erection of a court of appeal, which shall mean either division of the Court of Session where the appeal is from a civil jurisdiction, and the High Court of Justiciary or the Circuit Court where the jurisdiction is criminal. The second clause provides that any of the parties dissatisfied with the judgment of the justice or magistrate as being erroneous in point of law, or on the ground that evidence has been incompetently admitted or rejected, may apply in writing to get a case signed and stated for the determination of the court of appeal. The justices may refuse the application if made upon grounds that are frivolous, but they must certify to that effect; and when the application is made at the instance of the Lord Advocate they shall not have the power of refusal. Where the justices refuse a certificate, application for one may be made either to the Court of Session or the High Court of Justiciary, according as the case is of a civil or criminal nature. The court to which a case is transmitted shall now determine the questions of law arising upon it, and may either decide these or remit back to the justices, as they may consider proper; and all such orders shall be final. Notes of suspension are no longer to be necessary to bring any case under the notice of the Court of Appeal. Either party who avails himself of the right of a Court of Appeal shall be held to have abandoned his right of appeal to the Quarter Sessions. One of the most important sections in the new bill is that which repeals the sixteenth section of the Summary Procedure Act of 1864, which provides that it shall not be necessary to make a note of the evidence. Sheriffs of counties trying complaints under the Summary Jurisdiction Act are bound to do so in future, and so are justices, unless in complaints which they may be authorised to try by any special statute, or where the statute expressly provides that the evidence shall not be reduced to writing. The 28th section of the Summary Procedure Act of 1864 is repealed, and in place thereof it is provided that such cases shall be deemed criminal in which the justices are authorised to pronounce at once a sentence of imprisonment—or, secondly, to pronounce in his option a sentence of imprisonment or to impose a fine or penalty; and all other cases shall be deemed civil.

English Divorce Court.—Sir J. P. Wilde has dismissed a petition praying for the dissolution of a marriage entered into between two Mormons in the State of Utah, on the grounds of the adultery of the wife. The plaintiff had quitted Utah and abandoned the faith of Mormonism, but the wife refused to accompany him, and remained a Mormon, marrying co-respondent in Utah. His lordship held the petitioner was bound to prove that the marriage was a binding one, and was of opinion that a Mormon marriage was invalid in a Christian country.

Spring Vacation Arrangements, 1866.

CIRCUITS.

SOUTH.

LORDS JUSTICE-CLERK AND DEAS.

Ayr—Thursday, 12th April.
Dumfries—Tuesday, 17th April.
Jedburgh—Friday, 20th April.

HENRY JAMES MONCREIFF, Esq., *Advocate-Depute.*
ROBERT L. STUART, *Clerk.*

WEST.

LORDS COWAN AND JERVISWOODE.

Inveraray—Tuesday, 24th April.
Stirling—Thursday, 26th April.
Glasgow—Tuesday, 1st May, at 12 o'clock Noon.

GEORGE H. THOMS, Esq., *Advocate-Depute.*
WILLIAM HAMILTON BELL, *Clerk.*

NORTH.

LORDS ARDMILLAN AND NEAVES.

Dundee—Wednesday, 18th April.
Perth—Monday, 23d April, at 12 o'clock Noon.
Aberdeen—Friday, 27th April.
Inverness—Wednesday, 2d May.

JAMES ARTHUR CRICHTON, Esq., *Advocate-Depute.*
ÆNEAS MACBEAN, *Clerk.*

BILL-CHAMBER ROTATION OF JUDGES.

Wednesday, 21st March, to Saturday, 31st March—LORD MURE.
Monday, 2d April, to Saturday, 14th April—LORD CURRIEHILL.
Monday, 16th April, to Saturday, 28th April—LORD BENHOLME.
Monday, 30th April, to Friday, 11th May—LORD KINLOCH.

BILL-CHAMBER, 10*th March* 1866.

THE

JOURNAL OF JURISPRUDENCE.

SHERIFF COURT REFORM.

Mr. Baxter's Returns.

Since we last directed attention to the subject of Sheriff Court reform, a portion of the returns moved for by Mr. Baxter on 6th June 1864, and having reference to the state of the courts during 1863, have been laid before Parliament. The document is entitled, "Return of the Districts into which Scotland is divided for the purposes of the Sheriff Courts, showing the population, extent, and value of the property in each district, the number and value of the various actions brought therein, with the average length of time occupied, and expenses incurred in the actions for debt; the number of, and average length of time occupied in the appeals from the Sheriff-Substitute to the Sheriff, and other particulars." It is evident that a body of statistics of the character here indicated must prove of the greatest advantage in the discussion of all questions of Sheriff Court reform, and should be published annually, and not merely made the subject of occasional call. We regret, however, that the returns are not yet complete, the officials of certain counties having neglected to obey the injunctions of the House of Commons. The defaulting counties are seven in number, viz., Aberdeen, Edinburgh, Fife, Forfar, Kinross, Linlithgow, and Perth. These counties contain the important towns of Edinburgh, Dundee, Perth, and Aberdeen, and various other populous jurisdictions, and it is very much to be lamented that the officials have not furnished the returns from them in time to be presented along with those which have already been printed. We observe that Mr. Baxter has given notice of a motion upon the subject, but we trust that an early compliance with the injunctions of the House will render it unnecessary for him to proceed with that motion.

The returns, even in their present imperfect condition, are sufficient for the purpose for which we at present call attention to them, viz., as showing the imperative necessity for an immediate revision of the districts and emoluments of the Sheriff-Substitutes. In a recent number we pointed out the great inequalities that exist among these officials in the matter, both of work and of remuneration, and the more minute attention to the subject which the returns have enabled us to give, entirely confirms us in the justice and expediency of the changes we then suggested. We think that it is now made perfectly clear that at least twelve Sheriff-Substitutships might at once be suppressed with the greatest advantage to the public service, and an amount of public money would thereby be set free, which would enable the treasury without increasing the demands upon exchequer to give a substantial increase of salary to those of the Sheriff-Substitutes who have not participated in the recent augmentation. We give a tabular statement of the twelve Sheriff-Substituteships which we should gladly see abolished, together with such particulars from Mr. Baxter's returns as are sufficient to enable our readers to judge of the necessity of such seats of jurisdiction being retained.

That it is perfectly unnecessary to retain a resident judge at each of the twelve towns included in the above list is abundantly evident from a mere glance at the figures. In only one case (that of Falkirk, of which we shall speak in the sequel), does the population of the district exceed 25,000, and in one case it does not reach 8000. The idea of maintaining a judge for such a microscopic jurisdiction is simply absurd, and we should much have wished that the county of Kinross had not been one of the defaulters, in order that we might have had some idea how there can in it exist even the semblance of business. The plea of overwork as an excuse for disregarding the orders of Parliament will surely not be advanced in this case.

We give a table shewing the amount of business in the different districts, which we think should be absorbed. We have added, printing the name in italics, those relating to one or two others, that our remarks may be the more easily followed.

Name of Sheriff-Substituteship.	Population.	Valuation for Income-Tax.		No. of Solicitors.	Salary of S. S.	Ordinary Court Actions.							Small Debt.		Sequestrations.	Criminal Business.		
						For Debt.		Total Sums sued for.		Ad facta præstanda.		No. of appeals to Sheriff.						
		Sched. A.	Sched. B.			Litigated.	In absence.	Above £25.	Under £25.	Litigated.	In absence.		Litigated.	In absence.		Judicial Examinations.	Summary Trials.	Tried by Jury.
Argyll—																		
(*Kintyre*),	15,397			8	£500	2	12	£557	£29	0	14	2	52	82	0	62	79	12
(Inverary),	45,183			10		17	50	2604	585	12	78	25	869	844	2	57	66	8
(*Tobermory*),	15,796			8		10	21	598	269	5	89	8	191	188	0	8	47	0
(Fort-William), }	4,783			8 }		0	1		19	0	5	0	4	8	0	4	21	0
Inverness-shire—					500													
(Fort-William), }	6,703	83,600	5,776	8 }		0	2		89	0	5	2	29	27	0	23	86	0
Bute,	16,331	59,500	13,900	4	525	9	20	695	202	5	0	5	265	176	4	39	85	8
Clackmannan,	21,450	70,525	43,959	7	525	17	24	2690	240	10	11	8	157	189	0	28	104	8
Inverness-shire—																		
(Lochmaddy),	18,853	15,885	530	1	500	9	8	535	79	2	12	8	79	46	0	7	18	0
Kinross,†	7,977			6	500	No Returns from this County.												
Nairn,	10,065	27,529	6,834		500	8	8	200	104	2	4	44	97	84	8	19	20	5
Peebles,	11,408	91,791	13,608	5	500	5	12	575	92	2	0	8	79	47	0	18	78	7
Ross—																		
(Tain and Cromarty),	20,318	57,144	12,415	6	550	14	19	2749	177	9	86	23	876	289	8			
Selkirk,	10,449	62,798	39,531	11	500	0	4	119	87	0	0	7	45	28	0	84	101	0
Stirling—																		
(Falkirk),	34,628	198,300	92,360	18	600	38	41	8698	805	2	5	19	870	473	8	69	495	15
Falkirk and Stirling,	91,926	401,822	172,499	40		91	92	19,463	772	17	15	50	948	1068	6	134	819	51
Glasgow—(½ *of*),	113,783	699,234	871,959	53		814‡		29,622	1142	17	84	57	1870	2823	29	162	24§	59

† The figures given here are taken from the "Edinburgh Almanack."
‡ This includes decrees in absence.
§ Cases of this class, we understand, are treated as police cases in Glasgow.

Let us consider the case of each of the jurisdictions which we propose to suppress, and see how easily its work could be accomplished without overburdening the judge to whom it should be transferred. Commencing in the South, we find the little county of Selkirk with a population a little over 10,000. The Sheriff-deputeship will, on the occurrence of a vacancy in either county, be amalgamated with that of Roxburghshire, with a population of about 54,000; and one Sheriff-Depute, with one Sheriff-Substitute, will be amply sufficient for the care of 64,000 inhabitants, the county towns of Jedburgh and Selkirk being connected by railway, and within an hour of each other. This arrangement would also have the effect of remedying a local inconvenience which arises from the manufacturing town of Galashiels being situated partly in each county, and which has been the source of such embarrassment that the Lord Advocate, if we mistake not, is under pledge to promote legislation on the subject.

On a vacancy occurring in the Sheriff-Deputeship of Peeblesshire, that office is to be merged in the Sheriff-Deputeship of Mid-Lothian. Let the same course be followed with regard to the Sheriff-Substituteship, and the addition of 11,000 inhabitants will make scarcely any appreciable difference in the work of the three Sheriff-Substitutes of Mid-Lothian. It would give an average population to each of only 95,135—less than many of their brethren in other districts have to deal with. Indeed were Linlithgow, with its 38,645 inhabitants, also merged in Edinburgh, it would still leave a smaller population allotted to each than it is found that elsewhere a single Sheriff-Substitute can satisfactorily attend to.

The absence of returns from Perthshire makes it difficult to speak with precision, but we should suppose that the Dunblane district does not contain more than 30,000 inhabitants; so that if Clackmannan were annexed to it, the district would only contain about 50,000. Moreover, Clackmannan lies as it were in the very centre of the Dunblane district; for the Perthshire officials have, if we mistake not, in the discharge of their duties, to drive right across Clackmannanshire, from one side to the other, in order to reach Culross, which is under their jurisdiction. The distance between Dunblane and Alloa is but trifling, and easy railway communication exists between the two towns.

The county of Fife furnishes no statistics, but probably the Dunfermline district contains rather above 40,000 inhabitants. Kinross is only fourteen miles distant by railway, and an amalgamation of the two districts would give something like 50,000 for the Sheriff-Substitute to rule.

Stirlingshire is in a somewhat different position, as the Stirling district contains 57,298, and the Falkirk district 34,628, together a little above 90,000. The two towns, however, are within less than half-an-hour by railway, and 90,000 is by no means too large a populatiou for one Sheriff-Substitute to manage. It is desirable that there should be some prizes for men willing to undertake hard work, and a salary of £900 a year would probably at all times secure a first-rate man for the office. There is another possible way of dealing with the Falkirk district of Stirlingshire, and that is to combine it with the county of Linlithgow. This combination would throw only 73,400 under one Sheriff-Substitute; but it would be liable to the objection of the Sheriff-Substitute being under two Sheriffs—an arrangement which does indeed exist, and without inconvenience, in the case of Fort-William, about 5000 of the population of which district belongs to Argyle and 5000 to Inverness-shire. For districts, however, like those of Falkirk and Linlithgow, containing considerable mining populations, there might arise contingencies where a unity of purpose might be of consequence, which might not be attainable had the Sheriff-Substitute to consult the wishes of two principals. The same objections apply, though in a less degree, to the union of Clackmannan with Dunblane, and of Kinross with Dunfermline.*

Proceeding westwards we come to Dumbartonshire, united as to the Sheriff-Depute with Buteshire. The same process applied to the Sheriff-Substituteships would abolish that at Rothesay, and transfer its 16,000 inhabitants to the jurisdiction of the Sheriff-Substitute at Dumbarton, who has at present 25,000 under his care. The facilities of steam navigation would enable one judge to perform the duties of the combined counties without any inconvenience.

* It is no part of the purpose of the present paper to deal with the question of Sheriffs-Depute, but we cannot help thinking that without disadvantage Clackmannan and Kinross might be thrown under the Sheriffs of Perth and Fife respectively, and Linlithgow thrown under the Sheriff of Stirling. This would entirely obviate the difficulties pointed out above. Of course, were Linlithgow thrown into the Edinburgh district, the proper arrangement would be to put it under the Sheriff of Edinburgh. The salary thrown vacant would afford ample means for remunerating the Sheriffs on whom the additional work would be thrown. It will be observed that the *abolition* of Linlithgow as a separate district, does not form part of the scheme in the text.—ED.

The case of the Highland and Island districts is in many respects so peculiar, that it is with some diffidence that we offer suggestions for the amalgamation of districts. The extent is so great, and the population so scattered, that probably there must always be retained more Sheriff-Substitutes than are warranted by the amount of business transacted. At the same time, the present number of officials appears excessive, and we think the time has come when advantage may be taken of the increase of steam navigation to reduce their number considerably. Argyleshire and Inverness have at present between them seven Sheriff-Substitutes, three for each county, and one (at Fort-William) exercising jurisdiction over portions of both. We should propose the abolition of three of these, viz., Campbeltown, Fort-William, and Lochmaddy. We cannot help thinking that Argyleshire has been peculiarly unfortunate in the selection of Inverary and Tobermory, as two seats of jurisdiction. Had Lochgilphead and Oban been fixed upon instead, no one could doubt that there was no longer any occasion for maintaining Campbeltown and Fort-William. But we fear Lochgilphead must bend to the necessity of the Duke of Argyle predominating over the circuit and county town, and to this necessity the whole county arrangements will have to accommodate themselves. Even with Inverary for head-quarters, one Sheriff-Substitute could, no doubt at some personal inconvenience, to be compensated by an increase of remuneration, easily overtake the work of both the Inverary and the Kintyre districts. The former contains a population of 45,183, the latter contains only 15,397, and yields per annum in the way of business 2 litigated cases in the ordinary, and 52 in the small debt roll; of litigated actions *ad facta prœstanda, nil*, and of criminal trials 79 summary, and 12 jury trials. Surely there is no apology in this state of business for the maintenance of a Sheriff-Substitute. But we profess profound ignorance of the qualities of the whisky-making population of Campbeltown; it may be that nothing but the presence of the Sheriff prevents their drinking at home all the whisky they now send abroad, and running into all sorts of excesses. It may be also that the proper subdivision of the county would be to make the labours of the Sheriff-Substitute of the Southern district that mixture of Campbelton and Islay, the extreme virtue of which is so highly appreciated in the spiritual world beyond the county; in other words, to relieve the Inverary district of the Southern islands, Islay, Jura, Gigha, &c., and add them to Kintyre, abolishing the Tobermory substituteship, and adding that district to Inverary, transferring the ordinary Mull business to Oban, where the Sheriff of Inverary should hold an Ordinary Court once a fortnight, while Small Debt Courts might still be held in Tobermory. This arrangement would probably give the Sheriff-Substitute of Campbeltown jurisdiction over upwards of 25,000, leaving to the Inverary district about 55,000; a more equal division than would be produced by simply merging the Kintyre in the Inverary district, and the Fort-William district, with its population of 4,783, in Tobermory, with its population of 15,796, which would give a population of little over 20,000 to the Sheriff-Substitute. The particular subdivision of the county is truly an Argyleshire question, all we are concerned to show is, that two Sheriff-Substitutes could easily and effectively do the whole work of the county. In no view, however, should Oban be left as it is, with merely a few Small Debt Courts held there in the course of the year by the Tobermory Sheriff-Substitutes; from its increasing importance, soon still further to be enhanced by railway communication, it might well possess the advantages of an Ordinary Court, which either the Tobermory Sheriff-Substitute or the Inverary one, according as one division of the county or the other be adopted, could easily hold at such short intervals as might be necessary. If Campbeltown be added to Inverary, it might be deserving of consideration, whether the residence of the second Sheriff-Substitute should not be established at Oban, and his visits to Tobermory only occasional.

Let us now turn to Inverness-shire, the part of the Fort-William district belonging to which, containing a population of 6703, might quite well be undertaken by the Sheriff-Substitute of Inverness (who has at present only 46,909 under his jurisdiction), and the Caledonian Canal and Kingussie Railway afford sufficient facilities for the occasional visits which it would be necessary for him to pay in order to dispose of the two ordinary cases (both decrees in absence), and the 56 small debt cases (13 of which only were contested), which one year produced from the Inverness-shire district of Fort-William. The Small Debt Court held at Arisaig on the west coast, would naturally be thrown upon the Sheriff of Skye, who is within easy reach of it by steam. The Lochmaddy district, with its one solicitor (the procurator-fiscal we presume), might, but for the intervention of the Minch, well be annexed to Portree, which maintains three solicitors, and a visit from the Sheriff-Substitute a few times in the course of the year would dispose of the 9 ordinary and 79 small debt litigations which appear opposite its name in the returns. If the Minch be looked upon as an insuperable obstacle, let it be annexed to the Lews District of Ross-shire, which contains 21,000 inhabitants. The people of Harris, one-third of the population of the Lochmaddy District, having no ferry to cross, lie at anyrate more conveniently to Stornoway than to Lochmaddy, and of the remainder, about 9000, the great bulk are separated from the Sheriff at anyrate by many ferries; as the division of Argyleshire is a question for that county, so it might be referred to those immediately concerned to say whether the parishes of Uist and Barra should be annexed to the Lews or to Skye. The facilities of steam and postal communication point to the latter. Can it be doubted that the Sheriff of Skye, who seems to have but 9 litigated cases in his ordinary roll, would be thankful for the additional 6 which would probably be yielded by his share of the Lochmaddy District.

In the North of Scotland, as railway communication extends, the number of Sheriff-Substitutes might be materially diminished. Already Dingwall and Tain are brought into close proximity, and the latter jurisdiction, 20,318, might be annexed to the former, which has at present only 40,000 inhabitants. Nairn (10,065), in like manner, might be annexed to Elgin with its 44,218 inhabitants, even although the business in the latter Court appears to be considerably in excess of what the extent of population would lead one to expect, as it had 217 cases (134 of which were litigated) in 1863 in its ordinary, and 1234 in its small debt court, shewing, we may observe in passing, the entire inadequacy of the present salary of £550 as remuneration for the gentleman who fills the situation of Sheriff-Substitute.*

Another small county in the North claims our attention, viz., Kincardine. It has only 34,466 inhabitants, and its actions for debt amounted in a year to 57 (of which 38 in absence) in the ordinary, and 329 (of which 115 in absence) in the small debt court, indicating an amount of business plainly insufficient fully

* This case also illustrates the utterly capricious manner in which the salaries are fixed, although they are supposed to have some relation to the amount of work done. Thus, though the Sheriff-Substitute of Elgin has but the same salary as his brother of Easter Ross—he has more than double the population to look after, and double the duty to perform. His salary is smaller that those of the Sheriff-Substitutes of Sutherland and Caithness, while he has nearly as much work as the two put together.—Ed.

to occupy the time of the Sheriff-Substitute. The position of the county between the two great jurisdictions of Forfar and Aberdeen renders it difficult to annex it to either, and probably the best means of utilizing for the public service the spare time of the Sheriff-Substitute, and at the same time give a claim for increased remuneration, would be that he should relieve the already overworked Sheriff-Substitute of Aberdeen, by holding a weekly small debt court there. A similar arrangement in Lanarkshire, where the Sheriff-Substitute of Airdrie holds a weekly small debt court in Glasgow is, we believe, found to work well in practice.

We would again, before concluding, remind our readers that we do not advocate the abolition of a single *court*, nor even (except in remote Highland districts) the curtailment of a single day's sittings. All that we advocate is the abolition of superfluous *judges*. In every case, with the above exceptions, the seats of jurisdiction are so connected by railway or steam navigation, that the Sheriff-Substitute will easily accomplish visits to the annexed courts every week, or, if necessary, twice a week, leaving him ample time for his work in the jurisdiction where he resides. Criminal cases, except those of a very pressing nature, will be taken up at these periodical visits, and the whole machine of justice will go on, we are convinced, without the slightest derangement. The public will gain in the increased efficiency which comes to every man who is fully employed but not overworked; and the Sheriff-Substitutes will gain both by being supplied with full work, which many of those who are now more than half idle we know earnestly desire, and also by a substantial addition to their income, which the increased wealth and prosperity of the country, and consequent increase of expense in living, is every day rendering more desirable for men in their position.

Let us glance at the pecuniary results of the abolition of the twelve Sheriff-Substitutes in the table we have given. Their aggregate salaries amount to £5700 which, of course, will be available for distribution among those who remain, amounting to forty-four. Nine Sheriff-Substitutes, however (two in Edinburgh, four in Glasgow, and one each in Aberdeen, Dundee, and Perth), have recently obtained augmentations of salaries, raising their income, if bankruptcy fees be included, to different points above £800. These being deducted, leave thirty-five whose salaries should be raised. Of these, fourteen will be burdened with additional work, and the salaries thrown vacant would give each of them upwards of £1100 a year. This would, however, produce inequalities as startling as those which already exist. But let it be viewed in any way. If our readers think the salaries should be uniform, then the redistribution would raise all those at present under £800 a year to £760. If our readers think there should be still some graduation, the minimum might be fixed at £700, and there might be a gradually-ascending scale:—

10 at £700	. . . .	£7000
10 at 750	. . . .	7500
10 at 800	. . . .	8000
5 at 850	(Ayr, Kilmarnock, Paisley, Forfar, Stirling)	4250
	Amounting in all to	£26,750

The existing salaries amounting in all to £26,735.

In proposing the abolitions above mentioned, we do by no means consider that we are pressing the matter beyond reasonable bounds. On the contrary, we cannot help considering it a question whether several other appointments might not be dispensed with without any sacrifice of the public interest. For instance, the Sheriff-Substitute at Caithness might, without any severe pressure, take charge of the 25,000 inhabitants of Sutherland, a county which yields nineteen litigated cases in the ordinary, and a hundred and seventy in its small debt roll, and shews a total amount of criminal business embraced by ten summary cases and three jury trials—an amount of work which certainly we propose to make the country pay pretty dearly for at the rate of £700 a year.

We have already indicated that we see little difficulty in dispensing with Linlithgow, and the combination of Kirkcudbright and Wigton would only give a population of 84,533, 20 litigated cases in the ordinary roll, 9 litigated actions *ad facta præstanda*, 553 litigated small debt cases, and under the head of crime an aggregate of 150 summary, and 23 jury trials.

What would a Glasgow Sheriff-Substitute think of these figures?*

* We have given one quarter of the Glasgow work at the foot of the table, showing the amount of business in the districts proposed to be absorbed, in order that the reader may see at a glance the contrast. We have also given the aggregate work of the two districts of Stirlingshire, which would be by very much larger than that in any of the other districts which we propose to create by amalgamation, yet how much smaller is it than that of Glasgow?

We have thus reserved ample margin to support our case. If it be thought that either Campbeltown or Lochmaddy should be spared, that will not disturb our figures, or if it be thought that we have fixed our minimum too low, or that we have not raised enough to a higher scale, the means are at hand without asking a penny from the public purse to meet either view.

Such briefly is the pecuniary result of the scheme of abolition and fusion which we advocate. It is a question for government, whether the abolition should be made at once, or whether it should be allowed to come into operation by the lapse of time, and the gradual occurrence of vacancies. The former course would cause a temporary demand upon the public purse, but perhaps is the preferable course, as the other or gradual scheme would involve such a number of readjustments of salary as might occasion a good deal of trouble, and perhaps some ill-feeling. That some such scheme of abolition and fusion as we have sketched is absolutely necessary we cannot doubt, and the mode of carrying it out is comparatively of little importance.

Mr. Baxter's returns offer a perfect mine of materials for Sheriff Court reform, but until we are in possession of complete statistics from each court, we refrain from further comments. As soon as the complete returns are before us we shall return to the question of Sheriff Court reform, and consider some other questions which the returns even in their present defective state press upon the attention of every one who at all masters their details.*

* Since these remarks were in type another series of Sheriff-Court Returns has been issued in answer to an address moved in 1864 by Sir William Dunbar. The whole of Mr. Baxter's returns are repeated in this paper, and the returns extend over the years 1861, 1862, and 1863, instead of being confined to the last year. Some additional items of detail are also embraced in the new returns, but none of the defaulting counties seem yet to have furnished the information required from them. The result of the additional returns appears to confirm the soundness of the conclusions arrived at in the foregoing article, although, as might be expected, in some districts the average of three years shews a somewhat different amount of business from that shown in the table. Thus, in Kintyre, the average number of litigated cases (combining ordinary actions for debt and *ad facta præstanda*) is 8 per annum, and the average in the Small-Debt Court is 64. The average number of summary criminal trials is 64, and of criminal cases that actually proceeded to trial by jury is 4. On the other hand, Sutherland shows an average of only 9 litigated causes in the ordinary roll, and 118 in the small-debt.

THE FRENCH BAR.

Much has been done of late years, both here and in England, to improve the educational qualifications of aspirants to the Bar, and to put an end to a system which afforded very slender guarantees for the attainments of those whom it admitted to the rank and privileges of advocate; and it is now generally felt and admitted that we have acted wisely in thus requiring a longer period of study from the candidates for forensic honours, and in subjecting them to a stricter and more searching examination. But on some subjects of great interest and utility, possessing—one would imagine—special claims upon the attention of the legal profession, much ignorance still prevails even among our best informed advocates. For example, how few of them possess extensive or accurate information concerning the history and constitution of the Bar, even in those countries of Europe with which our intercourse is most constant and friendly; although such a subject might naturally be expected to recommend itself strongly, both to those who already belong to our Bar, and to those who are looking forward to joining its ranks. A striking example of the prevailing ignorance on this subject is given by Mr Jones in his interesting "History of the French Bar." "I recollect," he says, "not long ago, hearing a gentleman (learned in the law) publicly make the following erroneous and unjustifiable assertion with respect to the members of the French Bar. He stated that, being on a visit to Paris, his curiosity naturally led him to the Palace of Justice, that is, to the courts, where he saw the French Barristers sitting in the hall behind a black desk, evidently *touting* for business. He expressed himself much disgusted (as well he might be) at such a state of things, and clearly entertained a most contemptible idea of the French Bar, as well as of everything connected with it. This gentleman was most attentively listened to by his professional brethren around, by whom his ready assertion was as readily received, and no doubt believed, and necessarily produced that effect which it was intended to convey in the minds of his hearers. Here, then, is an instance of the great danger of discoursing on a matter with which one is totally unacquainted. This gentleman had simply confounded an ignoble class of men, a class only known to the world as public scribes, with an honourable, highly educated, distinguished body, which can boast of having for its associates such men as Berryer, Chaix-d' Est-Ange,

Paillet, Billault, Bethmont, Baroche, and many others of like distinction and social standing. He had merely confounded the public scribe with the lawyer, the jurisconsult, the advocate, the orator, the statesman, and in his error it is to be feared he was believed, that he led others astray, that he made converts."

In the following sketch of the French Bar we hope to be able to shew that no Bar has been more fertile in men distinguished as jurists, orators, judges, and statesmen;* that none has taken a more active and prominent part in legislation; that none has had greater influence on all the chief political movements that have modified or revolutionized the state of parties or the face of society; that none has afforded more striking examples of civil courage and devotion; that none has more highly appreciated learning and talent; that none has more jealously watched over its honour, or more rigidly maintained its discipline; while, at the same time, none has ever been more honourably distinguished by the closeness of association and feeling of brotherhood existing among its members. It is interesting to observe the important part taken by the Bar in all the chief political movements recorded in the French annals, from the earliest times down to our own days. In the dawning of civilization, before the establishment of modern judicial institutions, we find advocates appearing to assist in its development and progress; we see them engaged in moderating the fury of judicial combats, and also acting as pacificators in the earlier commotions which distracted France, and not unfrequently falling victims to their devotion. In the contests between the rival factions of the Orleanists and Burgundians, in the League, and in the Fronde, their influence was strongly felt; and their share in the great revolution, and in the numerous political changes that have since taken place, is thus eloquently commemorated by M. Pinard in his work on the Bar. "What power, what party has not had need of advocates? What class, during the last half century, when the career of ambition has been thrown open to all, has given more orators to the tribune, more statesmen to the council, more victims to the scaffold? Where has there been more moderation,

* Even in the Church, members of the French Bar have risen to high honours. Guy Foucault—styled the luminary of jurisprudence from his remarkable knowledge both of the civil and the canon law—was raised to the Popedom in 1265, under the title of Clement IV.; and two other famous advocates—Pierre de Fontebrac and Pierre de Fusigny—became Cardinals.

more devotion, more enlightenment, more courage? . . . In the Constituent Assembly, Thouret, Barnave, Chapelier, these fathers of French liberty, who died for her, were advocates. There were also advocates in the Convention, such as Petion, Buzot, Vergniaud, Guadet, who were misled as great souls are misled, and who fell victims to the spirit of revolution. Under the empire, the Emperor availed himself of the services of advocates, although he disliked them. Portalis, Tronchet, Bigot, Duveyrier, Berlier, and some others, were advocates. The functionaries of the empire, the councillors, the administrators, had almost all belonged to the Bar. The Restoration itself, which had the highest classes at its devotion, went to seek assistance among the ranks of the Bar: Lainé, de Serres, Martignac, eloquent orators, whose names the Bar should preserve with pride, and who all three expiated with their lives the unpardonable crime of being wiser and abler than those whom they wished to serve, were advocates. The Revolution of 1830, which had some cause to be dissatisfied with the Bar, did not the less confide to advocates, almost exclusively, the task of representing and defending it. The list would be too long of those whom it enlisted in its service. . . . . M.M. Dupin, Teste, Sauzet, Barthe, Persil, Martin (du Nord) Hébert, Berryer, Mauguin, Marie, Odillon-Barrot, Dufaure, Billault, warriors issuing from the same camp, have gone forth to combat under opposing banners."

We propose, in this and subsequent articles, to give a summary of the history of the French Bar, dwelling a little upon the more important epochs in that history, and upon the career of some of the most illustrious advocates, concluding with a brief notice of the constitution, position, and prospects of the Bar under the government of Napoleon the Third.

The Gauls were subject to Rome for more than 450 years. No other nation was so completely assimilated to the imperial model; and in the code and constitutions of Justinian we continually meet with rescripts directed *præfecto prætorio Galliarum.* Judicial tribunals were established in the seventeen provinces into which the country was divided, and the eloquence of the bar was assiduously cultivated, so that we find in Juvenal's 15th Satire

"Gallia causidicos docuit facunda Britannos,"

St. Jerome too, in one of his epistles, mentions the "exuberance and brilliancy of Gallic eloquence" (ubertatem Gallici nitoremque sermonis), and the poet Ausonius records the names of twelve illustrious orators of Bordeaux and Toulouse. The profession of Advocates was held in the highest honour, and those who exercised it successfully, arrived speedily at wealth and distinction. The Frankish invasion of Gaul dissolved the connection between that country and the empire, shattered the stately fabric of the Gallic bar under the Roman dominion, and introduced a ruder and simpler system of laws. Of the times that followed the barbarian invasions we have but scanty records. We possess no information concerning the French bar during the 6th, 7th, and 8th centuries. Charlemagne conceived the idea of completing and reforming the laws of France, but did not live to carry out his design, though he issued a series of decrees known as Capitularies, in which, amid all their imperfections, may be traced the work of a master-mind. In a capitulary, dated 802, he specially recommends the interests of justice, and ordains "ut comites et centenarii, omnes ad justitiam faciendam compellerent; ut judices secundum scriptas leges juste judicent, non secundum arbitrium suum." In the Capitularies also occurs the first mention of the profession of Advocate, enacting "that none should be admitted therein but men mild, pacific, fearing God, and loving justice, upon pain of elimination." For a time Charlemagne's great genius succeeded in raising society from the abyss of ignorance and the dominion of lawless force. But his work—entirely personal—perished with him, and evil became again paramount. The ancient civilization almost entirely disappeared; war was perpetual; and for one Amadis there were a thousand bandits sporting with the lives of men and the honour of women. Absurd ordeals dignified by the name of the judgments of God, and judicial combats, usurped the place of regular justice. A law of Gondebaud king of the Burgundians, promulgated in 501, expressly authorised and regulated these combats. It is known as *la loi Gombette* and is couched in the following terms. "We have learned with grief that the obstinacy of pleaders and a censurable thirst for gain have corrupted the administration of justice among our subjects to such an extent, that, in the majority of cases, they are not afraid to make oath upon subjects of which they are entirely ignorant, or to perjure themselves in matters with which they are acquainted. Wishing to destroy such a criminal custom, we ordain, by the present law, that when a law suit shall arise among our subjects, and the defender or accused shall have offered to deny on oath that he owes what is demanded of him, or that he has done what is imputed to him, the suit shall terminate in the following manner: Our will is that, if the party to whom the oath would have been offered, refuses it and declares, confident in the truth of his cause, that his adversary may be convicted by force of arms, the judges deny not the combat." Some wise and good men did indeed exert themselves to put an end to the barbarous custom thus legalized, and Agobard Archbishop of Lyons counselled Louis le Debonnaire to repeal what he denounced as "damnosam et damnabilem legem." But the practice was too much in accordance with the mingled ferocity and superstition that characterised the time to be easily put an end to, and the judicial combat was not finally abolished by law until 1566. Under Louis the seventh the practice had risen to such a height that in a law relating to the city of Orleans it was found necessary to forbid it for a matter less than 5 sols. So that for a sum of £2 15s.—the equivalent of 5 sols at the present day—and upwards, the lives of one or both of the litigants might be risked in mortal combat. Philip Augustus in the end of the 12th century, and after him Saint Louis, attempted to put a stop to the trial by combat. The latter—by a law of 1260, and afterwards in the second chapter of his Establishments published in 1270, before his departure for the crusade—substituted proof by witnesses for the barbarous practice of wager of battle, and from this time it began to decline; though, with the tenacity of life peculiar to abuses of all kinds, it survived for nearly three centuries longer. Philip the Fair relaxed the stringent measures of Saint Louis, and allowed the judicial combat in cases involving capital punishment. Advocates played an important part in the singular ceremonies preceding the combat, and their duties are prescribed and regulated by a law of Philip the Fair in 1306. The challenger was bound to bring his accusation before the judge, personally, or by his advocate; and the advocate's mission was one of no slight danger, as, if he did not take care to speak in the name of his client, he was held to have offered the combat in his own person, and might be obliged to do battle with the opposite party. He was therefore bound to weigh well his words, to exculpate his client, and to demand from the judge permission to offer the combat. The extraordinary mixture of legal formalities, religious ceremonies, and barbarous superstitions which distinguished these judicial combats is highly curious, and strikingly illustrative of the spirit of the age in which they prevailed. We therefore translate from the Style Book of Dubrueil the speeches made by the advocates for the parties, and the orders by the judge of the combat. The advocate for the appellant addressed the Court in the following terms:—" I have to state before you against my Lord so and so whom you see there, on behalf of my Lord so and so here present, nothing in which there is villany; for in all my life I have never seen in the said Lord anything but good and honour, but what I am about to say and set forth against him, I say as the advocate of the Lord so and so, my client; and although he has instructed me, and wills that I say and set forth accordingly, and will bear me out in your presence if it pleases him, he has given me his instructions in writing and substance, and I hold them in my hand; for of myself I should never do this; for the aforesaid Lord has never done me any wrong, nor I to him that I know of, but only right and honour, as I am here to state. But this is my cause, and otherwise it could not be maintained to the desired conclusion; and as you know better than me that every advocate ought to say what supports the cause of his client, especially we who are bound thereto by oaths, and also it is right that every one should do his duty. Wherefore, my Lords, I beseech you of your good pleasure that you will graciously grant what I demand; and, at the same time, I pray my Lord so and so that he will pardon me; for God aiding me, in all other things I will serve him; but in this special case it is necessary that I do my duty, for I am bound thereto." After these introductory precautions, indispensable to the personal safety of the advocate, the President of the Court replied to him: "But state your quarrel, and take care that you say nothing in which there is villany, although it make in favour of your cause; for the Court forbids you to do so." The appellant afterwards stated his conclusions according to the following formula: "Having thus set forth my cause, as you, my Lords, have heard, I thus conclude —that if the said so and so confesses the things that I have set forth to be true, I require that you adjudge him to have forfeited body and goods to our Sire the king for the reasons aforesaid, or that you punish him with such penalty as the customs of the country ordain, or the nature of the cause set forth demands; and if he denies, I affirm that my Lord so and so cannot bring sufficient proof by witnesses or otherwise. But he will prove it by himself or by his champion in the lists, as a gentleman, provided with horse and arms and other things necessary, useful, or convenient for a wager of battle, and in such case, according to his nobility, I throw down his glove." On uttering these words the advocate threw the glove into the centre of the Court. The advocate of the opposite party then brought forward all his reasons of defence to induce the rejection of the wager of battle; and then added, "And in case that the Court should think that the statement made by the other party is sufficient to support the wager of battle, my client denies the facts set forth; on the contrary, he affirms that he who has caused these allegations to be made lies, and that he is ready to support this by himself or by his champion, and thereto pledges his gage." Then the accused said to the Court before giving his gage, "My Lords, I affirm, that in all that so and so has made to be set forth and vouched against me by his advocate accompanied by the delivery of his glove, he has lied like a rascal, saving the honour of the court; and I deny all that he has set forth and stated against me and support my advocate in what he has said in my defence; and maintain that in case the court finds good grounds for the wager of battle, I shall defend myself, notwithstanding what the advocate of the opposite party has said to the contrary, like a good and loyal gentleman, as I claim to be, and as one who has done no wrong in the matter urged against me, and there lies my gage." After the defiance thus given and accepted, a regular minute of the proceedings was drawn up; the judge authorised the combat, and the parties pledged themselves to appear on the day appointed. On that day the king of arms, after having summoned the combatants, beginning with the challenger, published the police regulations according to law. The combatants, by themselves or by their advocates, made protestation in terms also regulated by law; and the combat was preceded by oaths and religious ceremonies in presence of the advocates of the parties. Then the herald-at-arms gave the signal, the members of the court retired, leaving to each combatant a bottle full of wine and a loaf. The advocates also retired; their ministry was over; and the combatants were left, in the words of the formulary, "to do each the best that he shall be able." The victor gained his cause and left the lists with honour. The vanquished was handed over to the marshal, "to do justice on him according to the king's pleasure." Certainly the advocates of the 19th century have good cause to congratulate themselves on being exempted from the risks to which their predecessors were liable in the 14th An ill considered speech may still lose a cause; but then, a careless word might compel an advocate to throw aside the robes of peace and to do battle for his client, not only metaphorically, but in the most literal sense of the words. Both clients and advocates have a danger the less; and though law still ruins many a man, it no longer assists and authorizes him to cut the opposite party's throat, or put his own in peril.

THE MONTH.

The Law of Partnership.—We have much pleasure in directing the attention of our readers to a treatise just published on the Law of Partnership and Joint-Stock Companies from the pen of Mr. Francis W. Clark, advocate. There is no department of the law which admitted and stood more in need of patient study and elaborate exposition. For the theory of the partnership relation, as it exists in the law of Scotland, touches the results of speculation, the facts of history and all possible developments in practice. Nowhere is the affinity between the Scotch and Roman jurisprudence more apparent. Nowhere does the law more exhibit that it grows along with the history and the habits of the nation. And yet it cannot be said that the subject has ever been treated, in this country at least, with the consideration to which it is entitled. No doubt much in the law of partnership is of recent growth, whether as regards direct legislative enactment, or what is evolved from the life and experience of the country. But even leaving these topics out of view, there is no doubt that the subject with which Mr. Clark deals is both in its historical and dogmatic aspects, to a great extent, untrodden ground.

It is not too great a compliment to Mr. Clark to say that, while in his choice of theme he has shown his sense of a great professional want, he has laboured to supply it in a manner that does the highest credit to himself personally, and will cause his work to be received in legal circles with the utmost satisfaction. It is out of our power at present to enter at any length upon the merits of such a recent publication. A detailed notice of the aim and execution of the work must be left for a future number. But it is a simple act of justice to Mr. Clark to take the earliest opportunity of expressing the favourable impression which, upon a general perusal of his book we have formed, and to recommend it to the notice of the profession. It appears to us that the subject admits, and that the occasion might have been taken, by one so competent to the duty, of a more speculative form of treatment than that to which Mr. Clark commits himself. But Mr. Clark may readily excuse himself on the ground that there was so much to do in the way of statement of legal principle, that there was little scope for theorizing, and there is no doubt that in one very important department of the work, its historical exposition, the execution leaves nothing to be desired. The object of the treatise is very clearly and concisely stated in the introduction, to be to examine the law applicable to the various forms which the partnership relation assumes in Scotland, in so far as they are applied for purposes of mercantile gain. A very wide field is in this way brought under review, comprehending the principles that underlie private partnership, the point where our law touches more closely than in any other upon the Roman law, and makes greater divergence than in any other from the English, un-incorporated joint-stock companies, companies formed under the Letters Patent Act and the Registration Acts, without attaining limited liability, corporate bodies with the full privileges of the Registration Acts, companies formed by Royal Charter or incorporated by Act of Parliament, and companies that possess aggressive powers under special acts. The record alone of the legal principles, and the decisions that have been pronounced under these heads is a narrative of no ordinary length, exciting the surprise that bulky as the work is, it should not be more. But Mr. Clark's clear apprehension, and his vigorous and terse expression are apparent when the reader observes with what laboriousness and perspicacity every application of legal principle has been traced, and is detected in quarters where generally they would be least looked for. Mr. Clark indulges too very happily, and always under subordination to practical aims, a strong analogical faculty, and his work has the merit of exhibiting at one and the same time a trustworthy and available exposition of legal doctrine, and a high standard of professional and of general intellectual cultivation.

We do not hesitate to predict that the work will take a high place in the profession. We do not detect a single omission that would impair its influence for practical uses. Every reference has been anxiously verified, and if it would seem that Mr Clark has made a liberal use of English authorities, it is clear that he has done so under the guidance of a sound judgment, and under rules that are very exact and rigorous in construction. There is, in truth, no part of the book that more commends itself to our acceptance than the clear perception and strong hold which it has of the genius of the law of Scotland, as distinguished from that of England, in spite of all their statutory similarities. And the work will not be found more practically useful than satisfactory to all who entertain a sense of the intellectual elevation of their profession, and desire to see its topics treated in a scholarly and dignified way. There is no reluctance to enunciate legal doctrines boldly, when it can be shown that they have the sanction of principle and authority; and Mr Clark's dicta will generally be found upon examination to be good for all they say. With the style of the book the reader will experience a hearty satisfaction. If disposed to be hypercritical we should say that we have observed a certain fastidiousness in the selection of choice and educated language. But most people will not consider that a fault in an age when so much tawdriness is palmed off upon the world in the shape of law literature. We think that there is now and then repetition in Mr Clark's book which might beneficially be avoided, and too frequent a use of stereotyped Latin law language.

Court of Session Rolls.—From the rolls for the ensuing Session of the Court, it appears that there are 62 cases depending in the Outer House before the Lords Ordinary. In the First Division there are 125 cases before the Court, 13 are summary, 66 ordinary, 4 are at *avizandum*, and 1 is before the whole Court. In 41 cases the causes are not ready, and the parties are not moving. 61 cases are before the Second Division: 8 are summary, 23 ordinary, and in 30 parties are not moving or the cases are being prepared. The Court meets on Saturday, 12th May.

Bills in Parliament—Feuing of Glebes.—A bill with a view of enabling ministers to let or lease, feu or sell their glebe lands, has been introduced into Parliament by Sir James Fergusson, Major

Walker, and Mr. M'Lagan. It is proposed that a minister may, with the consent of the Presbytery, grant a lease of any part of his glebe for a period not exceeding eleven years. Leave to feu may be got by application to the Court; but the consent of the Presbytery and of the heritors to the application must be previously obtained. The fourteenth section of the bill provides that in granting authority to feu, the Court are to make the following directions.

(1.) The payment of the feu-duties to the minister until his entire income from the benefice shall amount to a sum equal to at least one-half more than his income therefrom at the date of the said order, in the whole to the sum of £400 per annum at least, and which said payment is in the Act called the Ministers' Fund.

(2.) The payment of the feu-duties, if any, after providing for the Ministers' Fund to form a fund called the Parish Fund, for providing additional spiritual supervision in the parish, and the mode and manner in which the same is to be applied.

It is proposed to confer on conterminous proprietors a right to feu or purchase the glebe lands in fee simple after an order has been pronounced by the Court. Proprietors are to appear before the Court and express their willingness to do so, and when there are two conterminous proprietors desirous to obtain the lands, the highest bidder is to be preferred.

The *Valuation Bill,* to which we referred in our last number, has been thrown out of Parliament, and the *Writs Registration Bill* remitted to a Select Committee.

The Lunacy Acts (Scotland) Amendment Bill now before Parliament, was rendered necessary in some degree by the expiry at 1st August 1866, of the time for which, under the Acts 20 & 21 Vict. c. 71, and 27 & 28 Vict. c. 59, the appointment of the Deputy Commissioners was to subsist; but it has been thought proper to tack to the clause continuing that appointment various important provisions affecting the treatment of insane persons in asylums. Some of the clauses are causing a good deal of discussion, while others are clearly calculated to prove beneficial. Section fourth provides very properly that the granters of medical certificates on which the Sheriff's order for the reception of ordinary lunatics into an asylum proceed shall neither of them be officers of that asylum. The Edinburgh physicians in a memorandum which they have drawn up on the subject have made the most feasible suggestion we have yet seen for giving effect to the desire of the medical profession for some protection against groundless actions by lunatics, or persons whom they have taken for lunatics; viz.—that every application for a warrant to confine a lunatic should be laid in the first instance before the Sheriff, by whom the medical reporters should be named. Acting under the Sheriff's remit they would have the responsibility and the protection of officers of Court. Though the alarm of the doctors seems unnecessarily great if compared with the sufferings of the profession, this suggestion deserves consideration not only in their interest but in that of the public, who will certainly suffer if the respectable medical men become frightened to grant certificates as to lunatics. The matter will fall into the hands of the poorer, most ignorant, and least scrupulous members of the profession. By section sixth it is provided that, orders granted shall remain in force notwithstanding the patient's absence from the asylum for fourteen days when he has left or escaped, or for three months when he remains under the care of the officers of the asylum.

The seventh section affords a new guarantee against improper detention in asylums. At present the Sheriff's order has no natural determination, except by the recovery or death of the lunatic; but this section proposes that it shall not remain in force for more than three years after the admission, unless the superintendent shall, on each first of January after the expiry of the three years, certify on soul and conscience that within a month preceding the date of the certificate he has carefully reviewed and considered the case, and is of opinion that the continued detention of the patient is necessary for his own welfare or the public safety.

Section eighth provides that pauper lunatics discharged on probation, under section 16 of 25 and 26 Vict. c. 54, shall remain during the period of probation subject to inspection by the Commissioners, and shall not during that period be taken off the poors'-roll without the sanction of the Board, under a penalty.

The penalties imposed on inspectors in this and the following sections are not novelties in the Lunacy Acts, but they appear to proceed on an erroneous, or at least inconvenient principle. No inspector would do what is here forbidden except on the order of the Parochial Board; and thus any fine imposed would really be imposed on the Parochial Board, or rather on the funds raised by assessment, of which they are administrators. The idea of keeping inspectors, who are thoroughly under the control of the Board of Supervision, to their work by means of penalties is in itself rather ridiculous, but it is especially out of place when the penalty is affixed, not to a personal omission, as in Section 112 of the original statute, but to an act which must generally, if not always, be done in the execution of orders received from their immediate superiors. It is said that no fines have hitherto been imposed by the Commissioners under the existing act, so that the question who shall pay, has not arisen, any more than the question who shall win in a conflict between the Board and the Board of Supervision, or a Parochial Board backed by the Board of Supervision.

The 9th, 10th, and 11th Sections contain provisions for the removal of unrecovered lunatics, not being dangerous lunatics, detained in asylums. In the present acts there is no distinct regulation for this purpose. In practice it is said the sanction of the Lunacy Board is nominally required for such removals; but in fact the discharge of pauper lunatics is obtained simply by taking their names off the poors'-roll. The bill proposes to authorise the discharge of any pauper lunatic, not being a dangerous lunatic committed under the 15th Section of 25 and 26 Vict. c. 54, on the production to the superintendent of a copy minute of the Parochial Board certified by the chairman, ordering his discharge or removal. But the superintendent may make a written representation to the Lunacy Board that such lunatic is "dangerous to himself or the public, or otherwise not a fit person to be discharged," upon which it shall be lawful for the Board to prohibit his discharge. Such removal, when it takes place, is to be notified to the Board by the Inspector of Poor, together with its date, the house to which the lunatic is removed, and the nature and amount of the parochial allowances made to him; and any subsequent change in like manner must be intimated. The Board may at any time order such lunatic to be replaced in an asylum, and it shall not be lawful for the relatives of any pauper lunatic ordered by the Board to be removed to an asylum to take him off the poor's roll without their sanction. Pauper lunatics may also, by order of any Parochial Board responsible for their maintenance, be removed from the poor's roll, and entrusted to any private party who shall undertake to provide for their care and treatment; but the Lunacy Board may, on a report from the superintendent of the asylum stating his opinion that "such removal will be injurious to such lunatic, or a risk to the public," or, "on any grounds which the Board may deem satisfactory," authorize their continued detention at the expense of the Parochial Board.

So far as these sections provide for information being given to the Lunacy Board of changes in the treatment of lunatics their provisions are all right, but when they interfere with the question whether the relatives are to take a lunatic off the poor-roll or not, they give a power which cannot with propriety be committed to any committee of doctors whatever. The Parochial Boards are at present amenable to two authorities—the Board of Supervision and the Sheriff—and nothing but confusion can arise from introducing a third. By all means let information be given to the Lunacy Board, and let no change be made till a reasonable time after they have received it, but let their interference be through the Board of Supervision, or more properly still through the Sheriff. We understand the grounds on which the superintendents are allowed to object to removal, but we do not understand those on which the Lunacy Board may. If they satisfy the Sheriff "on any other grounds," we have no objection to the detention, and even see that it would be better to go to the Sheriff before the lunatic's discharge, rather than apply to him half-an-hour after for an application for readmission, which they could do just now; and to give a Board, not supposed to have any knowledge of legal rights, power to declare that the Parochial Board shall continue to be responsible for the maintenance of lunatics whose friends wish to remove them and provide for them, seems rather absurd.

Section 41 of the Act of 1857, regulating the reception of a single lunatic in a private house, and section 43 bringing under the cognizance of the Board lunatics kept or detained in private families, although members of the family or relatives, are repealed. In lieu thereof, section 12 requires that every person receiving into his house "any person as a lunatic for gain," shall, within fourteen days, apply for an order of the Sheriff or the sanction of the Board, and in the case of pauper lunatics the inspector of poor shall make the application, which may be granted, in the latter case, on one medical certificate. The section further provides for the inspection and visitation of such lunatics. The important words of the former Act, "unless such house shall be the dwelling place or temporary private lodging of such lunatic," are omitted; and thus, it is objected, inquisitorial and oppressive powers are conferred on the Board. It is made necessary to intimate to the Board every transitory attack of insanity where the patient lives in lodgings, or for which the proper treatment is change of scene and air. Puerperal mania, for example, seldom lasts more than a month or six weeks, and a brief visit to a watering-place, its proper treatment, will be possible under this Act only by permission or under the inspection of the Board, for otherwise the lodging-house or hotel-keeper is subject to a fine of twenty pounds. The 13th section appears to place under more stringent conditions the interference of the Board with lunatics in private families, not kept for gain, chiefly by obliging the Board to obtain the consent of the Secretary of State or Lord Advocate, before they can visit or inspect any such lunatic suspected to be subjected to coercion or harsh treatment. Failure to intimate such cases to the Board is no longer to be an offence punishable by fine or imprisonment.

The 14th section provides, that with consent of the District Board of any district, which has provided district accommodation, or without such consent where no accommodation has been provided, any Parochial Board or Boards may "assess *themselves*" (a manifest error which requires correction), for the erection of an asylum for their own pauper lunatics, which asylum shall require a licence from the Lunacy Board, and shall give such parishes exemption from future district assessments to such extent as the Board shall think fit. It is on this section we believe that the chief conflict of opinion will be found to exist. On the one hand, it will be said that this measure merely reinstates the authorities who had shown themselves incapable previous to 1857, and whose mismanagement was the cause of the great public scandal which led to the Act of that year. That Act transferred from the parishes to District Boards, consisting of persons supposed to be less influenced by considerations of mere expense, the entire control of pauper lunatics. Its purpose was that all lunatics should be sent to the royal or chartered asylums, and, where these were not available, to the district asylums for the erection of which it furnished machinery. This principle was seriously affected by the Act 25 & 26 Vict. c. 54, which sanctioned the reception of pauper lunatics in poor-house lunatic wards to be licenced by the Lunacy Board without the order of the Sheriff, and allowed arrangements to be made for receiving the lunatics of any county, district, or parish in any public, private, or parochial asylum beyond the limits of that district. It is objected that this clause is a farther step in the same direction. Every parish, it is said, will be able to have its own little madhouse, in which its lunatics may be caged at the lowest price. On the other hand, it is urged that in some cases the District Boards have failed in the duty for which they were created of providing accommodation for their pauper lunatics, and the undue extension and mismanagement of poor-house lunatic wards, is guarded against by requiring the concurrence of the District Board to the erection of the new asylums where a district asylum already exists. It is only where no district asylum exists, and no accommodation has been secured elsewhere under the Act of 1862, that any encroachment will be made by Parochial Boards, and that will be owing to the failure for nine years to carry out in any way the intentions of the Legislature.

We are not disposed to overestimate the capacity and the philanthropy of the parochial mind, but we believe that under the supervision of the Board of Lunacy the condition of poor-house lunatic wards in Scotland is not (with certain exceptions, in which licenses have lately been withdrawn) so unsatisfactory as the objectors to the bill would have us suppose. They are admittedly superior to those of English workhouses, over which the English Lunacy Commissioners have no jurisdiction. But it is not the less to be lamented that a necessity should have arisen for breaking in upon the principles laid down in 1857. The public is entitled to a full explanation of the circumstances connected with the failure to supply the requisite house room for lunatics under the present acts. It is said that the existing royal asylums are aggrieved by having only the worst and most expensive cases entrusted to their care, while the ordinary cases are retained in the poor-house lunatic wards. This is said to be the source of controversy between the authorities at Morningside and the local officials in the Lothians; but the former excuse themselves by the statement that more than a year ago they referred the whole question of terms to the Lunacy Board. Surely the matter might have been settled by fixing two rates, one for patients requiring more care and treatment, and another for simpler cases. If this section should eventually be approved by Parliament, it would be well to add the usual powers for borrowing and paying the debt by instalments in thirty instead of ten years. This power the proposed clause of reference to the Poor Law Act will not give.

Section 15 extends to others than dipsomaniacs the power of voluntarily submitting to treatment for mental disease as boarders in asylums. The 16th Section introduces a regulation similar to one which has existed, in England so far as regards private patients, since 1862, viz., that every letter addressed by a patient in an asylum to the Board, or their Secretary, or the Commissioners in Lunacy, or any of them, shall be forwarded unopened, and that every letter from those persons to any patient and marked "private," shall be delivered unopened. The Edinburgh College of Physicians in a "Memorandum" upon the bill, object to this provision as tending to "foster distrust in the minds of the patients in an asylum, and very subversive of discipline."

The principal provisions of the remaining Sections (17-24) are for giving the Lunacy Board power to interfere by summary application to the Court of Session, for the protection of lunatics having judicial factors; for enabling district boards to provide superior accommodation for lunatics not paupers; and for empowering the Sheriff to authorize the discharge of any dangerous lunatic on certificates by two medical men approved by the Procurator-Fiscal. Why not appointed by the Sheriff, the proper judicial officer for dealing with such delicate matters?

The question is suggested by this, the fifth Lunacy Bill since 1857, whether the time is not approaching, or already come, when the legislation on the subject should be consolidated in a single statute. The acts are not administered by lawyers, but chiefly by medical men and inspectors of poor, and their provisions surely ought to be as clear and acceptable as words can make them. And if a well-considered measure of consolidation were prepared, with our present lights, some important improvements might be made, both in the substance and the form of our Lunacy Law.

AT the annual ceremony of Graduation in the University of Edinburgh, the degree of Bachelor of Laws was conferred on the following gentlemen:—Mr William Frederick Hunter, advocate; Mr Andrew Jackson, M.A.; Mr Thomas M. Mure, M.A., advocate; Mr Alexander Thorburn; and Mr Æneas T. G. Mackay, B.A., Oxon., advocate.

THE

JOURNAL OF JURISPRUDENCE.

LAW STUDIES.

No. II.—LAW DEGREES AT THE ENGLISH UNIVERSITIES.

STRANGE as it may appear, it is nevertheless a fact, that at neither of the ancient universities of England do the law degrees, technically so called, afford so complete a guarantee for acquaintance with those branches of learning, which are intermediate between the speculation of the closet, and the practice of the forum, and thus form the immediate groundwork of a lawyer's training, as the degree in arts in the moral sciences department at Cambridge, of which we spoke in our last article. If the scheme of study for this degree has a fault, that fault, as we have seen, lies in its very completeness, or, in other words, in its attempting too much. The ordinary Cambridge bachelor of law escaped far more easily—too easily indeed it is thought—for, like other creatures of an easier-going age, he has been trodden down in the hurry of our day, and will soon be abolished. No doubt he has many faults; but the worst fault alleged against him is that he is merely a sort of bachelor of arts, who sails under false colours, and has got a trick of running into port without duly submitting to the right of search. In consequence of this allegation, on 3d June 1865, a so-called "grace" or statute of the university declared that he should henceforth be called by his true name, and that a special examination in law should in future be recognised as one of the avenues to the ordinary degree of bachelor of arts. The ordinary degree of bachelor of law being thus rendered unnecessary, a subsequent "grace" of 2d Nov. directed that, saving existing interests, it should be discontinued. This arrangement was declared to have reference to all students whose residence at the university commenced on or after the Easter term 1865; and the last ordinary degrees in law, still open to those whose residence began previously to that period, will be conferred in June 1868. But it is the ordinary bachelor of law only who has been thus struck down, or absorbed as it were by what we should call the faculty of arts. His robuster brother, who takes honours, is still spared; and the nature of his examination consequently becomes a subject of interest for us. So far as we can gather them, the final arrangements with reference to him appear to be these: He has to pass two general examinations, common to all students who aspire to any degree whatever:—1st. The so-called "previous examination," or "little go," which is open to all students who have entered on their third term; and 2d. A general examination, held towards the end of the Easter term in each year, open to all who have entered on their fifth term. So far he is on common ground; but these conditions fulfilled, in place of one of the five special subjects now open to those who proceed to the ordinary degree of B.A. (of which law is one) he must now choose the examination for the law degree *with honours.* It is in the character of this latter examination then, it would seem, that we must seek the touchstone of the legal training of the modern bachelor, and we consequently turn with interest to the subjects prescribed for the present year. They are these:

"I. Roman Law. *For Translation;* Gaii Commentarii, and Justiniani Institutiones; Cicero, Oratio pro Quintio; Digest, Lib. 10, tit. 3, De Communi Dividundo, and Lib. 17, tit. 2, Pro Socio.

II. English Law. Joshua Williams's Law of Real Property. Blackstone's Commentaries, Vol. III.

There will be a paper on each of these books.

III. English History. The Constitutional History of England, from the termination of the Commonwealth to the end of the reign of George II.

Special reference must be made to the leading statutes cited by Hallam, and to the two following trials: That of Bushel, reported, &c., and that of Ashby *v.* White.

IV. International Law. Kent's Commentary (Vol. i. part i.)

N B.—There will be three papers of questions.

(1). On Roman Law, (having reference to the subjects above mentioned)

(2). On General Jurisprudence, which will be taken from Austin's Province of Jurisprudence, vol. i., and Bentham's Principles of Civil Legislation.

(3). A problem paper containing hypothetical cases, and abstract points of Law, Roman, English, and International."

Now in all this we see no guarantee whatever for high legal training, or even for solid preparation for the special studies of the Jurist, the Statesman, or the Diplomatist, in after life. The translation of such books as Gaius' and Justinian's Institutes, without any special preparation at all, ought surely to give little trouble to a man who takes a degree of any kind at Cambridge, to say nothing of a degree with honours. Then what would a student of law, in any other European country except England, think of such a subject as general jurisprudence being represented only by such names as Austin and Bentham! To say nothing of the one-sidedness of their method, their own want of acquaintance with the attitude which scientific jurisprudence had assumed on the Continent, even in their own day, is notorious; and if they did not know themselves what had been done while they lived, they can scarcely be expected to teach others what has been done since they died.

The subjects, in short, are precisely such as any ordinary English law student, whose horizon was bounded by the three seas, and who had received no scientific training whatever, would be likely enough to select for himself; and he would be a student of very little energy or ambition if he did not succeed in mastering them pretty fairly as a relish to the pipe-of-peace with which he composed his thoughts after the labours of a day in Chambers, or the distractions of a Committee-room of the House of Commons. But the aspirant to legal honours at Cambridge does not necessarily rest contented with a Bachelor's degree. A Bachelor of Law may take the degree of Master of Law, by incepting, as in Arts, at any time after the completion of three years from his inauguration. The creation of Masters of Law takes place, without their personal attendance, on commencement Tuesday. Bachelors of Arts and Masters of Arts may also take the degree of Master of Law; but they must pass the same examination as candidates for the degree of Bachelor of Law. A Master of Law of five years' standing may proceed to the degree of Doctor of Law; he is required to keep an Act in the following manner:—"The Regius Professor of the faculty shall assign the day and hour when the exercise shall be kept; The professor, or some graduate of the faculty, who is a member of the senate deputed by him, shall preside over the exercise; The candidate shall read a thesis, composed in English by himself, on some subject approved by the professor; the professor, or graduate presiding, shall bring forward arguments or objections in English for the candidate to answer, and shall examine him in English, *viva voce*, as well on questions connected with the thesis as on other subjects in the faculty of a more general nature; the exercise being made to continue at least one hour; Public notice of the Act shall be given by fixing on the door of the university schools, eight days at least before the assigned time, a written paper specifying the name and college of the candidate, the day and hour appointed for the exercise, and the subject of the thesis. Copies of the notice shall be delivered also, at the same time, to the vice-chancellor and to the professor. Candidates for the degree of Doctor of Law pay to the professor for keeping their Act a fee of £10, 10s." Now this exercise may be a great effort, or it may be no effort at all. That the latter part of the performance means something, will not be doubted. But as regards the thesis, and the disputation, and above all the *viva voce* examination, where, in the general case, the examinee is a member of the bar of five years' standing at least, and the examiner very possibly his junior, that these are anything more than forms, is what no one who has seen anything of similar proceedings elsewhere, will readily believe.

As regards the Cambridge law degrees, as a whole, the conclusion at which we arrive is, that they are good things, in the sense of being, *in the meantime*, very much better things than nothing at all. But viewed as guarantees for an acquaintance with scientific jurisprudence, in any high sense, they are wholly inadmissible; and as a preparation for the strictest and narrowest career of professional life, they are by no means equal to a training in ethics, logic, and political philosophy, such as the moral sciences *tripos* affords. Take the first of these subjects—ethics—alone. Any man who has "got up" the moral dialogues of Plato, Aristotle's Ethics, Cicero de finibus and de officiis, Clarke on the Attributes, and on Unchangeable Morality, Butler's Sermons, Dugald Stewart on the Active Powers, Paley's Moral Philosophy, Whewell's Elements of Morality and Lectures on the History of Philosophy, Kant's Ethical System, and Fichte's Ethical System (which are the works prescribed), is not only far more highly educated as a man, but far more in a condition to enter, with advantage, on the special studies of a lawyer than the Bachelor, the Master, or even the Doctor, who has graduated after the fashion we have described. Indeed, the whole of the legal studies at Cambridge strike us as very much like non-professional playing at professional work; and we should suppose that the result stood to what is, or ought, afterwards to be done in London, pretty much in the same relation in which volunteer drilling stands to the drilling of the line.

Nor is the case at Oxford at all different. There, too, jurisprudence and modern history are recognised as one of the modes in which the degree of B.A. may be taken. Responsions and the first public examination having been passed, students have their option of going out in one of four schools, called the schools of Literæ Humaniores, Scientiæ Mathematicæ et Physicæ, Scientia Naturalis, and Jurisprudentia et Historia Moderna. The student who selects the latter school must offer himself for examination *either* in English history, from the Conquest to the accession of Henry VIII., together with that part of English law which relates to things real; or in English history from the accession of Henry VIII. to the death of William III., together with that part of English law which relates to persons and things personal; being at liberty, however, to substitute Adam Smith's "Wealth of Nations," or some other approved work on Political Economy, together with the History of British India, for either portion of English history, and Roman law for either portion of English law. This latter option, of course, is intended to meet the case of candidates for the Indian civil service. For honours, the subjects of examination are "Modern History as far as the year 1789, and jurisprudence. Candidates must bring in one of the two portions of English law mentioned above, or Roman law, and they may bring in both. Those who do not bring both English and Roman law, must bring in either international law, or some approved work on political economy."

This examination, it must be remembered, is not for a law degree, strictly speaking; but only for a degree in Arts, taken in the Law school. With reference to the Law degrees, it is provided that "no one may be admitted a student in Civil Law until he has passed all the examinations required for the degree of B.A. 1. Candidates for the degree of B.C.L. must pass an examination which is held every year, in full Act Term, by the Regius Professor of Civil Law, the Vinerian Professor of Common Law, and some other person, who must be a Doctor of Civil Law, or a Bachelor of four years' standing in that faculty, nominated by the Vice-Chancellor, and approved by Convocation. It is conducted partly in writing, partly *viva voce*, in the four books of the Institutes of Justinian, or some part of them; and in some work illustrative either of the Institutes, or of the *science* of Civil Law." What the Science of Civil Law, as distinguished from the Institutes, may signify, is a subject on which we shall not hazard a conjecture; nor shall we affect to be enlightened by the subsequent information that it is contained in Heineccius's Recensiones, or in Vinniius's quatuor libri Institutionum, "or some other work of this sort, of which the Regius Professor is to give public notice six months before." On this side of the Tweed, we have been in the habit of imagining that, if the Institutes have any meaning at all, it is that of exhibiting the skeleton of the Civil Law, viewed as a science.

2. "A Bachelor of Civil Law, wishing to proceed to the degree of Doctor, is required to read publicly, within the precinct of the schools, in presence of the Regius Professor, a dissertation composed by himself, on some subject pertaining to Civil Law, approved by the Professor, and to deliver him a copy of it." If the word *Civil* had been omitted in prescribing the subject of the Thesis, and the candidate bound simply to read an essay on some subject "pertaining to Law"—the Doctor's "promotion" might have had something approaching to the character of a reality. But a provision which brings him into competition with the civilians, years after he has terminated the very mild course of Civil Law study in which he originally engaged, necessarily reduces the whole proceeding to a form; thereby, however, placing it, as we have said, on a footing of equality with promotions for the degree of Doctor of Laws in every University of which we have ever known anything.

One advantage which Oxford unquestionably possesses over most Universities elsewhere, and all other Universities in this country, is that it possesses two Professorships in this department so endowed as to render it possible for the Professors really to devote themselves to the duties of their Chairs. These are the Chichele Professorships of International Law and Diplomacy, and of Modern History, founded by ordinance of the University Commissioners in 1854, and each endowed with a stipend of £750 a year. The Chair of Moral and Metaphysical Philosophy, moreover, which closely borders on this side of learning, is one of the best in the University, being maintained by a stipend of £600 a year.

But in both Universities the great defect, obviously, is the want of a Faculty of Law, in the separate and complete sense attached to that member of the body-academical in the continental Universities and, in theory at least, in our own. So long as they confine themselves to preparing their pupils for the special studies which they are to pursue in a different atmosphere, and stimulated by different influences, no action can be more valuable than that of these two ancient seats of learning. But it is with law just as it is with medicine. Oxford and Cambridge can no more produce a jurist, than they can produce a physician, or an operative surgeon. Even the more general branches of professional study, so soon as they undertake to deal with existing human affairs, cannot be pursued apart from the more special. Anatomy and physiology are inseparably bound up with pathology and materia medica. Constitutional and International Law cannot be studied,—and even general Jurisprudence can scarcely be adequately illustrated,—apart from Municipal Law, Criminal Law, and forms of Civil procedure. The defect is one which can never be supplied effectually, and which, in our opinion, ought not to be attempted to be supplied at all, at the University towns. The real corrective is the formation of a complete school of law, of a legal University (if we may apply the term, without contradiction, to a single Faculty) in London, in connection with the Inns, Chambers, Courts, and other legal appliances, now about to be gathered together in the neighbourhood of Lincoln's Inn Fields. The formation of such an institution—an institution which should deal with the "Social Sciences" in the largest sense, is a scheme which has long been ardently cherished by some of the most enlightened members of the English Bar and Bench. In our next article we shall endeavour to describe what has been accomplished or is being attempted toward its realization.

THE SHERIFF OF GLASGOW AND SHERIFF-SUBSTITUTES.

Sir Archibald Alison has been making a speech—an event not in itself to be considered remarkable; and yet the speech is a very remarkable one. He spoke from the bench, but not in the exercise of judicial functions; therefore, without detriment to his judicial character, he might, if he pleased, ignore his own remark, that "perhaps the most important qualities any judge can have are suavity of manner and gentlemanly demeanour." The occasion of the speech was a sufficiently ordinary one, and we should not have been surprised if even he had allowed to pass in silence such a circumstance as Mr. Archibald Lawrie, advocate, taking his seat as interim Sheriff-Substitute, in room of Mr. Sheriff Smith, who has got leave of absence for some months on account of bad health. But because Mr. Lawrie was an advocate, instead of a Glasgow procurator, Sir Archibald tells us he only refrained from declining to sanction his appointment, because he felt he could not do so "without a slap in the face to Mr. Lawrie." We can assure Sir Archibald that it was a great mistake to refrain from doing what was right out of any delicacy towards Mr. Lawrie, as that gentleman has earned for himself such a position and character at the bar as to make him equally independent of any "slap on the face" he could give, and of his offensive patting on the back, and telling the public that "his manner, his appearance, and general demeanour, are extremely prepossessing."

We have, however, little interest to inquire into the Sheriff's standard of good taste and good feeling, as displayed in his allusions to Mr. Lawrie, and we cannot trust ourselves to deal with, nor do we choose even to quote, the most unbecoming of his references, still more to Mr. Smith, his fellow-labourer on the Glasgow bench for twenty years. But Sir Archibald Alison's speech has a wider than any merely personal interest, for he enunciates a general principle as that which is to guide him in the exercise of the large patronage committed to him for the public good.

"No one knows better than I do that the judicial appointments to this Court in general can best be made in favour of gentlemen who have practised before it. I know perfectly, in my own experience, that a very considerable amount—I would even say a great amount—of practice at the bar in Edinburgh affords hardly any adequate preparation for the business of this Court, and the reason is that the business of the one Court is quite different from that of the other; and that the great qualities here, even required more than legal acumen, are knowledge of the world, knowledge of human nature in all its grades, and knowledge of the wants and necessities of the various classes of society unknown elsewhere, but which have such an important influence upon the business transacted in this place. I have no hesitation in saying, however, that with a view to a permanent appointment, if Mr Smith should be unable to return to his duties in the beginning of October, I shall not look beyond this Faculty; and I have no hesitation in saying that there is a gentleman now in my eye in whose talent and knowledge, and gentlemanlike manner I have the most entire confidence."

Passing over the circumstance that these remarks were called forth by the interim appointment of a gentleman, born in Glasgow! and trained for years in a Glasgow writer's office!! we cannot at all sympathise with the view, that among procurators alone are to be found fit occupants of the Sheriff-Substitute bench. Time was when these officials were not necessarily lawyers at all, and were remunerated with pittances of £60 and £70 a year. When the remuneration was increased, the qualification of having at least the knowledge of law implied in being a procurator before some court was required, and the more important substituteships came to be filled by members of the bar, who on the other hand ceased to hold, what used to be, and what even sometimes is, the more lucrative office of sheriff-clerk. Now the qualification of membership of the bar has ceased to be the exception, and become the rule, and with such manifest good effect, that there is little danger of progress otherwise than in a direction opposite to that pointed at by Sir Archibald. We do not say that the Sheriff of Lanarkshire, or of any other county, if predetermined not to seek a fit man, or if he engages in his search with either a man, or a beam, in his eye, may not make an unfortunate selection from the bar; but we do say, that if any one of them comes to the bar with an honest purpose to find a man of *proved* fitness, he will succeed, and no man knows this better than Sir Archibald, for among the members of the bar who have sat on the Glasgow bench have been, and are, men possessing judicial talent of the very first order. We will go further in our objection to the principle laid down, and say, that if procurators are to be selected to preside over Sheriff Courts, they should be sent to districts other than those in which they have practised, and totally dissevered from their local associations and connections.

It may be said in reply, that the bench in Edinburgh is supplied from the bar, but then the bar is not local any more than the business transacted in the supreme courts. Both are collected from every province of the country. But even assuming the correctness of Sir Archibald's estimate of the value of intimate local knowledge derived from personal associations, there is no part of the country for which the bar cannot supply a substitute with such local knowledge unimpaired—but with his local prejudices rubbed off. We believe, therefore, that generally the safest course, and that most palatable to the highest-toned procurators throughout the country, will be to choose sheriff-substitutes from the bar, as the branch of the legal profession which undoubtedly possesses the highest social status, and the highest culture. From it young men of tried experience may be appointed without the risk of exciting public dissatisfaction or local professional jealousy. But the emoluments of the office will not tempt the best and most successful men among the local procurators to abandon a lucrative business;—and to take a man of standing, but second rate position is most mischievous, while the difficulty of putting a promising young man from a local society to preside over his brethren and fathers in the law is manifest.

It is really amusing, at this time of day, to hear Sir Archibald announcing as a discovery, "that knowledge of the world, and knowledge of human nature in all its grades," are required for the bench even more than legal acumen. But when he speaks of these qualities as if required only for the Glasgow bench, and capable of being picked up only in a writer's office on the banks of the Clyde, and as necessarily lost by experience, he merely shows the narrowing effect upon the intellect, of being confined too long to one circle, and in that occupying a central position, in which he is necessarily isolated from all equal and unrestrained communication with the men of his own pursuits. We say this, because we believe Sir Archibald to have been speaking in simplicity and honesty. Unwearied devotion to the duties of his office, and unvarying courtesy to all who ever come in contact with him in business, have secured him so well-deserved a popularity with the procurators of his court, as to raise him above the suspicion of having spoken to curry favour with his audience. But the whole tone of the speech exhibits Sir Archibald so completely in a new character, that it is just possible that he was trying on a little waggery with his procurators. We should have liked to have been present to see whether he embraced the whole procurators present in one comprehensive 'all-in-my-eye' glance, or concentrated his gaze on the "gentleman *now* in my eye;" but whatever he did, we are much mistaken in the Glasgow procurators generally, and the gentleman whom report names as the "man in my eye" in particular, if they did not, one and all, blush for the exhibition of their Sheriff.

We admit that the Sheriff-substitute bench has, from time to time, been occupied, nay, is now occupied, by members of various societies of procurators, possessing high magisterial and judicial qualities. We deny that present or past experience of that or any other bench, warrants any other presumption than the one which is now well established on both sides of the Tweed, that, as a rule, the bar affords the best training for judicial office. We admit that, as the law at present stands, Sheriffs are not only at liberty, but bound to look through all bodies, with the statutory qualification, in order to find out the best man, and that it is, as a general rule, proper to tell any one holding an interim appointment, that the fact of his doing so confers no title to a permanent one. But, because we object to a Sheriff's choice being hampered, we deny that it is decent for him, as a dispenser of important public patronage, to say, nine months before an expected vacancy, "I have a man in my eye," to the exclusion of others, or another, of whom he can say as he said in this case, "I am quite sure that he will answer all the hopes and expectations of myself and of the faculty." How can Sir Archibald be sure, or expect the public to suppose that he cares to be sure, that the "man in my eye" is the best man to be had, if he openly professes to reject trial alike of him and of others as a test of fitness.

New Books.

A Treatise on the Law of Partnership and Joint-Stock Companies, according to the Law of Scotland. By FRANCIS WILLIAM CLARK, Advocate. 2 vols. Edinburgh: T. & T. Clark, 1866.

IN our last number we directed attention to the appearance of this book. We were not then in a position to give anything beyond a brief and very general sketch of the aim and the character of the work. It is our intention to attempt a fuller and more exhaustive notice now, but the ground over which Mr. Clark has travelled is so extensive, and he has so carefully gleaned and utilized the materials that came upon his path, that we cannot hope to be able to present, even with the largest space at our disposal, anything like a complete or satisfactory analysis of his labours.

We have already expressed our regret that one, who is obviously so competent to the duty, should not have attempted to give his work a more speculative cast. No doubt it is very true, that now-a-days, a work which is to be practically serviceable, must, in the main, concern itself with the dogmatic treatment of a subject, and we are not insensible to the alliance existing between crude and elementary thought and inaccurate knowledge on the one hand, and the habit of abstract speculation on the other. But it is just because Mr. Clark's knowledge is so comprehensive, and it is evident that he has carefully studied his subject, and seen it in all its bearings, that we experience the regret that he has not set before him a wider and more ambitious aim.

No author ever had a better opportunity than lay before him of producing a work that should be permanently valuable as a philosophical exposition of its subject-matter. For it is no injustice to Mr. Bell, and no disparagement of his great work, to say that it has a comparatively small pretension to this character. Stair's treatment of the subject, in accordance with the habit of his mind, is more of the character which we have indicated that a work to be long serviceable should assume, but there is no branch of law which has been more modified than the law of partnership by the action of modern constitutional history, and by the usage and the experience of modern life; none, accordingly, that stands more in need of a careful speculative and historical review. Of the strictly historical part of the work we have already expressed our approval, but even that is not altogether satisfactory. For Mr. Clark seldom travels beyond the history of his own country, and when he leaves it it is for the most part to represent the law of partnership as an outcome from and an aggregation of modern mercantile usages. This is not to say that he has not apprehended the spirit of the Scotch system, or the points in which it differs from the English. On the contrary, the leading characteristic of the Scotch law of partnership, that it recognises a *quasi persona* in an unincorporated mercantile firm, and among other results admits of questions being raised between the firm and its own partners, is held up to view and illustrated to an extent, and in such a variety of form, which seem to us to involve a quite unnecessary elaboration. Beyond a very general statement that the theory of the law of Scotland is modelled upon that of Rome, Mr. Clark seems to ignore the Roman law altogether. The convergence of the Scotch and Roman jurisprudence is nowhere more apparent than in this branch of law, and although a practical treatise, which Mr. Clark's is intended to be, cannot dispense with a detailed examination of Acts of Parliament and of forms and styles, it was, we think, worthy of the subject and necessary to a complete execution of the aim which Mr. Clark set before him to enter upon an analysis of the great legal theories and ideas upon which the system of partnership law is built. Perhaps Mr. Clark does not care much for the Roman law. The reverential way in which he speaks of the English system, of its elasticity and power of adaptation to the practical wants of a great mercantile community, would seem to point in this direction. And, no doubt, Mr. Clark has secured merits to his book by strict adherence to this practical view. But, we think, it would have improved the symmetry of his work, and enhanced its ultimate value, if he had stood upon a more comprehensive and elevated platform.

It is necessary to a proper understanding and appreciation of the execution of Mr. Clark's book to bear in mind the object which he has set before him, that being, as he explains it in the introduction, to examine the law applicable to the various forms which the partnership relation assumes in Scotland, "in so far as they are applied for purposes of mercantile gain." Any allusion made to associations not having gain for their object is purely incidental, and is only used for purposes of illustration. The plan of the treatise appears to us to be at once simple and exhaustive. After an introduction entitled, from its point of view, to the highest praise for its brevity and conciseness, Mr. Clark proceeds, in his first book, to deal with the constitution of society. Here he has occasion to deal with the purposes for which partnerships may be constituted, with the parties who may enter into and sustain the relation, with partnerships and corporations, and with the formation of companies at common law and under Acts of Parliament. Under the latter head he takes the opportunity of showing the different forms in which registered companies may be formed under the Act of 1862, and under the Companies Clauses Consolidation (Scotland) Act of 1845. No part of this section of the work strikes us as more effective than the chapter in which he states the general characteristics of partnerships and corporations, and the points in which these differ respectively in England and in Scotland. Here Mr. Clark points out the recognition by the Scotch system of a *quasi persona* in the firm, apart from the partners of which it is composed, and its rejection by the law of England, and the consequences that spring from that relation. Here also he explains how, on the other hand, the history of corporations has been very much the same in both countries, as both are acted upon by the constitutional history of the Empire. The distinction between a formed and contemplated partnership, is clearly and succinctly stated, and with just as much elaboration as would seem to be required for practical purposes. But surely Mr. Clark is disposing in too summary and light a fashion of the important question of the evidence of partnership by devoting to it only a page and a half. And we should have preferred to have seen a fuller examination of the Scotch authorities than a statement of the English. Questions of this kind are constantly arising in the Inferior Court, and we fear that their exact bearings are but imperfectly understood.

In the second book Mr. Clark deals with the Constitution and Management of Partnerships and Companies, in which, following an exact and logical order, he takes up in the first place the constitution of companies registered under Acts of Parliament and common law companies, following them successively through their various elements of capital, property, liability, and management, and concluding with a clear and terse expression of the extinction of company obligations and the liability of partners for company debts. Under the chapter titled "Powers of Partners, Directors, and other Officials," Mr. Clark supplies us with a very succinct analysis of a difficult and intricate subject, although his treatment is not above the charge of being guided rather more than is desirable from the English point of view. No doubt questions of pledging and mortgaging are of more frequent occurrence in England, and these principles have there received an application and extension which are almost unknown here, but partnership law in regard to bills and notes is, at least, a subject of paramount importance here, and it does not bulk in Mr. Clark's work in such large dimensions as we would like to see it. In this part of the work, too, is largely apparent what we took occasion to make the ground of objection in our introductory remarks,—we mean the complete subordination of the Roman law, and the undue prominence given to the theory of the law of England. The law of Scotland, in these points almost more strictly and directly than any other deduced from the Roman, which rests upon the four leading principles of Compensation, Novation, Delegation, and Prescription, affords scope for an interesting and useful exposition of some legal notions that have both a frequent and wide application, but Mr. Clark does little more than point out the rules of practice as illustrated by leading cases, and when he elaborates his subject, it is generally to point out the technicalities of English principle or procedure. The third book is devoted to the "Rights and Obligations of Partners and Companies," and its leading, and in our opinion most excellent feature is an analysis of the Lands Clauses Consolidation Act, and its auxiliary measure the Railway Clauses Consolidation Act. This department has been prominent for some time in the practice of the law, and as there is every prospect from the state of the country, that, for some time at least, it will be even more so, Mr. Clark's summary is well timed and well worthy the attention of those who are concerned with such matters. The fourth book, which treats of judicial proceedings, appears to us to be the best executed in the work, particularly the chapters on the mode of suing corporations and companies, that on judicial pleading, and the concluding chapter on diligence, which is somewhat magnificently introduced by a few general remarks upon "Executorials." The idea will naturally occur that a chapter on pleading, in which an attempt is made to lay down general practical rules for the guidance of the profession, is somewhat gratuitously introduced into a treatise on partnership law, but its appropriateness, or, at least, its justification, would seem to lie in the exactness which is necessary in dealing with this relation. Mr. Clark's remarks at the same time form a very suitable complement to the useful collection of forms which he has brought together in the Appendix. Without agreeing with all that Mr. Clark says upon this subject, and while we could have wished to see a greater attempt to trace and to explain the similarity which undoubtedly exists in this branch of law[a] between the civil process of England and that of the Romans, than the mere statement that the system which has been adopted for ages in England, "probably prevailed in ancient Rome also" there is much that Mr. Clark says, which, we think, well worthy of attention and consideration. He points out very clearly the differences between special pleading and pleading at large.

"According to this latter system, both parties to the action are allowed to make such averments as they deem necessary to bring their respective cases fully before the Court, without being much controlled or guided by technical rules or recognised *formulæ*; and when the record is closed, the questions of fact or law which form the real subjects in dispute, are extracted by the Court from the materials it furnishes, after hearing the views and arguments submitted by the contending litigants. This system of procedure, which has been termed pleading at large, has much to recommend it in theory, and would no doubt work well in practice if the pleadings were always framed by men of sound legal knowledge and long experience in forensic practice; but since these qualifications cannot always be secured, it frequently produces records of a confused and irrelevant description, in which the real points at issue are hard to be discovered, if indeed they have not been omitted altogether. As a palliative to these evils, which are probably inseparable from every system of pleading at large, important amendments were formerly allowed to be made on the initial writs, and elaborate and argumentative written pleadings were allowed or encouraged after what might be properly termed the record had been completed. These corrections, which in some form or other appear to be necessary adjuncts to a system of pleading at large, tended in a certain degree to abate the evils in question; but being found to be accompanied by others of equal magnitude, they were ultimately abolished by statute.

"As matters now stand, the existing system of pleading in Scotland appears to combine the disadvantages both of special pleading and of pleading at large, without the benefits peculiar to either. On the one hand, the pleader is required to state his case from the outset with all the exact relevancy which a system of special pleading demands, but affords mechanical means for attaining; on the other, he is required, in conformity with the principle of pleading at large, to exercise his own judgment in the original statement of his case, but is not allowed to make such subsequent amendments as the efficient working of that system of pleading seems to demand. In a considerable number of cases, when the issues involved are simple, the evil consequences of this mixed system do not make themselves sensibly felt; but in cases of intricacy, such as those which frequently arise when the partnership relation is involved, an error of judgment in the preparation of the initial writs frequently produces much unnecessary delay, and ruinous expense at subsequent stages of the cause, and sometimes even eventuates in a total miscarriage of justice. To obviate these possible contingencies, the following suggestions are submitted as practical guides in the preparation of pleadings."

And further on,

"The system of pleading at large may, under proper regulations, be made to work with tolerable success in courts where matter of fact is ascertained by the judge or on commission; but it seems altogether unsuitable where this has to be done by the intervention of a jury. Accordingly, it never existed in England, and it would seem that it found its way into Scotland at the time when the trial by assize in civil causes was falling into disuse. It is remarkable that in criminal procedure, where trial by jury was retained, the libel has always continued to be framed in conformity with the principles of special pleading. When jury trial in civil causes was reintroduced into this country, it was conceded on all hands that the existing forms of pleading were entirely inapplicable; but instead of importing for the preparation of such causes as were designated for jury trial the English forms of special pleading, or providing some machinery whereby the record might be so adjusted as to be sent like a criminal libel to the knowledge of the assize, the legislature, for reasons which appeared cogent at the time, directed that the questions of fact should be artificially extracted from the record, prepared in accordance with the existing forms, and should be laid before the jury in the form of issues. The evil consequences of this half measure have continued to make themselves felt down to the present day, and form one great cause of the aversion and distrust with which trial by jury, in itself the most searching and efficient mode of ascertaining fact ever invented, still continues to be regarded in Scotland. However well a record may be framed, it is always a matter of more or less nicety to extract from it all the questions of fact which are pertinent to the cause, and to cast them into the distinct yet brief forms of expression which an issue requires. When this process has not been attempted till after the record is completed, and more particularly where the pleadings are loose and confused, the task often becomes extremely difficult, sometimes hopeless. Even when it has been accomplished in appearance, it sometimes turns out when too late that the adjusted issue does not exhaust the matters of fact actually in dispute, or applies to something similar but different. Ruinous expense, and occasional miscarriage of justice, are the consequences to the litigants. From the complexities incident to causes involving the partnership relation, such results are more to be apprehended in that class of cases than in any other.

These observations show that Mr Clark has reflected much upon this subject, which some time ago engaged much the attention of the profession with reference to proposed changes in the practice of the Court of Session. The following admonitions may be very sound, and we dare say are very much required, but we should not have looked for them in a treatise on Partnership Law :—

"In the first place, the practitioner should consider whether the state of matters complained of admits of any remedy by judicial intervention; for, as we have already seen, there are some cases in which the courts will not interfere between a company and its members. If the case appears to be one for judicial intervention, he should next set himself to ascertain what is the proper remedy in the particular circumstances, since it will generally turn out that one remedy only is competent, and that even where there are several, one is greatly to be preferred to the others, as being the most commodious, speedy, and effective. While making up his mind on these matters, and at all events before any proceedings are taken, he ought to satisfy himself as to what propositions in fact and what propositions in law it is necessary to make out in order that the remedy contemplated may be obtained. The best and surest method of doing this, is to draw out in a logical form the legal principles which, if sound, warrant the conclusion of the action he proposes to raise, and to state in the form of issues the propositions in fact which, if established, will allow those legal principles to come into play. If, after due consideration, it appears that the facts or the law of the case will not warrant the conclusions necessary for the legal remedy contemplated, he ought to consider whether some other remedy is not available; but if none such is to be found, his duty appears plain—to advise his employer that the case should not be proceeded with."

We have already said, the aim of Mr Clark's book is to deal solely with companies that are associated for purposes of mercantile gain. A result of this, and what but for the plan of the work, would seem an omission, is, that in treating of the manner in which companies may sue and be brought into Court, there is almost no notice whatever of the law applicable to the numerous class of unregistered bodies who league themselves for purposes of insurance and protection. Of the remaining part of this book,—the law of diligence as applicable to companies,—we are sorry that the space at our disposal does not allow us to give extracts.

In the 5th Book, Mr Clark treats of the dissolution of companies, and the work is concluded with a valuable Appendix, which contains forms of articles of copartnery, observations, practical suggestions upon these, and the various statutes relating to the subject-matter of the treatise. From Mr Clark's observations on articles of copartnery, we make the following quotation. Its length, we hope, will be excused by reason of the good sense and practical sagacity by which it is throughout pervaded:—

"Simplicity, clearness, and brevity ought to form primary characteristics of all partnership articles. It should be remembered that the object of reducing the contract to writing is not only to settle disputes when they arise, but to obviate as far as possible the likelihood of their arising. The articles ought therefore, in many respects, to form as it were a code by which the *socii* may learn their rights, duties, and liabilities, what they ought to do, from what they ought to abstain. But for the same reason, all complicated provisions should be avoided, as ministering only to obscurity, to misconception, and to litigation.

"As the contracting parties are not generally laywers, all legal technicalities should, if possible, be shunned. This should be carefully observed by the Scottish practitioner, whose legal phraseology is not generally understood over by far the greatest portion of the British Empire. If a contract couched in Scotch law language comes to be made the subject of litigation in English, Irish, Colonial, or American courts, its construction may give rise to much embarrassment and unnecessary expense. Nor are such technicalities at all necessary. Legal phraseology is not the language of mercantile men. The only cases in which the employment of technical words seem necessary are in the clauses of registration, and in relation to Scotch heritage, the conveyance of which requires the use of the word *dispone*. Similar observations apply to technical phrases connected with a particular trade or business. Their use has often occasioned much difficulty; for not only do they frequently bear a different meaning in different localities, but they are sometimes altogether unintelligible beyond the particular locality where the contract is framed.

"Intending partners sometimes adopt a form of partnership contract which they have found in use among others in a similar line of business, without considering whether its provisions, however well adapted for the purposes for which they were framed, are at all suitable for the circumstances of their own case; and even where they avail themselves of the services of a law-agent, they frequently give him instructions too general and indefinite to enable him to discharge his duty in an efficient manner. Such loose practices are fraught with danger to the future prosperity of the company; and it may be said with truth, that the concern would in many cases work more successfully without written articles at all, than when fettered with provisions unsuitable for its character and purposes, or at variance with the real intention of its promoters.

"When the successful prosecution of the business or undertaking for which a private company is formed is interrupted by dissensions among the partners, it will often be found that this is attributable to their having entered into a contract, the real nature of whose provisions, as expressed in the written articles, was entirely misunderstood by some, or perhaps by all of the contracting parties, who, if they had fully realised the meaning and effect of what they signed, would either have declined to enter into the partnership at all, or would have required its provisions to be materially modified. Intending partners ought therefore, before entering into the contract, to consider maturely whether the proposed articles are in all respects suitable for the purposes they have in view; and each one of their number should take especial care that the true import and effect of the articles adopted are fully understood, not only by himself, but by the others, before the contract is finally executed. . . . It must also be observed, that if the articles come to be the subject of litigation, the Court will construe them in accordance with their plain meaning and legal import, unless where, by a course of practice, it clearly appears that they originally bore, or were afterwards intended to bear, another construction. This is an additional reason why, in private partnerships, the use of technical phrases should as far as possible be avoided; since by the adoption of such language the partners may commit themselves to a construction essentially different from what they really intended.

"The most effectual means of ensuring that the provisions will be fully understood and carried out in their integrity, by whomsoever they may come to be applied, is to make them as simple in themselves and as little divergent from the common law as possible. If they are complicated, or at variance with what the law if left to itself would provide, it becomes extremely difficult to express them with the necessary clearness and binding force; they are apt to generate misunderstandings between the partners;

and circumstances often emerge, not contemplated at the time, to which they are plainly inapplicable, but in which they will create much unnecessary embarrassment. Of this kind may be instanced complicated provisions as to sharing profits, *e.g.* that one partner shall receive a larger share of profit in one branch of the business than another; that his share shall increase or diminish with reference to certain contingencies; that he shall receive a salary in addition to his share of profits: provisions as to management at variance with the common law, *e.g.* that certain partners shall not be entitled to inspection of the books except under certain restrictions; that certain partners, though they share profits, shall be excluded from taking part in the management: provisions as to the introduction of third parties into the concern under certain conditions, and in certain circumstances: provisions as to making contributions at future periods, or in certain contingencies: provisions that the partnership shall determine *ipso facto*, or at the option of parties, on the occurrence of events about which there may be a difference of opinion: provisions as to winding up, realization of the company estate, or division of the assets, on principles at variance with those of the common law. Provisions of the kind alluded to are of no unfrequent occurrence in contracts of copartnery. They should always be avoided. Some of them, such as those excluding from inspection of the company books, are plainly inoperative. The others are objectionable, not only as involving embarrassing complications, but as having a tendency to destroy that harmony of action which is essential in partnership.

It should never be forgotten, that if parties have not full confidence in the honour, integrity and common sense of each other, they should not enter into the contract of partnership. Attempts to make up for the want of these requisites by stipulations in writing are almost always nugatory; and penalties seem very much out of place in a contract, the very essence of which is exuberant trust. If the partners are really suitable to each other, they will discharge their respective duties from a sense of mutual interest, all the more efficiently and zealously that they are not fettered by artificial regulations and compulsitors. If they are unsuitable, the sooner the relation is dissolved the better. If any one of them has ulterior views, and is void of honourable principle, no provisions which the ingenuity of a lawyer can frame will keep him to his duty, and secure the benefit of his services or connection, while guarding against his fraudulent intentions.

"In conclusion, it may be noticed that partnership articles, however comprehensive or exhaustive, are not in law understood to embrace all the mutual rights and obligations of the *socii*. Much must always be left unprovided for, and will be defined and enforced by well-known legal and equitable principles. Nor will conventional provisions receive such a literal interpretation as would involve obvious and gross injustice. The courts, it is true, will not allow the alleged intention of parties to defeat the plain terms of their written agreement; but, at the same time, they will construe these terms in accordance with the purposes of the contract, and will, if possible, reject a construction which would give occasion to fraud, or the taking of unfair advantage. It must also be observed, that as any article, however fundamental it may appear or be declared to be, may be altered by the consent of all the partners; so this consent may be evidenced not only by writing, but by a contrary course of practice and dealing, provided it be sufficiently marked and of sufficiently long continuance.

"The following matters should be fixed with clearness and precision in all articles of copartnery, as they appear to be essential fundamentals of the contract:—

"1 The nature of the business.

"2. The social name; that is, the 'firm' or 'style' by which the company is to be known, and under which it is to contract.

"3. The principal place at which the business is to be carried on.

"4. The date of commencement and the period of endurance.

"5. The capital, and the amount of contribution to be made by the partners respectively.

"6. What is to be deemed company property, and what (if any) separate estate, the use of which only is to be given to the company.

"7. The mode and proportions in which profits are to be shared and losses apportioned.

"8. The amount which each partner shall be entitled to draw out from time to time.

"9. The mode in which accounts are to be kept, and balances struck.

"10. In what cases the partnership may be dissolved; and what shall *ipso facto* operate a dissolution.

"11. In what way the company affairs shall be wound up.

"12. The appointment of arbiters.

"13. A clause of registration, and a testing clause.

"These appear to be the only provisions necessary in ordinary circumstances to the proper working of a private partnership; and in the absence of any of them it can hardly be said that the articles are complete. If the persons chosen to be partners are at all suited to enter into that relation with each other, these provisions, simply and clearly expressed will generally be found amply sufficient for all practical purposes, and more likely to conduce to harmonious working than articles which contain provisions of a more extensive and minute character. In some cases, however, additional provisions may be found advisable, in consequence of the nature of the business, or the mode in which it has to be carried on. Under this class may be instanced the following:—

"1. Restrictions on the right of subscribing the company firm.

"2. Provisions as to continuance of the company notwithstanding the death, bankruptcy, or retirement of a partner.

"3. Power to assume new partners.

"4. The appointment of managing partners, or the limitation of the agency to particular individuals.

"5. Provisions as to apprentices, agents, or servants.

"Beyond these, numerous clauses will be found in books of styles, and in other forms extensively used. Some of them may occasionally be found of importance; but of the great majority it may be said, that they are at best useless, and too frequently minister to embarrassment, misunderstanding, and litigation."

We have already expressed our opinion of the artistic execution of the work. Mr Clark informs us that he has studied compression as far as possible, and that is throughout apparent. It is evident that Mr Clark has striven to give all possible polish to his style, and but for a little fastidiousness, there is no doubt that he has succeeded, and that his work is to be admired as much for its elegance as for its ability and completeness. We cannot, on a fuller perusal of Mr. Clark's book, withdraw our objection to his constant use of quoting stereotyped Latin law phrases. In pleading, this is often very effective, but in composition it has always struck us as an ungraceful ornament. Upon the whole, we have no hesitation in expressing our highest approval of Mr Clark's work, and we hope that it will find its way into every public and private law library. We cannot conclude without a word of recognition of the handsome and enterprising manner in which the publishers have performed their share of the work.

THE SUMMARY PROCEDURE BILL.

THIS Bill has been much canvassed, and met with little favour at the county meetings. We give below the best defence of the bill and the fullest discussion of its principle, which we have seen, in the speech of Mr. Fraser, Sheriff of Renfrewshire, at the county meeting on 30th April—when it was resolved to send back for reconsideration the recommendation of the Standing Committee to petition parliament against the bill. Reconsideration did not alter the views of the Standing Committee.

The following are the material portions of the speech :—

"The bill has been very greatly misunderstood. Its object is merely to simplify procedure, and to abolish a system of process which is at once expensive, cumbrous, and technical. In various of the petitions which have been industriously communicated to the Commissioners of Supply, it is said that at the present moment there is no right of review on the part of the Supreme Court of any judgment of the Justices of the Peace. That statement is inaccurate. Under the existing law, the judgment of a Justice can be reviewed, if not to the same extent, at least to nearly the same extent, as it is proposed to give that right under the Summary Procedure Bill. His judgment cannot be reviewed upon facts; and it is not proposed to give any right of review upon facts; but if a Justice of the Peace admits incompetent evidence, or rejects competent evidence, or does not observe the forms pointed out by the special statute under which he is acting, or if he misconstrue the Act which he professes to administer, then in every one of these cases the Court of Session or the Court of Justiciary (according as the case may be civil or criminal), may quash his judgment. £50 frequently are required to liquidate the accounts in obtaining a decision under our present cumbrous mode of procedure in the Justiciary Court. But that expense and that procedure are simple as compared with what takes place in the Court of Session. In that Court you may have to run the gauntlet of the Outer House, then of the Inner House, upon an appeal, and at last the House of Lords (for every civil case may be appealed); and a record must be made up before a judgment can be given upon a simple question as to whether a Justice of the Peace has construed rightly an Act of Parliament, whether he has exceeded his jurisdiction, or whether he has admitted incompetent evidence, or refused competent evidence. The object of the new bill is merely to get rid of this obsolete system of pleading, and to substitute in its place one short paper which states the point to be decided, and upon which there shall be one decision, and no more, by a Supreme Court. Its main purpose is to get rid of the note of suspension in the Court of Justiciary, of the summons of reduction and of the record in the Court of Session, and to substitute a simple case, embodying nothing more than the question of law which has been stated to the Justice, and upon which he may have had difficulty. Such a case could be stated upon the face of a sheet of paper, not occupying twenty lines, whereas, according to the present procedure the matter is expanded into a long record. The whole of the clauses in the Act of Parliament are intended to do nothing more than effect that rational reform. The only other question is in reference to the 19th clause, which gives for the first time a clear and intelligible definition of what is to be held as criminal, and what is to held as civil. The procedure allowed by the bill has been in existence in Scotland for the last thirty-six years; and that which is now denounced as a measure intended for no other purpose than to put money into the pockets of Edinburgh lawyers has been worked since the year 1827, and with every advantage to the public. The Revenue Act of Parliament of that year (7 and 8 Geo. IV., c. 53 and 84), authorised the Justices of the Peace to state a case for the opinion of the Court of Exchequer in any question of law. The point was stated in about twenty lines, and the judgment of the Court of Exchequer was easily obtained. I refer to one case as an example of the working of this law where on a difficult question they were puzzled, and themselves desired to be guided by better opinions than their own, (*Watson* v. *Simpson*, 19 D. 380). The form of procedure of stating a case is the form for the opinion of a superior court, is the form allowed by the Assessed Taxes Acts; by the Valuation Acts; by the Adulteration of Food Act (1860); by the Herring Fisheries Act (1860), and other Acts. In short, it is a form at once simple, inexpensive, and easily worked, and has been gradually superseding our old wordy form of pleading. That this was an admirable reform was at last set at rest by the success which has attended the "Act to improve the administration of the law, in so far as respects summary proceedings before Justices of the Peace," (20 and 21 Vict., c. 43), which is now the law of England and Ireland. The present Summary Procedure Bill is just a transcript of this Act, with such necessary alterations as are required in consequence of the difference of our legal terminology from that of the law of England. That this Act has been a great success in England and Ireland, I need scarcely tell you. I find one of the most experienced writers on the law of summary proceedings before Justices of the Peace thus writing of it. I refer to Mr Oke, the clerk to the Lord Mayor of London, and who has had as much experience of the English Act as any man living. He says:—" Previous to this Act, *which has been found most beneficial*, it was always felt as a great blemish in our law, that there is no such power as is given by this statute, and no means of getting at the merits of a case, or of reviewing the decisions and proceedings of justices acting within their jurisdiction." Now, in the year 1864, it was thought that what had proved good in Scotland for thirty-six years in revenue cases, and had proved good in England in general summary proceedings would prove good in Scotland also in general prosecutions. With the concurrence of the Bar, the Lord Advocate introduced a bill to give us in Scotland the benefit of this English law. I cannot tell by what grievous blunder it was, that the clauses of the present bill, which were part of the law of England, were omitted from that act, as it was introduced into the House of Commons. But so it was. And when the attention of the Lord Advocate was called to the subject, the omission was immediately remedied by the insertion of the clauses in committee. Then uprose a great noise and clamour. The eleven clauses that were added were immediately denounced, notwithstanding that they were then the existing law of England and Ireland. It soon appeared through whose instrumentality this was effected. Three or four Justice of Peace clerks appeared in London, besieging the doors of Scotch members of Parliament. The Duke of Buccleuch is all-potent in the House of Lords, and apparently some persons who thought their interests would be affected by the new clauses converted the Duke, who intimated to the Lord Advocate that he would oppose the bill if these clauses remained. I regret much that the Lord Advocate did not at once decide to throw the bill overboard. Without these clauses it was an abortion, and has been the source of needless litigation. At the same time I am glad to say that the authors of the stratagem have been defeated. In some of the first questions which arose under it, it was pleaded that there was no remedy, however erroneous the Justice might be in point of law; and thus, if this view were correct, we would have law administered to the lieges in every county according to the views taken by each particular Justice in each county of poachers and teetotallers. This condition of things could not be tolerated in a civilised country; and the Court of Justiciary have fortunately been able to see their way to set aside (although under a cumbrous form of process) judgments of the Justices of Peace which were manifestly erroneous in point of law. Now, all that the Summary Procedure Bill professes to do, is simply to enact that a case may be demanded from the Justice of the Peace upon a question of law; which case is to be laid, not before a Judge in the outer House of the Court of Session, from which it has to run the whole course of appeal to the Inner House,—and from thence to the House of Lords; but it is at once to be laid upon the table of one of the divisions of the Court of Session, or upon the table of the Court of Justiciary, according as the case may be civil or criminal, and the judgment of each of those two Courts is to be final. The right of appeal to the House of Lords is absolutely taken away. It is said, however, that the bill imposes a great hardship on Magistrates, who, if they refuse a case, may be found liable in costs. Now the man who wrote that must have been unfit for his profession as a lawyer through gross ignorance, or he must be unfit for it because of an incapacity to state the matter truthfully. The award of cost to be made by the Lord Ordinary, if he sees proper to order a case where the Justice of Peace has refused it, is not against the Justice, but against the respondent—the other party in the case. This is no new law. It is merely copied from the English and Irish Act. It is a gross misrepresentation to say that the bill authorises the Court to award expenses against Justices. In some of the petitions, it is stated that no complaints whatever have been made against tho Summary Procedure Act of 1864, and that it has worked beneficially. Now, that Act, so far as it goes, is a very good statute, and it is not proposed to repeal it. It is only proposed to add to it clauses which were originally in it when it passed the House of Commons, and were only withdrawn in the House of Lords in consequence of the opposition got up by a combination of olerks to the Justices of the Peace, who have used—in the petitions which they have got country gentlemen to sign—language towards the members of the Bar in Scotland, at once 'disgraceful and discreditable, and which I will not demean myself by replying to."

THE MONTH.

The Case of Charlotte Winsor.—The final determination of the fate of this unfortunate woman, who has for the last twelvemonth been made the subject of an *experimentum in corpore vili*, will be a great relief and satisfaction to the public mind. The circumstances of the case will be still fresh in the recollection of our readers. She was, nearly a year ago, indicted on a charge of child-murder, committed under circumstances of unprecedented and unnatural depravity; and although additional evidence was obtained at the second trial, there is no doubt whatever that the proof led at the first was amply sufficient to warrant a conviction. The jury, however, to whom she was remitted do not appear to have had the same clear opinion, and they deliberated for five hours without being able to arrive at the unanimous result which the law requires. At the end of that time, they were discharged by the Judge, there being reasons, in his opinion, requiring that step—in the first place, the fact that the proceedings of the Court were entering upon Sunday morning; and secondly, that he had to open the Assizes at Bodmin on the following Monday. After a lapse of many months, the prisoner was again put upon trial, and the evidence of the mother of the child, who was arraigned on the same indictment, having been admitted, a conviction followed. Execution of the sentence was then attempted to be averted, on the ground that she had, according to our phrase in Scotland, "tholed her assize," and that, having done so at the first trial, she was illegally tried a second time. This objection was brought before the Lord Chief Justice and three other Judges sitting in *banco*, by means of a writ of error, which was issued, as is required by law, with the consent of the Crown. After a very full argument the Court, without any difficulty, repelled the objection; and the Home Secretary having declined to commute the sentence of death which had formerly been passed, the unhappy woman was again drawn, after the interval of many months, into the contemplation of her approaching doom. Again, at the last moment, on the ground that the Irish Judges in a recent case had arrived at a different result from the judgment of the Queen's Bench, the convict was a second time respited, and the satisfaction of the extreme penalty of the law was made contingent on the fate of a writ of error to the Exchequer Chamber, for which the Attorney-General granted his *fiat*.

The interest of the case for our pages lies, of course, in the discussion which followed upon the writ of error. But we do not hesitate to express our opinion that the idea of putting the convict to death at the close of the deliberations in the Queen's Bench was simply barbarous. The objection to the validity of the second trial was either a good or a bad one. If it was bad, and we think as the Court held that it was clearly and obviously so, the Crown should have withheld its consent from the writ of error; and it was anything but mercy to yield to the most anxious solicitations of the prisoner, assuming these to have been put forward. If it was a good objection, that is to say, in the form in which the question here rises, if there were reasonable grounds for the opinion that it might prevail, it was right that the Crown should provide every facility for the determination of a question of the greatest practical concern to the whole community. No doubt the step taken was at the instigation of the prisoner herself; and she need not have done so. But who will so strictly construe a struggle made for life? And it must not be forgotten that the act upon which the writ of error was based, was not an act of the prisoner's own doing, or of those who were acting for her. No one is allowed to profit by his own wrong, and, in the circumstances, the maxim does not seem to be improperly extended by being applied to a case where the wrong consists in a false view of the law. But whether right or wrong of the second trial, the Judge was the cause, and not the prisoner. Independently, however, of all such considerations, we hold the opinion in full consciousness of the views which we have in a previous number of this Journal expressed in support of the maintenance of capital punishment, that the execution of a sentence of death should not, under any circumstances, be held *in dubio* for such a period as occurred in the case of Charlotte Winsor. The enormity of the crime does not appear to us to be in any way a consideration relevant in support of a different view. The law does not recognise degrees in the severity or aggravation with which the sentence of death shall be carried out. And who will say that death, with the contemplation of it for ten months, is not an infinitely greater punishment than when its anticipation is limited to the short period which the law, with questionable mercy, admits to give an opportunity for repentance and forgiveness? It appears to us to be clear beyond the possibility of argument, that whenever delay such as we are now speaking of has occurred, it must be regarded as a miscarriage of the law, for which it would be inhuman to hold any one responsible.

On the merits of the legal question we feel that there is occasion for just as little doubt. It is not pretended that the validity of the discharge of the jury raises anything more than a rule of practice, and was a question which fell entirely within the discretion of the judge. The judge of the Queen's Bench decided that the discretion of the presiding judge in discharging the jury was well exercised; but holding it to be matter of discretion, they said they could not have reviewed what had been done, even if they had thought otherwise. It does appear that the practice in the English law has varied, and that there was a period when a similar discharge of the jury would have been declared illegal. But the law has in recent times gone back on its more equitable and practical rules. And, accordingly, the Lord Chief-Justice said it was impossible for the judge to have followed any other course in the circumstances, without doing what would have been upon other grounds liable to challenge. If he had received the verdict of the jury on Sunday, he would have committed an illegal act, because it is idle to say that the receiving of a verdict from a jury is not a step judicially taken; and, according to the English law, Sunday is *dies non juridicus*. If he had confined the jury till Monday, the assizes at Bodmin must have been delayed; and, more important still, the jury must have received refreshments, which, again, is opposed both to the principle and the practice of the English law. It is true that the English law holds, as ours does, and that of every civilized state, that no person shall be twice put in peril of his life. But that has no meaning, unless it is taken to include the verdict of the jury. Until that has been returned no question of double peril can exist, because it is only on the verdict of the jury that sentence can be pronounced.

It does not appear that any question of the kind could arise in Scotland, at least in the precise form in which it occurred in England. For the difficulty which led to the discharge of the jury in the case of Winsor was the unanimity required by law, at which they could not arrive. But we have no doubt whatever that if through illness of the judge, or of a juror, a trial proved abortive, it would be perfectly competent to proceed with a second. The case would be different if the suspension of the proceedings could be referred to any fault of the prosecutor; such as the absence of a witness rendering it impossible to close the case with any hope of a conviction; or the breaking down of the evidence in any other way, or its inapplicability to the indictment, or a flaw in the indictment itself. In all these cases the prosecutor and the prisoner must be held to have fairly joined issue; and it would be an endless source of injustice and oppression if any other rule were admitted, even exceptionally. A prisoner would, under these circumstances, be entitled to acquittal, not on the ground that he had tholed an assize, or, at any rate, not according to the application of that principle in its proper and primary sense; but simply because a miscarriage had occurred, from the consequences of which the law would not relieve the Crown. Nor would the other difficulties which determined the judge to discharge the jury have been operative in Scotland. A judge may order refreshments to be provided for the jury; and he may also receive their verdict upon Sunday, as was done by Lord Moncrieff in the case of Rosenberg, and by Lord Deas in the case of Reilly. In the former case, the validity of the verdict to infer sentence was brought up on a certification to the High Court of Justiciary; but the counsel for the panels declined, in the state of the authorities, to urge the objection; and, accordingly, it may be held to be as much settled in our law as, we humbly think, it has always been in reason and common sense, that no such difficulties as were pleaded in the case of Charlotte Winsor will be entertained here.

Capital Punishment.—The labours of the Commission

appointed to consider the operation of the laws as to Capital Punishment have resulted in a bill introduced into Parliament by the Lord Chancellor by which it is proposed to give effect to the leading provisions of the report. We have already taken occasion to comment upon the report itself, and as the Lord Chancellor's measure embodies its principal recommendations, our views are substantially already before the public. The classification of murder as that of the first or second degree, according as it is established by evidence that it is committed with or without malice aforethought is retained and the punishment of death is to be awarded only when the crime is impressed with the former quality by the verdict of the jury. It is unnecessary to recapitulate the views which we have already expressed upon this subject. Our leading objection is that it is impossible in nine out of ten cases to evidence to the satisfaction of a jury, or at any rate to such an extent as would induce them to embody their conviction in a verdict, whether the element of malice is present in the crime or not, and yet the tenth case in which its presence can be affirmed may involve the least guilt of all. But if it might reasonably be anticipated that there should be, as it has actually appeared that there are, differences of opinion upon this point, we think there can be little room for doubt that it is a blot in the bill as it was in the report, that the element of malice is to be made the subject of a separate finding by the jury. Our notion is that the attribute of the crime should not be separated from its substance by legal definition, which is done both in the report and the bill; but here we have the aggravation that it is not only separated in definition but in practical form. And the latter will create practical difficulties which the other might not. For will not, in nine out of ten cases, again, a jury hesitate to declare the fatal word when they know that the whole responsibility of a man's life or death devolves upon them. No doubt it may be said that the discharge of their duty lies in a clear and cognizable path which can neither be mistaken by third parties nor themselves. But why should the burden of a duty so repugnant to natural feeling be thrown entirely upon that body in the administration of the law, which is the only one that is deprived of the consideration that operates to a certain extent to relieve its irksomeness? And apart altogether from this view of the case, it is quite clear that the requirement of the act opens the door of escape wider than it is at present for those who hold opinions against the justice or expediency of punishment by death. That is not fair to the report of the Commissioners upon which the bill of the Lord Chancellor is avowedly founded, because the result reached by the majority, after a deliberate balancing of opinion and an anxious sifting of most voluminous evidence is, that in certain specified cases, capital punishment should be retained. The provision of the bill accordingly will operate—and that too in the most practical form—against the very purpose for which the Commissioners were empowered and the report was issued, which was to allay the doubts which were supposed to prevail as to the propriety of capital punishment.

In accordance with the recommendation of the Commissioners the Chancellor's Bill proposes to restore to the Judges the power for some time suspended of recording, instead of pronouncing, sentence of death. This is a technicality of English procedure which has no application to Scotland, but the slightest examination of the grounds upon which it is rested shows that the proposal is absolutely untenable. Virtually, the result of it is to abrogate the functions of the Jury, and to constitute the Judge supreme arbiter of the destinies of life and death. No doubt it is derogatory to the dignity of the law, and it is calculated to impair its usefulness, that an execution should be threatened which obviously cannot be carried out. But surely the remedy for this anomaly is to be found in the fountainhead; in some arrangement or adjustment of the law, that will secure a verdict upon which it is not necessary that a capital sentence should follow. The theory of the law in capital cases is, that the Judge has only one duty to discharge when the Jury have pronounced an unfavourable verdict, and that the remission of sentence is the prerogative of the Crown, and of no less authority. But the judicial function sought to be restored is a subversion of this constitution altogether. No doubt it will be said that the character of the English bench is a sufficient guarantee that the power will be exercised with a due regard to the interests of justice, and under submission to the principles of law and the dictates of common sense. But it has never been the genius of English law, or the policy of English government, to subordinate a system to the results of individual action, however much these may commend themselves by their prudence and vigour.

Other two of the leading recommendations in the Report are adopted in the Bill. The Commissioners, without dealing in a special manner with the question of infanticide, suggested that it should be made a crime to inflict injuries upon a child within seven days of its birth, and that it should not be necessary to adduce proof that the child was born alive. This provision is transferred to the Bill, and although there can be no doubt that the remedy is quite inadequate to the evil which it is intended to meet, and it is to be regretted that more attention has not hitherto been directed to a subject which is every day beginning to wear a graver social aspect, there is good ground for the hope that the change will operate beneficially. We do not find ourselves in a position to speak of the remaining feature of the Bill with the same approval. We refer to the proposal to substitute private for public executions. The Lord Chancellor, in explaining his measure to the House, announced that he had changed his views upon this subject, that whereas, during the progress of the Commission, he firmly held the opinion that the law could not dispense with the deterrent influence of a public execution, he is now as firmly satisfied that it would be strengthened by losing hold of the corrupting concomitants by which it is attended. It is impossible not to admire the candour with which the highest law-officer of the Crown calmly admits the action of free discussion upon his mind. But it does not appear to us that the evidence, when fairly interpreted according to its true value, not its mere bulk, admits of the construction which is put upon it by the majority of the Commissioners, and by the Bill, and seeing that the conflict in the evidence was strengthened by the dissent of an influential minority, we think that action upon this point was in the meantime undesirable and unnecessary.

Bankruptcy Law Amendment Bill, England.—During the month a Bill for the Amendment of the Bankruptcy Law of England has been introduced into the House of Commons; but this bill is in many respects liable to grave objection, and will not, we hope, be allowed to pass in its present shape. We have already from time to time pointed out the abuses of the English system, and made suggestions for its amendment, which we have reason to believe have met with the approval of the mercantile community in England. But the supporters of the bill now in Parliament, while they profess to adopt the Scotch system, stop short in the removal of abuses, and introduce evils which do not exist in our law. The points specially requiring reconsideration are so well stated in a Petition which we understand has been presented to the House of Commons by the Bristol Chamber of Commerce, that we think it unnecessary to do more than to refer to the four objections to the bill which they have set forth. They object—

1. To the proposal to abolish the power of Imprisonment for Debt on final process.

2. To the omission of any provision for administering the estates of deceased insolvents.

3. To the proposal in the said bill to provide for two offices, under the heads of "Accountant General" and "Comptroller," the duties of which are fulfilled by one officer only, under the Scotch Law. And,

4. To the proposal to establish an indiscriminating rule by which every Bankrupt, however unfortunate, would be prevented from obtaining his discharge, unless with the assent of every creditor, under the fixed period of six years; or unless his estate should realise a dividend to all his unsecured creditors of not less than six shillings and eightpence in the pound.

In support of these objections they state that—

Even under the Scotch Law, in about one-fifth only of the cases passing through the Courts do the estates pay so much as six shillings and eightpence in the pound to unsecured creditors, after paying the losses and expenses of winding-up. This proportion, if the same in England would leave four-fifths of the Bankrupts uncertificated and dependent on their relations and friends for six years.

By the Scotch Law for discharge of Bankrupts, greater scope is allowed for discriminating between the unfortunate and the culpable insolvent (at the discretion of their creditors) than is provided in the said bill, and the time of suspension is limited to two years, unless in such cases as the Court may, after hearing opposing creditors, consider to be deserving of a longer suspension.

The Foreshore—Crownright.—The action against Colonel Maclean of Ardgour, in which the Crown claim right to the sea-shore between high and low water mark, as belonging *jure coronae* to the hereditary revenue of the Crown, has been abandoned, the Crown having moved the Court in the Single Bills to refuse their Reclaiming Note. It would not appear that there is any significance in this step beyond a conviction that in the state of the evidence it was impossible to urge the case with any hope of a favourable judgment. An action at the instance of the Crown against Lord Seafield, claiming the right of Salmon Fishing in the sea opposite his Lordship's lands, in Banffshire, has been abandoned also.

THE

JOURNAL OF JURISPRUDENCE.

THE FRENCH BAR.

(Continued from the May No. of the Journal).

We closed our former paper on the French Bar with an account of the peculiar and perilous duties which advocates had to discharge, in connection with those judicial combats which harmonized so well with the mingled ferocity and superstition characteristic of the middle ages, but which gradually disappeared before a more enlightened faith, and a more advanced civilization. In the present article we shall trace the progress of the bar from the comparative barbarism of these iron times. We shall see it acquiring a compact organization and increasing in influence and importance, in proportion as men began to perceive the superiority of science to brute force, and to prefer the systematic administration of law both to the chance-medley of wager by battle, and to the no less absurd trial by ordeal, where the ends of justice were at any time liable to be defeated by the tricks of priestcraft.

The Establishments of Louis the ninth, published in 1270, afford the first example of anything approaching to a regular code of French law. They borrow much from the existing consuetudinary laws of the country, from the Civil and from the Canon law; and it is evident that such a compilation could only have been drawn up by learned and experienced jurisconsults who probably belonged to the French Bar. The Establishments are contained in two books, divided into a hundred and ten articles. Nearly the half of the first book is occupied with matters relating to feudal law, and with regulations concerning civil and criminal procedure, drawn from the customs and from the Roman law;

but by far the most important point is the introduction of proof by witnesses in all matters, civil and criminal, which gave the first blow to the judicial combat and to trial by ordeal. The fourteenth chapter of the second book of the Establishments, contains several regulations of great importance, with regard to the profession of advocate. Thus one rule provides, that all arguments calculated to injure the opposite party, should be spoken courteously, without abusive language either as to fact or law; and another forbids the advocate to make any bargain with the party for whom he pleads for a share of the matter in litigation. A subsequent law of Philip the Bold, published in 1274, imposes upon advocates the obligation of taking an oath, that they will only take charge of those causes which they believe to be just—the refusal to take the oath being punished with interdiction. The second and third articles of this law treat of the fees of advocates, which were to be proportioned to the importance of the cause and the skill of the pleader. The fee was never to exceed 30 livres turnois, equivalent to about £27 of our money. Advocates were to swear that they would receive nothing above that sum, directly or indirectly, and they were liable to be declared infamous, and to be perpetually interdicted for any violation of this oath. A subsequent law of the same monarch seems to imply that, at that period, the pleadings were not public; for it provides that no persons except those necessary for the conduct of the cause shall enter the court. Nor does the Roman law then appear to have had much authority in France, as an article of the same law enacts, that no advocate shall found upon the written law where the consuetudinary law exists. In 1291, Philip the Fair renewed the enactments of Philip the Bold, concerning the fees of advocates, and the prohibition to receive anything beyond the amount fixed by law, and added to it a recommendation to them to be exact in the discharge of their duties, and to avoid the use of abusive language in their pleadings.

By far the most distinguished advocate of the age of Saint Louis, was Guy Foucault, afterwards Pope, under the title of Clement IV. He was born in Languedoc, about the year 1200, devoted himself to the study of law, went to Paris, and became the most distinguished pleader of his time, and one of the royal council. He took orders after the death of his wife, was made Bishop of Paris in 1250, Archbishop of Narbonne in 1260, and Pope in 1265. He seems to have been thoroughly free from the vice of nepotism, which disgraced the character of so many Popes, as the following curious letter to his nephew, Pierre Legros, sufficiently proves. He thus addresses him,—"Be content with your present position; let your brother and other relations be so also, and let them not come to the pontifical court without being summoned, unless they wish to be sent back covered with confusion. Do not seek for your sisters husbands too much above their own rank. If you marry them to the sons of simple knights we shall give them a dowry of 300 livres turnois. . . . . As to our own daughters, we will that they marry those whom they would have had, if we had remained a simple priest." In a letter to Charles of Anjou, who had become King of Sicily, Clement IV. shews himself possessed of ideas with regard to the administration of justice far in advance of the age in which he lived. "Select," he says, "some wise men to reside in your palace, who, on each day set apart for the administration of justice, shall decide on causes, and intimate to you their decisions, in order that you may confirm them, or send them back to those who have judged them." Afterwards he says, "Have men of substance for your judges, men with clean hands. Make them publicly swear to administer justice without respect to persons or nationality. In order that justice may be freely administered, leave the magistrates to discharge the duties of their office, and do not bring before yourself, at the instigation of certain persons, suits commenced before them, unless under circumstances of grave and pressing necessity. Let law-suits follow their regular course, and let those who think themselves aggrieved have the right of appeal." A stain has been left on the memory of this great man by the counsel which he is said to have given to the same cruel and fanatical Charles of Anjou, to whom the above letter is addressed, and who consulted him with regard to the fate of his unsuccessful rival, Conradin, the last scion of the royal house of Hohenstaufen. The Pope is said by several writers to have answered, "vita Conradini, mors Caroli; mors Conradini, vita Caroli," an answer which sealed the fate of the captive prince. M. Gaudry, in his Histoire du Barreau Francais, denies the truth of this imputation. But when we consider the long struggle for power between the Popes and the great German race of the Hohenstaufen; the undying and deadly hatred of the Papacy against all who opposed its pretensions; and the respectable character of the writers who relate the story of Charles' application, and the Pope's answer;

we are scarcely prepared entirely to exonerate the great French advocate and Pope from the charge brought against him.

Another distinguished Advocate of the age of Louis the ninth, was Philip de Beaumanoir, who wrote about 1283 a work entitled *des Coutumes de Beauvoisis*, in which a great variety of legal matters are treated with much ability. The 6th chapter is entirely devoted to advocates, and contains some curious rules with regard to pleadings, fees, &c. Among other things, he recommends them to hear their adversaries' statements with calmness and patience and to be brief in their pleadings. It appears that those convicted of false witness, excommunicated persons, and those in the habit of insulting the Judges and the parties in a suit, were, at this period, refused admission to the profession of Advocate. The Judge also had the right of refusing to allow advocates, whose incapacity was known to him, to plead before him. He could likewise, on the application of parties, appoint them an advocate, whose fees should be regulated by usage, and who was bound to accept such an appointment unless he could state satisfactory reasons for refusal. Upon the whole, therefore, the French Bar in the time of Saint Louis appears to have received a distinct organization, and to have been subjected to a strict discipline. Another famous Advocate who flourished in the reigns of Louis the ninth and Philip the Bold, was Yves de Kermartin who was born in Brittany in October 1253, and died 16th May 1303. He was canonised as Saint Yves in 1347. By some authors—such as Loisel, Rittiez, and others—he is considered the patron Saint of Advocates; but M. Gaudry thinks that that honour belongs to Saint Nicolas, who was received as the patron of the legal faculty in France five years before the canonisation of Saint Yves. The last great name that we shall mention among the founders of the French Bar, is that of Guillaume Durand author of the *Speculum Juris*, a treatise on the whole science of law. He was distinguished as a poet and theologian as well as a lawyer, and such was the respect in which his legal knowledge was held in his own days, that he was termed, not merely *jurisconsultus*, but *jurisconsultissimus*. His great work contains many useful and eloquent remarks upon the profession of the Bar; and abounds in noble thoughts expressed in vigorous language, which show that he had true and elevated conceptions of the duties of those charged with the administration of justice. He is fond, for instance, of repeating the maxim,

"*Tutius est condemnandum absolvere, quam absolvendum condemnare,*"—a maxim too often violated in the days in which he lived. Under Philip the Bold, the Ecclesiastical Courts attempted to arrogate to themselves the regulation of the profession and fees of advocates, with the view of thus gaining the ascendency in civil matters over the French kings, and also in order to punish the advocates for their courageous and successful resistance to the famous Bull of Gregory the seventh, infringing the liberties of the Gallican Church. And here it deserves to be mentioned to the honour of the French Bar, that, from first to last, they uniformly resisted the encroachments of the Papacy upon the independence of the French throne and the liberties of the Gallican Church. As we advance in our narrative, we shall meet with many memorable examples of their honourable and patriotic opposition to the ecclesiastical usurpation, which would fain have turned the whole of Europe into a vast theocracy.

The reign of Philip the Fair is one of the most important in the history of France. He made the Parliament stationary, which formerly had followed the person of the King, and thus greatly increased the power and influence of the Parisian Bar, and gave a strong impulse to the science of Jurisprudence. The study of the Roman law, the emancipation of the serfs of Valois, and the regular keeping of the Registers of Parliament, date from his reign. With the assistance of some able and learned lawyers, such as Enguerrand de Marigny, Nogaret, Plasian, and others, he was able to make head alternately against the encroachments of the Papacy, the feudal law, and the great vassals of the crown. The regular keeping of the archives of the Grand Court of Parliament was ultimately provided for by a law of Philip the Long, which enacted, that "there shall be kept a book called *Journal*, in which shall be continuously inscribed what has been done in our council." Since that period, the Registers of the proceedings of the French Court of Parliament have been regularly kept, and the Imperial Archives contain more than 10,000 volumes, arranged according to their chronological order, from 1254 to 1790. The Advocates Library in Paris possesses one of the principal abridgments from this immense collection, comprised in 225 volumes, and extending, with some gaps, from 1383 to 1790. In speaking of this latter series of records, M. Gaudry remarks,—"The history of the Parisian Bar is found there almost entire; it is, in spite of its imperfection, one of the most precious collections." A law of 13th

Feb. 1327, made more particular regulations with regard to the duties of members of the bar than had previously existed. They were obliged to make oath that they would diligently and faithfully discharge the duties of their office; that they would not knowingly take up unjust causes; that if they discovered any cause to be unjust after they had undertaken it, they would forthwith abandon it; that they would immediately intimate to the King's Court if anything in any of their causes affected his Majesty; that they would not knowingly introduce matters impertinent to the case, or state or insist upon customs which they did not believe to be true; that they would to the utmost of their power endeavour to expedite their cases; that they would not seek delays or knavish subterfuges; that, however important the case, they would not receive, under any pretence, more than thirty livres tournois as a fee for their services; that, for a case of average importance, they would receive less, and for a case of trifling moment, much less, according to the nature of the case and the quality of the persons. Such was the nature of the oath imposed upon advocates admitted to plead before Parliament; and we think it will be generally admitted that it shews a very fair appreciation of the duties of the Bar, considering the times in which it was framed. A resolution of the Parliament of Paris, following upon a royal ordinance of March 1344, gave a still more specific organisation to the Bar, and provided for the creation of a novitiate, or period of probation, for those who intended to become advocates. Three classes of advocates are noticed in this resolution—consulting advocates, pleaders, and listeners. Of these, the first were the highest in professional rank, being at least of ten years' standing. They wore a robe of black silk, covered with a scarlet mantle lined with ermine. The pleaders wore a violet gown, the listeners a white one. An ordinance of King John, in 1363, ordained that advocates should sign their papers, "that the knowledge and skill of the advocates of our court may appear more clearly, and that they may be more strongly stimulated to write, in a brief, able, and substantial manner." It is further provided that they shall not be heard more than twice in the same cause, and that they shall not repeat, in their replies or duplies, what they have already said, unless it be absolutely necessary. Thus, even at this early period, the right of reply, and even of duply, was considered as one of the greatest privileges of the Bar; and the right of defence seems to have been as well provided for in the stormy days of King John, when France was exhausted and crippled by the English wars, as it now is, when she is in a position to give law to Europe under the imperial despotism of Napoleon the Third. The advocates in Paris were held in high honour by the Court of Parliament. "They are," says Pasquier, "honoured with the furred hat, which is the true mark of the magistrates of the palace, and they also give to the more ancient among them a seat on the *fleurs-de-lis* with the King's Counsel." Advocates of high standing were often consulted by the judges upon difficult questions. In the old style of Parliament, they are termed *conseillers au parlement*, and in the sixteenth century they still preserved the costume belonging to that office; for, in 1515, on the occasion of the entry of Mary, sister of the King of England, into Paris, when the Parliament resolved to go to meet her in scarlet robes and furred hats, the president sent to summon the advocates "to join themselves to the Court, well mounted, and clothed in robes of scarlet and furred hats."

Among the famous advocates of the fourteenth century, may be mentioned Pierre de Cugnières, who possessed the confidence of Philippe le Bel, and who is said to have written the famous answer of Philippe to the outrageous claims of Boniface the Eighth. The Pope wrote to the King:—"*Scire te volumus quod te in spiritualibus et temporalibus subditum habemus; aliter autem credentes hæreticos habemus.*" To which the monarch replied, in terms said to have been drawn up by de Cugnières, and certainly more remarkable for vigour than politeness:—"*Sciat tua maxima fatuitas, in temporalibus nos alienis non subesse; secus autem credentes fatuos et dementes reputamus.*" Pierre de Cugnières raised for the first time the question of appeal in error against the decisions of the ecclesiastical courts; and his determined opposition to the Court of Rome made him be very generally deemed a heretic. He died in 1356. Guillaume de Nogaret, another advocate, also signalised himself by his opposition to the Papal claims. Philip sent him, along with Sciarra Colonna, to arrest the Pope. He surprised him at Agnani, made him prisoner, and carried him to Rome: and Boniface soon afterwards died of grief and rage, having previously, however, taken care to excommunicate Nogaret. Benedict XI., successor to Boniface, continued the excommunication. Nogaret appealed to a General Council, and was at last absolved by Clement V., on condition that he should make a pilgrimage to the Holy Land.

He died in 1313. Raoul de Presles, poet, historian, and advocate to Charles V., is generally supposed to be the author of the *Songe du Vergier*, in which, under the semblance of the greatest respect, the temporal pretensions of the See of Rome are attacked with the utmost vigour.

In the early part of the fifteenth century, France was torn by the quarrels of the rival factions of the Orleanists and Burgundians, of which the first act was the assassination of the Duke of Orleans, the King's brother, in Paris, in the Rue Barbette, by order of the Duke of Burgundy. An advocate, Guillaume Cousinot, displayed extraordinary courage in venturing to plead the cause of the widowed Duchess of Orleans before the Parliament against the assassin, the terrible John the Fearless, Duke of Burgundy, whose troops occupied Paris. His courage, however, did not communicate itself to the court; and the King granted letters of absolution to the murderer of his brother. In 1418, the Burgundians possessed themselves of Paris, and, in concert with the populace, who favoured them, took an atrocious vengeance upon the Orleanist or Armagnac party. On 26th May, fifty or sixty Orleanists were put to death, and the prisons were crowded with all who were suspected of favouring their faction. On the 12th June, the populace attacked the prisons, and massacred all the prisoners to the number of 1500 persons; among whom were the Chancellor—Henry de Marle—four presidents of Parliament, twenty-three councillors, and forty-one advocates. In 1418, only sixteen advocates were left in Paris; and justice had almost entirely disappeared in the midst of massacres and rebellion. The following year, the Duke of Burgundy was assassinated on the bridge of Montereau in presence of the Dauphin. In 1422, upon the death of Charles VI., the King of England took possession of the throne; and in the registers of Parliament in 1425, are to be found several edicts and ordinances in the name of Henry King of France and England. In 1436, the English were driven out of Paris, and the Court returned to it after eighteen years' sojourn at Poitiers; and in 1439, Guillaume Cousinot, the intrepid advocate above-mentioned, received the reward of his devotion by being made president in Parliament. In the last-mentioned year Paris was ravaged by a deadly pestilence. The King and Court fled from the city; but the Parliament and the advocates determined to remain at their posts, and many of the latter fell victims to their sense of duty.

Charles VII. made many regulations with regard to the French Bar. In one, dated 1446, we find it enjoined upon advocates to be as brief as possible in their pleadings and writings, on pain of an arbitrary fine; and in another, dated 1453, they are recommended to be moderate in their fees, both for pleadings and writings, which seems to shew that the old regulations restricting them to 30 livres tournois had fallen into disuse. Shortness of pleadings is also enjoined; and, from the repetition of this injunction in almost all the ordinances, it may fairly be inferred that the long-windedness of the Bar had been found a serious obstacle to the efficient administration of justice.

The pragmatic sanction of Charles VII. had recognised the supremacy of councils, the freedom of ecclesiastical elections, the abolition of the reservation of benefices, annats, and other rights claimed by the popes, and the restriction of the effects of ecclesiastical censures. It was, of course, highly distasteful to the See of Rome; and Louis the Eleventh—a prince as superstitious as he was cruel, treacherous, and unscrupulous—determined to undo the work of his father, and an ordinance of revocation was prepared in 1461, in which it is declared that the Pragmatic belongs to a time of schism, and is a work of seduction contrary to the authority of the Pope. The Parliament and the bar, however, faithful to their old traditions, refused to register this ordinance; and Jean de Saint-Romain, an advocate and procureur-général, had the courage to tell Cardinal Balue, then prime minister of Louis XI., that "he betrayed the interests of the King." The affair was not pressed; and when, three years afterwards, Louis again brought the matter under the notice of Parliament, an answer, couched in twenty-nine articles, was returned, and it was declared that the new ordinance "was dangerous, and contrary to the laws and to the interests of the kingdom."

Some important regulations with regard to the Bar belong to the reign of Charles VIII. By one of 1490, it is forbidden to admit to the profession of advocate any one who has not studied in a recognised university for five years, and who has not been found properly qualified. By a subsequent ordinance, the buying of any judicial office is strictly forbidden, under pain of severe penalties. The reign of the selfish, voluptuous, and unprincipled Francis the First was disgraced by the establishment of the torture and the interdiction of the free defence of accused persons. Criminal proceedings were made secret, and the functions of the *parquet*, or public prosecutor and his subordinates, were separated from those of the Bar, so that members of the latter were deprived of the hope of being rewarded for their services by being promoted to the rank of crown counsel. The ordinance of Villers-Cotteret (August 1539) was good in only one respect—its introduction of the French language into judicial proceedings. Its other provisions above-mentioned, depriving the accused of the benefit of counsel and of free and open defence, were highly objectionable. Another great evil received the sanction of law during this reign. The purchase of offices was legalised. A bureau was opened for their sale; and what had formerly been considered an abuse was now openly and universally practised, to the great detriment of justice and of the public service. Francis was desirous of gaining over the Pope, in order to further his designs upon Italy; and in order to do so, concerted with him a concordat which was to overturn the Pragmatic Sanction of Charles VII. But Parliament and the Bar, as formerly, were jealous of the interference of Rome with the independence of France and the liberties of the Gallican Church, and strongly protested against the proposed concordat, and resisted its registration. Again and again, they refused to agree to it, in spite of the remonstrances and anger of the King; and, in a solemn sitting held 24th July 1517, the advocates Bouchard, Jean de Lantier, and Olivier Alligret pled against it with great ability and the utmost boldness. At length, however, after six months' resistance, the royal will prevailed, and the obnoxious concordat was registered.

The pride and delicacy of feeling of the French Bar were deeply injured by an ordinance of Henry III., known as the ordinance of Blois, one article of which enjoined them to inscribe with their own hands, beneath their signature, the amount they had received as fees. They had previously been in the habit, from time immemorial, of receiving their fees without any acknowledgment, and they refused to submit to this regulation, which was allowed to remain unexecuted. However, under Henry IV., the Parliament, forgetful of the good understanding which had always subsisted between it and the Bar, listened to the representations of Sully, who complained of the enormous fees paid by a noble relative,* and made an order that the provisions of the obnoxious

* This noble relative was the Duke of Luxemburg, who complained that an advocate had demanded 1500 crowns for an important cause, or a sum nearly equal to £500 in the present day.

ordinance of Blois should be enforced. The result was a protest, famous in the annals of the French Bar. Their repeated and respectful remonstrances having been ineffectual, the advocates went, two and two in a body, to lay down the functions of their office, deciding upon "voluntarily abandoning the profession of advocate rather than obeying a law injurious to their honour." Four hundred and seven advocates thus solemnly protested against the ordinance of Blois. When the Parliament met, there were no advocates to plead. Justice was at a stand-still, and the capital on the verge of an outbreak. In this awkward dilemma, Parliament applied to the King to extricate them from the embarrassment they had been led into by their own shortsighted obstinacy; which that great monarch did by confirming *pro forma* the order of Parliament, but, at the same time, reinstating the advocates in their functions, and authorising them to plead *as they had previously done;* so that the Bar were successful in carrying their point. During the time the matter was undecided, there were no pleadings from 21st May to 20th July—all the advocates adhering to their resolution of voluntary deprivation in preference to dishonour.

A similar secession and similar instance of independence,—though not quite so unanimously carried out, nor so successfully persevered in—occurs in the history of the Scottish Bar. It is thus narrated in Brunton and Haig's "Historical Account of the Senators of the College of Justice."

"In February 1674, the Court were about to decide a cause depending between the Earl of Dunfermline, and the Earl of Callender and Lord Almond, in favour of the former. Lockhart (afterwards Lord-President), who acted as Counsel for Lord Almond, advised his Lordship to appeal from the Court to Parliament, and accordingly the latter appealed, and in presence of the Judges gave in his appeal. This unexpected proceeding highly surprised and offended the Court. Resting on the statute of James II., which declares that all causes decided by the Court, then called the Session, shall be final, and that of James V., by which the sentences of the Senators of the College of Justice were declared to be of the same validity as those of the former Lords of Session; they considered the appeal as illegal, and resented it as disrespectful. They accordingly addressed the King on the subject, and, after narrating the acts on which they grounded their opinion, pointed out the dangerous consequences which would ensue if appeals were to be permitted, and their decrees rendered thus ineffectual and illusory. To the King the right of appeal contended for was peculiarly disagreeable. He knew well the hold which the decisions of the Supreme Court gave him over the fortunes of his subjects, and that it was much easier to nominate pliant Judges than to procure the return of subservient members of Parliament. A letter was therefore written to the Court, approving of their conduct, expressive of the royal determination to support them in the exercise of all their privileges, and directing them to make enquiries as to who had been the contrivers of the scheme. The Lord Almond and his Counsel were, on the receipt of this letter, ordered to attend the Court on the 26th of February. His Lordship still adhered to his appeal, but refused to swear if he had done it with or without advice. His Counsel were then called, and two of them upon oath denied all knowledge of the appeal, but the other four, including Lockhart, refused to swear, as inferring a breach of confidence between them and their clients. The Court unanimously repelled the objection, and ordained them to give their oaths on the following day. They were then heard at greater length on their reasons for refusing to swear, which having been again overruled, they were of new commanded to make oath, and again declined. The dignity of the Court was now fully committed, but, as the Session was at a close, they contented themselves with sending the King a narrative of what had taken place. A royal letter, dated the 19th May, was sent down at the opening of the Summer Session, declaratory of the King's abhorrence of the appeals, and containing instructions to the Court to intimate to all advocates, writers, and other members of the College of Justice, 'that none of them presume to advise, propose, plead, speak, or suggest anything that doth express or import the changing of any of the decreets and sentences of the Lords of Session with injustice, whether in the terms of appeals, protestations, supplications, informations, or any other manner of way, either publicly in the exercise of their functions, or privately in their ordinary conversation with their clients,' under the pain of deprivation. The King also directed that nothing further should take place with regard to the advocates who had refused to swear as to their knowledge of the appeals, provided they would now disown the same, but that if they refused to disown the appeals, they should be debarred from exercising the functions of an advocate in time coming. The Court intimated the contents of this letter to the whole body of advocates on the 23d June, and the rest having been then removed, Sir George Lockhart, Sir John Cunninghame, and Mr. William Weir, were required to obey the letter, in so far as they were concerned. Continuing still resolute, they were deprived on the following day, and immediately left the house, followed by almost the whole body of the Faculty. The Court had not calculated on this unanimity and firmness, and for some time vainly tried to break it by threatening proclamations. The advocates still absented themselves. One division of them, headed by Sir George, enjoyed themselves at Haddington, the other, with Sir John Cunninghame, resided at Linlithgow. It was now resolved to try stronger measures, and a letter was addressed by the King to the Court on the 12th December, in which, after mentioning that as yet none of the advocates had been petitioned to be restored, 'whereby, and by their whole carriage in this matter, we are convinced that in a factious way they doe forbear to give or offer satisfaction, each for himself severally, till they all come in jointly together, upon such terms as they think fit, which is a dangerous preparative, and highly prejudicial to our service;' the King promises, for the encouragement of those advocates who had remained, that he will not allow a greater number of the absentees to be re-admitted than the number of those who had continued, and declares, on the word of a prince, that such of the advocates who had withdrawn, and who should not petition for their re-admission before the 28th of January following, should never be admitted at any time thereafter. Even this did not produce submission. On the contrary, the advocates, under the direction of Sir George Lockhart, on the last day fixed for receiving their petitions, gave in one to the Privy-Council, justifying the use of protestations for remeid of law from various statutes; but offering, if the Judges would, by an Act of Sederunt, 'plainly and clearly declare that protestations for remeid of law to His Majesty and Estates of Parliament were, and are, in themselves unlawful, and that the Parliament cannot thereupon renew and rescind their decreets if they find just cause, the petitioners will so far defer to their authority, as to be concluded thereby, and satisfy what was prescribed and required by the Lords of Session as to that point.' This pleading highly offended the Privy-Council, who sent it to the King as a most seditious paper, and Sir John Cunninghame, Lockhart, and Sir Robert Sinclair, were therefore sent to London to appease the King, which, however, they were not then able to accomplish. A process was raised against the advocates before the Privy-Council (20th February 1675), to which defences were lodged by Sir George Mackenzie and others, which may be seen in his memoirs of Scotland. According to his own statement, having discovered that Lockhart and others at London were waiting the issue of this process, before deciding on their future conduct, he called the advocates together, and recommended submission, adding, 'It was no dishonour to submit to their Prince, ceding being only dishonourable among equals, and never being so, when the contest was raised by those who designed to make them knaves and fools. All such tumults tended to sedition, and sedition to war, in which advocates not only became losers, but insignificant.' This reasoning prevailed, and the advocates yielding, were re-admitted. Deserted by their associates, Lockhart and his friends in London were soon afterwards obliged to follow their example. The King declared himself satisfied with their submission in a letter to the Court, dated 11th December 1675, and Lockhart and his colleagues were re-admitted on the 28th January 1676." That the advocates were in the right throughout this struggle it seems scarcely possible to doubt; and the right of appeal, for which they contended, was acknowledged and established, soon after the revolution, as a salutary control over the Court of Session.

Pierre Séguier and Christophe de Thou were two of the most eminent advocates of the 16th century. Both were eloquent and successful pleaders, but in different styles. The one was short and pointed; the other, fluent and diffuse. Of Séguier it was said, *Multa paucis;* and of De Thou, *Pauca multis.* The Séguiers were a famous family of the robe. Pierre Séguier was King's advocate, and afterwards a president in Parliament; and the same honours were held by his son Antoine; while Pierre Séguier, the second of the name, became Chancellor of France. De Thou was raised to the high dignity of first president of Parliament in 1562. He was the father of the celebrated historian Jacques-Auguste de Thou. Olivier, Jean Lemaistre, François de Marilhac (who defended Anne Dubourg and the Prince of Condé), Simon Marion, Antoine Arnaud, Omer Talon (the first of the name), and Etienne Pasquier, were also among the eminent advocates who have left the traces of their talents and virtues in the annals of the sixteenth century. Antoine Arnaud, born in 1548, preferred the career of the Bar to the office of advocate-general or a place in the King's Council. His most celebrated pleading is that against the Jesuits in 1594. He was so famous for his eloquence that Henry IV., wishing to gratify the Duke of Savoy, took him to the Parliament where Arnaud was pleading; and so charmed was the King with his speaking, that he sent him the brevet of Councillor of State that same day. The respect and popularity that Arnaud enjoyed were immense. He had the greatest nobles in the realm for his clients, and they were in the habit of coming to his house to consult him. He married the daughter of Simon Marion above mentioned, and became the father of twenty children, of whom ten died in infancy. His four sons were distinguished by their talents and virtues, and his six daughters embraced a religious life at Port-Royal, under the direction of *la mère Angelique*, one of their number, who was abbess at eleven years of age. The great Arnaud, the youngest of the sons, also retired to the abbey of Port-Royal, which became the nursery and school of Jansenism, and the refuge of many distinguished men.

The advocates of Paris had the principal share in arranging, and putting into shape and order, the different systems of consuetudinary law existing in various parts of France. This important work was commenced about the middle of the fifteenth century, under the reign of Charles VII. The *Coutume de Ponthieu* was the first drawn up, under Charles VIII. in 1495; the others were published in the sixteenth century, under Francis I., Charles II., and Charles IX. The *Coutume de Paris*, drawn up in 1510, was almost entirely the work of the Bar, and so was its revisal in 1580, which was performed by Montholon, Versoris, Pasquier, Antoine Loisel, Simon Marion, and Louis de Sainction, all members of the Bar.

The sixteenth century was not specially distinguished for the good taste and eloquent style of its judicial pleadings. They were too often disfigured by a strange marquetry of French and foreign words, more curious than correct, and overloaded with long quotations from a variety of authors, sacred and profane, which were intended to display the learning of the advocate, but which materially interfered with the progress and effect of his argument. Many great writers on the science of jurisprudence, and many distinguished teachers of its principles, flourished in France during the sixteenth century, among whom we may mention Budé, born in Paris in 1467, and died in 1540. He was termed "the splendour and ornament of the realm, and the restorer of the Roman law." His commentaries on the Pandects, written in a somewhat barbarous latinity, are his principal work. He was so absorbed in his studies that he had no time or attention to bestow upon anything else; so that, being informed on one occasion that a fire had broken out in his house, he coolly replied, "Tell my wife; I don't meddle with domestic affairs." Charles Dumoulin —1500–1566—was another great jurisconsult of this era. His decisions were more respected than the decrees of Parliament, and the most learned lawyers deferred to his opinion. His religious views were very unsettled. In 1542 he became a Calvinist, afterwards adopted the Lutheran creed, and ended by returning to the bosom of the Romish Church. The brothers Pythou, of whom Pierre was author of the famous *Traité des Libertés de l'Eglise Gallicaine*, and Antoine Loisel, author of the *Dialogue des Avocats*, and *Institutions Coutumières*, also deserve mention; but the most illustrious lawyer of the period belonged not to Paris, but to Toulouse. We allude to the famous Cujas—1522–1590—one of the most learned commentators who have ever illustrated the Roman law. He left behind him seven folio volumes of treatises on different subjects relating to the civil and canon law. Alexander Scot, a native of Aberdeen, was one of the most eminent of the disciples of Cujas. He was deeply learned both in the civil and canon law, and held the position of judge in the town of Carpentras. An excellent edition of the works of Cujas was published by him, and he also wrote a Greek grammar, which passed through a number of editions. He died in 1615.

During the sixteenth century, Protestantism made rapid progress in France, in spite of the severe measures adopted to extirpate it. In June 1559, Henry II. issued an edict pronouncing against Protestants "the penalty of death, without limitation or remission." The first sufferer under this monstrous edict was Anne du Bourg, an upright and fearless magistrate, who was put to death with circumstances of atrocious cruelty, merely for having spoken in his place in Parliament against the edict. He had for defenders the advocates Pierre Robert, François de Marilhac, and

Antoine Dulac. On the 24th August 1572, occurred the memorable and infamous massacre of St Bartholomew, in which Taverny, Duterrieu, Robert, and some other advocates perished. Only one advocate, Jean Ferrier, is mentioned as having taken part in the horrors of the scene. Christophe de Thou, however, then first president of Parliament, and formerly a member of the Bar, approved of the massacre. "He made," says Père Daniel in his History of France, "a great eulogium upon the prudence of the King, who, on so important an occasion, had most usefully put in practice the maxim of his predecessor, Louis XI., that to know how to reign, one must know how to dissemble; that it was the only means which the King could adopt to anticipate a dangerous conspiracy formed against the whole royal house." Shortly after St Bartholomew, took place the formation of the famous Catholic League, in which we find several advocates—such as Louis d'Orleans, Caumont, Menager, and Lemaistre—playing important parts. Louis d'Orleans and Jean Lemaistre were the most distinguished members of the Bar who supported the League, to which they became advocates-general. In 1589, the King and the Leaguers were at open war, and the former transferred the Parliament to Tours, notwithstanding which the Parliament at Paris continued its functions. In August of that year, occurred the assassination of Henry III., which was speedily followed by the war between Henry IV. and the League. The honour of having restored peace and good government to France belongs, in a great measure, to Jean Lemaistre, advocate-general, and afterwards first president to the League. He entered into a secret correspondence with Henry IV.; and, after having assured himself of his willingness to abjure Protestantism and of an amnesty, he communicated with several influential men, and having ascertained their sentiments, convoked an extraordinary meeting of the court over which he presided, where resolutions were passed condemnatory of handing France over to the rule of any foreign prince or power under pretext of providing for the safety of the Romish faith. In carrying out these resolutions, which risked the lives of all who passed them, Lemaistre was zealously supported by another advocate, Michel de Marilhac, who, though a leaguer, was strongly opposed to the designs of the Spaniards against the liberty of France. The surrender of Paris to Henry IV. was also powerfully aided by certain members of the French Bar; and, in 1594, the advocates and procurators took the oath of fidelity to the new sovereign, and renounced all leagues and associations. In May of the same year, the Parliament, which had been held at Tours and Chalons, during the troubles that had distracted the kingdom, returned to Paris, and the administration of justice resumed its regular course. In 1595, a famine caused by the ravages of the civil wars, brought on a violent pestilence in Paris, and all who could fled from the city. But the court of Parliament and the Bar determined to act as they had formerly done during the plague of 1437. They remained firm at their post; and seventeen magistrates and twenty-two advocates fell victims to their devotion.

FRIEDBERG ON THE CONSTITUTION OF MARRIAGE.

Das Recht der Eheschliessung in seiner geschichtlichen Entwicklung. Von EMIL FRIEDBERG, Doctor der Rechte und Privat-Docent an der Universität zu Berlin. Leipzig, 1865.

DR. FRIEDBERG informs us that this work, a historical view of the legal doctrines and legislative enactments as to the constitution of marriage, was undertaken on the suggestion of his friend and teacher, the late Professor Richter of Berlin, well-known as editor of the *Corpus Juris Canonici*, and as author of a standard work on Ecclesiastical Law. Although it includes only a portion of what we describe as marriage law—touching only incidentally on the law of divorce and the patrimonial rights depending on marriage—it is, within its own limits, by far the most complete and satisfactory summary of the progress of European jurisprudence and legislation which we have seen, and cannot fail to be of the highest value both to the Commissioners who are now investigating the marriage laws of the United Kingdom, and in the discussions which their Report will occasion.

We do not mean to say that it is a book which will live and take a high rank in legal literature. It has too much German cumbrousness, too many mere narratives of bootless controversies and discussions, too little literary workmanship as distinguished from industry and learning, to entitle it to any position higher than that of a collection of materials to some extent arranged and ticketed for the use of others. It is, however, a very good collection of materials, with here and there a plain and succinct summary of the results which the author has arrived at in his examination of a particular period. We regret, for the sake of our own legislators and controversialists, that it is written in German, and that it is too extensive and too disjointed for us to be able to give a connected and intelligible *resumé* of all its contents. We shall endeavour, however, to give such an account of them, and such extracts, as our space permits, and as we hope will encourage some of our readers to independent study of the history of the marriage laws of Europe.

Dr. Friedberg passes lightly over the earliest Christian period, already fully occupied by Bingham, Augusti, and Klee, and begins his proper labours with the development of doctrines in the middle ages, illustrating, in particular, by poetry and by other documents which do not usually form part of legal studies, the great gulf between the requirements of the ecclesiastical theory of marriage and the ordinary life of the people. He then surveys the changes resulting from the Reformation, both in the Roman Catholic Church law as settled by the Council of Trent, and in the different countries of Protestant Europe. His fourth book treats of the rise and progress of civil marriage in all the countries of Europe. A hundred and thirty pages are devoted to England, and would do great credit to the knowledge and industry of any British lawyer. Indeed these pages contain the most complete history of British legislation on this subject which exists; and, among other recommendations, we may remark that the foot notes form a very full index to all the parliamentary debates on this subject since the middle of last century. The author has sought the materials for his work in personal visits to the countries whose legal development he traces, and his pages teem with proofs of his diligent use of their libraries and archives.

It was natural that marriage between Christians should very early acquire a religious character, and be brought into some connection with the Church. But although, like many other important private transactions in a society whose code of morality and even of laws was materially different from that of the new religion, marriages were generally entered into after obtaining the sanction of the Church, and although, even in the time of the fathers, the Church appears to have co-operated or to have lent its sanction in the inception of the matrimonial contract, yet, even after special nuptial solemnities had been introduced, the declaration of matrimonial consent continued separate from the religious ceremonies. It was only in the rituals of the eleventh and twelfth centuries that it was uttered in presence of the priest and at his demand, it was only then that the benediction assumed the character of a confirmation of the marriage, and was closely connected with the exchange of consent. It is remarkable that the Greek ritual which even in its present form bears marks of extreme antiquity, still knows no declaration of consent by the spouses.* The ecclesiastical solemnity of marriage was not therefore an act constituting marriage, but only one of sanctification, acknowledgment, and confirmation of a marriage which previously existed. And marriages which were disapproved by the Church, such as second marriages, and those of divorced persons, lacked every ecclesiastical sanction, without losing thereby full civil validity. Dr. Friedberg recapitulates the evidence of the fact, which has strangely enough been questioned, that while the Christian Church down to the Council of Trent never ceased to insist on the priestly blessing as a laudable and wholesome accompaniment of marriage, it always recognised the legal validity of clandestine marriages.

Dr. Friedberg traces the growth of the *mundium* of the old Germanic tribes into the law of dower, the price originally paid by the husband to the relations of the wife for her *mundium* (*i.e.*, the privileges arising to him out of the legal guardianship or *tutela* which he acquired over her), being in course of time secured to her as a provision in case of widowhood. The marriage was constituted by the formal transfer of the *mundium* and the settling of the *dotalicium*, and was purely a civil contract; but consummation seems to have been considered necessary to its full effect, and the author ascribes to the influence of Germanic ideas, the tendency of the canon law as distinguished from the Roman law, to give prominence to the carnal connection of the spouses. The wife in the words of the Sachsenspiegel entered into the power of the husband, "when she went into his bed." So deeply rooted in the popular mind was the notion of its necessity that in 1330 a Council of Würzburg found it necessary to forbid the laying of the bride in the bed of a bridegroom who had died immediately after the wedding, in order to go through the form of consummation ("dass die Beschlagung der Decke vor sich gehen lasse"). With "the bedding," as we should say in this country, were connected all the

* *Daniel Codex Liturg.* iv., 528 foll. Leips. 1847.

symbols and usages relating to the expression of consent. The married people were presented with food and drink, and driven to bed with blows. Down to the sixteenth century the *concubitus* in marriages of persons of princely rank was as public as the nuptial solemnity itself; and usages of this kind are referred to as existing in Germany in the seventeenth and eighteenth centuries.* So far as regards the form of marriage, there seems to have gathered around it a variety of customs interesting to the antiquarian, but of little value to the lawyer, especially the employment of a *Fürsprecher*, attorney, or procurator, who occupied an important position, and seems to have been a kind of predecessor of our "best man" or "groomsman." Marriage was, with these tribes, a purely civil affair, although not in the sense that it was entered into in presence of state officials. Its essence consisted not in the presence of witnesses, nor in the acts of the Fürsprecher, for these might be wanting, but in the expression of consent, which, as we see, might be inferred from circumstances.

* Consummation in some countries was required as well as the solemnity in church in order to the constitution of absolute marriage with full civil effects. "Jus autem Saxonicum non solum celebratas nuptias, sed etiam thori maritalis ingressum prorsus exigit." Wesenbec. in Tit. Dig. de Sponsal. n. 9. Swinburne p. 235. See also Bluntschli *Deutsches Privatrecht*: "Marriage was preceded by espousals which were entered into in presence of the family, and were connected with the alienation of the tutorial right which had hitherto pertained to the bride's father, but for the future was to belong to the husband. For the purpose of transferring this tutorial power—at least among the Franks—the agreement was concluded before the tribunal (*mallum*), whence the terms *Gemahl* and *vermählen*. The bridegroom paid a price for it (the *meta*, Muntschatz), which was afterwards—for the most part—handed over to the wife herself. The espousals created a personal and family relation between the spouses. The bridegroom was not allowed capriciously to repudiate the bride, without incurring a penalty. Otherwise there was no compulsion to complete the marriage. If a child was begotten between espoused persons it was regarded according to the old law in all respects as a child born in wedlock, not as a *Brautkind*; for no precise form was as yet required for the constitution of marriage, and the spouses became married persons at the moment when, according to the old proverb, "die Decke Mann und Weib beschlagen hatte." (*Cf. Aeneas Sylvius*, Hist. Fred. III. p. 36. Jussit (Fridericus III.) teutonico more stratum apparari jacentique sibi Leonoram in ulnas complexusque dari, ac praesente rege cunctisque proceribus astantibus superduci culcitram. Neque aliud actum est nisi datum osculum. Erant autem ambo vestiti, moxque inde surrexerunt. Sicque consuetudo Teutonicorum se habet cum principes primo junguntur). That is the case only with ordinary espousals, entered into openly before the family, not with secret espousals." As to the effect attributed to consummation even where, as with us, the maxim *consensus non concubitus facit matrimonium* is received in its largest sense, compare Lord Meadowbank's opinion that "where no consummation of a first marriage had taken place, no lawyer had ever entertained a doubt that the children of the second would be legitimate." Bell's Put. Mar. p. 6. And as to the effect of *concubitus* as evidence of matrimonial consent, See Fraser, Pers. and Dom. Rel. I. 225; *Elder* v. *M'Lean*, 8 S. 56.

The early English law differed in no material respect from the German law. Strutt, for instance,* has a picture of a marriage showing the relations of both the parties, but no priest. The marriage services which have come down from the Saxon period show how gradually the Church succeeded in enforcing its demands. In the oldest, which Dr. Friedberg cites from Schmid's *Geschichte der Angelsachsen*, the priest occupies a very subordinate place. Later he becomes the principal personage, as in the old rituals of Salisbury and York, asking the parties at the church-door as to their consent, and asking the husband what *dos* he means to bestow on the bride. But even in these rituals the act constituting marriage, the giving away of the bride, is performed by her father or relations, although it is observable that the questions as to the "settlements" are put by the priest, and the interchange of consent is made an integral part of the religious act. The mention of the church-door as the place where the bride was *endowed*, marks, in those times, the prevalence of ecclesiastical marriage. Thus says the wife of Bath—

> "I was a worthy woman all my life,
> Husbands at the church-door had I five."†

The statute 2 and 3 Edw. vi., c. 1, introduced marriage *in* the church, although a verse of Herrick seems to indicate the continuance of the ancient custom after the Reformation. The author remarks, that in England also clandestine marriages were frequent, as the numerous prohibitions of them sufficiently prove; but it is characteristic that in these mention is almost always made of the priest who solemnized such marriages, and that lay marriages are not specially forbidden in England. They did occur, however, very frequently in the form of *handfastings*, which are frequently alluded to in poems of the 16th and 17th centuries. It is remarkable to find the ring and the giving of gold or silver, a usual symbol in those marriages without clergy, introduced into the religious ceremony. "This shows," says our author, "how the church endeavoured to combine the popular customs which it could not abolish with the religious act in order to accommodate the latter to the people. This policy of the church, everywhere revealed in the reception of purely worldly acts, to which some religious significance or other had then to be ascribed, shows how hard the church deemed the contest with hostile custom to be,

* *Horda Angel-Cynnan*, vol. I., fol. 13, fig. 13.
† See *Brand's Popular Antiq.* (ed. Ellis, 1849) II., 134.

how it neglected no means in order to carry out the desired religious marriage, and how little this was spontaneously desired by the people."

One of the most interesting passages in the book, is that relating to the English marriage customs of the middle age. The old dramatists are largely cited. Shakespeare is referred to for his carricature of the ecclesiastical ceremony in the *Taming* of the Shrew;

> "When the priest should ask—if Katherine
> should be his wife,
> Ay by gog's—wouns', quoth he, and swore so loud,
> That all amazed, the priest let fall the book.
> . . . .
> But after many ceremonies done,
> He calls for wine:
> A health, quoth he, as if he had been aboard,
> Carousing to his mates after a storm:
> Quaff'd off the muscadel and threw the sops
> All in the sexton's face; having no other reason—
> But that his beard grew thin and hungerly,
> And seems to ask him sops as he was drinking.
> This done he took the bride about the neck
> And kiss'd her lips with such a clamourous smack,
> That at the parting all the church did echo."

The Yelverton case is the authority for a statement, that in Irish Roman Catholic marriages it is to this day, usual, and even essential, that the bridegroom should give the priest a piece of gold; and the *Daily Telegraph* of 10th Aug. 1864, proves by a paragraph, entitled, "Selling a Wife for a Shilling," the lingering belief among the English peasantry that a man can sell his wife, a possible relic of the old law of *mundium*.

Dr. Friedberg discusses with great perspicuity the question as to the legal effect of irregular marriages in England. He observes, that in other European countries medieval law is unimportant for the decision of the questions of to-day, and that the learned, who alone in such countries attempt to trace in the rubbish of the past the growth of particular institutions, have never doubted the validity of such connections, especially as the church, the only competent judge, constantly recognized them as binding. Both of these matters are different in England. Precedents of old date are still appealed to, and the question of the validity of informal marriages in the middle ages has in our own times been the subject of keen discussion in the Supreme Court of Appeal.*

* *The Queen* v. *Millis*, 10 Cl., and Fin. 534.

"English Courts and English practice," he says, "will perhaps be bound by that decision, but for us and for legal science it can hardly claim a higher authority than any other learned opinion, and all the less because I have no hesitation in declaring it to be erroneous," p. 48. To lawyers not the least interesting part of this book will be the examination of the argument of Chief Justice Tindal to prove the absolute necessity of marriage in *facie ecclesiæ* in England previous to 1753. Much of the argument on the other side is already familiar in the letter of Sir John Stoddart, and on the judgment of Lord Brougham in the same case. The author states the results of the inquiry thus:—"The church, which was alone competent to determine whether a marriage was lawfully contracted or not, which in other countries judged the question of law and the question of fact together—as indeed they could not reasenably be separated—held all *sponsalia de præsenti* to be true marriages, punished those who avoided the celebration before the church, or cohabited before it took place, allowed a suit for celebration of marriages not entered into in *facie ecclesiæ*, just as was the case in other countries, and as was entirely in conformity with the principles of the Canon Law. Thus the English *Ecclesiastical* law is in no way distinguished from the common law of the church. But the Courts of the *Common Law* exacted quite other requisites, if not for the *validity*, yet at least for the *efficacy* of matrimonial engagements. For them it was not sufficient that there was cohabitation with the purpose of begetting children, (*marriage in possession*), nor even public espousals (*matrimonium de facto*), according to the ancient rules of law; they required that the act should have been performed in a chapel, in a church, they required ecclesiastical, in other words, the only public authentication then possible. There was a very plain reason for this. In the secular courts the neighbours of the parties decided as jury; it was for them to find whether a marriage existed or not. Intimate as they were with all the circumstances of their neighbourhood, they could know that fact only when they had seen it by unmistakeable public signs, when the pair had gone to church before their eyes. The essential matter to them was not the mere priestly co-operation, but the *public* religious act, the public "going in the church and in the street." * They would undoubtedly have declared a union contracted in a room with all the requisites of the church service to be concubinage, with the same distinctness

* See "*The Christian State of Matrimony*," p. 43, *Anno.* 1543.

as they regarded a pair publicly married in the church as husband and wife in spite of all possible impedimenta.

"The consequences in regard to informal marriages were:—They were perfectly good in law; he who, having contracted such a marriage, entered into another, was guilty of bigamy, and his marriage was necessarily annulled *ratione precontractus*. The wife, however, could neither claim dower, nor the husband obtain any right to her estate, for on that point the secular courts were the judges. In regard to the legitimacy of the children born of such connections, a distinction was to be made according as the parents, or one of them were, or were not, still living. In the former case, there was still access to the spiritual court, so that the legitimacy of the child might be assured; but, in the latter case, and that is another logical inconsistency, they were held illegitimate, since the lawfulness of the connection was presumed in favour of the deceased only in so far as regarded its subsistence in point of fact,—so far, in short, as the decision on the question of fact, and therefore by the jury, could be obtained.* Thus, the child of a bigamous marriage *in facie ecclesiæ*, was declared *legitimus hæres* of his father, if his parents were dead, while, in the opposite case, he was dedeclared *adulterinus*."

In France, as in England, the *dos* was fixed at the church door, and the fact that many of the *coutumes* recognised the patrimonial consequences of marriage only when the priest's benediction had been pronounced, leaves no doubt that marriage *in facie ecclesiæ* was very usual, and indeed necessary for some effects. The proproverb, "Boire, manger et coucher ensemble c'est mariage ce me semble," proves, however, the prevalence and recognition of informal contracts. Dower seems, in Brittany, to have depended on the bedding or consummation, and D'Argentré gives the maxim, "Femme gagne son douère à mettre son pied au lict." There existed in the Gallican Church forms for blessing the marriage-bed. During the *concubitus* it was a custom in some districts for the guests to sing the "Veni Creator Spiritus" at the window of the bridal chamber, which is somewhat suggestive to modern readers of a celebrated Conte of La Fontaine.

An overwhelming mass of evidence shows how, in the earliest periods of modern European history, there was no recognized necessity for marriage in the face of the church, and how very gradually the ecclesiastical ceremony became usual. In

* Y. B. 42 Edw. III. 1388: Law Mag. for 1846.

Germany especially it seems to have been long an inveterate usage that the *concubitus* should precede the blessing of the church, and that without much objection on the part of the hierarchy. The author also remarks, that the custom which still exists among the lower classes under the name of the "Komm and Probenächte (trial nights), Kiltgehen, &c." (that is, that those who proposed to enter into marriage should previously have carnal intercourse with each other), prevailed in the middle age even among the higher ranks. Thus Count John the Fourth of Hapsburg slept half-a-year with Herzland of Rappolstein, to whom he was betrothed, and was rejected by her on account of his inability to perform certain conjugal duties (mit ir nie geborte in der Mossen als ob'er ein Man were, p. 84.) The humble people in Scotland, and in some districts of England, who don't marry the women with whom they have had connection till time shows whether "it hauds," only follow a practice handed down to them from knights and ladies of old. An anecdote of Louis I. of Bavaria and the Countess Ludmilla von Bogen, appears to prove that the ladies of that country and age, were quite as well acquainted with the law of marriage as modern "pursuers" in Scotland. The Duke long sought with fair words the love of this beauteous and crafty dame. After many coy denials she fixed a day on which he should receive the wished for favour, admission to her chamber. Meanwhile she caused a screen, or curtain, to be hung before her couch, adorned with a beautifully executed picture representing three armed knights; and on the appointed day she hid behind the screen three real knights, her friends and accomplices. When the Prince came, supposing that he was alone with the lady, he resumed his importunity, and she agreed to grant his wish if he would take her *de præsenti* for his wife, "before these three knights as witnesses." Thinking the three painted figures of little account in such a matter, he promised without hesitation, upon which she pulled aside the screen, and invoked the three real knights to bear testimony to the declaration of the Duke. The spouse thus ensnared, hastily departed, and absented himself for a-year; but at length he wedded the lady, like a Christian, solemnly, before the church, (p. 89).

Dr. Friedberg describes the extreme disorder and perplexity which the facility of contracting marriage had produced at the time of the Reformation, and which was not counteracted by its natural corrective, facility in obtaining divorce. This was a subject of much solicitude to both the great parties in the 16th century. There is no exaggeration in Luther's description in the Table Talk* of the distress of those who came to the Confessional, to bewail the vexations and griefs of the bigamous union in which that state of the law had involved them. "Quæsitum est," says Erasmus, "an etiam solo nutu possit contrahi matrimonium, et responsum est posse. Quaesitum, an literis scriptis coëat matrimonium, responsum est coire. Quaesitum est, an signo, veluti si quis nummi fracti dimidium det puellae, responsum est coisse matrimonium. Quaesitum est, an per procuratores inter absentes coëat matrimonium, responsum est, coire, si procurator a certa persona de contrahendo cum certa mandatum acceperit. Quaesitum est, an facto fiat ratum matrimonium, veluti si iuvenis dicat: Si me habes pro coniuge da basium; responsum est coire. Quaesitum est, an silentio coëat matrimonium, veluti si puellae pater dicat patri iuvenis: Do filiam meam uxorem filio tuo: rursum proci pater respondeat, Et ego filium meum do maritum filiae tuae, si nec iuvenis, nec puella contradicat, sed tantum obticescat uterque, ratum erit matrimonium."

Some abatement of these evils was found, for Roman Catholic countries, in the celebrated decree of the Council of Trent, "de Reformatione Matrimonii," of which it was said, that a council might well have been held for its sake alone. This decree making marriage a purely ecclesiastical matter, annulling informal contracts, and making the priestly function and the sacramental nature of the solemnity of the essence of the thing, was the subject of keen discussion, which may be read in the histories of Sarpi and Pallavicini. It was undoubtedly a usurpation on the part of the church; but it must be judged in its relation to the condition of society at the time. The provinces of church and state were then undefined; there was almost a fusion, there certainly was a *confusion* of the two powers, and it was only in the course of the centuries that these notions underwent that process of separation which is not yet completed. According to the ideas

* "They came to me or to another in the Confessional and said: 'Lieber Herr, I have a wife whom I espoused in secret; what am I to do about her at all? Help me, lieber Herr Doctor, lest I despair. For Greta, to whom I was first betrothed, is my true wife. But this Barbara, whom I afterwards married, is not my wife and yet must I live with her? The one I may not have, whom I would fain have, if it could be; but now I cannot, for I have another, and she too has another man; yet none knoweth that she is my wife, but God in heaven only. Oh, I am damned, I know no remedy.'"

of that time, it was the duty and the right of the church to regulate marriage in all its consequences; the church alone had the power to do so. Who will blame her if she obeyed the call of that duty, and exercised that right? The Tridentine rule is authoritative only in the countries where it has been published, and many European countries, especially the minor German states, while they adopt its provisions, still regard marriage as a civil contract, and the priests as state officials, who, in celebrating marriages, perform a civil rather than an ecclesiastical function. This was the view of the Emperor Joseph II., whose *Ehepatent* of 1783, was the foundation of the Austrian marriage law till the Concordat of 1855 restored the Tridentine law in its entirety.

The author next proceeds to review the progress of legal theory as to the constitution of marriage in Protestant countries. But our space forbids us to enter at present on this subject or on his elaborate history of the development of the modern idea of "Civil Marriage."

TWENTY-SEVENTH REPORT ON PRISONS IN SCOTLAND.

The Annual Report to the Home Secretary by the managers appointed under the "Prisons (Scotland) Administration Act," in continuation of those of the late General Board of Prisons, was laid before Parliament at the commencement of the session, and has recently been printed and circulated. It presents the usual immense mass of statistics with regard to each prison in Scotland, and in addition to a detailed statement as to the condition of the General Prison in Perth, which is under the immediate control of the managers, contains their observations upon the points which they deem worthy of notice in prison administration throughout Scotland. There are in Scotland 68 prisons, containing 3286 cells for criminal, and 168 cells or rooms for civil prisoners. The average daily number of prisoners for the year ending 30th June 1865 was in the criminal 1306 male and 1112 female, and in the civil department 60 male and 2 female prisoners. The total number in confinement during the year (including recommitments) was 17,099 male and 11,411 female criminal prisoners, and 727 male and 29 female civil prisoners. The number of commitments during the year was 25,015, in contrast with 19,701 during the year ending 30th June 1862, since which time the criminal commitments have been steadily increasing, while before that there appeared a considerable decrease on the average of the five years ending 1861, as compared with that of the five years ending in 1856. One of the most distressing features in the statistics is the enormous number of previous imprisonments which had been undergone by the prisoners received during the year. No fewer than 12,167 had been previously imprisoned in the same prison as that to which they were committed during the year, and 282 prisoners had been previously imprisoned the surprising and almost incredible number of fifty times *and upwards*. On examining the details as to these previous imprisonments, some curious and apparently inexplicable facts appear. The 282 prisoners who had been previously fifty times and upwards in prison are divided between the two sexes in the most unequal ratio of 8 males to 274 females. Whether this is to be explained by the greater incorrigibility of the female delinquent, or the mistaken kindness of judges in pronouncing sentences of shorter imprisonments upon females than upon males, we cannot say. The prisons, too, throughout which the 282 incorrigibles are distributed are six in number, viz., Edinburgh, Dundee, Airdrie, Perth, Paisley, and Greenock; and of these Edinburgh had 180 (including all the 8 males), leaving 102 females for the other five. The most surprising fact is that Glasgow is conspicuous by its absence in the column headed "Fifty times and upwards."

The details as to imprisonment on civil process are of interest at present when it is proposed in England entirely to sweep away that time-honoured institution. The number of civil prisoners *received* during the year was 672, of whom 24 were females; and of those only 48 males and 2 females were imprisoned for debts exceeding £100. The number imprisoned for "other causes" than debt, including those *in meditatione fugæ*, and those imprisoned under decrees *ad facta prestanda*, was 49, all males. Even if imprisonment for debt shall come to be abolished (a step which we recently took occasion to state would, in our opinion, be most inexpedient), it will, we conceive, be necessary always to retain the power of imprisonment *ad factum prestandum*, as in such cases as refusing to restore sequestrated effects, declining to obey the orders of a judge to deliver up a deed or the like, it is impossible that any substitute can be found for the plain compulsator, "You must stay in prison till you do it." It is satisfactory to find that no females have vindicated the character of the sex for obstinacy by going to prison rather than do what they have been ordered to perform.

One of the most important duties which, in our opinion, the prison managers have to perform is to report as to the due observance of the regulations in regard to the regular visitation of prisons by the local boards. The best governor is the better of the stimulus afforded by frequent visitations by members of the board; and if any abuse exists, a system of visitations, regular as to their number, but uncertain as to the time at which they are paid, is the only infallible means of detection and check. The regulations approved of by the Secretary of State provide for a monthly visitation at least of each prison, and a table in the report before us shews the manner in which the regulation has been obeyed. We regret to say that the result is not at all satisfactory, in 23 prisons the number of visits provided for by the rules not having been made. Some of the prisons in which the rule has not been observed are small, and this in some instances is stated as the reason for the non-observance of the rule. It appears to us that the fewness of the prisoners, so far from being a reason for few visits being paid, is the very reverse. The chances of abuse are reduced to a minimum in large establishments, where the numerous prisoners necessitate the employment of a large staff, all acting as checks upon each other. But in the case of a small prison, with its single governor, matron, and warder, the eye of the visiting members of the board cannot be too frequently upon them. In some of the counties the board seem to perform their duties of visiting in a most conscientious manner, not resting content with the minimum number of visits required. Thus the prison of Ayr was visited 36 times; that of Edinburgh, 23 times; Cupar, 50 times; Dunfermline, 35 times; Glasgow, 18 times; Lanark, 26 times; Hamilton, 20 times; Airdrie, 19 times; Kirkcudbright, 21 times; Dingwall, 21 times; Dornoch, 28 times in the course of the year; and in many other instances the minimum number of visits was exceeded.

The general management of the prisons of Scotland during the period embraced in the report appears on the whole to have been satisfactory. The following somewhat mysterious paragraph gives the only hint of anything being found wrong:—

"Circumstances having led to the supposition that there was irregularity or misconduct on the part of one or more of the officers of the prison of

Ayr, you (*i. e.* the Home Secretary) issued, in the month of July (1864, we presume), an order, under § 58 of the Prisons Act, for an inquiry on oath into the condition and management of that prison. The managers, as a body, are not responsible for such inquiries, the results of them being reported to you by those of their number who conduct the inquiries. In this instance the investigation was conducted and the result reported to you by the Crown agent and the stipendiary manager, and it seems to be only necessary here to state that the County Board took prompt and effective steps for the removal of any source of risk to the discipline of the prison."

There was only one escape during the year. A man who had voluntarily surrendered himself as a deserter was committed to Huntly prison. He appeared, however, soon to have repented of his act, as he contrived to escape, the vigilance of the keeper being naturally not so great towards a prisoner who had come under his care in so peculiar a manner. In two days after his escape he was captured, and we presume again was committed to Huntly.

The report contains the usual details with regard to the General Prison at Perth, which is under the more immediate control of the prison managers. That great establishment, the growth of many years, appears now to be complete, and consists of two departments—the penal and the lunatic. The latter department, in its complete form, has been occupied only since 12th January 1865, and the managers report that they "have every reason to be satisfied with this establishment and its adaptation to its special purpose. It was rendered necessary by the enlargement of the classes for which the old lunatic department was available. This enlargement was made by statute, for the purpose of comprehending all lunatics who, by their conduct, have shewn themselves so dangerous to the public that they must not only be detained in custody, but should be under the charge of a Government department." In this department are confined, in the first place, all prisoners who have become insane in the General Prison, their removal to the lunatic department being effected upon medical certificate. In the second place, all persons placed at her Majesty's disposal on the ground of insanity, either at the time when they committed the offence charged against them or at their trial, are in the first instance confined in this department, and are removed from it only if her Majesty should think fit otherwise to dispose of them. In the third place, the managers have the power of removing to this department from a local prison any prisoner who becomes insane; but this power is exercised only where the case is of such a nature as will justify them in applying to the Secretary of State to exercise his statutory power of detaining in the General Prison an insane prisoner after the expiration of his sentence. It is evident that the second is the most important class of the prisoners detained in the lunatic department, and the gravity of the offences committed by them in their frenzy renders it a very difficult and delicate task for Government to deal with them. We have the evidence of the governor that several of this class are now quite sane, others are subject only to occasional attacks of insanity, and both classes "are very importunate on the subject of regaining their liberty." It appears, however, to be a rare thing to liberate such prisoners on their convalescence; and probably public opinion will, on the whole, justify Government in its reluctance to restore to society a man who has had the misfortune (for such, logically considered, it is), while in a state of insanity, to take the life of a fellow-being. All appears to be done for the unhappy inmates which it is possible in the circumstances to do. The "department" partakes more of the nature of an asylum than a prison, and the inmates are allowed every indulgence which can be granted consistently with their safe custody. The lunatic department had an average of 41 inmates daily throughout the year.

The criminal department of the General Prison had an average daily number of 652 inmates. Except that about one half of these are undergoing sentences of penal servitude, the discipline and management of these prisoners does not differ much from that observed in the local prisons. Of course, however, in the great central establishment there is a completeness of organization which cannot be expected to exist in the smaller prisons. The discipline and management seem on the whole to have been admirable, the health of the prisoners very good, and the number of deaths only two. The following paragraph may probably excite the indignation of the "Scottish Reformation Society."

"The managers have had under consideration how far it might be desirable to encourage or permit visits to prisoners by persons of superior education and position, professing to have in view the moral or religious improvement of the prisoners. The question assumed a practical shape in respect to a portion of the prisoners, by a proposal that certain ladies belonging to a religious sisterhood of Roman Catholics, should visit female prisoners of their own persuasion. With your sanction the managers have allowed the visits of these ladies under such restrictions as they thought advisable. This arrangement, which has existed since the month of June, without any results detrimental to the general discipline of the prison, is

still merely experimental, leaving open the question whether the admission of such visitors, who are not under the control of the authorities of the prison, shall be provided for in special regulations to be recommended for your approval."

We can scarcely doubt that on further experience it will be found that these visits exercise a salutary effect upon the Roman Catholic prisoners, and we trust that the good example set by the ladies referred to will be speedily followed by some of their Protestant fellow-countrywomen.

The report this year contains an appendix consisting of a "Report on the Prison Dietaries in Scotland, prepared under instructions from the Right Hon. the Secretary of State for the Home Department." The reporters are Prof. Christison and Mr. Thomson, the Resident Surgeon of the Perth General Prison. Some changes had recently been made in the English Prison Dietaries, and one object in remitting the subject to the consideration of the reporters, was, that these gentlemen might examine into the comparative advantages of the Scotch and English system. The main difference between the two systems appears to be the substitution in Scotland of oatmeal porridge and milk for the considerable quantities of animal food allowed to prisoners in England. The English authorities in their recent change have not adopted the Scotch staple, and it is contemptuously spoken of by them as "a combination of milk and meal similar to that which is successfully employed in England to fatten pigs." Upon this Dr. Christison and Mr. Thomson remark,—"This is not a fit occasion for controversy, if it were, it would be easy to show that the statements of that report must have been written in ignorance of the important enquiries, of the nature both of scientific analysis and practical observation, which have been communicated to the public at different times during the last twenty years by the Prison Managers of Scotland and their predecessors relative to Prison Dietaries." The result arrived at by the two reporters is, that the present scale of dietaries in the local prisons in Scotland is sufficient, and no more than sufficient, for adult males on longer sentences than 14 days; that it may be slightly reduced for females, and juveniles, and short sentence adult males; and that in the General Prison there should be a slight reduction in the dietary for females in the reformatory classes. Within the last few weeks a new dietary has been promulgated in the Scotch Prisons, giving effect we presume to the conclusions of Professor

Christison and Mr. Thomson, and it is satisfactory to believe that the happy medium has now been ascertained between pampering and starvation, and that the criminal population will, while in prison, be kept alive and in good health, without being fed in a manner which an honest working man is unable to afford for himself and his family.

The whole of the report of the Prison Managers is deserving of attentive consideration, and contains many details of interest in addition to those we have briefly indicated.

THE MONTH.

Proofs by Commission.—Our readers are aware that this is a subject in connection with which we have steadily insisted against the existing practice of the Court of Session. We are happy now to be able to state that there seems an immediate prospect of deliverance from the evils and abuses which it has engendered, and which it is not using strong language to say, amount to a professional scandal. The question has been taken up at two recent meetings of the Faculty of Advocates. On the first occasion a resolution was passed unanimously, that it was desirable that an act should be carried through Parliament, enacting that proofs should not as now be taken by a commissioner, but should proceed before the Lord Ordinary. On the propriety, indeed the necessity, of this rule, there was no suggestion of diversity of opinion in the faculty, the feeling being universal that the proposed reform has been neglected, or at least unduly delayed. It would be repeating a thrice-told tale to state the grounds upon which this measure commends itself to general acceptance. But we think it right to say, that the feeling of the faculty was on that point so unanimous, that everything was avoided in the discussion that might have the effect of postponing the accomplishment of a reform admitted on all hands to be in itself beneficial, and to make acknowledgment of an obvious truth necessary to the very existence of the Court of Session. It is, of course, impossible to be indifferent to the fact, that in dealing with this question the faculty are bordering on the confines of a very difficult and delicate problem, in other words, are indirectly raising and bringing prominently into view the question of jury trial. But it was not intended by the faculty, and in the present divided state of opinion it is not desirable that that point should be made the subject of controversy. It is, in the meantime, sufficient to know, that all are agreed that the present system of delegating to a commissioner a duty that should be undertaken by the Lord Ordinary is unwarrantable, and stands imperatively in need of amendment. The resolution of the faculty was confined strictly to cases where ordinary proof by commission would be allowed. At a second meeting, however, the faculty went one step farther. By the Court of Session Act, 13 and 14 Vict., c. 36, parties may of consent have issues tried by a Lord Ordinary, whose verdict has all the formality which attaches to the verdict of a jury. The faculty have suggested that it should be within the option of parties by consent to try any of the causes enumerated as peculiar to jury trial, by proofs of the facts before the Lord Ordinary. This of course would deprive the conclusion at which he may arrive of all formality; but we see no reason why, if parties choose, they should not be allowed to have recourse to this mode of settling their disputes. We trust, however, that this extension of the proposed alteration may not lead to endangering the leading proposal, viz., that of having proofs by commission superseded by proofs taken before the judge, who is in the first instance to decide the cause. Every change proposed in the mode of administering justice provokes so much discussion, that one always dreads lest a change which every one recognises as an improvement be postponed by being coupled with others as to the value of which public opinion is not yet settled.

Sheriff Court.—Two cases having an important bearing on the jurisdiction of the Inferior Court were argued during the month. In the High Court of Justiciary an attempt was made to quash a conviction for theft obtained in the Sheriff Court at Glasgow, on the ground that the Sheriff had laid down bad law to the jury, had refused to make a direction asked by the agents of the panel, and had declined to note his refusal to do so. The Court sustained the conviction, mainly on the ground that there is no authority, either in law or practice, to review the proceedings of the Inferior Court in criminal proceedings; and it would be difficult to take exception to the judgment of the Justiciary Court as so rested. But the Court proceeded to express, or at least to indicate, an opinion, that the law laid down by the Sheriff was not bad. The Judges were not unanimous on this point, and we think it is matter for regret that so important a question should be raised and almost decided incidentally. The question in dispute is, whether a previous conviction is admissible as evidence of guilty knowledge, to confirm the inference deducible from the *res gestæ* of the case. The prevailing practice of the Court has been, we should have said, to withhold such evidence from the jury as evidence on the substantive charge, and to consider proof of previous conviction as a consideration for the Judge to hold in view in pronouncing sentence, not for the jury to regard in arriving at their verdict on the principal charge. And so much does this view harmonise with the logical theory of our law, that every man is to be presumed innocent until he is proved guilty, that a desire has frequently been expressed that the practice which prevails in England of proving convictions after the verdict of the jury has been returned, should be adopted in this country. It is difficult, on the other hand, to dispute that a good deal may be said on the other side of the question. In the other case to which we refer, the Second Division have decided that an action of reduction, except in the way of exception as provided by the Bankruptcy Law Amendment Act, is not competent in the Sheriff Court. It is certainly taking very narrow ground to say that a form of process which is competent by way of exception shall not be competent by way of action. But there is no doubt that the strict construction which the Court have put upon the statute is in accordance with the general theory that declaratory actions are incompetent in the Inferior Court. It is well that the question has been raised, and an authoritative judgment pronounced, for we understand that there is a practice in some Sheriff Courts to the contrary, and it is notorious that there are at least two volumes containing forms of styles which are observed in the practice of these Courts.

Writs Registration Bill.—We have much pleasure in calling attention to an admirably clear and concise pamphlet on this subject, from the pen of Mr Donald Beith, W.S. Mr Beith contrasts the Bill of the Lord Advocate with Mr Dunlop's Bill of 1865, and gives his support to the former, as tending to reduce the number of registrars, and thereby lessen expense, as well as to add security generally to the system of registration of land rights. It is quite impossible within our limits to advert to the details of the discussion. Mr Beith's remarks are well worthy of perusal, and will be found eminently practical and useful.

Legal Appointments.—The appointment of Mr Charles Morton, W.S., Crown Agent, in room of Mr Murray, had hardly taken when the Ministry resigned. Mr Andrew Murray has been appointed Agent for the Commissioners of Woods and Forests in room of Mr Donald Horne resigned.

Bills in Parliament.—The Lunacy Act Amendment Bill, to which we some time ago called attention, has passed into law. A measure has been for some time before Parliament which might have been expected to attract greater notice from the bearing which it has upon important interests in Scotland. Its title being called the Crown Lands Bill may afford some explanation of the comparative silence which the press has observed in regard to it. Its leading provision is to transfer to the Board of Trade the management of the fore-shore, and to withdraw the powers of the Commissioners of Woods and Forests. We observe that a Bill has been brought in to diminish the expenses and delay in decisions as to the settlement of paupers in Scotland. Everything, of course, that has a tendency to reduce expense is to be commended, and there is no doubt that the parochial funds of the country have been recklessly employed for no better purpose than to obtain decisions on nice points of law. And the delay of the Court of Session bears injuriously upon that class of cases as much as on any other. But we are at a loss to discover a reason why they should be singled out to receive a preference. Indeed there are no cases which in a certain sense stand less in need of expedition; for the paupers whose settlement is in dispute have no interest in the issue of the cause, they being provided for and maintained during its progress, and the parishes would seem just to have as little, for they have claims for past advances against the party who is ultimately found unsuccessful, although undoubtedly some inconvenience to individual ratepayers arises from the changes in the occupancy of land which are taking place every year, rendering it desirable to have all current expenses cleared off as nearly as possible year by year. Nor can we forget that no preference can be given to those public boards except at the expense of delay to ordinary suitors whose all may be at stake in the litigations in which they are concerned. The Court before whom proceedings in this matter under this bill are to take place, is to consist of any three of the Lords Ordinary of the Court of Session.

The Breadalbane Case.—The Court, by a majority of ten to two, have decided this important case in favour of Glenfalloch, the party in possession.

THE

JOURNAL OF JURISPRUDENCE.

LAW STUDIES.

No. III.—LONDON.

It is scarcely possible to imagine conditions more favourable to the formation of a great school of law than those which, to a stranger's eye, appear to exist in the metropolis. When you pass from the bustle of Holborn, or the roar of Fleet Street, into the quiet precincts of Lincoln's Inn, or the monastic Courts of the Temple, you can scarcely believe that such a school has not existed for ages. Even when you are persuaded that it is not, you still ask, why should it not be? For many centuries these spots have been the local habitation of a proud, powerful, rich, ambitious brotherhood, bound together by many cherished associations and by the ties which common interests and common pursuits engender,—a brotherhood which numbers in its ranks every class of person, from the humblest attorney's clerk to the president of the House of Peers,—whose branches shoot upwards and whose roots strike downwards in every conceivable direction, and whose mere *fiat*, sincerely spoken, would actually suffice, at any moment, to call such an institution into existence. Those who belong to the highest branch of this fraternity—who are in priest's orders, so to speak—are the persons by whose instrumentality, if at all, such a school must be created, and for whose benefit it would mainly exist. Of these many are very learned, after the English conception of learning. Some are accurate scholars, thoroughly acquainted, not with the languages only, but with the institutions and opinions of the classical nations. To these acquisitions of their earlier days, they have added, since they joined their profession, an intimacy with the civil life of England to which no man but a lawyer ever attains. Others again, trained as mathematicians, have become conversant with the latest discoveries of physical research; and are able to bring to bear on other departments of study those habits of methodical and concentrated effort which are the most valuable results of such pursuits. The vast majority of them are gentlemen and men of the world, beyond any other class of persons of which this country, or any other country in the world, can boast. Of these men, thus endowed and thus circumstanced, not one half engage,—and a very large proportion never seriously wish to engage,—in practice. They are men of fortune and of leisure, who have joined the body mainly for the attractions which its society offers; or else they are men whose ambition, from the first, has sought its gratification in learned occupations or in political life, to both of which careers the bar opens avenues to its members which are closed against the laity without.

To such a profession, and to such individuals as we have here described, a school of scientific jurisprudence, dealing, not with the narrower professional learning only, but with philosophy, history, politics, and economics, and this not in the abstract forms in which they are suitable subjects for academical prelection, but in their more immediate applications to the existing conditions of English life, offers advantages so great, so obvious and so readily attainable, that few things, as we have said, are more mysterious than that they should have failed for ages to secure them. Apart from all more material advantages, it is obvious that such a scientific nucleus would vastly enrich and beautify the life even of those who did not directly participate in the labours which it engendered, and increase their value in the eyes of the rest of the community. The gown and the coif would regain the reverence which they owed originally to the general intellectual pre-eminence of their wearers, quite as much as to their special skill. Why then has it not been created?

Many immediate answers might be given; but the ultimate answer lies in peculiarities of our national character so strange as to be inconceivable to foreigners, and so deep-seated and familiar as generally to escape our own observation altogether. To define them, or to trace them to their historical, ethnological, and other sources, is impossible here; but perhaps they may be described as a sort of vague terror for the systematical and reasoned, and a passionate clinging to the immethodical and irrational in our whole social organization. Just as many theologians are afraid to be learned in case they should cease to be pious, so almost all Englishmen are afraid to think or to reason on the laws which govern society, lest they should become convinced of the desirableness of greater freedom, or of the necessity of more perfect order, than is compatible with the constitution of society as it exists, or with what they believe to be British traditions. This propensity, rooted in national temperament and national circumstances, was vastly strengthened by the spectacle which Continental Europe presented towards the close of last century. From causes having very little analogy to any that ever were operative amongst us, France was then led to reconsider the whole subject of her political and social organization, and she reconsidered it rashly and hastily, and arrived at conclusions which all true Englishmen have ever since seen excellent reasons to repudiate. But the inference which all true Englishmen drew from this occurrence was one which, though warranted to some extent for the time being, becomes, as a permanent rule, untenable and almost unstateable—the inference, viz.: that men ought never to reconsider such matters, or to reason about them at all—that all "discussion of first principles" leads necessarily to error, and that, if we must "progress," the only safe course is to progress in the dark, to follow the stream, and to go we know not whither! Now that such a rule of conduct would be very likely to be called in question, were a great central school of jurisprudence and politics founded in the metropolis is obvious, and this consideration, (for we cannot call it a reason,) has all along formed and forms still, we believe, the great objection to it in many honest minds. So long as such studies are confined to the universities they are regarded as tolerably safe, because, from the youth of those by whom they are carried on, they are necessarily fruitless for immediate action; and before the time for action comes they are generally forgotten. But introduce them amongst men who are already mingling in the great world of London, and their influence on public opinion and on legislation would be inevitable, and nobody could tell what might become of it!

But though these views in the main have prevailed, they have not prevailed wholly. Some few eccentric and fanciful individuals have had the hardihood to maintain that human reason might be of service in the conduct of human affairs, and that reason might be fostered by thought and knowledge. Nor has this heresy been altogether barren of results. Persons in high places have been smitten with it, and something has been done, in the double direction of offering assistance to legal students, and enforcing its acceptance. Our present purpose is to enquire very briefly to what this something amounts?

With this view, the first document to which we turn is the "Consolidated Regulations of the several Societies of Lincoln's Inn, the Middle Temple, the Inner Temple, and Gray's Inn," which constitute the four Inns of Court "as to the admission of students, the mode of keeping terms, the calling of Students to the Bar, and the granting certificates to practice under the Bar, and Legal Education."

As to the admission of students, the rules are:

1. "That every person, not otherwise disqualified, who shall have passed a Public Examination at any of the Universities within the British dominions, shall be entitled to be admitted as a student to any Inn of Court, for the purpose of being called to the Bar, or of practising under the Bar, without passing a preliminary examination."

This regulation (which of course exempts graduates in Arts of all the Scotch Universities) is subject to the following restriction. "No Attorney at Law, Solicitor, Writer to the Signet or Writer of the Scotch Court, Proctor, Notary Public, Clerk in Chancery, Parliamentary Agent, or Agent in any court original or appellate, Clerk to any Justice of the Peace, or person acting in any of these capacities, and no Clerk of or to any Barrister, Conveyancer, Special Pleader, Equity Draftsman, Attorney, Writer to the Signet, or Writer of the Scotch Courts, Proctor, Notary Public, Parliamentary Agent, or Agent in any Court original or appellate, Clerk in Chancery, Clerk of the Peace, or of any officer in any Court of Law or Equity, or person acting in the capacity of any such clerk, shall be admitted a Student at any Inn of Court for the purpose of being called to the Bar, or of practising under the Bar, until such person shall have entirely and *bona fide* ceased to act or practice in any of the capacities above named or described; and if on the Rolls of any Court, shall have taken his name off the Rolls thereof."

This prohibition, it will be observed, does not strike at the members of the Scottish Bar, who may keep their terms in England whilst practising their profession in Scotland. But those of them who are not graduates of a British University are, to all appearance, subject to the preliminary examination imposed by the following clause, even though they should have passed the very much more stringent literary test now imposed for the Scotch Bar, or though they should have taken a degree in a foreign University. "Every other person applying to be admitted as a Student to any Inn of Court, for the purpose of being called to the Bar, or of practising under the Bar, shall, before such admission, have satisfactorily passed an examination in the following subjects, viz. :—

(*a.*) The English Language,
(*b.*) The Latin Language, and
(*c.*) English History."

Inasmuch as the preliminary examination for the Scotch Bar, in the case of candidates who are not graduates in Arts, now amounts to something very little short of the pass examination for a degree at Oxford or Cambridge, it is difficult to imagine anything more unreasonable than that a Scottish advocate going to England should be subjected to such an examination as this; and there surely is a still greater absurdity and a still more flagrant violation of the *Comitas Gratium* in imposing it on a German Doctor of Philosophy, or a French Bachelier ès Lettres! But the English are "a peculiar people;" and no amount of ignorance of the doings of their neighbours, on their part, need surprise us. What does surprise us, however, is the manner in which a sort of instinctive tendency to do the right thing in the wrong way, helps them out of difficulties which would have been fatal to a more directly logical race. We doubt whether a German, a Frenchman, or a Scotchman, would have been likely to frame so wise and liberal a provision as the following—

"Provided that the Board of Examiners hereinafter mentioned shall have power to report any special circumstances to the Masters of the Bench of the Inn to which any person may desire to be admitted as a student, for the purpose of being called to the Bar, or of practising under the Bar, and that the Masters of the Bench of such Inn shall have power to relax or dispense with this regulation, in whole or in part, in any case in which they think the special circumstances so reported, or otherwise ascertained by the bench, justify a departure from this regulation."

The provisions which follow have reference to the Board of Examiners.—That it shall be a joint board, appointed by the four Inns, each Inn appointing four members: that these Examiners shall be remunerated as the Council of Legal Education shall appoint, and that two Examiners shall be a quorum, &c. The form of admission is then given, and it is provided that each Student, on applying for it, shall pay the sum of one guinea.

As to *Keeping Terms* the regulations are that—Students of the said societies who are graduates of British Universities shall be enabled to keep terms by dining in the halls of their respective Societies, any *three* days in each term, whereas those who are not graduates must eat twice as much, or in other words, "must dine in the halls of their respective Societies *six* days in each term." Moreover, "that no day's attendance in the respective halls shall be available for the purpose of keeping term, unless the Student attending shall have been present at the grace before dinner, during the whole of dinner, and until the concluding grace shall have been said." In the character of these social arrangements, at once genial and orderly, we recognise what has always been the most precious element in English Academical life. Long may they endure! Even the imposition of the double grace, viewed as an intimation that the citadel of the profession is still in the keeping of Christians and gentlemen, has a value in our own day far beyond that of an antiquarian custom.

The educational provisions as to calling to the bar are, that no student shall be eligible "who shall not have attended during one whole year the lectures and private classes of two of the Readers, or have been a pupil during one whole year, or periods equal to one whole year, in the Chambers of some Barrister, Certified Special Pleader, Conveyancer, or Draftsman in Equity, or two or more of such persons, or have satisfactorily passed a General Examination." The second course here still offered to students, that, viz., of passing a year in chambers, is too familiar to require any explanation. The first and third are comparative innovations, and as they apply to applicants for certificates to practise under the Bar, as Special Pleaders, Conveyancers, and Equity Draftsmen, as well as to those who look to an immediate call, it therefore becomes doubly interesting to inquire what is the nature of the legal training which they really involve.

The whole educational arrangements for the bar are placed under the guidance of a standing council, called "The Council of Legal Education," consisting of eight Benchers, two of whom are nominated by each Inn of Court. To this council is "intrusted the power and duty of superintending the whole subject of the education of the students, and of arranging and settling the details of the several measures which may be deemed necessary to be adopted." The legal year is divided for educational purposes into three terms, of which the first extends from the 1st of November to the 22d of December, the second from the 11th January to the 30th of March, and the third from the 15th of April to the 31st of July. On the important subject of Readers, we shall quote the Regulations in full:—

"That for the purpose of affording to the Students the means of obtaining instruction and guidance in their legal studies, five Readers shall be appointed, viz.:—

1. A Reader on Jurisprudence and Civil and International Law, to be named by the Society of the Middle Temple.

2. "A Reader on the Law of Real Property, to be named by the Society of Gray's Inn.

3. "A Reader on the Common Law, to be named by the Society of the Inner Temple.

4. "A Reader on Equity, to be named by the Society of Lincoln's Inn, and

5. "A Reader on Constitutional Law and Legal History, to be named by the Council of Legal Education."

In the appointment of these Readers, and the distribution of the subjects assigned to them, two distinct objects are plainly visible. The first Reader and fifth are devoted to the higher and more general training of the legislator and diplomatist, the second, third, and fourth to the stricter and more definite training of the Jurisconsult and the Judge. In the recognition of the first of these objects as falling legitimately within the scope of a course of "Legal Education," a very decided step has been made towards widening the borders at once of the science and of the profession, as hitherto understood in England, and bringing the conclusions of systematic study and consecutive thought to bear upon subjects which, notwithstanding their primary and pre-eminent importance, it has been too much the habit of our nation to abandon to the guidance of what seemed to be present expediency, or what was felt to be present impulse. The existence of this tendency is rendered still more apparent from a subsequent provision, to the effect that "a separate course of lectures on International Law shall be delivered, and shall for the present be delivered by the Reader on Jurisprudence and Civil and International Law."

That so many separate subjects should all be handed over to one Reader, as "Jurisprudence," which, if it means anything at all, means, we presume, the philosophy of the science as a whole,* and "the Civil Law," which means, no doubt, the Civil Law of Rome, and International Law, or the *Jus inter gentes*, shows of course how very imperfect these arrangements still are. That the same man should do justice to them all, even in separate courses of lectures, is very unlikely, and would not be expected of him in any University where a proper faculty of law exists. But he will probably do pretty fair justice to one, or even two of them. Jurisprudence and International Law are naturally allied, and are bound together moreover by the old academical tradition, which has united the "Law of Nature and Nations," and rendered the literature of the two subjects well-nigh inseparable. He who is read in the one subject can scarcely be to seek in the other; though we should be sorry to accept the fact of his being conversant with both as a guarantee for his being a Civilian (or vice versa) in anything more than a very general and popular sense. But though such observations cannot but occur to any one at all acquainted with the constitution of the legal faculties in continental Universities, every one must feel that for a long time to come it would be very unwise to be proud or fastidious about such matters in this country. Let us accept with thankfulness what instalments are attainable, and rejoice that the subjects in question are henceforth to form part of the legal instruction offered to Englishmen.

With reference to the more strictly professional branches we find the following very enlightened directions:—"That it shall be part of the duty of the Reader on the Common Law to give instruction in his lectures on the subject of the office and duties of Magistrates," and that "The Readers on Common Law and Equity shall have particular regard to the Law of Evi-

* Such, judging from the prospectus of Lectures for the Michaelmas Term, 1865, is *not* the meaning attached to it by the Reader. In the subjects there announced, no place is assigned to Jurisprudence at all, in the strictly scientific sense; but the field, as we have said, is so vastly beyond what any one labourer can possibly cultivate, that the Reader is amply justified in selecting the portion of it that suits him or his audience best.

dence in their Lectures, and other instructions, to their Students." The duties of all the Readers, in accordance with the arrangements of the English Universities, are in a great measure tutorial. From the provision, that each Reader shall deliver two courses of lectures in each term, it is obvious that these courses must be mere sketches. It is not therefore unreasonable that the additional duty should be devolved on him of forming private classes, "for the purpose of giving instruction in a more detailed and personal form, than can be supplied by general lectures, and affording to students, generally, advice and directions for the conduct of their professional studies." For these Private Classes fees are paid by the students in addition to the fixed sum of £400 a-year, which each Reader receives from the Common Fund. These emoluments, though greatly more respectable than those of the Professors of the corresponding branches in our own University, are altogether inadequate to induce men of ability to devote themselves permanently to the learned side of the profession; and it will probably be found that in this circumstance more than any other the weakness of the new system consists. The most promising men will be continually abandoning the work just when their services are beginning to be most valuable and most valued; and the greatest improvement we can suggest is that the Readerships (we prefer the time-honoured title of Professorships) be made permanent appointments, with endowments of not less than L.1000 or L.1500 a year.

In the month of July of each year, Voluntary Examinations on the subjects of the several courses of lectures are held, and as an additional inducement to students to attend and make themselves proficients in the subjects of the lectures, exhibitions have been founded, and are conferred on the most distinguished students. We fear that some such direct and material inducements to the prosecution of study as the English Bar have offered, are indispensable to the proper working of any such educational system as they have sought to institute; and in the hope that the Bar of Scotland may imitate their example, we shall quote the sections in which they intimate their good intentions:—

1. "That five of such Exhibitions shall be given to members of the Advanced Classes in the Common Law, in the Law of Real Property, and in Equity, and the most proficient among the Students in Jurisprudence, the Civil Law, and International Law, and the Students in Constitutional Law and Legal History, every year,

and be thirty guineas a-year to endure for two years, making ten running at one time.

2. "That three of such Exhibitions shall be given to members of the Elementary Classes in the Common Law, in the Law of Real Property, and in Equity, and be twenty guineas a-year, to endure for two years, making six running at the same time; but to merge on the acquisition of a superior studentship."

So much for the lectures and other means of instruction, and the inducements to attend them. Last of all, come the *General Examinations* previous to being called to the Bar, for which the following are the leading provisions:—

"That General Examinations shall be held twice a-year, for the examination of all such Students as shall be desirous of being examined previous to being called to the Bar, and such examinations shall be conducted by at least two members of the council, jointly with the five Readers."

"That as an inducement to Students to prepare themselves for such examination, Studentships and Exhibitions shall be founded of fifty guineas per annum each, and twenty-five guineas each per annum, respectively, to continue for a period of three years, and one such Studentship shall be conferred on the most distinguished Student at each General Examination, and one such Exhibition shall be conferred on the Student who obtains the second position; and further, the Examiners shall select and certify the names of other three Students who shall have passed the next best Examinations, and the Inns of Court to which such Students as aforesaid belong, may, if desired, dispense with any terms, not exceeding two, that may remain to be kept by such Students, previously to their being called to the Bar. Provided that the Examiners shall not be obliged to confer or grant any Studentship, Exhibition, or Certificate, unless they shall be of opinion that the Examination of the Students has been such as entitles them thereto."*

"That, at every call to the Bar, those Students who have passed a General Examination, and either obtained a Studentship, an Exhibition, or a Certificate of Honour, shall take rank in seniority over other Students who shall be called on the same day."

* These latter Studentships, Exhibitions, and Certificates of Honour have been in operation since 1853, and we learn that the men who have obtained them have generally done well in the Profession, thereby falsifying the predictions which were made before they were established, that professional distinction would be found to turn mainly on qualifications which an examination could not bring out.

These are strong inducements certainly, but still it must not be overlooked, that these are *inducements* merely, and not absolute *requirements*. There is "a screw loose" in this ingenious and enlightened system of training and education, which, if we are not misinformed, does much to render its whole operation inefficacious. The old back-door to the profession, the broad road through "the Chambers of some Barrister, Certified Special Pleader, Conveyancer, or Draftsman in Equity," has not been closed; and more, we believe, would be effected towards the encouragement of scientific training, by striking out the second Clause from the 15th Regulation, and by securing, by adequate remuneration, the assistance of a class of permanent teachers, than by all the Studentships, Exhibitions, and Exemptions that can be offered. There is no reason why work in chambers should not count for something. Let it be accepted in place of attendance on one or more of the practical courses. But so long as it is admitted as equivalent to a knowledge of General Jurisprudence, the Civil Law or the Law of Nations, the Bar of England can never be a learned profession in any strict and proper sense.

THE FRENCH BAR.

(Continued from the July No. of the Journal.)

In the present and in a subsequent article, we shall trace the history of the French Bar from the beginning of the 17th century, or reign of Louis the Thirteenth, to the great revolution of 1789. But before doing so, we shall pause for a little, in order to examine the constitution of the Parliament of Paris, with which the bar was so intimately connected. The Parliament, though forming one great body, was divided into several departments. At its head, was the Great Chamber, composed of the first President, of nine presidents—termed *présidents à mortier*, from the black velvet cap, ornamented with gold lace, which they wore—of twenty-five lay and twelve clerical councillors. The crown officials in the Great Chamber, consisted of the first advocate general, the *procureur général*, two other advocates general, and fifteen substitutes. The chief registrar had the rank of councillor. The presidents *à mortier* were all considered the substitutes of the first president. They took his place in his absence, and each of them might preside over the whole assembled Parliament. The most celebrated advocates practised before the Great Chamber. The first president, when necessary, fixed hearings of seven hours where petty causes were decided. The younger advocates, and those of inferior standing in the profession, devoted themselves to these hearings, until their reputation entitled them to take part in the more solemn and important audiences. The crown counsel held consultations in their department, to judge of affairs remitted to them from the court, and even of disputes arising between the chambers of Parliament. Besides the grand chamber, there were three chambers of inquest, each composed of two presidents and twenty-five councillors, and a chamber of petitions with two presidents and fourteen councillors. There was also *la Tournelle*, in which criminal affairs were settled, so called, either because the magistrates of Parliament sat there by turns, or because the judges who composed it held their sittings in a tower of the Palace termed Tournelle. This Court was held every three months, and was composed of twelve lay councillors of the grand chamber, of two councillors of each of the chambers of inquest, and of three of the chamber of petitions. It thus appears that the members of the Parliament of Paris were not merely temporarily divided into different chambers for the administration of justice. They really occupied different positions; and although they were all councillors with the same prerogatives, the councillors of the grand chamber regarded themselves as the true Parliament. All these judges, however, met together on great occasions. But, in the *lits de justice*, the presidents of the Court of inquests and those of the Court of petitions, alone sat with the grand chamber; the simple councillors of the Court of inquest and of that of petitions, taking rank after the first advocate of the King, the *procureur général*, and the two other King's advocates. The territorial jurisdiction of the Parliament of Paris was very extensive. Originally it extended as far as the royal authority, for the King himself was held to judge in his Parliament. Afterwards, it was considered to extend over whatever was not comprehended within the jurisdiction of the other Parliaments of France. But, in addition to this, it asserted its title to take cognizance of whatever appeared to affect the interests of the realm. Police, religion, finances, taxation, and many other matters, were all held to come within its province; so that there were few affairs of importance in which it could not interfere. The most valuable of its political privileges was its right of remonstrance against the registration of laws, and even of absolute refusal. This right of registration and of remonstrance was one of the most glorious and important privileges of the ancient Parliament, and was always strenuously maintained and defended by the French Bar. It was a check upon despotism, to give to virtuous and independent magistrates the right of pointing out to their sovereign the evils of laws which he wished to promulgate, and of indicating the real wants of the country. The absolute refusal of registration in extreme cases is more open to objection; and the ancient annals of France seem opposed to the right of Parliament to place an absolute veto upon a law. The ordinance of Philip the Fair, of March 1302, which rendered the Parliament stationary, created a Court of justice, *propter expeditionem causarum*, not a political or legislative body; and so with the ordinances of Philip the Long, Philip of Valois, and others which followed them. The claim of the Parliament of Paris to refuse the registration of laws gave rise to the famous *lits de justice*, which proved most injurious to the interests of the monarchy. In the early days of France, the sovereign regarded himself as the supreme judge of his subjects, and when the Parliaments were made stationary, and the King came to preside in them, he occupied a throne termed *lit* or *lit de justice;* and especially when it was necessary to procure the registration of a law in spite of the opposition of Parliament, he came to hold a *lit de justice.* Thus, when it happened that the King compelled the registration of fiscal or other laws bearing severely upon the people, which were opposed by the Parliament on the ground of the public good, the odium of such unpopular measures fell upon the sovereign, and the royal dignity was seriously compromised. After Louis the Fourteenth assumed the government of France, the *lits de justice* became almost useless. The royal supremacy and the servility of Parliament made legislation go smoothly, and by the ordinance of August 1667, the highest Court of the realm was formally deprived of the right of refusing the registration of laws.

At the point at which we have now arrived in the history of the French Bar, it will be advisable to bestow a short time in considering the office of the public prosecutor (*le ministére public*), and the relations subsisting between him, his subordinates and substitutes, and the French Bar.* The origin of the bar and of

* For an account of the present relations subsisting between them, see a paper by the writer of the present article, entitled "*The French Bar and the Public Prosecutor,*" in the Journal of Jurisprudence for May 1861.

le ministére public is the same. M. Gaudry traces the latter back to the officers who were termed *procuratores Cæsaris, patroni fisci,* whose duty it was to guard the interests of the Prince and of the treasury. But its true origin is coeval with the ordinance which established the Parliament of Paris as a fixed and stationary Court. It was then found necessary permanently to attach to it eminent men charged with watching over the good of the kingdom and the interests of the Prince, and these were originally selected from the ranks of the bar. The office of advocate-general and *procureur général* in the Parliament were of the highest importance and dignity. In point of rank, the first advocate-general occupied the foremost place; after him came the *procureur général,* and then the other King's advocates. When it became customary to sell public appointments to defray the cost of foreign wars and supply the luxury of the Court, the office of *procureur général* was often disposed of to the highest bidder, or transmitted, like an inheritance, on payment of a good round sum, and meritorious advocates ceased to be elevated to it as a reward for their services. The office of advocate-general was at first still more closely connected with the bar than that of *procureur général.* Previously to the 14th and 15th centuries, all the advocates of the Parliament of Paris called themselves advocates-general (*generaliter advocati*), meaning by that, advocates of the public. The King chose one among their number to watch over his interests, but those so chosen were still so much regarded as simple advocates, that we find them sometimes assigned by Parliament as defenders to parties along with the ordinary members of the bar. Pierre d'Acy, Jean Desmarets, Jean Pastorel, Jean Lecocq, were thus appointed to act as defenders while holding the office of King's advocate. Even at a much later date, in the time of Francis the first, the advocates of the King were still simple advocates. In 1499, a law was made forbidding the crown counsel to consult or to plead for parties against the crown; but they might still freely exercise their functions as advocates in all cases in which the King was not interested. Even in the last days of the Parliament, the advocate-general took pride in considering and terming himself the general or head of the bar. We shall afterwards see when we come to consider the modern French Bar, how completely the relations of the bar and of the public prosecutor have been changed since the revolution; how entirely they are now separate, and often hostile; the one standing up for the free defence of the accused, and claiming the right of contending against the prosecution with equal arms, the other assuming an air of superiority, striving to infringe and limit the immunities of defence, and attempting to exact from the bar a degree of deference inconsistent with its independence, and altogether unworthy of its long line of glorious traditions.

We now return, after these necessary digressions, to the proper history of the Bar, from the beginning of the 17th century until the revolution. We have seen that the most ancient regulations with regard to the Bar, imposed upon its members the obligation of taking an oath, and of inscription upon a roll, in order to notify the names recommended to the confidence of the public and of the judges. But it is somewhat strange that more than 300 years elapsed, after the date of these regulations, before a formal and regular roll of the Bar was kept. In 1687 there is a roll, containing 366 names, said to have been recorded by the batonnier, or president of the Bar, in August of that year; but the name of the batonnier is given neither in the roll nor in the title, and it was not until 1696 that a regular roll of advocates began to be kept. From a pretty early period in its history, the Bar of Paris was accustomed to arrange itself by benches, in order that its members might meet and confer more easily. These benches were placed in the great hall of the Palais de Justice, or in the adjacent galleries. In 1711, the advocates, formerly divided into eleven benches, were arranged in twelve. The first was composed almost entirely of seniors, and a few seniors were placed at the head of each of the others, after whom came the younger members, according to the date of their admission into the order. This organization, however, was found to be very imperfect; and in 1780, the 5th bench contained 101 advocates, the 7th nine, and the 8th seven, while the 10th had ninety-five, and the 12th ten. In 1781, a reform took place, and the order was divided into ten columns, each containing an almost equal number of advocates, from fifty to sixty. Each column elected two deputies, whose functions lasted for two years, and who might be re-elected. These deputies from the different columns, along with the former presidents of the bar, constituted the council of the order, elected its presidents, watched over its roll, and maintained its discipline. The advocates were further divided into three classes—listeners (avocats écoutants) pleaders (avocats plaidants), and consulting advocates (avocats consultants). According to the ancient practice, the young licentiate from the university was presented to the Court by one of the seniors of the Bar, and the president administered to him the oath to observe the laws, which he took standing upright, in his gown, with uncovered head, and right hand uplifted; in short, the ceremony of the oath seems to have been very similar to that observed at our own Bar. A minute of the taking of the oath was then drawn up and signed by the senior, or, as he was termed in the older times, the god-father of the young jurist. After taking the oath, the advocate might assume the gown, but he had not yet the right of pleading. He entered upon a period of probation, called the stage (le stage), which, by a decree of May 1751, was extended to four years. Upon the lapse of this period, his name was inscribed in the roll of advocates, upon the report of one of the chiefs of his bench or column. The pleaders (avocats plaidants) were highly respected, and had the right not only of appearing in the Courts of Parliament, but also in all the inferior judicatories. The mutual exchange of papers was considered one of the courtesies of the profession; and, before pleading, the advocates were in the habit of making extracts from their briefs, containing the facts of the case, and communicating them to the opposite counsel. Pleading and consultation for the poor was one of the established rules of the ancient bar, and every week nine advocates met in order to hold gratuitous consultations on the causes of the poor. The advocates, as at present, spoke with their heads covered, except when they pled before the King's council. The consulting advocates—advocati consiliarii as they are termed in the old ordinances—held the highest rank at the Bar. They gave their advice to the pleaders, they regulated the affairs of families, and were entrusted with many matters of the highest moment. They had a bench set apart for them in Parliament, and were entitled to a seat on the fleurs de lis. The head or president of the French Bar was, and still is, termed batonnier. This title dates back to the middle of the 14th century; but, for a long time after that period, it was an office of little importance. The name is derived from an ancient usage, according to which the staff (baton) of the banner of St. Nicolas, the patron of the confraternity of advocates, was carried at the head of the order in procession and ceremonies. He who carried it was termed batonnier. So late as 1602, however, the dean (doyen) held the first place at the French Bar, the batonnier only the second. The latter is mentioned for the first time as the head of the order in 1687; and it is only since July 1693 that he has had a legal title to be considered the head of the Bar. Formerly, the senior member of the order by date of inscription on the roll, used to be elected batonnier. But as the great age of the advocate thus chosen, often unfitted him from efficiently discharging the duties of an office requiring watchfulness and tact in no ordinary degree, the order determined to give up this principle of election. The batonnier is chosen for one year only; but since 1830, it has been usual, at the close of his first term of office, to re-elect him for a second year. The batonnier has the privilege of making his business appointments at his own residence, even with those who are his seniors at the Bar. The title of dean (doyen) belongs to the senior member of the Bar inscribed on the roll; but it confers no other privilege than that arising from seniority. The batonnier, along with the former batonniers, and the deputies from the columns, form a council which meets in the advocates' library, and whose chief object is the preservation of the discipline of the order. The batonnier himself adjudicates upon trifling complaints against members of the bar; but, if the matter is of consequence, he reports it to the council. If the suspension of a member, or his erasure from the roll, is to be deliberated on, the batonnier, after examining into the matter, reports to the Crown Counsel, and their decision is registered. In the most important and serious cases, the Court is petitioned to give judgment in terms of the requisitions of the batonnier, and the conclusions of the Crown Counsel. At the expiration of his term of office, the batonnier makes up the roll of advocates, with the assistance of the former batonniers and the deputies, and deposits it in the register before the 9th of May.

During the reign of Louis XIV., the eloquence of the pulpit attained a splendour never surpassed. Bossuet, Massillon, Bourdaloue, and other great preachers composed discourses destined to immortality; and, in the domain of poetry, Racine and Corneille were not less illustrious. The eloquence of the Bar also soared to a higher flight than it had ever previously attained, though it contended on unequal terms with that of the pulpit, as the topics treated of in the latter are of interest to all men in all ages, whereas the greater number of judicial causes, relating only to private persons and special circumstances, possess in comparison but an ephemeral and passing interest. But occasionally judicial eloquence too was distinguished by its grandeur and independence;

for example, in that speech of Omer Talon's, where he said, "The ears of kings are in their knees; they hear only those who prostrate themselves; the greatness of their position, which they know right well, and in which they are brought up, makes them impatient of the slightest contradiction." Boileau mentions Patru, an advocate, among the best prose writers of the period; and Fourcroy, another advocate, was termed the French Hortensius by those in the habit of listening to the eloquence of Bossuet and Bourdaloue. D'Aguesseau has pronounced a splendid eulogium upon the forensic orators of this period, though La Harpe speaks in somewhat contemptuous terms of their performances. The example of D'Aguesseau, in his eloquent but florid discourses upon the character and eloquence of the Bar, pronounced at the close of the seventeenth century, was upon the whole of evil effect. These discourses, splendid as they are, are overcharged with imagery, and introduced a pompous and declamatory style which is disagreeably conspicuous in the forensic oratory of the subsequent century.

The Parliament and the advocates of Paris played a conspicuous part in the troubles of the Fronde which took place during the minority of Louis XIV. and the ministry of Mazarin, the subtle and intriguing, but weak successor of Richelieu. In 1645, several edicts were presented to Parliament, against which the members of that body strongly remonstrated. The reply of the Chancellor Seguier to their statement, that their consciences forbade them to register the edicts, is worth recording. "There are two consciences," said the Chancellor, "one a state conscience, which must be accommodated to the necessity of affairs; the other, a conscience relating to our private actions"—certainly a highly convenient doctrine, and one admitting of great latitude of interpretation. In 1648, a *lit de justice* was held, and the edicts presented for registration were still strenuously opposed; Omer Talon, in opposing them, used the following eloquent and courageous words:—"Sire," he said, "for ten years past the country has been ruined, the peasants reduced to sleep upon straw, seeing their furniture sold to defray the taxes, to maintain the luxury of Paris, which they are unable to pay; millions of persons have been compelled to subsist upon bread made of bran and of oats, and have no other defence but their innocence. These unfortunates have neither goods nor land, nothing but their souls, which they retain only because they cannot be sold by auction." What a terrible picture of the state of France, of the overgrown luxury of the capital, and the misery of the provinces —apoplexy in the head, paralysis in the extremities—do those words of the great Advocate-General present to us! Two of the most prominent members of Parliament—Blancmenil and Broussel —were soon after arrested and imprisoned by the Court for their resistance to the edicts. But the populace flew to arms and demanded their release; and then was made the first essay in barricades, which have since played so important a part in the numerous revolutions of France. On this occasion, the Court was compelled to yield and release the prisoners; but the struggle at the barricades was the commencement of the strife of the Fronde which distracted France for more than five years. The most remarkable circumstance connected with the Bar that occurred during the Fronde was the exile of Omer Talon by Cardinal Mazarin, and his speedy return, forced upon the reluctant minister by the firmness of the advocates. When that upright and able magistrate gave up his functions, the Bar refused to appear and plead, and nothing could shake their resolution. The Cardinal then issued a decree, and procured its registration, empowering the procureurs to plead, even in appeal cases, instead of the advocates. But Pomponne de Bellièvre, the First President, represented to the King that, as the procureurs were but imperfectly acquainted with questions of law, the cases would be but ill conducted. One advocate only, named Rosé, yielding to the influence of Fouquet, then procureur-général, made his appearance to apply for judgments by default. The first president was obliged to pronounce them, but he forbade the registrar to give extracts of them. It seemed as if the long stoppage in the administration of justice in 1602, previously noticed, were about to be renewed. The populace began to murmur, and affairs wore such a threatening aspect that Mazarin was at last compelled to request Omer Talon to resume his functions. Upon this, the advocates immediately returned to their duties; but the unhappy Rosé was regarded as a cowardly deserter, with whom his brethren could hold no communion, so that he was forced to quit the palace, and soon after died of grief.

One of the most splendid instances of civil courage during the Fronde was that given by Mathieu Molé, first president of parliament, who had incurred great odium in certain quarters for the share he had taken in bringing about the peace of Ruel. At the moment when that peace was about to be signed, those opposed to it stirred up a portion of the populace against the Parliament; and while they were deliberating about the ratification of the treaty, the palace was surrounded by an infuriated crowd, who broke in upon the deliberations, and attempted to intimidate the members by the most terrible threats. The president especially was menaced with death. But he preserved the most perfect calm in voice and manner, and refused to attempt to make his escape. "The Court," he exclaimed, "never conceals itself; if I were assured of death, I would not be guilty of that cowardice, which would only add boldness to the seditious; besides, they would easily find me in my house, if they knew that I had feared them here." Then, after having proclaimed the ratification of the treaty, he descended into the midst of the excited crowd, and proceeded through them with a firm step and fearless look, regardless of their cries and menaces. One of them clapped a pistol to his head. Molé looked the ruffian in the face and coolly said to him, "When you have killed me, I shall need only six feet of earth." Cardinal de Retz, in his memoirs, thus speaks of this grand act:—"If it were not a species of blasphemy to affirm that there had been any one in our time braver than the great Gustavus and the Prince of Condé, I would say that it had been Molé, the first president. He preferred the good of the State to everything, even to that of his family, to which he appeared to be much attached."

Even after the majority of Louis XIV., the Parliament opposed the royal authority, removing it from Paris to Pontoise, and, in concert with the Duke of Orleans and the Prince of Condê, protested against the orders of the King, though several times repeated; and in this opposition they were, as usual, warmly supported by the Bar. At a later period, Louis took the unwarrantable and unprecedented step of suppressing the registers of Parliament from 1648 to 1652, in order to destroy all trace of opposition to his supreme authority. He certainly encountered no further check during his long reign, for Parliament passed, in a somewhat undignified manner, from extreme independence to extreme servility, till it became a mere passive instrument of the royal will. In 1693, in conformity with an ordinance of Parliament, the first roll of advocates, containing 240 names, was made up and deposited in the register; and ever since that date it has been regularly continued. For a long time the members of the

Bar pleading before the courts had the title of *Sieur;* but, in 1699, the Court decided that for the future they should be called *Maitre*, the title which they still bear.

We shall now proceed briefly to notice some of the more distinguished advocates belonging to the French Bar during the course of the seventeenth century. Denis Doujat, the first batonnier whose name has been preserved, enjoyed so high a reputation that he was elected batonnier in 1617, when only thirty-nine years of age. Another advocate of the same name, Jean Doujat, was distinguished as a jurisconsult. He was a member of the French Academy, and author of several works, of which the principal are a history of the canon law and a history of the civil law. He died in 1688. Louis Servin, first simple advocate, and subsequently advocate general, was highly distinguished for his eloquence and for his resolute and independent spirit. When Louis XIII. came to hold a *lit de justice* in February, 1620, in order to compel the registration of certain edicts which Parliament had declined to register, Servin addressed him in the following plain-spoken terms:—"Sire, we hold it very strange that your Majesty proceeds to the verification of our edicts by so extraordinary a method as to come to your court of Parliament, contrary to the ancient forms preserved from time immemorial. . . . To-day, seduced by evil councils, you come into your Court, to deprive us of the means of deliberating with freedom of conscience. . . . If the presence of your Majesty compels us to pass beyond all these considerations, it shall be under protestation." Six years afterwards, Louis held another *lit de justice*, to procuré the registration of eight edicts, which had in view the creation and revocation of certain offices, and the establishment of taxes upon a number of articles of consumption. Cardinal Richelieu, the author of the edicts, was present; but Servin—who spoke for the procureur-general—was not on that account the less free in his remonstrances. He had just pronounced the words, "You will acquire a more desirable glory by gaining the hearts of your subjects, than by subduing our enemies," when he was seized with an apoplexy, and fell expiring at the feet of the King, and in the presence of the Parliament, on whose behalf he was protesting against the royal edicts. He died on the field of honour, in March 1626.

A parallel to this noble conduct of Servin, may be found in the spirited resistance of the Judges of the Court of Session, to

James the sixth, about twenty years previously. A well known minister—the Rev. Robert Bruce—had been deprived of his stipend by the King. He sued the Crown before the Court, and obtained a judgment in his favour. The King appealed, came to the Court in person to press his suit, and commanded the Judges to give a decision in his favour. The President, Sir Alexander Seton, then rose and said—"My liege, it is my part to speak first in this Court, of which your highness has made me the head. You are our King; we your subjects, bound and ready to obey you from the heart; and, with all devotion, to serve you with our lives and substance; but this is a matter of law, in which we are sworn to do justice, according to our conscience, and the statutes of the realm. Your Majesty may, indeed, command us to the contrary; in which case I, and every honest man on this bench, will either vote according to conscience, or resign and not vote at all." Another of the Judges—Lord Newbattle—then rose and observed, "That it had been spoken in the city, to his Majesty's great slander, and their's who were his Judges, that they dared not do justice to all classes, but were compelled to vote as the King commanded; a foul imputation to which the lie should that day be given; for they would now deliver a unanimous opinion against the Crown." James in vain threatened and remonstrated. The Judges, with only two dissentient voices, pronounced a decision in favour of Mr Bruce, and the baffled monarch had to leave the Court "muttering revenge and raging marvellously."

In 1618, the greater part of the Palace of Justice was destroyed by a fire; but the King gave a commission to the celebrated architect, Jacques de Brosse, to repair the damage done by the conflagration, and to him is due the construction of the grand hall, 250 feet in length, and 90 in height—now known as the *Salle des pas perdus*—which serves as a promenade for the pleaders, and as a place of resort for all the habitués of the Palace. We have already mentioned Charles Bonaventure Fourcroy, born at Noyon in 1625, and admitted to the Bar in 1645, of which he became one of the most distinguished ornaments. It was said of him, by an excellent judge, "The Bar has perhaps never had, in the same person, and in so high a degree, the science of the jurisconsult, and the talents of the orator." He died in 1691. Pageau and Erard, two of his contemporaries, occupied a position at the Bar only second to that of Fourcroy. Among the great Judges of this epoch, who originally belonged to the Bar of

Paris, we may mention Achille du Harlay, admitted to the Bar in 1656, and raised to the dignity of first president of Parliament in 1689; Francois-Michel Letellier, advocate in 1657, and afterwards Minister and Secretary of State; Michel Chauvillart, who arrived at the same honours; and Chretien de Lamoignon, admitted to the Bar in 1693, and made president in the Parliament of Paris in 1706. Nicolas Boileau—a great name in the field of literature—deserves also to be noticed. He was inscribed on the roll in 1656, but made a very poor appearance as a pleader, and soon afterwards left the Bar.

We have already seen how important a part was taken by the members of the Bar, during the 16th century, in introducing order and method into the confused mass of consuetudinary law existing in various parts of France. Nor were their labours less conspicuous and useful in the 17th century. In 1665, a Council, specially charged with the reformation of the laws, was formed by Louis XIV., upon the suggestion of Colbert. It was composed of several eminent magistrates and councillors of state, and was directed to take the opinion of certain eminent advocates, of whom the King indicated Barthélemy Auzannet, Jean Marie L'Hoste, Louis-Philémon Ragueneau, Jean de Gomont, Antoine Bilain, and Joseph Foucault. This council, and the chosen advocates, held conferences twice a week, and sat for fifteen months. The result was an ordinance, drawn up by Hotman, master of petitions, and Auzannet, which was submitted to Parliament in January 1667; and, after receiving some modifications, passed into a law in April of the same year. It related principally to the form of procedure, and was rapidly followed up by other ordinances, regulating a variety of important matters in civil and criminal law. But the injustice and severity of the latter, as regulated by the infamous ordinance of Villers-Cotteret, was not in any way mitigated; and the proceedings still continued to be secret, and the accused to be denied the right of defence by counsel. The ordinances on the French marine, and on the Colonies, suggested by the genius of Colbert, were in great part prepared and drawn up by advocates; so that, in every part of the revised legislation, their aid was regarded as indispensable. But the revision of the laws was not the only benefit conferred on the science of jurisprudence by Louis XIV. In 1679, he established a school of law in Paris, where, though the civil law had been privately taught, there had previously been no recognised and official institution for imparting legal instruction. Several distinguished jurists flourished during this reign; the greatest of whom was unquestionably Jean Domat, born at Clermont in Auvergne in 1625. In his youth he was long resident in Paris, was closely allied with the Port Royalists, and received the last sigh of Pascal, whose intimate friend he was. The first edition of his great work on the civil law appeared in 1689. It is still an authority, and affords an admirable example of the fundamental principles of Roman law applied to French manners and legislation. Domat died in Paris, in 1696, at the age of 70. It is to an advocate of this century—d'Etienne Gabriac de Riparfonds—that the Bar of Paris owes the foundation of its library, and the institution of the admirable custom of the conferences of doctrine held therein. Riparfonds possessed a noble collection of books, and this he bequeathed by will to the bar,* at the same time expressing his desire, "that his brethren should meet together from time to time in the place where the library should be deposited, in order to discuss points of law." The library was formally opened in May 1708, in presence of d'Aguesseau, procureur général, M. M. Lenain, Joly de Fleury, and Lamoignon, advocates general, and of Nivelle the batonnier. Mass was celebrated by Cardinal de Noailles, and an oration was pronounced upon Riparfonds, who is termed "the most famous consulting counsel of his time." The first conference was held in December 1710, it having been previously agreed that the discussions should take place on questions sent to that benches by the batonnier some days before, in order that every one might come prepared. They were held thereafter every fortnight, and many great advocates and judges honoured them with their presence. Thus, the advocates general Lamoignon, de Chauvelain, and Joly de Fleury, were frequent attenders, and the procureur général d'Aguesseau not only attended, but proposed questions, and took part in the discussions. M. Bellart, one of the most eminent advocates of the present century, thus eloquently describes these conferences, at which, in addition to the discussions on points of law, gratuitous consultations were frequently given to the poor. "It was there, in these fortnightly re-unions, that young aspirants learned how to regulate their forward ardour by the advice of the old chiefs of the bar, who showed how zeal must be tempered by modesty, and the will submitted to the yoke of

* About the same date and with same purpose as foundation of Advocate' Library, Edinburgh.

a salutary discipline; it was there that glory and probity, the brilliant qualities, and the modest virtues, blended in the most touching fraternity, rendered homage to their mutual success, of which every one was proud and no one jealous, because it was the common property of all. It was there that talent itself would not have ventured to seek absolution for having violated the law of duty; and there that we early learned that horror of acting dishonourably which became the rule of the rest of life. These re-unions presented the affecting spectacle of friendly rivals, suspending their debates to lavish upon each other a sincere courtesy, champions illustrious for their many triumphs, conferring on equal terms even with mediocrity, and raising it to their own level. . . . . We there beheld orators entrusted with the most important interests, and jurists devoted to the most abstruse studies, forgetting both their long array of clients and their profound science, to hear with simplicity, and disentangle with patience the diffuse, and often obscure narratives of peasants, women, and all sorts of poor people, who left them enlightened as to their rights, better disposed to come to a peaceful understanding, and not unfrequently with their necessities relieved."

Review.

LOTTERIES, *Past and Present, Legal and Illegal.* By W. B. DUNBAR, Assistant Procurator-Fiscal, Dundee. Revised by Dr BARCLAY, Sheriff-Substitute, Perth. Edinburgh: James Nichol. Pp. 18.

IT will be no recommendation to most of our readers that this pamphlet is a revised reprint of articles printed in the sectarian periodical known as "The Bulwark." We are glad, however, to say that in its present form Mr Dunbar's little work contains only about two pages on the matter of Roman Catholic lotteries, and that he frankly admits the equal illegality, and urges the discontinuance of those "set in operation in connection with bazaars in Scotland, by Protestant clergymen of various denominations;" which, he observes, however, "are of a local character, and have not, rather curiously, incurred the odium attached to the systematic and universal Roman Catholic lotteries." Whatever may have been the origin of the pamphlet, it is very creditably executed, and gives a short and clear statement of the past legislation, and existing law, on the subject of which it treats.

Mr Dunbar points out the extensive and questionable use of lotteries for commercial speculations of different kinds, notwithstanding their illegality; as, *e.g.*, in sweepstakes on horse races, and to attract subscribers to periodicals, purchasers of sewing machines or of the photographs of the National Photographic Association, as well as in other schemes :—

"Besides occasional lotteries got up for special purposes, there is a regular class of men who subsist entirely by the lottery system, travelling from town to town, and disposing of cheap and showy merchandise by means of the "wheel of fortune," in shops which they open for the purpose. Occasionally, the authorities give these erratic and illegal merchants notice to quit, under threat of prosecution; but a prosecution is rarely instituted. If their calling is discouraged in one place they avoid the penalties of the law by simply removing to another place,—and thus they go the round of the three kingdoms. The process of interdict is not sufficiently speedy or effectual to curb the career of these adventurers. In various towns in Scotland, there are regular weekly raffles or lotteries for various kinds of property, got up by needy individuals. Concerts and other entertainments which have not in themselves sufficient elements of attraction, are made to pay by attractive prizes or presents being distributed to the audience by lottery, tickets for which are presented gratis. Our fairs are infested with well-known characters who ply their vocation in various illegal games of chance, among which the "lucky lottery" finds a place. The General Police Act in Scotland empowers magistrates to deal with this class of offenders as having no *lawful* means of gaining their livelihood. Their practices, however, are generally winked at by the police, and it is rarely that a magistrate is called upon to exercise his power. Some persons may think it unfair and invidious to include these vicious games and lotteries in the same category with lotteries for sacred purposes; but they all find their level on the same ground of illegality."

Our author raises the question whether the exception to the general prohibition of lotteries in favour of Art Unions should be continued ; but, although the Art Union principle may have been abused, public opinion will not now admit of the withdrawal of the exceptional privilege. It may be desirable, however, that some more stringent measures should be taken to prevent abuses. Mr Dunbar's view of the remedy is that :—

"No further legislative measure is necessary to arm the executive, so far, at least, as the wide-spread schemes advertised in our newspapers are concerned. The remedy for these exists in the present state of the law, which only requires to be enforced. The procedure, however, might certainly be simplified, and at same time rendered more speedy and effectual, if *prosecutions were authorised by local officers in any place where the law is violated*, instead of confining such prosecutions to the courts of the metropolis. It may safely be affirmed that if *private* prosecutions were still lawful, the present extensive lottery system would not have existed. Private prosecutions, however, are not now unfortunately authorised; the law officers of the crown only can enforce the law, and upon them the duty devolves, and the responsibility rests, of its proper administration. The provisions of the Acts of Parliament of 1836 and 1845, before noticed, affixing a penalty of £50 to the printing and publishing any advertisement or notice of any lottery not authorised by law, are of the simplest possible character for putting an end to the graver class of illegal lotteries, by preventing all publicity as to their existence; and in the enforcement of these provisions no difficulty can be experienced. The like penalty might properly be extended by the legislature to *all persons who dispose of tickets* for such illegal lotteries.

"In regard to local lotteries in the shape of subscription sales, raffles, or otherwise, these can, as we have seen, be effectually prevented by the process of interdict at the instance of the fiscals, unless where the offenders are of the erratic class. To deal efficiently with these persons, a legal measure of a more speedy and potent character is necessary, and it is worthy the consideration of our legal officials whether such a measure should not be applied for from the Legislature. Unless some such measure is obtained, they may safely carry on their illegal practices with impunity. As for our small offenders at fairs and markets, we commend them to the care of the police, who have sufficient powers under the Police Acts to prevent them carrying on a profitable trade."

We are inclined at present to object to the introduction of the system of private prosecutions, which would merely put a new means of persecution in the hands of the Scottish Reformation Society, whose advertisements adorn the cover of Mr Dunbar's book. But, on the whole, the pamphlet will do good service in calling attention to a subject which, we fear, is somewhat neglected by our public authorities.

THE MONTH.

Legal Education.—At a meeting of the Faculty of Advocates, held on the 18th inst., a resolution was, by a considerable majority, passed to the effect, that the whole law curriculum of the University of Edinburgh should hereafter be made incumbent on candidates for admission to the Bar. A motion, which was at the same time before the Faculty, with the view of dispensing with compulsory attendance altogether, and leaving qualification to be tested by examination only, was, without much difficulty, rejected. A remit was made by the Faculty to a Committee to carry the principle of the resolution into effect, which, we understand, have since been deliberating on the subject. The curriculum of the University of Edinburgh was taken as a standard, because it is the most complete in Scotland, but there is no intention of creating a monopoly in its favour. The other Universities, so far as the subjects of examination are national, are to be admitted to the same privilege; and, as to the others, the certificate of any foreign University will be received, if it be approved by the Dean and his Council. The object of this qualification is to meet the cases, such as Oxford and Cambridge, where the courses of lectures, on many subjects, are merely nominal, and which obviously could not be permitted to rank on the same footing with the other Universities, where the teaching extends over a protracted session.

The Game Laws.—A good deal of attention has been attracted during the month, and some very unnecessary controversy raised by the bill which is now in Parliament on the subject of the Game Laws. One would have expected that the ground of complaint would have been that the bill did not go far enough, yet in some quarters it has been received with as grave an apprehension as if it was going to create a revolution. The truth is, that the bill does next to nothing, at least in the way of direct enactment. For its leading, and it may almost be said its sole provision, is, that in the absence of express reservation by the landlord of the right to hares and rabbits, a tenant shall be entitled to kill or destroy them. Now it is quite obvious that this leaves the tenant very much where he is at present, that is, at the mercy of his landlord. Farms must be let, and any price will be paid for them, and accordingly the landlord is in a position to dictate his own terms. But although the bill does little or nothing in the way of direct enactment to introduce changes upon the existing law, it will prove beneficial by drawing public attention to the subject in the most powerful and legitimate form in which this could be done, and thereby putting landlords in a condition favourable for them to realise the growing feeling of the country, that the Game laws, as they at present exist, are often worked in an unjustifiable and oppressive manner, and that they cannot long continue to be administered on their present footing. More than this, looking to the angry spirit which has been imported into the controversy, and the attitude of contending interests, it would not, perhaps, be prudent to attempt at present. That any settlement of the question on such a narrow basis as forms the limits of this bill, can ever prove a satisfactory and a permanent one is, of course, not a thing to be dreamt of. But a great deal will be done towards the final adjustment and reconciliation of the various interests involved by first ascertaining how far parties are likely to go in the way of concession and demand.

Husband and Wife.—An exceedingly important case, falling under this head of the law, has been decided during the month by the Second Division. The Court adhering unanimously to a judgment of the Sheriff of Aberdeen, have found that a son-in-law is bound to aliment the indigent parents of his wife, even though he is not in any way *lucratus* by the marriage, and in the particular case held the defender liable to re-imburse a parochial board in advances made for that purpose. The *ratio* of the decision is that, as the wife would be liable before marriage in the obligation *ex jure naturæ*, it devolves upon the husband after marriage, because marriage transfers to him all the wife's debts and obligations, whether these are at the date prestable or not. The subject is of such importance that we shall take an opportunity of recurring to it.

International Law.—In the case of Clements *v.* Macaulay, Lord Barcaple has pronounced an important judgment, refusing to give effect to an action of accounting, brought by one citizen of the State of Texas against another, in respect of a joint adventure which, along with others, they entered into during the late civil war in America, its object being to supply munitions of war to the Confederate Government. The ground of judgment is, that the action involves a recognition by the Court of the independence of the Confederate Government, which is an incompetent step, seeing there has been no recognition by the Government of the country. The action having been dismissed, the pursuer has reclaimed, and an interesting discussion may be expected to follow.

Western Bank Cases.—In these cases the Court, with the view of simplifying the questions at issue before putting to the jury the question of the defenders' negligence, have remitted to an accountant to report on the books of the bank. A motion by the pursuers for leave to appeal to the House of Lords was refused.

Bills in Parliament.—The Writs Registration Bill has been withdrawn, Mr Walpole, the new Home Secretary, undertaking to introduce a similar bill next session. The Parochial Buildings (Scotland) Act Amendment Bill, which extends the powers granted by 25 & 26 Vict. c. 58, so as to include within the powers to borrow and grant bonds conferred by that bill the price of buildings already erected which may be purchased for parochial purposes, including the purchase of feu-duties, has passed.

The Salmon Fisheries (Scotland) Bill, and the Summary Procedure Bill, have also been withdrawn.

Just as we go to press, we learn that the Law of Evidence in Civil Causes Act, introduced at the suggestion of the Faculty of Advocates in order to dispense with the present system of taking proofs by commission, substituting the system which has worked so well in consistorial causes, has narrowly escaped a similar fate. At the last moment, after the Bill had passed through the House of Commons, and had been read twice in the House of Lords, a section of the Society of Writers to the Signet made strong representations to the Lord Advocate, in regard to certain parts of the Bill, which they considered objectionable or defective. They objected especially to the provision, at the end of the first clause of the Bill, that the proof shall be taken continuously in like manner as in jury trials in civil causes, with power to the Lord Ordinary to adjourn on such grounds as justify adjournment in the case of causes set down for jury trial. It was also urged that the Lord Ordinaries' blank days should be abolished, in order that more of their time might be available for the taking of proofs, and that it should be made lawful, when a proof is begun at the end of a session, for a Lord Ordinary to sit during vacation for the purpose of concluding it.

We believe that a deputation met with the Lord Advocate and fully discussed these and other matters. The objectors finally agreed to waive the last two points, which it was represented could not fairly be introduced into the bill at this late stage. The Lord Advocate agreed to recommend that the first clause of the bill should be modified so as not to require the diets of proof to be peremptory. We sincerely trust that nothing may occur to prevent the passing of a bill which is so necessary, not only to the efficient conduct of business in the Court, but also to prevent the scandal of having a large staff of able and diligent judges spending the next winter session in comparative idleness.

Legal Appointments.—In consequence of the advent to office of the Conservative Government, the following new appointments have been made:—Mr. Patton has become Lord Advocate, and Mr. E. S. Gordon, Solicitor-General. The Advocates-Depute are

Mr. Broun, Mr. Millar, Mr. Adam, and Mr. Blackburn; and Mr. Roger Montgomerie is the Advocate-Depute in the Sheriff Courts. Besides these, the following appointments have been made:—Mr. John Marshall, Jun., Counsel to the Treasury; Mr. Scott, Counsel to the Offices of State; Mr. Gloag, Counsel to the Admiralty; Mr. Skelton, Counsel to the Accountant in Bankruptcy; and Mr. D. B. Hope, Counsel to the Board of Ordnance; Mr. T. G. Murray, W.S., is Crown Agent; and Mr James Hope, D.K.S., Solicitor to the Treasury.

Calls to the Bar.—The following calls to the Bar have been made during the month:—Adam Gibb Ellis, Esq.; John Maitland, Esq., B.A., Oxon.: Peter Alexander Speirs, Esq., B.A., Cant.; Alexander Gibson, Esq., M.A., Edin.; John Alexander Reid, Esq., M.A., Glas.; and James Lutyens Mansfield, Esq., B.A., LL.B., Cant. Mr J. Badenach Nicolson has been appointed Secretary to the Lord Advocate.

The sheriffship of Perth, vacated by Mr Gordon, has been conferred on Mr Tait, who is succeeded as Sheriff of Linlithgow and Clackmannan by Mr George Monro.

The last mentioned appointment cannot be allowed to pass entirely without comment, as it is one which lawyers of every shade of political opinion will hail as a tardy recognition by his party of Mr Monro's able and honourable discharge of his duties as an advocate, and of the position which he has long held at the Bar.

Extended Sittings.—An Act of Sederunt has been passed extending the next winter session of the Court of Session. The sittings of both Divisions of the Court will begin on Thursday November 1st, instead of Tuesday November 13th.

General Council of Procurators.—The Judges of the Court of Session having approved the regulations and bye-laws as to the admission of persons applying to be admitted as Procurators to practise before any Sheriff Court in Scotland, a meeting of the General Council took place in Edinburgh on July 13th. The first diet of examination of intrants was appointed to be held at Glasgow on Thursday, Sept. 13th, at eleven A.M. The following office-bearers were appointed:—President, Mr J. F. Murdoch, P. F., Ayr; Vice-President, Mr J. B. Baxter, P. F., Dundee; Secretary and Treasurer, Mr J. W. Barty, P. F., Dunblane; Special Councillors, Mr James Mitchell, D.F., Glasgow; Mr A. M. Caird, P.F., Stranraer; Mr James Watson, P. F., Linlithgow; Mr Robert Watt, Solicitor, Airdrie; Mr T. Falconer, Solicitor. The public prosecutors are well represented in this list.

VACATION ARRANGEMENTS.

Box Days.

Thursday, 30th August; Thursday, 11th October.

BILL-CHAMBER ROTATION OF JUDGES.

Autumn Vacation, 1866.

Saturday, 21st July, to Saturday, 4th August 1866,	Lord Ormidale.
Monday, 6th August, to Saturday, 18th August,	—— Barcaple.
Monday, 20th August, to Saturday, 1st September,	—— Mure.
Monday, 3d September, to Saturday, 15th September,	—— Curriehill.
Monday, 17th September, to Saturday, 29th September,	—— Benholme.
Monday, 1st October, to Saturday, 13th October,	—— Kinloch.
Monday, 15th October, to Saturday, 27th October,	—— Ormidale.
Monday, 29th October, to Saturday, 10th November,	—— Barcaple.

AUTUMN CIRCUITS, 1866.

WEST.

Lords Justice-Clerk and Deas.

Stirling—Wednesday, 12th September,
Inverary—Thursday, 20th September.
Glasgow—Monday, 24th September, at twelve o'clock noon.
James Adam, Esq., Advocate-Depute.
Robert L. Stuart, Clerk.

NORTH.

Lords Cowan and Jerviswoode.

Dundee—Tuesday, 11th September.
Perth—Monday, 17th September, at twelve o'clock noon.
Aberdeen—Friday, 21st September.
Inverness—Wednesday, 26th September.
John Millar, Esq., Advocate-Depute.
William Hamilton Bell, Clerk.

SOUTH.

Lords Ardmillan and Neaves.

Ayr—Tuesday, 11th September,
Dumfries—Friday, 14th September.
Jedburgh—Wednesday, 19th September.
R. B. Blackburn, Esq., Advocate-Depute.
Æneas Macbean, Clerk.

THE

JOURNAL OF JURISPRUDENCE.

SCOTTISH RECORDS.*

It is no part of the functions of this journal to rejoice in any change of Government; but as a change has taken place, we may express a hope that a more liberal, or rather a more just, spirit may prevail at the Treasury, in regard to Scotch matters, than has been displayed by the late ministry. It would be easy to produce a long catalogue of Scottish grievances against this department of the Government, but it would be difficult to select one more unanswerable than the case of the Lord Clerk Register.

He superintends an important national department which yields to the exchequer a clear revenue of many thousands a-year. At the instigation of men of the greatest influence, position, and learning, he proposed that a certain portion of the documents under his care should be made accessible to the public, and that £2000 a-year out of the surplus revenues of the department should be devoted to that purpose. This seems at first sight a very moderate and a very proper proposal; but to Mr. Gladstone, through Mr Frederick Peel, it appeared a very clever thing to agree to the expenditure of only half the requisite sum, and limit the allowance to five years.

Had the proposal been a novel and purely Scotch idea, we could have understood such an economist as Mr. Gladstone being determined to crush it, quite irrespective of its merits. But the scheme is in part a continuation and completion of one long ago

* Copies of correspondence between the Right Hon. the Lord Clerk Register of Scotland and the Treasury, respecting the publication of a Series of Scottish Records. Ordered by the House of Commons to be printed 1866.

sanctioned—of the publication of the records of our Parliament, and in part the adoption of a scheme now for many years in operation in England, under the able superintendence of the Master of Rolls. Had the publication of the English records been conducted with the funds of some special department, and the demand made by the Lord Clerk Register been for money from the public purse, we could have understood, though we could not have approved of, the spirit which dictated the conduct of the Treasury; but in point of fact the case is precisely the reverse of that which we have put. The English publications are issued at the expense of the public purse; all that is asked for Scotland is leave to expend part of the surplus revenues of the department to which important State documents belong, in making these documents accessible to the public.

The contemptible proposal of the Treasury was answered by Sir W. Craig with a force and a spirit worthy of the high office he holds—

"Considering the number of calendars, chronicles, and memorials in the Register House which ought to be published, and that the Scottish series of these historical records will be of the highest interest and importance, this would be actually trifling with what ought to be a national work. Besides, if these records are worth publishing at all, they cannot be published too soon, that the present generation of literary men may have the advantage of them; and it is a most unwise and false economy to restrict the grant, so that no one living can hope to see anything but a fragment of the series. This would give such intense dissatisfaction in Scotland, and would be so discreditable to the Government and the Register House, that if the grant is not to be increased it had better be withdrawn. I must again also remind you that I am only requesting that a portion of the surplus revenue of the Register House should be applied to the publication of the historical records it contains. Although the estimate for the Record Office is £22,000, while the fees received are only £700, the Master of the Rolls has for years had grants for calendars, &c., of £5450 (which in the estimates just printed are increased to £6260, with which he has published thirty-three volumes of calendars and sixty volumes of chronicles and memorials, among which there is only one Scottish work, of no value. While, therefore, there has not only been already such an extensive publication of the English records, but the Master of the Rolls is still receiving so large a grant for continuing it, it is certainly not unreasonable that the Register House should have returned to it a grant of only £2000 out of its own surplus revenue of upwards of £5000 for the publication of the records of Scotland for which nothing has as yet been done."

The following account of the publications, for effecting which arrangements are in progress, is selected from various papers submitted to the Treasury:—

"When the fifth and sixth volumes of the Scottish Statutes were published, the Registers of the Parliaments from 1639 to 1650 were not known to be preserved, and their ordinances and proceedings could only be given from the scanty and unauthenticated sources which are described in the editor's prefaces. The original registers—authenticated by the signature of Sir Alexander Gibson of Durie, the Lord Clerk Register for the time—have since been discovered in her Majesty's State Paper Office in London, whither they had been carried about the year 1654, and are now in her Majesty's General Register House at Edinburgh. Their importance was so manifest that Mr. Thomson lost no time in having them transcribed, in order that they might be printed, and substituted for the two volumes which had been issued before their discovery.

"This intention has not yet been carried out, but its fulfilment is obviously necessary to complete the series of the Acts of the Parliaments of Scotland. Not only do the original registers contain much important matter which is not to be found in the printed volumes, but these volumes, compiled as they necessarily were from very imperfect materials, are certainly not an authentic record of the statutes of the time. When it is remembered that the registers which have been recovered contain the Parliamentary record of the great struggle between the Crown and the Legislature in the reign of King Charles the First, nothing need be said of their interest or importance to the constitutional history of the country. But it may be added, that they contain many private or personal Acts which materially affect still existing interests. One of these (appearing only by its title in the printed volumes, but recorded at length in the original manuscript register) served lately to terminate a litigation between two counties."

In regard to the formation of a General Index of the Scottish Acts of Parliament—a work which is now proceeding under the direction of Professor Innes—that antiquary says, in a memorandum addressed to the Lord Clerk Register:—

"The lawyer has long felt and complained of the want of such an index, and the historical student would have made louder complaints if he were not in a manner kept in ignorance of the contents of these volumes by its want.

"Of the 11 volumes, as they stand at present, only one has an index of matters. The other 10 large volumes, recording the proceedings of the Scotch Parliaments from the return of James the First from England in 1424, to the Union of the Kingdoms in 1707, thus containing the legislation of three centuries, and the chief and best materials of the national history, have no such help for consultation. They are of course in chronological order; but the student searching for a law of unknown date, or tracing the progress of legislation on any subject, or investigating facts, manners, opinions, must wade through whole volumes, with no better assistance than the short imperfect titles of the several Acts. Even these are wanting for large classes of Parliamentary Proceedings, as distinguished from actual statutes; and I need not explain how greatly a complete *Index Materiarum* would facilitate the labours of the lawyer, give more accuracy and precision to the researches of the historian and legal antiquary, and lay open to the student a vast collection which is at present almost unused from the want of it.

"Such an index, though so long delayed, formed an essential part of Mr Thomas Thomson's plan, as he himself states in his report to the Lord Clerk Register for 1814, that the work should be concluded by 'a complete and digested index.' But no such index can be complete or satisfactory without including the Acts of Parliament 1639-50, the authentic record of which was not discovered till after the date of that report, and has not yet been printed.

"Independent of the wish to see perfected the published record of the legislation of Scotland during the whole of its separate existence, I know no period of more historical importance than the precise portion embraced by these lately recovered volumes, so long lost to the world. They furnish the record of Parliament during a time of great conflict of opinion, when all principles of Government and Church were called in question; and at no time is it of more consequence to have the proceedings of the Legislature given in the most authentic and authoritative shape."

Mr Skene has undertaken to edit a work entitled "Chronicles of the Picts, Chronicles of the Scots, and other Early Memorials of Scottish History," of which he says—

"It will contain all the chronicles, annals, and other memorials of Scottish history antecedent to our first formal historians, and comprising, to a great extent, the materials from which these historians compiled their works. It is essential to the historian that he should have the remains of our earliest historic literature presented to him in the oldest and purest form in which they now exist, unaffected by the influence of writers who used them in support of their own historical theories. They consist, to a great extent, of documents which are still in manuscript, and have never been printed; and, to some extent, of documents printed in the appendices to various historical treatises, and thus existing only in a very scattered shape, while they are in general very inaccurately printed, and, where there are several manuscripts, not always from the best manuscript."

In January last Mr Joseph Robertson wrote to the Lord Clerk Register, offering to edit

"The accounts of the Lord High Treasurer of Scotland during the reign of King James the Fourth (A.D. 1488—A.D. 1513), as part of the Scottish series of chronicles and memorials in preparation under your Lordship's direction.

"These accounts (he says) are among the public records of Scotland in the Register House. They have been so carefully preserved, that only the transactions of a few years have perished; and this loss I propose so far to supply from the accounts of other great officers of the Crown, also preserved in the Register House, for which likewise, where necessary, I would draw other elucidations of the accounts of the Lord High Treasurer."

Prcfessor Innes also edits "A Volume of the Antiquities of Scotch Trade." He writes:—

"I propose that the text of the book should consist of two parts.

"(1.) The book of accounts of Andrew Hallyburton, Conservator of the Privileges of the Scotch Nation in the Netherlands, and himself a merchant carrying on trade there, chiefly with correspondents in Scotland, at the end of the 15th century. This ledger, which is preserved in the Register House, fills a large folio volume, in the original binding, and in excellent condition. The dates of the entries extend from 1493 to 1503, and it is by far the oldest of merchants' books extant in Scotland. It shows what were the manufactures, the articles of export and import, the money used, the banking, the exchange, of Scotch trade with the Continent, three and a half centuries ago.

"(2.) A tariff of the customs authorised to be levied on articles exported and imported into Scotland in the year 1612. This, which is also preserved in the Register House, is an authentic warrant, bearing the subscriptions of the King (James VI.) and the Lords Auditors of his Exchequer. It is the earliest perfect code of custom regulations of Scotland extant; and as it is very full and minute, it enumerates all the commodities of our trade, and throws much light on life and manners two and a half centuries ago."

Of the importance of these publications, it would seem unnecessary to have laid before the Treasury any testimonials beyond the mere explanation of their character, but the result shows that even the weightiest have been insufficient to convince such economists as Mr. Gladstone and Mr. Peel of the importance of an effort towards making our national records available, and the starving process is continued.

The correspondence between the Lord Clerk Register and the Treasury has been laid before Parliament, and we cannot help thinking that if the new Treasury officials maintain the attitude of their predecessors, it will be the bounden duty of the Scotch members, as a body, to see to the immediate reduction of the fees for the registration of deeds. The purpose of the exaction of these fees is not the increase of the revenue, but the remuneration of the officials. There may be some apology for keeping up the fees beyond the point necessary for this primary purpose, provided the surplus be expended in making the contents of the Register-House more available for the public; but if this legitimate object be denied, then the country should make one united and common effort to secure the utmost possible reduction of the fees.

We cannot better take leave of the subject than by the following extract from the last letter by the Lord Clerk Register to the Treasury, with which the correspondence closes:—

"You will perceive that after providing for the formation of the Index to the Acts of the Parliaments of Scotland (the most important work we have to perform), I can only defray the expense of editing three chronicles or memorials in two years, while I cannot undertake the preparation of a single volume of Calendars of State Papers, the allowance for which by the Record Office is about £500 per volume.

"I enclose a memorandum, which shows the vast store of manuscript documents the Register House contains, which are almost unknown, and many of which, if calendared, would be of the greatest value for the elucidation of the history of Scotland. I should certainly only propose to publish the most important of them, and I can assure you that the selection would be made with the greatest care, and on the best advice; but I beg you to keep in view that the labour of compiling a calendar from old manuscripts is so great that it frequently takes some years to prepare a volume. There ought, therefore, to be several in progress at the same time (as there are in the Record Office), but if the grant were increased to £2000, I could easily arrange that the payments to be made in any year for calendars, or chronicles and memorials, should always be within the limit of the grant.

"The best evidence of the general satisfaction which the prospect of the publication of a series of Scottish records has given, and of the interest taken in it, is the fact that many of the most distinguished literary men in Scotland are willing to give their assistance as editors. Besides the volumes which the Treasury has sanctioned, and which are being prepared by Mr. Skene, Professor Cosmo Innes, and Dr. Joseph Robertson, I have great pleasure in informing you that the Duke of Argyll, Lord Lindsay, Mr. Stirling, of Keir, M.P., Mr. David Laing, Professor Sir James Simpson, Mr. Hill Burton, &c., have agreed to edit, with historical prefaces, works of the series which have been proposed to them, but which can only be undertaken as the grant at my disposal will permit. If it is not increased, and the publication of these historical records is consequently delayed, the disappointment will be extreme, while the contributions of many of these editors, all of them men of very remarkable acquirements, will probably not be obtained.

"In fact, the whole question is, whether the present or future generations are to have the benefit of these publications."

"SPARKS FROM THE JURIDICAL ANVIL."

It is a great mistake to suppose that the reports of our Law Courts are of interest only to the legal profession, and are repulsive to the general public. There are few decided cases but what throw some light on a nation's history and traditions, and form an epitome of the men and manner of the time. There are especial seasons when the bench is adorned by men of high renown in the paths of philosophy and literature—men who illustrate and illuminate the arid region of abstract legal doctrines by the features of the *Belles lettres.* Some such periods form a sort of Augustine age in our Law Courts, and for a time our law reports may justly be classed with the polite literature of the day.

With this fact in our view we have curiously devoted a spare hour to one volume of our reports, from which we select a few of the brilliants which adorn its pages, and may at some future season add to the number by taking up some other volume, which doubtless will yield as abundant and choice a crop, which may thus be saved from oblivion.

No. 1.—In a case in the House of Lords (5th August 1834), a parish minister appealed from an adverse decision of the Court of Session in a dispute with his heritors about cutting down some trees. Lord Brougham, then Chancellor, observed—"There must be an end to such appeals as these, otherwise the appellate jurisdiction of this House will be a curse instead of anything else. There is nothing like a point of law here, and the expense of this appeal cannot be less than £100."

Mr. Sergeant Spankie—"I am happy to say the party is very rich."

Lord Chancellor—"That is a good thing. It is only right your Lordships should make him pay; but the blame is not always imputable to the party himself but the adviser, and I only wish your Lordships could get at him and make him pay."

No. 2.—In a jury case (24th July 1834) where a deed of settlement was reduced framed by an agent in his own favour, on the ground of incapacity in the testator. The Lord President (Hope), charging the jury, remarked—"You are told that there is nothing in the poor old man mistaking one shop door for another; but then he actually walks in and remains in an apothecary's shop, smelling with all kinds of drugs, and mistakes it for a clothier's! He might have mistaken the door, but he could not have mistaken the gallipots." "I say that no man who had respect for his own character—no man who thought for a moment or was sensible of what was for his own interest, would have acted as this agent did. But there is an oft repeated proverb—*Quem Deus vult perdere prius dementat*—that is to say—whom God wishes to destroy he first distracts—the agent was not aware of all the consequences that would follow from that conduct, or he would have avoided it, but he so mixed and mingled himself with the deed that it speaks fraud on the face of it, and I agree with that English judge, that when the deed is taken by the agent in his own favour, it raises a strong presumption against the deed."

No. 3.—In a jury trial (Nov. 1834), a deed of settlement was sustained, which was challenged on the ground that it was executed under the influence of Monomania.

Lord President (Hope) in his charge to the jury, observed, "The most extraordinary of all delusions—the most wonderful and unaccountable to man in his sound mind—is that which has been stated by the learned counsel who last addressed you, and yet it is a very common one; it is that which occurs in many people, mistaking their own identity, and believing themselves to be different sorts of beings, or different persons from what they really are! One naturally says, is it possible that the human mind can mistake itself, or that a man can believe himself not to be what he actually is? Yet it is so, and one cannot but marvel much even at that which is a common sort of delusion. We find it generally the case, that those labouring under such a delusion are found to be supposing themselves greater than they really are, or greater than they really, by human possibility, could be raised to. You invariably find that such persons are always imagining themselves to be Princes, Kings, or Emperors. Nay, often they imagine themselves God Almighty himself, or our blessed Saviour. I have known several instances of that nature. I remember the case which is mentioned in that judgment and opinion of Sir John Nicholl, in the decision of the cause Drew *v.* Clark; but I find he had not had before him the right edition of it. I heard it from Mr Erskine, who was himself one of the counsel in the cause. He told me the true story was this,—that a man was brought before a jury to be cognosced, as it is called, and he answered before the jury the various questions put to him, so sensibly, and in such a composed manner, that the jury when they heard him, stared and wondered how any party could bring such a case as his before them. Mr Erskine, however, it appears, had got his cue upon the subject of the particular species of delusion, and the proper mode of touching upon it, so as to discover it; and after the other counsel had addressed the jury, he rose, and, previous to addressing them, asked leave of the individual himself, sought to be cognosced, to put a few additional questions to him. To this the party had no objection; but says he (the counsel) before doing so, 'I ought to fall down on my knees, and humbly ask your gracious forgiveness for daring thus to put questions to such a high, mighty, and supreme character as you avowedly are.' 'Stop (says the other), rise up, and fear not, thy sins are forgiven thee;' thereby showing at once the truth of what was suspected, viz., the fact of his actually imagining himself to be our Lord and Saviour. I had an extraordinary instance of a similar nature occurring a considerable time ago to myself, at my own Chambers in Hill Street, where a gentleman was announced as wishing to speak to me; he was a young man, and, as I supposed, was calling upon business. I accordingly saw him, and found him to be one of the genteelest looking persons I ever saw in my life. I asked him to sit down immediately, when he began to speak. I supposed he had some letter or petition to present to me; but finding that was not the case, I rose and said, 'I am just preparing to go to the Court, and may I beg to know what your demands are?" Upon this he stared with astonishment, and said, 'What! don't you know me?' 'No; I don't at present recollect you, sir,' after looking firmly and stedfastly at him. 'That is very odd," says the gentleman. Then I observed, 'It may be odd to you, but as I have no recollection whatever of ever having seen you, it would be more odd if I did know you. Let me know who you are, and then I can ascertain how it is that I should not recollect you. Let me know who you are in the first place?' 'I am Jesus Christ,' says he. 'Then,' says I, 'I really was not aware of that, but as I have not time to receive communications, I beg leave to postpone the interview, as I have to go to the court immediately, and therefore you must allow me to withdraw at present.' He accordingly walked out of the room, and I soon afterwards found he was a person who had actually made his escape from his keepers, who were in pursuit of him. In fact, he was an insane or deluded person, who had escaped out of the custody of keepers who were waiting outside for his return. Besides these instances, we hear of many other delusions of a very extraordinary nature. There is one case upon record for instance, of a very honest gentleman who believed himself to be a tea-pot. How he managed that in his own mind, I really don't know; but, upon various occasions in the day time, he stood up with one hand turned round in this way to represent the handle, and with the other, in an attitude to represent the stroup of the tea-pot. There also have been instances of other descriptions of delusive ideas; such as persons imagining that some parts of their bodies were made of glass, or that their whole frame is made of china. In short, the delusions of the human imagination are quite unaccountable, and there is no end of them."

No. 4.—In an advocation from the Dean of Guild Court of Glasgow, it was held (15th Nov. 1834), that that court had no jurisdiction in cases of obstructions on a street. Lord President

(Hope) "If the Dean of Guild had jurisdiction in this he would have jurisdiction to prevent my carriage standing on the street—*Lord Gillies.*—Or to prevent half-a-dozen carts driving abreast with the carters all riding, *while the Police are walking about as if they had nothing to do with the matter.*"

No. 5.—Bill of Suspension was passed of a decree of removing at the instance of an heritable creditor against a proprietor (15th Nov. 1834), *Lord Balgray,* "I never heard of anything like this—an heritable creditor to bring an action of removing in this way. I never saw anything so out of shape and so extraordinary. *I will venture to say there are few proprietors in Scotland who might not be turned out of possession of their estates in ten days if this doctrine were sanctioned.*"

No. 6.—In a case (19th Dec. 1834) of a reduction of the lease as granted between conjunct and confident persons being brothers. Lord Jeffrey remarked, "The causes of favour are infinite, and many of them stronger than brotherly affection—an old school-fellow—a political partizan—a boon companion—a skilful flatterer—are in fact more generally favourites than brothers—and no law can consistently interdict the latter from advantages which may be legally conferred on the former."

No. 7.—In a case of filiation and aliment (17th January 1835). Lord Glenlee remarked—"When a person is in a dilemma and does not know what to do, the best way is for him *to do nothing.* But that rule is applied only to men of years, not to a *youth* who may have thought that it was necessary to do *something.*"

No. 8.—In an application for an interdict by a minister and kirk-session of a parish church against the undue interference of magistrates with the ringing of the church bell (7th Feb. 1835). Lord Meadowbank observed—"I conceive that with the single exception of the King's Chapel Royal, the bell of which was transferred by royal charter to an Episcopal Chapel in Edinburgh, where it still is, *no body of dissenters are entitled to a bell.* This is not a new idea. An attempt was made in Fife some time ago to put up a bell at a dissenting meeting-house. Opposition was given, however, and the law officers of the Crown (including the late Lord President Blair), gave a clear opinion *that no dissenting body were entitled to have a bell at all, and the attempt was consequently abandoned.*" Lord Medwyn—"I am of the same opinion with all your Lordships, and I would scarcely have occupied the time of the Court with any observations, but for the peculiar situation in which I am placed as the only dissenter on the bench. Being satisfied, however, that it is a *privilege* of the Established Church to summon its worshippers by a *great* bell, I am for continuing the interdict." "Even if there were no proper church bell but a town's house or court bell, I would not be for allowing it to be rung for the meeting of dissenting congregations."

No. 9.—In a case of nuisance (7th March 1835). Lord Cockburn reported the bill of suspension, with the following note:—"The Lord Ordinary reports this case in consequence of the reference made by both parties to the views of the Court, when the former application for an interdict was advised. He has only to state, that on the day on which the bill was presented, he visited the premises in the absence of both parties, and that if he had disposed of the case himself, that visit would have made him grant the interdict. On that day there was a very considerable quantity of dung—no want of swine—and a public privy as close as possible to the public road—all in a very offensive condition, and all in a south-westerly direction to the premises of the complainer."

No. 10.—In construing a will (21st May 1835) the following legacy was given:—"The whole of the furniture in her own bedroom, and *any other* she may choose for furnishing her house." The question arose whether "*any other*" was limited to another bed-room, or to other furniture sufficient to furnish her house. Two judges were for the first reading, but the majority were for the second, and the decision was so given.

No. 11.—An apprentice barber bound himself to work holiday and week-day. He refused to shave customers on the Sabbath. The magistrates of Dundee held him bound. Lord Jeffrey held him not bound. The Inner-House (19th May 1835) reversed, the Lord Justice-Clerk (Boyle) dissenting. But the House of Lords returned to the judgment of the Lord Ordinary. Per Lord Jeffrey—"It is ridiculous to speak of a public shaving shop as an establishment of such necessity as not to admit of interruption for a single day in the week. If the apprentice had refused to shave the head of a lunatic, or one whose skull had been fractured, the cases would have been parallel. The pretence of usage—especially such a partial usage as is alleged—is irrelevant in a question of illegality by violation of public law."

FRIEDBERG ON THE CONSTITUTION OF MARRIAGE.

Das Recht der Eheschliessung in seiner geschichtlichen Entwicklung. Von EMIL FRIEDBERG, Doctor der Rechte und Privat-Docent an der Universität zu Berlin. Leipzig, 1865.

[*Second Notice.*]

PROTESTANTISM did not, like Romanism, attain to a fixed and uniform doctrine in matrimonial matters. The Protestant ecclesiastical law was essentially a continuation of the ante-tridentine, but its development was affected by many circumstances. In the great controversies which have repeatedly raged as to "civil marriage," the authority of Luther has been invoked by the advocates of ecclesiastical rights as well as by their opponents. Dr. Friedberg examines his various statements with some minuteness, and notwithstanding various contradictions in his writings, concludes that he held marriage to be essentially a secular matter (ein weltlich Ding.) "He did not content himself, like the medieval schoolmen,* with recognising the secular along with the ecclesiastical side of marriage, but he demanded, before all things, that its constitution should be subject to rules laid down by the civil magistrate, and he desired the jurisdiction in matrimonial causes, as well as the legislation concerning marriage, to be left to the State." At the same time that he called it "ein weltlich Ding," Luther guarded himself from degrading marriage according to the notions of that time. In other passages he enlarges much on the sacredness of the institution, and its divine origin and symbolism, as indeed was natural in one who repudiated clerical

* Cf. *Thom. Aquin. contra Gentes*, C. IV., c. 78. "Considerandum est, quod quando aliquid ad diversos fines ordinatur, indiget habere diversa dirigentia in finem, quia finis est proportionatus agenti: generatio autem humana ad multa ordinatur, scilicet ad perpetuitatem alicujus boni positivi, puta populi in aliqua civitate; ordinatur etiam ad perpetuitatem Ecclesiae, quae in fidelium collectione consistit: unde oportet, quod hujusmodi generatio a diversis dirigatur. In quantum igitur ordinatur ad bonum naturae, quod est perpetuitas speciei, dirigitur in finem a natura inclinante in hunc finem: et sic dicitur esse naturae officium. In quantum vero ordinatur ad bonum politicum, subjacet ordinationi civilis legis. In quantum igitur ordinatur ad bonum Ecclesiae, oportet, quod subjaceat regimini Ecclesiastico," etc. The practice of the later jurists was less liberal. Take, for example, one of the Canonists best known to Scottish jurisprudence. Covarruvias, in discussing the doctrine started by Bartolus, that the secular judge may deal with a matrimonial question *incidenter, si controversia in facto non in jure consistat*, concludes thus—"Unde consultius res agetur si oblata incidenter, super matrimonio vel alia causa ecclesiastica, quæstione etiam facti, coram sæculari judice, is cujus interest ad ecclesiasticum judicem accesserit ab eoque petierit ut illius quæstionis cognitionem assumat, atque judicem laicum inhibeat, ne in ea etiam incidenter procedat; tunc enim si judex sæcularis nondum coepit id negotium tractare, ecclesiasticus citatis his quos id tangit, eandem incidentem causam expediet."—*De Matrimonio*, ii. 8, 12, 10.

celibacy. But the contrast between the secular and the religious, the political and the ecclesiastical, was in the early days of Protestantism not yet visible. The State was in many things the ally of the new religionists; it was no longer, as in the middle ages, unholy, as being part of the unholy world outside the holy Church. After the Reformation, the State was invested with a moral character and functions, and secular matters within its administration ceased to be unholy. The secular and the ecclesiastical were no longer opposed to one another, because the State now included the Church, and made it an integral part of itself. It was no degradation, therefore, for marriage to be a secular thing, and to be cared for and regulated by princes who were the Church's nursing fathers and nursing mothers, and who ranked their duties to the Church even above their duties to the State.*

* We get curious glimpses here and there in this book into the medieval theories of the relations of Church and State; but they are little more than glimpses, the author referring for ampler details to his little work "*De finium inter Ecclesiam et Civitatem regundorum Judicio quid medii ævi Doctores et Leges statuerint*" (Leipzig; Tauchnitz.) "Throughout the middle ages," he says, "the Church had absorbed nearly all spiritual interests, and the State was neither admitted to have the right, nor was it endowed with the power of interfering with anything beyond the merely material. The Church had claimed for itself divine origin, and held itself and its influence to be co-extensive with the sphere of the spiritual (des Geistes); the State was not in itself holy—Gregory VII. said kings sprung from the devil—(Epist. lib. 8, cp. 21 in Mansi Con., tom. 21) and it received the divine blessing in an indirect way, only in so far as it accommodated itself to the requirements of the Church, and obeyed them, just as the body obeys the commands of the soul (Comp. c. 23. C. xxiii. qu. 5.) Nay, this view of the subordinate position of the State, which degraded it into a mere instrument of the Church, was declared without a blush, by princes themselves, to be the true one (Frederick II., at least, adopted without protest the comparison, so frequent in ecclesiastical writers, of the State and the Church with the sun and the moon); although even in the earliest period of the middle ages a reaction was observable in the theory, and although their actual relations never exactly corresponded with the theory." The great effort of the Reformers was to keep Church and State apart, as Occam, Dante, and others had urged of old. But their views were not logical or homogeneous. They were unanimous and consistent only in rejecting the previous domination of the Church. On one side they denied the right of kings to intermeddle with ecclesiastical affairs, and strove according to their abilities against it (See a letter of Luther, *anno* 1543, (in De Wette Luther's Briefe, &c., Berlin, 1825 v. 596.) "Satan pergit Satan esse. Sub Papa miscuit ecclesiam politiæ, sub nostro tempore vult miscere politiam ecclesiæ. Sed nos resistemus Deo favente et studebimus pro nostra virili vocationes distinctas servare;") and on the other, they accommodated their doctrine without more ado to the circumstances in which they were placed, when the march of events had left their theory behind. The sovereigns of Germany were sufficiently zealous in Church politics, and their interest was of such importance to the success of the great religious revolution, that they could not easily be disregarded as a merely secular power. Hence the conception of the Christian State and the Christian magistrate, (of which some traces were already to be found in Huss and Tauler,) "the theory that kings were the holders of a divine office, instruments of a divine will, that, like the Old Testament kings, they were guardians of the divine laws, *custodes utriusque tabulæ*." Such a State and such rulers necessarily obtained a certain authority, even in matters where an ethical or quasi-religious element had formerly excluded the State, and without lowering the dignity of marriage, might, one would suppose, have regulated the law matrimonial, and directed the proceedings of its courts.

In his views of the substance of the law matrimonial, Luther differed materially in one or two points from the Canon Law. The ecclesiastical ceremony he regarded as good and desirable, though he did not pronounce it absolutely necessary. The essence of marriage he placed in the consent of the spouses, and this consent, if expressed openly and unconditionally, he held as constituting marriage even without the presence of the priest. He allowed the same effect to the conditional and secret expression of consent when followed by *copula carnalis*. He admitted no distinction, however, between *sponsalia de præsenti* and *de futuro*. It seems also (p. 210, 226, &c.) that he denied all effect to espousals without the consent of parents, even when followed by *copula*. In this lay the main difference between his theory and that of the Canonists, and the great cause of dissension between him and the contemporary Protestant jurists who adhered to the principles of the old Papal law, and against whom he often expressed himself with extreme bitterness (pp. 188, 226.) He intended, indeed, to write a book against them, but was dissuaded from doing so by the Elector of Saxony. The great Reformer having been removed by death from the controversy, the lawyers remained victors, and the Canon Law, which Luther would have consigned to the dust-heap, continued for some centuries longer the chief storehouse of jurisprudence for the Protestant Church.

It was indeed but a natural result of the arrangement by which matrimonial causes were placed under the jurisdiction of special Courts, that the ancient law was in all material points preserved; and as these Courts were mainly composed of ecclesiastics, or at least of jurists trained in the learning of the Canon Law, marriage came gradually to occupy a position contrasted with, and yet curiously like that which it held in Catholic countries. "According to the Canon Law the matrimonial jurisdiction was claimed by the Church because marriage was a sacrament; among Protestants it almost became a sacrament because the Church exercised matrimonial jurisdiction," (p. 192.) This erroneous view of marriage* called forth the

* The sacramental notion of marriage had already been violently assailed by the Reformers, especially by Calvin, e.g., "Et quis tandem finis aut modus? nihil hac ratione sacramentum non erit. Quot in scriptura parabolæ sunt et similitudines, tot erunt sacramenta. Quia etiam furtum sacramentum erit: quandoquidem scriptum est: Dies domini sicut fur." And again he adverts to the contradiction between the sacramental theory of marriage and the celibacy of the clergy. "Quam absurdum est, arcere a sacramento sacerdotes? Si a sacramento se arceri negent, sed a coitus tantum libidine, non ita mihi elabuntur. Nam et coitum ipsum partem esse sacra-

censures of many distinguished writers, both theologians and jurists, and John Samuel Stryk wrote a special work, "de Reliquiis Sacramenti in Matrimonialibus," (Halle 1711), in which he pointed out the consequences of the theory.

It is impossible for us to follow Dr Friedberg through his long review of Protestant doctrine on this subject, or to give even a sample of his notices of such writers as Melanchthon, Erasmus, Sarcerius, Bidembach, Beust, Schneidewin, Vultejus, Bullinger, Beza, Chemnitz, Spener, Havemann, Gerhard, Mevius, Brunnemann, Carpzow, Schilter, Samuel Stryk, Johann Samuel Stryk, Pufendorf, Brouwer, Samuel von Cocceji, Thomasius, Böhmer, and fifty others, of whose names we have hitherto been happily ignorant. Neither shall we follow him in his notices of legislation and practice during the centuries subsequent to the Reformation. It will be enough to sum up in his own words the results of his narrative of the development of Protestant opinion.

"Marriage in *facie ecclesiae* was not made a dogma, or a binding and absolutely necessary ecclesiastical institution. Neither could it be referred to a special command of the Deity, and although such an attempt was made, *e.g.* by Carpzow and some very late theologians, it was almost universally regarded as erroneous in the eighteenth century, and the same view must be maintained as the scientific and correct one in the present century also. Here of course we entirely put aside the question how far such a divine command, even if it existed, could claim an outward authority in the state.

Marriage *in facie ecclesiae* has rather been appointed by the State, and the priest in marrying is essentially the delegate of the State. His solemnization has moreover no efficacy in constituting marriage if the State refuses to recognize it, or if it takes place under conditions which the State, though not the Church, regards as impediments to marriage.—(Böhmer, J. E. P. iii., 1300 foll., Thomas., Diss. Ac. I., 665.)

"In the 16th century the ecclesiastical ceremony was regarded only as an act confirmatory of the marriage already contracted by *sponsalia*. *Matrimonium inchoatum* and *consummatum* were distinguished, and in regard to their dissolubility, they were placed on the same line; the consummation of marriage was effected by *copula* as well as by the priestly benediction; by either the spouses became one flesh, *in short there was no ecclesiastical constitution of marriage, but nothing beyond an ecclesiastical confirmation of marriage.*

mentum tradunt." Luther was highly indignant because lawyers persisted in applying Canon Law rules to matrimonial matters, and so retaining and prizing the popish filth which had been cast out of the Church with so great an effort. It would be curious to trace the causes which have produced the phenomenon now to be seen in Scotland, of an ultra Protestant clergy defending against modern encroachments a system of marriage law originally elaborated by the labour of successive Popes, and now forming almost the only remnant of Romanism in our national institutions.

"In the seventeenth century also this theory was the prevailing one, although the opinion already gained ground, that the ceremony in the church made the marriage, a view which obtained the predominance in the course of the 18th century.

"From that time it was first possible to speak correctly of an ecclesiastical *constitution* of marriage.

"Still however the theory of *sponsalia de praesenti* comes into conflict with the necessity of the ecclesiastical solemnity, and at least Böhmer recognized espousals followed by *copula* as true marriages. For this case at least the ceremony before a priest is therefore only confirmatory of marriage. The practice of compulsory solemnization, which has continued down to our own times, rests upon the same principle, and is in truth only a consequence of the doctrine that the ecclesiastical solemnity constitutes no marriage.

"The absolute necessity of marriage in the face of the church, was now, on the contrary, but rarely asserted, and the civil marriages in use in Holland were universally declared not to be inconsistent with the Protestant law and the statutes of the church.

"The last step was to declare that *sponsalia de praesenti* even where *copula* had followed, were binding only if entered into before the priest and followed by the benediction. It was the modern legislative enactments establishing the ecclesiastical ceremony as the only form of constituting marriage, which chiefly led to the adoption of this theory. By these enactments for the first time, and therefore only at the end of the last and the beginning of the present century, was the quality of absolute necessity thoroughly impressed on the solemnization in the face of the church in Germany, although it has been falsely claimed since the time of the Reformation.

"The doctrine as to Brautkinder (*i.e.*, children borne by a bride, *sponsa*,) which is even yet particular law, and indeed a subject of controversy, (Vangerow, Lehrb. d. Pand, § 413, Arndt. Lehrb. d. Pand, § 476, Puchta Pand, § 41) may be regarded as the last remnant of the old doctrine of the constitution of marriage.

"The tendency of legal theory finally, which was hostile to the ecclesiastical ceremony, as it was to everything ecclesiastical, had no important influence so far as regards the constitution of marriage on German practice or legislation.

"It has still to be remarked that the full civil effects were generally allowed to a marriage, only if the *concubitus* had taken place, and that therefore the mere priestly benediction was not sufficient for this end. This deserves a prominent mention in connection with the objection that espousals have never been identified with marriage, because the former have never had the patrimonial effects of the latter. These effects as we have said, did not always take place even after the blessing of the priest, and therefore nothing is thereby proved."

The Fourth Book of Dr Friedberg's work, occupying somewhere about three-fifths of his volume, is a history of the progress of "Civil Marriage." The author treats separately of the various countries of Europe and America, beginning with England. He gives in pages 309 to 478, a history of the marriage laws of England, Scotland, Ireland, and the United States, since the Reformation, which is fuller and more convenient than any that exists elsewhere, and without a translation of which we do not hesitate to say that both the inquiries of the Royal Commission now sitting, and the discussion that must follow the conclusion of these inquiries, must be carried on under great disadvantages. We earnestly recommend some one of our legal brethren to devote the leisure of the long vacation to the work of preparing a translation of this part of the book, or, still better, a small book founded on Dr Friedberg's, containing almost all this portion of it, and a judicious selection from the remainder. It would be very important to have an abridgement in English, with improvements and additions, of the latter part of the book, which comprises the details of the legislation and discussions on this subject in foreign countries during the last and the present centuries.

It is impossible, in the space to which we are confined, to enter on the large subject which this Book embraces. The author traces the course of the English marriage law from the entire absence of form which existed under the regime of the Canon Law, till it arrived at a degree of formalism such as has never been known on the Continent, and which could only have grown up to supply the want of a law of divorce. "For," he says, "as the unloosing of the marriage tie was nearly impossible, necessity taught men to find a remedy by annulling it" (p. 436). The law of Scotland is sketched more shortly, but with as much insight and accuracy as can be expected from a writer who appears not to be acquainted with Mr Fraser's "Personal and Domestic Relations," or with any recent cases, except newspaper reports of the Yelverton case. Dr Friedberg declares himself against the existing law of Scotland:—

"Secret marriages," he says, "wherever they have not been extirpated by the severity of the law, have produced crimes of all sorts, the most serious improprieties, and danger to the whole moral life of the people. We had to point out the unhappy condition of the middle ages in our account of the ante-tridentine law, and it may easily be calculated to what extent such disorders must reach in the more complicated relations of a civilized age.

"Although in other countries the seduction of females, whether major or minor, may never be entirely prevented by statutory provisions, and although only the morality which arises from culture may afford a sufficient protection against this evil, yet a marriage is not entered into by the mere fact of that seduction; unchastity is not so identical, or at least so nearly connected with marriage as it is in Scotland.

"And what an inducement to the irregular satisfaction of the passions is to be found in this informal law! The maiden is silenced by some soothing words, which perhaps she wrongly takes for a promise of marriage, or by a formal betrothal is made more disposed to be seduced, and the man seeks to overcome her scruples by the cheap pretence that he really intends to enter into a matrimonial connection, not perhaps now, but afterwards; and then, having easily attained his purpose, treacherously forsakes the girl. And that is a favourable case; for how often may the false pretence, the deception, have been in the thoughts of the seducer from the first!

"But what family is safe when the twelve-year old daughter, whose bodily and mental immaturity makes her fitter for the nursery than the nuptial couch, can without form or preparation, without the assent of either parents or guardians, enter into a lifelong connection; when boys of the age of fourteen are exposed without any defence to the wiles of covetous or wanton women?

"And then how pitiable is the condition of those who in good faith contract a marriage, with public proclamation and solemnities, but are afterwards declared concubines, and their children bastards, because the other spouse, who is perhaps dead, had, it may be fifty years ago, in an unguarded moment, contracted a secret marriage!"

These are the ordinary objections to the Scotch marriage law, which it is not the purpose of the present article to discuss. It strikes us, however, that as Dr Friedberg states them, some of these objections might very easily be turned into arguments on the other side. It is right to add, that Dr Friedberg, after referring to the various attempts to alter the law, and the strenuous resistance to these attempts, acknowledges "that the Scotch marriage law does much less mischief in Scotland than it would cause in any other country. Long custom has brought the people for the most part into the habit of regular marriages, and makes irregular marriages on the whole but rare exceptions."

Dr Friedberg, in summing up the results of his survey of the legal history of Europe, believes that for the last three centuries all civilised countries have been tending in different ways towards the same end, civil marriage. The ecclesiastical marriage, as it everywhere prevailed, reconciled the interests of Church and State, and was a fit expression of the moral character of the matrimonial relation. But the law which was wholesome and adequate in simpler times became oppressive and injurious in a more complicated state of society. Various causes combined to make it inevitable that the ecclesiastical solemnity as the *only* mode of contracting marriage should be relinquished. The unity of

Christian faith had disappeared. Romanism was no longer powerful enough to enforce the observance of one religious ceremony, and Protestantism was compelled by the very nature of its being to tolerate different confessions within its borders. This tolerance was indeed of slow growth. At first it was said, "Let those religious acts which are bound up with the welfare and security of the State be withdrawn from the strife of sects. Let men worship God as they will, but let them contract their marriages before that priest whom the State entrusts with the function." But by degrees culture and increasing sensibility for religious independence has been removing one by one such restrictions upon the principles of toleration. Preachers of every sect were allowed to officiate in the nuptial ceremony, in this country only very lately. But this remedy was not sufficient. Many religious societies had not a regular organisation, and wanted any official to whom the charge of the marriage ceremony could be given.

"Then the legislator again became conscious of the original nature of marriage. It was not of a character so essentially ecclesiastical that in every case it must be suffered to fall into the hands of the Church. Protestant teaching had openly enough proclaimed that marriage was a secular contract, that it was only the laws of the State which had allotted to the Church the regulation of marriage, and that in doing so they had been in accord with the general opinion and the wants of society. It was no act of injustice towards the Church, but a mere act of justice towards its citizens, if, again following public opinion and the requirements of the age, the State now resumed what was its own function. On the other hand it was not right to offend the majority for the sake of a few, and to take away the ecclesiastical constitution of marriage from all who were still truly attached to it in order to liberate a few."

Hence a new law of marriage, confined within the narrowest possible limits, which Dr Friedberg calls, throughout his book, "*Noth-civilehe,*" civil marriage for cases of necessity, or subsidiary civil marriage. This first departure from ecclesiastical marriage was made in the United Provinces in the course of the sixteenth century, and in France immediately before the Revolution. It was taken not merely from motives of tolerance, but also as the only means of avoiding a conflict between church and state. The pretensions of the church to the exclusive control of matrimonial matters had been revived. Romanism was enabled by its organisation to assert again in defiance of the claims of the state the maxims of the Canon Law, as altered by the Council of Trent; and its doc trine of the sacramental nature of marriage furnished a convenient theoretical basis for such claims. The Protestant clergy also had forgotten or renounced the doctrine of the fusion of church and state, which had so long been preached and practised, and had adopted an almost sacramental theory of marriage. Hence civil marriage was adopted only as a remedy for conspicuous evils; in order, for example, to facilitate mixed marriages between Jews and Christians, or between Protestants and Roman Catholics.

Theoretical speculation also led to the doctrine of civil marriage. The Reformation revived the doctrine of the dualism and separation of Church and State, as it was held in the infancy of Christianity; but as the State had previously been over-ridden by the Church, so now the State was for the most part too powerful for the Church, and it was long before this doctrine led to any practical result. Indeed, as we have already indicated, the State and the Church were in reality more closely connected in early Protestant times than they had been before the Reformation, with this difference that the State had the predominance. As the ancient theory revived and gained strength, the Church, which could not now hope "to set its foot on the neck of the State," had to content itself with proclaiming its own freedom and equality.

"Only once before the end of the 18th century had an attempt been made to carry out practically the distinction of the ecclesiastical and civil power. This was not made from any anti-ecclesiastical disposition, which sought to banish religion from common life, and deny to the Church all outward action; but, on the contrary, from an excess of piety, striving to make the church more devout and spiritual, and liberate it from the frivolous concerns of the world. Hence the position assigned to marriage. It had originally belonged to the province of the State. Church and State being separated, it necessarily followed the State, and was to be entered into with forms and conditions prescribed by the State. Thus arose the *obligatory* civil marriage of the English Commonwealth."

Cromwell's marriage law, which was in force over all the British islands, was a consequence of the Puritan effort to restore the whole Church constitution to the apostolic pattern, and to get rid of every form or ceremony which might recall the times of Paganism or Popery. It introduced civil marriage, says our author in another passage, "because that system deprived the clergy of a considerable source of revenue, and thus drove away hirelings from the service of the church; it took the matrimonial jurisdiction from spiritual functionaries and transferred it to justices of the peace, because no secular jurisdiction pertained to the clergy; it prohibited the marriage ring because it was of heathen and Romish origin." * The writings of Milton show the principles on which this legislation, which was of course repealed at the Restoration, was founded.

When this theoretical view of civil marriage again received practical expression, the impulse was not derived from a regard for the interests of religion and the church, but rather from profound dislike to both.

> "The civil marriage of the French Revolution sprung from a desire not to make the Church less worldly, but to make the State less ecclesiastical. (Man wollte nicht so die Kirche entweltlichen, wie den Staat entkirchlichen.) The modern German civil marriage stands between these two tendencies. It would be incorrect to ascribe it either to hatred or affection for the church. It is historically false to connect it either with the French or English model. . . . The separation of the spheres of ecclesiastical and political action is an almost undisputed maxim of modern Constitutional Law. Church and State must be left free to continue their development alongside of one another, unembarrassed by the artificial tie which has hitherto confined and hampered the growth and prosperity, sometimes of the one and sometimes of the other. If this theory be regarded as practicable, it leads as an inevitable consequence to civil marriage.
>
> "Marriage is the basis of the family, and therefore of the State; it is the most important institution that the State has to regulate and watch over. If it is the duty and the will of the church to withdraw from every political influence, the State cannot commit to her the regulation and control of marriage. It would then give up its own function, and place its most important institutions at the arbitrary disposal of a corporation whose sphere transcends its own rights and powers. Hence it insists on the political character of marriage, fixes the legal conditions of its validity, and leaves it to the choice of the individual and his religious necessities, to come to terms with the requirements of the Church."

From these principles have sprung not only the *obligatory* civil marriage of France and the Rhineland, but also the *facultative* or *optional* civil marriage of England. For the story of the de-

* Comp Butler's Hudibras III., 2., 303 :—

"Others were for abolishing
That tool of matrimony, a ring,
With which the unsanctified bridegroom
Is married only to a thumb,
(As wise as ringing of a pig
That used to break up ground and dig);
The bride to nothing but her will,
That nulls the after marriage still."

Our author quotes (p. 329) an amusing specimen of the squibs produced by this legislation; but its wit is too broad for our pages. See Flecknoe's Diarium (1656) p. 83.

velopment of these and other varieties, we refer to the book before us.

The controversies which the author had in view in his own country were different from that which now chiefly occupies us in Great Britain. On the Continent the great struggle has been, as it was in England, between the ecclesiastical and the secular theories of marriage, between the marriage in which the sacramental character predominates, and that in which the political and social aspects are alone regarded,—between the marriage which the Church reckoned peculiarly her own, and marriage as an institution of the State. In Scotland, on the other hand, the controversy now is between the optional purely civil marriage and the ecclesiastical marriage with registration, co-existing, as in England, and that *natural* system of marriage, as it may be called, to which the ecclesiastical law, during its supremacy, allowed a subordinate and unauthorised existence, which has from various causes survived in Scotland to the present day, which has become so much a part of our national life, and has apparently produced so few of the evils which have been laid to its charge elsewhere, that it remains doubtful how far the progress of legal assimilation will be able to affect it.

The subject-matter of both controversies, however, is the same, —the proper mode of constituting marriage, or, in other words, of providing the necessary proof of marriage; and no one will be fully armed for either side of the controversy between English and Scottish lawyers, unless he has furnished himself from the arsenal of Dr. Friedberg with some of the weapons which have been wielded in other countries, and in our own island, by the redoubtable champions of other generations.

THE MONTH.

Jury Trials.—Since our last publication the jury sittings of the Summer Session have taken place, and the cases depending before the Court have, as a general rule, been of more than ordinary importance. At the same time the exceptions were sufficiently numerous to justify us in directing attention to a practice which has become but too common in the Court; we mean the practice of trying by jury all questions that are set apart for that method of ascertaining facts, irrespective altogether of the magnitude of the case, either in respect of public interest, or of pecuniary conclusion. It is surely a burlesque upon legal procedure, that after a lengthened investigation, and the addresses of four counsel, and a judicial exposition of the evidence, twelve gentlemen should enter a public court and solemnly announce, as the result of their consultation, that they find for the pursuer and assess the damages at £3. Yet such a spectacle was exhibited at the recent sittings of the Jury Court, and there were other cases whose proportions did not vary much from the dimensions we have just stated. No wonder that jury trial is an unpopular institution in this country! Such cases would drain the strength of any system, however great its strength and vigorous its vitality; one that is wearily sustaining a valetudinarian existence will by such processes speedily meet its death-blow. Of the cases of importance calling for special notice that which stands prominent above all others is of course the North Esk Pollution Case. There are many considerations which will render it for a long time to come a *cause celebre*. As the Lord Justice-Clerk observed, seldom if ever have parties brought to the question at issue such a resolute determination to exhaust all the resources from which material bearing on the point in controversy could be extracted. An interest, too, although we think it is a spurious one, was lent to the case from the accidental circumstance that the pursuers were proprietors of large territorial possessions, and the defenders persons who represented more immediately the capital and the industry of the people. Tried as the question was at the crisis when a Liberal ministry was defeated, and supplanted by a Conservative one, and one party of course, by accident, being represented by the leaders of the Bar acknowledging one political faith, and the other by the leaders who profess its rival, the action had in some of its aspects the appearance of a political contest. But it would be a great mistake, and a great misfortune, if the significance of the case should be lost sight of in presence of such purely personal considerations. To the profession the case is of importance, as deciding a point which, if ruled by principle, is likely afterwards to repeat itself in questions of practice: we refer to the form of issues under which the case was tried, and under which, as interpreted by the Court, the question put to the jury was— whether each and all of the mill proprietors on the river had materially contributed to its pollution? The jury found for the pursuers on all the issues, and the result of the verdict accordingly is, that a lower heritor complaining of the pollution of the river opposite to his lands, is entitled to complain in a process comprehending all against each superior heritor who has contributed in a material way to the gross pollution, which is the subject of dispute. But the chief value of the case lies not in the verdict of the jury, but in the charge of the judge; and it is satisfactory that so important a question came to depend before so great a master of exposition as the Lord Justice-Clerk.

In the case of Urquhart *v.* Bonnar, a curious result was attained, which we hope we shall never see repeated in this country. A jury in a question involving the relations between a medical man and his patient, found for the pursuer for a third time. The first division of the Court, upon a hearing after the first trial, upset the verdict, as contrary to evidence. This step was repeated when a second jury had proved as recalcitrant as the first, and found for the pursuer. Will it be repeated a third time, as the jury have thrice affirmed the same view of the evidence? We do not see how it can be avoided, for it seems to us that the Court have placed themselves in a dilemma; and if it is considered that this is a course too invidious and high-handed to be adopted, there is only another horn which they can accept, and upon which we humbly think they must be impaled. If the view of the evidence taken by the first jury was a reasonable one, or, to state the proposition more in accordance with the theory of jury trial, was one which a body of twelve men of average intelligence might be fairly enough expected to take, then the Court, in our opinion, by upsetting the verdict of the jury on the ground that it was contrary to evidence, usurped its province. For it is peculiarly the province of a jury to pronounce upon disputed facts; and if verdicts are to be set aside on the ground merely of a difference of opinion between the jury and the Court, then is the system of jury trial already at an end. If, on the other hand, the view of the evidence taken by the first jury and repeated by the succeeding two was not a reasonable one,—was not such as twelve men of average intelligence could, under any circumstances, be expected to take, but was, on the contrary, grossly absurd and outrageous,—then, under the reserved power which the system of jury trial gives to the Court to deal with verdicts of this kind, it would seem to be the duty of the Court to rectify the error just as often as it is perpetrated. We should be glad to have it pointed out where one may logically halt between these two positions.

The Nuisance Acts.—We think it advisable, in unison with the combined efforts that are being put forth in all directions to promote sanitary precautions, to call attention to the excellent series of regulations issued by the Board of Supervision, in virtue of the powers conferred upon them by the Statute 19 and 20 Vict., c. 10, part II., sec. 24 and 26, put in operation in all parts of Scotland by the Orders in Council of the 4th day of June 1866. These regulations have been put into the hands of all the representatives of public bodies, and the leading officials throughout the country; and it is not necessary that we should recapitulate them here. But it may be important to notice that questions of this kind, so far as they have legal bearings, fall to be determined, for the most part, by "The Nuisances Removal (Scotland) Act, 1856," 19 and 20 Vict., cap. 103, and "The Police and Improvement (Scotland) Act, 1862," 25 and 26 Vict., cap. 101, "Part VII., Promotion of the Public Health." The local authorities under these Acts are different according to the different circumstances of communities. Sometimes it is the Town Council; sometimes Police Commissioners or Trustees exercising their functions; sometimes the Parochial Board. Considerable penalties are imposed by these Acts, and it is a provision of one of them which ought not to be overlooked—for there is no guarantee that statutory local authorities will always discharge their duty—that if the local authority fails in its performance, it is competent for any two householders residing within the district, or the Inspector of Poor of the parish, or the Procurator-Fiscal, or the Sheriff, or Justice of Peace Court of the county, or of the Borough Court, to apply to the Sheriff, in order to enforce the provisions of the Acts, or the directions and regulations of the Board of Supervision.

Shareholders in Limited Banking Companies.—So much misapprehension has existed in regard to the recent decision of the Court of Appeal in Chancery in the case of *Overend, Gurney, & Co. (limited), exparte Grissell*, that it is necessary to state briefly the true import of the judgment. When the company stopped payment, Mr Grissell held 80 shares, nominally of £50 each, on which £15 per share was paid up. He was also a creditor of the company for £1500 of deposits. A call of £10 being made, Mr Grissell disputed his liability to pay it, and claimed to set off the amount of it against his deposit, so that he might stand as a creditor of the company for £15,200; or otherwise, that his dividend should be calculated on the whole £16,000, and the amount of the call deducted from the dividend. "Both applications," says the Lord Chancellor, "may be regarded as raising the question whether, a shareholder who is also a creditor of a limited liability company, is entitled either to set off or have credit for so much of his debt as is equal to the amount of calls which have been made upon, but not paid by him, and to receive a dividend on the balance." Kindersley, V. C., applied to the case the general principle of partnership law, that partners creditors of a company cannot receive anything from the company estate until all its public creditors have been fully paid. The Order made by his Honour was that Mr Grissell must pay up the call before receiving any dividend; but the principle of the decision went to this extent that he could receive no dividend till all the creditors of the company, not shareholders, were paid in full, and that he must in the meantime pay all calls. On appeal this wide application of the common law was negatived. The question was held to depend entirely on the construction of the Companies' Act 1862. That Act recognizes members of the company as creditors, *e.g.*, in § 38, (7), and § 101; and they are thus, under § 133, entitled to satisfaction of their debts out of the property of the company *pari passu* with the other creditors. The Court of Appeal holds 1) that "they cannot be required to pay up the full amount remaining unpaid on these shares," for, by § 75, until the call is made, though there is a debt, that debt does not accrue due till a call is made. 2) That the amount of the call not being paid cannot be set off against the debt. By the 101st section a set off on an independent contract is allowed to the member of an *unlimited* company against a call, although the creditors have not been paid, evidently because he is liable to contribute to any amount till all the liabilities of the company are satisfied; but in the case of a *limited* company this might be paying him 20s. in the pound, while the other creditors were only receiving a small dividend, it would withdraw from them a part of the fund applicable to the payment of their debts. Hence calls must be paid before such a creditor can share in a dividend. When they are paid, a shareholder stands upon the same footing as other creditors with respect to a dividened on a debt due to him by the company, and will receive a dividend on his whole debt, without any deduction on account of his liability to future calls.

Report of the Parliamentary Committee on the Law of Master and Servant.—The Select Committee of the House of Commons on the Law of Master and Servant has issued its report. Its principal recommendations are, that all cases in this branch of the law should be publicly tried before two or more magistrates or the Sheriff; that procedure should be by warrant to cite, and failing the appearance of the defendant the Court should have power to grant warrant to apprehend; that punishment should be by fine, and failing payment by distress or imprisonment; that the Court should have power in its discretion to order fulfilment of the contract, and to exact security therefor; that the Court should still have power to imprison "in aggravated cases of breach of contract causing injury to person or property;" that the arrest of wages in Scotland in payment of fines should be abolished. The Committee add that they are not prepared to recommend, as suggested to them, that in all cases of breach of contract between master and servant, it should be competent to examine the parties as in civil cases, although the offence be punishable on summary conviction.

Appointments.—George Burnett, Esq., advocate, who has for some time held the office of Lyon-Depute, has been appointed Lord Lyon King-at-Arms. John Hunter, Esq., has resigned the office of Auditor of the Court of Session, and Edmund Baxter, Esq., S.S.C., has been appointed in his room.

Colonial Appointments for the Scotch Bar.—This journal has repeatedly asserted the claims of the legal profession in Scotland to a more liberal share of legal appointments in the colonies than has hitherto been accorded to it. It is satisfactory to learn that Lord Advocate Patton has taken up this matter, and that in consequence of his representations the Colonial Office has already placed two nominations in his gift, viz., to the judgeship or chief magistracy of the Gold Coast, now vacant, and to that of Gambia, shortly to become vacant. A Scotch advocate will probably not covet very much an appointment on the west coast of Africa; but we trust that this prompt attention to the Lord Advocate's claim betokens the end of the unjust neglect under which the Scotch bar has too long suffered in this respect. It is also matter for congratulation that we have now a Lord Advocate willing to interest himself in the prosperity of the profession to which he belongs.

An Examination for the Degree of Bachelor of Laws of the University of Edinburgh will be held on the 23d, 24th, 25th and 26th of October. Candidates must leave their names, with evidence of their being graduates in arts, and certificates of attendance on the necessary courses of lectures, with the Secretary of the University, not later than Sept. 30.

Curriculum of Study and Examinations of Procurators.—The General Council of Procurators have issued a curriculum of study for persons applying for admission as procurators, and regulations as to the subjects in which they shall be examined. The office-bearers with three other members of the General Council shall be examiners, and diets for examination shall, if required, be held on the second Thursday of January, the second Thursday of April, and the second Thursday of September in every year, at Edinburgh, Glasgow, and Aberdeen. Applicants for admission after 1st January 1868, shall produce evidence of having attended University classes of Scots Law and Conveyancing, but this shall not apply to any person under indenture at 5th July 1865 (the date of the passing of the Act), or who had prior to that day completed the term of his apprenticeship. The examinations shall be partly written and partly oral, and shall consist of two parts. Part I., General Knowledge: embracing English Composition; Histories of Rome, England, Scotland; Geography; Arithmetic; Book-keeping; Latin; any Book of the Æneid, or of Cæsar's Commentaries, to be selected by the applicant; Logic, or, in the option of the applicant, Mathematics—first three books of Euclid. Part II., Law, and Legal Training and Practice; (1) Scots Law, including Criminal Law and the Law of Evidence; (2) Conveyancing; (3) Forms of Process both in civil and criminal cases. Applicants to have the option of being examined in the two parts at one or different diets. They must give twenty-one days' notice to the secretary of their wish to be examined, and at the same time transmit their discharged indenture or other evidence of apprenticeship; a certificate of any examinations passed during apprenticeship, with certificates of attendance at classes, and five guineas as examination fee. If an applicant on examination is found not duly qualified, he may apply again, on paying an additional guinea.

THE

JOURNAL OF JURISPRUDENCE.

LAW STUDIES.

No. IV.—Scotland.

Of the four Universities of Scotland, that of Edinburgh alone possesses a Faculty of Law that makes any pretension to completeness. It is true that in Scotland, as everywhere else, the study of the Civil and Canon law was embraced in the original scheme of the older Universities. The Papal Bull of Benedict XIII. provided for it at St. Andrews in 1413; and in the second erection of St. Mary's College in 1553, the Canonist, who was to be in Priest's orders and *Sacrorum Canonum licentia decoratus*, was enjoined to teach the Canon Law five days a-week. But the St. Andrew's Canonists and Civilians have long been silent, and they and their offices must be sought for only amongst the picturesque and stately traditions which cling to that storied seat of learning. The original Constitutions, both of Glasgow and Aberdeen, contained similar provisions; and both of these Universities still boast of a legal Faculty. But if the maxim *tres faciunt collegium* be applicable to a faculty, there is no real Faculty of Law in either of them; for the so-called Faculty of Law in Glasgow consists of two, whilst that of Aberdeen is represented by a single professor.

In Edinburgh, though *professores jurium* are mentioned in the Charter of Constitution of James VI., in 1582, their establishment does not appear to have been one of the primary objects of the institution, and they drop in only incidentally as it were, before referring to the *quarumcunque aliarum liberalium scien-*

Great War,—just as the use of Gladstonian claret, as an article of ordinary family consumption, revived in Scotland, the moment that the duty was removed,—and the number of members of the Bar, at the present time, who have studied abroad is very considerable. But what was once the rule is still, and probably will always continue to be, the exception—an exception so rare as not materially to affect the general character of the body, or to act in any degree as a satisfactory substitute for home study. Nor does foreign instruction, even when resorted to, serve the same purpose as in former times. From its exceptional character, and from the fact that Scotch professors are no longer at hand to aid their youthful compatriots abroad, it is no longer communicated in so systematic a manner, and rarely for so long a period, as to secure its full scientific advantages, whilst from the gradual divergence of the Law of Scotland from the continental systems it does not possess the same value for practical purposes as, formerly.

But though we are very far from calling in question the importance of foreign study even in our own day, we have dwelt upon its prevalence in former times not so much for the purpose of urging its revival, as because we believe that it furnishes the true explanation of the facts, otherwise disparaging to our country, of the late foundation of the Faculty of Law in the University of Edinburgh, and the incomplete character that still belongs to it. Whilst matters were in the position we have described; whilst Latin was the common language of the learned, and Scotland, as regarded her judicial arrangements, and even her higher intellectual life, a sort of outlying province of continental Europe, a local School of Law was really in a great measure superfluous. Even after the cultivation of the modern tongues had given a local character to learning abroad, and British influences had gained the ascendancy in Scotland, such a school might not unreasonably be still regarded for a time as merely supplementary. The highest class of persons who studied the laws still followed the ancient custom. As regarded them, the function of a National School was accomplished if it enabled them to adapt their foreign studies to national uses. The training of the inferior branches of the profession, again, was mainly practical, and scarcely called for the services of a complete Faculty of Law.

Such was the position of affairs, and such probably the state of feeling on the subject, up to the period of the Union. When that event occurred, the intimate ties which bound Scotland to the Continent were finally loosened, and the formation of a School of Law in the University of Edinburgh henceforth became an object of national concern. That it has not been more perfectly accomplished is a subject of regret, but of regret which must be largely mixed with thankfulness and national congratulation when we reflect that, in its present condition, it is, very much, the nearest approach to a complete School of Law of which this country can boast. For this fortunate circumstance we are no doubt indebted to the fact that the learned and enlightened tastes which our ancestors had derived from their own foreign studies, induced them to lay the foundations of the institution not in practice, but in theory. Had they begun at the other end, the error would have been irretrievable; for what we develope with such difficulty, we should have found it impossible to plant. But the two first chairs which *they* endowed were, not Scotch Law and Conveyancing (which we fear might have been the case with their descendants), but the Law of Nature and Nations—"the fountain of justice and equity," as they denominated it, and the Civil Law!

But the good seed fell on a barren age. The generation which succeeded them was inferior to them. The elements of social disorder which soon after burst forth in the American War and the French Revolution, were already fermenting and deranging the organic development of European life. When these events occurred, the passion for a rude chaotic equality took possession of the minds of those who in better times would have constituted a really progressive party. Levelling of all distinctions was assumed to be the only remedy for the inconveniences which began to arise from feudal distinctions which had become effete, and all inquiry into the finer relations between liberty and order, and the deeper laws of society, was regarded by both parties not with disfavour only, but with suspicion. The study of the law of Nature and Nations languished, and the chair, whilst filled by a professor of great eminence,* fell into abeyance. The chair of Civil Law, being partially protected by the examination which the Faculty of Advocates has always imposed, held its ground but feebly supported and miserably endowed. The practical chairs which were added—the chair of Scotch Laws more par-

* Alan Maconochie, the first Lord Meadowbank.

ticularly—have attracted large classes, and have frequently been filled by men of real eminence, but their holders could not, of course, contribute very materially to the importance of the Faculty as a School of Scientific Jurisprudence.

Such was the position of affairs in the University when the Faculty of Advocates, on the 25th January 1854, "Resolved, That a committee be appointed to consider the existing regulations applicable to the qualification of Intrants into the Faculty, and the expediency of making any alterations on those regulations." The very interesting Report from which we have already quoted, for which the Profession and the country were indebted to the unwearied labours of the convenor, Mr. Fraser,* was presented on the 11th July following. The practical suggestions with which the Report concludes, were the result of many meetings, and of a very careful consideration of the vast mass of materials which had been collected. These suggestions, with very slight modifications, were embodied in the existing "Regulations as to Intrants," and constitute the present educational code of the Scottish Bar. But before placing this document before the reader, we shall quote two or three sentences illustrative of the spirit in which it was framed. "The Faculty of Advocates," say the reporters, "is essentially a *learned* profession, and has ever held a high position as to learning among the Faculties of Law in Europe. Amid the general diffusion of education, and the increased knowledge of all ranks, it is certainly incumbent upon a body so renowned to maintain a character for learning upon other grounds than traditionary respect. It is possible to treat law as a mere mechanical art, and it is also possible to argue a case without knowing Latin; and if it were enough to become a body of mere case-lawyers, contented, in argument, with simply placing before the Court an accumulation of Scotch authorities, applied with the tact derived from a knowledge of Practice, then philosophical knowledge would not only be useless, but an encumbrance. Treating law on this footing, the mind is apt to confuse the law itself with the forms and routine which alone too often constitute the study and the practice of a lifetime. Such have not hitherto been the principles upon which the Scottish Bar have acted; and these are not the

* The Committee were—The Dean (Inglis), the Solicitor-General (Maitland), Mr. Penny, Mr. Moir, Mr. Dundas, Mr. Patton, Mr. John T. Gordon, Mr. Fraser, Mr. James Lorimer, Mr. W. G. Dickson—Mr. Fraser, Convener.

times for lowering the standard of qualification. America is an example and a warning." Recent events have given, both to the example and the warning, a significance which they scarcely possessed in 1854, and they may probably prove not less instructive to the reader than they did to the Faculty. Here is the example—"Speaking generally, no attendance at schools, colleges, classes of philosophy, or other specific course of instruction, is required of one seeking admission to the Bar. No lectures on law are required to be attended. Only one examination is had, which is on applying for admission to practice, and refers to professional knowledge merely." And this, on very high *American* authority, is the warning:—"There is a gradual change for the worse coming over the Bar, as a body of gentlemen. Among them learning is not quite as much respected as it was. Practical tact, adroitness, the arts of playing the demagogue before courts and juries, are becoming more available in the waning influence of learning, and want of some degree of legal rank. By the old plan" (abrogated in 1845 in the State of New York, which till then had accepted four years of classical studies as equivalent to four years of clerkship, and imposed other conditions favourable to culture), "some learning was insured, some service with superiors, which tended, if not to subordination, yet to a forbearing deference. Some unfit men were shut out. The people and the Courts, however, are the chief sufferers; the magnates of the profession are not; nor are there wanting sufficient inducements to learning and study." We must not withhold the concluding touches of the picture, though they render it more than doubtful if the inducements would seem sufficient to the magnates of the profession anywhere but in America. "The salaries of the judges are low; the tenure of their office short. They are appointed by election. And now it is with difficulty that men of independent professional condition can be induced to go on the bench; and it may safely be said that the bench is not above, if equal to, the body of the bar. The result of this is conflicts of decision, and great uncertainty, and an entire absence of submitting to any judgments not rendered by the Courts of last resort; and these are acquiesced in, not from authority so much as from necessity. Juries disagree, and judges have small influence to guide them in any matter involving popular feeling." The concluding reflection of the writer is, that "these are not pleasant prospects," and the Committee was deeply impressed with its justice. Feeling that the ballot-box, which in former times had given to the Faculty something of the character of a learned club, had become a sham, that the entrance fees, once considerable, had been greatly lowered by the depreciation of money, they arrived at the conclusion that the Institutes of Justinian and a "Title from the Pandects" were no longer adequate protections to themselves against the inroads of unsuitable candidates, and consequently declared themselves unanimously of opinion "that evidence, both of general and legal learning, should be afforded by every candidate for admission to the bar." "The proper evidence of general scholarship" they pronounced to be "a University degree." "But such a test as this the Committee are unwilling to require absolutely and exclusively, as it might bear hard upon persons of humble family and straitened circumstances." As, in the case of such persons, "all that ought to be insisted upon is proof of the possession of the requisite liberal education, the course which seemed most expedient to the Committee was "to subject the candidate to an examination upon certain branches of general knowledge, conducted by men to whose hands it may be reasonably and safely entrusted." The subjects to which they recommend that the examination should be confined were the following:—*First,* Latin; *Secondly,* Greek; *Thirdly,* Ethical and Metaphysical Philosophy; *Fourthly,* Logic, or (in the option of the candidate) Mathematics." The Law course recommended extended to two years attendance at a University; and embraced the various subjects then taught at the University of Edinburgh. In accordance with these suggestions, slightly modified by the subsequent discussions in the Faculty, regulations were issued which up to this time have regulated admission to the bar.

In farther pursuance of the objects which the Faculty of Advocates had in view in the new regulations, the University Commissioners shortly after undertook the task of improving and developing the Faculty of Law in the University of Edinburgh. They slightly increased the endowments of the chairs, though leaving them still so slenderly provided for that their tenants, in several cases, would consult their pecuniary interests if they were to accept macerships of Justiciary, and would in almost every case be great gainers by becoming Sheriff-Substitutes. But in all respects, except those in which the parsimony of the exchequer constrained the good-will, and set at defiance what are believed to have been the strongly-expressed remonstrances of the Commissioners, their provisions were in the highest degree liberal and enlightened. As we conceive it to be of the utmost importance that these provisions, and more particularly the arrangements for graduation in law which the Commissioners adopted, should be more accurately known and more maturely weighed by all branches of the profession than they have yet been, we have no hesitation in reprinting, *in extenso*, the following passage from the General Report:—

"Degrees in law," say the Commissioners, "have for a long period been granted by the Universities of Scotland as honorary distinctions only. Considering, however, that the legal education of the country is for the most part carried on in the Universities, and that in some of them the Faculty of Law occupies a very prominent position, we regarded it as of the highest consequence that a course of study and examinations for degrees in that Faculty should be established. In Edinburgh, in particular, instruction in Law forms a most important feature of the University system, and the numbers of students is very considerable, amounting at present to about 260. In this University the strongest reasons presented themselves for giving to the Faculty of Law a more extended constitution than it possessed when we began our labours; and a consideration of these grounds justified, in our opinion, the course which we adopted of reviving the chair of Public Law, which for some years had been in abeyance, and of imparting a new character to the Professorship of History, which, as a chair in the Faculty of Arts, directed to the purposes of general education, had not been successful in attracting students."

The Commissioners, after referring to the recommendation contained in the Report of the Faculty of Advocates, from which we have already quoted, and a corresponding memorial which the Faculty submitted to Government, to the effect that the scheme of University instruction in law should comprise courses of lectures on International Law, both public and private, and also a course of lectures on Constitutional Law, thus proceed:—

"To these recommendations of the Faculty of Advocates we were naturally disposed to attach the greatest weight; and after a careful consideration of the subject, we resolved to follow the course which our ordinance, No. 23, subsequently embodied, of directing that the professor of the revived chair of Public Law should lecture on International Law, and of assigning to the Professor of History, whom we introduced as a member into the Faculty of Law, the department of Constitutional Law, and History. By the same ordinance, we also required the Professor of Civil Law and the Professor of Scots Law to deliver courses of lectures during the summer, in addition to their usual winter courses.

"By these arrangements, the system of lectures in the Faculty of Law in the University of Edinburgh has been established on such footing as to give students the opportunity of obtaining complete instruction in the various departments of law. We were therefore encouraged in considering the subject of graduation in law, to regard it as no longer impossible to prescribe such a course of study for the degree as should secure to it importance as a mark of high legal education."

After stating that they had called into their counsels both the Faculty of Advocates and other legal bodies in Scotland, the Commissioners proceed :—

"The conclusion at which we arrived, after much consideration, was, that there should be one degree in law conferred after examination; that that degree should be granted only to graduates in arts; *that it should be considered as a mark of academical, and not of professional distinction;* and that it should, therefore, be subject to such conditions as would imply a more extended course of legal study, and the possession of *higher attainments than are ordinarily required for mere professional purposes.* The introduction of a degree of this high character which the enlarged constitution given to the Faculty of Law in Edinburgh now renders possible, appears to us likely to be instrumental in elevating the standard of legal education in the country.

"The general ordinance, No. 75, for the regulation of degrees in law, is based on these views. It provides that the degree of Bachelor of Laws shall be conferred only on graduates in arts; and that the course of legal study for the degree shall extend over three academical years, and include attendance on a distinct course of each of the six departments of Civil Law, Law of Scotland, Conveyancing, Public Law, Constitutional Law, and History, and Medical Jurisprudence. *The examiners*, who are to be six in number, *are directed, in judging of the qualifications of candidates, to have special regard to their acquirements in public law and constitutional history.* Attention to this provision we consider of importance, with a view of securing, as far as possible, that the degree shall not be regarded as a mere test of professional knowledge.

"The University of Edinburgh, in which there is now a professor in each of the six branches above specified, is the only University in which the whole of the course of study can be prosecuted. But each of the Universities of Glasgow and Aberdeen affords the means of completing a part of the necessary course; and a provision of the ordinance enables a student to proceed to a degree in one University, although one of his three years of study may have been spent in another.

"The ordinance provides that the degree of Doctor of Laws shall be conferred, as heretofore, as an honorary degree only. With the usage of the Universities in that respect, we thought that there was no occasion to interfere."

During the very short period that has elapsed since their enactment, the operation of these regulations has, on the whole, been highly satisfactory. Five gentlemen graduated in law, at the end of last winter's Session, and there is every reason to believe that, before many years, the degree of LL.B. will be regarded as a passport to practice, quite indispensable for all the higher professional positions. The enlightened provision in the

Procurator's Act (28 and 29 Vic., c. 85, sec. 5), by which the degree is made equivalent to and adopted as a substitute for all examinations whatever, holds out good hope that it is already taking hold of the profession generally throughout the country. In one respect only has the expediency of the ordinance been questioned. It has been said that the condition that every candidate for the law degree shall present himself in the wedding-garment of a graduate in Arts, operates as a positive prohibition of all but the wealthier members of the profession, and renders it impossible that legal should ever become co-extensive with medical graduation. Absolutely there can be no doubt that the Commissioners were right. It is only by placing such a preliminary barrier before its portals that the sanctity of the Temple of Jurisprudence can be preserved, and the reverence for its ministers maintained. But relatively to the present position of the profession throughout the country, the argument for modification possesses much plausibility. If the question be between a humbler form of graduation, and no graduation at all, there is much to be said for the former alternative, and the following scheme suggests itself as worthy of consideration :—

1st. That two Sessions of attendance in the faculty of Arts, with a corresponding examination, embracing, we shall say, the Classical Languages, Junior Mathematics, Logic and Ethics, together with a full curriculum of Law, should entitle candidates to come up for the degree of LL.B

2. That a higher degree of D.C.L., distinct from the honorary degree of LL.D., which has long been dissevered from the Faculty of Law in everything but in name, should be instituted; and that all Bachelors of Law, *who were also Graduates in Arts*, should be eligible for this degree, after the lapse of five years, without further examination.

Other analogous schemes have been proposed, and we throw out that which for the present occurs to us the most feasible, only for the purpose of showing that if the object of extending graduation to the inferior branches of the legal profession be regarded as desirable, a way to it may be found.

When the University Commissioners began their labours in 1858, the most flagrant deficiencies, though not the only ones in the Law Faculties of our Scottish Universities, were the following courses of lectures—all of which are held essential to such a Faculty in the continental Universities, and several of which, at such Universities as Berlin, and Bonn, and Heidelberg, are represented by several professors.

1st, A course in which the science is mapped out, and its skeleton, so to speak, is presented to the student. This course, which in Germany is called Legal Encyclopædia (juristische Encyclopædie), and which we might perhaps most aptly characterise as the Institutes of Jurisprudence, is usually a preliminary one, serving as an introduction to the study, though occasionally it takes the form of an ultimate résumé, which is presented to the student at the termination of his career. In the former case, in which its utility is most obvious, it corresponds to the old *conspectus*, the function of which, in the Medical Faculty, has been familiar in this country since the days of Dr. Gregory, and is still discharged by the Institutes of Medicine.

2d, The Philosophy of Law, in which the absolute character of the science is vindicated, its relation to ethics is explained, its sources are examined, and, in short, the question how it comes to be law at all, is attempted to be answered. This, of course, is the old Law of Nature, the *first* subject for which our ancestors provided, but the teaching of which had gone into abeyance since the French Revolution.

3d, The Law of Nations, the *Jus inter Gentis*, public and private.

4th, Public Law, or the relations between the citizen and the State—the ancient *Jus Publicum, quod at statum rei Romanæ spectat.* It is this branch of the science which we inaccurately talk of, and inadequately characterise, as Constitutional Law.

5th, Political Economy, or the doctrine of the acquisition and distribution of material wealth, with a view to the promotion of human well-being.

This latter subject, though nominally attached to the chair of Moral Philosophy, and placed in the Faculty of Arts (probably in consequence of the accident of its greatest modern cultivator having been a Professor of Moral Philosophy), has no more, nay, has *less*, relation either to that chair, or to that Faculty, than any other branch of the science of Jurisprudence; and it is in the Faculty of Law that it finds its place in all completely organised Universities. As the old arrangement, however, was left undisturbed by the Commissioners, it has remained outside of the Faculty of Law in Edinburgh, and is taught by the Professor of Moral Philosophy in a separate course of lectures. The other subjects we have mentioned, though not in a perfectly regular or symmetrical manner, have all been admitted into the Faculty of Law, which, as now constituted, covers nearly the whole field of Jurisprudence, and forms, as we have said, the nearest approach to a complete School of Law in this country.

The fourth of the subjects above enumerated, viz., Public Law, belonged, in all reason, to the chair which bore its name. But under the designation of Constitutional Law, this subject, in its historical aspects, at all events, had been assigned to another chair, that, viz., of Constitutional Law and History; and as, apart from its historical aspects it could not be taught at all, it was practically removed from the chair to which it was nominally assigned. The question then came to be, to what extent ought the lectures to be delivered from the resuscitated Public Law chair to embrace the three remaining subjects? By the ordinance (No. 23) of the Commissioners, the only *obligation* imposed on the professor was, that he should "deliver a course of not less than forty lectures on International Law, during the winter session of the University, yearly." But the provision in the General Ordinance (No. 75) "for the regulation of Degrees in Law," that "the examiners, in judging of the qualifications of candidates, should have special regard to their acquirements in Public Law and Constitutional History," seemed to contemplate a wider range of teaching. This conclusion was strengthened by the explanatory clause in which the Commissioners state that "attention to this provision we consider of importance with the view of securing, as far as possible, that the degree shall not be regarded as a mere test of professional knowledge." Now, even public international law is "professional knowledge," though knowledge belonging to the profession of the diplomatist and the statesman, rather than of the municipal lawyer; whilst private international law is professional knowledge, in the stricter and narrower sense, which the Commissioners probably attached to the phrase. In this position of affairs, the determination of the question rested ultimately with the Government; for it depended on the nature of the commission that should be issued, and the full title which should be given to the chair. The whole subject, we have reason to know, was maturely considered at the time by the Lord Advocate, himself one of the Commissioners, and his Lordship's ultimate determination was, that the old name of the chair should be revived, and that the whole of the duties which had belonged to his predecessors should devolve on its new occupant. The commission of the present holder of the chair accordingly constitutes him professor, not of International Law simply, but of "Public Law and the Law of Nature and Nations."

Three of the lacking subjects were now provided for in Edinburgh;—the Professor of Constitutional Law and History was appointed to teach the *Jus publicum*; a sort of *Dominium Eminens* in it, (except as regarded Constitutional History,) being left with the Professor of Public Law; and to the Professor of Public Law were assigned the two subjects of Natural Law, or the Philosophy of Law (what is called General Jurisprudence in England), and the Law of Nations.

But the first of the subjects we have mentioned—the first in the chronological order of study, and not the least in practical importance—was left out in the cold. Nobody was instructed to tell the student, at the outset of his career, what the science was that he was expected to study. What did it include? how was it subdivided? what was the relation of its several branches to each other? in what order ought he to study them? and where was he to look for the best and most reliable information regarding them? These were questions which would naturally present themselves at the very threshold to any intelligent student, and the value which is attached to their being answered to him, not in Germany only (where for the last half century the press has positively teemed with encyclopædias), but in the other learned countries of Europe, the following passage from the preface of M. Pellat's French edition of Falk's Encyclopædia will sufficiently demonstrate:—"In 1838, M. de Salvandy, Minister of Public Instruction, proposed to the Commission, on the higher legal studies, the following amongst other questions:—'Ought we to introduce into our schools those encyclopædic courses which in Italy and in Germany bring together and review the whole science? In that case, ought we to follow the example of the majority of Foreign Universities, and place them at the commencement of the studies of the Faculty of Law; or reserve them for the conclusion, according to the practice of some of the others. In 1840, another minister, M. Cousin, answered the question by creating "a general *Introductory* course to the study of the law;" and he thus expressed himself, in presenting to the king (Louis Philippe) the scheme of the ordinance which established a chair for the teaching of that subject in the Faculty of Paris (*Moniteur*

Universal, 30 Juin. 1840):—"For a long time past all those whose opinions are worth listening to have been calling for a preliminary course of lectures, the object of which should be to enable the younger students to find their place in the labyrinth of Jurisprudence, which should give a general view of all the parts of the science, mark the distinct and special object of each of them, their reciprocal dependence, and the links by which they are so closely bound together—a course which should determine the general method to be followed in the study of the law, with the particular modifications which each branch demands—a course, in fine, which should indicate the more important works which mark the progress of the science. Such a course would elevate the science in the eyes of young persons by the character of unity which it would impress on it, and would exercise a happy influence on the labours of pupils, and on their moral and intellectual development."

How the want has in fact been supplied, we reserve for another number.

ON THE DIVISION OF THE ANN OR ANNAT BETWEEN THE WIDOW AND CHILDREN OF A MINISTER.

There are not a few matters of practice in which much diversity exists in different parts of the country, and as to which there is unfortunately no distinct authoritative rule to reconcile this variance. The division of Ann as between the widow and children of a deceased minister is one of these matters. In some districts the division is made equally between the widow and children; in other parts, the stipend, so far as forming the Ann, is treated in the same way as the outstanding stipend due at the time of the minister's death, and as part of his moveable succession and executry, and as such one-third only is given to the widow, and the remaining two-thirds to the children, or other next of kin.

The provision had its origin in Popish times, when neither widow nor children of ecclesiastics could, *as such*, be recognised in law. No such questions as to division between these parties could, therefore, then exist, and the next of kin could alone be recognised, and would claim and receive amongst them equal shares of the fund. In those times the patronage and preference of the favoured few received the name of *nepotism*, whilst perhaps in point of fact, though not in law, *filiusism* might have been the more appropriate denomination of the protegés of Churchmen.

The earliest Statute on the subject appears to be the Act 1546, passed the third Parliament of Queen Mary, and is as follows:—"At *Monktoun-hall* (?) the aucht day of *September*, the zeir of God, ane thousand five hundreth and fourtie seven zeires. The quhilk day my Lord Governour, with advise and consent of the Prelats, Kirkmen, Earles, Lordes, Barronnes, and all uthers Patrones of benefices, baith spiritual and temporal, understandand that the haill bodie of the realme, is passand forwarde at this time, to resist our aulde enemies of *England*, cumming in this realme to invade the samin: Ordainis, that quhat-sum-ever kirkman that happenis to be slaine in this present armie, hurte to the death, or takis seicknes in the samin, and dies in the said seicknes gangand, remainand, or cummand therefra: That the nearest of the said Kirk-mennis kin, sall have the presentation, provision, and collation of his benefice that time allanerly: And the samin to be disponed to the nearest of his kin, that happenis to be slaine, or decease, in manner foresaid, maist able therefore: And the profites of their benefices, with the fruites speciallie on the grounde, *with the annat thereafter*, to perteine to them and their executoures alsweil Abbotes, Priores, and all uthers Religious-men, as all uthers Kirk-men."

Another Act almost in the same terms, though passed under somewhat different circumstances, is the Act 1571, c. 41, in the reign of James the Sixth, which is in the tesms following:—"Anent Kirkmen that happenis to be slaine in our Soveraine Lordis service, in *defence of his hieness* authorities: Item, Our Soveraine Lorde, with advise of his Regent's Grace, the three Estaites, and haill body of this present Parliament, hes statute and ordained, that in case ony our Soveraine Lordis trew lieges, beneficed men happinnis to be hurt, slayne, or wounded to the death, and thereafter of the saidis hurtes, or woundes to die in our Soveraine Lordis service, and in defence of his Authoritie, at ony time, against the foirfalted and declared Traytours, presently being within the Castel and Burgh of Edinburgh, and uthers, his Majesties open and manifest enemies, resisters and conspiratours against his hienes authoritie, during all the time of the open and manifest resistance thereto, that the *nearest of the said Beneficed mennes kyn*, abel and qualified, sall have the presentation, provision, and collation of his benefice, for that time allanerlie. And the samin to be disponed to the nearest of his kyn, that happenis to be slayne, or decease, in manner foresaid, being alwaies abil and qualified therefore as said is. And the profites of their benefices, with the fruits speciallie on the ground, *with the annat theirafter to perteine to them and their executors*, alsweil Abbottes, Priores, as well uther Kirk-men.".

These singularly-worded statutes recognise the Annat as then existing, and their scope seems to be confined to members of the Church *militant*, who in those days were worthy of the name, and who usually wore mail underneath their cassocks; and so, when striking their breasts in solemn protestation of peaceful aspirations, often occasioned their "*consciences to clatter*" the reverse.

The earliest case on the question is one reported by Durie, p. 88, 9th Decr. 1623, Colonel Henderson's bairns. It is there noted—"Annat of benefices pertaine to the *Executors of the defunct*, and may be evicted for the deceased's beneficed person, his debts, by his creditors, albeit it useth not to be confirmed, nor comes under the defunct's testament."

The next case is also reported by Durie, 19th July 1626, the Earl Marischal against the relict and bairns of the minister of Peterhead—"In that case the Lords found that, if a minister die before Michaelmas and after Whitsunday, the *relict and heirs* are entitled to the *whole* of that year's profits and rents of the benefice; but where he died after Michaelmas, they were entitled not only to the whole of that year's rents, but also the half of the subsequent one." The case of Earl Marischal is fully reported by Durie, Appendix to Morrison, p. 21.

This case was followed by another case, 28th Dec. 1628, the Bairns of the Bishop of Galloway *v.* Couper, Mor. 470, where it was recognised "that the annat pertained to the *relict and bairns*, conform to the ordinance of the Act which provides the funds of the benefice for the year after the late incumbent's decease, *to pertain to his* wife and bairns."

The next case is 16th June 1629, Smeiton *v.* the Relict of the late Minister of St. Bothans, Mor. 461. The contest in this case was between the newly-inducted minister and the widow of the last incumbent, as to what formed the annat; and the Lords found "that the late minister dying in April, before any of the terms came, no part of that year's stipend was due to him for that year, and consequently could not be claimed by *his relict and bairns* by any other right but as *the annat*, by virtue whereof *only* it was found to pertain to *them* and not otherwise." The purport of these decisions is correctly noted on the margin of the last cited case, thus—"The annat extended to a whole year *more* than the defunct had right to *proprio jure*." This indicated that the annat was not executry, but was payable to the relict and bairns and next of kin *in their own rights*.

The next case in the Books is 26 July 1661, Kér *v.* Parishioners of Cardine, Mor. 462. The son of a deceased minister (who died in Novr.) sued the succeeding minister and parishioners for Annat. The Pursuer maintained that the annat, as being *in bonis defuncti*, but indulged by the law to the wife, bairns, and nearest of kin, to the defunct minister, and so originally *their right*, the same needs no confirmation. The Lords found that "the Annat needed no confirmation, but did only extend to half a year more than the defunct had right to *proprio jure*."

The decision in the case of Smeiton was authoritatively repeated July 1662, in Wemyss *v.* Parishioners of Lasswade, Mor. 462, and the Lords found "that a minister dying in January, the following year's stipend is due to *his Executors as Annat*." The same case seems again to appear on page 472 of Morrison.

In the case 19th July 1664, Scrimgeour *v.* Executors of Murray, Mor. 463, it is noted "that it fell into consideration whether the annat would only belong to the wife, there being no children, or half to the wife and half to the nearest of kin. The Lords thought it would divide *equally* betwixt them, though it was not resolved whether it needed to be confirmed, or would be liable to the defunct's debts." The same parties again appear in a different question (Mor. 464.) The widow now pursued the Executors of her husband, and "craved the annat as belonging *wholly* to her, seeing there were no children, and annat being in favour of the wife and children, the nearest of kin could have no part thereof. The Executors answered that the annat was introduced in the time of Popery, when the clergy had no wife nor bairns, and so did still most properly belong to the nearest of kin who would get it if there were neither wife nor bairns. The Lords found the annat to divide betwen the relict and the nearest of kin." This implied an *equal* division between the widow and nearest of kin.

In the case 6th July 1665, Colville *v.* Lord Balmerino, (Mor.

464), the Executors of a minister sued for the stipend of 1663, which had been paid by the Heritors to the successor of the minister in the charge. The minister died in Jany. of that year. The defender pled that "annat is only due to the wife and bairns of the defunct, and this minister had none." The Lords found that the whole year's stipend belonged *to the Executor as nearest of kin.*" This could only have been as annat conform to the decision in Smeiton's case.

As there appears thus early to have been a variance as to the exact *amount* of Ann payable on the decease of a minister, the following statute was passed 23d Aug. 1672, in the reign of Charles the Second. (The statute will be found quoted on page 462 of Morrison's Dictionary.)

"Act for the Ann due to the *Executors* of Bishops and Ministers.

"The Kings Majesty, judging it necessary, for the good of the Church, that such a stated and equal course be taken for clearing and securing the Ann *due to the Executors* of deceast Bishops, beneficed persons, and stipendiary ministers, as may be suitable to the interest of the Executors, and no discouragement or hinderance to the planting of the vacand Benefices; doth, therefore, with advice and consent of His Estates of Parliament, Statute and Ordain that in all cases hereafter, the Ann shall be an half year's rent of the Benefice or Stipend *over and above what is due to the Defunct for his Incumbency*, which is now settled to be thus, viz. —If the Incumbent survive *Whitsunday*, there shall belong to them for their incumbency, the half of that year's Stipend, or Benefice, and for the Ann the other half; and if the Incumbent survive *Michaelmas*, he shall have right to that whole year's rent for his Incumbency; and for his Ann, shall have the half year's rent of the following year. And that the Executors shall have right hereto, without necessity or expenses of a confirmation."

This Act was passed merely to settle the *amount* of the Ann, and not to provide as to its division amongst the parties who might have right thereto. Though stating that it is due *to Executors* it as clearly recognises it as not being *Executory, and as such not requiring confirmation.* The word *Executors* must, therefore, be taken as meaning *next of kin* in the absence of relict and children.

The first case which occurred after passing of the Act 1672 is 16th July 1673, Ker *v.* Parishioners of Morumside, Mor. 471.

The relict pursued for the whole year's stipend, as annat, her husband having died in April. "The defenders alleged no process until the annat were confirmed, because it would belong to the minister's executors, and be subject to his moveable debts. It was answered that the annat being due after the minister's death, was not in *bonis defuncti*, but was granted to his nearest friends *ex gratia*. The Lords found no necessity of confirmation of the annat."

The next case in order of time is 22d Jany. 1679, Spence and Clerk *v.* Craig, Mor. 465. The relict, as executrix of the minister, confirmed the annat, and was sued by the legatees of the minister. The widow pled that "she had the *sole* right to the annat in respect there were no children, and that it was not in *bonis defuncti*, nor due to the defunct for his service, but a privilege indulged by law in favour of his nearest relations, so needs no confirmation, and if he have no bairns *all belongs to his wife*, which excludes his nearest of kin. It was answered that the annat being a favour to the successors of beneficed persons, though it need no confirmation, yet it must belong to the nearest of kin as well as to the wife, which is cleared by the late Act of Parliament 1669 (sic ?) "anent annats," declaring them to belong to executors without confirmation; therefore the executors can only be accountable to the wife for the half where there is no children. The Lords found the answer relevant," thereby sustaining the claim of the executors for one-half of the annat. This decision repeated that given in the case of Scrimgeour, which was before the statute 1672, thereby clearly holding that the statute made no alteration in the law of divisions at least between the wife and the next of kin.

The next case in the order of time is 18th March 1686, Alexander *v.* Cunningham, Mor. 470. A minister having no children assigned the annat to his brother's son. His sister competed as nearest of kin, and alleged it was not the defunct's but, being given in the time of Popery, when churchmen were neither allowed (?) wives nor children, it belonged to the nearest of kin. "The Lords preferred the nearest of kin." Harcarse in reporting the same case states that it was pleaded for the sister "the annat was not in *bonis defuncti*, but designed by way of charity to the relict and nearest of kin." Answered for the assignee, "by the Act 1672 the annat is mentioned as due to the minister and his executors, and so is at his disposal." Replied, "The said Act clears only what is the annat, and not whom it is due to, and by the Act 1647 (?) it is due to the nearest of kin. And though the Act 1672 mentions executors, that is upon supposition that the nearest of kin were executors."

The next case is 7th Feb. 1694, Donaldson *v.* Dr Brown of Dolphinton, Mor. 471, where it was found the annat was a legal gratuity, that could not be burdened with the minister's debts, not being in *bonis defuncti*.

In the case 8th Feb. 1709, Shiels *v.* the Town of St Andrews, it was contended for the defenders that as annat was "a gratuity introduced by law in favour of ministers' relicts and children left commonly poor, it has only place where the stipend is payable out of the teinds, and not in royal burghs, where the ministers are paid out of the common good." The Lords, by a plurality, found all stipendiary ministers included in the Act 1672, whether paid by money or victual, and therefore found annat due to a brother and executor of the late minister of St Andrews.

The same question, as in the case of St. Andrews, arose between the widow of one of the ministers against the magistrates of Edinburgh, and the same decision was there repeated, 9th June 1714, Mor. 467. In the pleadings it was mentioned that "the annat was in use with us before the Reformation, as appears from the 5th Act of the Parliament 1546, but the extent and boundaries of it were never clearly settled till done by the Statute 1672."

The decision in the case 14th July 1747, Macdermit, is the only one which raises some difficulty as to the division between relict and children. It is very shortly reported by Kilkerran, and repeated by Morrison, p. 464, in these terms—"It being controverted between the relict and the children of Mr. John Macdermit, late second minister at Ayr, whether the annat belonged to the children, *per capita*, or if the children were only entitled to the one-half equally amongst them, and the relict to the other half," the Lords found the children were only entitled to the one half.

It is matter of surprise that, notwithstanding the diversity of authority in the institutional writers, and consequently the practice throughout the country, there appears no decision in the books since the case of Macdermit in 1747.

Lord Stair, writing in 1681, after the Acts 1669 and 1672 (of which it is not unlikely he was the framer), lays it down that "the annat *divides* between the relict and nearest of kin if there be no bairns." But he gives no opinion as to the division between bairns and the widow (B. 2, T. 8, S. 34.) Mr. Brodie, in his edition of Stair, makes no note on the text under this head.

Sir George M'Kenzie, in his Institutes, lays it down that the annat is *equally* divided between the relict and children (B. 1, T. 5, S. 16.) Sir George repeats the same opinion in his Observations on the Statutes, p. 150.

Forbes, in his Institutes, in 1722, p. 56, states "that the annat is *equally divided* between the relict and the children."

Bankton, T. 8, S. 204, cites the statute 1672, and declares that, "if the deceased left a wife and children, the annat divides *between her and them by equal portions*, she getting one-half and they the other."

Erskine, in his Institutes, (in 1733, B. 2, T. 10, S. 66), explains the annat "as borrowed from Germany. In several Protestant churches there, as of Pomerania, Frankfort, &c., a year's rent of each parochial benefice was soon after the Reformation by Luther given on the incumbent's death as a gratuity to *his wife and children*, besides what was due to himself for his incumbency, to which they gave the name of *annus gratiæ*. In Saxony, Bavaria, Magdeburg, &c., only six months' stipend was allowed." After tracing the decisions, and noticing the statute 1672, as fixing the *extent* of the right, the learned jurist adds (S. 67)—"Writers differ about the *proportions by which* the ann is to be divided between the incumbent's widow and children. Some affirm that the widow ought to draw no more than an equal share with any one of the children, and some that the one-half of the ann goes to the widow by herself, and the other to the children, among whom it is proportioned *in capita*, which last opinion is supported by a decision July 1747, Children of Macdermit (Dicty. p. 464). But if we set aside that authority, a third opinion may perhaps be more agreeable to the Act 1672, which gives the right to executors, without the least mention either of widow or children; for if it be given to executors, it ought to be governed by the rules of succession in executry, by which one-third of the ann would, like other moveable subjects, go to the widow, where there are both widow and children, and the remaining two-thirds be divided among the children, *per capita*." It is worthy of note that Mr Erskine does not cite the authors before his day who held different opinions on the point, and they are now nowhere to be found. Lord Ivory on this passage writes—"This opinion is contrary to all the authorities, excepting perhaps Stair (B. 2, T. 8, S. 34), where the mode of expression is not free from ambiguity." Lord Ivory cites all the opposing authorities, and seems to think Mr. Erskine, in his Principles, to be of a different opinion. Mr. Erskine, in the earlier work of his Principles, states, "if the annat were to be governed by the rules of succession in executry, the widow, in case of no children, would get one-half; the other would go to the next of kin; and where there are children, she would be entitled to a third, and the other two-thirds would fall equally among the children. And the Court of Session, probably *led by the general practice*, have in this last case divided the ann into two equal parts, of which one goes to the widow, and the other among the children *in capita* (1747, Children of Macdermit.")

It is remarkable how subsequent authors have been led in the direction indicated by Mr Erskine's doubts.

Hutchison, Writer on Ecclesiastical Law (vol. 2., p. 477, 3rd ed.), adopts Erskine's view of the division of annat in all cases as of Executry.

Bell in his Law Dictionary (1838) states that "the rule for dividing the ann between the widow and the children does not seem to be very clearly fixed. But Erskine inclines to adopt the same rule of division which would be followed in regard to executry, that is, to give one-third to the widow and two-thirds to the children *per capita*."

Connel on Tythes (p. 91) states—"The right of Ann, as now understood, was unknown in times of Popery, and seems to have been introduced into Scotland in the reign of James the Sixth, by an ordinance of the Bishops, in consequence of a letter to them from the King." For this, he refers to the case of Earl Marischall as reported by Durie. Mr Connel proceeds to observe "that before the Act 1672, it was debated whether the widow was entitled in a question with the nearest of kin, to the whole or the half of the annat, and by the case of Scrimgeour, she was found "right to a half only." He then cites the Act 1678, and the case of Macdermit, and the opinion of Mr Erskine that this decision is not agreeable to the terms of the Act 1672, because subjects which go to Executors, suffer a separate division when there are a wife and children, and a wife gets only a third of this; and the learned author concludes thus, "the ann never belonged to the minister at all, but is declared by the Act to accrue to his

conceived, and the question raised by Mr Dunbar is, whether in carrying it out we have not gone too far in favour of the accused. The favour for the liberty of the subject, and the presumption of innocence are so great, that there is hardly a conceivable irregularity which has not led to a prisoner's escape —and that not merely when the irregularity has regarded substance, as, for instance, the accused receiving all the information and notices guaranteed by statute, but also as to his receiving them authenticated by the proper party, whether an important official or a mere servant of the Court. Most, however, of these grounds of escape, where substance was not involved, have been swept away by Sir William Rae's Act, 9 Geo. IV., cap. 29, § 6.

Mr Dunbar, however, while acknowledging the great value of that piece of legislation, holds that the course of decisions since its date has continued to be far too favourable to the prisoner, and with a view to removing fatal technical grounds of objection still existing in our ordinary criminal proceedings, he makes the following important suggestions :—

"*First*—No formal objection whatever which could have been stated *in limine* should be allowed at an after stage of the trial.

"*Second*—Where, during the course of a trial, a necessary witness, supposed to be present, is found to be absent, or a witness is found to be intoxicated, or otherwise unable to give evidence, the Court should have power to adjourn or direct a new trial.

"*Third*—Clerical errors in the record should be allowed to be corrected when the error is palpable, and the correction can be made before the conclusion of the proceedings.

"*Fourth*—Where an innocent irregularity in the assise takes place, through no fault of the prosecutor, and by which the prisoner has suffered no prejudice, the verdict and sentence should stand, or a new trial be allowed.

"*Fifth*—If the proof disclose a discrepancy as to time, place, mode, or other essential particular libelled in the indictment, the prisoner should not escape on a verdict of *not guilty*, but the error should forthwith be corrected and the trial completed; or, if the interests of the prisoner require it, a new trial should be allowed.

"*Sixth*—Even in cases where the prisoner has taken the benefit of the Act 1701, any clerical error or omission in the criminal letters should not have the effect of liberating the prisoner, but the error should be rectified or the omission supplied.

"*Seventh*—Where the charge in the indictment is held to be irrelevantly laid, the prisoner, where he has taken the benefit of the Act 1701, should be detained till correct criminal letters are prepared and served.

"In the circumstances sixth and seventh above stated, the prisoner might still, in many cases, be brought to trial within the limited time under the

Act 1701. If any prisoner, whether he has taken the benefit of the Act or not, has suffered lengthened detention in consequence of informality in the libel, this should be taken into consideration in determining the punishment in case of conviction."

An important section of Mr Dunbar's work is devoted to the cases where a power of review—whether on the merits or in respect of want of jurisdiction in the inferior courts—is exercised by the Supreme Courts. Practically, in this class of cases the mischief arises from the powers conferred on justices; they are felt to be a body of judges who require minute guidance, as little as possible is left to their discretion—the statutes are directory in the minutest procedure—schedules are provided according to which the court must walk. If the justices fail to do so, the higher court must. Mr Dunbar's suggestion in this matter, which perhaps calls more pressingly for remedy than the other, is, that the Supreme Court should have power to amend informal sentences by supplying what is defective, deleting what is improper, and putting them into proper form, or remitting to the inferior magistrates to do so.

We have not time to follow Mr Dunbar through his discussion of all these points. He is substantially sound, temperate, and judicious, though we cannot help thinking that his views are somewhat toned by his experience as a prosecutor, and that he is here and there willing to sacrifice something of what is due to the liberty of the subject, to permission of slovenly and careless discharge of duty on the part of those whose part it is to frame indictments and carry through trials.

EXTRADITION OF PRISONERS.

A VERY remarkable case is said to have occurred in Canada under the Extradition Act,—one of which, if the facts at all resemble the allegations, we are likely to hear more. The statements made are these:—About the end of July M. Lamirande, a French subject, was at Montreal, where the Consul-General of France demanded his surrender, under the Extradition Treaty, on a charge of having committed "forgery," by defrauding the branch of the Bank of France at Poictiers, by making false entries. He was arrested on a Governor-General's warrant, obtained by a French detective through the French Consul at Montreal, and on the 22d of August was committed to prison by a police magistrate, who held that a *prima facie* case had been made out against him. Next day notice was served that the prisoner would on the following day, the 24th, apply to the Court of Queen's Bench for a writ of *habeas corpus*, and an order of discharge. On that day, accordingly, the prisoner's counsel appeared before Judge Drummond in support of the petition, and the learned Judge intimated an opinion in favour of the prisoner, and was about to issue the writ, when the counsel for the prosecution asked for an adjournment, in order that he might reply to the arguments brought forward for the prisoner. At first the prisoner's counsel demurred to the adjournment, on the ground that the prisoner might meanwhile be taken beyond the jurisdiction of the Court. Mr. Pommville, the prosecuting counsel, is said to have expressed indignation that so dishonourable an intention should be imputed to his clients, and ultimately the prisoner's counsel agreed to the adjournment. That night the French detective got an order signed by the Deputy-Sheriff, grounded upon an instrument signed by the Governor-General, and the prisoner was hurried into a train and carried beyond the jurisdiction of the Court, before any steps could be taken to effect his rescue. The document on which the Deputy-Sheriff signed the order is alleged to have been a false record, to which the Governor-General's signature had been obtained on false pretences. M. Lamirande may be the greatest villain unhung, but that does not in any degree affect the merits of the question so far as the British Government is concerned. A foreigner who had sought asylum, and the legality of whose extradition was at the moment *sub-judice*, was carried off and deprived of that asylum under the guise of a legal warrant. On the day after Lamirande had been thus kidnapped, Judge Drummond issued the writ of *habeas corpus*; but of course the gaoler was unable to produce the prisoner.

THE

JOURNAL OF JURISPRUDENCE.

JUDGE OR JURY?

UNDER THE EVIDENCE SCOTLAND ACT, 1866.

It is remarkable that one of the most important statutes affecting Scottish judicial precedure since 1815 should have been carried through Parliament at the end of a session, almost unnoticed by the public, and, so far as we are aware, without undergoing any discussion whatever, except that which it received at two meetings of the Faculty of Advocates. It is perhaps equally remarkable that, during the three months which have elapsed since it received the royal assent, there should have been an entire absence of speculation as to its probable influence on the administration of the law. And yet it is an Act which, even if it should fail to increase the sum of litigation in the Court of Session, may double the work of the Lords Ordinary, which will change the aspect of the Outer House by filling it with witnesses from all parts of Scotland every day of the session, and which (say some) virtually abolishes trial by jury in civil causes. We do not say that the Act now under consideration is a circuitous attempt to effect this object; but it will certainly put the Scottish system of jury trial to the test. It will either abolish it, or it will produce reforms of very great magnitude, both in the statutory rules of procedure and in the conduct of causes by professional men. Whatever may be the result in this respect, we are certainly arrived at the beginning of very great changes; and it does not necessarily imply a profound admiration of this statute, if we account it a fortunate thing that a Whig and a Tory Lord Advocate were found to agree in thinking that proof by commission was a bad thing, and that perhaps if a stab could be quietly inflicted on jury trial, no one would after all be very greatly the worse for it.

The rapid working off of the causes in the Debate Rolls of the Outer House under the regulations of the Act of Sederunt of July 15, 1865, was the immediate occasion of the passing of the Act. It may be that the marked change in the Outer House Rolls was to some extent a temporary phenomenon, arising from the operation of the 11th section of the Act of Sederunt, which requires either renunciation of probation or an order for proof at closing the record, itself, by the way, one of the largest reforms effected for many years, and one of which this Act is but the natural consequence. The fact of there being a probability or even a possibility of the Lords Ordinary having time themselves to take the proof in most of the causes depending before them was enough to doom to death that practice of proof by Commission which originated when the Court, sitting as one chamber, could not possibly hear *in presentia*, or by the instrumentality of Lords Ordinary on Oaths and Witnesses, the proof in every case, and which became too deeply rooted to be supplanted by an imperfectly contrived and imperfectly worked system of trial by jury.

It was therefore proposed in the Parliament House, that steps should be taken to substitute the Outer House judges for Commissioners in the taking of evidence in ordinary cases. In consistorial causes that change had been effected five years before, with the most satisfactory result; and the use of shorthand notes had been found to contribute in an unexampled degree both to expedition and certainty in the attainment of justice. Why, it was naturally asked, should the same system tried with such success in the annual forty matrimonial causes, not be "beneficially applicable" to all cases of disputed facts? No one thought of proving the negative, and it was moved at a meeting of Faculty, and unanimously agreed, that the Lord Advocate and Dean of Faculty (Moncreiff) should be asked to introduce a bill on the subject. Its ostensible and declared purpose was to abolish the absurd and much abused system of proof on commission, by substituting for it the method of leading proof before a judge in the manner authorized by the Conjugal Rights Act. How far it has effected this end, and what more it is likely to do, will appear in the course of a brief analysis of its provisions.

In order to understand the bearing of the statute, it is necessary to keep steadily in view the modes in which, until 10th August last, disputed facts could competently be ascertained in the Court of Session. Apart from Consistorial Causes, and the novel methods authorised but not practised under 13 and 14 Vict. c. 36, §§ 48, 50, two manners of inquiry were practically available—Jury Trial and Proof on Commission.

By 6 Geo. IV. c. 120, § 28, (applied to the Court of Session by 1 Wm. IV. c. 69, § 2), the following actions are held as appropriate to be tried by jury, namely:—

Actions for Injury to the Person, whether real or verbal; Injury to Moveables, or Land where the title is not in question; Damages for Breach of Promise, Seduction or Adultery; of Damages for Delinquency or Quasi Delinquency of any kind; against Shipmasters and Owners, Carriers by Land or Water, Innkeepers or Stablers, grounded on the principle of the Edict *Nautæ, Caupones, Stabularii;* of Nuisance; of Reduction on the Head of Furiosity and Idiotcy, Facility and Lesion, or Force and Fear; on Policies of Insurance; on Charter parties and Bills of Lading; for Freight; for Carriage of Goods by Land or Water; for Wages of Masters and Mariners of Ships or Vessels.

In all causes not enumerated above, the 13th and 14th Vict. c. 36, made it competent for the Lord Ordinary, but only with consent of both parties, or after obtaining the leave of the Inner House on a verbal report made on the motion of one party, or for the Inner House when the cause depended there, to appoint the evidence to be taken by commission; and the Court could competently allow proof by commission even in any of such enumerated causes, except where the action was for Libel; for Nuisance; or properly and in substance an Action of Damages.

In all cases in which issues have been adjusted,* it is competent under § 46 of the last cited Act, though it is now unusual in practice, where both parties consent, to try the issues before the Lord Ordinary without a jury, and his findings in fact are final. The result of experience has been, that this mode of arriving at a conclusion is not popular. Thus by 13 and 14 Vict. c. 36, the facilities for jury trial were greatly increased, and on the other hand proof by commission was made competent in many causes appropriated to trial by jury by 6 Geo. IV. c. 120, and the Lords

* Even in enumerated causes, see, *e.g.*, *Balfour* v. *Wordsworth*, 9th July 1854, 16 D. 1028; *Hood* v. *Williamsons*, Feb. 8, 1861, 23 D. 496; where damages were concluded *for*.

Ordinary were empowered in all cases to try issues and special questions of fact without the aid of juries. In short, the general scope of that Act was very much to enlarge the choice of litigants as to the mode of proof. Still it remained, to use the words of Lord Justice Clerk Inglis, "the general rule that cases involving questions of fact should go to a jury, and parties who wish a proof on commission instead of a jury trial, need to show special cause to induce the Court to allow it." *Cameron* v. *Kerr*, July 6, 1861, 23 D. 1257.

The immediate occasion of the introduction of jury trial was the multitude of appeals on questions of fact with which the House of Lords was overwhelmed. But the true cause lay in the inherent defects of the system of proofs by commission,—the want of control over the conduct of the proof by the commissioner, which resulted in intolerable delays, and sometimes in worse abuses, and the necessity imposed on the judge of deciding the facts without having seen one of the witnesses. These evils were, indeed, partially cured by the introduction of jury trial; but it is perhaps one of the strongest arguments that can be urged against that object of English idolatry, at least as it has been administered in Scotland, that with no rival but this wretched system of commissions, it should after fifty years of probation continue to be distrusted and detested by a large class of the people. But though some abatement of the evil was found in restricting the number of causes in which proof before a commissioner was competent, abuses were still frequent, and delay was still the characteristic of Court of Session procedure. It was not surprising, therefore, that when a favourable opportunity occurred, some prominent Scotch lawyers should desire to abolish entirely the evil thing. It was natural, too—whether it was expedient or not on a large view of the question, we do not here inquire—that they should seek to do so by substituting for it not trial by jury, but trial by judge, which has been largely used under the Act 13 and 14 Vict. c. 36, and which with additional improvements has been in operation for five years in matrimonial causes.

Let us see how this has been done by the Statute which has just been passed, 29 and 30 Vict., c. 112. After a preamble, referring to the expense and delay in the administration of justice, produced by the practice of taking proofs by commission, the first section enacts that, "except as hereinafter enacted, it shall not be competent in any cause depending before the Court of Session to grant commission to take proof." The last words, we need hardly observe, save all commissions already granted.* The abolition is as wide and complete as possible, unless, indeed, the exceptions are found to be unreasonably extensive. These are contained in sec. 2. It is there provided that it shall be competent to the Court, or to the Lord Ordinary, to grant commission

1. To take the depositions of havers:

2. "Upon special cause shown, or, with consent of both parties," "to take the evidence in any cause in which commission may, according to the existing law and practice, be granted."

3. To take the evidence of witnesses residing beyond the jurisdiction of the Court, or who are physically unable to attend the Diet of Proof.

4. The existing practice as to granting commission to take the evidence of aged and infirm witnesses to lie *in retentis* before a proof has been allowed, is not to be affected by the Act.

The second head of the exception is not excusable. It reduces the language of the Act to absurdity, although, it may be, there still remains a useful piece of legislation. Let us combine the preamble, and the first clause of section 1, with this second exception "hereinafter enacted," and see how the Act will read.

"Whereas the practice of taking Proofs by Commission in the Court of Session in Scotland is productive of unnecessary expense and of great delay; be it therefore enacted—

"I. It shall not be competent in any cause depending before the Court of Session to grant Commission to take Proof.

"II. Provided always that it shall be competent to the judges of either division of the Court, or to the Lord Ordinary, * * * upon special cause shown, or with consent of both parties, to grant commission to take the evidence in any cause in which commission to take evidence may, according to the existing law and practice, be granted."

In other words, because Proofs by Commission are productive of unnecessary expense and delay, be it enacted that the Court may, if they please, perpetuate this creation of unnecessary expense and delay. Nay, more, it would rather seem that the Lord Ordinary's power of granting Proofs by Commission is absolutely extended and made as large as that of the Inner House. Unless this Act is construed with reference to the 13th and 14th Vic.

* See Donald v. Donald, Nov. 12, 1861, 24 D. 25.

c. 36, as an Act *in pari materia*, and the Court *applicando singula singulis* hold the relative powers of "the judges of either division of the Court," or of "the Lord Ordinary," to be unaltered as regards the cases in which proof may be granted according to the existing law. At all events the Lord Ordinary requires in future neither the consent of parties, nor the leave of the Inner House—but may act either on special cause shown, *or* of consent, not only where he could grant commission formerly, but even where the Inner House has had conferred upon it at least in express words, no such power, namely, in cases of libel, nuisance, and damages—as we shall see when we come to section 4.

The words "special cause" in this second, and also in a subsequent section, may mean very much or very little. The words were thrust into the Act at the last moment, it is reported, on the urgent remonstrances of a committee of the Writers to the Signet; and in yielding to them the Lord Advocate has in a great measure rendered the measure self-contradictory and illusory. The words give a large discretion to the judges, and according as they construe and work the measure will be its success or failure. The discretionary power conferred by the Court under the Act 13 and 14 Vict., to allow proof by commission in certain of the causes enumerated in the 6 Geo. IV. c. 120, has hitherto been exercised very sparingly;* and, even of other cases, a fair proportion has been tried by jury. The policy of previous Acts has been rather to encourage trial by jury, and it cannot be said that the judges of the Court of Session have failed to give jury trial a fair chance of establishing itself in public confidence and favour as against proof by commission. Now that we have an Act encouraging proofs before judges, we do not doubt that they will fairly and wisely use the discretion entrusted to them as between the various manners of taking proof which are now competent. The additional labour imposed on themselves by the new method of trial will certainly have no influence in making the judges in the Outer House more favourable to proofs by commission, and the greater expense and delays which attend proofs before a commissioner, not to mention other disadvantages, will prevent agents and counsel from having recourse to it, except in very special circumstances. Even when parties consent, it does not seem to be imperative, though it is competent, for the Lord Ordinary to grant proof on commission; and an interlocutor of a

* *Watt* v. *Watt*, June 5 1857, 19 D. 787.

Lord Ordinary allowing proof on commission, on special cause being shown, may, it would seem, be reclaimed against. It may no doubt be contended that the construction of the Sheriff Court Act, sec. 15, adopted by the First Division in *M'Douall v. Brown*, July 13, 1865, 3 Macph. 1079, is applicable to the case. The words of the statute construed in that case were precise—"on showing good cause to the satisfaction of the Sheriff why no procedure had taken place." The Act, however, contained a very precise limitation of the privilege of review, and it was held that there was no power of appeal from the Sheriff-Substitute to the Sheriff, or the Court of Session. In the Act before us there is no exclusion of review, and it rather appears that such an interlocutor on special cause shown, whether under this section or under section 4, falls under the 14th section of the Judicature Act, allowing review by the Inner House of any order of the Lord Ordinary for the ascertainment of facts which do not require to be ascertained by jury trial, but excluding appeal except on leave expressly granted, and reserving the effect of any objection to the course of proceeding in any final appeal on the merits.

The third section provides that, "where proof shall be ordered by one of the divisions of the Court, such proof shall be taken before any one of the judges of the said division, or of the Lords Ordinary, to whom the Court may think fit to remit, in one or other of the modes above provided in section first hereof, and his rulings upon the admissibility of evidence, in the course of taking such proof, shall be subject to review by the division of the Court in the discussion of the report of the proof; and when the Court shall alter any finding of the Judge rejecting evidence, they shall, if they think the justice of the case requires it, remit to have such evidence taken." Does this exclude the device, sometimes found useful in practice, of sealing up questions and answers of doubtful competency, to await the decision of the Court? We believe this has been done by the Lords Ordinary in taking consistorial proofs only in two or three instances, in cases which never came before the Divisions, and probably it will be quite competent for Lords Ordinary taking proofs under this Act to follow such a course. We see no other escape from expensive miscarriages if it be found that the Lord Ordinary has gone wrong, as there is no provision for reviewing a Lord Ordinary's ruling in a question of evidence, except under section 1, under a reclaiming note against a final interlocutor disposing of the merits

This third section concludes with a provision that, "where a reference to oath is made and sustained; either by the Lord Ordinary before whom the cause depends, or by one of the Divisions of the Court, the deposition shall be taken in one or other of the modes above provided." There can be no doubt of the propriety of this enactment, so far as it goes; but what is to happen when the deponent cannot be brought up before the Court? Is such a case covered by the exceptions in the second section? That depends upon whether sustaining a reference and granting commission to take the deposition falls under the category of "allowing a proof." If it does, then this addition to section 3, as it stood in the Bill originally introduced, is superfluous; if it does not, then it is defective.

The fourth section is that the propriety of which will probably cause the keenest controversy; because it alone clearly touches the great question as to the merits of jury trial. No doubt there is a reading even of the 1st and 3d sections which would strike at jury trials. The new method of taking proofs is to take effect under the one wherever "proof is allowed," and under the other wherever "proof is ordered," and trial by jury is undoubtedly a mode of taking "proof"—but the whole tenor of the act shows that what is dealt with is "proof" as distinct from jury trial. The preamble shows that proofs on commission were the special subject of the anxiety of the legislature, nor could there be a doubt upon the subject but for the fact that the provisions of section 4 are an excrescence, and are wholly in excess of the purpose set forth in the preamble, having reference to the very cases in which the unnecessary expense and delay of proofs on commission were excluded and in which proof by jury trial alone has hitherto been thought competent. This fourth section enables the Lords Ordinary, "if special cause be shown," or "with consent" of litigants,—who agree in disapproving of jury trial as an instrument for ascertaining the truth, or in disliking the expense which in our present practice appears to be inseparable from it, or who think that verdicts are so liable to be overturned in the present day,* that a final judgment is more

* If Jury Trial was ever well thought of in Scotland, it was about 1830, when the Faculty of Advocates and the Writers to the Signet both reported in its favour. One cause of this appears from the Returns laid before Parliament under the Jury Court Acts, which show that while 500 causes had been tried in the Jury Court from 1815 to 1830, only seven new trials had been granted on the ground that verdicts were contrary to evidence. Contrast with this the present practice as to granting new

likely to be obtained from the House of Lords than from the Court of Session co-operating with juries,—to select the new mode of taking proof even in those cases of libel, nuisance, and damages, which, formerly, no prayers of parties and no expediency in the special circumstances—nothing in short but a compromise—could withdraw from the cognizance of twelve men in a jury box. That the appropriation of the enumerated causes to jury trial was truly a monopoly in favour of that mode of trial, except so far as relaxed by the 49th Section of the Court of Session Act, was the understanding equally of the bench and the bar. It was so laid down in Livingstone *v.* Matthew (Feb. 7, 1852, 14 D. 456), soon after the passing of the Court of Session Act.

Even in December last (Magistrates of Rothesay *v.* M'Kechnie, Dec. 14, 1865 ; 4 Macph. 214), we find the Second Division engaged in a deliberation which implied that in the Outer House none of the actions appropriated to trial by jury, by 6 Geo. IV. c. 120, could, even of consent, be sent to proof on commission ; but we have since been instructed by the Lord Chancellor, with the concurrence of Lords Cranworth and Westbury, in the case of Bickett *v.* Morris (July 13th 1866), as follows :—" It appears to me that this is one of the actions appropriate to the Jury Court under the 28th Section of the Scotch Judicature Act. . . . The cause ought, therefore, in regular course, to have been remitted to the Jury Court, and the Lord Ordinary had no authority to order the proofs to be taken by commission. But it was quite competent to the parties to agree that the proof should be taken by commission instead of a jury" If, as we suppose we are bound to do, we must accept this subversion of our preconceived ideas as furnishing for the first time to Scotland since 1825 the true reading of the statutes relating to jury trial, then, as regards the competency of trying any of the excepted causes " of consent " by a proof instead of a jury, Section 4 makes no change ; but it points to the Lord Ordinary, instead of a commissioner, as the person to take it, and allows jury trial to be dispensed with, not only " of consent," but also " if special cause be shown ;" and it seems to remove a doubt indicated by the

trials. We lately commented on a case in which a third trial was allowed, two previous verdicts in favour of the pursuer having been set aside as contrary to evidence. And it is notorious that in almost every trial in right of way cases, such as Jenkins *v.* Robertson and Jenkins *v.* Murray (the Elgin and the Bannockburn cases), the jury disregard the law laid down, and the verdict is, as a matter of course, overturned by the Court.

House of Lords in Bickett *v.* Morris, whether if jury trial be dispensed with "of consent," the judgment of the Lord Ordinary be subject to review. Such a course will no longer be a proceeding by the Lord Ordinary "without authority," and the power of reclaiming to the Inner House and of appealing to the House of Lords not being taken away, we must presume that it subsists. Why the language of Section 3, empowering the Inner House to order proofs, and to order them to be taken by one of the Inner House judges, was not repeated in Section 4, it is difficult to perceive.

However this may be, parties and the Lord Ordinary have now, subject to correction by the Inner House, power to abolish civil trials by jury.

We do not mean to say that we are in the least apprehensive of any attempt to reach such a result. But jury trial will be put to the test in a way in which it never was tested before. It will no longer be compared with the most dilatory, expensive, and unsatisfactory mode of proof ever devised. For the future, as we said before, trial by jury will have to compete with trial by judge, under the most advantageous conditions; cheapness and expedition will be immensely in favour of the latter; and will, we suspect, greatly outweigh in the estimation of the public and the profession, the thoroughness of investigation, which is, perhaps, the most unquestionable merit still belonging to jury trial. Cheapness, expedition, and certainty, must be restored to this latter system, before it can attain to the same popularity in Scotland which it is alleged to possess in England.

We need say little as to the mode of taking proof introduced by this statute. Section 1st is in its latter clauses nearly a transcript of the 13th section of the Act 24 & 25 Vict. c. 86 (The Conjugal Rights Act). The differences are :—1. It authorizes the diet of proof to be fixed in the discretion of the Lord Ordinary, either during session or in vacation. 2. The Lord Ordinary may dictate to his clerk or shorthand writer, instead of noting with his own hand, the documents adduced. 3. It would seem from the silence of the Act, that a note of evidence tendered and rejected, or objected to and admitted, made by the clerk or shorthand writer will be sufficient for the purposes of review, whereas the Conjugal Rights Act requires such note to be made by the Lord Ordinary himself. 4. There is more apparent precision in the new Act as to the grounds on which a proof may be adjourned.

It is said, "The proof shall be taken continuously in like manner as at jury trials in civil causes before the Court of Session in Scotland, but with power to the Lord Ordinary to adjourn the proof upon such grounds as causes set down for jury trial may according to the existing law and practice be adjourned or postponed, or on such other special grounds as to him shall appear sufficient, and under such conditions, if any, as he shall think proper." The words following "adjourned or postponed," were added, as was mentioned in the August number of the *Journal*, while the bill was passing through Parliament. The discretion of the Court in refusing or granting postponements of jury trial does not appear to be assisted by many positive rules; and cannot, we should suppose, be either extended or limited by the words, "or on such other special grounds," &c.

It was perhaps superfluous, though it may be justified on the ground of providing against possible emergencies, and of deviating as little as possible from the model suggested, to authorize in section 1 the use of the three methods of taking proof allowed by the Conjugal Rights Act. With the exception of two or three cases before Lord Mackenzie soon after the passing of that Act, every consistorial proof has been taken with the aid of the short-hand writer; and we believe that no one anticipates that any of the other courses now made competent will be adopted in time to come either in consistorial or ordinary proofs. If they are still to be competent, it would have been well, in the two manners of writing down the evidence which are not now used in practice, to dispense with the necessity of reading it over to the witness, and having it subscribed by him. Why should this be done any more than at a jury trial?

Section 5 empowers the Court of Session to pass Acts of Sederunt for carrying into execution the purposes of the Act, and it is to be hoped that such an Act will soon be issued. It will be desirable that expense should be saved, delay prevented, and efficiency secured by a strict interpretation of the concluding portion of the first section of the Act relative to adjournments. The grounds of adjournment may probably be specified,—we should hope with more precision (as well as in better English) than in the Jury Court Act of Sederunt of 1841. The laxity of that provision in regard to trials by jury has been prevented from working much mischief by the wisdom of the Court; but what works well enough in the Inner House may have very different results where the same discretion is entrusted to a number of single Judges. A great variety of practice exists under the corresponding clause of the Conjugal Rights Act, which has been interpreted at some bars with considerable laxity, and also in trials before the Lord Ordinary, under the 13th and 14th Victoria, c. 36. Thus, in Hood *v.* Williamson, we find the Lord Justice-Clerk remarking, "I see the trial began on 26th January, and did not conclude till 4th February—that is nine days. One does not suppose that the trial was going on all that time; but there were three days on which the trial was going on, and these were not three continuous days, which was a clear violation of the Act of Parliament." To provide against such delays is absolutely necessary, in order to follow up the admirable and stringent Act of Sederunt of last year. It is important that agents both in town and in the country with whom the preparations for the trial rest, should know that their evidence must be forthcoming at once, and that there will be no room, as in proofs on commission, for bringing up witnesses in detachments, as may be convenient for the witnesses, or as the progress of the proof seems to require additional evidence on special points. The professional man who has a proof to lead must now, as in a jury trial, take a large general view of his whole case, founded on reliable precognitions, must make up his mind at the beginning what witnesses he will adduce, and have them all in the Outer House on the day fixed. One provision an Act of Sederunt might well contain; namely, that where the proof is allowed in the Outer House, counsel shall speak on the evidence as soon as both parties have closed their proof. Half the benefit of the Act will be lost if the freshness of the impression produced by seeing and hearing the witnesses is allowed to wear away from the minds both of counsel and Judge. Besides, this continuity of procedure would save much expense in additional fees to counsel, and (where no reclaiming note is lodged), in copies of the evidence. It would also promote efficiency, by necessitating closer attendance by senior counsel. If the speeches are heard at a different diet, senior counsel will speak from the printed proof instead of their own notes, and will rarely attend at the leading of evidence, though of course they will pocket a fee all the same.

Such an Act should lay down a rule either forbidding, or providing absolutely, in Outer House cases, for taking and sealing up the evidence of which the competency is disputed, under suitable conditions as to expenses.

It would further be very desirable to require the Lords Ordinary and the Court itself, in every judgment, to separate the facts from the law, as is done at present, under § 40 of the Judicature Act, in interlocutors of the Court on proofs taken in inferior Courts. Of course, one important reason for such separation does not exist in this case, for this Act does not enact that the judgment of the Inner House shall be final on matters of fact. But it is always well that such separation should be made. The Court of review must always exercise a certain reserve in altering the findings in fact of a judge who has himself taken the evidence and seen the witnesses; and in itself the practice conduces to perspicuity. Besides, it would greatly narrow the area of discussion in the Inner House on reclaiming notes, and in the House of Lords on appeals, if the particular findings in fact objected to could be pointed out.

We do not say that without such an Act of Sederunt this Act cannot have a fair trial, but certainly, having regard to the wide discretion committed to Lords Ordinary, to our experience of the loose hand with which they held the reins of procedure till the recent Act of Sederunt was passed, and to the excellent working of that Act, we are entitled to presume that such an Act of Sederunt would greatly strengthen the hands of the Lords Ordinary in carrying out this new Act. Its structure, our readers will gather, we do not much admire. It is one of those statutes which demonstrate the necessity of there being a department charged with the preparation and with the revision, as altered in Parliament, of all bills before they finally pass into law. Still we look upon the Act as a great boon. No mode of ascertaining facts is arbitrarily imposed upon the country—it will be left simply to the Court and to parties, with the aid of experience, to discover the best mode. The presumption continues to be in favour of trial by jury. Where issues are settled in any case the trial may proceed of consent before the Lord Ordinary without a jury. Where issues are not adjusted, the presumption will be in favour of trial before the Lord Ordinary or an Inner House judge on the record, to which parties may ask leave to have recourse to wherever they agree in preferring it to jury trial, and which the Lord Ordinary or the Court may impose upon them where they do not consent. Least favoured of all the methods comes proof on commission, which parties may consent to; but as to which the Court will probably exercise its veto except in very special cases. In future there is no case of disputed facts which may not be tried by jury,* and on the other hand there is none that must be so tried—that may not be tried by a Lord Ordinary; and again, wherever proof on commission is now competent it will still be competent. The consent of parties figures largely through the Act, but is nowhere made to control the discretion of the judge to whom is left the final determination of the mode of investigation.

INFANTICIDE.

It was hardly to be expected that so tempting an opportunity as the question of infanticide should have been avoided by the social reformers of Manchester. But it was not unreasonable, in a subject pregnant with such important interests to the prosperity, and almost the life of the community, to look for something more than the morbid sentimentalism by which the discussion was disfigured, and in which it ended. And all such discussions must prove similarly resultless so long as the question is dealt with, or at least is mainly dealt with, in its social and not its legal bearings. *It has* a very important social aspect, and it is just from that quarter that the most danger is to be apprehended, because, as such, it deals with elements in the consideration and treatment of which, experience has shown that men are more apt to be guided by feeling than by the dictates of sound reason and sober sense. It is quite true that until the question has been considered socially, it cannot be held to be placed upon a permanent or satisfactory footing. But what possible object can be supposed to be attained by such rhapsodies as those in which most of the speakers indulged at the Manchester Congress? Dr Mary Walker, of New York, complacently assuming the superior morals of her own countrymen and countrywomen, suggests that the evil is to be repressed by familiarising the members of her sex with the shortcomings of their wayward and erring sisters. It is difficult to find, or at

* We must except under the Lunacy Acts Amendment Act (29 and 30 Vict. c. 51 § 24) issues in any action at law against any medical person in respect of any certificate granted by him under the Lunacy Acts, which must in future be tried by the Lord Ordinary without a Jury.

least to state, an answer to such views, when that does not commend itself to one's own proper feeling and good sense. No proverb is more true, or more frequently verified, than the saying that "familiarity breeds contempt;" and if ever the women of England, or of any country, come to regard the crime of infanticide, and those by whom it is directly perpetrated, with any other feelings than the uncompromising indignation and aversion with which they are now visited, it is impossible that there will be any other result than an increase of the evils complained of. This is no preaching, nor approving of the "Stand back, I am holier than thou" doctrine. When facts assume the startling proportions which statistics have recently disclosed as to the sacrifice of infant life, it is no time to dally with considerations that have their origin at best in mere sentiment. Another speaker, the Rev. Mr Solly, proposed that every act of criminality should of itself be held to constitute marriage, and that the parties, if previously married, both, or either of them, should be liable in a prosecution for bigamy. This ingenious theory we are quite willing to leave to the indignant retort of Mr Montague Chambers, who pointed out that no scheme could be more fruitful of all the evils which it is the object of the crusade against infanticide to express. Even Dr Lankester, competent as he is to pronounce an opinion on the question, is not above the charge of having lost sight of its practical bearings, in the contemplation of its social, or rather its moral relations. It is quite right that society should hold and express a very strong opinion as to the guilt of a seducer. It is also true that the power of society in this respect is greater, in far more directions, and in a higher degree, than it has ever yet been exercised. But these are quite obvious truths, which stand in no need of perpetual inculcation. And good as is the intention of those who are continually harping on this side of the question, it is undoubted that more evil is produced by the agitation than would result from at least comparative silence; and this for two reasons, because, in the first place, men, in these matters, however much they may be guided, will not be ruled, and secondly, because the remedy proposed is utterly inadequate to cope with the evil to which it is applied. When the conclusion has been reached that infanticide is a crime, which society has a strong interest as well as a clear duty to repress, we are very far indeed from the heart, and indeed but little beyond the confines of the question. It is only when we have considered and clearly ascertained the attitude of the law and of its administration, that conditions will be found possible for the settlement, or even the elucidation of the subject.

We purposely include the administration of the law, for it will form at least a part of the object of our remarks to show that much of the evil complained of is a direct result of defective administration. The law of England is in all substantial respects the same as that of Scotland. Infanticide, according to law, is the unlawfully taking away of the life of a person, and it is a result which seems to follow logically from this definition that the law requires the complete separation of the child from the mother as a necessary condition of the possibility of the crime. In this rigour of the law many are prepared to see all the difficulties of the question. And it is impossible to deny that the law's position is anomalous. For it is a strict deduction from it, which is confirmed by daily practice, that whatever injuries may be inflicted on the child in the progress of birth, these are not cognizable by the law until there is complete birth, and thereby a legal person. That there should be any danger of such wickedness passing unpunished by reason of the tolerance of a legal fiction, is a thing of course to be regretted, and yet it is difficult to see how the result can be avoided. The tenderness of infant life, and the difficulties that occur naturally in attempts at its preservation, make it necessary that there be a law which shall exclude the possibility of mistaking every case of natural for artificial violence. And the theory of the law, which requires the complete separation of the two *personæ*, is eminently a step in this direction. It requires the jury to be satisfied that the child has had a separate existence of its own before violence was done to it, as an indispensable condition of the perpetration of it murder. At the same time, it may be doubted whether in this case the law does not err both by reason of the rigour of its principle and the rigour of its administration. It is so easy to simulate natural violence, that it is often difficult to say—and the strictness with which medical evidence is interpreted in courts of law aggravates the difficulty—when death has been caused by the violence incidental to delivery, or by artificial application. But although a difficult question, it is not by any means one on which it is impossible to have a clear and distinct opinion; and any person who is familiar with this department of criminal law must have noticed the impatience with which medical witnesses regard the scepticism which is so commonly imported into their vocation. There is not a more frequent spectacle, none, in our opinion, is more derogatory to the dignity and usefulness of the law, than the flimsy grounds on which many a flagrant case of infanticide goes unpunished—we regret to say too often—through want of firmness in the direction from the bench. The medical witnesses of the Crown—and they are for the most part the most approved and competent in the district—have sworn in a case to their unhesitating conviction that death has been caused by artificial violence, and that, that being absent, the child would have been born into the world in its ordinary and healthy state. How often is it seen that because they are unable to affirm the question put with so much confidence now-a-days by the merest tyro in defence, "Will you swear that the injuries, which in your opinion were the cause of death, were produced after complete birth, and not during its progress?" the jury are told by the presiding judge that unless every possibility of natural death is excluded, they cannot proceed to so solemn a conclusion as finding a panel guilty of infanticide. No doubt this statement is accompanied by the stereotyped precaution, that nothing is to receive effect but doubts that rest upon reasonable grounds; but this is dwelt upon with such unnecessary elaboration, that the vacillation of the Court is communicated to the jury, with a result that is a matter of universal observation and regret at every Circuit Court. The difficulty in the way, in our opinion—or at least a great part of it—is, that a habit of exaggeration has been acquired by all concerned as to the danger which every case presents of confounding violence with the action of nature. No doubt the crime is committed generally with the utmost secrecy, and there is the additional disturbing element that is absent from other forms of crime, that there is naturally a simulation of symptoms that are referable to very different causes. But do we not trust in other matters, even when the consequences are more appalling than any that follow on a conviction for child-murder, to the action of our honest, ordinary convictions? Is there any greater or more fearful working in the dark than to ascertain the guilt of a person charged with murder when the evidence relied upon is purely of a circumstantial order? Yet every day there are convictions upon such evidence, and they are known to be entirely satisfactory. Why, in child murder, may not the jury be trusted to act upon their common sense convictions? There is no case in which the possibility of error can be excluded. And there juries have the advantage which is often wanting in other cases, of being able to ground their own conviction on that of others, which is doubtful in its expression only by reason of a false fastidiousness, and is the conviction of those who are the most competent to pronounce an opinion on the subject. We are bold to say that many of the unfortunate results which are so much deplored, and which pave the way for so many others, arise directly out of this bugbear of complete birth that is so often held up before the jury. Let the law be—proceeding on logical grounds we cannot suggest a better—that the jury must be satisfied that there has been a complete living separation of the two persons. Surely that is a large enough concession to the rigour of legal principle. Why is this indispensable fact not to be ascertained in precisely the same way that other facts are? by trusting to the conviction of the jury formed upon the whole evidence? We do not deny that in theory the law acknowledges it must be so ascertained, but, practically, we say it introduces a rule so strict and unbending in its application as to make it impossible to arrive at any judgment at all. And it is thus that it appears that much of the evil complained of is to be ascribed to bad administration. Let the measure of evidence required to sanction a conviction for child murder be as strict as it may be—the prevailing notion is that it is fully strict already—but do not impose upon the evidence by which it is to be established, conditions under which, evidence is in no other case, cannot in truth be properly apprehended. Practically, this is done by the manner in which the law is stated to the jury.

We have set before us the endeavour to show that the law is defective both in the strictness of its principle and the rigour of its administration. The strictness of principle consists in requiring the jury to find as an antecedent fact preliminary to the consideration of the subsequent evidence that there has been separation of the child from the person of the mother. We can see no reason why there should be such disintegration of the various parts of the evidence. It is quite true that to establish the person of the child is naturally the first step in the inquiry. But, by taking the import of one part of the evidence apart from the import of the whole of it, there is an obvious danger of its being judged by different, or at least unequal, standards, and we can admit no other criterion but what conveys to the jury an unhesitating conviction or fails to satisfy them. Over and above the difficulty that is caused by the direction of the bench, by the concentration of the mind upon one particular fact, instead of relying upon the inference deducible from the evidence as a whole, we think, an additional difficulty is introduced into practice by the habit which has been insensibly acquired of applying to infanticide a stricter method of construing the evidence than obtains in other forms of crime. We believe that this is in great part induced by the anxiety that is born of its increasing prevalence and of the doubts that are so largely entertained as to its real cause, and the best measures that can be proposed for its abatement. But we cannot admit that this fastidiousness is to be commended. The responsibility lies with the jury to say whether or not they are satisfied of the guilt of the prisoner, and it appears to us that the difficulties incidental to the investigation are so obvious, so apt to divert the minds of men into the channel in which it is complained they are so often found to run—that no deterring influence should be laid in the way of a fair and reasonable conclusion.

W. A. B.

LAW STUDIES.

No. V.—Conclusion.

Were *we* then still to forego these advantages, and was such a subject to continue to be ignored by a Faculty of Law now professing to embrace the whole science, and to grant a degree which, it was hoped, might in time take rank beside those of the Continental Schools of Jurisprudence? Was the student still to be permitted to wander into the science at his own sweet will, to spend half his time in discovering how he ought to have spent it, and in finding out, perhaps very imperfectly even at last, what without difficulty could have been told him at first by any second year's student at a German University? No one was commissioned, or even authorised, to teach it in a separate course; and to separate courses, involving additional demands both on the time and the means of students, there were obvious and valid objections. The only remedy seemed to be that it should be embraced in one of the other courses; and as it lay nearer to the philosophy of law than to any of the other authorised subjects of teaching, the most feasible provisional arrangement appeared to be that it should be dealt with by the Professor of Public Law in the portion of his course which was to be devoted to the Law of Nature. The method which has been adopted has been :—

1. To explain in general the relation which subsists between Natural Law, viewed as an aggregate of the principles of the Science of Jurisprudence as a whole and positive law; and in particular between Natural Law and International Law; and to obviate some difficulties which arise from the different senses in which the terms *jus naturale* and *jus gentium* are used by the Roman writers and by ourselves.

2. To enquire into the sources of Natural Law, in the double sense of the fountain from which it derives its authority, and the means by which we become acquainted with the import of its teaching.

3. To investigate the Rule of Life, first in its general aspect, and then in its special manifestations.

4. Having examined the ultimate sources and ultimate objects of the science, to trace its *proximate sources*, still considered as a whole, but no longer apart from its concrete manifestations.

5. Under the head of the proximate *objects* of the science, the various branches of Positive Law are enumerated. One of these only, viz., international, is discussed in detail, first in its public, and then in its private relations, but the territories covered by the others are marked out. By this means, a survey of the whole field of Positive Law is ultimately presented to the student, not indeed a developed system of Natural Law, in the sense in which Natural Law was attempted to be worked out by the jurists of last century, and in which some modern writers again profess to deal with it, but very much in the sense which we have mentioned, of an Encyclopædia or Complete Scientific Conspectus.

The latter portion of the course, though, as we have said, of a strictly professional character, deals with a branch of professional study which possesses many claims on the interest of the student of general jurisprudence, whilst the first part supplies him with what has been very well described as the major-premise of his syllogism. Of the necessity of an acquaintance, with these branches, to any one who aspires to the character of an educated lawyer in the higher sense, no one whose opinion is of any value is likely to doubt.

The utility to a municipal lawyer of anything beyond a very general acquaintance with Public International Law is not so immediate. But it must be borne in mind:—

1. Even in Scotland, where no Prize Courts exist, very recent experience reminds us that municipal lawyers may be called on to advise, and to practice, in cases which involve an acquaintance with Public International Law.

2. The municipal lawyer is a citizen, and frequently becomes a legislator, and in both capacities is frequently called upon to deal with subjects which involve a knowledge of this branch of jurisprudence.

3. The various branches of the diplomatic service, taken in conjunction with the consular service, open to the educated youth of this country a wider field of honourable and lucrative employment than almost any other.

As the Faculty of Advocates in 1856 lost no time in giving effect to the enlightened views of the Committee, and required of intrants evidence of the most complete legal training which the Scottish Universities then afforded, so now that they have seen in operation the further development of the Law Faculty of the University, obtained, in answer to their repeated demands, through the aid of the University Commissioners, they have resolved to require of all candidates for admission to their body that they shall have attended in Edinburgh, or elsewhere, a series of lectures embracing as wide a range as that now furnished by the Law Faculty of the University of Edinburgh. The necessary changes in their regulations, pursuant on this resolution, have not yet been made public. The existing regulations, are as follows :—

1. Every Intrant shall be deemed duly qualified in general scholarship if he produce evidence that he has obtained—

(1.) A degree in Arts from any British University.

(2.) Such degree of a Foreign University as shall, in the opinion of the Dean and his Council, be evidence of the same amount of scholarship as that afforded by the degree of Master of Arts in a Scottish University.

(3) In the event of the Intrant not having graduated as above he shall undergo an examination on the following subjects :—

1. Latin. 2. Greek, or (in the Intrant's option) any two of the following languages—viz., French, German, Italian, Spanish.

3. Ethical and Metaphysical Philosophy.

4. Logic, or (in the Intrant's option) Mathematics.

On the expiry of a year, Intrants qualified as above may proceed to their examinations in Law, provided (1) that, during the year before such examination, he shall not have engaged (except with the sanction of the Dean and his Council) in any trade, business, or profession, either on his own account, or as assistant to, or in the employment of another; and (2) that he shall have been a pupil for at least one Session in a class of Civil Law; and classes of Scots Law, Conveyancing, and also Medical Jurisprudence (and, it may be presumed), Public Law, and Constitutional Law.

As regarded the so-called Public Examinations, no change has been, or is likely to be made on the old regulations; and the time-honoured usages of the Latin Thesis, the public disputation, and the final admission by ballot are still retained. As links between the present and the past, these are not useless, and we rejoice at their retention; but as substantial tests of qualification, or even of acceptability to the brotherhood, they are of no value.

No one, however, who glances at the above statement will doubt that the private examinations now furnish very ample guarantees both for the literary and professional qualifications of Intrants, and this conviction will be strengthened by contrasting them with the requirements for the English Bar, as narrated in our previous article. J. L.

THE MONTH.

Death of Mr Ivory.—We regret to have to intimate the death of Mr James Ivory, so long known to the public as Lord Ivory, which occurred during the last month, at his residence, in Edinburgh. He was born in 1792, at Dundee, and received his early education under Mr Duncan, afterwards Professor of Mathematics at St Andrews. After passing through his curriculum at the University of Edinburgh, Lord Ivory was called to the bar in 1816. He was appointed an Advocate-Depute in 1830; in 1832 he was appointed Sheriff of Caithness, and in the following year he was transferred to the Sheriffdom of Bute. In 1839 he became Solicitor-General, and soon after was raised to the Bench of the Court of Session, on the retirement of Lord Glenlee. In 1849 Lord Ivory was appointed a Justiciary judge, which office he filled till the spring of 1862. In the autumn of that year, in consequence of impaired health, he resigned the whole of his judicial duties, and has since lived in almost entire seclusion. He took a considerable share in party politics, and more especially his name was associated with the subject of Burgh Reform. He was one, and nearly the last, of those Whigs who derived manifest pleasure in the sunny evening of long official lives in recalling the chill of the cold shade of opposition, but to whom it never occurred that possibly to men of different political views, the sacrifices for party and principle which resulted in a sheriffdom after sixteen, and the bench after twenty-three years at the bar, might not seem very severe. Although enjoying a considerable practice at the bar, Lord Ivory's defects as a speaker prevented his attaining the position of an eminent pleader. As a judge he never allowed fair-play to his clear and vigorous intellect. With a great knowledge of law—both of principle and of decision—his first impressions of a case were generally sound, but in his anxiety to be fully satisfied in his own mind, he acquired so much of the habit of doubting as materially to impair his usefulness while sitting alone in the Outer House. When he took his seat in the Inner House—in the First Division—the necessity of keeping pace with his brethren materially diminished the evil effects of this peculiarity, although no judge in modern times has so frequently sheltered himself under the old form of *non liquet* even in cases in which he expressed views of much originality and value. But in this position another besetting sin developed itself. In his youth he had made Form the subject of study the most minute and the most scientific, and in his old age his strong hold of Form became his weak point. In that large branch of Inner House business which formerly consisted in the administration of entailed and other estates, no petition was ever in the roll without the counsel, who was to support it, going up to the bar wondering what technical objection Lord Ivory had discovered, for certain he was that his Lordship had some difficulty to state. Had he confined his objections to statutory procedure, where so often form is truly substance, he would have rendered great service. But in no case could he resist a technical point, and even in ordinary civil causes, he would—"as an old formalist"—start off upon some technical point where others had been dealing with the merits. But here, too, he would often hit a blot on which the whole case really depended. Thus, had his view been taken in the M'Millan cause, the last judgment would have been the first, and the cause, in the shape in which it was brought, would have terminated two years earlier than it did. Though we cannot shut our eyes to these peculiarities, they were but peculiarities, and left us notwithstanding a learned, able, and valuable Judge, many of whose decisions are full of instruction, and will be often quoted long after these minor defects have been forgotten. The fact that a judgment had been pronounced and interlocutor signed, did not in the least exhaust his interest in a cause, and months afterwards we have known of his re-writing, and re-casting, and re-touching the language of his judgment, still doubting whether the legal principles involved were expressed with sufficient accuracy. He was a warm-hearted genial man, a sound lawyer, and an honourable upright Judge.

Legal Appointments—The Sheriff-substitute of Glasgow.—We regret to learn that Sheriff Smith has, owing to continued indisposition, felt it necessary to withdraw from the duties of the office he has so long and so acceptably filled.

Sir Archibald Alison has conferred the vacant appointment on a man long "in his eye"—Mr Galbraith, for some time a law lecturer in the Andersonian Institution in Glasgow. In Mr Galbraith, Sir Archibald Alison has found an intelligent and accomplished Substitute, who will, we trust, now that he is in the eye of the public, bring an energy to the discharge of his important and laborious duties which will justify all that has been somewhat indiscreetly said by his patron in his behalf.

Sheriff-substitute of Dundee.—We regret also to learn that Sheriff Ogilvie of Dundee has been obliged to apply for temporary leave of absence on the score of bad health. Mr Robert Berry, advocate, has been appointed to act in his place.

Business in the Court of Session.—After a long vacation, more than ordinarily free of legal incident, the Court will resume its extended, on the 1st of November, and its ordinary, sittings on the 12th of that month. We are glad to say there is a prospect of increasing business in the Court. The calling lists on the second Box-day contained 151 cases, being 15 more than for the corresponding period last year. From the first number of the Rolls of the Court of Session, 1866-67, it appears that there are 51 causes in the Debate Rolls of the Lord Ordinary. The First Division Rolls contain 11 summary causes, put out in the Summary Roll of Tuesday, Nov. 13, and following days, and 24 summary causes not ready for hearing, or in which parties are not moving. Of ordinary actions, there are 60 in the Printed Roll of this Division; 3 cases at *avizandum*, and 19 causes not ready for hearing, or in which parties are not moving. The Second Division has 1 cause in the Summary Roll; 22 summary causes not ready for hearing, in which orders are current or parties not moving. We understand that there is the prospect of a considerable amount of work for the Registration Appeal Court, there being an unusually large number of appeals.

THE

JOURNAL OF JURISPRUDENCE.

CRIMINAL RESPONSIBILITY OF DIRECTORS OF PUBLIC COMPANIES.

Recent events, both in England and Scotland, have drawn public attention to the question whether Directors of Railway, Banking, and other public companies, may be made to answer in the Criminal Courts for mal-practices in their official capacity. In considering this question in the following paper, it must be distinctly understood that our only purpose is to deal with principles and not with persons; and if, in illustrating any point, we should happen to put specific cases which may be thought to bear an analogy, more or less close, to those reported in actual life, it is our most anxious desire to avoid expressing any opinion as to the truth of the charges which have been made against any individuals. It is for the constituents of the accused, and for the public authorities alone to deal with such matters. Our province is quite different.

The director of a public company is essentially a trustee, and it is from a consideration of his fiduciary character and duties that his responsibilities, alike to his constituents and to the general body of the public, can be best appreciated. At the same time, the trusteeship of a director has not a few peculiarities of its own, and these tend in no small degree to embarrass the question of his criminal, as they have always done of his civil, responsibility. It is a comparatively simple thing to define the duties of a private trustee, and, by consequence, to state his responsibilities and the redress, civil and criminal, which may be obtained if he neglects them. It is far more difficult to attempt precise definition either of the duties or the liabilities of those who have the conduct of great public undertakings. We are far from saying that *in foro conscientiæ* that which is wrong in a private trustee can be right in a director of a public company. But undoubtedly public opinion is more tolerant in regard to the doings of the latter than in regard to those of the former; and as in this class of cases especially public opinion affects not only the minds of jurymen, but the sources of the law itself, it is plain that the sufficiently ascertained rules in regard to the liabilities of private trustees afford only an uncertain light as to those of public directors.

If we were to attempt to define the duties of the director of a public company, we would say, that he is bound to give such an amount of time and attention to the concerns of the company, that he shall be able, individually, or with the aid of his colleagues, to exercise a general control over all its affairs, and over the officials engaged in conducting the details of the undertaking; in particular to see that its property is efficiently protected and maintained, its accounts accurately and honestly kept, and its relations with its members, its creditors, and the money-lending public, perfectly open and just.

If such be the duty of a director, it is evident that there may be various classes of mal-practices of which he may be guilty. In the first place, he may be guilty of mere vulgar peculation, putting into his pocket, or applying to his private use, the money or other property of the company. This is not a case which would occasion any difficulty under the criminal system of Scotland, for under the category of breach of trust and embezzlement, such an offender would speedily be brought to justice. In England, however, until the year 1857, it would not have been competent to institute criminal proceedings in such a case, for by the common law of that country trust property is held to be the property of the trustee and not of the beneficiary; and hence, though a civil action for recovery of the funds misappropriated would have lain in a Court of Equity, no redress could be obtained in a Criminal Court. As Attorney-General Bethell said, in moving for leave to introduce the Fraudulent Trustees Bill of 1857: "He knew no other code in Europe in which fraudulent breaches of trust were not held to be proper subjects of criminal punishment. In all other countries it had been deemed a proper principle of law to hold the violation of confidence, or the betrayal of trust, reposed by one man in another, to be one of the greatest aggravations of crime; but he must beg the House to observe in our law there was this peculiarity, that fraud or theft, when accompanied by breach of trust, was divested of its criminal character. If a man stole £500, he would be punished by the criminal law; but if a man upon his death-bed called in a friend and told him, 'I propose to make you executor to my will, and commit to you all my property for the benefit of my widow and children,' if the man accepted the trust, proved the will, and then robbed the widow and the orphans of their property, the law said that he was not a criminal, but a debtor. That which to the mind of every man rendered the act most odious and most abominable, according to our law, stripped it of its wicked character, and we said to the man, 'It is not a crime which you have committed, it is only a debt which you have incurred.'" The Fraudulent Trustees Act, however, was passed (20 and 21 Vict. c. 54), and the law of England is now substantially the same as our own in regard to fraud perpetrated by private trustees, and the more direct swindles of public directors.

But there are other cases of far greater delicacy in which directors may act wrongfully, and in which it is by no means easy at first sight to say whether they have or have not brought themselves within the reach of the criminal law of the land. It will be sufficient for our present purpose to notice one or two of these.

The directors of a banking company are, it may be, desirous to effect an amalgamation of their undertaking with that of another company, either as purchasers or sellers. In either case it is for the advantage of the company that its affairs should appear prosperous, so that the terms of the amalgamation may be favourable. Or, the directors of a railway company may be anxious to borrow large sums of money on easy terms, and for this purpose it will be desirable that they should be enabled to shew a flourishing front to the money-lending public. Or, to take one more case, it may be the policy of the directors of any public company to induce the public to buy largely and readily a new issue of shares, and for this purpose to shew that a handsome return may be expected upon them. In every one of these cases the readiest mode of attaining the object in view is to shew a favourable balance-sheet, and to declare a good dividend. The balance-sheet and the dividend may be called the *pulse* of a public company, and if there is no reason to suspect the use of *stimulants*, the public *feeling* them, may regulate their transactions by the indications of internal health and prosperity thereby afforded.

Nor is such conduct on the part of the public the mere fruit of commercial experience. It is distinctly justified by statutory regulations. The Companies Clauses Act of 1845 (8 and 9 Vict., c. 17) provides: sec. 119—"The books of the company shall be balanced at the prescribed periods, and if no period be prescribed, fourteen days at least before each ordinary meeting; and forthwith, on the books being so balanced, an exact balance-sheet shall be made up, which shall exhibit a true statement of the capital, stock, credits, and property of every description belonging to the company, and the debts due by the company at the date of making such balance-sheet, and a distinct view of the profit or loss which shall have arisen on the transactions of the company in the course of the preceding half-year; and previously to each ordinary meeting such balance-sheet shall be examined by the directors, or any three of their number, and shall be signed by the chairman or deputy-chairman of the directors." Sec. 124—"The company shall not make any dividend whereby their capital stock will be in any degree reduced. . . ."

But what if these regulations are neglected, and, for some purpose, personal to the directors themselves, or for the supposed good and aggrandisement of the company, the books are tampered with, the balance-sheet does not exhibit a *true* statement of capital and of profit or loss, and, as the probable and intended result, dividends are paid out of capital or by unlawfully burdening the earnings of future years? Other companies and the public generally are deceived, transactions are entered into which are quite irrevocable, a collapse comes sooner or later, and it may be widespread ruin is the result. Can the directors who have done this wrong be made criminally responsible for it by the law of Scotland?

Before endeavouring to answer this question, it will be instructive to state what the present law of England is on the point.

It is not necessary to carry our inquiries farther back than the year 1857, in which, as we have already mentioned, the Fraudulent Trustees Act was passed. When the Bill was introduced, the Attorney-General Bethell said: "There were other breaches of trust of a more dangerous character, because of more extended influence, committed by persons who did not stand in exactly the relation of a trustee, but which required the introduction of some particular law, in order to meet delinquents who might at present remain untouched. He alluded to those persons who, in the prosecution of those great undertakings which were almost peculiar to this country, had formed companies, and had placed themselves in the position of directors or managers of these companies. The next set of clauses which he proposed to introduce into the Bill had been framed to meet the delinquencies which, he regretted to say, were so frequent and so gigantic, of persons standing in that situation. In those cases in which such persons fraudulently and openly appropriated sums of money, there could, of course, be no doubt as to their liability to prosecution; but these appropriations were for the most part much too cleverly executed to render it necessary that they should have recourse to a proceeding so clumsy and common as a direct and manifest fraud. Their appropriations of money were, as the House was well aware, effected through the medium of false accounts and fraudulent representations. He had, therefore, introduced into the bill a series of clauses under whose operation, if they should pass into law, the act of keeping false accounts, of making false entries, or disguising the nature of those transactions, by means of untrue representations, should be made criminal. He had also framed two other clauses, which would embrace in their operation that extensive system of fraud which was produced through the medium of false representations, coupled with acts to give a colour to those representations, such as fraudulent statements of the affairs of a company, the payment of dividends out of a fictitious capital (*sic in* Hansard), or other wrongful acts, which went to the perpetration of great public cheats. Whether the law, as it stood, was or was not sufficient to meet such cases, there could be no harm whatsoever in making the particular mode of robbery to which he referred the subject of a direct criminal enactment."

To some of the provisions of the measure there was a good deal of opposition, but the clauses affecting directors who should "cook" the accounts of their companies, met with universal approval, and were passed without a word of dissent. Accordingly, when, four years afterwards, a statute (24 & 25 Vict., c. 96) was passed consolidating the law of larceny in England and Ireland, the clauses of the Fraudulent Trustees Act in regard to directors above referred to were included in it, with some trifling verbal alterations. It will be sufficient to quote the following clauses:—§ 82. "Whosoever, being a director, public officer, or manager of any body corporate or public company, shall, with intent to defraud, destroy, alter, mutilate, or falsify any book, paper, writing, or valuable security belonging to the body corporate or public company, or make, or concur in the making, of any false entry, or omit, or concur in omitting, any material particular in any book of account or other document, shall be guilty of a misdemeanour . . ." § 84. "Whosoever, being a director, manager, or public officer, of any body corporate or public company, shall make, circulate or publish, or concur in making, circulating or publishing, any written statement or account which he shall know to be false in any material particular, with intent to deceive or defraud any member, shareholder, or creditor of such body corporate or public company, or with intent to induce any person to become a shareholder or partner therein, or to intrust or advance any property to such body corporate or public company, or to enter into any security for the benefit thereof, shall be guilty of a misdemeanour . . ." The punishment of these misdemeanours is, by § 80, declared to be that the party convicted shall "be kept in penal servitude for any term not exceeding seven years and not less than five years, or be imprisoned for any term not exceeding two years, with or without hard labour and with or without solitary confinement." The law of England is, therefore, clear, and under it it is manifestly not necessary that any personal benefit to be derived from the fraud should be proved against the director or directors concerned in it. Indeed, if the Royal British Bank case, tried in 1858, is to be taken as a precedent, the most complete ignorance of the mal-practices on the part of one or more of the directors will not save them from a criminal prosecution, though it may mitigate the punishment to be awarded in the event of a conviction.

Originally it was intended that the Fraudulent Trustees Act should apply to all parts of the United Kingdom, but as it passed it was expressly declared "not to extend to Scotland." What then is the common law of Scotland on the point?

Admittedly, there is no precise precedent, no director of a public company having ever been placed at the bar of a criminal court to answer for his official mal-practices. It has, however, always been the boast of Scottish criminal lawyers that their system is an elastic one, and that it is capable of accommodating itself to changing times and crimes. That this boast is not unfounded may be seen by a perusal of Hume's chapter on "Falsehood and Fraud" (i. 137-178), in which he shews that "our common law takes cognizance of, and competently punishes all" false and fraudulent practices, while in England "its more artificial and punctilious system of law has obliged our neighbours to guard against them as they arise (in which shape the remedy is always imperfect) by successive provisions of the legislature. Two recent illustrations of this peculiarity of our system, bearing too on the particular question now under consideration, may here be mentioned. In the case of *H.M. Advocate* v. *Reid and Gentles*, 23d Sept. 1857, 2 Irv. 704, a charge of breach of trust and embezzlement was sustained and a conviction followed,—the *species facti* being that the accountant and teller of a bank facilitated or concealed the embezzlement and appropriation to his own uses, by the bank-agent, of certain sums of money deposited in the bank. The jury expressly found "that neither of the panels received one farthing of the money," and yet a sentence of eighteen months' imprisonment was pronounced on both of them. See also the earlier case of *H.M. Adv.* v. *J. and J. Christie* 12th March 1841, 2 Swinton 534. Again, in the case of *H.M. Adv.* v. *Paton*, 22d Sept. 1858, 3 Irv. 208, an indictment was sustained which charged the panel with falsehood, fraud, and wilful imposition, in so far as that, in order to obtain certain prizes offered by an agricultural society, he inflated portions of the skins of the cattle exhibited by him; that he affixed to them false or artificial horns, for the purpose of improving their appearance, and that one of the prizes was awarded to him. It does not require a very lively imagination to apply this last case to the one we have in hand.

It is not immaterial to observe, that in the Civil Courts the responsibility of directors for the consequences of fraudulent balance-sheets and fictitious dividends has been clearly recognized, and on the ground that the case was laid, as Lord Colonsay, now Lord-President M'Neill, said, "on fraud amounting even to delict," one shareholder has been held *in titulo* to sue and to select one of the alleged wrongdoers without calling his colleagues. See *Leslie* v. *Lumsden*, 17th Dec. 1851, 14 D. 213, and 19th June 1856, 18 D. 1047, and *Tulloch* v. *Davidson*, 3d June 1858, 20 D. 1045, affd. 23d Feb. 1860, 3 Macq. 783; and although in the former case the action was ultimately dismissed on account of want of specification in the condescendence, it was throughout admitted that it was generally relevant.

Perhaps, however, the clearest light on the subject is afforded by the speeches of Lords Campbell and Brougham in Burnes v. Pennell, 16th July 1849, 6 Bell's App., 541. In moving the judgment, affirming that of the Court of Session, Lord Campbell said:—"I repeat that it is most nefarious conduct for the directors of a joint-stock company, in order to raise the price of shares which they are to dispose of, to order a fictitious dividend to be paid out of the capital of the concern. Dividends are supposed to be paid out of profits only, and when directors order a dividend to any given amount, without expressly saying so, they impliedly declare to the world, that the company has made profits which justify such a dividend. If no such profits have been made, and the dividend is to be paid out of the capital of the concern, a gross fraud has been practised, and the directors are not only civilly liable to those whom they have deceived and injured, but, in my opinion, they are guilty of a conspiracy, for which they are liable to be prosecuted and punished. There can be no doubt that a conspiracy by falsehood (as by a fictitious dividend), to raise fictitiously the market value of shares of a railway company, or any other joint-stock company, that the Queen's subjects may be deceived and injured, and that at their expense a profit may be made by the conspirators, would be an *indictable offence.*" Lord Brougham took the same ground, and observed—"I view with the greatest severity the conduct of railway directors, in declaring dividends which can only be paid out of capital, because I consider that it is, of itself, a most vicious and fraudulent course of conduct. It is telling the world that their profits are large, when it may be their profits are *nil*, or that their losses are large, with no profits. It is a false and fraudulent representation by act and deed, much to be reprobated; and I go the full length of what my noble and learned friend has laid down, that it would be a just ground, if a course of conduct of this sort were pursued, coupled with such circumstances as clearly to shew a fraudulent intent, for proceedings of a graver nature against these parties."

It may be thought that these observations (made, be it remarked, in the House of Lords sitting as a Scotch Court of Appeal), would not apply to cases where the motive for "cooking" could not be traced to any direct pecuniary benefit to be derived by the director or directors engaged in it, but where the motive may be supposed to be the improvement of the credit of the company and its aggrandisement at the expense of the public, or of its rivals. We cannot assent to this. It is trite law that the proof of a motive is quite unnecessary to the proof of a crime. The proof even of a motive, not itself unworthy, will not relieve from criminal responsibility.* If I forge a man's signature to a bill and obtain money on it, it would be no defence to me against a prosecution for forgery, that I devoted the proceeds to charity or even to the furtherance of some object which, in my opinion would benefit him with whose credit I had made free. My conduct in so acting may not be so despicable, as if I had applied the money wholly to my own uses, but it is no less cognisable by the criminal law.

There seems to us, therefore, nothing to hinder the application of the observations of Lords Campbell and Brougham to the case of directors "cooking" their accounts for the real or supposed good of the company.

Of course we are well aware that even if we have brought the argument satisfactorily to this point, many most difficult questions remain behind. What, it may be asked, is to be reckoned a fraudulent tampering with or "cooking" of accounts? Considerable difference of opinion, we know, exists as to the proper way of charging expenses, of forming suspenses, and of estimating profits. Taking advantage of this a good many irregularities may doubtless be perpetrated with impunity. Still, there are certain well-ascertained principles acted on in all good accounting, and, as we have seen, expressly recognised by the Companies Clauses Act, which, if they are transgressed, and undoubtedly they often are so, will subject those who wilfully and fraudulently disregard them to criminal prosecutions. To give but one instance, that used by Lord Campbell,—we entertain no doubt that if directors declare fictitious dividends, that is to say, dividends which have not been fairly earned, for the purpose of raising the company's credit and inducing the public to rely on it, they may be subjected to criminal proceedings for so doing.

It frequently happens that the boards of public companies contain one or two leading spirits, the remaining members being mere ciphers, selected an account of their ornamental qualities only. These *dummies*, however, would not be safe from criminal proceedings, if they sat quietly by whilst their colleagues were "cooking" the accounts. Ignorance may be criminal as well as

* See the case of *Charles Grant*, 1 Hume 172, note.

knowledge. Gentlemen of this class ought to abstain from undertaking duties which they systematically neglect, but if they do undertake them, and their accepting office implies that they do so, they may be surprised some day to find themselves placed at the bar of a criminal court, and subjected to pains and penalties. Several of the Royal British Bank directors found themselves in this unpleasant predicament.

As to the particular categories under which peccant directors could be prosecuted, there cannot be much difficulty. Those who have been actively participant in the mal-practices could be indicted for breach of trust, or falsehood, fraud, and wilful imposition. While those who by their carelessness permitted the mal-practices to be carried on, could be indicted for breach of trust or culpable neglect of duty. The framing of the indictments would unquestionably be a matter of very great delicacy, and the proof would be laborious and difficult. But we entertain no doubt that the common law of Scotland is, as it stands, perfectly strong enough to bring to justice in our criminal courts the class of wrong-doers with whom we have been dealing, as well as those more vulgar offenders with whose trials we are familiar. That these are not new views, taken up for the nonce, any one may satisfy himself who chooses to refer back to previous articles in this journal.

MEETING OF THE SOCIAL SCIENCE CONGRESS.

As on former occasions, we subjoin a very brief abstract of the papers bearing upon the Amendment of the Law, which were read before the National Association for the Promotion of Social Science, at its October meeting, in Manchester.

Lord BROUGHAM'S introductory address contained the following reference to the state of the law:—

"It is, however, manifest that as long as there is no judicial department, nothing effectual will ever be undertaken for the great matter of law amendment. What is everybody's business is proverbially nobody's business; and the heads of the law are quite enough occupied in administering it as at present constituted, beside that they are unfortunately, for the most part, averse to any change. Many years have now elapsed since our eminent colleague, Mr Napier, after he had ceased to be Chancellor of Ireland, carried in the House of Commons an address for the establishment of a judicial department, which received a favourable answer from the Crown; and, if the promises then given had been performed, the institution would, beside many other advantages (among the rest, the affording an efficient council to the Home Secretary in the discharge of his most delicate and difficult duty of advising the Crown on the remission of punishment), have assured the undertaking of the needful improvements in our legal system. Our learned and excellent colleague, Sir E. Wilmot, has prepared a plan for a Law Amendment Department, the particulars of which, it is to be hoped, he will transmit, should his judicial duties unfortunately prevent his attendance at the Congress. The same negative which applies to the formation of a judicial department must unhappily be given as to almost all other law amendments. Among others the important subject of reconcilement has been once more passed over. The great success of conciliation in other countries, especially in Denmark and the Danish colonies, render this repeated postponement truly vexatious. The report of the Commission for Inquiry into the great subject of capital punishment has been printed, and is most important from the great body of information which it contains both on this and other countries, and it offered an almost solitary exception to the blank of the late session; for the material recommendation of the report against public executions has been adopted by Parliament after a somewhat warm opposition in the Upper House. The more this subject is considered, the expediency of the change thus introduced into the execution of the criminal law will be more fully admitted. The great defects in the law of evidence, so often pointed out, still remain not only without remedy, but without any real defence. The great amendment in the law of evidence, by the act for examining parties, would be rendered complete, if also extended to cases in the Divorce Court. Of the many deficiencies of the late session, one was the not passing an act to amend the optional clause in the County Courts Act. The importance of the jurisdiction of these courts has long been admitted even by those who were at first averse to them. The number of suits which they determine is prodigious, and so far they are a relief to the superior courts, and a most valuable benefit to the suitors. To the late improvements in our county and borough gaols it is reasonable to attribute the greater part, if not the whole, of the diminution of crime during the last half year. The employment of Sir Walter Crofton by the Home Office in carrying the Act into operation has been most beneficial. One sees with astonishment and indignation, in cases before magistrates in the country, intoxication urged in extenuation of offences, whereas it is a gross aggravation. No magistrate is entitled to suffer one such word to be uttered before him on the part of the accused. Any magistrate is bound to stop the party or his advocate the instant he begins on this, and to tell him that if intoxicated, he must suffer a punishment more severe, and the magistrate is further bound to take it into his consideration when the prosecutor has stated it in explaining the circumstances of the case. It is undeniable that a most wholesome effect would be produced by the general impression being made that drunkenness, though by law it may be not liable to punishment, except by small pecuniary penalty, yet makes offences to which it has given rise more severely punishable."

EXTRADITION OF CRIMINALS.

The special question under this head was, 'How may the extradition of criminals be best secured consistently with the right of asylum?' After the reading of papers, a long and not satisfactory discussion followed. Its import was that there were four conditions to be held in view in any attempt to establish extradition treaties—(1) The punishment of crime so that it should be impossible for a criminal to escape merely by removing to another country; (2) The maintenance of the right of asylum to persons charged with political offences; (3) The establishment of a Board of Inquiry to investigate and report upon fabricated charges; (4) Provision for extradition and afterwards trial within a fixed time.

INTERNATIONAL COPYRIGHT.

A paper on this subject was read by Mr Anthony Trolloppe, pointing out that there is no law securing copyright between this country and America, although such law exists between England and some states in the Continent, such as Saxony. In the discussion which followed, an unanimous feeling of the justice and expediency of such a law was expressed, and the chairman of the section, Mr Dudley Field, of New York, stated, as regards America, that it was not a question for state legislation, but for Congress, and that the remedy was to try to get Congress to pass an Act securing the right in the same way as Acts were passed in the British Parliament.

BANKRUPTCY LAW.

Several papers were read upon this subject, having immediate reference to the law of England, the special question being, "The principle on which a Bankrupt Law should be founded." A great preponderance of opinion was expressed, to the effect that the English system of special jurisdiction in bankruptcy was radically unsound; that the Scotch system, which vests the bankrupt state in a curator for all the incorporated creditors, was preferable, and that, upon the whole, with certain alterations in details, it might be satisfactorily adopted in England.

CODIFICATION OF THE ENGLISH LAW.

A paper on this subject was read by Mr Hastings, who argued for codification to the limited effect, that a digest of the case laid should be prepared mainly for the assistance of the county judges who do not enjoy the assistance of a law library, and whose jurisdiction is every day being enlarged. Mr Dudley Field pointed out that the great difficulty in codifying the laws of a country was the separation between law and equity, but thought that these might be readily forced in England. In the course of the discussion, opinions were expressed that nothing short of a complete code, such as the Code Napoleon, would be of any practical avail.

DISPOSAL OF PROPERTY FOR CHARITABLE PURPOSES.

Three papers were read upon this subject, the general import of which was, that all restrictions should be removed from the disposition of property, except when it was left for charitable purposes that were inconsistent with public policy. Mr Hare recommended that all land devised for charitable purposes should be sold within a fixed period not exceeding ten years from the date of the conveyance, and that the proceeds of the sale should be invested under the direction of the department of charities. In the course of the discussion, an opinion was expressed in favour of the Scotch system, where the only restriction to which the testator is liable is that which is imposed upon all real estates.

LIFE SENTENCES.

Two papers were read on this subject on the special question, "Is it desirable to carry out life sentences to the utmost, and if so, in what cases, and under what form of discipline." The first clause of the question was answered by comprehending in the class to which this punishment should be extended, (I.) People who have perpetrated death in a fit of passion, and those convicted of murder, who have been repreived by the Crown. (II.) Convicts whose repeated convictions after punishment for felony or grave misdemeanour, show to be incorrigible. The plan of treatment proposed in the leading paper involved the following positions:—1. Certainty of the literal execution of the sentence, the abatement of the full punishment forming the exception, and not the rule. 2. The elimination of hope from the convict's mind, as regards the chance of his eventual liberation from prison, but not in respect of the amelioration of his position in prison. The particular plan suggested was that convicts should be placed, on their first entering prison, in as heavy irons as nature can bear, and should be permitted, by good conduct, to work themselves into milder punishment. 3. Treatment in prisons specially set aside for such convicts. A long discussion followed, in which the opinion was expressed that the proposed scheme was objectionable by reason of its cruelty and severity. The following resolutions were carried.—1st. That the altered circumstances of this country, with regard to transportation, render it necessary that the treatment of life-sentenced convicts should be revised, and that such steps be taken for the protection of society as will cause their liberation to be the exception, and not, as heretofore, the rule. 2d. That the opinion of those qualified to judge induces the conclusion that the retention of this class of prisoners, under these circumstances, in the ordinary convict prisons, would be attended with danger to these establishments, and be detrimental to the prisoners themselves, and that it therefore appears to be absolutely necessary to institute a special prison for the purpose, if possible, on some island near our own shore, in which a special treatment could be carried on suitable to the peculiar position of the inmates.

INFANTICIDE.

A paper on this subject was read by Dr Lankaster, but his treatment, as also the general purport of the discussion, had rather a social than a legal bearing. One suggestion was made, and afterwards censured, intending to promote the very evils complained of—that sexual intercourse should be held as *ipsum matrimonium*, and if the guilty parties were previously married they should be liable to be prosecuted for bigamy.

CRIMINAL TREATMENT.

Under this head the attention of the Association was called to those measures recently adopted by the Magistrates in Gloucestershire. The first was a return of all convictions with a description of each prisoner, and an antecedent paper, "giving all that could be ascertained of his history, so that men not known to have been previously convicted received a lighter sentence. The second was a proposal that to secure certainty of punishment, and thus to deter from the commission of crime, it should be the practice in ordinary cases (excluding murder, highway robbery, burglary, &c.) to punish a first offence with ten days' imprisonment, a second with twelve twelve months, a third with seven years, and the fourth with as long a term as the law would allow. The third measure had respect to vagrants, and was designed, while assisting those travelling in search of work, to discourage professional tramps. Each vagrant on leaving a workhouse was furnished with a passage to a workhouse twenty miles off on his way to his alleged destination (or a less distance if necessary), but if he diverged from this route he was required to do four hours work when he next obtained relief.

UNITED DIGEST OF THE LAWS OF ENGLAND AND SCOTLAND.

A paper was read upon this subject by Mr MACQUEEN, Q.C., so far as we have observed, the first that has boldly demanded that in any digest all the assistance should be taken derivable from the law on this side of the Tweed. —"Notwithstanding the example of Foreign States and of despotic Governments, the predominating sentiment of this country is against codes. But we have the authority of great names in favour of digest, and to this we may probably some day attain. Of such a digest the delineations and definitions would be verified by references, so that the text and the authorities might be compared and construed together. It ought not, he said, to be confined to England. It should embrace Scotland. The work must be concurrent. A contemporaneous exposition of the laws of both countries, by presenting differences and resemblances, will give rise to the most useful of all criticisms—that of contrast and comparison. As a whole, the Scotch law is excellent. So is the English law. But each has defects from which the other is free. Now, with respect to the laws of Scotland, Lord Bacon noticed 'how near,' as he expressed it, 'they came to our own.' The jurisprudence of each continues in a great measure still the same. Personal freedom depends on the temper of the existing Government, or rather on the discretion, peradventure the caprice, of the Lord Advocate. It is a grave question whether it be fitting and consistent with the dignity of a great and intellectual people that their political rights should depend on the clemency of the Government. The marriage laws of Scotland, and of the whole empire, are now undergoing investigation by a Royal Commission. I will, therefore, say nothing of them except that when settled the digest must unfold them. Our northern neighbours have had for two centuries what we are only now trying to acquire—a satisfactory system of registration. To imitate their code of bankruptcy will next session form the study of the Legislature. They do not set law and equity in opposition to each other, but by one high tribunal administer both. Their criminal law is admirable. The impossibility of appealing against wrong convictions and wrong acquittals is a blemish not peculiar to Scotland. The Scotch have no grand juries; they don't desire to have them. They have no coroner's inquests, nor do they feel the want of them. But they have public prosecutors, which the English have not. And they have allowed always that which the English have allowed only recently and reluctantly—counsel to prisoners. In the event, therefore, of a united digest, the borrowings will be pretty nearly balanced, and the advantages reciprocal. To digest the law of England alone, without any reference to Scotland, would be a pretty sure way to widen the existing segregation; but to digest the two systems harmoniously together would be to realise quickly that amalgamation which was desiderated by Bacon at the union of the Crowns, and desiderated by Somers at the union of the kingdoms. Ireland cannot be overlooked in a work essentially imperial.

AN INTERNATIONAL CODE.

Mr David Dudley Field of New York, delivered an address on an International Code. With regard to many subjects falling within the scope of the international regulation both during peace and during war there was great uncertainty. On the subject of re-capture at sea, there were different rules applied in America, England, France, and in other states. The case of the Alabama was viewed so differently, on different sides of the Atlantic, as to complicate the relations of England and America. Expatriation and allegiance were likewise subjects fraught with dangerto the relations of nations. Extradition of Criminals, Patents, and Copyrights were also matters requiring international regulation. The right of search, the right of access by river to great inland seas, were questions of the same class; and like the diminution of the horrors of war by abolishing war on private property could only be settled by an International Code. Such a code might be drawn up by a conference of diplomatists and signed as treaties,—or codes might be prepared by a committee of publicists embodying the matured judgments of the best thinkers and most accomplished jurists, and then the assistance of the different nations might be obtained. The Association might lead the way by appointing a committee to prepare the outline of such a code—and after that was approved they might invite the co-operation of Professors of Universities and publicists throughout the world, and fill up the scheme. It would be a great honour to the Association to take the initiative in such an undertaking, and add to the glory of England.

THE MONTH.

Death of Sheriff Ogilvy.—Sheriff Ogilvy, of Dundee, died on the 22d ult. We believe that, in the large and important legal district over which he presided, there will be but one feeling as to the heavy loss which has been sustained by his death. He was a man of rare attainments, combining in a degree not often seen, a special talent for philosophical speculation, with great practical shrewdness and sagacity. No province of literature was inaccessible to him. All who knew him professionally, knew him as a most accomplished lawyer. Always abreast of the current jurisprudence of the day, he was fond of research into the more recondite sources of legal learning, which had an attraction for him just because they were curious and unfamiliar, and because, perhaps, they might chance to throw light on some favourite historical or philosophical speculation. Those who enjoyed familiar intercourse with him can best testify to his originality as a thinker, and to his acuteness and humour in colloquial controversy, into which he was always ready to enter with unaffected zest, though without any taint of acrimony, and in which a slight tinge of eccentricity added an increased relish to his discourse. They can also bear testimony to his reliableness as a friend. It is now upwards of six years since Mr Ogilvy was transferred, with the unanimous approbation of the public, from Forfar to Dundee, and his merits thoroughly justified his promotion. His recent situation was probably the most laborious judicial office in Scotland, and yet, though he put through his hands more work, perhaps, than any one of his brethren, it is doubtful whether work of a similar kind was ever better done. He will be long remembered by his fellow-townsmen in Dundee as a public-spirited and beneficent citizen, while the whole circle of his own profession will unite with them in lamenting the loss of an accomplished scholar, a learned lawyer, and a most successful and conscientious judge.

Notes on Points of Practice decided during the past year.—We have already noticed the effects of the larger changes which have been within the last year effected in the procedure of the Court of Session, either by its own wise sensitiveness to public opinion, or in consequence of the representations made by the profession to the Legislature. It may be useful now to note briefly a few of the principal decisions of the Supreme Court relating to practice. Under the Act of Sederunt July 1865, two decisions have been reported as to the provision (in section 12) that all appointments for lodging or adjusting of issues shall be peremptory—*Anderson* v. *Glasg. and S.W. Railway Company*, Dec. 20, 1865, 4 M. 259; *Guardian Assurance Company* v. *Wallace*, June 6, 1866, 4 M. 796. It has been held that the periods appointed cannot be prorogated by consent of parties, but that the Court has power to receive the issues, apparently on some special cause being shown. On the former of these occasions the Lord President, for the second time (see *Burden* v. *Mitchell*, 29th Jan. 1856, 18 D. 339), elucidated the law as to prorogations of consent; and traced the history of that doctrine in order to show that it has no reference to the giving in of an issue, which "is not a pleading in the cause; it is a mere memorandum of what the party suggests as the question to be tried." The judgment is chiefly valuable for the remarks on the most elementary principle of our system of pleading, a principle so systematically neglected that the exposition of it by so high a place must be regarded as a signal service to the law. We cannot do better than quote it:—

"There can be no difficulty for a party, if his record is properly framed, to extract the proper issue for the trial of the cause; for I do not understand how any one can frame a record properly without having in his mind the issue he wishes to try, and selecting from the materials before him those, and those only, that are pertinent to that issue. To throw into a record all matters directly or indirectly connected with the case, or having any possible bearing on it, is not the right way of framing a record; it may save the trouble of thinking at that stage, and relieve from the labour of selecting and arranging the materials; but it is not the right way of framing a record, and it multiplies the subsequent labour and risks of miscarriage, and adds greatly to the expense. A party should, while preparing the record, have the issue he wishes to try steadily in view, and direct his materials to that end; and if he has done so, there can be no reason, after the record is closed, for prorogating the time for lodging issues, unless under very special circumstances indeed, *e.g.*, the illness of his counsel, or the like."

Similar advice is given in the chapter on "Pleadings" in Mr Clark's valuable book on Partnership and Joint-Stock Companies —a chapter which suggests the utility of a larger treatise on the subject of pleading.

Reference should be made to the strictness which both divisions of the Court have properly used in dealing with reponing notes against decrees by default. The case of *Mather* v. *Smith*, Nov. 28, 1858, 21 D. 24, in which a party was three times reponed, has been a stock precedent in such applications. The Lord President says, that the Court there went very far, and that he is "not disposed to give it that character," and a second reponing note was refused in respect no sufficient grounds had been stated, *Pearson* v. *M'Gavin*, May 29, 1866, 4 Macph. 754. The Second Division a fortnight later went a step farther, and pronounced a judgment intended to "form a useful precedent," to the effect that "when a reclaiming note is presented by a party praying to be reponed against a decree by default, it is not a matter of course that he shall be reponed, even on the condition of paying full expenses. It is always a matter for the discretion of the Court."—Per Inglis, J.C., in *Arthur* v. *Bell*, June 16, 1866, 4 Macph. 841. In *Arthur* v. *Deuchar*, May 12, 1866, 4 Macph. 705, a reponing note against a decree by default in a suspension in the Bill Chamber, where answers had been lodged, was refused as incompetent. "There is no such a thing as a decree by default in the Bill Chamber."

The *Antermony Coal Company*, March 7, 1866 and June 30 1866, 4 *Macph*, 544 and 1017, has been acquiring a place in the annals of the law similar to that long held by the Culcreuch Cotton Company. It has, or rather had, two partners, one of whom is abroad. The remaining partner suing Wingate and Co. in the company name, was met by a motion that a mandatary for the absent partner should be sisted. This was refused on the ground that a solvent partner was in the country. Subsequently, in revised defences, the plea of want of authority to use the name of Walter Wingate, the absent partner, in the instance was raised and repelled. This gave occasion for an authoritative *resumé* of the doctrine of suing by descriptive firms with joinder of three partners. The general doctrine was stated nearly as it has been laid down by Mr Clark (p. 537 sqq.). The majority of the Court was inclined to hold the instance in this case good, even if one partner (there were but two) should disclaim. The fact, however, that the absent partner was also a defender, as a partner of the firm sued, enabled Lord Deas to rest his judgment on the narrower ground, that " where a party is liable as defender he is not entitled to refuse to become a pursuer if his concurrence be necessary to the validity of the action." His Lordship also founded on the absence of actual disclamation by Wingate; and the other Judges, though also relying on larger principles, seemed to concur in thinking these specialties sufficient for the decision of the particular question raised. The first appears to be an example of the principle of personal bar so largely applied in this class of cases both in Scotland and England (see *Clark*, p. 544 sqq.). But it may be asked, why should that principle apply here, the defender not being Wingate the partner of the Antermony Company, but Wingate and Co., a separate *persona*, consisting of Wingate and G. C. Bruce, the individual really defending? This seems to justify the majority in referring their judgment to a more general principle.

In *Paterson* v. *Moncrieff*, May 15, 1866, 4 *Macph.* 706, trustees stated as a defence to an action by the representatives of a child of the truster, that they had, living the children, elected as their tutors and curators nominate, to take certain provisions under the settlement in lieu of legitim. The Lord Justice-Clerk, in his judgment repelling this defence, laid some stress on the fact that the trustees had never entered upon the office of tutors and curators in the manner prescribed by the Act 1672 c. 2;

and therefore had never put themselves in a position to renounce the right to legitim, if that were competent to them (which in the circumstances was very doubtful). It is believed that very many tutors and curators nominate altogether neglect to make up inventories as required by the statute—the consequences of which, though the rule of the Roman law, *Tutor qui repertorium non fecit, dolo fecisse videtur*, is not received in Scotland, may be very serious both as regards themselves and their pupil. It is worth considering, whether the simpler forms introduced by the Pupils' Protection Act for tutors at law and tutors dative might not be beneficially extended to all tutors. At least the necessity of having recourse to the Inner House in all cases where the next of kin reside out of Scotland might be removed, and as Mr Fraser (*Parent and Child*, p. 198) suggests, it might be made competent for the Lord Ordinary before whom the process depends to dispense with citation of next of kin.

The Second Division has pronounced some useful decisions on points of Sheriff Court practice. We formerly noticed (Journal for July) the case of *Dickson* v. *Murray*, June 7, 1866, 4 M. 797, in which it was held that the provisions of § 10 of the Bankruptcy Act 1856 and § 9 of the Bankruptcy and Real Securities Act 1857, do not make reductions under the Acts 1621 and 1696 and at common law competent in the Sheriff Courts. In *Murphy* v. *M'Keand*, Feb. 15, 1866, 4 M. 444, Sheriffs were warned of the mischief which "arises from granting interim interdict where the circumstances do not warrant such a course of procedure." The excessive indulgence practised in adjourning diets of proof for the accommodation of agents was also reproved and it was held in point of law that an interlocutor reviving allowance of proof is the same as one allowing a proof, and may therefore be appealed under sec. 19 of the Act. The jurisdiction of the Sheriff in questions of possession of heritable subjects is elucidated in *Maxwell* v. *Glasgow and S.-W. Railway Company*, Feb. 16, 1866, 4 M. 447; and his jurisdiction in summary removings in *Nisbet* v. *Aikman*, Jan. 12, 1866, 4 M. 284. In *Byres* v. *Forbes*, Feb. 7, 1866, 4 M. 388, the Second Division adopted the strong measure of ordering a trial by jury, and refusing to look at a proof which had been led in the Sheriff Court before a Commissioner, on the ground that it was incompetent under sec. 10 of the Sheriff Court Act. The parties had acquiesced in this form of procedure, and it might perhaps be held that the doctrine of the House of Lords in *Craig* v. *Duffus*, 6 Bell 308, *Mag. of Renfrew* v. *Hoby*, 2 Macq. 478, and in the late case of *White* v. *E. of Morton*, July 13. 1866, 10 Journ. of Jur., Dig. of Cases, 201, should have been applied here. The case having been taken out of the ordinary course of judicial procedure "by consent of parties, the judgment of the Sheriff-Substitute being in reality that of an arbiter, would in this view have been final. What then would have become of the subsequent judgments of the Sheriff, Lord Ordinary, and Court of Session? It would seem, from *Morris* v. *Bicket*, in the House of Lords, July 13, 1866, 10 Journ. of Jurispr. Dig. of Cases 190; 1 Law Rep. Sc. and Div. Ap. 47, that the defender, having appealed to the Sheriff, was barred from objecting to the competency of any subsequent process of review at the instance of the pursuer, who was the advocator. It may therefore be suggested that it was not "incompetent" for the Court to look at the proof in question, although it may have been competent for it to refuse to take cognizance of proceedings which had once been taken out of the ordinary course of judicial procedure." The House of Lords, however, did not on this ground refuse to look at the proof in *Morris* v *Bicket*.

Legal Appointments.—Mr. W. A. Parker has been appointed chief judge and magistrate of the Gold Coast. Mr. Parker was called to the bar in 1853. His predecessor has been promoted to Penang—a principle the recognition of which by the Foreign Office will certainly secure a higher stamp of judge than in times past for the less valuable of our Colonial appointments.—Mr. J. Guthrie Smith has been appointed Sheriff-substitute of Dundee in room of Mr. Ogilvy. He thus returns to the county in the rural districts of which he gave so much satisfaction when Sheriff-substitute at Forfar.

Winter Circuit.—The Glasgow Winter Circuit has been fixed for 26th Dec., at half past twelve o'clock. *Judges*, Lord Deas and Lord Ardmillan; *Advocates-Depute*, Mr. R. B. Blackburn and Mr. Roger Montgomery; *Clerk*, Mr. Æneas Macbean.

SCOTCH CASES

DECIDED IN THE

HOUSE OF LORDS, COURT OF SESSION, COURT OF JUSTICIARY, &c.:

WITH

SELECTIONS FROM ENGLISH DECISIONS

VOLS. IX. AND X. OF JOURNAL OF JURISPRUDENCE,

FROM 20TH JAN. 1865 TO 20TH DEC. 1866.

EDINBURGH:
T. & T. CLARK, LAW BOOKSELLERS, GEORGE STREET.
GLASGOW: SMITH & SON. ABERDEEN: WYLLIE & SON.
LONDON: STEVENS & SON.

MDCCCLXVI.

TURNBULL AND SPEARS, PRINTERS, GEORGE STREET, EDINBURGH.

DIGEST OF DECISIONS

OF SCOTCH AND ENGLISH CASES,

1865–66.

COURT OF SESSION.

FIRST DIVISION.

Susp. and Lib., JACKSON *v.* SMELLIE.—*Nov.* 22.

Meditatio Fugæ.

In this case, Smellie had obtained from the Sheriff of Lanarkshire a warrant of imprisonment against Jackson as *in meditatione fugæ*. Jackson, having been imprisoned, presented the present suspension and liberation upon two grounds :—

1. That in the original petition presented to the Sheriff, Smellie only stated that Jackson was '*in meditatione fugæ*, and about to leave Scotland' without paying the debt claimed, 'whereby she (Smellie) will be defeated or disappointed of her claim,' and did not state that Jackson intended to leave Scotland to *avoid payment* of the petitioner's claim. It was argued that an intention to evade payment was of the essence of *meditatio fugæ*.

2. That there was no proof of intended flight. The Lord Ordinary refused the note of suspension ; and to-day, the Court, while holding the proof of intended flight to be extremely narrow, adhered in the whole circumstances of the case.

Susp. and Int., LORD LOVAT AND OTHERS *v.* TAIT. DITTO *v.* MACKENZIE.—*Nov.* 23.

Fishing—Mode of Exercise of Right.

These were applications for interdict at the instance of Lord Lovat and several other proprietors having right to the salmon-fishing on the rivers Ness and Beauly and Loch Ness,—the first against Archibald Tait, salmon-fisher, residing in Inverness ; the second against R. G. Mackenzie, Esq. of Flowerburn, in the county of Ross. The petitioners averred that the respondents have been and still are in the habit of fishing for and taking salmon, and other fish of the salmon kinds, by means of stell nets or other fixed engines or machinery, in the estuaries of the Ness and Beauly ; and on the ground that such a mode of fishing is illegal, and in contravention of the Acts regulating salmon-fishing, and injurious to the petitioners' rights of salmon-fishing, they asked that the respondents should be interdicted from continuing it.

The respondent Tait, in his answers to the petition, averred that in fishing he employed the ordinary net and coble. One end of the rope to which the net was attached was held by a man on shore, whilst the net was paid out from the stern of the coble. During stormy weather and strong tides, a drag or weight was attached to the seaward end of the net for the purpose of keeping it in position, and the coble returned to shore with the rope. The net was not in any way fixed or made stationary, and after the return of the coble the net was drawn by means of the ropes in the usual manner.

The respondent Mackenzie, after describing the manner in which he paid out the net, averred—'The net is not fastened to any stake, or fixed or permanent thing in the water, nor is the net itself kept fixed or stationary throughout the operation of fishing, though, for the purpose of steadying the net, a stone or light anchor is sometimes attached to the outward end of the net.' He also averred that stell-fishing could be practised without such a stone or anchor, in which case the net continued moving during the entire operation of fishing.

The Lord Ordinary (Barcaple) passed the notes to try the question, but refused interim interdict.

Against this interlocutor the petitioners reclaimed, but to-day the Court (Lord Deas dissenting) affirmed the Lord Ordinary's interlocutor, and refused interim interdict.

The majority of the Court thought the statements of the respondents not very satisfactory, especially those of the respondent Mackenzie, which were so vague and indistinct as almost to be reconcilable with those of the petitioner. If this had been the season for fishing, they would have been disposed, in Mackenzie's case at any rate, to grant interim interdict; but as it was inexpedient to deal with the cases differently, and there could be no salmon-fishing till February next, by which time the parties might be in a position to take their stand on their final statements, their Lordships thought it was the safer course to leave matters *in statu quo*, seeing that the application could be renewed when the statements of parties were made more specific.

Lord Deas was of opinion that interim interdict should be granted. He read the respondent Mackenzie's averment as in substance that his net was not fixed or stationary *during the whole period* of its use in fishing, and therefore that it was fixed during a part of the period. That was just an admission of the statements of the petitioners on which the application was founded, and they were therefore, he thought, entitled to interim interdict.

The respondents asked expenses, which were refused.

Napier *v.* Glasgow and South-Western Railway Company.—*Nov.* 25.

Interdict—Railway and Canal Traffic Act, 1854.

This was a petition by Mr J. R. Napier, shipowner, Glasgow, founded on the Railway and Canal Traffic Act, 1854, complaining of certain alleged undue preferences given by the Glasgow and South-Western Railway Company to the owners of the steamer 'Oscar' over him as owner of another steamer called the 'Lancefield,' and praying for an interdict against the company continuing these preferences. It appeared that for some time prior to September 1864, the petitioner was engaged in running a steam-vessel called the 'Lancefield,' for the carriage of goods, cattle, and passengers between Ardrossan and Belfast, in connection with trains running between Glasgow and Ardrossan, on the respondents' railway, under an arrangement with the railway company. Through tickets for passengers were issued by the respondents at through rates at Glasgow and Paisley, available for the whole journey by rail to Ardrossan, and by the steamer to Belfast, and similar tickets were issued at Belfast, or on board the steamer, to parties travelling between Belfast and those towns; the railway company's proportion of the through rates being only one-fourth of the gross fare, and being in every case lower than the local rates charged to passengers travelling between Glasgow or Paisley and Ardrossan. There was a similar arrangement for through rates of freight or carriage for goods and live stock. Mr Napier continued to run his vessel between Ardrossan and Belfast till the beginning of September 1864, as the only steam-vessel trading regularly between these ports in connection with the railway. About that time, some communications passed between him and the railway company relative to a removal of his vessel to the harbour of Troon; and the company, becoming apprehensive that he might remove his vessel from Ardrossan to that port, entered into an arrangement with the owners of another vessel called the 'Oscar,' whereby they agreed to give the same facilities and advantages to the owners of that vessel as they had previously given to Mr Napier, upon their undertaking to place that vessel upon the station, and to sail it between Ardrossan and Belfast on alternate days, as Mr Napier's vessel had done. In September 1864, the 'Oscar' was put upon the station to run on the same days on which Mr Napier's vessel had been in use to run between those ports; and upon this being done, he altered the days of sailing of his vessel, so as to avoid sailing on the same days as those on which the 'Oscar' sailed. On this being done, the same facilities were continued by the railway company to Mr Napier as he had previously enjoyed, until the beginning of October, when orders were issued by the company to discontinue those facilities; and since then they have refused to issue through tickets, or to charge through rates, but have insisted on charging local rates for all passengers and goods between Glasgow or Paisley and Ardrossan which are to proceed from that port to Belfast by Mr Napier's vessel.

The Lord Ordinary decided that in so acting the railway company placed Mr Napier at an undue disadvantage, and conferred an undue preference and advantage on the owners of the 'Oscar,' in contravention of the Railway and Canal Traffic Act, 1854, and granted interdict.

The Court to-day unanimously recalled this judgment, and held that the second section of the Railway and Canal Traffic Act applied only to continuous communication by railway and canal, and did not apply to the case of a railway terminating at the sea; and further, that the arrangement which the railway company made in this case with a particular steamer was a legal and perfectly reasonable one.

Pet., Jarvie, for Recal of Sequestration.—*Nov.* 25.

Sequestration—Competing Petitions.

Messrs R. and J. Jarvie, rope-spinners, Stobcross Street, Glasgow, presented this petition for the recal of a sequestration granted under the petition of John Ronald and Co., John Ronald, jun., and John Templeton, merchants, Glasgow, with concurrence of a creditor, in so far as it operated as a sequestration of the estates of Ronald and Co. and John Ronald, jun. On 3d August last, Messrs Jarvie presented a petition for sequestration of these estates, with their grounds of debt and diligence showing bankruptcy; and on the same day the Lord Ordinary pronounced a deliverance, granting warrant to cite the parties, in terms of the Bankruptcy Act, to appear in Court on the seventh day after citation. That interlocutor being the first deliverance, was recorded in the Register of Inhibitions. The citation was given on 9th August, but on the 15th the bankrupts themselves presented a petition for sequestration, without giving notice to Jarvie and Co. This sequestration was granted, and it was recorded as a first deliverance in the Register of Inhibitions.

The Court were of opinion that the bankrupts were not entitled to take that proceeding, as endangering the rights already acquired by the creditors under the petition presented by Jarvie and Co. on 3d August; and they recalled the interlocutor of 15th August *in hoc statu*, and remitted to the Lord Ordinary, with the view of conjoining with the petition presented on 3d August, and ordering sequestration of new.

THOMS *v.* THOMS.—*Nov.* 25.

Issues—Fraud—Essential Error.

The object of this action, in which Mr John Thoms, Sea-View, St Andrews, was pursuer, was to reduce a general disposition and settlement, by which the deceased Mr Alexander Thoms, of Rumgally, near Cupar-Fife, left his whole property to the defender, Miss Robina Thoms, his illegitimate daughter. Mr Alexander Thoms was infeft as heir of entail in the estate of Rumgally, a property worth about £25,000: he was never married, and the next heir entitled to succeed under the entail was the pursuer; but it now appears that the fetters of the entail not having been directed against the deceased as institute, he held the property at his absolute disposal. It was maintained for the defender that it passed to her under his general settlement, and she is now in possession of it, the Court having some time since refused to appoint a judicial factor. The pursuer alleged that the deceased was not aware that he held the estate in fee-simple, and only intended to convey to his daughter, the defender, the other property of which he was possessed; and he further averred that the defender and Mr Charles Welch, writer, Cupar, who prepared the settlement, fraudulently obtained that deed from Mr Thoms, on the pretence that it conveyed nothing but his personal or moveable property, which was small in comparison with the estate in question. The pursuer proposed to take three issues: 1*st*, Whether the general settlement was granted by the deceased under the belief that it did not convey the lands of Rumgally; 2*d*, Whether it was granted under essential error; and 3*d*, Whether, in so far as it imported to convey these lands, it was fraudulently impetrated from the deceased by the defender and Mr Welch, on her behalf, or by one or other of them.

The Court to-day disallowed the first two issues, but granted the third.

M'Clelland *v.* Brown's Trustees.—*Nov.* 28.

Appeal—Expenses.

In this case a majority of the whole Court had found that marriage-contract trustees, who had invested the trust funds in the Western Bank, did not incur any personal liability on the bank's failure. The House of Lords, on appeal, reversed this decision (except as regarded Dr Buchanan, one of the trustees, with respect to whom the appeal was dismissed with costs), and ordered that the case should be remitted back to the Court of Session, with instructions 'to pronounce decree against the said respondents, except the said respondent Andrew Buchanan, in terms of the conclusions of the summons, etc., and to do farther in the said case as shall be just and consistent therewith.'

A petition to apply this judgment was now presented, praying the Court to decern in terms thereof, and to find the defenders liable in expenses, and to remit to the Lord Ordinary to decern for the same, and to proceed with the cause. The explanation of this latter clause given by the pursuer was, that he meant to ask the Lord Ordinary to find Buchanan liable to the extent of the unexhausted trust funds, if any. The pursuer contended farther that decerniture in terms of the libel, which was directed by the House of Lords to be done, necessarily carried expenses.

To-day the Court held that under the order of the House of Lords, 'to do farther in the cause as shall be just and consistent,' they would be entitled to pronounce an interlocutor assoilzieing Buchanan. On the question of expenses, they were of opinion decerniture in terms of the libel did not necessarily carry expenses; that in a case like the present, when judgment had gone against the party who had been supporting the judgment of the Court below, and when the House of Lords had made no mention of expenses, it must be held that expenses had been intentionally omitted.

Bathie *v.* Bathie.—*Dec.* 9.

Divorce—Circumstances held not to infer Adultery.

This was an action of divorce at the instance of William Gordon Bathie, sometime shoemaker in Dundee, against Mrs Grace Lamb or Bathie, his wife. The ground of action was the alleged adultery of the defender with Nicholas White, auctioneer in Leith, who was called as a co-defender. The case for the pursuer was, that he and his wife had lived separate since 1858; that from January 1859 to the date of the raising the present action in 1863, the defender lived at various places, and kept lodgings, and that the co-defender invariably lived with her. There was no direct evidence of adultery having been committed at all, or even of improper familiarity between the defender and co-defender at the place where the adultery was alleged on record; but there was evidence tending to show that White occasionally called the defender Mrs White, and that they might, at a different place from that averred, have occupied the same bedroom. There was also produced a certificate from the registrar of births to the effect, that the defender registered the birth of a child as illegitimate in 1859; and the co-defender, when asked whether he had committed adultery with the defender, declined to answer. The defender denied the adultery on record, and averred that she was obliged to leave her husband on account of his cruelty and intemperance, and that the co-defender's intimacy with her never exceeded friendly familiarity, and the conferring many acts of kindness upon her and her children. She led no evidence, but contended that the pursuer's case was not made out.

To-day the Lord President delivered the opinion of the Court (affirming that of the Lord Ordinary Mure), that the pursuer had not proved his case. They held that they could only find adultery proven at the place where it was averred on record; that the refusal of the co-defender to answer the question, whether he had committed adultery with the defender, was to be construed according to the circumstances under which the refusal was given, and that the certificate from the register of births must be kept out of view, there being no evidence to show that the entry was signed by the defender. The statute made the certificate equivalent to the principal register; but even if it was on the table, it would not prove, without evidence, that the signature to the entry was that of the defender. It was remarkable, if the adultery continued for such a time as was stated on record, that clearer evidence of it had not been available; and the suspicious circumstances of the case being explained on the footing that they were due to the familiarity and kindness of an intimate friend, they must hold that there was not sufficient evidence of the alleged adultery.

Report by Accountant in Bankruptcy, with Answers for A. B.—*Dec.* 9.

Bankruptcy—Breach of Statute by Trustee.

In this case the Accountant in Bankruptcy reported the respondent's conduct to the Court, in consequence of certain irregularities in his accounts as trustee on a bankrupt estate, connected with the retention in his own hands of part of the funds of the estate for a longer period than is allowed by the Act of Parliament. As the respondent had paid penal interest on the sums so retained by him, and no loss, therefore, had been caused to any one by his actings, and the estate under his charge had been wound up, the Court did not think it necessary to do more than express their sense of the great impropriety of the respondent's conduct, which, under other circumstances, might have led to his removal from the office of trustee. The Accountant had very properly brought the matter under the notice of the Court, and the respondent would be found liable in the expense attendant thereupon.

Kerr *v.* Thomson's Trustees and Others.—*Dec.* 13.

Trust-Disposition—Construction of Bequest.

The pursuer's uncle, Thomas Sproat, died on 30th January 1859, leaving a trust-disposition and settlement by which he appointed separate trustees for the realization of his estates in Scotland and Australia respectively. He appointed his Australian trustees, after the fulfilment of certain purposes in that country, to remit the residue to Scotland. By the second purpose of the deed he thus provided: 'I appoint my said trustee' (in Scotland) 'to invest the sum of £3000 sterling in Government or good heritable security, in their own names as trustees foresaid, and hold and retain the same, and pay the interest, dividends, and profits thereof to my niece, Mary Sproat Kerr' (the pursuer), 'only child of Peter

Kerr and Nicholas Sproat or Kerr, during all the days of her life; and that at two terms in the year, Whitsunday and Martinmas, by equal portions; declaring that the said interests, dividends, and profits shall be paid to the said Mary Sproat Kerr, exclusive of, and not subject to the *jus mariti* of any husband she may marry, and shall not be subject to, or liable for the debts or deeds of such husband, nor attachable by the diligence of his creditors; and that the receipt of the said Mary Sproat or Kerr alone therefor, without the consent of her husband, shall be valid and sufficient to my said trustees and all others concerned.' The fee of the sum was destined to the pursuer's children, if she had any, and, if not, fell into the residue of the testator's estate. Mrs Elizabeth Sproat or Thomson, sister of Thomas Sproat, and aunt of the pursuer, died on 7th March 1862, about three years after her brother Thomas. She had executed a settlement in April 1861, in which she left to the pursuer certain legacies, and a share of the residue of her estate. On 12th October 1861, she executed a codicil to her settlement, on the narrative 'that since the execution of the said settlement, my brother Alexander Sproat has returned from Australia, but I have received no statement of the affairs of my late brother Thomas; and, as the provisions contained in my said settlement in favour of my niece Mary Kerr' (the pursuer) 'were made under the impression, that, from the legacy bequeathed to her by the settlement of my deceased brother Thomas, she would be amply provided for; but as I consider it just that she should receive an additional provision from my estate, in the event of her not receiving the said legacy from the estate of my said brother Thomas Sproat.' On this narrative, she dispoues and conveys to the pursuer, in terms of present and absolute conveyance, the lands of Tonguecroft and others. She adds the following declaration:—'But declaring that, in the event of the foresaid legacy, bequeathed to my said niece by said brother, being paid to her within one year after my decease, then she shall have no right to the said lands hereby disponed; and the same shall be disposed of as provided for in the said settlement.' It appears that, when the year was drawing near an expiry, funds to the extent of £3000 were received in this country from the uncle's Australian estates; and on 7th March 1863, the anniversary of Mrs Thomson's death, a deposit in the following terms was made in the Bank of Scotland's branch at Gatehouse-of-Fleet:—'Received from Thomas Sproat, Esq., Rainton, for behoof of the trustees of the late Thomas Sproat, Esq., sometime of Geelong, for investment in favour of Miss Mary Sproat Kerr, £3000 sterling, which is placed to his credit on deposit-receipt.' The deposit-receipt was afterwards indorsed thus:—'Alex. Sproat, Thos. A. Sproat, the sole surviving and acting trustees of the late Thomas Sproat of Geelong.' The executrix of Mr Sproat, Rainton, the ostensible depositor, has declared she has no claim to the sum. And the deposit-receipt is said to be held by the agent for the trustees of Thomas Sproat, subject to their orders in the way of investment for the pursuer.

Miss Kerr has brought the present action, for the purpose of having it declared that, under Mrs Thomson's settlement and codicil, she is entitled to the absolute fee of the lands of Tonguecroft, etc., in respect the legacy bequeathed to her by her uncle had not been paid to her within a year after her aunt's death, and the event on which she was to have no right to these lands had not therefore occurred.

To-day the Court—recalling the interlocutor of the Lord Ordinary (Kinloch), Lord Curriehill dissenting—assoilzied the defenders.

Their lordships agreed in holding that Mrs Thomson's object was to secure a sufficient provision for the pursuer, and that she therefore fixed a term of twelve months from her own death, within which, if the pursuer's provision under her uncle's settlement was not made good to her, she would have the lands of Tonguecroft made absolutely her own. Nothing having come from Australia, where the staple of the uncle's fortune lay, she appeared to be afraid the provision would fall short.

The majority of the Court held that the deposit in the Bank of Scotland on the anniversary of Mrs Thomson's death was sufficient implement of the bequest in Mr Sproat's will, to satisfy the condition in Mrs Thomson's settlement, on the occurrence of which the pursuer was to have no right to the lands in question.

Lord Curriehill, on the other hand (concurring with the Lord Ordinary), held that under Mr Sproat's will the pursuer had a bequest of the interest of £3000; that no interest having been paid to her (although Mr Sproat had died in January 1859) up to 7th March 1863, the deposit of £3000 of that date could not be regarded as payment of the bequest, because, as the interest of that deposit would be required to pay the future interest due under the bequest, the arrears of interest could not be held to be paid without encroaching on the capital.

M.P., Brown's Trustees *v.* Patons and Craig.—*Dec.* 14.

Reduction—Force or Fear—Cautioner.

In this case, it was held that an averment by a married woman, that she was induced to subscribe a deed out of anxiety to prevent the incarceration of her husband for civil debt, was not relevant in a reduction, on the ground of force or fear. It was also held, that a person who subscribes a deed as a cautioner, after hearing another person who was named in it as a co-obligant refuse to subscribe, was barred from pleading that she was discharged, because the deed was not subscribed by all the proposed parties to it.

Clouston and Others *v.* The Edinburgh and Glasgow Railway.—*Dec.* 14.

Railway—Companies Clauses Act.

This was an interdict at the instance of several shareholders of the Edinburgh and Glasgow Railway Company against that company and its directors, by which it was sought to interdict the respondents from 'voting, paying, or applying the sum of £16,600 of the monies, funds, or revenues of the company, or any part of these monies, funds, and revenues, as a donation, gift, or present, by any name, or under any pretext,' to Messrs Latham, Jamieson, Thomson, Tawse, and M'Gregor, sometime officials of the said company, or to Mr Blackburn, sometime chairman of the directors; or from 'voting, applying, or paying any part of the said monies, funds, or revenues to all or any of these persons, otherwise than in discharge of legal obligations or debts justly due and resting-owing to them by the said company.' The grounds on which the interdict was asked were—(1) That the voting of the money as proposed was *ultra vires* of the company or its directors; (2) That by the 12th section of the recent Act amalgamating the company with the North British Company, the directors were bound to divide the assets among the shareholders after all 'claims' against the company are discharged; and (3) That the money was proposed to be voted, although in the notice of the meeting no intimation was made of the proposal to do so, as was necessary under the Companies Clauses Act.

Lord Curriehill, on 19th September last, granted interim interdict, and ordered answers; and on 25th September, after considering the answers and hearing parties, he passed the note and continued the interdict. His Lordship thought that the important question as to the power of the company to make donations to its office-bearers and servants for past services had not been settled by authority; and that the circumstances in which the question now arose were peculiar. No injury could arise by postponing the payment of the money until the question is settled. The respondents reclaimed.

To-day the Court unanimously adhered to Lord Curriehill's interlocutor, and continued the interdict. Their Lordships held, (1) That it was incompetent to vote the funds in the manner proposed at the meeting at which the motion was made, in respect no notice of the motion had been given; and (2) That under the Act amalgamating the Edinburgh and Glasgow Railway Company with the North British, the former company had ceased to exist, except for the purpose of paying its debts and dividing its surplus revenue; and the allowances proposed to be voted, not being debts but gratuities, they could only be paid out of the company funds with the consent of the whole shareholders.

INVERNESS AND PERTH RAILWAY COMPANY *v.* GOWANS.—*Dec.* 14.

Expenses.

This was an objection to the auditor's report on the pursuer's account of expenses. He had allowed a charge of £54, 2s. to the pursuers' agent for proceeding to London and attending the examination of a witness for the defenders, whose evidence was allowed by the Court to be taken to lie *in retentis.* The examination lasted for four days. It was objected for the defenders that it was unnecessary for the Edinburgh agent to attend the examination, and that a London agent should have been employed. The defenders founded in support of their objection on the cases of *Armstrong's Trustees* (12 S. 510) and *Lumsden* v. *Hamilton* (7 D. 300). It appeared that the Edinburgh agent for the defenders had also gone to London to attend the examination.

The Court repelled the objection.

The ordinary rule undoubtedly was, that a party was not entitled as against his opponent to the expense of such a charge as was objected to. It lay upon the pursuers to justify the charge. In this case the importance and propriety of having an Edinburgh agent was shown by what the defenders had themselves done; and it also appeared from the nature of the examination of the witness, who was a witness for the defenders, and was examined at great length as to details with which a London agent could not have made himself familiar.

HUNTER AND OTHERS v. THE CARRON COMPANY.—*Dec.* 15.

Fraud—Title to Sue.

The pursuer of this action is the trustee under the marriage contract of the late John Lothian, S.S.C., Edinburgh, and Mrs Mary Hunter or Caldwell or Lothian, his first wife, and also under the deed of appointment and settlement executed by Mrs Lothian relatively to her marriage contract. The residuary legatees under the settlement concur with the trustee in the action. The object of the action is to oblige the defenders, the Carron Company, to account for a large amount of profits said to have been realized by them between the years 1824 and 1846, during which period the pursuer's predecessor, Mrs Lothian, was a shareholder in the company; but which profits are alleged to have been fraudulently concealed and misapplied by the defenders, for the purpose and with the effect of keeping down the rate of divideud during the said period, and thus of withholding from the shareholders, and among them from Mrs Lothian, and the trustees under her marriage contract, profits which legally belonged to them.

The defenders contended *in limine* that the pursuers had no title to insist in the action, because, under the provisions of the marriage contract and Mrs Lothian's relative settlement, her shares of Carron stock had been made over to her husband, and after her death sold to the defenders, whereby the pursuers had been divested of all right to insist in the present claim.

The Lord Ordinary (Mure) repelled this plea, and found that the pursuers were entitled to insist in the action, on the ground that there was nothing in the transaction under which the defenders became the owners of Mrs Lothian's shares to show that they had acquired any right to the profits which had been realized by the Carron Company between 1824 and 1846, and of which it was alleged that the shareholders were fraudulently deprived.

To-day the majority of the Court adhered to the Lord Ordinary's interlocutor.

Lord Curriehill dissented, holding that when the shares were transferred to the defenders, all rights incident to them were transferred also.

Pet., MACALISTER.—*Dec.* 16.

Entail—Bond of Provision.

By bond of provision dated the 30th March 1813, the late Colonel Macalister of Glenbarr bound himself, his heirs, executors, and successors whatsoever, to pay to Mrs Macalister, his spouse, in liferent, and to Keith Macalister, his only son, in fee, the sum of £6000. The bond was gratuitous, revocable, and remained undelivered at the time of the granter's death in December 1829. Subsequently, in June 1829, the granter of the bond executed a strict entail of the lands of Glenbarr, in favour of the said Keith Macalister and a series of substitutes. The deed of entail contained, *inter alia*, a clause by which the entailer bound himself, his heirs, executors, and successors whomsoever, to relieve the entailed lands and the heirs of entail of all debts and obligements for which either the entailer or his ancestors were liable; and it further contained a clause by which the entailer revoked all former deeds of entail, settlements, or other conveyances of the entailed lands, excepting provisions in favour of his spouse. Colonel Macalister left no other testamentary writings. After the death of Colonel Macalister, it appeared that his debts exhausted the whole of his estates, heritable and moveable, with the exception of the entailed lands, leaving no funds available for payment of the bond of provision, which the petitioner, the grantee in the bond, and the institute in the deed of entail sought to have constituted a burden upon the entailed estate.

To-day the Court (Lord Deas dissenting) refused his application, holding that the entailer had sufficiently expressed his intention that the gratuitous bond should not be made a burden upon the entailed lands, which were made the subject of a special disposition.

MACFARLANE AND OTHERS *v.* ROBERTSON'S TRUSTEES.—*Dec.* 19.

Right of Way—Special Verdict.

This was an action of declarator at the instance of Malcolm Macfarlane and others of the inhabitants of Causewayhead near Stirling, against the trustees of the late James Robertson, Esq., of Easter Corntown, to have it found and declared that the road known as the Broad or Braid Loan, near the village of Causewayhead, bounded as described in the summons, is a public road, and that the pursuers and all others are entitled to the free use, possession, and enjoyment of the said public road, and all privileges therewith connected.

The road in question was averred to have formed part of the old highway or statute labour road between Stirling and Blairlogie. About the year 1806 the present Ochil turnpike road was made, and, as the defenders averred, the old road was then shut up, and has since been disused as a public road. The defenders further alleged upon record a title to the *solum* of the old road. They averred that the *solum* of the said road was allotted by the trustees to Sir Robert Abercrombie, and by him conveyed to their authors by charter in 1818. They further averred exclusive possession for forty years and upwards following on the said charter. They denied all right on the part of the public to the use of the said road, except the right of a footpath along the eastern side of it. The pursuers, on the other hand, denied that the said road had ever been either judicially or *de facto* shut up. They disputed the defenders' title, and averred that, so far as possession had taken place on their part, it was an illegal encroachment on the rights of the public.

The following issue was sent to a jury for trial of the cause:—'Whether, for forty years or for time immemorial prior to 25th October 1864, the road called the Broad or Braid Loan, near the village of Causewayhead, in or near the parish of Logie and county of Clackmannan, extending (here follows a description of the *termini* and boundaries of the road), has been used as a public road, connecting the parts of the said public highway from Stirling to Blairlogie adjoining the said points A and B.'

The following special verdict was returned:—

'Find that the road described in the issue was, from time immemorial prior to the year 1806, used as a public road for all purposes: Find that since the year 1806 the said road has not been used for horses, carts, or cattle; and further, find that the said road has since the year 1806 continued to be used as a public road for foot-passengers only, connecting the parts of the public highway from Stirling to Blairlogie adjoining the points A and B mentioned in the issue, and leave it to the Court to enter up a verdict for the pursuers or defenders in accordance with law.'

The pursuers, on 21st November last, moved the Court to apply the said verdict as a verdict for them. The defenders made a counter motion to have the verdict entered up as a verdict for the defenders. The pursuers contended the Court have nothing now before them but the verdict. By that it is found that the road in question was, from time immemorial prior to 1806, a public road for all purposes, and that since that time it has continuously been used as a public road for foot-passengers. There is no evidence to show shutting up of the road or adverse possession. On the contrary, the public have proved a possession inconsistent with such, viz. a possession and use of the road in its whole breadth and length. The defenders should have taken a counter issue to prove that the road was shut up, which they have not done. A public road does not cease to be such by mere disuse, there must be shutting up or adverse possession. At all events, the limited use of the road in the present case by the pursuers since 1806, must be held as sufficient to preserve to them all their ancient rights and privileges therein, and to keep up the character of the road as a public road.

The defenders contended, all that the verdict finds for the pursuers is that the road in question has been used by foot-passengers. That has not been disputed. The defenders have all along unreservedly conceded a right of footpath in the public.

At advising to-day, the Court were unanimously of opinion that the verdict should be entered up as a verdict for the defenders, subject to a right of footpath, and found the pursuers liable in expenses, subject to modification.

Thoms *v.* Thoms.—*Dec.* 19.

In this case, the judgment in which is reported under date 25th November, the Court to-day refused a petition by the pursuer for leave to appeal at present against the interlocutor disallowing the first two issues.

Ward's Trustees *v.* The Glasgow and South-Western Railway Company.—*Dec.* 20.

Act of Sederunt, July 1865—*Prorogation of Consent.*

In this case the record was closed in the Outer House, and an interlocutor pronounced appointing issues to be lodged. The pursuers failed to implement this order within the time fixed by the interlocutor, and thereafter moved the Lord Ordinary to allow issues to be received with the consent of the defenders. The Lord Ordinary (Kinloch) refused the motion, holding that the provision of the recent Act of Sederunt, that 'all appointments for the lodging or adjusting of issues shall be held to be peremptory,' deprived him of the power of granting it. The defenders did not exercise their right under the Act of Sederunt to take decree by default, and the pursuers reclaimed against the Lord Ordinary's interlocutor.

To-day the Lord President delivered the judgment of the Court. His Lordship, after referring to the several enactments under which the procedure in making up a record takes place, especially those under which prorogation by consent of the time for lodging papers was introduced, pointed out that while this was found to be expedient with regard to the papers forming the record, as time for getting additional information requiring to be stated in them might be necessary, the same consideration did not apply to issues, as the moment the record was made up and closed, there should be no difficulty in extracting from it the issue to try the cause. His Lordship could not conceive a record satisfactorily framed by a person who had not in his eye the issue he was ultimately to propose. There was therefore no necessity for delay in lodging issues, and it was inexpedient that any such should be allowed. He was therefore of opinion that the Lord Ordinary acted rightly in refusing to be controlled by the parties, and in rejecting the motion that the issues should be received of consent,—there being no speciality in the present case to justify the delay. As this, however, was the first case of the kind, and the parties might have been under a misapprehension, the Court would allow the issues to be lodged on the present occasion.

SECOND DIVISION.

M.P., Wilson *v.* Jeffrey and Others.—*Nov.* 17.

Testament—Legacy—Relations—Per stirpes.

By a codicil the testator provided, 'That on the death of Antoinette Aitken, my wife, . . . my whole household furniture shall be divided—one half among my relations, and the other half among the relations of the said Antoinette Aitken.' The question raised in the present action was, Who are the parties designated as 'my relations?' Henry Gardiner (a nephew of the truster, who was left a general legacy, for the payment of which there would be a shortcoming of funds if the legacy of furniture was valid) maintained that the bequest to the testator's 'relations' imported a bequest to all who could establish propinquity, however remote, and that the bequest was therefore void for uncertainty. The testator's next of kin, other than Gardiner, maintained that it was a bequest to the testator's heirs *in mobilibus*, and was therefore not void for uncertainty. The Court were unanimously of opinion that the bequest was a valid bequest in favour of the testator's heirs *in mobilibus;* and that the distribution fell to be made *per stirpes.*

M'Laren *v.* Clyde Navigation Trs.; M'Laren *v.* Harvey.—*Nov.* 17.

Valuation of Lands Act—Long Leases—Assessment for building Parish Church.

Where an assessment was imposed by a resolution of heritors for the purpose of rebuilding a parish church according to the real rent of properties within the parish, parties entered in the valuation roll as proprietors of lands and houses for the year in which the assessment was imposed, but whose connection with the subjects was that they held leases of them for more than twenty-one years, were sued as 'heritors, owners, or proprietors,' for the proportion of assessment effeiring to the annual value entered in the roll. The pursuer founded entirely upon the Valuation of Lands Act. The nature of the contentions of parties, and the decision, appear from the following abridgment of the opinion of the Court delivered by Lord Neaves: 'The question is, whether the provisions of the Act impose upon lessees, under leases of more than twenty-one years, a liability for this assessment, which but for the Act would not attach to them. The Court are of opinion that the Act has no such effect. The general purview of the Valuation Act seems to be explained in the title and preamble of the Act. It is not an Act for taxing parties. It is an Act merely for valuing properties. The warrant and nature of each assessment must be looked for in the original Act imposing it, and it is only the arithmetical ascertainment of its amount that the Valuation Act is intended to facilitate. The thirty-third section of the Act makes it imperative to take the real rent of any subjects from the valuation roll; but it is nowhere said that the roll is to be the rule as to the parties assessable. The entry of a person's name upon the roll is no ground of liability unless he is otherwise liable, and its omission from the roll is no ground of exemption if he is not otherwise free. But it is said that under the *sixth* section there is a new liability imposed. The leading object even of this section is to fix the mode of estimating the yearly value of heritages. With respect to that matter, a distinction is drawn in the section between leases of a longer and a shorter duration, the line being drawn at twenty-one years in ordinary subjects, and thirty-one years in the case of minerals. The main purpose of this distinction is, that in the shorter leases the actual rent shall be taken as the true value, which it will probably be; while in the longer leases it is not necessarily to be taken as the value, it being thought probable in many cases that the present value may there be different from the rent. We should not naturally expect an alteration of liability under a clause which professes to deal merely or mainly with the estimate of value; but if such a change were intended, it ought at least to be explicitly set forth. But it is said that, when in these longer leases the actual value is taken and not the actual rent, this is an injustice or a hardship to the proprietor, who might be assessed at a rate greatly exceeding the benefit received by him from the subjects; and on this account it is argued the enactment in the sixth section has been introduced, that the lessee under the long lease "shall be deemed and taken to be also the proprietor of such lands and heritages in the sense of this Act, but shall be entitled to relief from the actual proprietor," in manner therein mentioned. There is some apparent plausibility in this view; and it may be a hardship in some cases that the heritor should pay an assessment according to the actual value, and not according to the rent he receives. But the clause, according to the pursuer's interpretation of it, would create more injustice than it could possibly remedy. If equity had been the object of the clause, it would have taken into view, not the original duration of the lease, but the period for which it had still to run at the time of the valuation and assessment. It may be hard that a proprietor, at an early part of a long lease, shall pay an assessment according to the actual value of a subject which he is to be kept out of for one hundred years, and for which he is only to get in the meantime a nominal rent. But, on the other hand, it would be as hard, or much harder, that every tenant in a lease longer than twenty-one years should, even in the last year of his possession, pay a great share of the expense of building a church from which he is not to derive the slightest benefit, and for which he was in no respect liable by the law as it previously stood, and as contemplated when the lease was entered into. Such an inversion of the rights of parties, and such an alteration of a voluntary contract, would be eminently unjust, and is not to be presumed to have been intended. Again, there are many cases where the hardship may lie the other way from what the pursuer urges. The tenant, though paying a small rent, may have begun by paying a large grassum; or he may be bound, as generally happens in a building lease, to leave buildings on the ground such as will be a great boon to the landlord. To lay upon the lessee the church assessment would, in such circumstances, be most inequitable. Yet none of these considerations are here taken into view, although they were manifestly essential if equity was the object of the clause. It seems much more probable that the object of the sixth section was merely some matter of convenience in the collection of assessments, without its being intended to effect any change of ultimate liability. Upon the whole, the only safe and sound construction of the statute is, that it does not impose on the defenders a liability to which they were not previously subject, and consequently that they must be assoilzied from the conclusions of the actions.'

MURRAY'S EXECUTORS *v.* FORBES.—*Nov.* 21.

Sheriff Court—Proof by Commission.

In a Sheriff Court action for money contained in a deposit receipt by the Union Bank to the deceased, indorsed by her to the defender, and the amount of which had been uplifted by him, but had not, it was alleged, been accounted for by him to the deceased or the present pursuers, a proof was led by commission, and the defender was assoilzied. In an advocation, held incompetent under sec. 10 of the Sheriff Court Act to take the proof by commission, and that it should have been before the Sheriff himself. Issues ordered.

KIRK *v.* BROWNS.—*Nov.* 22.

Proof—Trial by Jury.

The chief question in this action of removing, was whether the pursuer was barred from pleading a clause in a lease excluding assignees and sub-tenants, by her own acts and those of her agents, in receiving rents from the defenders and recognising them as tenants. The question came to be, whether the evidence of the pursuer and her daughter, or that of her law-agents, was more worthy of credit. Proof having been led by commission, the Lord Ordinary found that the pursuer was barred from pleading the clause of exclusion. On a reclaiming note, the Lord Justice-Clerk briefly stated the facts of the case, and delivered the judgment of the Court as follows:—This is a pure question of fact. We are all very decidedly of opinion that this question should have been tried by a jury, and that its not being so tried is a very grave miscarriage. And since we are obliged to discharge the functions of a jury, we avail ourselves of the form of verdict usually returned, and simply find for the defenders. The form of interlocutor will be to adhere to the Lord Ordinary's interlocutor.

Miller *v.* Hunter.—*Nov.* 24.

Process—Expenses—New Trial—Excessive Damages.

In an action of damages by a tenant against a landlord for being wrongously prevented from taking a waygoing crop, the pursuer obtained a verdict in his favour, which was overturned (23 March 1865, 3 Macph. 745) on the ground that the damages awarded were excessive. On a second trial, the jury awarded a smaller sum. The case came before the Court upon the question of expenses, and it was held that there had been in the first trial a very grievous miscarriage on both sides. The defender had been to blame for what he maintained in point of law; while the pursuer, by estimating his damages, through his witnesses, on a fundamentally erroneous principle, chiefly produced the excess of damages allowed by the jury. Hence neither party should get the expenses of the first trial. As to the discussion upon the rule, the circumstance that it was obtained and maintained upon two grounds, on one of which the defender was successful and on the other unsuccessful, led to the same result. In the fact that the new trial was granted on the ground of excessive damages, there was nothing very special, so as to make a different rule applicable from that which would apply where the verdict was contrary to evidence. There was only this peculiarity, that if the ground for granting a new trial is excessive damages, the party obtaining a new trial is not entitled to expect a verdict the other way; and it is only fair to consider that he has substantially succeeded in his object in the second trial, if he has obtained a reduction of the amount of damages. Expenses of the record and the second trial only were awarded to the pursuer.

Macbride *v.* Clark, Grierson, and Co., etc.—*Nov.* 24.

Partnership—Cautioner—Relief.

In a cash credit bond the admitted co-obligants, along with a company and its individual partners, the principal debtors, were James Gemmell, James Munn, and Clark, Grierson, and Co. as a company. The partners of the latter company, Robert Bland Clark and William Grierson, also signed the bond. The principal debtors having become insolvent, the present action was brought by Munn's judicial factor, to have it determined whether R. B. Clark and William Grierson signed merely as partners and in corroboration of the company obligation, or, as he contends, added their individual obligations to that of the company. The pursuer contends that there are five cautioners; the defenders that there are only three, the partners of Clark, Grierson, and Co. not being also bound as individuals. The Lord Ordinary (Jerviswoode) found that Mr Clark and Mr Grierson had superadded their personal obligations to that of the firm; and to-day the Court adhered, holding the case to depend on the construction of the particular bond. The first question was, Who are bound to the bank? There were nine parties bound conjunctly and severally, and the bank would be entitled to charge any one of them to pay the whole sum. It was provided that, even if there should be a change of partners in the principal debtor, the company of Anderson, Son, and Clark, all the parties to the bond should remain bound as before. Now, if these individuals, William Anderson, John Anderson, and Francis Clark, ceased to be partners, and others came in their places, the firm would be liable; and William Anderson, John Anderson, and Francis Clark would still be liable *personally*. If so, it was hopeless to contend that any other construction could be put, in a question with the bank, on the obligation of the other company. But it appears that the principal debtor is the firm of William Anderson, Son, and Clark. Now that raises a somewhat different question. It was argued that if there are five cautioners, then there must be eight cautioners, because William Anderson, John Anderson, and Francis Clark are bound as cautioners just the same as the other parties. But the answer was, that in a question of relief they were the principal debtors, and individually bound in relief. The obligation must be construed in the same way as in a question with the bank. If these are all bound *in solidum* to the bank, the relief must be estimated in the same way. William Grierson must have relief not only against Munn, but against his own firm and his partner. The moment you fix the meaning of the obligation as between the bank and the whole obligants, you lay the foundation for the construction of the obligation as between all the parties.

Lord Benholme concurred, but was not aided by the preliminary construction of the obligation as to a change in the firm. It was difficult to see how the parties could ever bind another company from their own.

X. and Y. *v.* Q.'s Trustee.—*Nov.* 25.

Expenses—Sequestration—19 *and* 20 *Vict. c.* 79, *s.* 126.

The trustee on a sequestrated estate rejected without inquiry a claim by a firm in whose employment the deceased bankrupt had been from 1849 to 1855, for monies of which they alleged that they had been defrauded by under-summations of sums received, and over-summations of sums paid by him as their cashier. On appeal, the Lord Ordinary after proof remitted to rank the appellant in terms of his claim, finding the trustee liable in expenses. The trustee reclaimed, contending that he should not be found liable in expenses. The majority of the judges regarded the case as one peculiarly well suited for investigation by the trustee himself, under the powers given him by the 126th section of the Act, rather than for judicial investigation. It was no doubt a peculiar claim, a very long time having elapsed after the bankrupt left the claimant's office. But the affidavits gave in effect all the facts now before the Court. It appeared to be the policy of the 126th section to encourage the trustee and creditors to have extrajudicial examinations wherever they were competent, and likely to lead to a settlement of the claim. This extraordinary power of citing parties and putting them on oath would not have been given to the trustee except for the purpose of enabling him to get all the light he could get by judicial investigation. If the trustee had here done so, the proof, consisting only of explanations by the partners and their clerks of the way in which the business was carried on, could have been got without any expense at all by the trustee himself. If the trustee and creditors want to take the chance of an appeal, which may sometimes be expedient, they must incur the usual penalty of failure.

Lord Benholme differed, holding that under the 126th section the trustee and creditors were entitled to take any way they thought proper for ascertaining the justice of a claim.

App., LATTA *v.* DALL.—*Nov.* 28.

Sequestration—Affidavit—Rectification—19 *and* 20 *Vict. c.* 79, *ss.* 51, 60.

In a competition for the office of trustee in a sequestration, the Sheriff, who had not been present at the meeting of creditors, allowed an affidavit which had not valued and deducted the obligation of the co-obligant in a bill, to be rectified under the 51st section of the statute. Held that although, by sec. 60, the valuation of securities, etc., is to be made 'before voting,' yet it was the imperative duty of the Sheriff to order rectification of any kind of error or omission. As to the time when this could be done, there was an apparent contradiction in the statute; but it was plainly intended that the Sheriff should have the same power to consider the votes when reported to him by the preses as if he had been present at the meeting. It lay with him, and not with the creditors, to declare the election (*Miller* v. *Duncan*, 18 March 1858, 20 D. 803. See *Gibson* v. *Greig*, 17 Dec. 1853, 16 D. 233). As to the mode of rectification, it was not necessary for the Sheriff to make any written order; and he would have done more wisely, and would at all events have prevented this appeal, if he had merely intimated that he required the affidavit to be amended.—Appeal dismissed.

SUTHERLAND *v.* DOUGLAS' TRUSTEES.—*Nov.* 29.

Succession—Legacy—Conditional Institution.

The late Mrs Douglas of Orbiston directed her trustees to make over to Mrs Esther Monro or Sutherland, wife of Alexander Sutherland, certain debts or sums to the extent of £1000, 'declaring' in very express terms that it should not be subject to her husband's *jus mariti*, 'being to remain as an alimentary fund free of any such debts and deeds; and in the event of the said A. S. surviving his said wife, he shall be entitled to enjoy the interest of the said sum during his life, and upon his death it shall go to the heirs of his said wife; which declaration my said trustees are requested to carry into effect.' Mrs Esther Sutherland and her husband both predeceased the testator, her husband predeceasing her. Mrs Janet Sutherland, their daughter, and her husband brought this action to establish their claim to the said sum. The trustees maintained that the legacy had lapsed by the testator's predeceasing Mrs Monro or Sutherland; that the legacy was to her, and that the liferent to her husband and the declaration as to her children were merely qualifications of it. The Court held, that the only question being whether the words of the deed provide, (1) in the event of Mrs Sutherland predeceasing, a conditional institution in favour of her heirs, subject only to the liferent of her husband, or (2) a legacy in her favour, to come into operation only in the event of her surviving, with a substitution of her heirs, the former construction must be adopted as, on the whole, the more rational. The presumption *in dubio* in such a case was in favour of conditional institution, rather than of substitution; and there was not enough in the words of the clause to overturn that presumption. The legacy was to Mrs Sutherland absolutely, with protection against the *jus mariti*, and with power of disposal. If she had taken and not disposed of it, it would have gone to her heirs under the burden of the liferent; and so, when she predeceases, it still goes to her heirs as conditionally instituted.

BALLANTYNE *v.* BALLANTYNE.—*Dec.* 1.

Nullity of Marriage—Interim Aliment.

In a declarator of the nullity of a regular marriage raised by a husband against his wife, on the ground of a previous irregular marriage contracted by her with another, who was also called as co-defender, the defender moved for interim aliment. Interim aliment had been allowed by the Lord Ordinary (Ardmillan) in 1861, on the authority of English cases, and the cause had since proceeded in the Outer House on that footing. Decree of nullity had now been pronounced by the Lord Ordinary, against which the defender was reclaiming. The pursuer argued that this decree reversed the presumption in favour of the person who was in the possession of the status of his wife, and that aliment should not now be awarded. The Lord Justice-Clerk said, if it were necessary to decide as to the competency of such an application, he should hesitate to dispose of the motion without further consideration; but it was enough here that the Lord Ordinary had annulled the marriage, and refused the defender expenses. Lords Benholme and Neaves had not much difficulty about the competency, because, when a husband brings an action of this kind against one who is enjoying the status of his wife, she is entitled to protect herself at the expense of him who has the control of all her estate, at least at the commencement of a cause; but, in the circumstances, they concurred in refusing the motion.

KINLOCH *v.* CLARK.—*Dec.* 1.

Reparation—Road Surveyor—Road Trustees—General Turnpike Act.

Mrs Kinloch and her husband sued Clark, road surveyor for the Glasgow and Shotts Trustees, for reparation for injuries sustained by the female pursuer through falling into a large hole, open space, or abrupt declivity, on the footpath along the road through the village of Holytown, which is under the charge of the defender as surveyor. The Sheriff-substitute, after proof, assoilzied the defender; but the Sheriff (Alison), on appeal, found him liable in damages. The defender advocated, and contended that he was not liable for a mere omission in having failed to remove or fill up an existing hole or declivity. The pursuer founded on the General Turnpike Act, 1 and 2 Will. IV. c. 43, s. 101, which enacts that 'if the surveyor of any turnpike road, or any contractor, or other person employed on such road, . . . shall lay on any such road any matter or thing, or shall knowingly permit to remain on any part of such road any matter or thing, which shall endanger the safety of any passenger, or shall dig any pit, or make any cut on any turnpike road, without sufficiently fencing the same, such person shall for every such offence forfeit and pay a sum not exceeding £5, *over and above the damage sustained thereby*, and expenses.'

The following cases were referred to:—*Findlater* v. *Duncan*, 1839, House of Lords, M'L. and Rob. 911; *Young* v. *Davies*, 8 Eng. Jur. 286; and *M'Kinnon* v. *Penson*, 8 Exch. 319.

The Court held that the accident had been occasioned by a contraction of the footpath on which the pursuer was walking, caused by the turnpike road having been raised above the natural level, and by the necessity of making a cart entrance to some houses adjoining at a lower level. This operation was done before the defender became surveyor. The accident was produced entirely by the malconstruction of this footpath, and not by any other circumstance, such as by the footpath having got out of repair. Upon these facts, the question is whether the pursuer is entitled to recover against the surveyor, on the ground that he failed to perform a duty incumbent upon him. The 82d, 94th, and 116th sections show that it is incumbent on the trustees to keep in repair the footpaths along the road, and fence them; and the question is, whether that duty is imposed also on the surveyor. If we take the relation between him and the trustees as at common law, we must look to the nature of the contract. From the evidence as to employment, apart from the statute, it appears that the surveyor had no power to spend money at his own hand in *improving* the road, and that his whole duty consisted in the supervision of contractors, *i.e.* of contractors with the trustees. He had no power to employ men as his own servants, and was not different from any other ordinary servant of the trustees. At common law, a servant so employed is not liable for his employer's failure of duty. So far as there was a failure of duty, it was on the part of the trustees. The funds of the trust cannot indeed be applied to pay damages for wrong done by them; but if the trustees have committed any personal injury, they are just as liable as any other person. The only point decided is, that they are not answerable *as trustees*, and cannot defray out of the public funds in their hands such a charge as this. In the Act of Parliament there is nothing more directly bearing on the question than sec. 101 (cited above). It comprehends all persons employed in any capacity whatever, even mere day-labourers; and the whole section is concerned with *personal fault*. It does not describe any special duty laid on the road surveyor, and refers to a general class of faults of commission which any one may be guilty of. Upon the whole, the 101st section, so far from supporting the pursuer's contention, proves that the whole view of the statute was to make every one answerable for his own faults, and not for those of any one else.

WALKER *v.* SIMPSON.—*Dec.* 1.

Sheriff Court Act, sec. 10.

Observed, that adjournments of diets of proof in the Sheriff Court, which bore to be made of consent of parties, were in violation of the 10th section of the Sheriff Court Act, which requires them to be embodied in interlocutors stating the reason of adjournment.

HIGH COURT OF JUSTICIARY.

TAGUE *v.* SMITH.—*June* 10.

Poor Law Amendment Act, 1845 (8 *and* 9 *Vict. c.* 83), *sec.* 80—*Complaint —Summary Procedure—Penalty.*

The Poor Law Amendment Act, 1845, provides (sec. 80), that any person deserting or refusing to support a wife or child 'shall be deemed to be a vagabond, and may be prosecuted criminally before the Sheriff at the instance of the inspector of the poor, and shall, upon conviction, be punishable by fine or imprisonment, with or without hard labour, at the discretion of the said Sheriff.' A complaint against Tague, who was in the position contemplated, prayed the Sheriff 'to decern and adjudge the said Tague as a vagabond, to forfeit a "fine not exceeding £10 sterling," "and in the event of failure to pay the same, to grant warrant to imprison" him "for such period, not exceeding sixty days, as your Lordship shall fix, unless paid, or to decern or adjudge the said Tague to be imprisoned in the common jail or house of correction of Dumbarton, and for such period, not exceeding sixty days,"' etc. Tague having been brought to trial, was convicted and sentenced to thirty days' imprisonment. The proceedings before the Sheriff were in the summary form authorized by 9 Geo. IV. c. 29, secs. 19 and 20: 'Where the prosecutor shall in his libel conclude for a fine not exceeding £10, together with expenses, or for imprisonment in jail or bridewell not exceeding sixty days.' Tague having been imprisoned, brought this note of suspension, arguing that the respondent was not entitled to limit the penalty prayed for in his complaint, so as to make the summary procedure of 9 Geo. IV. c. 29 applicable to the case. He was bound to bring under the view of the Sheriff all the alternatives of punishment which might be imposed under the statute—*Thomson* v. *Wardlaw*, 23d January 1865, see index. In any case he was not entitled to omit all mention of 'hard labour,' which was an element of the statutory penalty—*Ferguson* v. *Thow*, 30th June 1862.

The suspension was refused with expenses; Lord Deas remarking: 'The view I take is that hard labour, as expressed in the 80th section of the Poor Law Act, is additional punishment. It is not expressed so as to be a necessary part of the statutory punishment to be awarded. I do not think, therefore, that the prosecutor here was bound to conclude for a sentence of imprisonment with hard labour.'

STANLEY *v.* JOHNSTON.—*Nov.* 7.

Warrant to apprehend—Suspension.

Warrant to apprehend the advocator for examination was granted by a justice of the peace under the Summary Procedure Act, upon a complaint by the Procurator-fiscal, alleging that the advocator had fired a gun from a boat upon a river across a highway, to the annoyance of a passenger, in contravention of the 96th sec. of the General Turnpike Act. This suspension and advocation of the proceedings was brought, in which it was objected that the warrant to apprehend was incompetent, the 110th sec. of the Turnpike Act authorizing citation of persons contravening it, and sec. 111 authorizing a warrant of apprehension only where the justice was satisfied that such warrant ought to be granted. The Summary Procedure Act authorized such a warrant only 'where apprehension is competent.' The Court were of opinion, that whether the objection was well founded or not, the present suspension was premature. The suspender should appear and state his objection as a dilatory plea which might be sustained. The Court would not interfere until it was known whether the inferior court would go wrong.

CRAIG *v.* GREAT NORTH OF SCOTLAND RAILWAY COMPANY.—*Nov.* 20.

Conviction—Railway—Travelling without Ticket—Summary Procedure Act.

The Railway Company, with concurrence of the Procurator-fiscal, charged the complainer with travelling without a ticket, or at all events with failing to deliver up his ticket or pay the fare when required to do so, in contravention of the bye-laws of the company made in pursuance of the provisions of the Railway Clauses Act. There was an alternative charge of obstructing and impeding the company's officers, in contravention of 3 and 4 Vict. c. 97. The Sheriff-substitute of Aberdeenshire convicted him 'of the contravention first charged, of having failed to deliver up his ticket.' The Court were very clearly of opinion that the conviction was bad. The offence under the bye-laws consisted in travelling without having paid the fare and obtained a ticket, or at all events in not delivering up the ticket or paying the fare when required. The Sheriff's conviction said nothing of refusing to pay the fare. This was not a matter of form, falling under the operation of the 33d section of the Summary Procedure Act, but of substance. The second member of the contravention did not consist of having failed to deliver up his ticket, but of that *and* of refusing to pay the fare. The conviction was therefore quashed.

BUIST *v.* LINTON.—*Nov.* 20.

Edinburgh Police Act—Inspector of Markets—Relevancy.

Mr Robert Buist, cattle-salesman, Lauriston Place, complained in this suspension of a sentence pronounced in the Edinburgh Police Court. The complaint stated that the panel did, 'in the premises at Lauriston Street, Edinburgh, occupied by him, annoy and interrupt Robert Wilson, an inspector, and Robert Reid, an assistant-inspector of markets to the city of Edinburgh, and did use opprobrious epithets towards them, whereby they were annoyed and disturbed.' The complainer objected that the charge stated no offence, either at common law or under the police or other statute, and that therefore the Magistrates had no jurisdiction. The Court held unanimously that the complaint contained no allegation of any offence at common law or under any Act of Parliament. Apart from the character of inspectors of markets belonging to Wilson and Reid, and the character of cattle-salesman belonging to Mr Buist, and any relation arising from such characters, no one would venture to say that this was a good charge, or that any criminal prosecution is competent for annoying and disturbing persons within the accused's own premises, if they have no right to be there. The only thing that gave the case of the respondents any appearance of relevancy was that this was a proceeding for the protection of persons in the discharge of a statutory duty, and reference was made to sections 113 and 114 of the Edinburgh Police Act. The 113th section defines the duties of inspectors of markets. A further provision in section 114 is intended to aid the inspectors in these duties, and lays upon the keepers of slaughter-houses, markets, shops, stalls, etc., and upon cowfeeders, an obligation to allow the inspectors access to their premises, under a penalty of 40s. Mr Buist was not the keeper of a slaughter-house, stall, shop, or market, and just as little was he a cowfeeder. In short, the sections were totally inapplicable to the case of a cattle-salesman who deals in live cattle. It was of the greatest importance to observe that Wilson and Reid were not said to have been there in the discharge of any duty, and even if it had been so said, it was necessary to ascertain whether they *could* be there in any official capacity; and it was evident from the statute that there was no duty which could have led them to a cattle-salesman's premises. The conviction was therefore suspended.

CIRCUIT COURT OF JUSTICIARY.

AYR, *Sept.* 27.

BAIRD *v.* ROSE.

Summary Procedure (Scotland) Act, 27 *and* 28 *Vict. c.* 53—*Complaint —Process—Appeal—Amendment.*

Held that a complaint for breach of certificate by a publican had not been framed in conformity with the directions of the Summary Procedure Act (Scotland), and appeal sustained, but case remitted with directions to amend the complaint.

GLASGOW, *Oct.* 4.

Proof, BAIRD *v.* DOWNIE.

A Crown witness having stated that on one occasion she had written a letter to the panel's dictation, containing statements in regard to the paternity of a child of the panel, the Advocate-depute, without attempting to prove that the letter was irrecoverable, asked the witness what the panel had told her to write. Held the question was a competent one, as affording evidence not of the contents of the letter, but of the panel's statement.

GLASGOW, *Oct.* 6.

GLEN *v.* COLQUHOUN AND OTHERS.

Salmon Fisheries (Scotland) Act, 1862—*Res Judicata.*

A complainant tried under 11th section of the Salmon Fisheries (Scotland) Act, 1862, may be tried again under the 27th section upon the same *species facti.*

REGISTRATION APPEAL COURT.

(Before LORD KINLOCH and LORD ORMIDALE.)

STIRLINGSHIRE, *Nov.* 29.

GOW *v.* WATSON.

Held that a member of a building society, enrolled under 6 and 7 Will. IV. c. 32, who had bought a dwelling-house from the society by public sale, and had occupied it for more than a year, was entitled to be registered as a proprietor, although a large part of the price had not been paid to the society, and no formal conveyance granted, his title standing merely on the 'conditions of sale,' the act of preference, and the books of the company; and although the sale was voidable on his incurring a certain amount of arrears on the instalments of the price.

DUMBARTONSHIRE, *Nov.* 22.

KENNEDY *v.* DONALDSON.

The proviso in sec. 9 of the Reform Act—' No sub-tenant or assignee to any lease for fifty-seven or nineteen years shall be entitled to register or to vote in respect of his interest under such lease, unless he shall be in actual occupation of the premises thereby set'—applies to a sub-lease for ninety-three years.

Nov. 23.

YOUNG *v.* LINDSAY.

Held that the Reform Act (secs. 7, 9, and 11) does not allow to connect periods of occupancy in counties, and that no change was introduced by the County Voters Act, 24 and 25 Vict. c. 83, s. 42.

FERGUSON *v.* M'CULLOCH.

Claimant held entitled to have his name retained on the roll, where his grandfather, father, and himself had possessed for seventy years, and paid ground-rent, the receipts having been produced and proved; where his landlord deponed that all the subjects in the neighbourhood were let for leases of ninety-nine years, and that he deemed the claimant's father and himself to be lessees; and where a lease in favour of the claimant for ninety-nine years was produced, setting forth the term of entry as at Whitsunday 1792, and dated 21st September 1865.

Held that the claimant's name having been for some time on the register of voters, it was for the objector to establish sufficient grounds for having it expunged. The question was, whether there was a sufficient written title; and it was plain, from *Emsley* v. *Duff* (3 Macph. 854), that a very slender written title is sufficient as between landlord and tenant. Here there was identification of the ground, and proof that in 1792 it was let on a long lease along with certain adjoining portions of ground, and a plan which must be held to be the landlord's plan.

Nov. 25.

BLAIR *v.* BARTIE.

The husband of a lessee in a lease for ninety-nine years is not entitled to be enrolled.

Nov. 29.

KINNIBURGH *v.* DONALDSON.

Subjects belonged to the claimant and appellant, and his father, as *pro indiviso* proprietors. The father was sequestrated in 1850, and his share exposed for sale by the trustee in 1854. The claimant was the highest offerer, and the usual minute of preference and obligation to grant bond for the price was executed. It did not appear that the bond was granted or the price paid, but the claimant continued in possession. Held that non-payment of the price did not void the sale; that whatever right the seller may have had to demand the bond at the time, he must now be held to have waived his right; and anyhow the minute of enactment, followed by possession, constituted a good written title.

DONALDSON *v.* GRAHAM.

Held that the tenant of a dwelling-house, who occupied it throughout the year, except two months, when he let it furnished, had not had such occupancy as is required by sec. 9 of the Reform Act.

WADDELL *v.* MACPHAIL.

A tenant who entered into possession on 1st August held not to have been in possession for twelve months previous to the 31st July following.

Dec. 2.

M'CULLOCH *v.* FREELAND.

A free yearly liferent annuity of £10, 10s., secured upon heritable property without any personal obligation, does not entitle a claimant to have his name on the register.

M'CULLOCH *v.* SMITH.

The same held, where there was a 'liferent yearly ground-annual rent.'

DICK *v.* WADDELL.

Continuous occupancy under sec. 9 may exist, although the claimant had held a house for successive periods of three and two months, and one month; and the rent being of the requisite amount, it is not necessary that the contract under which it is received should be for a year.

M'CULLOCH *v.* SHARPE.

A claimant held not divested, though his creditors were receiving the rents of the subjects under a decree of maills and duties.

Expenses.—In the appeals from Dumbartonshire, the Court taking into consideration the facts that all were conducted by the same counsel and agents, and that many of them did not need separate discussion, awarded £2, 2s. of expenses in each case.

ENGLISH CASES.

CARRIERS BY RAILWAY.—Under section 7 of 17 & 18 Vict. c. 31,—which provides that no greater damages shall be recovered from a railway company for loss of or injury to a horse than £50, unless the person sending or delivering the same shall at the time of such delivery have declared it to be of a higher value, in which case it shall be lawful for the company to demand and receive reasonable percentage upon the excess of the value so declared, and which shall be paid in addition to the ordinary rate of charge,—the knowledge of the company as to the value of a horse, not derived from a declaration to that effect by the sender, does not give the company any right to demand such increased rate of charge under the above section. To entitle the company to demand such increased rate, the declaration must be made with an intention by the sender of the horse that it should so operate.—(*Robinson* v. *The South-Western Rail. Co.*, 34 L. J., C. P. 234.)

CHARITY.—The Hospital of St John at Bedford appeared to have been founded, or reconstituted, in 1280, 'for the support of two or three brethren, the most advanced of whom was to hold the place of master; and for the relief of the poor of Bedford.' The mastership of the hospital had, from the earliest mention of the parish of St John, been inseparably united with the rectory of the parish. From the year 1280 to 1374, the master was elected by the brethren; but in 1444 a vacancy was filled up, on the presentation of the Mayor of Bedford, and from that time the united mastership and rectory had always been filled up on the presentation of the mayor, or the mayor and burgesses; but there was no evidence to show by what right these presentations were made. The corporation seal of the hospital was still in existence, and leases were granted thereunder, and small payments were made to ten poor persons, called beadsmen. It was held, by the Master of the Rolls, that the long exercise by the mayor of the right to present to the mastership could not supersede the original trusts; and that as well the property of the hospital, as the right of presentation to the mastership, remained subject to these trusts. And on appeal the Lords Justices affirmed the decree so far as it related to property of the hospital, but held that the corporation could not be treated as trustees of the right of presentation to the mastership.—(*The Attorney-General* v. *The Master and Co-Brethren of the Hospital of Saint John, Bedford*, 34 L. J., Ch. 441.)

POWER.—The will of a testator, who gave property to three persons as trustees, contained a power providing that, if the trustees thereby appointed should depart this life, or decline or become incapable to act in the trusts, it should be lawful for the surviving or continuing trustee or trustees, his executors, administrators, or assigns, to appoint one or more person or persons to be a trustee or trustees in the room of the trustee or trustees so dying, declining, or becoming incapable to act therein. Two of the trustees disclaimed. The third acted, but subsequently, being desirous of retiring, appointed two new trustees, and conveyed the trust estates to them. This appointment was held invalid, the retiring trustee not being a continuing trustee within the terms of the power. The word 'declining,' in a power so worded, covers the case of a trustee who, after having acted, refuses to act any longer.—(*Travis* v. *Illingworth*, 34 L. J., Ch. 665.)

MURDER ON THE HIGH SEAS.—The prisoner was one of the crew of a ship which was built in Holstein, from whence she sailed to London. All the officers and crew were foreigners. R., the registered sole owner, was an alien born, but described in the register as 'of London, merchant.' The ship sailed from London, and under the British flag. While on the voyage, the prisoner killed the master on board the vessel when several thousand miles from England, and 200 miles from any land. On the trial of the prisoner for murder, these facts were proved; and no evidence was given that R. had been naturalized or had obtained letters of denization. It was held, there was no evidence that the ship was a British ship, and that consequently the prisoner could not be convicted in England for this offence.—(*R.* v. *Bjornsen*, 34 L. J., M. C. 180.)

COLLISION AT SEA.—The enactment of the Merchant Shipping Act Amendment Act, 1862 (25 and 26 Vict. c. 63, s. 54), fixing the limit of liability of the owner of a ship 'in respect of loss of life or personal injury caused by the improper navigation of his ship to persons carried in another ship,' extends to the crew of such other ship as well as to other persons carried thereby; and such liability consequently is measured by and extends to the sum of £15 per ton of the wrong-doing ship's tonnage.—(*Glaholm* v. *Barker*, 34 L. J., Ch. 533.)

CONTRIBUTORY.—In October 1846, A., in the belief that he must take shares in order to qualify for the office of director which he had accepted in an assurance company, applied for and had certain shares allotted to him. Understanding shortly afterwards that no qualification was necessary, he thenceforward repudiated the shares, refusing to execute the deed of settlement or to pay calls. No dividend was ever received by him. In 1855, after intermediate communications, he offered to pay a specified sum on being released from all further liability; and the directors, who were empowered by the deed of settlement to compromise disputed claims, passed a resolution accepting his proposal. This resolution was confirmed at a general meeting of shareholders, but no notice had been given of the intention to confirm the arrangement or of its terms, nor were the terms stated in the circular subsequently sent to the shareholders, containing the directors' report and the resolutions passed by the meeting. A.'s name had been originally put upon the register of shareholders, and was never removed. In 1861 the company was wound up, and the Master of the Rolls put A. on the list of contributories; but the order was, on appeal, discharged by the Lords Justices, their Lordships holding (there being no ground for imputing fraud, collusion, suppression, or concealment) that whether A. was originally liable as a shareholder or not, the arrangement under which he had been released must stand as a *bonâ fide* compromise.—(*Re The Agriculturist Insur. Co., ex parte Belhaven*, 34 L. J., Ch. 503.)

CONTRIBUTORY.—A. filled up a blank form of application, by which he agreed to accept a certain number of shares in a company, or any less number which might be allotted to him; and he paid a deposit, for which he received a banker's receipt. No shares were ever allotted; but he never made any formal claim for repayment of his deposit, which the company used. The company was wound up before it had commenced its intended operations, and A. was placed by the Master of the Rolls on the list of contributories. But on appeal it was held by the Lords Justices that the contract was only to accept shares when an allotment should have been made, and that until allotment there was no complete contract, and consequently that A. was not a contributory.—(*In re The Adelphi Hotel Company Lim.* (*Best's case*), 34 L. J., Ch. 523.)

CONTRIBUTORY.—A., upon his appointment as agent to a limited assurance company, agreed to take shares upon the terms that payment for them should be deducted from his commission as agent; and no deposit was ever paid by him upon them, but he was registered as the holder of the shares. The company very soon after his appointment dismissed him, but, as he contended, wrongfully. On the winding up of the company, the Lords Justices, reversing a decision of the Master of the Rolls, held that the company's cancellation of A.'s appointment as agent, whether justifiable or not, could not operate as a cancellation of A.'s agreement to become a shareholder, and that (subject to any question of account as to payment for the shares) A. was liable as a contributory.—(*In re The Life Association of England Lim.* (*Thomson's case*), 34 L. J., Ch. 525.)

INFANT (*Minor*).—The Court will not take a child of tender years from the custody of its mother on the ground that the mother's religion differs from that of the deceased father, and that such change of custody is requisite to the training of the child in the father's religion; but the Court, in the circumstances of the case, declared that the child ought to be brought up and educated, when capable of receiving religious education, as a member of the church to which the father had belonged.—(*Re Austin and Austin* v. *Austin*, 34 L. J., Ch. 499.)

PATENT.—It is sufficient to constitute user of a patented article, that the same sort of benefit, however temporary and indirect, has been in fact derived from it as would arise from it in its ordinary use. It is immaterial whether the use of the article be active or passive.—(*Betts* v. *Neilson*, 34 L. J., Ch. 537.)

FOREIGN DIVORCE.—A., an Irishman by birth, resided at the Cape of Good Hope from 1842 to 1862. During the earlier part of this period he served in an English regiment stationed at the Cape; during the latter, in the Cape Mounted Rifles. In 1850 he married at the Cape B., and in 1852 this marriage was dissolved by a sentence of the Colonial Court on the ground of B.'s adultery. In 1852 he married C., in the lifetime of B., and in 1863 he died intestate. An application by C. for administration to A. as his widow was opposed on the ground that A. was a domiciled Englishman at the date of his first marriage, and therefore that the sentence of divorce pronounced by the Colonial Court was inoperative. It was held, that as upon the evidence there was no proof that

A. was a domiciled Englishman, or that his domicil was not at the Cape, the sentence of divorce must be treated as valid. *Quære*, Whether, if A. had been a domiciled Englishman, the divorce would have been invalid in England.—(*Argent* v. *Argent*, 34 L. J., P. M. A. 133.)

Bills and Notes.—Defendant, a British subject resident in Florence, signed two promissory-notes there, as joint and several maker with his brother in London, to whom he sent them by post. His brother then also signed them, and delivered them in London to the payees. It was held that the cause of action arose when the notes were delivered to the payees in this country, and that defendant could therefore be sued here under sec. 18 of the Common Law Procedure Act, 1852.—(*Chapman* v. *Cottrell*, 34 L. J., Ex. 186.)

Carriers by Railway.—An attorney, going by railway to attend a county court, took in his portmanteau documents and bank-notes for use in certain causes in which he was engaged as an attorney. The portmanteau was carried under the private act of the railway company without charge as passengers' 'ordinary luggage;' it was missing at the end of the journey, and not recovered for some days. It was held, these articles were not 'ordinary luggage' of the attorney as a passenger, and that the railway company were not liable in damages for the consequences of the temporary loss of them.—(*Phelps* v. *The London and North-Western Ra. Co.*, 34 L. J., C. P. 259.)

Carriers by Railway.—Plaintiff took a ticket from defendants from C. to N. Plaintiff, after waiting a long time, was told by a porter that the train was late in consequence of an accident, and the train eventually arrived an hour and a half late. The consequence was, that plaintiff was late for the train at G., which would have carried him on to N. The train-bill was not put in, but only some correspondence in which defendants repudiated their liability on the ground that by the train-bills they gave notice they would not be liable for the trains keeping time. It was held, there was no evidence of a cause of action.—(*Hurst* v. *The Great Western Ra. Co.*, 34 L. J., C. P. 264.)

Charter-party.—A. of Alexandria bought coals of B. of London, which were to be delivered at Alexandria, price to be paid on delivery of bill of lading, less balance of freight payable at Alexandria. B. chartered C.'s ship to carry the coal: 'Coal to be delivered on freight being paid; . . . freight to be paid on unloading and right delivery of cargo, less advances in cash at current rate of exchange; . . . half the freight to be advanced by freighter's acceptance at three months on signing bills of lading; owner to insure amount and deposit with charterer the policy, and to guarantee the same.' The bill of lading was signed. B. gave his acceptance for the half freight, the receipt of the half freight was indorsed on the bill of lading, and the bill of lading was indorsed in blank by B. and given to A. The average length of the voyage was two months. Before the ship arrived, B. became insolvent; and on arrival of the ship, and before the acceptance was due, the master refused to deliver the cargo to A., unless the whole of the freight was paid, or payment guaranteed. A guarantee was given by D. for A. under protest, and the cargo was delivered; D. then, by A.'s direction, refused to pay. An action was brought in the Consular Court against D., who then, by A.'s direction, paid under protest. A. repaid D., C. knew nothing of the arrangement between A. and B. It was held, that A. was entitled to recover the half freight from C.—(*Tamvaco* v. *Simpson*, 34 L. J., C. P. 268.)

Damages (*Reparation*).—On a contract to sell cotton of a certain quality at a certain price, to be delivered at a future time, the measure of damages for non-delivery is the difference between the contract price and the market price at the time limited for the delivery; and the buyer cannot recover for the loss of profit which he would have made by carrying out a re-sale at a higher price made in the interval between the contract and the time for delivery.—(*Williams* v. *Reynolds*, 34 L. J., Q. B. 221.)

COURT OF SESSION.

FIRST DIVISION.

Nelson *v.* Black and Morrison.—*Dec.* 21.

Issue—Privilege—Malice and Want of Probable Cause.

The defenders, on 25th December last, presented a petition to the Sheriff of Fife, setting forth that, in the course of their precognitions in regard to the accusations against certain persons of having conspired for the purpose of taking the life of the Rev. James Pitt Edgar, minister of Dunbog, or of doing him grievous bodily injury, and of having sent him threatening letters, they (the defenders) had recovered documents showing that the pursuer among others had been engaged in said conspiracy and in writing and sending said threatening letters, and praying for a warrant to search his house and those of the other alleged conspirators, for all documents and articles tending to establish their guilt. The Sheriff granted the warrant as craved. It was executed against all those against whom it was directed except the pursuer. A few days after it was granted it was withdrawn as against him. In a suspension of the warrant, at the instance of the other parties, the Court of Justiciary, on 30th June last, set it aside as illegal. The pursuer now brings the present action of damages in respect of the alleged slanderous statements in the said petition.

The case was reported by the Lord Ordinary on the question whether the pursuer must put in issue, malice and want of probable cause.

It was contended for the pursuer that it was not necessary to insert malice and want of probable cause, as the warrant had been held by the Court of Justiciary to be illegal, and the application for it by the defenders having thus been *ultra vires*, they had no privilege in making it.

The Lord President, after explaining the nature and position of the case, said—Procurators-Fiscal have certain duties to discharge in the interests of justice, and in regard to them they are protected, unless it is shown that they acted maliciously and without probable cause. It is said that the pursuer in the present case is not bound to take this burden of proof, because the warrant which the defenders asked and obtained was an illegal warrant, and so, it is argued, they had no privilege in making the statements upon which they did ask it. Questions of nicety and difficulty arise in such a case, as to how far a Procurator-Fiscal is outwith the ordinary protection accorded by the law when he concludes a petition by asking something which he is not entitled to demand, and these questions must be determined by the nature of the illegality in the demand. If it be something beyond all law and reason to search repositories, that is one kind of illegality; if, on the other hand, it is merely illegal to search them in the way asked and granted, that is a different kind. The one illegality touches the substance of the proceedings, the other points to some error or omission in the same or want of caution in carrying them out. Were the illegality of the first kind, the pursuer might be entitled to an issue without malice and want of probable cause; but if the illegality be of the second order, I am of a different opinion. I think this comes under the latter class. Under this application it was competent to the Sheriff to have granted a legal warrant. For example, had he limited the search to particular documents, or appointed it to be carried out under his own eye, I am not prepared to say that would have been an illegal warrant. Now, although that has not been done, I do not think that the defenders' application was out and out, and in substance, contrary to law. Therefore, I am of opinion that the pursuer must take upon him the burden of showing that the defenders' statements were made maliciously and without probable cause.

Cuthbertson v. Cuthbertson.—*Jan.* 18.

Reference to Oath—Intrinsic and Extrinsic.

The question in this case, which was an action of accounting, was whether the defender was entitled to charge against the pursuer an alleged debt of £180, said to have been incurred by him to the deceased George Cuthbertson. The existence of the debt was referred to the pursuer's oath. In his deposition he admitted that he borrowed £180 from the deceased George Cuthbertson, for which he gave him an I O U. But he added, "within three weeks, according to my best recollection, after I had borrowed the £180, I went up to the Bazaar Market in Glasgow, and held out £180 to him, saying, 'here is your money,' and asked him to give me up the I O U. He said that he did not want it, and 'I make you a compliment of it.' I asked him what was to come of the I O U. He said he would either destroy it or bring it to me; and he never asked the money from me after that." The pursuer says, I never saw the I O U since I granted it.

The Lord Ordinary (Kinloch) held that the foregoing statement in the pursuer's deposition was intrinsic of the reference and negatived resting-owing of the debt, and therefore found that the defender was not entitled to charge it against the pursuer.

The Court adhered to the Lord Ordinary's interlocutor.

Anderson v. Scottish North-Eastern Railway Company.—*Jan.* 20.

Title to Sue—Assignation.

This action was originally raised by John Anderson against the Scottish North-Eastern Railway Company for the reduction of an arrestment of his stock by the company.

The point now before the Court was whether Mr Watt, who had obtained an assignation to the stock from Mr Anderson, and had been sisted as a party to the action, was entitled to insist in the same.

The Lord Ordinary (Jerviswoode) in respect that the assignation contained no assignation to this action, and farther in respect that Mr Watt had not been registered as a shareholder in the company, dismissed the action.

The Court unanimously recalled the Lord Ordinary's interlocutor, holding that the right to insist in the present action was carried by the general assignation to the stock, and that Mr Watt was entitled to try in the action whether he had a right to the stock in virtue of his assignation.

Pet., Hugh Swan.

Minor—Curator ad litem.

This was a petition for the removal of a trustee, and the appointment of a factor on the trust estate. One of the parties called as a responent in the petition, and to whom it was intimated, was a minor. He made no appearance; and to-day the counsel for the petitioner suggested that a curator *ad litem* should be appointed to him. The Court, however, thought this unnecessary in the case of a minor who had not appeared, and therefore granted the prayer of the petition.

Pet., The Duke of Athole for Authority.—*Jan.* 12.

Disentail—Consents.

The question in this petition was whether the entail, under which certain of the Athole estates are held, was to be held to be of the date of the trust deed directing them to be entailed, or of a subsequent private Act of Parliament obtained by the late Duke. The question was of importance to the petitioner, as if the entail was to be held to be of the date of the trust deed, it would then be competent for the petitioner to disentail the lands with the consent of the three next heirs entitled to succeed, which had been obtained. If, on the other hand, the entail was to be of the date of the private Act, the land could only be disentailed with the consent of the heir who, if in life at the Duke's death, must succeed, and who, to make his consent available, required to be of the age of twenty-five. As the petitioner has no family no such consent could at present be obtained.

The Court held that the entail was to be held to be of the date of the trust deed, and, therefore, that the estates could be disentailed with the consents already obtained.

The Greenock Harbour Trustees *v.* Stewart's Trustees.—*Jan.* 12.

Title—Bounding Charter.

In the beginning of the present century, the deceased Roger Stewart, feued from Sir M. Shaw Stewart, a piece of shore ground, on which he built a warehouse. After the purchase, the Greenock Harbour Trustees feued the ground seaward of Stewart's feu. The space between the buildings was used by Stewart as a place for lumber for many years, and was afterwards enclosed by him, and let out to tenants, and certain buildings of a temporary character were erected thereon. The present dispute arose in consequence of the pursuers having, with a view to using the space northward of Stewart's feu for harbour purposes, taken possession of it. Stewart's trustees thereupon raised an action of removing, in which they averred that the space in question was included in their feu contract, being the *solum* of a bulwark originally constructed by Stewart to protect his feu from the sea, and the right to erect which was included in the contract. The harbour trustees met the action by a counter action of declarator, that the said space was included in their feu contract, in which they averred that the possession had all along been by them. The two actions were conjoined, and proof led, from which it appeared that the possession had truly been with Stewart's trustees.

The Court, affirming the Lord Ordinary (Kinloch's) interlocutor, held that Stewart's charter was a bounding charter, and that, as the harbour trustees' charter made Stewart's feu to be their boundary, the space in question fell within their title.

Munro *v.* The Caledonian Banking Company.—*Jan.* 16.

Bond of Caution—Suspension—Issues.

This is a suspension of a charge by the Caledonian Bank on a bond of caution for a cash credit of £200, signed by Munro and others. The grounds of suspension averred are, that the suspender was induced to sign the bond by false and fraudulent representations on the part of the principal in the bond—Robert M'Intyre, formerly parochial schoolmaster and inspector of poor for the parish of Kincardine—who represented that the suspender, by signing the bond, would merely become cautioner to an insurance company for £40, to be borrowed on a policy of insurance on his (M'Intyre's) life. It is also averred that the bond was not signed by Munro in presence of the persons who subscribe it as instrumentary witnesses. The suspender proposed to take issues on both grounds of suspension.

The Court allowed an issue to try the question whether the instrumentary witnesses saw the bond executed by the suspender, but disallowed the issue in regard to the false and fraudulent representation under which the bond was alleged to have been signed, holding that that, although true, would be no ground for suspending the charge at the instance of the bank; and the Lord President observing that, if it were otherwise, a bond of caution would be of little value.

M.P., Niven (Kirkland's Factor) *v.* Stocks and Others.—*Jan.* 16.

Trust Deed—Construction.

The late William Kirkland, innkeeper and coachmaster at Kinross, by his trust disposition and settlement conveyed his whole estate to certain trustees. He directed his trustees to hold his estate for behoof of his daughter, Mary Kirkland or Stocks, in liferent, and after her death to divide the same amongst her children on their attaining twenty-five years of age. In the event of his said daughter dying without issue, or of any children she might have dying before attaining twenty-five years, he directed his trustees to realise his whole estate and divide it equally among his brothers and sisters. Mr Kirkland thereafter executed the following codicil:—"I hereby so far vary and alter the foregoing settlement as to declare it is my will that in the event my daughter shall have no other child lawfully begotten than my present grandson, James Stocks, my said grandson, even though he shall have attained the age of twenty-five years, shall have no more than a liferent interest in the estate thereby conveyed, unless he marries and has lawful issue, on the occurrence of both of which events my said trustees will be bound to denude of this trust in his favour in the terms before specified."

The truster died in 1836, survived by his daughter, Mrs Stocks, who had an only child, viz., the James Stocks mentioned in the foregoing codicil. He now claims the whole of Kirkland's estate as heir at law. Kirkland's brothers and sisters, on the other hand, maintain that the judicial factor on the estate is bound to hold it for the purpose of paying the liferent of it to Stocks until—(1) he marries and has lawful issue, or (2) the liferent provided to him lapses by his death, without his having married and had lawful issue, in which case it would fall to them, the truster's brothers and sisters.

The Court, recalling the interlocutor of the Lord Ordinary (Ormidale) held (1) that under the trust-deed the testator's grandson (the claimant

Stocks) had right to the fee of the estate on attaining twenty-five years of age, and in the event of his dying before twenty-five the fee belonged to the testator's brothers and sisters; (2) that by the codicil Stocks' rights were restricted to a liferent, and by his survivance of the age of twenty-five the only condition on which the testator's brothers and sisters were to have the fee had been rendered impossible, and (3) that in these circumstances the testator had died intestate, *quoad* the fee, which therefore belonged to the claimant Stocks as heir at law.

M.P., National Bank *v.* Bryce and Others.—*Jan.* 20.

Bank Cheque—Donation—Proof.

The fund *in medio* in this case was a sum of £281, standing at the credit of the late Matthew Young with the National Bank, at 5th February 1863, the date of Mr. Young's death.

The sum was claimed by Miss Mary Bryce. Her statement was to the effect, that Mr. Young had boarded in her house for some time before his death, and had incurred a considerable debt to her for board and lodging, and for cash advances and outlays. On 4th February 1863, the day before Mr. Young died, he filled up and gave to the claimant a cheque on his account with the National Bank for £321, telling her that she was to pay herself out of the contents, and retain the surplus.

Mr. Young's executors also claimed the fund, stating their belief that Mr. Young's object in sending for the balance of his account before his death, was to place the money in the hands of his father, and that he did not intend donation to Miss Bryce.

The Lord Ordinary, Jerviswoode, was inclined to sustain the claim of Miss Bryce, but appointed parties to lodge issues.

The Court unanimously sustained the claim of Miss Bryce.

The Lord President said, that the question was whether, believing the statement made by Miss Bryce, the Court was to give effect to it, as a donation attempted to be proved by parole evidence. Now, there were many circumstances connected with the position of the parties which might be looked to, and which might be proved by parole. There was the fact, that Mr. Young boarded in the claimant's house, and was indebted to her for board and lodging, &c. Taking all these facts and circumstances, together with the existence of this document, Miss Bryce's statement was very materially supported. The fact that the payment was made on deathbed was in no way against this claim, nor the fact that Mr. Young had considerable means otherwise. They were rather in favour of it. He had made a settlement, and if he had wanted to make in it a regular bequest to Miss Bryce, he would have had to employ an agent, which he might not feel inclined to do, and he therefore took a very natural way of giving the money. He drew out what he supposed to be the entire amount of his funds in bank, by mistake over-estimating the amount. It was hardly conceivable that the sum to be drawn out was for his own use, and the defender's story, that the money was to be a donation to Mr. Young's father, was not very credible, for it was a very curious way of making a donation to the father, by giving a cheque in favour of Miss Bryce.

MORGAN *v.* MORGAN.—*Jan.* 20.

Promissory Note—Stamp.

The question in this case was whether certain documents were promissory notes, and, being unstamped, were null under the stamp laws, or, assuming that they were not promissory notes, whether they were I O U's, or bonds requiring to be stamped. The documents were in the following terms:—

"1st September, 1853.

"Dear ——,—I was favoured with your letter of yesterday, prefixing letter of credit on the Western Bank for three hundred and ninety-seven pounds, which, with the interest due to you at last Whitsunday, and the interest thereon since that date, makes up five hundred pounds, which I have received in loan from you, to be repaid in December next, but hope you won't be too strict as to the time of repayment, as it will depend much upon the price of Clydesdale Bank stock, as I am averse to sell at present prices.—Yours truly."

"14th October, 1845.

"Dear ——,—I have borrowed from you one thousand pounds sterling, which I hereby bind and oblige myself to repay to you at Whitsunday next, with interest at the rate which shall be paid on money lent upon first heritable security. And I also engage to grant you, if required, satisfactory heritable security for the above sum.—I remain, &c."

The Lord Ordinary (Kinloch), held that in neither document was there that simple promise to pay a specific sum at a definite date necessary to constitute them bills or promissory notes incapable of being now stamped. He further considered they were not I O U's, but documents of obligation requiring to be stamped, and therefore sisted process in order that this might be done.

The Court adhered, and on the same grounds.

WALKER *v.* THE TRADES LANE CALENDERING COMPANY.—*Dec.* 22.

Factory Acts—Appeal—Competency of.

The pursuer, Mr Walker, as sub-inspector of factories, presented, on 9th October, 1863, a complaint to the Justices of Peace for Forfarshire, accusing the defenders of certain breaches of the Factory Acts. The first charge was that of employing George Nicoll, a young person under the age of sixteen, without his name being previously registered, in terms of the Act; the second, that of employing the same George Nicoll, "time and place aforesaid," for more than nine hours a day, without a surgeon's certificate; the third, that of employing, "time and place aforesaid," fifteen young persons named, after six o'clock in the evening; the fourth, that of employing the same young persons during the night, "time and place aforesaid." The Justices convicted the defenders, and adjudged them "to forfeit and pay in respect of the offence first hereinbefore set forth, a penalty of £3 3s; in respect of the offence second hereinbefore set forth, a penalty of £2; in respect of the offence third hereinbefore set forth, the sum of £1 of penalty for each of the fifteen young persons illegally employed as therein mentioned, making in all the sum of £15; and in respect of the offence fourth hereinbefore set forth, the sum of £2 of penalty for each of the fifteen young persons illegally employed, as therein mentioned, making together the sum of £30, said whole penalties under the said several offences amounting in the aggregate to £50 3s." The defenders appealed to the Quarter Sessions, on 9th November 1863, the Justices in Quarter Sessions quashed the conviction on the ground, that the case did not fall within the provisions of the Factory Acts. The pursuer now sought reduction of this appeal, and of the judgment quashing the conviction, on the ground that the appeal was incompetent under the 69th section of 7 Victoria c. 15, which declares "That no appeal shall be allowed against any conviction under this Act, except for an offence punishable at discretion, or when the penalty awarded shall be more than £3." The pursuer contended that each offence charged must be considered separately, and that each young person must be held to constitute a separate offence, and that in this view the penalty awarded, except in the first-mentioned offence, must be held to be less than £3 in the statutory sense.

The Lord Ordinary (Kinloch) found that the appeal to the Quarter Sessions was competently taken, and assoilzied the defenders, on the ground that the defenders were charged, under a single complaint, with several breaches of the Acts committed at the same time and place, and as the aggregate penalties for these offences amounted to £50 3s, the case must be treated as one in which, in the sense of the Act, the penalty exceeded £3. The Court recalled this interlocutor in part, holding that four separate offences were charged, and that the penalty awarded in the second of these being only £2, that conviction could not competently be appealed. As to the others, they adopted the Lord Ordinary's judgment, the penalties in each being above £3.

Susp., Crow *v.* Fowlie.—*Dec.* 22.

Reference to Oath.

This was a case in which the suspender and another accepted a bill with one M'Farlane, they being the cautioners and he the real obligant. On the suspender being charged, he presented a suspension on the grounds that the debt in the bill had been already paid by the principal obligant, and condescended very minutely on the circumstances in which the various payments to account had been made. A commission and diligence was obtained to prove the suspender's accounts by the writ of the charger; but nothing was recovered which necessarily inferred payment. The Lord Ordinary accordingly repelled the reasons of suspension, and found the letters orderly proceeded. On a reclaiming note the Court adhered. The suspender then referred the whole cause to the oath of the charger, whose deposition the Court found amounted to *non memini* of circumstances which he could not reasonably be supposed to have forgotten, and accordingly held that the import of his oath was the same as if he had declined to be examined, construed it as affirmative, and suspended the charge.

SECOND DIVISION.

Aikman *v.* Nisbet.—*Jan.* 12.

Summary Removing—Question whether competent against a Disponer.

In a removing in a Sheriff-Court, the pursuer set himself forth as heritable proprietor of a dwelling-house, and produced a registered disposition in his favour. He acquired the subjects from the Commercial Bank, by whom they were sold under a cash credit bond granted to them by the defender. He set forth, in his petition, that the subjects in question were occupied by the defender "as tenant or possessor, or pretended tenant or possessor, under him," who had timeous warning, and he produced precept and execution of warning; and upon these grounds applied for summary ejection. In this suspension, the defender and complainer argued, *inter alia*, that this being an extraordinary removing to eject a proprietor from subjects belonging, or formerly belonging to him, the Sheriff had no jurisdiction.

Lord Justice-Clerk.—There is no irregularity in the pursuer setting out that the party in possession is either tenant or pretended tenant, of the subjects, for it might come out in the course of the proceedings that his title was open to objection; and there is no ground for supposing that a defect in the tenant's title would prove a good defence in such a removing. If the defender had alleged that he was proprietor, and had produced a competing title, there could be no doubt that the process would at once become incompetent in the Inferior Court. But Nisbet pleaded incompetency, on the ground that the parties never had stood in the position of lessor and lessee, which was an admission by him that he had not a good title of tenancy, and let in the alternative in the summons of pretended tenancy. It would be very rash for a pursuer to proceed upon the assumption that such a person as the defender had no title of tenancy, and turn him out without any warning. After such an admission as he has made, the defender's mouth is shut as to the objections which follow, for they apply to a warning which was not in the circumstances required at all. No doubt, he says, that the pursuer had no title, as he, Nisbet, *was* the proprietor. This is not an allegation that Nisbet *is* the proprietor. It is not said how or when he ceased to be proprietor, and there is no production of any title whatever. The case of Waterston *v.* Mason (8 D.) was referred to, and the proceeding of the Sheriff was said to run counter to it—on the ground that the summary removing of a tenant cannot be converted into an ejection of one who turns out to be a vitious possessor. But there is a material distinction. In that case the petition or summons in the Inferior Court libelled missives of lease on which the tenant possessed and had no alternative. Again, the question raised on the merits was a competition of heritable rights. Neither of these questions arises here. This is a proper removing against a party reasonably supposed to be a tenant, or in the position of a tenant; and who, when he admitted he was not so, left the Sheriff no alternative but to pronounce a decree of removing. It is not necessary to fix any general rule, except that a petition so framed is competent, and may proceed whether the party against whom it is directed has a proper title of tenancy or not.

The other Judges concurred in refusing the suspension.

Bain or Smith *v.* Smith.—*Jan.* 11.

Antenuptial Contract—Construction—Desertion.

This action, at the instance of a wife against a husband, was founded on a provision in an antenuptial contract, by which the husband became bound "to settle and secure a free yearly annuity in favour of the said Isabella Bain, to be paid during the subsistence of the said marriage, and during her natural life, in the event of her surviving after its dissolution by the predeceasing" of the husband, while she remained a widow allenarly, exclusive of the said husband's *jus mariti*, courtesy of Scotland, or other title, and of liability for his debts. The wife also asked that the husband should be ordained to invest, at the sight of the Court, a sum of £1248 which had come into his hands as her fourth share of her father's estate, and which he had not applied in terms of the said marriage-contract, which provided that she should enjoy a liferent of that share exclusive of *jus mariti*. It was pleaded, in defence, that the pursuer had deserted her husband, and was now living apart from him, and that she was not entitled to ask for implement of this contract while she herself was not performing her conjugal duties.

The Lord Justice-Clerk.—There was no doubt that where a wife was living separate from her husband, without a contract or decree of separation, she was in a state of desertion, unless the fault was on his side. But a woman in such a state was not entitled to come and ask for *equity* in any shape whatever. Hence she could not ask for aliment. This, however, was not an action in equity, but one to enforce the terms of a contract, which the Court was bound to enforce, unless the husband had a good answer. The question was whether it was a good answer to say that the wife suing on the marriage-contract had failed in the performance of her conjugal duties. Now, her duty to adhere to the *consortium vitæ*, and her other nuptial duties, were not constituted by this ante-nuptial contract, but by the more solemn consensual contract made in the face of the Church. The obligation in the ante-nuptial contract precisely fixes the terms and termination of the annuity. It is due during the subsistence of the marriage, and during viduity. The husband says the wife has violated not this contract of marriage, but the contract of marriage in another and more sacred sense. There is a different remedy for that, which consists in an action of adherence at the instance of the husband, not in his refusal to perform his obligations under the special contract. As to the sum of £1248, it was quite plain that the husband was bound to invest this so as to give precise effect to the terms of the marriage-contract.

The other Judges concurred; and the husband was ordained to state how he proposed to secure the annuity, and to deposit the £1248 in bank, subject to the orders of the Court.

Darsie *v.* Scealès.—*Jan.* 16.

Consistorial—Designation of Pursuer.

This was a declarator of marriage on various grounds, at the instance of "Eleanor Darsie, residing in London," against the representatives of the late Stewart Sceales, with whom she had lived in Edinburgh and elsewhere, between the years 1852 and 1859. The defenders moved, after the day for trial was fixed, that the pursuer should be appointed to furnish them with her present address. The Lord Ordinary (Ormidale) granted the motion.

The Court altered, and refused the motion on the ground that, although even such an unprecedented motion might be granted on special cause shown, yet no special circumstances were here alleged. It was true that the pursuer's designation was no designation at all, but the time had passed for objecting to that.

Lord Cowan differed, holding that the motion was made at a legitimate part of the trial. It was unprecedented, but it was also unprecedented that any such concealment of the pursuer's residence should be met with.

DUKE OF BUCCLEUCH *v.* MAGISTRATES OF SANQUHAR.—*Dec.* 8.

Teinds—Arrears—Bona fide Consumption.

The Duke, as titular, sued the defenders for arrears of teinds from 1830 to 1863. It was proved that down to 1810 only £5, 18s 2d a-year had been paid to the Duke's predecessors, and that nothing had since been paid. It was alleged that these payments had been under a tack or other agreement, and that the Duke having since 1810 been tenant of the defenders in certain lands of greater annual value, their teinds had been set off against the rent due by him, and were only sufficient to cover the amount of stipend localled on the defenders after the augmentation of 1822, and which had since been paid by the pursuer to the minister of Sanquhar. The chief contention was, that there had been a continuous use of payment to the amount of £5, 18s, or thereby, and that the remainder of the teinds had been *bona fide* consumed by the defenders. The Court held that till 1810 the payment had proceeded on a precarious instruction given by the then Duke of Queensberry, in 1726, to his chamberlain, which was purely gratuitous and revocable at the pleasure of the titular. The Lord Ordinary had founded his judgment on cases (*Stirling*, 1 Pat., Ap. 90, and *Scott*, Bell's fo. Ca., and M. 15,700), in which it was held that when a party took upon himself the character of titular, and in that character granted discharges for teinds, this was a colourable title under which the heritor might possess and consume surplus teinds. In the cases referred to the discharge had been granted by the minister, who, in so doing, necessarily assumed that he was parson, and had right to the teinds as such. But the minister of Sanquhar was a stipendiary, and payment to him for any length of time could not interfere with the right of the titular.

COWAN, &c. *v.* LORD KINNAIRD.—*Dec.* 15.

River—Upper and Lower Heritor—Alteration of Course Acquiescence.

In an action by an inferior against an upper heritor on a stream, for diverting water to supply a farm of the latter, it was admitted by the defender that the water was diverted, and was not restored; but pleaded (1), that about the time when the water was diverted, the defender in draining a marsh from which no perennial stream flowed, had so increased the water in the stream as to compensate for what he had taken off for the use of his farm; and (2), that the pursuer was barred by acquiescence from insisting in this action. The first defence was repelled, because the law distinguishes between the water of a *stagnum*, which is a precarious supply, and that of a perennial stream; and the water of the former can never be a sufficient compensation for a constant quantity drawn off from a running stream. The second plea was also repelled, because no facts and circumstances were stated in the record to support the averment of acquiescence. The defender maintained that in averring acquiescence, he must be understood to say that there were facts and circumstances to support this averment. But it was necessary according to the rules of pleading, to set out on record facts from which the acquiescence was inferred.

FINLAY'S TRUSTEES *v.* ALEXANDER.—*Jan.* 18.

Assignation of Legitim—Intimation—Equipollent.

A post-nuptial marriage contract conveyed to trustees all right, title, and interest which the wife or her husband had or might hereafter have in the succession or estates heritable or moveable of her father. One of the trustees was the wife's mother, who was sole executrix of the father. The marriage contract was recorded; and as part of the deed there was recorded a minute attached to it, signed by the wife's mother and another trustee, "We, the trustees within named and designed, do hereby accept of the office of trustee." *Held*, in a competition between the marriage-contract, trustees, and the trustee on the sequestrated estate of the mother, that this was an effectual intimation of the assignation. There could be no doubt that if anything technical were required in the intimation of an assignation this might not be quite correct, for it was rather an acknowledgment by her than an intimation to her. But there is no more satisfactory equipollent of intimation than the acknowledgment of the debtor.

EDINBURGH AND GLASGOW RAILWAY *v.* HALL.—*Jan.* 19.

Poor Law Amendment Act, § 37—*Assessment—Railway.*

In a suspension of a poinding for arrears of poors' rates on heritages belonging to a railway company. A remit was made to a man of skill to report as to what amount of deduction was proper to be made from the valuation of the suspender's lands and heritages in City parish of Glasgow in terms of the 37th sec. of the Poor-law Amendment Act (8 and 9 Vict., c. 83, sec. 37), which declares "that, in estimating the annual value of lands and heritages, the same shall be taken to be the rent at which, one year with another, such lands and heritages might in their actual state be reasonably expected to let from year to year, under deduction of the probable annual cost of the repairs, insurance, and other expenses, if any, necessary to maintain such lands and heritages in their actual state; and all rates, taxes, and public charges in respect of the same."

The reporter reported that deductions amounting in all to 38 per cent. ought to be allowed. The Lord Ordinary sustained, to a certain extent, objections by the Parochial Board and found that 28·60 per cent. was the proper deduction. On reclaiming the chief question discussed related to 5 per cent., proposed by the reporter to be added to the amount (24·85) otherwise allowed for maintenance and renewal of way. The reporter first ascertained from the company's books the sums actually so laid out for twelve years; but he thought that something more should be allowed. He found by an inquiry into the case of the Scottish Central Railway that what he calls the "life" of the railway should be taken at sixteen years—that is, that it would require a complete renewal every sixteen years. He found the sums actually laid out by the company were less than the proportion fairly belonging to the period now in question of the entire expense so estimated, and that only 50 miles out of a total mileage of 110 to 120 miles had been completely renewed in the twelve years over which his information extended; and he added a hypothetical 5 per cent. to cover the difference. The Court held, adopting the view taken by the Lord Ordinary, that the ground for adding this 5 per cent. was entirely fanciful and speculative;

that the fact, that in twelve years only fifty miles had been renewed, led to the inference that the sixteen years was too short a term for the life of a railway, rather than that extra expense would be incurred during the next four years; that the company, who were bound to furnish information as to the cost of maintaining the railway, had given the actual outlay for twelve years, which gave a percentage of 24·85 on the valuation; that under the Act there was no reason why that should not be taken, especially as the past cost was as good a foundation for the estimate as any other; and that in the absence of other grounds the Court must just take what the company had given as the basis of the deduction to be allowed. The 5 per cent. and some other items of deduction allowed by the reporter were therefore disallowed, and the total deduction under the Act fixed at 28·60 per cent. on the valuation.

EARL OF ROSSLYN *v.* NORTH BRITISH RAILWAY COMPANY.—*Dec.* 7.

Conveyance—Clause of Relief from Burdens—Construction—Teinds.

Held, in the locality of Dysart, that a clause in a disposition binding the seller to relieve his disponee, the North British Railway Company, "of all existing feu-duties, casualties, and public burdens, at and prior to the said terms of entry respectively, and also in all time thereafter, with the exception of poor-rates and prison assessment, which have been, or shall be, laid on the said railway company, in respect of the lands hereby disponed; which poor-rates and prison assessments, together with any augmentation of existing burdens, and all new or additional burdens to be imposed on the said lands, are to be paid by the said railway company from and after the foresaid terms of entry," &c., must be read with reference to the burdens on the subject conveyed, and did not import an obligation to relieve either from stipend already modified or future augmentations. It was not contended that the teinds were conveyed as well as the lands. Neither teind nor stipend is a burden on the *lands*, but on the fruits, and therefore the clause of relief is inapplicable to those burdens.

FORBES *v.* EDEN AND OTHERS.—*Dec.* 8.

Dissenters—Title to Sue Clergyman—Religious Body—Contract—Relevancy.

"A clergyman of the religious denomination known as the Episcopal Church in Scotland," and "minister of the Scotch Episcopal congregation at Burntisland," brought an action against a large number of clergymen, several of them holding the office of bishop in that communion, all as members of a General Synod, held at Edinburgh in the end of 1862 and beginning of 1863. His complaint against them was that, in making certain alterations on the Code of Canons, they had violated the constitution of the religious body to which both parties belonged, and thus committed a breach of contract. He alleged, further, that he could not conscientiously obey or conform to the altered code; and as by that altered code itself he is taken bound to do so, under heavy penalties, including degradation from the office, functions, and character of a clergyman, he had a material interest, personal and patrimonial, to challenge the legality of the alterations complained of, and to seek the protection of the law against their enforcement.

Held, that to the general relevancy of such an action no good objection could be stated, but that the pursuer had not put on record facts and circumstances relevant and sufficient to support the conclusions of the action It was observed by the Lord Justice Clerk that if a society, whether for secular or religious purposes, is bound together by articles of constitution, and an attempt is made to alter any fundamental article of the constitution, the general rule of law undoubtedly is, that the majority may be restrained, on the application of the minority, from carrying the alteration into effect. . . . . If the complaint here were at the instance of a mere lay member of the Scottish Episcopal communion, his interest and title to defend the constitution of the society might be seriously questioned; for he would be met with the ready answer that, as soon as the practice of the religious body became disagreeable to him, he was at liberty to bring his connection with it to an end. There are some weighty considerations which support the distinction between a lay and a clerical member of such a voluntary association. The possession of a particular *status*—meaning by that term the capacity to perform certain functions, or to hold certain offices—is a thing which the law recognises as a patrimonial interest, and no one can be deprived of it by the unauthorised or illegal act of another without having a legal remedy. Where a religious society embraces a numerous and wealthy section of the community, the position of a minister of religion in that society is an object for the attainment of which men are specially educated, and for which they throw away, it may be, other and more profitable prospects. When, therefore, one has been ordained a minister in such a communion, I hesitate to come to the conclusion that he has not obtained something which is of appreciable value even according to the vulgar standard of money. If, therefore, the pursuer can show that he became a minister in the Episcopal communion under one law, and now finds himself by the proceedings of the defenders under a new law, the enactment of which is a breach of the fundamental constitution of the society, which he cannot conscientiously obey, and which, if he disobey, he is liable to be deprived of his position as a minister, and of the character impressed on him by his ordination, I am not prepared to say that he is without legal remedy. That he has not yet been challenged for disobedience, and has suffered no actual injury, seems of little importance. If he can satisfy the Court that injury is surely impending, he is as much entitled to the exercise of preventive justice to stop the infliction of a wrong, as he is to reparation when the wrong has been done and the injury suffered. Holding these views as to the general nature of the action before us, I hesitate to adopt the course of reasoning in the note of the Lord Ordinary, and to give judgment against the pursuer solely or mainly on the ground that he has no sufficient title and interest to sue apart from a full consideration of the grounds of this complaint on its merits. I think we can scarcely do justice between the parties in this case unless we carefully consider what are the terms of the contract alleged to subsist between them, and what are the alleged breaches of that contract.

Lord Cowan remarked it was the province of the Civil Courts to redress civil wrongs; it was not their province, and had not been their practice, to interfere as courts of review with the theological dogmas or the internal regulations or discipline of religious sects or denominations. He concurred with the Lord Ordinary in saying that the canons of the Church were not enacted for the purpose of constituting a contract, but for the purpose of establishing and regulating its doctrine and discipline. . . . On the whole case, he was of opinion that no sufficient interest was stated by the pursuer to justify his demand on the Court to exercise its judicial powers in the matters complained of; and, second, that at any rate there is no averment in the record to support the demand in the summons on the alleged ground of want of power in the members of the General Synod of 1863 to act as they did.

The pursner alleged that the new canons of which he complained were not in conformity with the recognised constitutions of the Church. The pursuer's statement set forth, that when he was ordained, he understood that the Scotch communion office was the primary authority in his Church on the holy communion, and that by the new code of canons the forms of communion in the Episcopal Church in Scotland were substantially altered. If the pursuer's allegation was to be read absolutely, and to import that the recognised constitution of the Church had been altered by the introduction of new doctrine, the allegation would require to be followed up by some distinct and intelligent statement of the old doctrine, which had been changed, or of the new doctrine which had been introduced. The pursuer had shrunk, however, from making any such statement.

Lord Neaves said, with regard to the reductive and declaratory conclusions, the Lord Ordinary rests his judgment upon the ground mainly that the questions raised relate to an ecclesiastical matter which involves no civil right. I do not say that the Lord Ordinary's views in this respect are erroneous. On the contrary, I concur in them generally. But on one aspect of the case I entertain doubt, and wish to reserve my opinion. Suppose it could be held that the pursuer, as he alleges, was placed by the canons complained of in imminent peril of being deprived of his orders, that may involve a civil injury from which the pursuer might seek protection. Clerical orders conferred by a non-established church may have little or no civil effect in this part of the island. But they may possibly confer benefits elsewhere which may entitle the pursuer to have them preserved by the interference of a Civil Court. I should hesitate to throw it out on the mere ground that it involved no civil interest.

Pet.—COMMERCIAL BANK.—*Jan.* 17.

Sequestration—Notice of Meetings.

The Sheriff of Dumfriesshire sequestrated a bankrupt, and appointed the usual meetings for election of trustee and commissioners to be held, but, by mistake, the statutory period elapsed before the notices were inserted in the *Gazette.* In conformity with the course of practice established by the case of Garden, 10 D., 1509, the Court remedied the omission, by appointing new meetings to be held on certain days, ordering notice to be given in the *Gazettes*, and remitting to the Sheriff.

ENGLISH CASES.

AUCTION (*Sale*).—An auctioneer was instructed by the owner of premises to offer them for peremptory sale by public auction, at a named day and place. He issued handbills in which it was represented that the premises would be offered for sale by himself in such manner. It was also stated in the handbills, that the premises would be offered for sale by direction of the mortgagee, but without disclosing the mortgagee's name; and there was a notice at the bottom: 'For further particulars, apply to Mr Hustwick, solicitor, or the auctioneer.' Hustwick was the solicitor of the vendor. Plaintiff attended the auction, and made the highest bid, except that Hustwick bid a larger sum and bought in the premises. Plaintiff brought an action against the auctioneer; but it was held, that upon these facts there was no contract upon which the auctioneer was personally liable. (*Mainprice* v. *Westley*, 34 L. J., Q. B., 229.)

CHEQUE (*Bank*).—A cheque, payable to bearer, and stamped with a penny stamp, was on the 22d of June drawn by defendant and given by him to G. It was at the time dated the 22d of July. On that day G. indorsed it to W., who handed it to plaintiff, and received in return plaintiff's cheque for the same amount. Plaintiff took defendant's cheque without notice or knowledge that it had been post-dated. It was held, the cheque appearing to be correctly stamped according to its purport, and having been taken by plaintiff, without notice that it was post-dated, and innocently, he was entitled to recover upon it against the defendant.—(*Austin* v. *Bunyard*, 34 L. J., Q. B. 217.)

MARINE INSURANCE.—By a policy of insurance on a vessel against capture and detention, the assurers contracted 'to pay a total loss thirty days after receipt of official news of capture or embargo, without waiting for condemnation.' The vessel having been detained under an embargo within the meaning of the policy, it was held, that when the thirty days after receipt of official news of such embargo had expired, the assured was entitled to recover for a total loss, although before action, but subsequently to such thirty days, the embargo was taken off and the vessel was restored to the assured.—(*Fowler* v. *The English and Scottish Marine Insurance Co. (Lim.)*, 34 L. J., C. P. 253.)

RAILWAYS CLAUSES CONSOLIDATION ACT.—The effect of sec. 47 of the Railways Clauses Consolidation Act, 1845—which enacts that if a railway crosses any turnpike or public carriage-road on a level, the company shall erect and maintain sufficient gates across the road on each side of the railway. and shall employ proper persons to open and shut the gates, which shall be kept constantly closed across the road, except during the time when horses, carriages, etc., passing along it, have to cross the railway; and the person having the care of the gates shall, under the penalty of 40s., cause them to be closed as soon as the horses, etc., have passed through—is to make the road a highway only when the gates are opened by one of the company's servants; and if, there being no servant there, after waiting a reasonable time, a passenger open the gates, and attempt to pass through with his horse and carriage, and damage ensue to him from the gates swinging to, he is committing an illegal act, and the company are not liable for the damage.—(*Wyatt* v. *The Great Western Ra. Co.*, 34 L. J., Q. B. 204.

CONTRIBUTORY.—Certain reserved shares in a banking company were, in June 1864, offered by the directors to the existing shareholders, on the terms that the price of the shares was to be paid on the 1st of October then next, and that the shares would then be entitled to one quarter's dividend at the end of the year, but that, if paid before that time, interest at £5 per cent. would be allowed. A., a shareholder, agreed in July 1864 to take certain of the reserved shares; and in August he paid for them in advance. The manager informed him that a certificate would be given for the shares on the 1st of October; but on the 19th of September the bank stopped payment. It was admitted that the directors had gravely misrepresented the financial position of the company in their annual report, adopted by a general meeting in February. It was held, affirming a decision of Kindersley, V.C. (but *dissentiente* Lord Justice Knight Bruce), that the contract was to take the shares in *præsenti*, and that A. was a contributory in respect of the reserved shares agreed to be taken by him. Held, also (*per* Kindersley, V.C.), that A. could not be relieved on account of misrepresentations to which he was, as a shareholder, himself constructively a party; and (*per* Turner, L.J.) that, having regard to the lapse of time between the date of the report and the taking of the shares, the misrepresentations in the report could not be regarded as the proximate cause of A. taking the shares.—(*Re Leeds Banking Co., ex parte Barrett*, 34 L. J., Ch. 558.)

Contributory.—F. was the holder of fully paid-up shares in an industrial society formed with unlimited liability under the Industrial and Provident Societies Act, 1852. After the passing of the Industrial and Provident Societies Act, 1862, which repeals the Act of 1852, the society being in difficulties was registered under the Act of 1862 as a company with limited liability, for the purpose of being wound up, it having been held that a winding-up order could not be made under the repealed Act. Upon motion to settle the list of contributories, it was held that F.'s name must be omitted, notwithstanding there were debts contracted before the registration of the company with limited liability. The Companies Act, 1862, secs. 85 and 87, having taken away from the creditors their original remedy by action,—Semble, there were no means of enforcing F.'s liability to the debts of the company incurred before its registration with limited liability.—(*Re The Sheffield and Hallamshire Ancient Order of Foresters' Co-operative and Industrial Society* (*Lim.*), *Fountain's case*, 34 L. J., Ch. 593.)

Counsel have no authority to bind their clients in a suit to the terms of a compromise made out of court. Such compromise, if enforceable at all, must be the subject of a separate suit for specific performance.—*Green* v. *Crockett; Crockett* v. *Green*, 34 L. J., Ch. 606.)

Partners.—When a partnership is dissolved, each partner is entitled, in the absence of express agreement, to carry on business in the name of the old firm. —(*Banks* v. *Gibson*, 34 L. J., Ch., 591.)

Cruelty (*Husband and Wife*).—A husband's constant intoxication and open profligacy, coupled with some slight acts of violence towards his wife, and an attempt to cut her throat, held to constitute a case of cruelty.—(*Power* v. *Power*, 34 L. J., P. M. A. 137.)

Cruelty (*Husband and Wife*).—Where a husband treated his wife with neglect and indifference, ceased to have matrimonial intercourse with her, and carried on an adulterous intercourse with a servant in the same house where he and his wife were residing, it was held, that in the absence of any threats or acts of positive violence, his conduct did not amount to legal cruelty.—(*Cousen* v. *Cousen*, 34 L. J., P. M. A. 139.)

Charter-Party (*Shipmaster*).—A ship was chartered out and home at a lump sum; bills of lading to be signed by the shipowner or agent at any rate of freight, without prejudice to the charter. At an outward port the agent of the charterers advanced money to the master for the ship's use, on condition of the ship taking goods on the return voyage, under bills of lading making the freight payable to them (the agents), or their assigns at the port of delivery. It was held, the master had no authority to make such bills of lading, and that the shipowner retained his lien on the goods put on board for the freight.—(*Reynolds* v. *Jex*, 34 L. J., Q. B. 251.)

Game started and killed on the land of another, becomes the absolute property of the owner of the land, and not of the captor, even though it may be killed and carried away in one continuous act. *Quære*—Whether there would be any difference if the game were started on the land of one person and killed on that of another.—(*Blades* v. *Higgs* (House of Lords), C. P. 286.)

INSURANCE AGAINST FIRE.—A damage sustained by the atmospheric concussion caused by an explosion of gunpowder at a distance, is not a damage insured against by a policy for the payment of such loss or damage as should be occasioned by fire to the property thereby insured.—(*Everett* v. *The London Assur.*, 34 L. J., C. P. 299.)

MARINE ASSURANCE.—If a ship is submerged with cargo on board, and cannot be got out without raising the ship, the cost of raising is general average, to which the cargo must contribute. In such a case, in order to ascertain whether a ship is a constructive total loss, the sum to be contributed by the cargo as general average must be taken into consideration; and if, after deducting that sum, the remaining cost of raising, together with the cost of repairs of the ship, is less than her value when repaired, the ship is not a total loss. So held by Blackburn, J.; Shee, J., dissenting on the latter points.—(*Kemp* v. *Halliday*, 34 L. J., Q. B. 233.)

MASTER AND SERVANT.—A master cannot maintain an action *per quod servitium amisit* against a railway company for an injury to his servant whilst a passenger on the company's railway, caused by a neglect of their duty to safely carry the servant according to their contract with him as such passenger, unless the master was a party to such contract.—(*Alton* v. *The Midland Ra. Co.*, 34 L. J., C. P. 292.)

PRIVILEGED COMMUNICATION.—In an action of slander, laying special damages, it was proved that plaintiff, a trustee of a charity, asked C., by whom he was employed as bailiff, to obtain signatures to a protest against his being turned out of the trusteeship. C. asked defendant for his signature, which defendant refused; and on being pressed to give his reasons, said that he would not keep a big rogue like plaintiff in the trust; and he explained the reasons for his opinion, which were, that plaintiff had left the parish under discreditable circumstances, and without settling with his creditors, including defendant. He also added, that he was surprised that C. kept such a man on with his son. The whole of what was said about plaintiff's character was said with reference to the discussion whether it was proper that he should be continued as a trustee of the charity. In consequence of what defendant said, C. dismissed plaintiff from his employment. The jury found that defendant had not acted with malice. It was held that, assuming that the words were *bonâ fide* spoken with reference to the propriety of taking steps to retain plaintiff in the trusteeship, as they were pertinent to the question whether he was fit to be trusted or not, they were to be regarded as a privileged communication, and therefore that defendant was entitled to have the verdict entered for him.—(*Cowles* v. *Potts*, 34 L. J., Q. B. 247.)

COMPANIES ACT, 1862 (*Amalgamation—Rectification of Register*).—A shareholder in a company which is being wound up voluntarily, its business being transferred to another company in consideration of shares in that other company, cannot be compelled under the 161st section to take such shares even though he fail to notify his dissent from the resolution within seven days after the meeting at which it is passed. A name improperly placed on the register of shareholders may be erased under the 35th section, although the shares have since been forfeited, and the forfeiture entered in the register.—*Per* Romilly, M. R. (and Wood, V. C.).—(*Bank of Hindustan, etc.* (*Limited*), *ex parte Los*, 34 L. J., Ch. 609.)

COMPANIES ACT, 1862 (*Preference Shares*).—Where the memorandum of association provided that 'the directors may, with the sanction of the company in general meeting, declare a dividend to be paid to the shareholders in proportion to their shares;' and where, only half the shares being allotted, the directors had been authorized by an extraordinary general meeting to issue preference shares, held, *per* Westbury, C., that this was contrary to the articles of association, and *ultra vires*. Opinion, that the said issue, being one which essentially altered the basis of the company, could not be made legal by any exercise of the power of altering the articles of association conferred by sec. 50.—(*Hutton* v. *Scarborough Cliff Hotel Co.* (*Lim.*), 34 L. J., Ch. 643.)

CONTRACT (*Specific Performance—Time of Essence of Contract*).—Upon the sale of an estate by auction there was a condition fixing a period after the delivery of the abstract within which objections to title should be stated, and all objections not made within that time were to be held as waived. Held, that though it was not expressly so stipulated, time was of the essence of the contract.—(*Oakden* v. *Pike*, 34 L. J., Ch. 620.)

POWER OF APPOINTMENT.—A married woman having a power of appointment by will amongst her children, in consideration of a credit to one of her sons for the purposes of his business, covenanted with the son and the persons giving the credit that she would so exercise the power in favour of the son as effectually to appoint to him not less than £1000. Thereafter in her will she gave in the exercise of her power £1100 stock to the son, and directed him to pay it to the creditors. Held, *per* Kindersley, V. C, in conformity with previous cases, though doubting their soundness in principle, that the appointment was valid.—(*Coffin* v. *Cooper*, 34 L. J., Ch. 629.)

WILL.(*Construction*).—A testator gave his residuary estate among his nephews and nieces, and after directing the share of his niece E. G., and also a sum of £1000 which he had given her, to be held upon certain trusts, with an ultimate gift over, from the benefit of which as respected the £1000 he excluded a niece M. L., directed the shares of other nieces (including a niece M. B.), and also certain sums of £1000 given to them, to be held for their separate use respectively for their lives, and then for their children living at their respective deceases; 'but in case all the children of his said other nieces, or of any or either of them, should die either in their respective lifetimes, or after their deceases, under age and without leaving lawful issue,' then upon trust 'to pay, assign and transfer' their shares 'equally amongst all and every his nephews and nieces who should be living at such time or times, and to the issue of such of them as might be then dead, in equal shares and proportions (such issue to be entitled to its parent's share only), except as to the sums of £1000 given to his other nieces, which he directed should not survive to his niece M. L., but be paid in the same manner as he had directed the £1000 given to his niece E. G. in case of her decease without issue, or their all dying under age and without issue.' The gift over of E. G.'s £1000 was not made to take effect on E. G.'s death without issue, but in 'case all the children of E. G. should die either in her lifetime or after her decease under age, and without leaving lawful issue.' M. B. died without ever having been married. Held, that the gift over took effect as to her share and £1000; and semble, that even without the aid of the explanatory reference to the gift over of E. G.'s £1000, the gift over would have taken effect. Held also, *first*, that the word 'issue' meant children of the nephews and nieces, and not issue generally; *secondly*, that the gift to the issue of the nephews and nieces was an original gift, and not a gift by substitution; *thirdly*, that it was not necessary that the children who took a share should survive the tenant for life, or, the gift being original, their parents; and *fourthly*, that the children took as joint-tenants.—*Lanphier* v. *Buck*, 34 L. J., Ch. 650; see also *re Turner*, *ib.* p. 660.)

BILL.—A writing in the form of a bill of exchange, addressed to and accepted by the defendant, but without the names of either a payee or drawer, is only an inchoate instrument, and cannot be sued upon.—*M'Call* v. *Taylor*, 34 L. J., C. P. 365.)

LEGACY.—The mere erroneous recital by a testator that he has given something which he has not given does not create a gift. A will give a legacy of £1000 among such children of M. as should attain twenty-one. A codicil recited that the testatrix had by will given £1000 to F., a child of M., and directed 'the said legacy' not to be payable till F. attained twenty-one. Held that F. did not take a further legacy by the codicil.—(*Mackenzie* v. *Bradbury*, 34 L. J., Ch. 627.)

SALE OF LAND (*Right of Support from adjoining Land.*)—G. sold land in lots under conditions by which, *inter alia*, the purchaser of lot six was to build according to a certain elevation. The plaintiff, the purchaser of lot seven, altered, with G.'s consent, an old building on lot seven, by raising it several feet on the side next lot six. In consequence of excavations on lot six made by the defendant in the course of building in conformity to the conditions, the plaintiff's building fell. Held, that the excavations being made in terms of the contract with the vendor, the defendant, the purchaser of lot six, was not liable. Opinion, that the plaintiff, assuming his right to such support, lost it by raising the wall, and so increasing the superincumbent weight.—(*Murchie* v. *Black*, 34 L. J., C. P. 337.

Ancient Lights (*Right to Obstruct*).—A.'s house of three stories had an ancient window on each floor. He altered the windows in the two lower floors, leaving the window in the third floor unaltered. He also built two new stories to his house with windows intended to be permanent. A. did not intend to abandon any privilege of his ancient windows. B., the owner of adjoining premises, could not obstruct the new windows in the upper floors without also obstructing the old windows, and he built a wall obstructing all A.'s windows. A. afterwards blocked up his new windows, and sued B. for continuing the obstruction of the wall. Held, overruling previous cases, that B. had not at any time the right to build a wall which would obstruct the ancient lights in A.'s house, although the new windows could not otherwise have been obstructed. The right to an ancient light since the Prescription Act (2 & 3 Will. IV. c. 71) depends upon the statute, and does not rest on any presumption of a grant or licence from the adjoining proprietor.—(*Tapling* v. *Jones*, H. of L., 34 L. J., C. P. 342.)

Railway.—(*Lands Clauses Act*, 1845.—*Compensation for Loss of Trade.*)—A railway company during the execution of works under special act put a bridge on a highway over which passengers had to pass, and thus made the access to a public-house more difficult, causing a loss of trade. Held that the tenant could not claim compensation under sec. 68, on the ground that his land was injuriously affected; for (1) no action would have lain against the company had they not been authorized by their special act; and (2) the damage was to a personal interest, and the *land* was not injuriously affected. Previous cases overruled.—(*Rickets* v. *Metropolitan Ra. Co.*, in Exch. Chamber, 34 L. J., Q. B. 257.)

Railway (*Compensation for Injury to Shooting*).—One who has a right of shooting over lands by an agreement not under seal has no interest in the land to entitle him to compensation under sec. 68.—(*Bird* v. *G. East. Ra. Co.*, 34 L. J., C. P. 366.)

Damages (*Collaborateur*).—A workman in a coal mine received injury by the fall of a stone from the roof, which had lost its support in the ordinary course by the removal of the coal below. The underlooker was clearly guilty of negligence in not propping the roof, although the plaintiff had pointed out that it was necessary. The owners of the mine held not answerable for the injury caused to the plaintiff by the negligence of his fellow-labourer, there being no evidence to show that they were guilty of any want of proper care in the selection of the underlooker, or in putting the mine into proper order before the miners were sent down into it.—(*Hall* v. *Johnson*, in Exch. Chamber, 34 L. J., Ex. 222.)

Damages (*Contractor*).—The owner of a house employed a contractor to make a drain from his house to the main sewer under a local Act. The contractor fitted up the drain so negligently that it subsided and left a hole in a public footway into which the plaintiff fell. Held, by Exch. Chamber, that the owner of the house was liable for the injury.—(*Gray* v. *Pullen and Hubble*, 34 L. J., Q. B. 265.)

Negligence.—Where a machine is solely under charge of defendant or his servants, and the accident is such as, in the ordinary course of things, does not happen to those who have the charge of machinery and use proper care, it affords reasonable evidence of negligence in the absence of any explanation by the defendants.—(*Scot* v. *London Dock Co.*, in Exch. Chamber, 34 L. J., Ex. 220.)

POOR-RATE (*Exemption on ground of public purposes*).—The occupation of property which is liable to be rated under the 1st section of the 43 Eliz. c. 2, is an occupation yielding or capable of yielding a net annual value, that is to say, a clear rent over and above the probable average annual expenses necessary to maintain the property in a state to command such rent, and it is not necessary that the occupation should be beneficial to the occupier, so that trustees who are in law the tenants and occupiers of valuable property upon trust for charitable purposes, such as hospitals or lunatic asylums, are rateable, notwithstanding that the buildings are actually occupied by paupers who are sick or insane. The only occupiers exempt from the operation of the Act are the Sovereign, because he is not named in the statute, and the direct and immediate servants of the Crown, whose occupation is the occupation of the Crown itself; and the only ground of exemption from the statute is that which is furnished by the above rule. And consequently, when property yielding a rent above what is required for its maintenance is sought to be exempted on the ground that it is occupied by bare trustees for public purposes, the public purposes must be such as are required and created by the Government of the country, and are therefore to be deemed part of the use and service of the country.—(*Jones* v. *Mersey Docks and Harbour Board*, and *Mersey Docks, etc., Board* v. *Cameron*, H. of L., 34 L. J., C. P. 372; 35 L. J., Mag. Ca. 1.)

STAMP.—A notarial instrument in the form of schedule H. of the Titles to Lands Act (21 & 22 Vict. c. 76) is correctly stamped with a one shilling stamp, as being a 'notarial act,' in terms of 24 & 25 Vict. c. 91, s. 25, and not an instrument of seisin liable to a five shilling stamp under 13 & 14 Vict. c. 97, sched.—(*Lord Eglinton's Trs.* v., *Comrs. of Inland Revenue*, 34 L. J., Ex. 225.)

AUCTION.—An auctioneer and a puffer employed by him made eleven fictitious biddings against one another; a purchaser then made the first real bid, and the property was knocked down to him. The conditions of sale provided that the highest bidder should be the purchaser, but were silent as to any bidding on behalf of the vendors. Held, reversing the decision of the *Master of the Rolls*, that the fictitious biddings constituted a good defence to a suit by the vendors for specific performance.—(*Mortimer* v. *Bell*, 35 L. J., Ch. 25, 1 Law Rep. Ch. Ap. 10.)

BILL OF EXCHANGE (*Notice, Indorsement, "in need at, &c."*—A bill of exchange was indorsed, "In need, at S., P. & S.," S., P. & S. being London bankers. It was dishonoured by the acceptor, and on the following day was presented by the agent in London of the holder, who lived at Liverpool, to S., P. & S., and dishonoured. Next day the agent wrote to the holder, informing him that the bill had been dishonoured, and on the following day the holder sent notice to the indorsers:—*Held*, first, that the presentment of the bill to S., P. & S. was not notice to them of dishonour by the acceptor; secondly, that notice of dishonour to S., P. & S. would not have been notice to the indorsers, who were not made their agents for receiving such notice; thirdly, that a day could not be allowed for communication between the agent and the holder, and that consequently the notice to the indorsers was a day too late.—(*In re the Leeds Banking Co., ex parte Prange*, 35 L. J., Ch. 33: 1 Law Rep. Eq. 1.)

COMPANY (*Costs of re-investment—Lands Clauses Act—Abortive Attempt.*)—In a petition for re-investment of money paid into court by a railway company. Held, that if the purchase fails by reason of the Court disapproving of it, the purchaser must pay the costs; but in this case the Court had approved, though the purchase had failed for want of a good title, therefore the company must pay the costs as incidental to re-investment.—(*In re the Wisbeach, St. Ives and Cambridge Rail. Co., ex parte Rector of Holywell*, 35 L. J., Ch. 28.)

CONTRIBUTORY.—Shares in a joint-stock bank were purchased by a solicitor in the names of his brother and his clerk, who held as trustees for him; but there was no fraudulent object in thus concealing the name of the real purchaser. By the company's deed, it was provided that no trusts should be recognised; and no transfer of shares should be made without the consent of two directors. Held, that the beneficial owner was not liable to be placed on the list of contributories. —(*In re the East of England Banking Co., ex parte Bugg*, 35 L. J. Ch. 43.)

FAMILY ARRANGEMENT.—J. W. being seised and possessed of considerable real and personal estate, including stock-in-trade, died in 1831, having signed an unattested will, giving the whole of his property, subject to certain provisions for his widow, to his two sons. The will was not admitted to probate, but the two sons verbally agreed to carry out their father's intentions; and the elder, whose interest would have been the larger in case of an intestacy, declared that the property should not be "mine or thine, but ours." This arrangement was acted upon, and the business of the father was carried on jointly by the two sons for nearly twenty years, the evidence shewing that they acted in all respects as co-owners of the whole property, neither of the sons nor their father's widow ever having asserted their separate rights during that time. *Held*, that the course of dealing between the parties constituted a valid family arrangement which the Court would enforce.—(*Williams* v. *Williams*, 35 L. J., Ch. 12.)

INTERNATIONAL LAW.—Certain cotton, the public property of the Confederate States of America, was consigned by the Confederate Government to the defendants, a firm at Liverpool, in pursuance of an agreement, whereby the defendants were entitled out of the proceeds of the cotton to recoup themselves certain expenses incurred under the same agreement. The Confederate States having submitted to the United States Government, the latter filed a bill praying to have the cotton delivered up to them, and for an injunction and receiver. It appeared by the evidence that the defendants had, under the agreement, a lien upon the cotton to the extent of at least £20,000. *Held* by Wood, V. C., that the cotton was now the property of the United States Government, but subject to the obligations entered into respecting it by the *de facto* Confederate Government. The defendant Prioleau was appointed receiver, with power to sell the cotton; but he was required to give security for its value ultra the amount of the defendants' lien.—(*United States of America* v. *Prioleau*, 35 L. J., Ch. 7.)

STATUTE OF LIMITATIONS (*Same hand to pay and receive—trust of wife's next-of-kin.*)—Upon a marriage in 1818, a sum of £400 was handed over by the wife to the husband, who executed a bond for repayment with interest at the expiration of six months, if required by the trustees of the marriage settlement. The trusts of the settlement were to pay the interest to the husband for life, then to the wife for life, and then for the benefit of the children, but if no children, to transfer the trust funds to the next-of-kin of the wife. The husband died in 1853, leaving his wife his sole legatee and executrix, and the wife died in 1864. There were no children, and there had been no repayment and no demand:—*Held*, that the Statute of Limitations did not begin to run till the wife's death; and that the trustees were entitled to claim the £400 on behalf of the wife's next-of-kin against the husband's estate.—(*Mills* v. *Borthwick*, 35 L. J., Ch. 31.)

PATENT.—The inability of one of several joint-patentees profitably to use the invention without the consent of his co-patentees, as owners of a prior patent, does not entitle him to share with his co-patentees in the profits made by them from the use of the patent, there being no principle of law, in the absence of contract, to prevent any person not prohibited by statute from using any invention whatever, and no implied contract, where several persons jointly obtain letters patent, that no one of them shall use the invention without the consent of the others, or that he shall use it for their joint benefit. (Decision of the *Master of the Rolls*, 34 *Law J. Rep.* (N.S.) Chanc. 298, reversed.)—(*Mathers* v. *Green*, 35 L. J., Ch. 1, 1 Law Rep. Ch. Ap. 29.)

SPECIFIC PERFORMANCE (*Agreement*, *Consideration*, *Mistake.*)—J. in Calcutta, was tenant for life of real estate in England, with remainder to D. for life, with remainder to H. in tail. D. managed the estate. In June, 1863, J. became insolvent, and his property was vested in C., the official assignee at Calcutta.

On 6th August, C.'s agent in England applied to D. for information as to J.'s property in England, which D., after repeated applications, supplied on the 21st of October. On 30th October, C.'s agent having threatened at once to cut the timber on the estate, an agreement was signed by D. and H. and the agent, whereby it was agreed that C. should be entitled to the timber as if it had been cut and removed on 15th August; that D. and H., according to their present or future interests in the property, should carry out the agreement; that the agreement should not give C. any right besides what he had or could have exercised on the 15th of August, and that C. should not cut any timber before 1st December, 1863. J. died on the 24th of September, and his death was known to C. on the next day, but not to D. or H. or to C.'s agent, until November, 1863.—*Held*, by the *Master of the Rolls*, and *Lords Justices*, that the agreement was invalid for inadequacy of consideration, and on the ground of mistake; and by the *Master of the Rolls*, also, on the ground that the death of J. was known at the time to C., though not to his agent.—(*Cochrane* v. *Willis*, 35 L. J., Ch. 36, 1 Law Rep. Ch. Ap. 58.)

TRADE-MARK (*Colourable Imitation, Misrepresentation.*)—Misrepresentations in a trade-mark, amounting to a fraud upon the public, disentitle the person making such misrepresentations to protection in a court of equity against a rival trader; and, as a general rule, a misstatement of any material fact calculated to impose upon the public will be sufficient for the purpose: *e.g.*, a trade-mark representing an article as protected by a patent when in fact it is not so protected, or a trade-mark falsely representing an article as the production of an artist of special skill; or of a place of special adaptation. Though a man may assign his business and the use of his firm and of his trade-mark as belonging thereto, that proceeds upon the ground that the use of the name of the firm is not understood in trade to signify that certain individuals, and no others, are engaged in the concern. Though a man may have a property in a trade-mark in the sense of having a right to exclude any other trader from the use of it in selling the same description of goods, it does not follow that he can in all cases give another person a right to use it or to use his name, because he cannot give to them the right to practise a fraud upon the public.—(*The Leather Cloth Company (Limited)*, v. *the American Leather Cloth Company (Limited)*. (House of Lords). 35 L. J., Ch. 53.)

TRUST AND TRUSTEE—*liability of trustee for fraud committed on him by solicitor.*—A sole trustee committed the trust-fund to a solicitor to invest on mortgage. The solicitor appropriated the money; but he delivered to the trustee a fictitious conditional surrender of certain copyhold lands for securing the amount, but no receipt for the money was indorsed. The lands included in the pretended surrender were actually the property of the person by whom the surrender was expressed to be made, and of ample value. The solicitor regularly paid the interest on the money till his death, eight years afterwards, when the fraud was discovered:—*Held*, that the executor of the trustee was liable to make good the fund out of the assets of his testator. *Bostock* v. *Floyer*, 35 L. J. Ch., 23: 1 Law Rep. Eq. 26.

WILL (*Unity of vesting-Joint-tenancy.*)—Testator gave the interest arising from certain property to his niece for life, and after her death, the principal to go to her children or heirs for ever. Two of her children died in her lifetime; and it was held that the surviving children took as joint-tenants. *Ruck* v. *Barwise*, 35 L. J. Ch., 16.

COMPANY (*Winding-up-Companies' Act* 1862, 6 *Lease.*)—A company held a lease of quarries, containing no provision against assignment. In winding-up the lease was assigned to a purchaser. The lessor held not entitled either to have a sum impounded out of the assets of the company in respect of future rent, or to have the winding-up stayed during the continuance of the lease. *In re the Haytor Granite Co.*, 35 L. J. Ch., 29: 1 Law Rep. Eq. 11. The power conferred on the Court by sec. 147 of Companies' Act, 1862, to direct a voluntary wind-up to continue, but subject to its supervision, is absolutely discretionary. The summary jurisdiction of the Court under sections 118 and 165 is also discretionary. *Ques-*

tion,—Whether the 165th section applies to a voluntary winding-up. *Opinion*,—That the Court has no jurisdiction, where a company is being wound-up voluntarily, to make an order for winding it up compulsorily, on the petition of contributories. *Bank of Gibraltar and Malta*, 35 L. J. Ch. 49; 1 Law Rep. Ch. Ap. 59.

INTERNATIONAL LAW.—The carrying on of trade with a blockaded port is not a breach of municipal law nor illegal so as to prevent a Court of the *loci contractûs* from enforcing a contract of which it is the subject. *The Helen*, 35 L. J. Adm., 2: 1 Law Rep. Adm.. 1.

MARITIME LIEN.—A claim by a master for disbursements takes rank as a maritime lien, and is prior to the claim of a mortgagee of the ship. *The Mary Anne*, 35 L. J. Adm., 6: 1 Law Rep. Adm., 8.

ADMINISTRATION.—A woman, whose marriage had beeu dissolved on the ground of her husband's adultery and desertion, died intestate, leaving issue of the marriage one child, a minor. The Court decreed administration to the grandmother of the child, passing by the father, upon a copy of the decree dissolving the marriage being filed, and also copies of letters from him shewing that he was unfit to take the grant. In a grant of administration of the effects of a divorced woman the name by which the deceased should be described in the grant is that by which she was known at the time of her death. *In the goods of Hay (deceased)*, 35 L. J. Pr. and Mat., 3.

CHILDREN (*custody*.)—When a marriage is dissolved for misconduct of the husband, the Court, though it may deem him unfit to have the care of the children of the marriage, will not deprive him of his legal right to their custody in favour of the wife if she also is unfit to be intrusted with them; but will give the custody to some third person. *Chetwynd* v. *Chetywnd*, 35 L. J., Pr. and Mat., 21.

EVIDENCE.—The only evidence of the respondent's adultery was admissions made by her and the co-respondent; and the Court being satisfied that they were genuine, and that there was no ground to suspect collusion, dissolved the marriage. *Williams* v. *Williams*, 35 L. J., Pr. and Mat. 8: 1 Law Rep., P. and D. 29.

EVIDENCE (*Parol to explain ambiguity in codicil.*)—Testator executed a will and five codicils The fourth codicil revoked the first three; and the fifth confirmed the "said will and *four* codicils:"—*Held*, that there was sufficient ambiguity on the face of the codicil to render parol admissible to explain it; and as it appeared that testator intended to confirm his will and fourth codicil only, and that by mistake of the copyist of the draft the words "four codicils" had been substituted in the engrossment for the words "fourth codicil," that the will and fourth and fifth codicils only were entitled to probate. *In the goods of Thomson (deceased)*, 35 L. J., Pr. and Mat. 17: 1 Law Rep., P. and D. 8.

BUILDING CONTRACT (*Additional Work, Architect.*)—Defendants engaged plaintiffs to build a market-house, and the contract stipulated that no deviations in the way of extras or omissions should be made without the written authority of the defendants' architect; that no claim should be made for extra work without the written order of the architect, signed when the instructions for them were given; that if any dispute should arise as to the meaning of the specifications or contract, the architect was to define the meaning, and that his decision as to the nature, quality, and quantity of the works executed or to be executed should be final, and also his decision as regards the value of the extras and additions, which was to be regulated by the contract price. The architect certified that a certain sum, which included extras and additions, was proper to be paid:—*Held*, that neither party could raise the question of whether or not there was a sufficient order in writing; that a pump, drains, &c., though separately ordered, came within the meaning of "works connected with the contract," and that the architect's decision as to value was final.—*Goodyear* v. *the Mayor, &c., of Weymouth*, 35 L. J., C.P. 12.

CARRIERS BY RAILWAY (*Bye-law*).—A railway company must strictly comply with a bye-law on their part to entitle them to enforce it against a passenger. A bye-law provided that no passenger would be allowed to travel upon the railway without having first paid his fare and obtained a ticket, and that each passenger, on payment of his fare, would be furnished with a ticket, which ticket such passenger was to shew and deliver up when required by the guard or other authorized servant. A passenger, having three servants with him, paid his own and their fares, and was furnished with four tickets, for a certain train. He took his seat, with the tickets in his possession, in one part of the train, and the servants entered another part. The train was divided, and the servants were thus separated from their master. The part of the train in which the master was seated was first despatched, and before leaving he shewed the tickets for himself and servants. Afterwards, when the second part of the train was about to be despatched, the passenger's servants were unable to shew their tickets, and were not allowed to travel by that train:—*Held*, that the company could not justify their refusal to carry, inasmuch as the company had given the tickets to the master, and by the division of the train separated him from his servants.—(*Jennings* v. *G. Northern Ry. Co.*, 35 L. J., Q. B. 15; 1 Law Rep., Q. B. 7.)

CARRIERS ACT, (*Liability for Passenger's Luggage.*)—A railway company issuing a ticket for the conveyance of a passenger partly by land and partly by water are entitled to the benefit of the Carriers' Act, in respect of so much of the journey as is performed by land. The plaintiff arrived at the railway station, carrying a chronometer in his hand wrapped up in a handkerchief. He gave it to a porter, who in the presence of the plaintiff placed it on the seat of a carriage. Both porter and plaintiff immediately after left the platform together. After ten or fifteen minutes, the plaintiff returned and found that the chronometer was gone. *Opinion*, that the chronometer, at the time of its loss, was in the charge of the company as carriers, so that but for the Carriers' Act they would have been liable. —(*Le Conteur* v. *the London and South-Western Rail. Co.*, 35 L. J., Q. B. 40; 1 Law Rep. 2 B. 54.)

CARRIERS BY RAILWAY (*Packed Parcels—Different rates.*)—Plaintiff, a carrier, was in the habit of collecting small parcels, putting them together in one large package, and sending them by the defendants' railway, declaring them to be packed parcels. Defendants charged different rates of carriage for different classes of goods, and charged highest for "packed parcels." The company made plaintiff pay the packed parcel rate of charge. Plaintiff, finding that some others who sent packed parcels were charged for them at a less rate, sued the company for the alleged excess. On the trial, after giving the above general evidence, the plaintiff proved that, on a particular day he sent a specific parcel, for which he was charged the packed parcel rate. He, also, gave evidence that certain firms were in the habit of sending packed parcels to a large extent, and that they were not charged at the packed parcel rate, but at a lower rate; and he shewed that the practice of sending packed parcels had been so general as to be notorious among carriers; and also that on the reference of an action against the company in 1849, evidence of the generality of the practice of sending packed parcels was given in the presence of the company's then solicitor and their traffic manager. Plaintiff further proved that the company required a declaration from him as to the description of his parcels; but asked for and received no such declaration from other firms:—*Held*, in the Exchequer Chamber (*Erle*, *C.J.* dissenting) on a bill of exceptions, that such evidence was admissible, and that there was evidence on which the jury might find that parcels had been carried by defendants for other persons containing goods of a like description, and under like circumstances, at a less rate than such goods were carried by them for plaintiff, and also on which they might find that defendants knowingly and purposely charged plaintiff at a higher rate than other persons.—(*Sutton* v. *the Great Western Rail. Co.; and Sutton* v. *the South-Eastern Rail. Co.*, 35 L. J., Ex. 18.)

COURT OF SESSION.

FIRST DIVISION.

KERR *v.* MR. AND MRS. JAMES.—*Jan.* 23.

Suspension.

This was a suspension of a charge upon a decree *in foro* pronounced by Lord Barcaple on the 19th of July last in favour of the respondents, for an interim payment of £6000 out of a fund *in medio*, amounting at present to £13,000, and to which the respondents, "in virtue of the writings founded on in their claim," were by a judgment of the First Division in February 1858, found "to have right, under burden of the annuities" therein mentioned. The grounds of suspension were (1) That the decree was pronounced, and charge given by parties resident in England, without a mandatory having been sisted; (2) That the respondents had no sufficient title to grant a discharge to the complainer; (3) That the decree was disconform to and went beyond the terms of the judgment of 12th February 1858, which it was intended to carry out; and (4) That the money being in bank, the complainer was not in safety, and had not the power to make the payment, without a special warrant to uplift, which the chargers had failed to obtain.

The Lord Ordinary (Mure) refused the note of suspension. His Lordship held that in regard to the first three grounds of suspension they were competent to have been stated, but were omitted before the Lord Ordinary, when parties were heard on the motion for interim payment; and further that they could not be competently pleaded by way of suspension to a charge upon a final decree *in foro*, which the complainer, if dissatisfied with it, should have taken to review by reclaiming note. In regard to the fourth objection, his Lordship held the complainer would incur no risk by paying the money, and it had not been suggested that the Clerk of Court, who had the deposit-receipt, or the bank, had made any difficulty.

The Court, without calling on the respondent's counsel, unanimously adhered to the Lord Ordinary's interlocutor.

Pet., LAING *v.* NIXON.—*Jan.* 25.

Process—Commission to examine Defender to lie in retentis.

This was a petition for a commission to take the evidence of the defender, to lie *in retentis*, on the ground that he was above eighty years of age, and an important and necessary witness in an action which had been raised, concluding for £10,000 as the amount of damage which the pursuer alleged he had sustained, by having been induced to become and continue to be a customer of the defender, during a series of years, by false and fraudulent statements, representations, and concealment, made by the defender in regard to his price lists, and the way in which he carried on his trade.

The petition was presented after the summons had been executed, but before defences were lodged. The defender lodged answers to the petition, in which, besides denying the pursuer's allegations, he maintained that the application was an attempt to obtain a precognition upon oath of the defender, before the record was closed, and craved that the petition should be refused *in hoc statu*. The case was before the Court last week, when the pursuer, in support of his application, maintained that, by the Evidence Act, the parties to the cause were competent to be examined, and placed in the same position as ordinary witnesses; and that the defender being admittedly above the age of eighty, the Court should follow the ordinary rule applicable to witnesses of this age, and grant the commission. After hearing counsel, the Court, with the consent of the pursuer, delayed deciding the general point raised, until the defences in the action should be lodged.

Defences having been lodged, and the record closed, on summons and defences, the application for the examination of the defender to lie *in retentis* was renewed to-day, when the Court unanimously granted the prayer of the petition. The Court refused to compel the pursuer to lodge a minute consenting to waive his right to bring a new action in the event of his abandoning the present action; but ordered him to put in a minute, agreeing to hold the examination of the defender under the commission equivalent to his examination as a witness *in causa*, so as to preclude the pursuer from afterwards referring the cause to the defender's oath.

Farquharson v. Farquharson's Trustees.

Trust Deed—Construction.

The late Andrew Farquharson of Breda, in Aberdeenshire, died in 1831, leaving a trust-deed, by which he directed his trustees, *inter alia*, after payment of his debts and legacies, and without prejudice to his widow's liferent, to execute a deed of entail of the estate of Breda in favour of a certain series of heirs. The nearest heir male of Mr Farquharson, who was to be the institute under the entail to be executed, brought the present action of declarator to have it declared that the debts and legacies of the truster ought to be provided for by the trustees, either imposing them as a burden on the estate, or should be paid by a sale of a portion of the estate, "so that the existence of these burdens should not form any obstacle to the execution of a deed of entail." The pursuer averred that the burdens on the estate were of such an amount relatively to the rental, that if it was not to be entailed till they were all paid off by surplus rents, the heir of entail would be prevented from enjoying the estate for upwards of sixty years. The trustees, on the other hand, contended that under the present mode of management the burdens would be cleared off in a few years, and, in any view, that this must be done before the estate was handed over to the heirs of entail, that being clearly the intention of the truster. There is at present depending a process of multiplepoinding, in which the amount of the debts will ultimately be ascertained.

The Court held that the question before them was truly a question as to the construction of the trust-deed, viz., whether the truster intended to make his debts and legacies a burden on the fee or rents of the estate. It was quite competent for him to do either, and if it appeared to be his will that the estate should be cleared of debt before going to the heir of entail, that intention should receive effect. Looking to the terms of the deed, they were unanimously of opinion that such was the intention of the truster, viz., that he wished the estate not to be diminished by the debts and legacies. and not to be entailed until these were cleared off by the rents. That being so, the pursuer could not succeed in the present action. But that was apart altogether from the question whether, if it should turn out that the trust was at a dead lock from there being no surplus rental for application towards extinction of the debt, the Court would not, in virtue of its *nobile officium*, confer power of sale *ex necessitate*. Such a power unquestionably existed in the Court, to be exercised when absolutely necessary, but the pursuer was not in a position to show that the circumstances of the present case required its exercise. The decision now given, however, would not preclude a future application, if such became necessary.

The Inspector of Poor of Kirkconnel *v.* the Inspectors of Penninghame and Glencairn.—*Jan.* 27.

Poor—Industrial Settlement.

The question in this case was whether the pauper Janet Geddes or Candlish, wife of James Candlish, a labourer, had acquired a constructive settlement through her husband. The pauper became insane in the parish of Kirkconnel in May 1861, and her husband being unable to support her she was removed to the Southern Counties Asylum at the expense of the parish, and, with the exception of a short interval, has continued there up to the present time. Up to 1st November 1863 the outlay on her account amounted to £42, 16s 11d, for which sum, less £20 paid by the husband, with interest and all expenses since incurred, the pursuer sought relief against the defenders alternatively. It was not ultimately disputed that one of the two was liable, and a minute was lodged to that effect. Penninghame was the husband's parish of birth, but he was said to have acquired a residental settlement in Glencairn. It appeared that he came to Minnyhive in the parish of Glencairn, on 18th July 1854, and lived there in lodgings till 8th September following, when he left for a few weeks, being employed in harvest work in another parish. He returned on 14th October, when he took a house, and was joined by his wife and family on 6th November. They all continued to live there till Whitsunday 1858, when they removed to another house in the same parish, where the family remained till 4th or 6th November 1859, but the husband went on the 18th May 1859, to Creetown, which is not in the parish of Glencairn, and with the exception of two days in June, he did not return till the beginning of harvest, and in November 1859 he finally left with his wife and family. It further appeared that each year he was absent a few days during harvest time, but it was not disputed that he had supported his wife and family, both when he lived with them and was absent from them. The question, therefore, was whether there had been such continuous residence for five years as is required by the statute 8 and 9 Vict., cap. 83, to constitute an industrial settlement.

The Lord Ordinary (Ormidale), held that the husband's residence in Glencairn ceased on 18th May 1859, and in any view did not commence till 14th October 1854, while he was rather inclined to hold that it did not commence till 6th November 1854, when his wife and children joined him. His lordship accordingly assoilzied Glencairn, and decerned against Penninghame, the parish of birth.

The Court reversed this judgment, and decerned against the parish of Glencairn, holding that the husband's residence in that parish, counting from the period of his going there to the period of his leaving, having exceeded the statutory period of five years, and the interruptions by absence not having been of such a character as to dislocate its continuity, it had conferred upon the husband an industrial settlement therein.

Watt v. Menzies.—*Jan.* 27.

Issues—Expenses.

The pursuer sues Mr Menzies, omnibus proprietor in Glasgow, for personal injuries she sustained in Argyle Street, there upon being set down from one of his conveyances between the Cross and Anderston. She avers that, on asking to be set down, the guard, instead of stopping the omnibus, entered it abruptly, forcibly seized hold of her, and jumped with her in his arms to the middle of the street, and left her there. Before she recovered from her confusion, she was knocked down and injured by another omnibus. The defender proposed that it should appear in the issue that the pursuer was injured in consequence of the violent and reckless manner in which she was set down by the guard. The Court approved of the following issue:—

"Whether, on or about 6th June 1865, and in or near Argyle Street, Glasgow, in consequence of the parties in charge of an omnibus belonging to the defender, in which the pursuer was travelling as a passenger, failing to take due precautions in setting her down from the said omnibus, she was knocked down and injured by another omnibus through the fault of the defender, to her loss, injury, and damage."

Damages, £300.

Mr. Scott asked for expenses.

Mr. Clark explained that no copy of the issue now adjusted had been sent to defender before the second meeting for adjustment before the Lord Ordinary. A copy of another issue in the same case had, however, been sent, and it was to this, that defender objected before the Lord Ordinary. The issue now approved was a new issue lodged at the bar in the Outer House, which the defender had not then any opportunity of considering.

The Court refused pursuer's motion for expenses.

Pringle v. Bremner and Stirling.—*Jan.* 30.

Warrant to Search—Mode of Executing.

This is an action at the instance of James Pringle, millwright, Newburgh, Fifeshire, against the chief-constable of that county and one of the sergeants of police, arising out of the alleged mode of executing a warrant to search the pursuer's premises for materials supposed to have been used in constructing the cart wheel bush exploded near Dunbog Manse. The grounds of action are—(1.) That on 24th December 1864, the defenders came to the pursuer's house, stating they had a warrant to search the same, which they accordingly did; they, it is alleged, also searched the pursuer's repositories, examined all his private books and papers, and seized and took away a number of the same. The pursuer says they had no warrant for these proceedings. (2.) That the pursuer was on the same day apprehended by the defenders, and lodged at the Police Office at Cupar, all without warrant. For these proceedings he sues the defender for damages. The defenders do not aver that they had a warrant for the examination and seizure of the pursuers papers, or for his apprehension; but that, holding a warrant to search his premises for other articles, they accidentally came upon a number of papers which seemed to throw light upon a matter which was then under investigation by the Procurators-Fiscal and police, and which was connected with the matter in regard to which they were making a search. They therefore thought it their duty to take possession of the documents, and to take the pursuer into custody, and to take him to Cupar for examination before the Sheriff; which, however, in respect of the lateness of the hour, had to be delayed till the following day. It was not disputed by the pursuer that the after proceedings were regular and legal. But the pursuer says on record that the defenders did not accidentally come upon his papers in the course of their search for other articles, but that they, in the beginning of their search, proceeded to examine his books and papers.

The case was before the Court about a month ago for the adjustment of issues, when the main contention was whether the admissions on record raised a case of privilege, and the pursuer, was, therefore, bound to put in issue, "malice and want of probable cause."

The Court, considering that it was important to know the way in which the search for papers had been begun and executed—parties being at issue thereupon, and the record not supplying the information required—before pronouncing any judgment as to the issues, appointed the pursuer to state specifically what he alleged with regard to these.

The pursuer has since given in a minute containing the following additional statement :—

"On the occasion when the defenders came to the pursuer's house as aforesaid, the pursuer, who had been from home, arrived at his house just as the defenders had driven up. The pursuer's dwelling-house was situated on the side of a public road, and his workshop is separate, and at a short distance from it. The defenders informed the pursuer, immediately on his arrival, that they had a warrant against him; but they did not at this or any other time explain the nature of said warrant to the pursuer. At the time when the defenders informed the pursuer they had a warrant against him, they were all outside the house, and it was so dark that the pursuer could not have read the warrant. The pursuer did not after this demand exhibition of the warrant, because he did not doubt the statement by the defenders that they had a warrant of some kind; and he assumed that they could not exceed the limits of the warrant. After this the pursuer opened his dwelling-house, which the defenders entered, and a light was then procured. The defenders thereafter proceeded at once, and without further ado, to search the pursuer's writing-desk and the drawers which it contained. The defenders spent between one and two hours in ransacking the said writing-desk and drawers, and in reading and examining the MSS., books, letters, and papers which they found therein. The whole search made by them in the pursuer's dwelling-house consisted of the reading and examination of the pursuer's said books, letters, and papers. The pursuer is not aware whether the defenders ever made a search in his workshop."

To this statement the defenders have made the following answer :—

"Admitted that the pursuer was absent from his house when the defenders first arrived. Admitted that the pursuer's house is separate from his workshop. Admitted that the defenders informed the pursuer that they had a warrant; and explained that the defender, Bremner, produced it, offered it to the pursuer for his perusal, and explained to the pursuer its nature and contents. Denied that the defenders proceeded at once to search the pursuer's writing-desk. Explained that the defenders searched first other places likely in their opinion to contain wood or iron materials. Explained farther, that what the pursuer calls a writing-desk is a cabinet which had the appearance of a place where such things were likely to be. *Quoad ultra* denied."

The Court held that the statements on record by the pursuer were not exclusive of the truth of the explanation given by the defenders, viz., that in the course of searching for the articles specified in the warrant they had accidentally come on certain documents which they thought it their duty to examine, and therefore dismissed the action, on the ground that there was no issuable matter on record.

M.P.—North of Scotland Railway Company v. Mortimer and Others. *Feb.* 1.

Marriage-Contract—Provision—Vesting.

By antenuptial contract of marriage, entered into in 1830 between Mr Ludovick William Grant and Miss Helen Anderson, Mr Anderson bound himself, his heirs, executors, and successors, "to lay out at the term of Whitsunday or Martinmas that should happen next after his death, or as soon thereafter as circumstances would permit, the sum of L.2000, taken payable to the said Helen Anderson and L. W. Grant, and the survivor of them, in conjunct liferent for their liferent use allenarly, and to the child or children to be procreated of the marriage, whom failing, to the nearest heirs and assignees of the said Alexander Anderson in fee." The deed also provided that the said "sum of L.2000 shall bear interest from the date of the said Helen Anderson and L. W. Grant's leaving the family of the said Alexander Anderson." On 25th August 1831, a son, William Grant, was born of the marriage, who died in 1832, and there was no other child. Mr Anderson, the granter of the obligation, died in 1838, and was succeeded by his only son, James Andersen, as heir and residuary legatee of his father. Mr Anderson's (the son) estates were sequestrated in 1841, Mrs Grant died in 1862, and Mr L. W. Grant died in 1863, he having previously executed a trust-deed for behoof of his creditors.

The question raised in the present multiplepoinding is, whether the trustee on the sequestrated estate of Mr Anderson, the son and heir of the granter of the obligation, or the trustee for Mr L. W. Grant's creditors, are entitled to the said sum of L.2000, and that question depends on this other, whether the L.2000 vested in William Grant, Mr and Mrs Grant's son, in which case, at his death, it would be inherited by his father, and so now belong to the trustee for his creditors.

The Lord Ordinary (Mure) preferred Anderson's trustee to the fund, holding that it did not vest in William Grant, the only child of the marriage, in respect of his having died before the granter of the obligation, and therefore before it became enforceable.

The Court (Lord Ardmillan dissenting) adhered to the Lord Ordinary's interlocutor, though not adopting the grounds of his judgment. Their lordships held that, in the case of provisions in an antenuptial contract of marriage, the presumption is always against their vesting in the children till the dissolution of the marriage, and this presumption will be given effect to, if not counteracted by something in the deed. The only circumstance in the present case opposed to this presumption was the payment of interest to Mr and Mrs Grant during their lives. This the Court thought was not in itself sufficient to overcome the ordinary rule.

Lord Ardmillan held that the granter of the obligation was divested of the fee of the L.2000 on the marriage,—that it then passed to Mr and Mrs Grant as fiduciary fiars for any children they might have; and on the birth of their son William, that the fee vested in him.

Pet., J. H. Young.—*Feb.* 2.

Recorded Deed—Authority to send to England for Production in a Suit—Refused.

This is a petition by J. H. Young, merchant in Glasgow, praying the Court to warrant and authorise the Lord Clerk Register, or one of his deputies, to proceed to London with certain deeds recorded in the Books of Council and Session, and in the custody of the Lord Clerk Register, for the purpose of exhibiting them in the Court of Chancery, in England, as evidence in a cause depending there. The petitioner was not personally interested in the deeds, but it was proposed to use the narratives of the deeds in the English case, which involved a question of propinquity in disproof of certain allegations on which they threw light.

The Court refused the petition, holding that they were not warranted in authorising the transmission of the deeds to England, in respect it was impossible to guarantee that such a proceeding might not result in their destruction or loss, and the application was not at the instance of those having the sole interest in them.

Spinks *v.* Innes.

Bank Cheque—Fraudulent Impetration—Intoxication.

The summons in this case concludes for a decree against the defender for the sum of £100 sterling, being the principal sum contained in a bank cheque or draft, dated at Glasgow the 21st day of April 1864, drawn by the defender on the City of Glasgow Bank, and payable to the pursuer. It appears that the cheque, though dated Glasgow, was written and given to the pursuer in Alloa, where both parties were on the day of its date. The following morning the defender telegraphed to Glasgow to stop payment of the cheque, and the present action has consequently been brought. The pursuer's allegation is that the defender, being indebted to him to the extent of £100, gave him the cheque or draft in question in payment of his debt, which consisted of "advances of money made and services rendered by him (the pursuer) to the defender at various times during a long course of years." The defender's averment, on the other hand, besides a denial of his having been indebted to the pursuer, is to the effect that, when the cheque or draft in question was obtained from him by the pursuer, he (the defender) was in such a state of intoxication as to be utterly deprived of the use of his faculties; or, at any rate, that the pursuer taking advantage of his intoxicated condition, fraudulently impetrated from him the draft.

A proof having been led by both parties, the Lord Ordinary (Ormidale) held (1) that no value had been given by the pursuer to the defender for the cheque; (2) that when the cheque was obtained the defender was in such a state of intoxication from excessive drinking as to be easily imposed upon and taken advantage of; and (3) that the pursuer having taken advantage of the defender when in that state had fraudulently impetrated from him the draft. His lordship therefore assoilzied the defender.

The Court unanimously adhered. They held that the right of the pursuer to succeed in the present action depended on whether he had established his allegation that the cheque was granted in payment of a debt due to him by the defender. It was not averred that the cheque was given as a donation. They were of opinion that the proof, so far from establishing the debt, disproved it, and therefore, that the Lord Ordinary's interlocutor should be adhered to. They were of this opinion apart from the matter of the defender's intoxication when the cheque was granted. It appeared that a great deal of drink had been taken by the parties on the day in question, but it was a difficult question what was the precise degree of intoxication which relieved a person from liability for obligations undertaken by him. It might involve consideration of the amount and character of the drink, and of the temperament of the individual.

SMITH *v.* THE EDINBURGH AND GLASGOW RAILWAY COMPANY.—*Feb.* 3.

Railway Compauy—Amalgamation Act.

This is an action concluding for £3000 in name of damages and *solatium* for injuries sustained by the pursuer on 27th May last in a railway accident which occurred on that date at the junction between the railway from Milngavie and the railway between Glasgow and Helensburgh. The defenders pleaded that the action was incompetently directed against them, in respect of their amalgamation with the North British Railway Company, which took place on 1st August 1865.

The Lord Ordinary (Ormidale) repelled the plea, and sustained the competency of the action as law.

The Court (Lord Deas dissenting) adhered. The majority held that the cause of action having occurred prior to the amalgamation, and the Edinburgh and Glasgow Railway Company being still in subsistence (under the Acts regulating the amalgamation) as a separate company for the collection of outstanding revenue, and the payment of debts chargeable thereagainst, —and the claim in question being a claim falling to be liquidated out of the revenue of the old company,—an action for constituting it was properly directed against the present defenders.

Lord Deas dissented, on the ground that a claim like the present was not necessarily limited to the revenue, but might be chargeable against the capital, and the whole capital of the Edinburgh and Glasgow Railway Company having been transferred to the amalgamated company, they were the proper parties to call in the present action.

Pet., MRS. ELIZABETH AUCHTERLONIE OR KENNEDY.—*Feb.* 3.

Conjugal Rights Act—Protection of Wife's Property—Desertion.

This was a petition under the Conjugal Rights Act at the instance of a wife for the protection of property acquired by her during the alleged desertion of her husband. In 1849 the petitioner married Robert Kennedy, who was a shore porter in Dundee. At the time of the marriage the petitioner was a widow, and Kennedy a widower. Both had families, three of whom still reside with the petitioner, as well as a child of her marriage with Kennedy. In 1852, Kennedy, with his wife's consent, went to California, in the hope of increasing his means, and for two and a half years corresponded with his wife. From 1855 to 1863 there was no communication between them. In 1863 Kennedy wrote to his wife, expressing great affection for her and his family, and attributing his long silence and continued absence to reverses of fortune which he had encountered. In July 1864, before the present petition was presented, Kennedy wrote to his wife that he was to sail for home next day, and enclosed a bank bill for £180. He arrived at home two days after this remittance, and has continued to reside with his wife ever since, and does so now. During her husband's absence the petitioner supported herself and acquired by her industry some property, and it was for the protection of this property that the present petition was presented. The Conjugal Rights Act makes it competent for a wife deserted by her husband to apply to the Court for an order to protect against her husband and his creditors any property she had acquired by her industry, or succeeded to during her husband's desertion. The question, therefore, in the present case was whether the petitioner had been *deserted* by her husband.

The Court held (affirming the judgment of the Lord Ordinary), that desertion in the Conjugal Rights Act meant wilful desertion with a view to avoiding cohabitation, and as the absence of the husband was originally with the consent of the petitioner, and for the purpose of benefiting her and the family, and nothing had occurred sufficient to convert an absence so begun into desertion in the sense of the Act, the petition ought not to be granted.

Div., Mary M'Lean or Bonar *v.* Alex. Bowman.—*Feb.* 7.

Divorce on the Ground of Desertion—Circumstances in which Refused.

In this action Mrs. Bowman sued for divorce on the ground of desertion. In 1856 she was married to the defender, who is furth of Scotland, and who does not defend the action. After the marriage the parties lived together as husband and wife for about two years, when the pursuer, in consequence of intemperance and maltreatment on the part of the defender, left his house and returned to live in family with her father, with whom she has resided ever since. In April 1860 the pursuer obtained, in the Sheriff-Court, Glasgow, decree for certain sums of aliment and expenses against her husband. No part of said aliment or expenses was paid by the defender, and since its date he had broken up his establishment and disappeared from Glasgow, where he had previously resided. The pursuer has not since heard from him nor has she been able to ascertain where he resides, or whether he is in the country, but it is generally believed by his friends that he is abroad.

The Lord Ordinary (Ormidale) found that in law the pursuer is not entitled to a decree of divorce, there being no evidence that after she left her husband's house she was willing to return, or offered to adhere.

The Court adhered to this interlocutor. Their Lordships held that the remedy of divorce by the law and practice of Scotland proceeded on the assumption of the party applying for it being willing to adhere. Accordingly, the Scots Act 1573, cap. 55, provided that various preliminary steps, with a view to adherence, should be taken before the action of divorce could be brought. Although these steps might not now be necessary, having been expressly dispensed with by the Conjugal Rights Act 24 and 25 Vict., cap. 86, sec. 11, yet that the principle and theory of the law of Scotland remained the same. The remedy of divorce was, in our law, not for desertion, but for non-adherence. A case of great importance might be raised in circumstances similar to the present, where the wife was compelled to flee from her husband's house for protection, but that in the case before the Court the facts were scantily proved, and did not raise the important point pleaded for the pursuer, which the Court were not therefore called on to decide. They found that the proof adduced did not bear the interpretation that the pursuer had been willing to adhere and live with the defender as his wife since the time when she left him in 1860, but what proof existed rather showed that she was not willing to return to her husband. She had her remedy by an action of separation and aliment, and in this case, where the *onus* of proof lay on the pursuer herself, and she had failed to prove her readiness to adhere, she could not obtain the remedy of divorce, at all events on the proof as it stood. In referring to the authorities founded on by the pursuer, the Court declined to be guided in their interpretation of our Scots Acts 1573, cap. 55, by the interpretation of it, or of desertion, by American writers, and they remarked that, in England, divorce, as a remedy for desertion, was coupled with other things, and was made a ground of divorce by quite a recent statute. The remedy of divorce with us was given, not for desertion, but for non-adherence, and had been a ground of divorce for three centuries; and it was remarkable that, notwithstanding,—it was admitted for the pursuer that there was no precedent in our law showing that this remedy was ever sought for or obtained in such circumstances as this case disclosed.

The Crown *v.* Matheson.—*Feb.* 8.

Crown Charter—Reddendo.

Mr. Matheson, of Ardross, in July last, gave in a note for a Crown charter of, *inter alia*, the lands of Deluy in the county of Ross, lodging at the same time a draft of the proposed charter, which contained a *reddendo* clause in the same terms as in the five preceding Crown grants of the same subjects in favour of his authors. The proposed clause, besides obliging the vassal to pay to the Crown a specific duty of 6s. 8d. Scots annually, and £39, 8s. 4d. Scots at the entry of each heir, contained the following obligation of relief: "And relieving the heirs and successors of the late Earl of Cromarty of all feu-farms and feu-farm money, customs, augmentations, and grassums, payable from the said lands as proprietor of the Earldom of Ross, and which feu-farm duties, customs, augmentations, and grassums have been hitherto annually payable and paid to the Royal Treasurer of the county of Ross." The Crown now contended that this was a general *reddendo*, and as such struck at by an order issued by the Barons of Exchequer in 1802, forbidding the insertion in Crown grants of general *reddendo* clauses without the express authority of the Court, and therefore proposed to substitute for the obligation of relief a direct obligation on Mr. Matheson to pay the duties chargeable in respect of the lands of Deluy, and actually standing at this moment in the titles of the Duchess of Sutherland, the present representative of the Earls of Cromarty, whom Mr. Matheson admits his liability to relieve. To this Mr. Matheson objected—(1) That the proposed *reddendo* was not struck at by the order of 1802, inasmuch as it was sufficiently specific, the obligation of relief in no true sense forming a part of the *reddendo* clause; (2) That the Barons of Exchequer in 1826 and the Presenter of Signatures in 1854, by passing charters containing *reddendos* precisely similar to that in the draft, had admitted that this *reddendo* is not one to which the order of 1802 applies; and (3) That at all events the present summary process was not one in which this question could competently be raised—parties being at issue as to the duties payable in respect of the particular lands, and the Duchess of Sutherland, whose interests might be most materially involved, being no party to the process.

On 23d December last the Lord Ordinary (Ormidale) refused a motion by the pursuer to have certain specified duties inscribed in the *reddendo* clause of the charter.

The Court adhered to this interlocutor, reserving to the Crown, if so advised, to have their rights declared in a competent action in which all parties interested should be called.

The University of Aberdeen *v.* Irvine.—*Feb.* 8.

In 1629, Alexander Irvine, then of Drum, an ancestor of the defender, executed a last will and testament containing, *inter alia*, the following provision :—

"For the maintenance of letters, by their presents, I leave, mortify, and destinate ten thousand pounds Scots money, which is now in possession and keeping of Marion Douglass, my spouse, all in gold and weight, appointed for the use underwritten, of her own knowledge and most willing consent, to be presently delivered to the Provost, Bailies, and Council of Aberdeen, and to be bestowed and employed by them upon land and annual rent in all time hereafter to the effect after following, to wit, £320 of the annual rent thereof to be yearly employed hereafter on four scholars at the Grammar School of Aberdeen for the space of four years, ilk ane of them fourscore pounds; and £400 to be paid yearly to other four scholars at the College of New Aberdeen, and students of philosophy thereat, ilk ane of them ane hundred pounds during likewise the space of four years; and also I ordain to be given to other twa scholars who have passed their course of philosophy, being made Masters, and are become Students of Divinity in the said New College, 400 merks Scots money, viz., to each one of them 200 merks of the said annual rent during the space of four years also; and the odd 20 merks, which, with the dedications above specified, complete the said haill annual rents of £10,000, I ordain to be given to any man the Town of Aberdeen shall appoint for ingathering and furthgiving of the said annual rent to the said scholars, as is above designed; which scholars, of the kinds above written, I will and ordain yearly, in all time hereafter, be presented as my said executor, as my heir, and his heirs and successors, Lairds of Drum, to the Town of Aberdeen, Provost and Bailies thereof, and their successors, who shall be holden to receive them yearly upon their presentation, and shall stand obliged and compatible for the said annual rent to be employed as is above appointed in all time coming."

The testator died soon after executing this deed, and was succeeded by his son Sir Alexander Irvine.

When this legacy was communicated, on the testator's death, to the magistrates of Aberdeen, they declined to receive and administer it, on the ground, as stated in their minute of 9th May 1630, that they thought their doing so would make them liable for the sum of L.1000 Scots of yearly interest in all circumstances. And they requested the widow "to deliver the said L.10,000 to Sir Alexander Irving, now of Drum, his son, upon his acquittance to be given thereupon to her; to the end he may ware the same on profits to the use foresaid whereunto the same was destinate and left, and be comptable and answerable therefor, till such time as the Council and he may agree on reasonable conditions thereanent."

In 1633, Sir Alexander Irving brought an action in the Court of Session against the magistrates and various other parties, concluding, amongst other things, to have it found and declared "that it shall be leisome to the said complainer to ware and bestow the said sum of L.10,000 upon buying of land therewith, upon such easy prices and conditions as may be had therefor; and the said lands to be bought therewith, maills, farms, and duties of the same, to be mortified and destinated to the use of the said four scholars," &c., proportionally and *pro rata*, effeiring to the quantities of the annual rent of the said sum appointed to be paid to them by the said testament in case the said provost, bailies, and council of the said burgh of Aberdeen had received and employed the said sum for annual rent according to the said testament; and the yearly rent, profits, and duties of the said lands to be bought and conquest with the said sum, to be in place and satisfaction to the said ten scholars of the annual rent and profits of the said sum in all time coming." The summons contained a reservation of the right of presentation, and concluded that, on land being bought to the effect mentioned, the pursuer should be discharged of all liability for the sum in question.

A decree was pronounced, on 27th February 1663, in this action, in absence, ordaining Sir Alexander Irving to have retention of the money without interest till Whitsunday 1640, "at the which term decerns and ordains the said pursuer to provide for the use of the said ten scholars and bursars of the college and schools of New Aberdeen sufficient well-holden lands for employing of the said sum of L.10,000, worth in yearly rent to the sum of L.1000 money, which lands shall be bought and acquired by him heritably, without reversion, to the use and behoof foresaid, against that term, without further delay, according to the destination and mortification of the said Laird of Drum, and his mind specified in his latter will."

The mode in which Sir Alexander Irving gave obedience to this decree was, to mortify certain lands belonging to himself, including those of Kinmuck and others now in question, for the intended object, these lands being valued at the yearly rental of L.1000 Scots. This he did by his bond and deed of mortification (of which an extract from the Books of Council and Session is produced), bearing date 12th April 1656, and proceeding on a narrative to the above effect. On this narrative the deed declares:—

"Therefore, and to the effect the said ten scholars and bursars may be paid yearly furth of the maills and duties of the said lands, according to the division above written, I, the said Sir Alexander, for me, my heirs and successors, has mortified, destinated, and appointed, and by these presents, for me and my foresaids, mortify, destinate, and appoint the above written lands, maills, and others foresaid, with the pertinents, for the use and behoof of the said ten scholars yearly in all times thereafter, to the effect the maills, farms, and duties thereof may be paid to them yearly for their maintenance, according to the division above written; with power to them, and their curators in their name, to uptake the maills, farms, and duties of the foresaid lands for that effect."

The pursuers contend that the foregoing proceedings import that Sir Alexander appropriated to his own use the sum of L.10,000 Scots, and in consideration thereof, by the deed of 1656, mortified the lands of Kinmuck and others for the use and behoof of the pursuers, and the object of the present action accordingly is to have the pursuers' right to the said lands declared, which at the date of the deed were worth L.1000 Scots yearly, but are now said to be worth L.700 per annum. The defender, on the other hand, contends that the deed of 1656 was only a bond granted for the purpose of securing to the bursars the annual payment of L.1000 Scots, which sum he is and always has been willing to pay, as his ancestors have always done. The deed does not, he says, contain any absolute conveyance of the lands, and was never followed by possession, or acted on in any way; on the contrary, the lands have always remained in the possession of the Irvines of Drum, a part of that estate.

On 2d December 1863, the Lord Ordinary (Kinloch) found that, according to a sound construction of the testament of 1629, the decree of 1633, and the deed of mortification of 1656, the whole beneficial interest in the lands of Kinmuck was transferred and made over for behoof of the bursars, and that the pursuers were entitled to have this right declared and enforced against the defender as vested with the feudal title to the lands.

The defender reclaimed, and on 30th March 1864, the Court, after a debate, allowed to both parties a proof before answer of their respective averments on record. The proof was led, and the case having been again debated at great length, was advised to-day.

Lord Curriehill, who delivered the first opinion, after narrating the facts of the case, said the nature of the rights in favour of the bursars appear to be this. The testator directed his money to be paid to the Provost, Bailies, and Council of Aberdeen, to be invested by them upon land and annual rent, and to be paid in certain sums to the said bursars. If these directions had been executed in 1630, the rights in favour of the bursars would have been rights of annual rent, and each bursar would have had a separate right to a certain specific sum fixed by the testator himself. Such right would have been of a very different character from that of a right to the rent of land which varies, and must always vary in amount. Such a right to annual rents was at that date familiarly known in Scotch law. The bonds by which they were constituted were of two kinds, redeemable when intended as a security for a debt, and irredeemable when intended as a permanent security. They are also known in modern practice, though not so commonly employed—but their legal character is well known. These rights, although incorporeal, were, both in the manner of their infeftment and of their transmission, dealt with as ordinary feudal rights. If an annual rent of £1000 Scots had been originally granted in favour of the bursars, there can be no doubt that this would have been a complete fulfilment of the testator's intention. But two obstacles appear to have presented themselves. First, it appears that £10,000 Scots could not produce the requisite amount; and, secondly, the Town Council refused to accept the trust. But before intimating their declinature of the trust, they appear to have so far interfered in the management thereof as to have got the fund paid by the testator's widow to Sir Alex. Irvine; and ultimately they refused to accept this fund from him, although offered it in the presence of notary and witnesses. He then raised an action in the Court of Session. This action was of an unusual character. No decerniture was asked against any one. It merely stated the general circumstances of the case, and then went on to state that the money was lying idle, and the Court was therefore requested to confer on the pursuer a power to purchase lands to carry out the purposes of his father's will, or alternatively to allow the money to be consigned, that the Court might deal with it as it thought fit. Sir Alexander, the holder of the fund, made the above alternative proposals, while the Town Council appear to have made an extra-judicial proposal that the money should be allowed to accumulate for seven years, or until it should be sufficient to purchase feu-duties which would yield an annual return of £1000 Scots. This was a proposal not inconsistent with the intentions of the testator, because feu-duties are a species of annual rent. We have no information as to what took place at a conference, which it appears that the Court proposed that the parties should hold, nor indeed whether such a conference took place at all. The terms of the ultimate deliverance are somewhat obscure. The Court did not authorise an immediate purchase of land, nor on the other hand did they take any notice of the said extra-judicial proposal of the Town Council. The effect of what they did appears to have been this—that an arrangement was made that Sir Alexander should keep the £10,000 Scots until 1640 without paying any interest, and for his own behoof—that he should then provide land yielding £1000 Scots, and should then constitute a right of annual rent over the lands. There appears to have been some confusion in this judgment, but the real meaning appears to me to be what I have stated; and at any rate I do not think that the deliverance ought to or can be construed so as to innovate the right of annual rent, plainly contemplated by the testater, into such a precarious one as a right to rents must always be—such right being clearly at variance with the testator's intentions—more especially when the deliverance expressly bears that it is a carrying out of the testator's wishes. This arrangement imported that Sir Alexander and his successors were to have right to the fee, and that the bursars were to have right to the annual rent. The only remaining question is, whether Sir Alexander converted this right of annual rent into a right of fee by the bond of 1656. The phraseology of this bond is certainly obscure. But it is extremely unlikely that he had any such intention, and it is certain that he had no power thus to innovate the right of annual rent; and in the bond he expressly says that he is thereby implementing his father's testament, and the object of the deed plainly is to put the lands of Drum in the same position as if the bond had been granted by a third party. Moreover, he did not in point of fact dispone the fee to the bursars, or to any other party. Rights of annual rent were at that time available out of rents, maills, and duties. This had at that date been already settled by deliberate decisions. If Sir Alexander had in 1656 granted such right of annual rent, I think that the original testament and the deliverance of the Court would have been duly implemented. Has, then, anything occurred since to entitle the bursars, or any persons in their right, to demand the fee of these lands? The question depends principally upon usage; and after a careful examination of all that has since taken place I have not found anything which in my opinion entitles them to succeed in such a claim. In the first place, the right to the fee has all along been allowed to remain without question in the family of Drum. Second, the parties in possession of these lands have, except for a short and unimportant interval, arising from a feudal casualty, been the defender and his predecessors. Further, the pursuers have never levied any rents nor received any payments as landlords for this £1000 Scots. It is, moreover, a significant fact that part of this estate was at one time sold, and the price thereof was paid, not to the bursars, but to the defender's predecessor, and on the renewal of leases, grassums were received, which, were the pursuer's contention well founded, would have belonged to the bursars, but were, in point of fact, neither received nor claimed by them. Another and not unimportant incident is that, on 20th August 1813, the then laird of Drum wrote a letter to the University of Aberdeen to the effect that, in 1816, he expected to be able to make up the full sum of £1000 Scots, and the letter concluded by stating that, as his predecessor's original offer had been refused both by the University and the Town Council, he expected that they would now relieve him of all future claim on the lands, in case the rents should at any time amount to more than that sum. The Principal of the University accepted this offer, and in so doing he suggested that the town, having once refused the offer and declined to have anything to do with the fund, should now be held to be out of the field. The letter appears to have been recorded in 1822, for what purpose I know not, and I do not think it affects the question one way or another. His lordship then proceeded to examine various other points of usage, which it is not necessary to detail at length, and expressed his opinion that, on the whole, the usage did not appear conclusively in favour of either party, and certainly did not support the contention of the pursuers.

The other Judges concurred substantially on the grounds stated by Lord Curriehill, and accordingly the interlocutor of the Lord Ordinary was recalled, and the defender assoilzied with expenses.

SECOND DIVISION.

(Whole Court.)

FLEEMING AND OTHERS *v.* HOWDEN AND DUNLOP.—*Feb.* 2.

Entail—Devolution—Declarator—Competition

The late John Fleeming, the original defender in this action, was infeft as heir of tailzie and provision, in the estates claimed by the original pursuer, Lady Hawarden, on 1st May 1841. By the death of John, thirteenth Baron Elphinstone, on 19th July 1860, the succession to the Barony of Elphinstone opened to the said John Fleeming. By the entail under which

John Fleeming held the said estates it was provided—"That in case it shall have been any of the heirs of tailzie mentioned other than the heirs-male of my body, or of the body of Mr. Charles Fleeming, to succeed to the title and dignity of Peerage, then, and in that case, and how soon the person so succeeding, or having right to succeed, to my said estate, shall also succeed, or have right to succeed, to the said title and dignity of Peerage, they shall be bound and obliged to denude themselves of all right, title, or interest which may be competent to them of my said estate; and the same shall from thenceforth *ipso facto* accrue and devolve upon my next heir of tailzie for the time being, sicklike as if the person so succeeding and bound to denude were naturally dead." Lady Hawarden, as heir of entail next entitled to succeed to the said estates after the said John Fleeming, raised the present action, in which her only son is now insisting, against John Fleeming, and the defendor Dunlop for his interest, to compel Fleeming to denude of the estates in her favour, and also for the purpose of adjudging the said estates to belong to her in virtue of the entail, and of the opening of the succession to the title to the said John Fleeming. Dunlop was, during the lifetime of John Fleeming, and when the action was raised, in possession of the said estates, under a disposition in his favour by John Fleeming in 1859, which, though *ex facie* absolute, was truly a security for debt. Fleeming and Dunlop lodged joint defences. Fleeming having died on 13th January 1861; his estates were sequestrated on 7th July 1862, and the defender Howden was appointed trustee in the sequestration in July 1861. Lady Hawarden was served in special as heir of tailzie and provision of the said estates to the said John Fleeming, who died last vest and seised in them. With findings to the above effect in point of fact, and a finding that the entail was valid and effectual, this Division sent the revised cases for the parties to the whole Court for their opinions on the following questions:—

(1.) Whether the devolution of the estates provided by the clause of the deed of entail took effect *ipso facto* on the succession to the Peerage opening to Fleeming so as to entitle Lady Hawarden to immediate possession without any declarator?

(2.) Whether, assuming that the debt which the disposition to Dunlop was intended to secure is a subsisting debt. Lady Hawarden was, in competition with him entitled to the rents of the estates for the period between the succession to the Peerage opening on 19th July 1860, and the raising of this action, or for the period between the raising of the action and the death of Fleeming?

(3.) Whether Lady Hawarden was, in competition with the trustee on the sequestrated estate of Fleeming, entitled to the said rents or profits, or any part of the same?

The opinion returned by the Lord President, Lord Curriehill, Lord Ardmillan, Lord Jerviswoode, Lord Ormidale, and Lord Mure, was (1.) that on the succession to the Peerage opening to John Fleeming, the devolution provided by the deed of entail took effect so as to entitle Lady Hawarden to immediate possession of the estates, and to the rents without any declarator. The succession to the Peerage was not a contravention of any of the provisions or conditions of the deed of entail. It was not an act prohibited to be done, or an omission of anything that the heir in possession was enjoined to do. It was an occurrence of a character altogether different from those matters in reference to which the statute 1685 contemplates an action of declarator. It was not a penal irritancy; it was not, in the sense of the entail, or in any proper sense, an irritancy. It was a provision or condition for regulating the course of succession. John Fleeming took the estates, not only subject to the condition that if he succeeded to the Peerage (or it might have been if he succeeded to a certain other estate of greater value), the estates now in question should from thenceforth devolve on and accrue to the next heir, but also subject to an express obligation on him, as soon as the succession to the Peerage opened to him, to *denude*, which is tantamount to an obligation on him forthwith to *convey* the estates to the next heir. If John Fleeming refused to cede possession, an action at the instance of the next heir might be necessary, not to give her the right, but to enforce it, and compel implement of the obligation: nor could John Fleeming, by resisting such an action, prolong the period of his lawful enjoyment of the rents, or postpone until decree in that action the period when the rights of the next heir would commence.

(2.) That Lady Hawarden was entitled to the rents for the period between the date when the succession to the Peerage opened to John Fleeming and his death. When Fleeming's right ceased, that of Mr. Dunlop, derived from him, also ceased. This, we think, follows on principle, and from the terms of Mr. Dunlop's title.

(3.) That Lady Hawarden was, in competition with the trustee on the sequestrated estate of John Fleeming, entitled to the rents.

Lord Deas, Lord Barcaple, and Lord Kinloch returned separate opinions substantially agreeing.

The Lord Justice Clerk, and other judges at advising concurred in the views stated in the Lord President's opinion.

RICHMOND *v.* COMMON AGENT IN LOCALITY OF ORWELL.—*Jan* 26.

Locality—Surrender—Commonty.

In the locality of Orwell, Mr. Richmond of Colliston, gave in a minute of surrender of lands, including the teinds of a portion of the former commonty of Cuthil Muir, belonging to him, and allocated to him in a division thereof about 1774. He maintained, and the objectors denied, that these teinds were included in a sub-valuation in 1630. Mr. Richmond's titles since 1633, include parts, pertinents, and pendicles, but there is no mention of the common in the titles, and no information respecting it prior to 1774. The Lord Ordinary (Barcaple) found that Mr. Richmond had failed to show that the teinds in question had been valued by the valuation founded on, and sustained the objections to the surrender.

Mr. Richmond reclaimed; and the Court held that the record had been incompetently made up on the minute of surrender. A minute of surrender should be simple and unconditional. It should be in the terms of the valuation founded upon, and incapable of being objected to; while that in the present case involved the proposition, which is open to dispute, that the teinds of the lands in question were included in the valuation of 1630. That question ought to be raised in the form of objections to the interim scheme of locality, when it would be seen what other heritors were localled upon, and what they got under the decree of division. The Court recalled the interlocutor, and appointed the minute to be withdrawn.

App., Mackay, in Sequestration of Mackay.—*Jan.* 30.

Abandonment of Bankrupt's Estate—Duties of Trustee and Creditors.

A resolution having been passed at a meeting of creditors in a sequestration, abandoning the bankrupt's estate with a certain exception, Brownlee, a creditor, moved as a counter motion, that the estate should be realised and sold, and stated that he was prepared to offer and pay at least £15 upon the estate being (under the foresaid exception) conveyed to him either by public or private sale. The first motion was carried by a majority. The creditors having appealed, the Sheriff (Glassford Bell) found that there was no incompetency in the resolution, but that any creditor might demand an assignation of the abandoned claims for a sum paid, security being found to relieve the trustee and creditors of all expense and loss, and also for payment to the trustee of any surplus over 20s. in the pound of the debt claimed by the assignee in the sequestration; recalled the resolution, and found the trustee bound to grant the assignation. The bankrupt appealed to the Court of Session, which held that, while the Sheriff had gone too far in recalling the resolution, the former part of his interlocutor was right in point of law, and remitted to the Sheriff to appoint the trustee to call a meeting of the creditors to reconsider the motion to abandon the estate, together with the offer of Mr. Brownlee, and any others that might be made. It was not consistent with the rules applicable to bankruptcy to sustain the first resolution in the face of such an offer. But the Sheriff went too far in saying the trustee was bound to grant this creditor an assignation of the whole estate proposed to be abandoned. The fair result of recalling the resolution to abandon was to remit to the creditors to reconsider, in the light of Brownlee's tender, and of any other that might be made. The principle for the guidance of creditors is found in 2 Bell's Com., 415, where no direct authorities are given. There was, however, one case involving the principle laid down by Bell, that of Sprot *v.* Paul, (6 S., 1083). One lesson of that case was that, while a single creditor may protest against the abandonment, and propose to recover it himself, it is always a question of circumstances on what precise conditions he is to be allowed to do so, either as to using the trustee's name, or otherwise.

Lord Advocate *v.* Stevenson.—*Jan.* 23.

Succession Duty Act—Beneficial Interest.

On 5th June 1862, Miss Janet Rebecca Finlay died intestate, infeft in a house in Edinburgh. Her younger sister, Miss Wilhelmina Rutherford Finlay, was heir-at-law. Mr. Walter Stevenson was heir-in-heritage to both. Miss W. R. Finlay died 22d September 1862, without having made up any title, or enjoyed any benefit, or exercised any act of possession, unless it were a last will and settlement in favour of Clunie, executed upon deathbed, and admittedly ineffectual. Stevenson completed his title as nearest and lawful heir to Miss Janet R. Finlay, entered into possession of the house, drew the rents, and paid the two first instalments of succession duty as successor to the heritable estate of Miss Janet Finlay. The Board of Inland Revenue claimed duty also in respect of the said house as part of the succession of Miss Wilhelmina Finlay. A case was adjusted for the opinion of the Court, in which the questions upon these facts were—(1.) Whether under sect. 21 of the Act 16 and 17 Vict. 51, sect. 21, succession duty was payable by Stevenson in respect of a succession to the said house having been conferred on Miss Wilhelmina on the death of her sister? (2.) Whether such duty was payable by him in respect of a succession conferred on him on the death of Wilhelmina? Or (1.) Whether Stevenson's interest was, in the sense of the Act, the interest of a succession to Janet? (2.) Whether, in the event of its being held that Wilhelmina had, in the sense of the Act, an interest in the house as successor to her sister, the said Wilhelmina was not, in the sense of the Act, competent to dispose of a continuing interest in it.

Held that it was not intended to tax any interest which never came into beneficial possession. Wilhelmina's so-called succession was utterly barren, because she did not survive long enough to have a legal title to the fruits. Hence the first and also the second questions must be answered in the negative, and the first counter-question in the affirmative. It was not necessary to answer the second counter-question at all. The Crown was entitled to duty as upon one succession.

Duke of Buccleuch &c. *v.* Cowan and Others.—*Feb.* 6.

Process—Conjunction—Contingency.

Three actions of declarator and interdict at the instance of proprietors upon the river North Esk, against paper-makers who had works on the banks of the river, and who were alleged to have polluted the water by discharging refuse into it to the nuisance of the pursuers, were brought before the Court for adjustment of issues. In the course of the discussion the pursuers moved for conjunction of the actions. In the first action, (see 2 Macph. 653, Feb. 13, 1864), which was raised in 1841, and revived in 1863, there were originally seven sets of defenders, and it had reference to nine mills. The three first mills—those of Cowan & Co.—have continued in operation ever since, and their occupants have ever since been engaged, as is alleged, in polluting the stream. Four other mills dropped out of the action in consequence of the discontinuance of the works and other causes, so that on its revival it was proceeded with only against three sets of defenders representing five mills. The circumstances relating to the other actions are stated in the following abridgment of the Lord Justice Clerk's opinion: —There could be no doubt of the pursuers' right to go on against these parties, and to prove the pollution committed by them prior to 1841. But it was clear that from the long period during which the action was allowed to lie over, a number of paper-mills were not represented in the action at all; and the pursuers quite reasonably thought it desirable to bring into Court all the parties who subsequently to 1841 had come to be engaged in similar operations polluting the stream. They divided their proceeding against these into two actions—one relating to the mills above Hawthornden, from which all the pursuers complained that they suffered injury; and the other relating to those below Hawthornden, in which only the proprietors below that place on the stream were suing. This did not make much difference in the question before the Court. The consequence of the raising of the new actions was that, with two exceptions, all the mills originally represented by the defenders in the first action were now again represented by the defenders in the second action; and, in addition, another mill that of

Kevock, was represented in the third action, which was in existence previous to 1841, though its present occupier did not begin business till 1848. In these circumstances the motion for conjunction was made. It always appeared to his Lordship desirable that the question as to the pollution of the Esk should be tried once for all before one jury, and that all the parties interested in the matter should be represented. As to the competency, it was important to observe that, in the practice of this Court from a very early time, actions in any way connected were as much as possible brought together, and dealt with as much as possible in conjunction. The rules as to remits *ob contingentiam* go back to a very early period. They were recognised in the Act 48 Geo. III., c. 103, sec. 9. Though the words of that section are of large and comprehensive signification, they have been generally understood to mean that, where convenience required, an action should be remitted to another Judge before whom another action embracing similar issues should be depending. It did not follow that actions should be conjoined although so remitted. It might often be proper to sist one action and to proceed with the other. That is one thing which the Judge is enabled to do in consequence of the remit. If it is not desirable to keep the one action separate from the other, and if they have a natural contingency, the leaning of the mind of the Court has generally been to conjoin them, although that is always a matter of discretion. They may, for instance, be so complicated that embarrassment would arise from trying them all under one issue or at one time. If that is not so, if they raise one issue, then it is expedient that that should be tried once for all between all the parties interested. These are the general considerations that should influence the Court in disposing of such a motion as this. The object of the present actions is the same. The main question in all is, whether the defenders, paper-makers on the Esk, have, by discharging the refuse of their mills, polluted the stream to the nuisance of the pursuers, proprietors on the banks. All reasons of expediency are in favour of having the various actions conjoined.

The other Judges concurred, and decree of conjunction was pronounced, and issues ordered in the conjoined actions.

Sykes *v.* Wilson.—*Feb.* 2.

Patent—Issues.

Issues adjusted in an action of damages for infringement of a patent. Held that where there is no objection to the form of letters patent that should be made matter of admission in an issue of infringement. There are five different grounds of objection to a patent, which are the only possible defences against an action of infringement, except always the plea founded on a general denial of infringement. These are (1) That the subject-matter is not patentable; (2) that the patentee is not the first inventor; (3) that there has been prior use; (4) that the subject of the patent is not of general public utility; (5) that the specification is not framed in compliance with the Act. The first of these is a question of law and not of fact, and requires no special issue, though it cannot be determined before trial, because until the Court understands the specification it cannot determine what the subject-matter is. Counter issues allowed to the defender upon the other four defences. A separate counter issue of prior publication refused, the

Court holding that under the issue whether the pursuer was the first and true inventor, the defenders could maintain any objection to the claim of originality and true invention, except prior use, which was raised under another issue.

Pet., Gardner for Recal of Arrestments.—*Feb.* 3.

Arrestments—Competency—Recal—Delay.

The executor of a partner obtained judgment in 1848 against the former partners of the firm, of which their testator had been a member, for the balance of a sum in a bond for money advanced to the company. Payment was made under the decree to the law agents of the executor only on 14th March 1854. At that time an action of count and reckoning at the instance of another partner's executor against the partners of the company was in dependence, concluding also for relief *pro rata* of the obligation in the bond, and immediately on the money being paid to the agents, and on the same day, arrestments were used on the dependence of this action in the hands of the agents of the first partner's executor. Various proceedings and correspondence followed; and this petition was presented in November 1865. The Lord Ordinary (Barcaple) recalled the arrestments without caution. His Lordship had great doubt as to the competency of the arrestments, the action being for mutual accounting between partners, and not specially directed against the executor more than the other partners, and one in which he was not stated to be liable in any specific sum, or in respect of any definite ground of liability. He also considered the long delay since 1854 in following out the action a material element in the question. The Court altered, and refused to recal the arrestments, holding that, wherever there was a pecuniary conclusion, arrestment on the dependence was competent; and that, though delay might be a ground for recalling arrestments, sufficient ground had not been shown in the present case.

Potter *v.* Lawson or Potter.—*Feb.* 6.

Legacy—Payment—Proof.

The late John Potter died in 1844, leaving all his property to his son, James Potter, under burden of a legacy of £100 to his grandson, John Potter, son of the deceased William Potter. At this time John Potter, junior, was fourteen years of age. James Potter died in 1861; and the present action has been raised against his representatives by John Potter for payment of the legacy. The defence was that it had already been paid. No discharge was produced, but the defenders offered to prove his averment parole, and argued that, while parole evidence was as a general rule incompetent to prove payment, there were cases where the circumstances raised a presumption of fact in favour of payment. In this case the important facts were the long delay in claiming the legacy, and that the pursuer in a settlement with his creditors some years ago did not give up this claim as an asset, but, on the contrary, represented his uncle as his creditor; and a diligence was asked to recover documents in proof of these averments. The Court, without calling on the pursuer's counsel, adhered to the Lord Ordinary's interlocutor, refusing a proof, repelling the defences, and reserving to the defender a reference to the pursuer's oath.

CAMPBELL'S EXECUTOR *v.* CAMPBELL'S TUTORS.—*Feb.* 9.

Entail—Bond of Annuity—Liferent.

This was a claim at the instance of the executor of the widow of Lieutenant-Colonel John Campbell, heir of entail of Blackhall, who died in 1856, leaving a bond of annuity in favour of his widow, granted under powers in the entail "to provide and secure their lawful wives" in competent liferent provision out of the lands, and "to grant bonds and provisions for the same, not exceeding," &c. On this bond, his widow was infeft, and she survived till 1860. Colonel John Campbell was succeeded by Major Colin Campbell, who died in 1861. He had thus survived Col. Campbell's widow, at whose death it turned out that there were outstanding arrears of her annuity, and the present action was raised by her executor against a pupil heir in possession concluding for declarator that these arrears form a preferable charge upon the rents of the entailed estate. The action was maintained on the ground that the annuity was an entailer's debt, and that by the bond and infeftment a preference over the rents had been conferred both for the annuity and for arrears. The Lord Ordinary found that the pursuer had no claim upon the rents accruing subsequent to the death of Major Campbell.

Lord Cowan—The question is, whether the deed of entail gave powers to grant bonds of annuity, which, after infeftment, should constitute a burden on the entailed estate in a question with succeeding heirs. The entail contains the usual fetters, and no heir in possession—though no doubt a fiar—could shake himself free of them. But it is further provided that a liferent annuity, to be secured by infeftment, might be made in favour of a wife. But the annuity terminated with the life of the annuitant, and the infeftment terminated with it. The security must be made effectual out of the subject of it while the infeftment subsists, and not out of rents subsequently accruing, which are the property of another.

The Lord Justice-Clerk said—The true ground of judgment is, that this lady was a proper liferentrix, and not a mere annuitant with a security for her interest. A liferent is *jus alienæ rei utendi fruendi salva rerum substantia*, though it is with us a right of property and not a servitude. If she had had a liferent of the whole rents, she could obviously have attached only those which accrued during the subsistence of her liferent, and the principle is the same.

Lords Benholme and Neaves concurred, and the Court adhered to the Lord Ordinary's interlocutor, except that, instead of finding that the pursuer is not entitled to the rents "subsequent to death of Major Colin Campbell," it was made "subsequent to the death of the liferentrix."

HOUSE OF LORDS.

JACK *v.* ISDALE.—*Feb.* 12.

(In the Court of Session, March 31, 1864, 2 Macph. 978.)

Poor—Relief of Able-Bodied Poor—8 *and* 9 *Vict.*, *c.* 83, *s.* 68.

Mr. Isdale, a member of the Parochial Board of Dundee, presented this note of suspension and interdict, seeking to prohibit the Board from applying their funds to the relief of able-bodied poor who were unable to get employment. The First Division of the Court of Session ordered cases to be laid before the whole Court, when it decided by a majority of seven to six (all the Judges of the First Division being in the minority, with Lords Neaves and Barcaple), that a Parochial Board had no power to give relief to able-bodied poor out of the funds raised by assessment. The Inspector of the Parochial Board appealed; and it was contended that, although it was fixed, that the able-bodied have no right to relief, still they may, as was the case before the Act of 1846, be legitimate objects of the discretionary relief confided to the Parochial Board, just as it was formerly vested in the kirk-session. The right to relieve may exist though there may be no party having a right to the relief. In the case of *Adams* v. *MacWilliam* (Feb. 27, 1849, 11 D. 719; H. of L., March 26, 1852, 1 Macq. 120), the Court of Session held that there was no right in able-bodied men to demand relief. The case was brought by appeal to the House, and was affirmed. In that case, however, some of the Judges—Lord Moncreiff, Lord President Boyle, and Lord Jeffrey—said the right to relief was one thing, but the right to give relief was another thing. In *Petrie* v. *Meek* (March 4, 1859, 21 D. 614), the Court no doubt took an opposite view, but though there were *obiter dicta* contrary to the appellant's view, the point was not decided. The point here involved was one of practice, and the Parochial Boards throughout the country have ever since 1845 used their discretion in giving relief to the able-bodied; and the practice had been attended with the greatest benefit. Although the 68th sec. of the Act was carefully framed to exclude the legal right of the able-bodied poor to relief, the possibility of giving them relief was not thereby excluded. The terms of the section are, that "from and after the passing of this Act, all assessments imposed and levied for the relief of the poor shall extend and be applicable to the relief of occasional as well as of permanent poor, provided always that nothing herein contained shall be held to confer a right to demand relief on able-bodied persons out of employment."

Counsel for the Respondent were not called upon.

The Lord Chancellor (Cranworth) said, that his opinion turned chiefly, if not entirely, on the construction of the Act of Parliament; and hence it was necessary to see what was the meaning of the terms, permanent poor and occasional poor, in that Act. It was scarcely necessary to refer to reports of Parliamentary Committees, and of the General Assembly, to show that the term occasional poor included those who were disabled by temporary sickness, and also those who, though able-bodied, had fallen into destitution from their inability to get work. But the important matter was, what did the 68th section of the Scotch Poor-law Act say? If we were to read down to the proviso at the end of that section and stop there, one would have no difficulty in saying that able-bodied paupers were entitled to relief just as the permanent poor would be. But the section does not stop there, for there is a proviso that the able-bodied shall have no right to demand relief. Now, it had been already clearly decided, and he believed, perfectly well decided, by the all but unanimous judgment of the Court of Session, afterwards affirmed by this House, that no able-bodied man had a right to demand parochial relief in Scotland. It was said, indeed, in this case, that the able-bodied man did not demand relief, but merely to have it decided that the parochial board had a discretion to give such relief if it thought fit. But to admit such a right would be totally inconsistent with the provision of the same Act, for the 33d section says that it shall be competent to the parochial board to resolve that the funds requisite for the relief of the poor persons entitled to relief from the parish shall be raised by assessment. Now, the simple question is—Is this person a person entitled to relief? His Lordship could not distinguish between the right of persons entitled to relief and the right of the board to give the relief. The words of the 68th section are nothing if they do not mean that the board has no power to give the relief. Though the point was not directly decided in *Adams* v. *MacWilliam*, no one could doubt from what was said by Lord Truro and Lord Brougham that they were of opinion the two expressions meant the same thing. It could never be that this board could raise funds by assessment, and that though the able-bodied were not entitled to demand relief from such fund, yet the board were entitled to give them such relief whether demanded or not. The right to give relief must be entirely correlative to the right to receive or demand the relief.

Lord Chelmsford and Lord Kingsdown concurred. Affirmed.

LANDS' VALUATION APPEAL COURT.

The Assessor v. Gordon.—*Feb.* 7.

The Commissioners of Supply had sustained an appeal by Mr. Gordon, who had been assessed as proprietor of kelp shores in South Uist upon an annual value of £1000. The shores were not let to tenants. It was argued for Mr. Gordon that the manufacture of kelp was not a source of profit, but only carried on to provide occupation for small tenants; (2) That the ware did not grow on the rocks, but was drifted from the ocean; (3) That the profit of the manufacture was not a return from lands and heritages in the sense of the Act; (4) That only the value of the small portion of ware which remained after the estate is supplied with manure, &c., should be valued, amounting only to a fraction of £1000; (5) That no entry of the kind had been made in the valuation-roll in previous years. The Assessor maintained that the kelp shores were a pertinent of the land. Upon a case for the opinion of the Judges, their Lordships' decision was—"That the judgment of the Commissioners was wrong, and that the subjects should be valued at such sum of yearly rent as may be reasonably expected to be paid year by year by a tenant, to whom might be let the right of gathering and appropriating the ware growing and cast on the shore in question, together with the use of the shore for manufacturing kelp from the said ware."

The Assessor v. The British Seaweed Company.

The British Seaweed Company had also been assessed for kelp shores in North Uist upon a rent of £800. They submitted that, in terms of the lease or minute of agreement between them and the proprietor of the estate, Sir John Orde, they had a right to manufacture kelp upon the shore, but not an exclusive right to the ware, as there was a reservation in favour of tenants, and no lease of any lands or kelp shores. In the interpretation clause of 17 and 18 Vict., c. 91, the right to gather kelp or seaweed was not included under the words "lands and heritages." Seaweed was not, in fact, *pars soli;* and in law, the right to it stood upon an independent footing. The Commissioners sustained the appeal, but on a case for the opinion of the Judges, their Lordships were of opinion that the determination of the Commissioners was wrong.

COURT OF SESSION.

OUTER HOUSE.

FAIRBAIRN *v.* DUNDEE AND NEWCASTLE SHIPPING COMPANY (LIMITED.)

Feb. 10.

Merchant Shipping Act—Reparation—Notice to Board of Trade.

This action was brought by a widow to recover damages for the loss of her husband, a fisherman, who was drowned in consequence of his boat being run down at sea by the steamer of the defenders. The defenders pleaded, *inter alia,* that the pursuer, not having complied with the provision of the 512th section of the Merchant Shipping Act, 1854, that before any party can raise an action for damages arising out of the fault of the crew of another vessel, notice of the intention to raise such action must be given to the Board of Trade—was not entitled to bring this action. The Lord Ordinary repelled this preliminary defence, adding the following note:—

The 512th section of the statute provides that, where the Board of Trade has not already instituted an inquiry, no person shall bring an action unless the Board has refused to institute the same. In this case, an application was made to the Board of Trade on 13th October 1864, by Mr. Wilson, officer of the Board of Fisheries at Eyemouth, at the request of the fishermen of that place and relatives of the men lost, asking the Board to institute an inquiry. The Board took steps to get further information as to the matter; and thereafter, on 28th October 1864, they forwarded to Mr. Wilson a copy of the explanation of the master of the steamer as to the cause of the accident. The present action was not brought until September 1865, the Board having taken no steps in the interval. In these circumstances, the Lord Ordinary thinks it must be held that the Board refused to institute the inquiry. It appears from the recent correspondence, produced in process, that this is the view taken by the Board itself; and the Lord Ordinary thinks it the true construction to be put upon the facts of the case. The defenders found upon the special provision in the clause, that "the Board of Trade shall, for the purpose of entitling any person to bring an action or institute a suite or other legal proceeding, be deemed to have refused to institute such inquiry, whenever notice has been served on it by any person of his desire to bring such action or institute such suit or other legal proceeding, and no inquiry is instituted by the Board of Trade in respect of the subject-matter of such intended action, suit, or proceeding for the space of one month after the service of such notice." The defenders maintain that it was only by compliance with this provision that the pursuers could be entitled to bring the action, and that it was requisite that there should be notice of the intention to bring the action, and that it should be served upon the Board by the pursuers themselves or their agent. The Lord Ordinary cannot adopt this construction. He thinks it was intended to protect the rights of parties alleging injury, by enabling them to require the Board either to proceed with an inquiry or to leave the field open for an action by the private party. He does not think it was intended to derogate from the effect of the general provisions to the Board refusing

the form of application was the correct one, but held that no title having been produced by the railway company, in virtue of which the possession for thirteen years had taken place, they were not entitled to a possessory judgment, and therefore, that the question raised was truly one as to regulating possession, which could competently be disposed of by the Sheriff.

MORRIS *v.* GUILDRY OF DUNFERMLINE.—*Feb.* 16.

Guildry—Rules interpreted by prior usage—Ques. whether Guildry can make rules at variance with usage?

The pursuer in this action is a surgeon in Dunfermline. By the existing "Rules and Regulations for administering the revenue and managing the affairs of the Guildry of Dunfermline," which were approved of by the fraternity in 1852, it is provided that "sons and sons-in-law of Guild brethren," shall be admitted to the Guildry on certain specified terms, more favourable than those applicable to "any individual having neither by birth nor marriage any claim or title."

The pursuer admittedly married a daughter of Andrew Reid, a member of the Guildry. She died on 29th March 1862. In October of the same year the pursuer applied to be admitted to the Guildry, as the son-in-law of a Guild brother. He was refused admission in this character, on the ground that his privilege had been lost by the prior death of his wife.

The present action was brought for the purpose of having it declared that the pursuer was entitled to admission as a son-in-law.

The Lord Ordinary (Kinloch) held that the pursuer was a son-in-law of a Guild brother in the true sense of the rules of the incorporation, the death of his wife not having destroyed that character which previously belonged to him, and therefore decerned in his favour.

To-day, the Court recalled this interlocutor. They held that the regulations in question having only been entered into in 1852, and usage having been the only law of the Corporation prior to that date, the term "son-in-law" in the regulations fell to be interpreted according to the previous usage. It appeared from the evidence led, that no application by the son-in-law of a Guild brother for admission to the Guildry, after his wife's death, had ever been either refused or sustained; but it also appeared that there had been many persons in that position at different periods, whose interest it would have been to enter the Guildry, but who had not done so; and further, that several sons-in-law had been urged to enter during their wives' lives, in case the privilege might be lost by their deaths. The Court held that, in these circumstances, the preponderance of evidence was in favour of the view that, prior to the date of the regulations, and whilst the law of the Corporation was founded on usage, the general understanding had been that sons-in-law lost the privilege of admission, as such, by the death of their wives; and, that being so, that the term "sons-in-law" in the regulations, must be read in accordance with the previous understanding and usage. Their lordships had considerable doubt, though they gave no decision on the point, whether the Guildry could have made any regulations at variance with the law of the Corporation as fixed by immemorial usage.

SWAN *v.* PEACOCK.—*Feb.* 20.

Sequestration—Appeal.

This was an appeal by the trustee on the sequestrated estate of Walter Peacock, innkeeper, Lennoxtown, against a judgment of the Sheriff-substitute of Stirlingshire, reversing a previous deliverance of the trustee. A claim was made on the bankrupt's estate, by his sister, for L.139, 0s. 3d., alleged to be due to her by virtue of an agreement entered into betwixt the bankrupt and his father and mother in 1837, whereby the father and mother agreed to relinquish and convey their business to the bankrupt, and he agreed, *inter alia*, to pay to his sister L.100, "as a suitable consideration for her byepast services in conducting the said business." This sum was to be paid at the expiry of five years, with interest, and on 8th July 1864, the bankrupt granted a bill to his sister in implement of this obligation. He was sequestrated on 22d August 1864. The trustee repelled the claim of the sister, and his deliverance was reversed by the Sheriff-substitute, against whose judgment the present appeal was taken.

The trustee maintained (1) that the bill was null under the Act 1696, c. 5, being granted to a conjunct and confident person, and that within sixty days of bankruptcy; (2), that the terms of the original agreement were not such as to constitute an onerous obligation; (3), that the stamp was insufficient.

The Court, without calling for a reply, adhered *simpliciter* to the Sheriff-substitute's judgment, and dismissed the appeal.

COLLOW'S TRUSTEES *v.* CONNELL AND OTHERS.—*Feb.* 23.

Entail—Destination—Trust Deed Construction.

This is an action at the instance of the trustees of the late Gilbert Collow, Esq., to have it found and declared that two estates, called Auchenchain and Over Kirkcudbright, belong to them, in virtue of his trust-disposition and settlement, which conveyed to the trustees "all and sundry lands and heritages, goods and gear, debts and sums of money, and, in general, the whole estate, means and effects, heritable and moveable, real and personal, of whatever kind and denomination which shall belong to me at the time of my decease." This trust-disposition was executed on 31st March 1859, and Mr. Collow, the granter, died on 7th March 1863. It is admitted that the granter held the estates in question under an entail, by which they were conveyed to a series of heirs, whom, all failing, to the entailer's "own nearest of kindred, and their heirs and disponees whatsoever." At the date of the trust-deed one heir-substitute *nominatim* was in life, who was entitled to succeed Mr. Collow under the entail, and therefore there is no question that he had no power at that time to convey the entailed estates to his trustees. But it is also admitted that before Mr. Collow's death this heir-substitute died, and therefore the persons to take under the entail after Mr. Collow were the entailer's "own nearest of kindred, and their heirs and disponees whatsoever." The trustees maintain that by the death of the heir-substitute under the entail, Mr. Collow acquired right to the two estates in fee simple, and that they therefore were conveyed to them under the general clause in the trust-deed. This claim of the trustees is opposed by two persons, each of whom claims the character of "nearest of kindred" of the entailer, and who therefore contend—(1.) That the destination of the entail was not extinguished by the death of the substitute who intervened between Mr. Collow and the "nearest of kindred," and therefore that he had no power to convey the entailed estates to his trustees; and (2.) That even if he had the power it is clear from the trust-deed that he did not intend to do so.

The Lord Ordinary (Kinloch) adopted the latter contention without disposing of the former, and found that the trust-disposition and settlement did not, either in fact or in law, comprehend the entailed estates.

The Court, in substance, affirmed this judgment, but on the different ground, that the granter had not the power to convey the estates to his trustees. Their lordships held that the entail was at his death an effectual subsisting entail, the *predilecta successio* not having been exhausted by the death of the heir-substitute who predeceased Mr. Collow, as the ulterior destination to the entailer's "nearest kindred" was a sufficient designation of who was to be the next heir of entail. The whole of their lordships founded their judgments on the want of power in Mr. Collow to convey. At the same time, lest the case should be appealed,—and it might come to be of importance that their opinion should be known on the other question, viz., whether, assuming that Mr. Collow became fee-simple proprietor on the death of the substitute heir, his trust-deed conveyed the estates in question, they all, whilst thinking the question one of great difficulty, were of opinion, looking to the deed as a whole, that the truster intended to exclude the entailed estates from the general conveyance, and, therefore, that they were not conveyed.

M'Ewan *v.* Middleton.—*Feb.* 23.

Option—Time within which to be declared.

The pursuer and defender were partners as calenderers in Glasgow. The business was carried on in premises which belonged to the defender, and which were leased by him to the firm. They were burdened with considerable heritable debts. One of the loans over the property having been called up, the pursuer joined the defender in the security for a new loan, and, in consideration of this, the defender granted a deed to him containing, *inter alia*, the following clause :—"I bind and oblige myself, my heirs and successors whomsoever, to you and your heirs, that in the event of you and your foresaids exercising an option to that effect, and requiring me or my foresaids, *at any time within five years from the date hereof, or upon the* dissolution of our said copartnership, within the said period, and for payment as before expressed, to dispone and convey the subjects so acquired by me, to and in favour of myself, the said Lewis Stirling Middleton, and my foresaids, and John Thomson Henderson M'Ewan, equally, or your foresaids, betwixt us *pro indiviso* and our respective assigns," and so forth.

After a great deal of procedure before an arbiter appointed by the parties, the partnership was declared to be at end by a decree-arbitral, dated 11th December 1862. In one of the papers lodged by the pursuer before the arbiter he had stated that it had long become obvious that he would never exercise the option of requiring a conveyance of one half of the heritable subjects; and on 22d January 1863 the defender's agents in Glasgow, wrote to the pursuers' agents, that they understood Mr. M'Ewan had waived his right to take a half of the subjects, and if they did not hear to the contrary, in the course of the following day, they would proceed on that assumption. This letter was not answered till the 27th January 1863, when the pursuer himself wrote that he had been so busy he had not had time to look into the matter, but would give it his attention as soon as possible. On 28th January 1863, the defenders' agents replied that as he had failed timeously to exercise his option, he had lost the right to do so. On 30th January 1863, the pursuer replied that he did not agree with this view, and so the matter stood. The defender having ultimately sold the property at an unexpectedly high price, the pursuer, on 2d March 1863, wrote, exercising his option to take a half of the property, acquiescing in the sale, and claiming £760 as one half of the surplus price. The present action was to enforce this claim.

The Lord Ordinary (Jerviswoode) assoilzied the defenders.

The Court unanimously adhered to the Lord Ordinary's interlocutor,—holding that under the deed of obligation the *punctum temporis* at which the option fell to be exercised was the dissolution of the partnership,—that it was not necessary that it should be exercised on the very day of the dissolution, but within a reasonable period. That looking to the proceedings before the arbiter, and subsequent correspondence, the pursuer appeared to have intended, not to take a half of the property until after he heard of the favourable sale, indeed one of his statements on record acknowledged as much, and they were of opinion he was not entitled then to change his mind.

ORMISTON *v.* RIDPATH, BROWN, & CO.—*Feb.* 23.

Damages—Oppressive Action—Trade Protection Society.

The pursuer in this case sues the defenders for damages on the ground that, within a short time after a debt which he owed them was paid, he was served with a summons concluding for it, under which a decree was obtained, on which he was charged for payment. The defenders were not the active parties in these proceedings, although they were in their names, the matter having been entrusted to the Scottish Trade Protection Society. It was not disputed that the debt had been paid to this society a short time before the summons was served, but it was said that the whole thing was a mistake, in consequence of the business of the society being conducted in different departments, and the clerk who ought to have recorded the payment having overlooked it.

To-day the Court dismissed the action on the ground that there was no issueable matter on record.

The Lord President, after detailing the facts of the case, said he had no idea that a society like the Scottish Trade Protection Society could, by sub-dividing its work and carrying it on in different departments escape responsibility. It had no right to say that one hand did not know what the other was doing; it was just as responsible as if it were one person. It was clear the pursuer had great cause to be dissatisfied with their proceedings. It was great carelessness, and not very excusable neglect, which led to the action being brought into Court. The society had existed for some time, and his lordship believed its object was a good one, and if such a society were conducted in a careful and prudent manner it might be productive of much convenience and benefit as protecting the honest from the fraudulent? But, on the other hand, if conducted in a careless or negligent manner, instead of being beneficial it became positively evil and mischievous. His lordship did not say this society was in that state, but when an instance like the present was brought under notice, he thought it only right to give them this caution. But the question now to be determined was whether the issue was to be granted. He had great difficulty in granting one. He did not say that a person who was harassed by unnecessary, or, still more, by wrongful action, had not the power to obtain redress, and that in the form now sought; but he thought there was here a want of statements to construct a legal claim for damages. Some of the defences were extravagant. For example, it was said the pursuer should have reduced the decree, or have applied for a re-hearing. But there were some things which his lordship thought the pursuer should have done, and which he did not do. He did not give any valid reason for not going to the Court the day the action was brought. He might have a good reason, but if so, he had not stated it. He simply said that it was inconvenient for him to do so. Again, he did not aver that these proceedings of which he complained were taken in the knowledge that the money had been paid, and it was a very different thing to issue a summons of this kind in ignorance from what it would have been, had there been knowledge expressed or implied. On the whole matter he did not think that the conduct of the society was excusable, and some of their pleas were clearly bad, yet he was of opinion there were not sufficient averments to warrant the granting of an issue. The Court accordingly dismissed the action, but found neither party entitled to expenses.

THE BRITISH FISHERIES SOCIETY *v.* HENDERSON.—*Feb.* 27.

Police Assessment.

This is a note of suspension and interdict, at the instance of the British Fisheries Society, incorporated by Act of Parliament, against the treasurer to the Commissioners of Supply for the County of Caithness and collector of assessments imposed by them under 20 and 21 Vic., c. 72. The complainers pray for the suspension of a warrant by the Sheriff-Substitute of Caithness, dated 3d October 1864, for poinding their goods in payment of a police assessment for Pulteney Harbour. The ground of suspension is that the complainers, having the power, under certain private Acts of Parliaments, to appoint constables for Pulteney Harbour of their own, and having done so, they are impliedly, through these enactments, exempted from all liability for assessment under the General Police Act.

The Lord Ordinary (Lord Jerviswoode) refused the note of suspension, holding that there was no statutory provision in the Acts founded on by the complainers adequate to secure to them the exemption claimed; and further, that although in respect of local causes the Legislature had conferred special powers on the complainers to keep up a constabulary of their own within certain limits, it did not follow from that that they were in consequence to be exempted from the more general county assessments.

The complaimers having reclaimed, to-day the Court adhered to the Lord Ordinary's interlocutor without calling on the respondent's counsel.

DEWAR *v.* PEARSON AND JACKSON.—*Feb.* 27.

Reference to Oath—Competency of.

The Act 16 Vict. c. 20 sect. 5 provides that "the adducing of a party as a witness in any cause or proceeding by the adverse party shall not have the effect of a reference to the oath of the party so adduced: Provided always that it shall not be competent to any party who has called and examined the opposite party as a witness thereafter to refer the cause or any part of it to his oath."

To-day the Court held, construing the foregoing enactment, that, where a cause consists of two parts, one of which can be proved only by writ or oath, and the other *pro ut de jure*, it is competent to refer the former part to the oath of the adverse party who has been already examined as a witness in *causa* in regard to the other.

SECOND DIVISION.

INSPECTOR OF BARONY PARISH *v.* INSPECTOR OF DAILLY PARISH—*Feb.* 9.

Poor-Law Amendment Act, § 71—*Notice*—*Mora.*

This was an action of relief for the maintenance of a pauper belonging to the parish of Dailly. The pauper became chargeable on Barony Parish in February 1853. Notice was given to Dailly in August of the same year. In February 1854, she ceased to be chargeable, but became so again in November 1855. No new notice was given till 1860.

The Lord Justice-Clerk—The defences stated are want of notice and *mora.* The account begins in 1853, and terminates in 1854. No statutory notice was given to Dailly till 24th August 1853. The pauper got aliment from August 1853 to February 1854, but nothing afterwards for twenty months, till November 1855; and this is an important element in the case. It is averred and admitted that during this period no aliment was furnished by Barony Parish, because the pauper had ceased to be a proper object of parochial relief. The question is, whether another notice was necessary in order to preserve the recourse. We must give a fair interpretation to the 71st clause of the Act, which provides that in all cases written notice of such person having become chargeable must be given. I do not think notice is required after every break in receiving aliment. A person may be a month out of the workhouse without ever being restored to the position of a person of industry. But, on the other hand, I cannot adopt the pursuer's argument, that a notice once given lasts for the life of the person who had become chargeable. It was urged that there was no intelligible middle course; but I think the general rule may be laid down that, wherever it can be fairly and distinctly alleged that for a considerable time a person has ceased to be a proper object of relief—has become self-supporting—that if he again comes upon the parish, he is, in the sense of the Act, a poor person who has become chargeable; and I think notice was indispensable in this case. That defeats the claim between November 1855 and 1860, when notice was given. For the remaining periods the only defence is *mora.* It was said there could be no *mora*, because the parish, when called upon, repudiated its liability. But that must always be the case. But upon the question whether in the circumstances of the case there is foundation for the plea of *mora*, I am of opinion that there is not. There is nothing but the mere lapse of time, and that has never been held sufficient.

The rest of the Court concurred.

Susp.—GRAHAM *v.* M'CLELLAND (LIQUIDATOR OF WESTERN BANK).—*Feb.* 23.

Joint Stock Company—Contributory—Trustee—Transfer.

Colonel Graham suspended a charge upon a decree, obtained in a summary application by the liquidators of the Western Bank against him, as a contributory in his character of sole surviving trustee under the marriage contract of Mr and Mrs E. D. Sandford. The Lord Ordinary (Mure) passed the note, holding there was here a separate question, differing from that decided in Lumsden *v.* Buchanan, 22d June 1865, and requiring investigation on a passed note—viz., whether all the debts of the bank having, as was alleged, been already paid off, the liquidator could now take proceedings under the decree. The decree was pronounced without inquiry in a petition under the 19 and 20 Vict. cap. 47, sec. 104, art. 6, authorising the liquidators "to call on any of the contributories to the extent of their liability, to pay all or any sums they deem necessary to satisfy the debts of the company and the costs of winding it up." It was also maintained that Colonel Graham, having never signed the contract, but only the transfer, was in the same position as Dr Buchanan, who was assoilzied by the House of Lords; and further, that the charge on the suspender was to pay *in solidum*, while the decree represented him as jointly liable, along with other parties.

The Lord Justice-Clerk said—I should be sorry to pass the note of suspension, except on some relevant allegation. It is the policy of the Act to make the recovery of a call a very summary proceeding. The difference between this case and that of Lumsden is said to be, that the suspender has not subscribed the contract of copartnery, but only accepted and transcribed a transfer. I have no doubt the legal effect of both is the same. The two gentlemen who accepted expressly adopted in the transfer the provisions of the contract of copartnery. In the second place, it is said that the liquidator cannot enforce this decree, because the circumstances are changed, and all the debts in the company are paid. That is admitted by the respondent, with the qualification that at least he is in funds to do so. The question whether the decree can be made available for purposes of contribution, apart from the payment of debts, depends on 21 and 22 Vict. cap. 60. Section 5 is made applicable by section 14 to a voluntary winding-up. And in section 5, the decree is not restricted to cases where the debts are unpaid. It is as important an object to equalise the liabilities of the contributories as to provide for the payment of creditors. There remains a third plea. The decree proceeds upon a petition which contains a list of contributories, and the decree refers to that list. Colonel Graham, the suspender, is represented as jointly liable with other persons. The objection is, that the decree is not against these gentlemen jointly and severally. It is remarkable that only one of the gentlemen who signed the transfer appears in the decree, and the charge upon him is to pay *in solidum*. This is a much more difficult question than the other two, and I think we must pass the note for the purpose of trying that question.

The other Judges concurred.

TAYLOR *v.* MITCHELL.—*Feb.* 27.

Partnership—Reference to Oath—Bill Chamber.

Suspension refused of a charge by one partner against another, although the affairs of the company and the accounts of the partners *inter se* were still unsettled, on the ground that the debt charged for was truly the price of the suspender's admission into the concern. A reservation of the suspender's right to refer the whole cause to the charger's oath was inserted in the interlocutor, remitting the cause back to the Bill Chamber.

MACALISTER *v.* MACALISTER.—*Feb.* 28.

Lease—Warrandice—Damages.

The trustees of Macalister of Strathaird granted in 1834 a lease in favour of Jessy Macalister, a daughter of the testator, and Duncan Macalister, her husband, and the longest liver, whom failing, to their son Norman, and his heirs and assignees, for thirty-eight years, at the rent of £10. Duncan, his wife being dead, sublet, in 1842, for the twenty-eight years remaining of his tack to a younger son, Archibald. The Court found, after a long litigation (22d February 1859, 21 D. 560), that the sub-tack was *ultra vires* of Duncan, who had only a liferent interest in the tack. The representatives of Archibald now insisted against the representatives of Duncan for damages incurred through the eviction, founding on the obligation of warrandice in the sub-lease. The sub-tack was granted "for all the days, years, and space of twenty-eight years, being the remaining years still to run of the tack," &c., and contained the clause following:—"In the peaceable possession of which subjects hereby subset, the said Dr Duncan Macalister binds and obliges himself, his heirs and successors, to maintain and defend the said Archibald Macalister and his foresaids *during the space foresaid*, at all hands, and against all deadly, as law will." The Lord Ordinary held that Duncan acted on the assumption that he had an absolute right of tenancy, and had granted warrandice accordingly, and that his representatives were liable for damages. The Court adhered, the Lord Justice-Clerk remarking that clauses of warrandice are of very stringent obligation. Duncan, conceiving himself to have a larger right than he really possessed, or from some other motive, granted a sub-tack to Archibald. This sub-tack was said to be gratuitous. His Lordship was inclined to doubt this. The sub-rent was nearly double the original rent; and again, when a father makes over to a son a lease of this kind as a kind of provision, and thereby leads him to adopt the profession of a farmer, his Lordship doubted whether such a grant could be regarded as altogether gratuitous, even independently of the obligation to pay a higher sub-rent. Even assuming it to be gratuitous, the words "*for the space foresaid*" in the clause of warrandice, could refer only to the space of twenty-eight years. This was not a question of implied warrandice. If it had been so, and the deed were shown to be gratuitous, then it might have been held warrandice from fact and deed only. Stair and Erskine show that wherever warrandice is implied you are to be guided as to its extent by the nature of the right conveyed; where it is express, you are to be guided by the terms of the warrandice only. If a man with his eyes open, knowing the nature of the deed he is executing, and knowing it to be gratuitous, does bind himself in absolute warrandice, the obligation is to be enforced against him according to its letter. Hence it was not relevant to inquire whether Duncan had, or conceived he had, a complete right or not to the tack for the whole twenty-eight years still to run. Adhere unanimously.

HOUSE OF LORDS.

Leith Dock Commissioners, *v.* Miles, Inspector of North Leith.

(In Court of Session, June 17, 1864, 2 Macph. 1234.)

Poor—Assessment—Harbour—Res Judicata.

This was an appeal in an action raised by the Inspector of the Poor of the Parish of North Leith against the Commissioners. The pursuer sought to have it declared that their wharves, harbours, docks, warehouses, &c., are assessable to the support of the poor. The assessment in North Leith had for many years been imposed one-half on owners, and one-half on occupiers. The annual value of the Commissioners' property in the parish was estimated at £27,000, and the assessment for 1861 amounted to £2000; but they claimed entire exemption.

The defenders set forth that the property had been vested in them by Acts of Parliament, and that they had no beneficial interest whatever, but held it for the benefit of the public, and applied the whole revenues to the purposes specified by the statute. In 1830 and 1847, similar actions had been raised against them or their predecessors; and the Court held that they were not liable, except, in the latter case, to the extent of a sum of £7680, then payable by them to the city of Edinburgh, under a statute. The Commissioners appealed against that judgment, so far as related to the £7680, and the House of Lords altered the judgment (2 Macqueen, 28).

In this action the Lord Ordinary, and the First Division (Lord Curriehill *diss.*), held the Commissioners liable to assessment, and they appealed. In argument, the appellants endeavoured to distinguish their case from those of the Clyde Navigation Trustees and the Mersey Docks Commissioners (3 Macph., House of Lords, 100), decided last summer, maintaining that the former case as to the Leith Docks was *res judicata*, that, at all events, these Docks came within the exception left by the decisions of last year in favour of property held for public purposes connected with Government, and that, at least, some of the dues were not assessable. The Lord Advocate, in the course of argument, maintained that in *Adamson* v. *Clyde Trustees* there was no appeal to the House against the decision of the Court of Session relating to the Clyde Harbour itself. Therefore, the House had not yet decided that a harbour is a rateable subject. A harbour is not enumerated among the things stated by the Scotch Poor-Law Act to be assessable. It was not land in the strict sense, but was a *jus publicum*. It was an incorporeal right, and could not be included in the corporeal property enumerated in the Poor-Law Act.

The Lord Chancellor (Cranworth)—The point as to whether the trustees or commissioners of a harbour are rateable to the poor was fully argued before the House last year; and certainly the opinion arrived at was, that the trustees were liable to be rated to the full extent of their receipts or profits over and above expenditure. I do not wish to stop you from trying to make out some distinction between the Leith Docks and the Mersey Docks. It may be that you have grounds for that contention. Still, it is not on the principle that the harbour itself was not included in the Mersey case; for it was there clearly included, and what was decided was, that all these commissioners or trustees are rateable for the receipts coming to their hands, and that these receipts were to be deemed as profits, no matter whether the trustees were bound by statute to apply them to some specified purpose or not.

The Lord Advocate then argued that part of the money received by the Leith Dock Commissioners consisted of £7680, applied to the payment of the ministers of Edinburgh, in lieu of an old duty of a merk per ton, and that the House, in 1854, expressly decided that the appellants were not liable to the extent of that sum. In fact, the appellants were merely trustees as to that sum, and they applied the money for a charitable purpose. The judgment of the House in the Mersey case last year expressly left untouched the case of public charities.

The Lord Chancellor—We did not expressly decide last year that public charities were rateable to the poor, because that case was not before us; but probably the principle would extend to charities. The old theory on which charities were held exempt from poor-rates was, because it was said there was no occupier; but it was, I think, laid down in the Mersey case that in all such cases the trustees or managers are the occupiers, and therefore rateable as such.

The Lord Advocate—I certainly was not aware that it was considered that the Mersey case, which was decided last year, would rule the case of charities. Several years ago the Court of Queen's Bench expressly held that the buildings of Oxford University were exempt from poor-rate.

The Lord Chancellor—That was before the late decision in the Mersey case. Possibly you may make out that University buildings are in possession of the Crown. I say nothing as to that case; all I say is, that if the case of a University comes within the principle of the Mersey case, then it must now be ruled by that principle.

Counsel for the respondents were not called upon.

The Lord Chancellor said that this was a question of great importance; yet, after the elaborate examination which the same question received last year before their Lordships, it was not now attended with any difficulty whatever. An attempt had been made to distinguish the present case from that of the Mersey Board in three particulars; and it was well enough that the subject should have been brought before the House, because it could not be concealed that from time to time all the Courts of the country had gone wrong on this subject. He would not say that the House had ever decided the matter wrongly; for the cases had never come directly before the House. But all the Courts, and the greatest of modern judges, including Lords Mansfield, Kenyon, and Tenterden, had been under the error that public trustees and commissioners could not be rated in respect of the property vested in them, if they did not beneficially occupy it. That point was solemnly raised at last in the case of the Mersey Board; and, after an elaborate investigation of the whole subject by the House, it was finally decided that the trustees of these harbours, docks, and similar kinds of property, were rateable to the poor, in respect of their receipts derived from the property. That was so held on a correct construction of the statute of Elizabeth, which was the English Act relating to the poor; and there was no substantial difference in the language of the Scotch Poor-Law Act. They were all held liable, because the only persons exempted from rateability are the Crown, and the immediate servants of the Crown—as, for example, such a building as their Lordships' House would be exempt, because it was connected with the Government of the Crown. Therefore it was distinctly held that docks, wharfs, and such property, inasmuch as they had nothing to do with the Crown or public government were not entitled to any exemption. It might have been thought, therefore, that the very point now sought to be raised in the present case had been concluded by the case of the Clyde Docks decided last year. But on looking at the journals of the House, in order to see what was the judgment of the Court of Session then appealed from, it appeared that though in strictness the harbour dues were not held in that case to be included, still what was deficient in that case may now be taken to be supplied by the present case; and it must be taken henceforth as finally decided that in Scotland, as well as in England, the trustees of all public docks, harbours, and the like, were assessable to the poor in respect of their receipts from the property vested in them, whether these receipts were in the form of dues or otherwise, and no matter how the trustees are bound to apply these receipts. Then, as regards the point of *res judicata*, relied upon in the present case, it was much more plausible than substantial. The question raised in 1848 was whether the Commissioners were rateable to the poor, in respect of the receipts for the year 1846-47. The Commissioners resisted the action then raised, and pleaded that, because they held the property for public purposes, they were not liable in respect of the revenue of that particular year. It was decided that they were not liable; and however general may have been that decision in its terms, still it was only a decision as regards the revenue for the year 1846. It would be, indeed, a grievous misfortune if by any such action it could be concluded for all time to come, that the trustees of public property like this would be exempt from rateability on any ground whatever, and certainly no such effect as that can be given to the former judgment in 1854. Therefore, as the matter of the present action has not been concluded by any former judgment, the appeal fails on both grounds, and must be dismissed with costs.

Lord Chelmsford and Lord Kingsdown concurred.

Judgment affirmed, with costs.

Beckett *v.* Campbell and Hutcheson, Clerks to the Dumbartonshire Statute Labour Road Trustees.—*Feb.* 26.

(In the Court of Session, Jan. 22, 1864, 2 Macph. 482.)

Road Trustees—Obligation to repair Road.

The appellant, a proprietor of lands in the 8th statute labour district of Dumbartonshire, brought this action to have it found and declared that the road trustees were bound to keep the statute-labour roads in that district, including a road called the Langmuir Road, in proper and sufficient repair.

The Lord Ordinary (Kinloch), after remitting to a surveyor, found that the trustees had failed to perform their duty of maintaining the road, and that they were at least bound to put the road in repair for ordinary country traffic. The Second Division (Inglis, J.C., absent), recalled this interlocutor, and held that the trustees, under the provisions of their Act, were entitled to exercise their own discretion as to the extent of repairs or expenditure to be made on the road; and could not be controlled in the exercise of that discretion by the Court, and dismissed the action as incompetent.

The Lord Chancellor (Cranworth) said that, according to his construction of the local Act, it imposed on the trustees no general duty to repair, but merely to meet and consider what was the best mode of raising and expending the money which they were authorised to raise. If so, then no action could be raised against them for not doing that which they were not directed to do. There was another remedy provided by the statute; but these trustees were to have the final decision of such matters as the extent and necessity of the repairs confided to them.

Lords Chelmsford and Kingsdown concurred.

Affirmed, with costs.

Weller and Another, v. Ker's Trustees.—*March* 2.

(In the Court of Session, Dec. 19, 1863, 2 Macph. 371.)

Trust—Power—Personal Bar.

This was an appeal in an action of multiplepoinding and exoneration raised by the trustees of the late Robert Ker of Argrennan. The sixth purpose of the deed was that "the trustees shall hold the residue in trust for the use and behoof of Robert Ker, my eldest son, and the heirs whatsoever of his body, whom failing, to the second son," &c. Then the trustees were, on the sons in the order expressed attaining majority, forthwith to convey and make over to the said Robert Ker the said residue and remainder of his means and estate; and, in particular, to convey to the said Robert Ker the estate of Argrennan. The deed contained also this clause —"Declaring that, in case any of our said children shall marry or otherwise conduct themselves so as not to merit the approbation of my said trustees, or a majority of them accepting and acting at the time, the provisions hereby made in favour of said children so marrying or acting shall only belong to them in liferent for their liferent use allenarly, and to their issue or heirs above mentioned in fee; but it is hereby declared that a regular minute must be entered in the sederunt-book of the trustees expressing their disapprobation of the conduct of any of my said children, to restrict them to a liferent as aforesaid." In a codicil the truster directed his trustees not to convey the estate to Robert at his attaining the age of twenty-one, but only when he should attain twenty-five.

The truster died in 1854. Robert Ker, his eldest son, married when twenty-two, and the trustees entered in their minute-book an approval of his marriage. The marriage settlement proceeded on the footing of Robert's having right to dispose of the fee of the property, and was adjusted between the law-agent of the intended wife, and a lawyer who was agent both for Robert Ker and for his father's trustees. The minute of approval of the marriage was also adjusted by him at sight of the lady's law-agent. Just before Robert Ker attained the age of twenty-five, a majority of the trustees entered in their sederunt-book a minute disapproving of the son's conduct, and restricting his right in the heritage to a liferent. In this multiplepoinding claims were lodged for the marriage contract trustees of Robert Ker and his wife and for his creditors; and in a competition with a claim for the father's trustees.

The Lord Ordinary (Kinloch) held that the trustees had validly restricted the son's interest in the estate of Argrennan to a liferent.

The marriage contract trustees appealed. The respondents' counsel were not called on.

The Lord Chancellor (Cranworth) said, the grounds on which the appellants relied were three. First, that the power referred to did not apply to the eldest son at all, but this was an argument not much insisted upon, and indeed could not bear a moment's discussion. The second ground was more plausible, and was this—that, though the power given applied to all the children, still it could be exercised only as to the children on reaching majority, and did not extend to them between that age and till they attained the age of twenty-five. He (the Lord Chancellor) was at one time impressed with that argument, but on consideration he thought it was unfounded. He thought the true construction was that that power was not confined to the age of twenty-one, but was to endure for all the time the property was in the hands of the trustees, and until they conveyed it to the children. Then the only other question was whether the trustees, inasmuch as they had expressed their approval of the marriage, and not only the marriage, but take it that they had approved also of the settlement—could then divest themselves of the duty to consider the conduct of the child at the time that the property was about to be conveyed. By the law of England, it would be clear that they could not divest themselves of this duty; and though it was not necessary to say whether the law of Scotland differed from the law of England, still, if a testator gave to his trustees power to take into consideration the conduct of the children before conveying to them the property, it would be strange indeed if they could give up or discharge this power without ever exercising the discretion. But whether that was so or not, it could not be taken in this case that these trustees ever did divest themselves of the power. It was enough to consider what it was that was settled on the son's marriage. He purported to convey only the interest which he himself had under his father's will; but that must have been taken as subject to the power of the trustees still to exercise their discretion upon his conduct when it became necessary to do so. This power, therefore, must have been considered by all parties as still existing as a contingency, and nothing that was done excluded the trustees from exercising the power when the son should attain twenty-five.

Lord Chelmsford and Lord Kingsdown concurred.

Affirmed, with costs.

Strang *v.* Stewart.—*Feb.* 15.

(In Court of Session, March 31, 1864, 2 Macph. 1015).

Property—March—Sheriff.

In an action of declarator at the instance of the proprietor of one of two farms, which had formerly been parts of one estate, against the proprietor of the other, it was held in the Court of Session that the hedge and ditch separating them were not common property, that they did not together form a march fence between the properties, and that the regulation of the march fence belonged to the Sheriff. The pursuer appealed, maintaining that the hedge and ditch together formed the march.

The Lord Chancellor (Cranworth) said—The simple question was whether the interlocutor of the Second Division ought or ought not to be supported. Now the appellant, in his summons, seeks to have it declared that the hedge, together with the ditch, formed together the march fence, and was the common property of the appellant and respondent. That was what the appellant was bound to make out. By the law of Scotland it appeared that the Sheriff had jurisdiction, if there was no adequate boundary between two adjoining properties, to compel the owners to make one suitable to the circumstances, and to keep it in repair. That was a march fence. It was part of the law of Scotland at the same time, however, that if a boundary had formerly served as a division of fields when belonging to the same owner, then, after the fields on one side had been sold to a third party, it might be agreed to be treated as a march fence between the estates thus separated. That may be done by express agreement, or, if there is no express agreement, then if the parties had acted in such a way with reference to the boundary, that one may imply such an agreement, it would come to the same thing. Now, the state of the case is this: There was a hedge to the north, and a ditch to the south. The owner to whom the fields on both sides originally belonged sold the property on the north side to one Kennedy, who was now represented by the appellant; and afterwards he sold the property on the south side to the predecessors of the respondent. Since that date, the ditch had never been touched by the parties, but had been allowed to be choked up. The hedge itself had also gone to decay, and the cattle of both parties occasionally strayed through it. But during all that time it fully appeared that the cattle on both sides fed up to the roots of the hedge. The ditch was lost sight of altogether. Now, what the appellant is bound to establish is, that what was not originally a march fence became so by reason of the property on both sides being severed and sold to different parties. But there is a total absence of evidence to show that the parties so treated the subject. There was the very slightest evidence possible of some occasional repairs being done to the hedge. That may be doubtful so far as regards the hedge being treated as a boundary. But, as to the ditch, there was not a shadow of evidence that it was ever cleared out at the part expense of the parties, or was ever treated as the march fence or part of it. That being so, the interlocutor of the Court of Session must be affirmed.

Lord Chelmsford concurred.

Lord Kingsdown concurred, and said that the effect would be that the cause would go back to the Sheriff, who would have jurisdiction to decide what repairs should be made on the hedge, but the question of the ditch would be taken entirely out of his jurisdiction.

Affirmed, with costs.

COURT OF SESSION.

FIRST DIVISION.

Susp.—Learmont's Trustees v. Shearer.—*March* 3.

Arrestments—Heritable and Moveable.

The respondent brought an action against a Mr Learmont for payment of a debt, and arrested on the dependence, in the hands of Mr Learmont's father's trustees, on the supposition that they held funds belonging to him. Decree in absence was pronounced in this action. Thereafter, Shearer brought an action of furthcoming against the trustees, in which decree in absence also passed, and on which a charge was given. The trustees then brought the present suspension of that charge, on the ground, *inter alia*, that they had no funds in their hands belonging to Learmont. On inquiry it appeared that there were no moveable funds in their hands belonging to him, but that he was interested in an heritable estate conveyed to them by his father's trust-deed.

The Court (affirming the Lord Ordinary Ormidale's interlocutor) suspended the charge complained of, on the ground that, as the trust-deed contained neither directions nor power to sell the heritage, and there was no evidence that the circumstances of the estate made it necessary to do so, the *jus crediti* of Mr Learmont under the deed was heritable, and therefore not capable of being arrested.

Hodgson and Son v. Dunn.—*March* 3.

Sale—Contract of.

The present action was brought in order to enforce payment of the price of ten tons of turnip manure alleged to have been sold and delivered by the pursuers to the defender in May 1864, at the price of £7, 5s per ton. It is admitted that the manure was sent by the pursuers to the defender. An invoice of the manure, setting forth that it was bought from the pursuers, is admitted to have been sent and received shortly after. It is further admitted that the manure was taken possession of and used by the defender. The defence was in substance that the manure was not furnished on the credit of the defender, but on the credit of a Mr David Buchan, who is alleged to have been substantially the purchaser from the pursuers. What was said was, that the defender had entered into an arrangement with Buchan, by which he, the defender, was to supply Buchan with potatoes, and Buchan was, on the other hand, to supply the defender with manure. And it was alleged that Buchan bought this manure from the pursuers in order to fulfil his contract with the defender. The result was that Buchan, and not the defender, was the debtor of the pursuers. The action was brought in the Sheriff Court at Jedburgh. The Sheriff-Substitute (Russell) and on appeal the Sheriff-Principal (Rutherfurd) assoilzied the defender. The pursuer advocated, and the Lord Ordinary (Kinloch) recalled the Sheriff's interlocutors, and decerned against the defender. His lordship was of opinion that the defence was not established by the evidence; and that, on the contrary, the pursuers established their allegation of a direct contract with the defender. It appeared to be perfectly true that the defender and Buchan had entered into an arrangement of the kind averred. The defender was fulfilling his part of it by delivering the potatoes; but Buchan had failed to supply the manure engaged for. The defender was suffering inconvenience from this failure, and was anxious to procure manure. In this state of things he was waited on by Mr Fearby, the pursuer's agent, accompanied by Buchan; and these two persons being examined as witnesses, expressly declared on oath that the contract made by Fearby with the defender was a contract of direct sale by the pursuers to the defender; in other words, that the defender, being in want of manure, and not getting it from Buchan, supplied himself by purchase from the pursuers. It did not appear very probable that the pursuers would have trusted Buchan alone for the price; and their agent seemed to have had no authority to mix himself up with any barter of potatoes. At any rate, the two persons in question expressly deponed that the contract was one of direct sale by the pursuers to the defender. Against this proof, added to the real evidence of the invoice, and the delivery taken under it, the defender had nothing to offer but his own evidence in his own favour. The Lord Ordinary perceived no reason to doubt the good faith of the defender, and entertained a strong impression that he honestly believed the manure was to be charged against Buchan, and not himself. He further thought it probable that Buchan cherished this impression, by using language not always consistent with itself, by the use of which he endeavoured to stand well with both parties. But the Lord Ordinary found it impossible to concur with the Sheriffs in holding that the defender had established his defence, in opposition to the counter evidence, parole and real. On the contrary, he considered that the evidence made a good contract, under which the defender assumed the place of direct purchaser from, and direct debtor to, the pursuers.

The Court adhered on grounds similar to those held by the Lord Ordinary, with the exception of Lord Ardmillan, who was disposed to take a different view, on the ground that Dunn's evidence was the most trustworthy.

SECOND DIVISION.

The Queen *v.* Gilroys.—*March* 6.

Revenue—Brewer's Licence—Master and Servant.

This was a case stated by the Quarter Sessions of Lanarkshire for the opinion of the Court of Exchequer, under 7 and 8 Geo. IV. cap. 53. An information was laid before the Petty Sessions against the defendants, who are brewers, charging them with having retailed beer without a certificate and excise licence, in contravention of 24 and 25 Vict. cap. 91, sec. 12. They employed a servant to carry round beer in a cart to customers who had ordered it, and he had sold on the occasion charged, and apparently was in the habit of selling, bottles by retail, upon the high road from the cart. The justices convicted; but on appeal to Quarter Sessions, the defendants were assoilzied.

Lord Justice-Clerk—The first point insisted in by defendants is, that the case does not set out negatively that the defendants had not a license. I am unable to give effect to that. It lies on the defendants to allege and prove that they had a license. When the Justices find that a sale was made, and do not find that the defendants had a license, it is the same as if they found they had not. On the merits, the question is whether defendants made the sale or not. The place of sale is the place of business of the brewer in cases like this, where beer is sent out according to order. In the present case, the sale was made, not at the brewery, but in another parish, by a servant of theirs from a cart; and as the proceeds were not fully accounted for by him, but only as much as would have answered to a sale according to order, and it does not appear that they were aware of his proceedings—the question then is, whether his illicit sales were within the scope of his employment; and I cannot hold that they were.

Lord Benholme concurred on the merits, but thought the omission to state that the defendant had no license would have been fatal.

Advn.—Mitchell *v.* Scott.—*March* 8.

Relief—Cash Credit—Guarantee.

Scott sued Mitchell for relief from the conclusions of an action at the instance of the Clydesdale Bank against James Wood and Scott, in which the bank obtained decree against Wood and Scott for the balance on a cash credit account operated on by Wood, and for which he was liable to the bank under a letter of guarantee. The action of relief was founded on an obligation granted by the defender to the pursuer immediately before the opening of the credit account, and previous to the date of Scott's letter of guarantee, in these terms:—"As you have become security to the Clydesdale Bank for L.150 on account of Mr. James Wood, for the purpose of assisting him in his business, I hereby guarantee you against any loss by your so doing." A proof was led in the Sheriff-Court. It was contended for the defender that the guarantee undertaken by him could not be construed as a continuing guarantee for a cash credit, but was plainly a guarantee for a specific loan. The Court held that the letter of Mitchell was on the face of it a guarantee of a single transaction—viz., of a loan of L.150; that it was one of the most violent constructions ever put on a guarantee to hold this as an obligation to relieve Scott of the consequences of his liability in a cautionary obligation of such a continuing and most hazardous nature as that for a cash credit. The two kinds of guarantee were quite distinct, and nothing could demonstrate that more clearly than the fact that the bank did not advance one shilling on the credit account for more than a year after it was opened, the balance till then being always on the other side. Wood dealt with the bank according to the rules of cash credit accounts, and it was impossible to hold that all these were transferred into the simple obligation of guarantee undertaken by Mitchell. In Forbes *v.* Dundas (8 S., 865), there was an express guarantee of an overdraft that should be made on a cash credit account, and no particular time for making it was indicated. Although that was unquestionably a guarantee of a continuing nature, the Court had considerable difficulty in holding it applicable to the balance of a cash credit account. The Court advocated the cause, and assoilzied the defender (advocator).

COURT OF SESSION.

FIRST DIVISION.

ANTERMONY COAL COMPANY *v.* WALTER WINGATE AND COMPANY.—*March* 7.

Mandatory—Title to Sue—Process.

The pursuers describe themselves in this action as "The Antermony Coal Company, Antermony, Dumbartonshire, and Austen & Co. coalmasters at Hamilton and Glasgow, and Walter Wingate, coalmaster at Shirva, in the county of Dumbarton, at present in Australia, or elsewhere furth of Scotland, being the individual partners of the said firm of the Antermony Coal Company."

The defenders moved the Lord Ordinary (Barcaple) to appoint the individual pursuer, Wingate, who was abroad, to sist a mandatory. His lordship refused the motion.

The defenders reclaimed, and contended that a firm with a descriptive name had no title to sue except with the authority of three of the individual partners, and the only way of obtaining such authority in the present case was by granting the motion. For all that appeared Wingate's interest in the firm might be greater than that of the other two partners. If it was not known, and could not be discovered where he was, that might be a good ground for asking the Court to appoint a judicial factor, but it could not confer on the pursuers a title which they did not otherwise possess.

The pursuers replied that the defenders' argument rested solely on the want of title of the pursuers; but the plea on record to that effect had been repelled by the Lord Ordinary, whose interlocutor was now final. It appeared on the face of the record that the only party who was not here was in Australia. The two who appeared were in this country, and were solvent.

The Court adhered to the Lord Ordinary's interlocutor. They held that if want of authority from Wingate was to be founded on, there should have been a distinct statement on record to that effect, and a relative plea. The only plea stated on record under which such a contention could be maintained was the first, viz—No title to sue; and this plea had been repelled by an interlocutor, which was now final. Apart from this they were of opinion that the circumstances of the case, as disclosed on record, did not warrant the motion.

CAMERON *v.* MURRAY AND HEPBURN—*March* 8.

Master and Apprentice—Civil and Criminal—Sentence of Imprisonment in Absence—Competency of.

Murray and Hepburn, blacksmiths in Galashiels, presented an application to the Sheriff of Selkirkshire complaining that Cameron, who was bound to them under an indenture as an apprentice, had deserted their service, and containing the following prayer:—

"May it therefore please your Lordship to ordain a copy of this petition, and of the deliverance thereon, to be served upon the said John Cameron, and ordain him to lodge answers thereto within a certain short space, and thereafter, on this complaint being admitted or proven, to ordain him to return to his said service with the petitioners, and to grant warrant to officers of Court to imprison him in the prison of Selkirk, therein to remain aye and until he find sufficient caution acted in your Lordship's court-books, under a suitable penalty to return to the service of the petitioners, and to continue therein until the expiry of the term of his said apprenticeship, and to find him liable to the petitioners in expenses, and to decern therefor."

The Sheriff pronounced an interlocutor granting warrant for serving Cameron with a copy of the petition and the deliverance thereon, and ordaining him "if he intends to state a defence to enter appearance within four days after service; with certification, in case of failure, of being held as confessed, and the prayer of the petition being granted." The petition with this deliverance was served on Cameron, who did not appear. The Sheriff, thereupon, pronounced the following interlocutor:—"Having advised the foregoing petition and indenture produced in process, and no appearance having been entered on behalf of the respondent, within the period specified in the deliverance of 6th January, Finds, in terms of the said deliverance, that the said respondent must now be held as confessed: Finds the complaint proven; ordains the said respondent to return to his service with the petitioners; and grants warrant to officers of Court to apprehend and imprison the respondent, the said John Cameron, in the prison of Selkirk, therein to remain until the expiry of the term of his apprenticeship, or until he finds sufficient caution acted in the books of Court, to return to the service of the petitioners, and to continue therein until the expiry of the term of his apprenticeship."

Cameron has now brought the present suspension of this judgment on the ground (1) that the indenture between him and the respondents was not binding, his brother, who was to be his cautioner for the performance of his obligations therein, not having signed it; and (2) that the Sheriff's judgment was in effect a sentence of imprisonment for the rest of his apprenticeship, which had more than four years to run, as he was unable to find caution in terms thereof, and therefore had been incompetently pronounced in absence of the defender.

The Lord Ordinary (Mure) refused the suspension, and to-day the Court adhered.

The Lord President said he was satisfied the objection to the indenture was not a good ground of suspension. The failure of the complainer's brother to sign it might make the respondents *minus* a cautioner, but it did not relieve the complainer of the obligations which he had competently undertaken for himself. As to the other objection that the Sheriff's judgment had been incompetently pronounced, that also appeared to him not to be well founded. The application to the Sheriff was at common law, and not under the statute. It was a civil proceeding to enforce implement of a contract. He was of opinion, therefore, that it was competent for the Sheriff to pronounce an interlocutor containing the certification in his first one. It followed from that, that the complainer not having appeared (although it appeared from his statements he was aware of the terms of the interlocutor) the Sheriff was entitled to hold him confessed by his absence. There only remained therefore the question as to the defender's imprisonment. He was of opinion the sentence was quite competent, and its competency was the only matter before the Court. The same sentence had been pronounced in a great number of similar cases. Nor did he see that the apprentice was in a very favourable position to complain of its hardship. No doubt he said he was in prison, and could not get out because he could not find caution. But he did not say that he was willing to return to his service, and remain there. On the contrary, the proceedings indicated a persistent determination to desert his service. If he came to a better frame of mind, and satisfied the Judge Ordinary of his *bona fide* intention to return and complete his service, and of his inability to find caution, he did not say it would be incompetent for the Sheriff to hold the provision as to caution satisfied by a very limited security. That matter, however, was not at present before the Court.

A. *v.* B. & C.—*March* 10.

Bond of Presentation.

The present action, which is for aliment of an illegitimate child, of which one of the defenders is alleged to have been the father, was preceded by the arrest of that defender as in *meditatione fugæ*. The petition for arrest set forth, "that the petitioner has become pregnant with an illegitimate child, of which the respondent is the father, in consequence of sexual intercourse between the parties, on various occasions between the 8th and 27th days of August 1864." Under this application, one of the defenders in the present action granted a bond of presentation for the other defender (his son;) and the latter declared the Sheriff-Clerk's office his domicile for citation, all in common form.

It is now pleaded, that the bond of presentation, and domicile for citation, cannot be held applicable to the present action, because in the record in the present action the sexual connection is said to have occurred on the 11th and during the subsequent days of July 1864, not, as in the petition, between the 8th and 27th days of August 1864.

The Lord Ordinary (Kinloch) repelled this plea, holding that this discrepancy was not sufficient to vitiate the proceedings. The identity of the present action with that which formed the ground of the proceedings in the *meditatione fugæ* process was, he thought beyond doubt. The pursuer, in her petition, referred to an action to be raised for the aliment of a child with which she was *then* pregnant, and of which the respondent was the father, in consequence of a sexual intercourse, the locality of which was specifically described, and the present was just that action. It was a physical impossibility that there could be two children, the one conceived in July the other in August.

The defender reclaimed, and the Court, without calling on the pursuer's counsel, adhered to the Lord Ordinary's interlocutor.

Urquhart *v.* Bonnar.

Jury trial—Verdict set aside.

This is an action of reduction of an assignation of a policy of insurance on the life of the pursuer, on the ground that the assignation was granted by the pursuer under essential error induced through fraud and misrepresentation or undue concealment on the part of the defender. The case was first tried before Lord Kinloch and a jury in 1864, when the jury brought in a verdict finding that the pursuer was under essential error, but that there was no fraud, misrepresentation, or undue concealment. Lord Kinloch having explained that that was a verdict for the defender, the pursuer's counsel moved that they should be allowed again to retire, when they returned with a general verdict for the pursuer by a majority of nine to three.

In 1865 this verdict was unanimously set aside by the Court as being contrary to evidence. The case was again tried before the Lord President and a jury at the summer Jury Sittings of 1865, and the jury, by a majority of nine to three, returned a verdict finding that the pursuer was under essential error, induced through undue concealment on the part of the defender.

The defender moved for and obtained a rule to show cause why this verdict should not also be set aside as being contrary to evidence. Parties were then heard on the question whether the rule should be discharged or made absolute, and the Court took the case to avizandum. At advising, the Lord President said—This case comes before us on a motion to make a rule absolute for a new trial. There have been already two trials in the case, and this motion is for a third trial. That is an unusual but not an incompetent or unprecedented motion. The Court have considered very carefully and seriously the arguments on both sides, and have come unanimously to the conclusion that this verdict cannot stand, and that there must be a new trial, and that the question of expenses should be reserved.

Susp. and Inter.—MACINTYRE *v.* MACRAILD.—*March* 13.

Medical Practioner—Obligation not to practise.

The complainer, Dr Macintyre, is a medical man, residing in Fort William, but who, practising in Ballachulish, engaged the respondent as his medical assistant in August 1854. Some two months thereafter Dr Macintyre, who thought that his assistant was attempting to supplant him in his practice, obtained from him an obligation containing the following clause:—"I bind and oblige myself under a penalty of £500 in case of infringement on my part that, after my connection with the said Duncan Macintyre as his assistant has ceased, I shall not accept of the practice of the slate quarries in the case of its being offered to me to his exclusion and disadvantage at any future period, and that I shall never take advantage of any introduction or insight into his affairs the exigencies of my relations with him as his assistant require I should have and know, thereby settling down in his vicinity and practising to his detriment in opposition to him in any of the districts in which he practises his profession."

The respondent's engagement ended on 30th Oct. last, and he left the Ballachulish quarries on the 3d November. He however returned there on 3d December, having accepted an appointment as medical and surgical practitioner at the quarries.

The complainer brought the present suspension and interdict to have the respondent interdicted from practising at the slate quarries.

The Lord Ordinary granted interim interdict.

The respondent reclaimed, but the Court adhered, holding that the reclaimer was bound by the terms of his obligation, and must act in accordance therewith.

Pearson v. J. and G. Dewar.—*March* 14.

Advocation—Reference to oath—Competency.

This was an advocation from the Sheriff Court of Fifeshire. The Court some days ago pronounced in it the following interlocutor:—"Having heard parties' procurators on the question of expenses decided by the Sheriff, this being the only matter now insisted in by the advocator, as stated by his counsel at the bar, repel the reasons of advocation, and remit the cause *simpliciter* to the Sheriff."

The advocator now tendered a minute of reference of the cause to the respondent's oath, which the Court refused to sustain. Their lordships held that in respect of the preceding interlocutor the case was no longer in this Court, except for the purposes of having the expenses given against the advocator decerned for, and therefore that it was incompetent to refer it by a minute lodged here. They were of opinion, however, that it might still be competently referred by a minute lodged in the Sheriff Court. The advocator had abandoned his reasons of advocation *quoad* the merits, and *quoad* the expenses they had been repelled, and the case had been remitted *simpliciter*, so that it was now much in the same position as if no advocation had been presented, and, as it would have been competent to the advocator after the Sheriff's adverse judgment to refer to the oath of his opponent, they were of opinion that right had not been lost by what had taken place. Some of their lordships stated that if they had been of opinion that the reference was incompetent now in the Sheriff Court, that would have influenced their opinion as to its competency in this Court, because they were clear it must be competent in the one Court or the other any time before extract.

A. v. B. and C.—*March* 17.

Gaming Debt.

The pursuer in this case alleges that her son, who is now dead, and whose executrix she is, was for some time previous to his death in a very weak state, both of mind and body, and was so addicted to the use of stimulants, that he was generally, more or less, in a state of intoxication; that the defenders, taking advantage of his condition, induced him to play at cards, and won from him large sums of money; that the defenders did not wholly rely for their success in these games on her son's weak state, but by a system of preconcerted signals and other unfair devices, made certain they should always win. The deceased granted bills to the defenders for the sums so lost by him, and paid these when due. The present action is brought for the recovery of these sums.

The defenders denied the whole of the pursuer's averments, and pleaded that no relevant ground of action had been stated. The case was reported by the Lord Ordinary on the adjustment of issues, and to-day the Court dismissed the action as irrelevant.

Their lordships held that the pursuer's statements, if true, disclosed a course of conduct on the part of the defenders which could not be reprobated in too strong terms. The question was, however, whether these statements disclosed a ground of action which could be entertained by this Court. They were of opinion they did not. They substantially came to this, that the pursuer's deceased son had lost money to the defenders at cards by their unfair play, and granted bills for the amount, which he had paid. The Court would not entertain an action to enforce payment of money won at cards, or to recover money lost at cards and paid, and the allegation here, that the money was lost through unfair play, could not make the action competent, because that involved an inquiry into what was unfair play—in other words, into the rules of the games played, which was a matter this Court could not take cognisance of. Further, it was not averred that the pursuer's son was in such a state of mental incapacity as to be unable to manage his own affairs, either at the time the money was won, or, what was more important, at the time when he granted the bills for the money lost and afterwards paid them. Their lordships therefore held that the action must be dismissed.

M'Neill *v.* Scott & Co.—*March* 17.

Breach of Interdict—Penalty.

This is a petition and complaint presented by Sir John M'Neill, G.C.B., residing at Granton House, with concurrence of the Lord Advocate, against Mr James Scott, merchant, Grassmarket, Edinburgh, and manufacturer of chemical manures at Granton. On 8th June 1865, on the application of Sir John M'Neill and others residing in the neighbourhood of Granton, Scott & Co. were interdicted, prohibited, and discharged from using their works at Granton "for the manufacture of chemical manures in any way which shall be a nuisance to the complainers (Sir John M'Neill and others), or which shall affect the health, or be offensive or a discomfort to the complainers or others residing in Granton House, Craigroyston, and Muirhouse, the residences of the complainers." In July 1865 Scott & Co. were found guilty of having committed a contempt of Court and a breach of the foregoing interdict. On that occasion no fine was imposed beyond the expenses of the suit. Sir John M'Neill now complains in the present application of a number of additional breaches of the interdict. The respondent's answer to the complaint is that he has done all in his power, and incurred great expense in order to prevent discomfort to the complainer, and even if any vapours have accidently escaped in the course of his anxious endeavours to obviate all cause for complaint, such accidental occurrences cannot be considered as a contempt of Court or breach of the interdict. He also stated his willingness to carry out any improvements which might be suggested by any man of skill to be appointed by the Court.

A proof was led by both parties, and the case having been debated some time ago, was advised to-day.

Lords Curriehill and Ardmillan held that the proof established three breaches of interdict, and therefore that the respondent must be found guilty of contempt of Court. At the same time, as it appeared that subsequent to the last breach he had stopped his works for some time and had incurred considerable expense in making alterations on them with a view to removing the nuisance, he was entitled to lenient consideration. It was necessary, however, that the Court should mark its disapprobation of the contempt of Court committed, though under extenuating circumstances; and therefore they fined the respondent in the sum of £5, to be paid to the Clerk of Court, to be handed by him to the treasurer of the Royal Infirmary, and also in the expenses of process.

Lord Deas dissented. He held that there could not be a breach of interdict without there being contempt of Court, and as he thought it was proved that on the occasions when there was a slight smell from the respondents' works, that occurred through accident or want of attention and not from design, he did not think a case of breach of interdict had been made out.

JAMIESON *v.* ANDREW.—*March* 20.

Liquidator—Lien.

The question in this case was whether Mr G. A. Jamieson, C.A., the official liquidator of the Garpel Hæmatite Company (Limited), is entitled to get delivery from Mr John Andrew, a solicitor in London, of the register of shareholders and transfers of shares to enable him to wind up the company, under the Companies' Clauses Act, 1862. Mr Andrew admitted that he had these documents, but declined to deliver them to the liquidator, on the ground that he had a lien over them for a sum of £768 19s 3d due to him as the solicitor of the company. In July last the Court, in virtue of its powers under the Winding-up Acts, appointed Mr Andrew to lodge the documents with the Clerk of Court, in order that inspection thereof in his hands might be obtained, and appointed the question of lien to be argued in writing.

The case was advised to-day, when the Court unanimously held that the liquidator was entitled to access to the documents in question. Looking to the provisions of the Joint-Stock Companies' Act (1856), which required the register of shareholders to be kept at the registered office of the company (which in the present case was in Ayrshire) to be open to the inspection of the shareholders, they were of opinion that it was incompetent for the company to pledge it with any one so as to create in the depositary a right of lien, more especially to send it for this purpose beyond the jurisdiction of the Court within which the registered office of the company was. As to the transfers, as these were the property of the individual shareholders, they were of opinion it was also incompetent for the company to pledge them, and they therefore allowed the liquidator to obtain the documents from the clerk on a borrowing receipt.

A motion was made on behalf of Mr Andrew that the Court should supersede extract of their judgment, for such a period as would enable him to present an appeal to the House of Lords, because if the judgment were given effect to in the meantime, and the liquidator obtained even a temporary possession of the documents, he would get all the information from them he required, and so render useless Mr Andrew's lien, if the court of last resort should hold that it existed.

The Court refused to express their judgment in any other than the usual terms.

SWANS *v.* WESTERN BANK.—*March* 22.

Heritable Title—Accretion.

The liquidator of the Western Bank sold to Messrs Swan, builders in Glasgow, the lands of Mount Florida and Hangingshaw, near Glasgow. The Messrs Swan, being dissatisfied with the title offered, brought a suspension of a threatened charge for payment of the price of the lands. In

1847, Mr Dixon, the then proprietor of the subjects in question, by an *ex facie* absolute disposition, conveyed them to the Commercial Bank, who were infeft. In 1849 and 1851, by a conveyance and a supplementary conveyance, he disponed them to Mr Johnston, his trustee, who, in April 1854, conveyed them to Mr Bunten, from whom they were acquired by the Bank. In March 1854 the Commercial Bank reconveyed them to Mr Dixon, who was thereafter infeft. The question in the present case was, whether Dixon having been divested of the lands by the conveyance to the Commercial Bank, at the date of the trust-deed to Johnston, which was the foundation of the Western Bank's title to them, the trust-deed and subsequent transmissions were validated by the accretion of the right subsequently acquired by Dixon from the Commercial Bank.

The Lord Ordinary (Barcaple) held that the trust-deed was validated by accretion, and therefore that the Messrs Swan were bound to accept the title offered by the liquidator of the Western Bank.

The Court adhered. They thought the conveyance to the Commercial Bank, though *ex facie* absolute, was truly in security, but even assuming that it was absolute, and that Dixon at the date of the trust-deed had no right to the subject, they were of opinion that on his being reinvested by the conveyance from the Commercial Bank, that reconveyance accresced to his disponee, there being no mid-impediment. This was an elementary principle of our law laid down by all the institutional writers, with the exception of Professor Bell, who expressed a doubt on the subject, and that doubt, they were of opinion, was not well founded.

Rennie *v.* Smith and Others.—*March* 23.

Guarantee—Extent of Liability.

The pursuer in this action is Mr John Rennie, mason and builder, Sauchiehall Street, Glasgow, and the defenders are Mr John Stevens Harkness, joiner, Anderston, Glasgow, as principal, and James Smith, architect in Glasgow, as his cautioner. The summons concludes against both defenders, jointly and severally, for payment of L.241 as the balance of an account for digger, mason, and brick work of two tenements at the corner of Elderslie and William Streets in Anderston of Glasgow, executed by the pursuers for the defender Harkness, amounting in all said account to L.1457. In July 1862 Harkness addressed a letter to the pursuer in the following terms :—"I hereby bind myself to pay you the following instalments for mason and brick works of buildings proposed to be erected in Elderslie and William Streets—viz., first instalment of L.100, on each tenement, when ready for first joists . . . . . ." The letter contained similar stipulations as to five other instalments to be paid at different stages of the work, and concluded, "and the balance when the work is completed." To this letter the defender Smith appended the following holograph note :—"Mr John Rennie—Dear Sir,—I hereby agree to see you paid the above instalments. I am, &c. (Signed) James Smith." The defender Harkness became bankrupt, and the question in the present case was whether, under the foregoing note, Mr Smith's liability, as cautioner for him, was limited to the specific instalments mentioned in Harkness's letter, or whether he was liable for the balance of the account for building operations over and above the instalments.

The Lord Ordinary (Jerviswoode) held that, according to the true and fair construction of Smith's note, he was liable for the balance of the account as well as the payments specially designated as "instalments."

The Court recalled this interlocutor, and assoilzied Smith, holding that there was no warrant for extending his guarantee beyond its express terms, viz., payment of the instalments.

SMITH AND GILMOUR *v.* CONN.—*March* 24.

Jurisdiction—Civil and Criminal.

The joint clerks to the Turnpike Road Trustees for the district of Irvine in Ayrshire, presented a petition and complaint to the Justices of the Peace for that county complaining of an alleged contravention of the Ayrshire Road Acts by Miss Conn, residing at Adela Cottage, Kilwinning. The contravention complained of was certain additions made by Miss Conn to a house belonging to her, situated on the side of the road leading from Irvine to Kellybridge. The prayer of the complaint was that the Justices would ordain Miss Conn to pull down and remove the additions and erections complained of, and further, fine her in a penalty not exceeding L.5, and not less than 20s., and, failing payment, grant warrant of imprisonment for four months. Miss Conn, in answer to the complaint, pleaded that the acts complained of did not constitute a contravention of section 12 of the Ayrshire Roads Act founded on, and further that the prayer of the complaint was not warranted, or within the powers conferred on the Trustees, by the said Act. The Justices, by a majority of four to two, sustained these preliminary objections, and dismissed the complaint. Against this deliverance the complainers presented the present advocation. The respondent pleaded, *inter alia*—(1), That the Court had no jurisdiction to entertain the advocation, in respect the proceedings were of a criminal nature; and (2), That the judgment of the Justices not having been appealed from in the manner provided for by the 14th section of 1 and 2 Will. IV., chap. 43, was now final, and not subject to review by advocation.

The Lord Ordinary (Mure) adopted the latter of these pleas, and dismissed the advocation as incompetent.

The Court adhered, but on the different ground that the proceeding, being of a criminal nature, the Court had no jurisdiction to entertain the advocation; expressing, at the same time, their opinion of the inconvenience resulting from the provisions of the Summary Procedure Act, which required cases to be taken for review before the Justiciary Court, for the disposal of which the forms of that Court were not well adapted.

HAMILTON *v.* TURNER AND THE MONKLANDS IRON AND STEEL COMPANY.—*March* 26.

Liability for Damage to Houses by Underground Mineral Workings.

The pursuer is proprietor of a house in the village of Armadale, built on ground fued in 1856 by Mr Dennistoun, the then proprietor of the estate of Barhauchlan, which now belongs to the defender, Mr Turner. Two years before the date of the feu Mr Dennistoun granted a lease of the gas coal on the estate to the Monkland Iron and Steel Company, and the pursuer avers that through their mining operations his house is coming down. This is an action of damages against Mr Turner, the superior, and his mineral lessees.

The Lord Ordinary dismissed the action as laid against Mr Turner, on the ground that the persons liable were those who did the damage, the Monklands Iron and Steel Company. But as against them he sustained the relevancy of the action, and ordered issues. This judgment was brought under review of the Court by both the pursuer and the Monklands Iron and Steel Company.

The Court recalled the interlocutor of the Lord Ordinary, and of consent appointed a proof of the facts to be taken on commission. Their lordships observed that no one was entitled to work minerals underground save in such a manner as might be consistent with the safety of the surface, and all reasonable and proper uses to which it might be put. But till the facts were ascertained, they would give no opinion as to whether the pursuer was entitled to recover from both of the defenders, or from the superior in part and the mineral lessees in part. It might be that only one of the defenders was liable, but which of them would depend on the proof.

CLAYHILLS AND OTHERS *v.* NORRIE AND OTHERS.—*March* 27.

Circumstances in which Trustee held bound to denude.

By feu-contract, dated in 1839, David Hunter, junior, wine merchant in Dundee, proprietor of the estate of Broughty Ferry, sold and disponed to Charles Norrie and others, as trustees for their own behoof in certain specified proportions, part of the lands of North Ferry. By the feu-contract Mr Norrie and his co-trustees bound themselves, as trustees and individuals, to pay to Mr Hunter, their superior and his heirs, &c., L.335, 14s. 9d. annually as feu-duty. Subsequent to the date of the feu-contract Mr Norrie and his co-trustees granted sub-feu rights of portions of the subjects in favour of various individuals, which contained obligations of absolute warrandice by the granters as trustees and individuals. The whole of the trustees for whose own behoof the trust was constituted, or persons in their right, have now obtained a vested interest in their respective shares of the trust subjects. The trustees are all now dead except Mr Norrie and another, and Mr Norrie having sold his share has now no beneficial interest in the subjects. In these circumstances the parties having right to the property have brought the present action to have Mr Norrie and his surviving co-trustee ordained to denude of the trust in their favour. Mr Norrie pleads in defence that he is not bound to denude of the trust until he receives a discharge from the over superior of the obligation undertaken by him in the feu-contract as an individual to pay the feu-duty of L.335 odds. The over superiors are a committee of the General Assembly, who decline to grant this discharge on the ground that they hold the superiority as trustees, and are therefore not entitled to grant it. The question in the present case is whether Mr Norrie is bound to denude of the trust without receiving this discharge.

The Lord Ordinary (Jerviswoode) held that he was not. The personal obligation undertaken by him in the feu-contract being still in subsistence, it might be annually enforced against him, and although he would have a right of relief against the beneficiaries, still his Lordship thought he could not be compelled to be satisfied with that, but was entitled to keep up the trust, so as to hold the subjects themselves in security for his relief from any claim for the feu-duty.

The Court, by a majority, recalled this interlocutor, and held that Mr Norrie was bound to denude. They were of opinion that as the trust was merely an *ex facie* trust, under which the trustees themselves were the beneficiaries, and was constituted only for the purpose of simplifying the feudal title to the subjects, and Mr Norrie had now no beneficial interest in them, he was not entitled longer to keep up the trust.

Lord Curriehill dissented, and agreed with the Lord Ordinary.

GREIG *v.* HERIOT'S HOSPITAL.—*March* 28.

Poor's Rates—Heriot's Hospital liable to pay.

The pursuer of this action is the inspector of the City Parish of Edinburgh, and the defenders are the Governors of George Heriot's Hospital. The question raised in the case is whether the building of George Heriot's Hospital, the site on which it stands, and the adjacent gardens aud grounds, are liable to be assessed for support of the poor. The pursuer contended that there was no ground at common law or under the statute for exempting the hospital, &c., from assessment. The defenders pleaded (1) that the hospital had been exempt prior to 8th and 9th Vic., cap. 83, and such exemption not having been taken away by that statute still continued; (2) that the hospital, &c., was exempt from poor-rates because it was a charitable institution and benefited and relieved the parish; also because it was a public charitable institution and benefited the public; and further, because the defenders were not owners and occupants in the sense of the statute.

The Lord Ordinary (Jerviswoode) repelled the defences, and the defenders having reclaimed, to-day the Court, at the close of the argument, adhered to the Lord Ordinary's interlocutor.

The Lord President said—I do not think that this is now an open question. The principle on which the House of Lords proceeded in the case of the Mersey Harbour & Docks Company, and also in more recent Scotch cases, must be held to apply here, and I also think that the grounds on which alone the Second Division held that the University of Edinburgh was exempt from the payment of these rates clearly show that no such exemption can be claimed in this case. I am not moved by the argument that there are here no owners or occupiers in the sense of the statute. We have here a beneficial occupation, and the parties assessable are not the boys of the Hospital but the trustees. Is there then any exemption because this is an educational institution, and not only educational, but charitable? I do not think that argument is of any weight. It would equally apply to any educational institution where the whole of the revenues were devoted to educational purposes, and no part found its way into the private pockets of the managers. Is it then a Crown or national institution? I think this can hardly be maintained. The private Act of Parliament (6 and 7 Will. IV.) entitled the trustees to apply the revenues to more extended purposes than was contemplated by the founder, but it does not give it a national character. It is quite a common proceeding to apply for a private Act of Parliament to enable parties to innovate on the original purposes of a trust, and this will not be refused by the Legislature if the case appear clearly to require it. I do not think that so far as the present question is concerned, the above Act is materially different in its consequences from an ordinary estate bill. Is the institution in itself national? I do not see how this case can be maintained. The funds were left by George Heriot for purposes which, though not local, were very limited in their character, and can in no sense be called national. No doubt it is said that the hospital has been recognised by Act of Parliament (1695) as "an ornament to the nation," and on that account exempted from certain excise duties. Now, I quite accept the meaning put on this expression by the reclaimers as the one really intended to be conveyed by the Act. I think it refers not to the building but to the institution generally, just as we talk of a man being an ornament to his country without any reference to his physical appearance; but we do not on this account exempt him or his property from the payment of these or any other taxes. The nation never had any voice in or control over the management of this institution from its foundation, and as a nation they have no property or interest in it. But it was farther contended that the hospital always has been exempt, and that this exemption has not been taken away by the Poor Law Act. Now, it is quite true that it has up to the present date never been so taxed. But, then, it must be remembered that the poor laws were long very loosely administered, and that great liberties were taking in granting or allowing exemptions, without much consideration as to the rights at common law or under the statutes; and the fact that it has not been taxed since the passing of the Act must just be held to be a continuance of this loose practice, and can give no claim for exemption on the ground of usage. Of late years the Act has been construed much more strictly and accurately than it was at first. On the whole, I have a very clear opinion that we must hold these subjects to be liable to be assessed for the support of the poor of the City Parish of Edinburgh.

The other Judges concurred.

Adv.—Morton *v.* Robinson.—*March* 30.

Sale—Failure to Deliver—Damages.

This is an advocation from the Sheriff Court of Lanarkshire. Robinson, a cattle-dealer in Lanarkshire, sued Morton, a farmer in the same county, for damages in respect of his failure to deliver to the pursuer 300 lambs, purchased on August 1863 at 16s 6d per head, to be delivered within or during the week of the ensuing Lanark lamb fair. A proof having been led as to the terms of the bargain, the Sheriff-Substitute (Dyce) assoilzied the defender. On appeal the Sheriff (Alison) recalled this interlocutor, and found the defender liable in damages, which he assessed at L.15.

The defender brought an advocation of this judgment, which was recalled by the Court, who returned to the judgment of the Sheriff-Substitute.

The facts of the case appear from the opinion of the Lord President, who said there was no doubt the parties met on 6th August, when a bargain was made for the sale of the defender's lambs,—not of a specified number, but of his stock for the season, whatever that might be, with the privilege of casting sixty. That was a common bargain. Delivery was to be at the farm, and the price was 16s 6d. So far all was clear. But the parties had difficulty in adjusting the time at which delivery should be taken. The purchaser proposed delivery in the week of the lamb fair, the defender, Morton, in the week preceding. Then a friend who was present suggested the 18th, the day of the fair. It was clear the defender did not object. The question is, whether it was further agreed that the delivery should be at any time in the course of the week of the fair. The evidence as to this was not clear. It was conclusive to this extent, that the defender passed from insisting on delivery in the week before the fair, but it was not clear whether the time was extended further than the 18th. The pursuer's action was on the ground that it was so extended. On 17th August he wrote to Mr Morton that he would lift the lambs on the Friday following. Morton, on the 18th, wrote to say he held it no bargain, in consequence of the lambs not being lifted on that day. The pursuer making this allegation as to the time, must establish it, for it was the basis of his claim for damages. The defender had reasons, apparently, for being strict in adhering to his time. As delivery could be taken any time on the 18th, he could not sell his lambs at Lanark fair. The only other fair was Carlisle market. Obviously it was a serious matter for the defender to run the risk of not selling there, and unless matters were put in train for despatching them immediately after the 18th, he would lose the market. If, therefore, the true understanding was that the pursuer was to have only till Tuesday, Morton was entitled to be strict. Prices appear to have improved, but it did not appear that the defender made much by that. He got 19s for his lambs, but he had to sell five score under 16s 6d, viz., four score at 15s 6d, and one at 10s. and he had to pay expenses, commission, and luck-penny. The pursuer considered the lambs worth 24s at Carlisle, and had sold them, not at Carlisle, but for the price that could be had at Carlisle, but had made a very safe bargain, not rendering himself liable for damages for failure to deliver. At Carlisle, too, though he seemed to think there had been a breach of bargain, he did not appear to be much disappointed. In these circumstances the Court thought the defender ought to be assoilzied.

BATTERSBY *v.* TOLAND.—*March* 31.

Sale—Action for Price.

The pursuer, a provision merchant in Liverpool, brought this action against the defender, provision merchant in Glasgow, for the sum of L.81, for bacon sold to the defender in December 1864, at the price of 47s. per cwt. The defence was that the price of the bacon was 37s., and that the bacon, being of inferior quality, was not worth more. After a proof, the Sheriff-Substitute decerned against the defender, finding it proved that, although the pursuer's letter to the defender in sending the bacon stated the price at 37s., this was evidently a clerical error for 47s., and must in the circumstances of the case have been known by the defender to be so, and that the defender having taken and used the bacon, was bound to pay the price at which the pursuer meant to sell it, or, at least, was bound to pay the market price.

The Sheriff (Alison) found for the defender, on the ground that the defender was entitled to act upon the pursuer's letter, as containing a correct statement of the price, and that the pursuer, by failing to correct his first letter, or send any invoice for five days after the bacon had been cut up and disposed of, had lost any right he might have had to have the price corrected.

Battersby advocated, and the Court returned to the judgment of the Sheriff-Substitute in favour of the pursuer.

SUTHERLAND *v.* M'BEATH.—*March* 31.

Lease—Encroachment—Interdict.

This was an advocation from the Sheriff-Court of Caithness-shire. M'Beath, tenant of the farm of Heathfield, petitioned in that Court to have Sutherland, tenant of a neighbouring farm, interdicted from encroaching upon the farm of Heathfield, and from taking possession of a piece of land within its boundaries. Sutherland averred that when he got his lease in 1858, he got besides the farm of Newlands, an additional piece of ground, being that claimed by the petitioner, under an agreement whereby a new boundary was fixed between this farm and that of the petitioner. After a proof, the Sheriff-Substitute found that, under his lease, M'Beath was entitled to possession of the ground in question, and granted interdict. On appeal, the Sheriff adhered.

Sutherland advocated, but the Court adhered to the judgment of the Sheriff.

SECOND DIVISION.

HERITORS OF CARRIDEN *v.* DUGUID AND OTHERS.—*March* 7.

Parish—Churchyard—Heritors—Feuars.

The whole heritors possessed of lands included in the old valuation-roll, and paying cess and other heritor's assessments, within the parish of Carriden, prayed to have the respondents, residenters in the said parish, interdicted from molesting or interfering with the complainers in the management and custody of the old kirkyard of Carriden, by forcing the gate of the churchyard, or otherwise effecting a violent entrance into the same, opening graves, and erecting or constructing headstones or other monuments or memorials of dead or living persons within said churchyard, without leave of or licence granted by the complainers or their predecessors, heritors of the said parish; or by any other fact or deed inconsistent with the legal rights of the complainers, as managers and custodiers of the said churchyard.

The Lord Ordinary (Barcaple) held that, if this were an illegal act the complainers had sufficient title to pursue the interdict as to forcing open the churchyard gate, even if they were not the whole heritors, individual heritors being entitled to check illegal encroachments on the churchyard (Ure *v.* Ramsay, 6 S., 916.) The Lord Ordinary thought interdict could not be granted against opening graves, which was the proper use that people having burying-grounds were entitled to make of it; and it would require a very special case of improper proceedings in regard to it to justify an interdict at all, and in any case it would require to be carefully qualified. The Lord Ordinary thought the heritors must have a control as to the erection of tombstones, &c. But as the prayer of the note required permission to be granted by the complainers or their predecessors—being the heritors paying cess—to the exclusion of all other heritors in the parish, and as his Lordship was not prepared, after the Peterhead case (4 Pat., 356) and Boswell *v.* Hamilton (15 S., 1148), and M'Farlane *v.* Monklands Railway Company (2 Macph., 519), to hold it clear that all owners of land and houses in a rural parish are not entitled to take part in the custody and management of the churchyard, his Lordship accordingly granted interdict against molesting the complainers in the management and custody of the parish, by forcing the gate of the said churchyard, or otherwise effecting a violent entrance into the same; allowed a proof to their respondents of their averments that there are many heritors having real rent in the parish besides the complainers, with reference to the interdict craved against erecting headstones, &c.; and, as to the remaining portions of the prayer, repelled the reasons of suspension, and refused the prayer, reserving the question of expenses. The Court, in respect of its being now admitted that, besides the complainers who pay on their old valued rent, there are persons in the parish (feuars) having real rent (but without indicating any opinion on the question whether or not feuars were entitled to share with other heritors in parochial management, or deciding whether the old valuation heritors have the exclusive right of management), recalled the Lord Ordinary's interlocutor, granted interdict against the respondents interfering with the *heritors* in the management and custody of the kirkyard, and against their forcing the gate of the churchyard, or otherwise effecting a violent entrance into the same, and erecting monuments, &c., without leave or licence granted by the *heritors;* found the complainers entitled to two-thirds of their expenses to the date of the Lord Ordinary's interlocutor, and the respondents to their expenses thereafter.

DUNN PATTISON *v.* DUNN'S TRUSTEES.—*March* 9.

Succession—Deathbed—Intestacy—Condition.

William Dunn of Duntocher executed a disposition and settlement of all his property in favour of his brother Alexander, and his heirs and his assigns whomsoever; "declaring, but without prejudice in any respect to, or limitation of, the rights and powers of the said Alexander Dunn, under and by virtue of the conveyance in his favour before written, to exercise the most full and absolute control in the disposal of the said estates and effects, either during his lifetime or by settlements or other writings to take effect at his death, that in the event of his dying intestate and without leaving heirs of his body, and of his not otherwise disposing of the subjects and estates hereby conveyed to him, the same shall fall and devolve, and, accordingly, I do hereby in these events, but under the burdens and provisions before written, dispone, alienate, and convey my said subjects and estates, heritable and moveable, to the persons, and in the terms, after mentioned." The testator accordingly provided and appointed that his lands in the parish of Kilpatrick should be divided into three portions, and should "fall and devolve" upon certain other parties, sisters and sister's children of the testator. The pursuer represents this class, and would be benefited by these ulterior provisions. William Dunn died in 1849. Alexander made up titles to his brother, and died in 1860, leaving a trust-disposition and settlement executed on death-bed. In an action at the instance of Alexander's heir-at-law, (M'Ewan *v.* Dunn's Trs., 3 Macph.), the Court found that the heir-at-law, being excluded by the deed of William, had no title to sue a reduction of the deathbed deed of Alexander. The pursuer, in the quality of heir of provision to Alexander Dunn under William Dunn's settlement, now raised this action to reduce Alexander

Dunn's settlement *ex capite lecti*, so far as it conveyed heritable property destined to him by William's settlement.

The Lord Ordinary (Jerviswoode) found that the pursuer had not set forth a sufficient title to pursue in respect of the conveyance by William Dunn to Alexander, "and his heirs and assigns whomsoever, and in respect of the exercise by the said Alexander Dunn of the powers of disposal conferred upon him." His Lordship thought it was the obvious intention of William Dunn to confer on his brother the most absolute right in, and power of disposal of, the subjects conveyed; and as the right of the pursuer to challenge the deed at all *ex capite lecti*, rested on his character as heir of provision under the very deed containing the primary destination to Alexander, "his heirs and assigns," the pursuer could not, consistently with the intent of the granter and the true character of the conveyance, assert a right here, the effect of which would be to annul and render nugatory those rights and powers conferred on his brother, which it was the direct object of William Dunn to protect.

The pursuer reclaimed; and the Court altered and sustained the pursuer's title to sue.

Lord Justice-Clerk.—This view of the Lord Ordinary proceeds on a misunderstanding of our judgment in the previous case. We were of opinion that the conveyance to Alexander Dunn was controlled to a certain extent by the after part of the disposition, and as most of us thought by the latter part of the dispositive clause, by which it is provided that, in certain events, the heirs and assigns of Alexander should not take; that if Alexander should succeed, and die without issue, and should not dispose of the estate in his lifetime, or by *mortis causa* disposition, then certain persons should come in as substitutes. I think, in conformity with the previous judgment, that we must hold that the destination to Alex. Dunn and his heirs and assigns is not sufficient by itself to exclude these parties, if the condition subject to which they take has been purified. But the Lord Ordinary finds that there was an exercise of the powers conferred on Alexander by which they are excluded. If Alexander had not been full fiar, but only entitled to a power or faculty of disposing of the lands, no doubt that power might have been exercised on deathbed; but he had the fullest power of disposal, and, in making the deed sought to be reduced, he was not exercising a special power, but his full *jus disponendi* as fiar. But it was contended further, that Alexander's deed was effectual as a conveyance of his moveable estate, and therefore that Alexander did not die intestate; and yet it was only in that event (of intestacy), among others, that the conditional substitution came into operation. But the event of intestacy means dying intestate as to each of the special subjects destined to the different substitutes. It could not be maintained that, if Alexander had sold one of the subjects conveyed to him, that would have evacuated the whole substitutions. Just as little, if he disponed *mortis causa* one subject, would that operate a defeasance of the whole substitutions. Still less are we to hold that, because Alexander may dispose of his moveables, he is thereby to be held as evacuating the substitution as to the heritage. But then it was contended further that Alex. Dunn had not died intestate at all, but had executed a deed which, though invalid, professes to dispose of his whole estate, and so he cannot be said to die intestate. If William Dunn had conferred on Alexander a power to defeat these substitutions even *in lecto*, that would be a good argument.

If he did not, it is not a good argument, because the deed *in lecto* is unavailing against the heir of provision, in whose prejudice it was made. But if William Dunn did confer on Alexander a right to defeat the substitutions *in lecto*, the defenders would be entitled to prevail. He made him full fiar during his life in every sense. But did he mean to make him anything more? I do not think he meant him to be exempted from the operation of any law limiting the right of owners to dispose *mortis causa* of their heritage. Whether one man can be held to provide that the public law of death-bed shall be abrogated in respect of another, in any particular circumstances, need not be decided here. He might, indeed, have validly made it a condition that a substitution should not take effect if Alexander should execute a deed disposing of the estates even on death-bed. But has he done this? There is no trace of such a condition. The conditions are :—(1) That Alexander should succeed; (2) that he should die without issue; (3) that he should not dispose of the estate during his life; (4) that he should die intestate; and the last cannot be held to mean that he shall not even attempt to dispose of the estate by a deed which is invalid.

The other judges concurred in sustaining the pursuer's title to sue.

Darsie *v.* Scbales—*March* 10.

Consistorial—Judicial Examination.

In a declarator of marriage, on the ground of habit and repute, the defenders moved the Lord Ordinary to ordain the pursuer to be judicially examined before fixing any diet for the proof. The Lord Ordinary refused the motion, and the Court adhered. Judicial examination was always an exceedingly delicate proceeding, especially in consistorial causes. In any other cases it would now hardly be attempted, because in other cases the parties are now competent witnesses. In no case had the motion been granted except where the case was surrounded with circumstances of very strong suspicion; and there was no example of such procedure in a declarator of marriage founded on allegations of habit and repute. There were very good reasons why it should not take place in such cases. These cases necessarily involved a very large inquiry into the whole life and history of the parties, and the proof necessarily would give the defender all the benefit he proposed to derive from the present inquiry.

Pet.—A. B. and Others.—*March* 13.

Sequestration—Declaring Sequestration at an end.

This petition, to have a sequestration recalled or declared at an end, was presented to the Lord Ordinary on the Bills by A. B. and his creditors at the date of the sequestration of his estates in April 1864. After intimation and service, and certain arrangements made with creditors, his Lordship, finding the case not to be within the procedure in the Bankruptcy Act, 1856, reported the petition with a note, setting forth that "sequestration was awarded in April 1864, and under section 48 of the Bankrupt Act, an abbreviate of the petition and deliverance was recorded in the Register of Inhibitions in the usual way. But beyond this, it does not appear that any proceedings have been taken under the statute. Immediately after sequestration had been thus awarded, negotiations took place between the petitioner and his creditors, which resulted in an arrangement by which the petitioner has been discharged of all his debts. This was, however, effected without the machinery of the Bankrupt Act having been called into operation. For none of the usual notices were inserted in the *Gazette;* no statutory meeting of creditors was held; no trustee was appointed; and there was no ranking of creditors in the sense of the statute. In these circumstances, the petitioner being anxious to have his sequestration judicially declared to be at an end, and the necessary marking upon the registers, has presented this application. But as the jurisdiction which the Lord Ordinary exercises in such matters is purely statutory, and the case is one which can scarcely be said to come within the provisions either of section 31 or 32 of the Act, which regulate the recal of the sequestration, inasmuch as there was no ranking of creditors in the sense of the statute, the Lord Ordinary doubts his jurisdiction to dispose of it." The Court appointed intimation of the deliverance awarding sequestration to be made in the *Gazette*, and a meeting of creditors to be held for the election of a trustee and commissioners. This interlocutor and the deliverance awarding sequestration were advertised; and on the day appointed for the meeting the agent for the petitioners attended at the time and place named for the meeting. No creditors appeared, and no trustee or commissioners were elected. A minute drawn up and certified by the petitioners' agent, setting forth these circumstances, was lodged in process, and the Court thereupon, on the motion of the petitioners, and in virtue of their *nobile officium*, declared the sequestration to be at an end, and the petitioner A. B. to be reinvested in his estates, and granted warrant for marking this deliverance in the Registers of Sequestrations and Inhibitions.

Advn.—Sim *v.* Sidey and Dewar.—*March* 15.

Reference to Oath—Loan—Extrinsic and Intrinsic.

This was an action by executors for recovery of L.220, alleged to have been cash advanced by the late Mr Gow to Sim in loan, on 29th November 1860. It was admitted that the advance had been made by a cheque, which had been cashed by the defender, and applied to his own purposes; but with the qualification that the money was paid and received by him in payment of services rendered by him to the deceased. Upon a reference to the oath of the defender, the Sheriff of Perthshire found the loan proved, and decerned in terms of the summons; but the Court reversed, and held the oath negative of the reference.

The Lord Justice-Clerk said—The question is, *Quid juratum est?* Apart from the question of extrinsic and intrinsic, it is impossible to hold that this party has proved that this money was advanced *in loan*, but on quite a different footing. But, then, it is said that the allegation as to the deceased owing money to Sim is extrinsic. This argument proceeds on a misunderstanding of the cases. When the question whether a sum was advanced by way of loan is referred to oath, it may be quite true that, if the defender cannot swear that it was advanced on any other footing, a presumption arises that it was advanced in loan. If a sum admittedly advanced was not so advanced in loan, there are only two possible alternatives—it must either have been a donation or payment of a previous debt; and if the defender swears that it was either of these alternatives, that is negative of the reference. Another class of cases is clearly distinguishable, where the oath of the defender resolves into a claim of compensation. That is clearly extrinsic of the reference, because there is no natural connection between the sum sought to be set off and that sued for. His Lordship then referred to *Lauder* v. *M'Gibbon and Medina* (M. 13,206), as being near the confines of the two classes of cases.

M.P.—Allardice's Trustees *v.* Ritchie, &c.—*March* 16.

Trust—Legacy—Vesting.

Robert Barclay Allardice of Ury left a trust-disposition and settlement, of which the second purpose was for payment of £3000 to David Stewart, his illegitimate son; the third for payment of an annuity of £100 to the mother of his two natural sons, and of an annuity of £200 to his daughter, Mrs Ritchie. The fourth purpose of the trust was for payment of £1000 to each of his three grandsons, who were in pupillarity at his death, "declaring that said bequests to the said Robert, Samuel, and David Ritchie, shall only be payable to them on their respectively attaining majority; but in the event of the previous predecease of their mother, my said trustees shall apply the interests of the said bequests, after that event, in alimenting and educating the said Robert, Samuel, and David Ritchie, until they respectively attain majority: which several sums and annuities I hereby leave and bequeath accordingly to the parties respectively before-mentioned." In the fifth place, the testator directed his trustees to make over the residue of his estate, heritable and moveable, to Robert Stewart, "with full power to my said trustees to apply the annual rents or interests of the foregoing bequests to my said two sons (that is, the illegitimate sons, David and Robert), in alimenting and educating them during their minority, and if found advisable, to apply the principal sums, in whole or in part, in purchasing commissions for them in the army or navy, or otherwise settling them in life; and declaring that, subject to the exercise of these powers, the bequest in favour of my said son, Robert, shall not take effect until he shall attain the age of thirty years complete, unless my said trustees shall be of opinion that it should take effect sooner." Samuel Ritchie died in the United States in April 1862, before attaining majority. Mrs Ritchie and her two sons were his heirs, *in mobilibus*, and as such claimed the legacy of £1000, as having vested in him *a morte testatoris*. The trustees raised this action of multiplepoinding to have it determined whether this sum of £1000 had so vested, and they claimed it in the multiplepoinding as part of the residue of the trust-estate, on the ground that it was not intended to vest in the legatee till majority. The Lord Ordinary (Jerviswoode) held that the bequest vested in Samuel at the death of the testator, and the Court adhered. The words of the bequest were the same as those of the bequests to the illegitimate children, as to which it was not suggested that vesting was postponed. The words previous to the "declaring" were words of complete gift in themselves. If the testator gave to trustees for the purpose of making payment, there was as complete a bequest as if it were made directly, without the intervention of trustees. It was impossible to adopt the contention that the condition as to payment at majority was the same as if it were part of the bequest,—as if the bequest and condition were blended together in one sentence. That view was quite inapplicable to the deed. It was the same as if he had said, "I leave and bequeath £1000, &c., but I direct that it shall not be payable till," &c. The provision as to the income of this part of the estate, was also most important as indicating the mind of the testator. The trustees were not in the same position towards these children as to the natural sons, to whom they were appointed tutors and curators; and accordingly the interests accruing during the mother's life were to be administered by her. But the testator took his trustees bound to step in on the death of the mother, which was a perfectly natural arrangement. It was not easy to understand how interest could run on a sum not vested.

CLEMENTS *v.* MACAULAY.—*March* 16.

Jurisdiction—Convenient Forum.

In an action of accounting at the instance of one joint adventurer against another who was the manager of the adventure, the defendant pleaded, *inter alia*, that this Court was not the competent and convenient forum. The adventure was entered into in 1862 in Texas, the pursuer being domiciled there. Three of the other adventurers belonged to New Orleans, and the other was a major in the Confederate Service. The last mentioned, one Moise, furnished a steamer on behalf of the Confederate Government, and the object of the joint adventure was to run the blockade with cotton from Texas, and bring return cargoes of munitions of war. The defender maintained that questions would arise as to the legality of the contract and other matters, which would be most suitably determined by the Courts of Texas or other American State, where the contract was made, and to the law of which the parties were all subject. The Lord Ordinary (Barcaple) sustained this plea; but the Court unanimously held that no sufficient case had been made out to lead this Court to sustain such a plea, its jurisdiction being undoubted. It was no unusual thing for questions of foreign law to arise in the course of a cause; but even if that were a good reason for sending parties to another forum, it did not exist here, the questions raised by the pleas being not questions of the municipal law of America, but of international law, as to which this Court was as well qualified to judge as any other. Moreover the defender, while maintaining the plea of *non conveniens forum*, had entirely failed to show what was the proper forum. The plea had never been sustained unless another competent forum was condescended on.

Susp.—NORTH BRITISH RAILWAY *v.* GREIG.—*March* 20.

(Heard before seven Judges.)

Poor—Assessment—Valuation—Railway—17 *&* 18 *Vict.*, *c.* 91.

The railway company claimed exemption from poors-rate alleged to be due by them for the refreshment-rooms, cab-stands, and book-stalls, at the terminus in Edinburgh. The Company contended that these subjects were included in the valuation made by the Assessor of Railways and Canals, and that they paid rates for them as part of their undertaking, and were not bound to pay separate rates for them because let to tenants.

Lord Curriehill, Lord Benholme, and Lord Cowan held that the conditions of lease of the refreshment-rooms had not the effect of making the apartments cease to be part of the station, and as such part of the undertaking. The company had expressly devoted the apartments to the use of its passengers, who were even secured in the exclusive use, the lessee not being entitled to allow any others besides passengers to intrude, and having reserved power to control the lessee and limited the prices to be charged, in their interest. Their Lordships held that the cab-stand and book-stalls were in the same position, being integral parts of the station.

Lord Neaves, with whom the Lords President, Justice-Clerk and Ardmillan concurred, said that by the Valuation Act, 17 and 18 Vict., c. 91, there were two modes of valuation according to the nature of the subjects, and it was often important to determine whether a particular subject should be valued separately, or held to be an adjunct of a railway or canal, so as to fall within the province of the special assessor. Any subject excluded from the ordinary valution must, in the first place, belong to the railway company; and, in the second place, must form part of the undertaking. It was not enough that subjects belong or lie contiguous to the railway; but it was their character and uses that determined the manner of their assessment. An inn, even within a railway station, would not be held part of the undertaking. A waiting-room, again, would be regarded as part of the railway undertaking. To which of these two classes was a refreshment-room to be assigned? It was not held by the railway company but by a tenant. Was there here a true tenancy in the legal sense? There was proof that the relation of landlord and tenant subsisted. The occupant was not a mere servant of the company, handing over the profits to them, dismissible at a moment's notice, subject to his claim of damages. The tenant in the present case could enforce his right of possession till the end of the term in the agreement. The case therefore came under the category of an inn. Again, the apartments were let for the purpose of carrying on a separate trade. Their Lordships doubted whether a railway company could on a large scale legally carry on such a business. Probably difficulty would be found in getting a license. As to the cab-stands and book-stalls, their Lordships were of a different opinion. In them there was not a proper tenancy, or a proper right of tenancy. There was only an exclusive privilege of supplying passengers using the company's premises with books and cabs. No permanent erection was let by the company (the lessee of the book-stalls having only the right to erect a temporary building), and the only right in regard to them was a right of access granted by the railway company.

There was thus a majority of four to three in favour of assessing the refreshment-rooms separately, and the Court was unanimous in holding that the cab-stand and book-stalls were part of the Company's undertaking, and fell under the valuation of the Assessor of Railways and Canals.

M.P.—Bell's Trustees *v.* Lowson and Flowerdew.—*March* 20.

Succession—Testamentary Writings.

Miss Bell conveyed her estate to trustees, reserving her liferent and power to alter even on deathbed. After her death four holograph papers were found in her repositories, written on separate sheets of letter-paper. They all bequeathed legacies to various persons or institutions, who were claimants in this process of multiplepoinding. In the first writing, after the truster's signature, were the words, "This is to be handed to Mr Reid to be added to my settlement." Mr Reid had prepared the trust-deed. The bequest of legacy in the second was preceded by the words, "To be handed to Mr Reid; a codicil to my deed. Should I be taken away suddenly, my trustees would act upon it the same as if it were written as a codicil to my settlement." The third and fourth writings, with unimportant exceptions, consisted only of lists of names and sums attached to them. A letter was admitted to have been written by Miss Bell to her agent, in the following terms:—"Miss Bell presents respectful compliments to Mr Thomson. She begs to acquaint him that she will be much disappointed if her late brother's matter is not completely settled by the term of Whitsunday, as she intends to make some alterations in her deed, and cannot do it until she knows what part of her brother's property falls to her share." It appeared from the proof which was led, that the testator had retained the trust-deed in her own possession from its completion by her man of business till her death; that it was found in a locked drawer in which she kept papers; that the four writings in question were found alongside of it; that there were also in the drawer other papers—such as deposit-receipts and certificates of railway shares, as well as documents of no value, including two earlier and superseded settlements; and that the four writings, though they were lying beside the trust-deed, were not wrapped up in it. The trust-deed was dated September 1853; the first writing in question, 17th March 1854; the second, 29th April 1856; the third, 20th February 1862; and the fourth, 20th March 1862. The testatrix's brother Samuel, who was to be liferenter of the whole estate conveyed by the trust-deed, had died in 1860.

The Lord Ordinary (Ormidale) held all the papers to be testamentary. The Court altered, and (Lord Benholme dissenting) held the second only to be a testamentary writing, and the other three to be ineffectual. The testatrix intended the second paper to be acted on if a certain event happened; but it was still to be added as a codicil to the will. It was to be testamentary only in a certain event. Was that condition purified? Where a paper had once obtained the character of a testamentary paper, it was a very strong thing to say that it was deprived of that character by the mere survivance of the testator for an indefinite time. The condition should be construed liberally, so as to mean, "Should I be taken away before carrying out the purpose I have indicated, of having these additions formally made to my will." The addition of this condition to the second paper clearly showed that the first was not testamentary. The first two papers depended on internal evidence. The facts in evidence were of some importance with regard to the other two; because they showed a change of circumstances which led Miss Bell to think of altering the whole plan of the original settlement. Then, in these two writings, there was almost nothing but a list of names and sums applicable to them. The other two papers were very good instructions to a man of business; but as to the two latter, no man in his senses could add to or alter a settlement on their authority alone. There was nothing like an expression of purpose in them. They were mere "studies for codicils."

BAILLIE v. HAY.—*March* 20.

Ferry—Burgh—Assessment.

The pursuer's estate of Redcastle lies entirely on the north side of the Beauly Firth; and under the same title he holds by Crown grant the ferry of Kessock. In order to enable him to exercise the right of ferry, he built piers on both shores. He brought this action to have it declared that he and his tacksmen were not liable to assessment, under the Inverness Burgh Act 1847, in respect of the pier on the south side, a structure of considerable extent, built below high-water mark, and as to some part of it, below low-water mark. The soil was not the property of the pursuer; but the Crown had not interfered to prevent the building of the pier.

The Lord Justice-Clerk observed, that the effect of the acquiescence of the Crown was not to create in Colonel Baillie any right of property in the ground on which the pier was built. Neither was there any property in the structure, except that, being proprietor of the ferry, and the pier being an adjunct of the ferry, he had a certain right in it as being necessary to the convenient use of that incorporeal right. If it should at any time happen that the pier were dissociated from the right of ferry, it would in no sense at all belong to Colonel Baillie. Every stone of it would be the property of the Crown. By the Burgh Act the Commissioners were authorised to assess for police purposes all lands, &c., and heritages of every description situated within the Parliamentary boundaries, and valued at more than £4. The 35th section also authorises assessments on tenants for lighting, and other purposes. His Lordship would have had great doubt whether the Act would comprehend such an incorporeal right as a ferry. That question did not require to be solved directly; but it was of consequence to observe that the ferry would not be included in the terms of the Act. Now, the pier being simply an adjunct, and inseparable from it so far as Colonel Baillie's right was concerned, the question was—Whether it could be made the subject of assessment as to that part of it between high and low-water mark, which was all that was within the boundaries defined in the Act? His Lordship thought a ferry was a highway as much as a road, and a road on land was an incorporeal right also. For the trustees are not proprietors of the soil, but are merely entitled to keep up the road on the surface of the ground for the use of the lieges. Apart from express legislation, it was difficult to see on what grounds a highway across the sea could be a proper subject of assessment, if a highway on land is not. If it was not easy to say the ferry could be assessed, how was it possible to assess what was only an adjunct of the ferry? Colonel Baillie could not use the pier for any purpose whatever but for the ferry, and he might be restrained if he went beyond that right. A ferry in a question of this kind was undistinguishable from a bridge, which forms part of a road. A bridge was not assessable, simply because it was inseparable from that aggregate of which it forms a part. Rights of ferry sometimes change their character. It might come to pass, if the firth were somewhat narrower, that this ferry should be superseded by a bridge, as was the case in *Cumming* v. *Smollett* (14 D. 885). There a proprietor of the ferry built a bridge, which came to be part of a turnpike-road, and he levied a pontage, which was sustained by this Court as a perfectly legal charge. There was no distinction between the pier here and the piers of a bridge.

The other Judges concurred; and the interlocutor of the Lord Ordinary was reversed, the Court holding the pier as well as the ferry not liable to assessment.

HOUSE OF LORDS.

Lord-Advocate, v. M'Neill.—*March* 23.

Revenue—Inventory-Duty—Bill—Donation—Proof—Onus.

(In Court of Session, Feb. 6, 1864, 2 Macph. 626.)

This was an appeal in an action for inventory duty on the estate of Mrs Margaret M'Neill, who died in 1844. She had in 1838 lent her son, Lachlan M'Neill, £6000, taking as security his acceptance of a bill of exchange payable one day after date, drawn by her. This bill she afterwards endorsed to her son Dugald M'Neill. After the death of Lachlan, the Crown made a claim against Dugald, who was executor both of his mother and of Lachlan, for inventory duty on the L.6000, treating it as the property of Mrs M'Neill. The question was whether that amount had been a donation to Dugald, or whether it was held in trust by him for the mother; if the former, no duty was payable; if the latter, it was. On the one side, it was alleged that the indorsement of the bill to Dugald amounted to a donation out and out, and therefore, it being no longer included in the estate of his mother, that estate was not liable to the duty in respect of it. On the other hand, the Inland Revenue contended that the indorsement of the bill was a mere colour or blind, and that Mrs M'Neill still retained control over the money, and received the interest.

The Lord Ordinary (Ormidale) held the respondent liable in duty. The First Division, however, recalled that interlocutor, Lord Deas dissenting.

The Lord Chancellor said there were cross actions—one by the respondent, Dugald M'Neill, and one by the Lord Advocate, on behalf of the Inland Revenue. It was, however, admitted that both cases depended on the question whether the L.6000 did or did not form part of the estate of Mrs M'Neill at the time of her death. That Mrs M'Neill once was possessed of this sum of money was not disputed; and that she had specially indorsed the bill to her son, the respondent, was also admitted. But the mere fact of writing on the back of a bill an indorsement is not sufficient to transfer the contents or the property in the bill. It must also have been delivered; for, until it was delivered, the property in the bill remained unchanged. The fact of indorsement was, no doubt, *prima facie* evidence of delivery; and if there had been no other evidence except the production of the bill, it might be sufficient. But in the present case the respondent had failed to prove that he was ever in possession of the bill during the lifetime of his mother; and the fact that since her death he has been in possession of it proves nothing, because, he being executor of his mother, he may have acquired it in that capacity. The *onus* was thus shifted, and the respondent was bound to prove that he had had the bill before her death. The original bill had been produced, and it contained on the back several markings of receipt of interest for seven years. Those endorsements would have been cogent evidence of his possession, if it could have been proved that they were made at the date which they bear. But there was no evidence whatever when the endorsements were written; and from their appearance their Lordships were satisfied they had been all written at one time, and probably were so written after the death of the mother, to settle some accounts between the survivors. Another remarkable thing was, that those indorsements stated that the interest was paid on the very day it became due for seven years running, though one of these days was Sunday. It was hardly credible that such could have been the true day of each receipt. If the respondent had been able to show that he had been in possession of the bill during his mother's life, then the question would have arisen, whether the fact of her so indorsing it, and of his holding it, amounted to evidence of a donation out-and-out, or merely of his being a trustee. In many cases, a transfer without consideration has been held not to alter the property in the thing transferred. Probably, as this was a negotiable instrument, the presumption of donation might have been more easily made than it would be as regards other property; but here there was no reliable evidence that the respondent had ever got delivery of the bill in his mother's lifetime.

Lord Chelmsford.—The first thing was, to ascertain on whom was the *onus* of proving the donation. Assuming the bill to have been properly indorsed by his mother, the respondent was bound also to prove delivery of the bill to him before her death. If he had done so, no further proof would have been required; but he gave no evidence whatever of having been in possession of the bill before the death of his mother. His sister never saw or heard of the bill. The indorsements of interest seemed to have been all written at one time. In these circumstances it was not unreasonable to infer that he had obtained possession of it only as executor of his mother. Then, one must consider the improbability of his having got the bill otherwise. The L.6000 formed the whole of the mother's property. She had by will bequeathed all her property to him, but subject to his paying his sister Bella L.1300; and it was not likely the mother would give away the only fund for making good that legacy. Then again, it seems, the mother kept her documents in a box; and it was not till after her death that this box was given to the respondent, and it no doubt contained the bill. Lord Kingsdown concurred. Reversed.

TEIND COURT.

App.—Cowan *v.* Cook, &c.—*Feb.* 28.

Valuation — Approbation — Dereliction.

In a process of approbation of a sub-valuation made in 1629—Held that the mere lapse of time was no objection to the approval of the valuation, for there was no prescription in matters of this kind. An augmentation having been made in 1793, and a locality fixed in January or February 1800, and no steps taken till now to obtain an approbation of the sub-valuation, circumstances in which the plea of dereliction was not sustained. Though the minority of a heritor, alleged to have abandoned his valuation, was not, as in prescription, a bar, it was a circumstance to be taken into account in the case.. Valuation approved, but without expenses against the defender.

ENGLISH CASES.

Railway Carriers (*Injunction*).—After the judgment in the action between the same parties, the defendants made no change in their charges, and plaintiff commenced another action against them indorsing the writ with notice that he should apply for a writ of injunction. He accordingly moved for an injunction to restrain defendants from charging him for the carriage of his goods otherwise than equally with all other persons, and at the same rate as all other goods of like description under the like circumstances. Held, that as plaintiff had an adequate remedy by action, and as there would be no appeal from the decision of the Court if an injunction were granted, and as an injunction might be applied for in a Court of Equity, or under the 17 & 18 Vict. c. 31 (the Railway and Canal Traffic Act), in the Court of Common Pleas, this Court would not grant the injunction even if it had the power to do so. And, semble, the grievance complained of by plaintiff was not a "repetition or continuance of a breach of contract or other injury," within the meaning of section 79 of the Common Law Procedure Act, 1854.—*Sutton* v. *the South-Eastern Railway Co.*, 35 L. J., Ex. 38, 1 Law Rep. Ex. 32.

Charter-Party (*General Average.*)—In a severe storm which plaintiffs' vessel encountered, her deck cargo of timber, which was lawfully stowed on deck according to the terms of the charter-party between plaintiffs and defendant (the charterer), broke adrift, and knocked against the pumps, so that the captain was compelled, in order that the crew might work the pumps and to prevent damage to the bulwarks and pumps, and for the safety of the ship and all on board, to throw a portion of such cargo overboard. *Held*, that such jettison was the subject of a general average contribution, from plaintiffs to defendant, it being both voluntary and to save all from the danger caused by the storm, which was common to the whole adventure. —(*Johnston* v. *Chapman*, 35 L. J., C. P. 23.)

Statute of Frauds (*Sale.*)—Letters passing between a principal purchaser and his agent to purchase goods, if they contain the terms of the contract, are a sufficient memorandum within the 17th section of the Statute of Frauds, to support an action by the vendor for the price.—*Gibson* v. *Holland*, 35 L. J., C. P.

Statute of Frauds.—An agreement to cash bills given on account of the price of goods to be supplied to a third person is an undertaking under the fourth section, and must be in writing. A contract to give a guarantee must be in writing as much as a guarantee itself.—(*Mallet* v. *Bateman*, Ex. Ch. 35 L. J.C. P.)

Industrial and Provident Societies Act, 1862.—Under the 6th section of 25 & 26 Vict. c. 87, which enacts, that "the certificate of registration under that act shall vest in the society all the property that may at the time be vested in any person in trust for the society." Held, that an action on a bond to trustees of an industrial society before the act, may, after registration under the act, be brought in the name of the newly-incorporated body.—(*The Queenshead Industrial Society* (*Limited*) v. *Pickles*, 35 L. J., 1 Law Rep., Ex. 1.)

Master and Servant (*Common employment*).—The rule which exempts a master from liability to his servant for injury arising from the negligence of a fellow servant employed with him for a common object, is not confined to a common immediate object, but embraces all cases where the "risk of injury from the negligence of the one is so much a natural and necessary consequence of the employment which the other accepts that it must be included in the risks which are to considered in his wages." A carpenter employed in a railway company and engaged in painting a shed at their station, is so necessarily brought into contact with the traffic of the line that risk of injury from the carelessness of porters employed to turn carriages on the turn-tables on the line is naturally incident to such an employment, and within the rule as to common employment. —(*Morgan* v. *the Vale of Neath Rail Co.*, Ex. Ch, 35 L. J.. Q. B.)

Merchant Shipping Amendment Act, 1862 (*Section* 67).—Sixty-five pipes of lemon juice were shipped on board defendant's ship to London, under two bills of lading, drawn to order, and containing the following clause: "Simultaneously with the ship being ready to unload the goods, or any part thereof, the consignee is hereby bound to be ready to receive the same from the ship's side; . . . . . and in default thereof, the master or agent of the ship is hereby authorized to enter the said goods at the Custom House, and land, warehouse, or place them in lighter, at the risk and expense of the said consignee." The ship arrived in London, and plaintiff, the consignee, was not ready till fifteen pipes had been landed; being then ready, he demanded delivery of the residue, but the master (though no additional expense would have been incurred) refused to deliver to him, and landed the residue at his expense, claiming a right so to do as he was not ready before any goods were landed. Held, that plaintiff was entitled to have the résidue delivered to him, both on the construction of the contract, and of stat. 25 & 26 Vict. c. 63. s. 67, sub-section 5.—*Willson* v. *the London, Italian and Adriatic Steam Navigation Company* (*Limited*), 35 L. J., C. P. 9.

Patents.—Letters patent were granted to W. for an alleged invention of fishes and fish joints, for connecting the ends of rails. The fishes were made of iron, with a groove on the outer surface, for preventing the square heads of the bolts passing through them and the rail from turning round, and also for procuring greater strength with an equal weight of metal. Grooved iron plates with bolts let into the grooves, had been previously used for fastening timbers placed vertically upon one another, or placed horizontally side by side. In one case of a bridge, a channelled plate with bolts had been used for fishing a scarf-joint where the ends of two timbers met together. Held, that there was no novelty in the patent, and therefore that it was bad; that the supposed invention had been in use previously to the date of the patent, not only in the case of the bridge, but for other purposes, and that a patent could not be upheld for the mere application of well-known mechanical contrivance to a purpose which was analogous to the manner or to the purpose in or to which it had been hitherto notoriously used or applied.—*Harwood (executor of Charles Wild, deceased), the Great Northern Rail. Co.* (House of Lords), 35 L. J., Q. B.

Principal and Agent.—The principal in a business who holds out an agent as ostensible principal, and carries on the business under the management, and in name of such agent, is bound by all acts and contracts of the agent incidental to the ordinary conduct of the business, and such liability to the public cannot be restricted by any private arrangement.—*Edmunds* v. *Bushell*, 35 L. J., Q. B. 20.

Railway (*Negligence.*)—Defendants' railway crossed a footpath on the level close to a station. At a turnstile for foot passengers, some few yards from the line, the view of the line was very confined, but at the point where a passenger would step on to the line, there was a clear view of 300 yards in each direction. A woman stepped on to the line immediately after a train had passed in one direction, and was knocked down and killed by another train coming in the opposite direction on the further line of rail. At least thirty-six trains passed the spot every day. There were caution-boards near the crossing, but no person was stationed there by the company to warn passengers of trains being due. A person who was near the spot while the deceased was waiting for the first train to pass, called out to warn her that another train was coming, which she could not see for the passing train, but she did not hear. *Held*, that there was nothing to shew that the company were guilty of negligence in not stationing a watchman at the crossing to warn people, or in not taking any other special precaution; and that they were not liable in an action brought by the husband of the deceased.—*Stubley* v. *the London and North-Western Rail. Co.*, 35 L. J., Ex. 3: 1 Law Rep. Ex. 13. Defendants' railway crossed a highway on a level close to a station. On each side were gates across the carriageway, and swing gates for foot passengers. By defendants' rules and regulations the carriage gates were always to be kept closed across the carriageway, except when opened to allow carriages to cross, and they were never to be opened until the gateman had seen that no train was due or in sight. A foot passenger crossing the railway was killed by an express train which passed the station without stopping. There was no servant of defendants at the gate or on the platform. The carriage gate on the side from which the deceased came was seen, after the accident, to be partly open. It had been seen shut half an hour previously, and there was no evidence of how it came to be open, or whether the deceased came through the carriage gate or through the turnstile. The train was four minutes overdue. There was a curve in the line, and the train would not be visible to a person at the gate till it came within 600 yards. The deceased was deaf. He was in the habit of coming to the station, and knew the times of the train. *Held*, in an action brought by the executors of the deceased, that a foot passenger who found the carriage gate open would be led to believe that no train was due, and that upon the whole case there was some evidence of negligence to be left to the jury.—*Stapley* v. *the London, Brighton, and South Coast Rail. Co.*, 35 L. J., 1 Law Rep. Ex. 21: Ex. 7.

WILL (*Vesting.*)—A., by will, gave an estate to his daughter H. during her life, and after her death to her sons in tail successively; and in default of such issue to his son J., in fee. A subsequent codicil, after reciting that he had devised the reversion in fee in this estate to his son J., and also that he had devised other estates to trustees for his use until he should attain twenty-one, and thereupon to him in fee for ever, declared his will to be, that in case his said son should die without leaving lawful issue of his body living at his decease, and before the said several estates should become vested in him by virtue of the said several limitations aforesaid, the estates should go over. J. survived the testator, attained twenty-five, and died without children. H. died unmarried many years after J. On the question, who was entitled on the death of H. to her estates, it was held, that the word "vested" in the codicil meant vested interest, and not vested in possession; consequently, that on the testator's death the estates vested at once in interest in J., subject to the estates of H. and her issue; and, therefore, on H.'s death without issue, passed to J.'s devisees.—(*Richardson* v. *Power*, Ex. Ch., 35 L. J., C.P. 44.)

BIGAMY.—It was proved that the prisoner and his wife had lived apart for seven years, when the prisoner married again. There was no evidence of the prisoner's knowledge of the existence of his first wife at that time. The prisoner was convicted; and it was held, the burthen of proof that he did not know that his wife was alive was not on the prisoner, and that the conviction could not be sustained. —(*R.* v. *Curgerwen*, 35 L. J., Mag. Ca. 58, 1 Law Rep. C. C. 1.)

POOR-RATE (*Exemption for public purposes*).—The occupation of property liable to be rated under the first section of the 43 Eliz. c. 2, is an occupation yielding a net annual value, that is to say, a clear rent over and above the probable average annual cost of the repairs, insurance and other expenses, if any, necessary to maintain the property in a state to command such rent, and it is not necessary that the occupation should be beneficial to the occupier; so that trustees, who are, in law, the tenants and occupiers of valuable property upon trust for charitable purposes, such as hospitals or lunatic asylums, are rateable, notwithstanding that the buildings are actually occupied by paupers who are sick or insane. The only occupiers exempt from the operation of the act are the Sovereign, because he is not named in the statute, and the direct and immediate servants of the Crown, whose occupation is the occupation of the Crown itself; and the only ground of exemption from the statute is that which is furnished by the above rule. And, consequently, when property yielding a rent above what is required for its maintenance is sought to be exempted on the ground that it is occupied by bare trustees for public purposes, the public purposes must be such as are required and created by the Government of the country, and are therefore to be deemed part of the use and service of the country. (*Jones* v. *the Mersey Docks and Harbour Board; the Mersey Docks and Harbour Board* v. *Cameron* (House of Lords), 35 L. J., Mag. Ca. 1.)

COURT OF SESSION.

FIRST DIVISION.

S. and J. Duff, Rossi, & Coy. and John Ross v. Kippen and Anderson.

May 15th.

Interdict—Proof.

The complainers in this case, who are engineers and boilermakers in Glasgow, seek to have the respondents interdicted from selling or removing the moveable machinery, apparatus, &c., at present within the premises No. 289 Garscube Road, Glasgow, and known as the Oakbank Engine Works. The alleged ground of the application for interdict is that the said moveables belong to the complainers, although the respondents hold an *ex facie* absolute conveyance thereto from the complainers' author, the right actually given by that conveyance being alleged to have been granted, merely in security. The respondents aver that they acquired an absolute right to the property in question by the said conveyance.

The Lord Ordinary (Barcaple) held that it was incompetent for the complainers to prove that the *ex facie* absolute conveyance to the respondents was granted merely in security, otherwise than by the writ or oath of the respondents.

The complainers having reclaimed,

The Court adhered to the Lord Ordinary's interlocutor.

The Breadalbane Case.—*May 16th.*

Declinature of a Judge.

The whole Court met in this Division to-day at 11 o'clock, for the purpose of disposing of Lord Kinloch's proposed declinature to take part in the decision of this case.

Lord Kinloch stated that he proposed to decline to take part in the decision of this case—(1) on the ground that the advocator (Boreland) was his nephew by affinity, being the son of his wife's sister, and (2) on the ground that the advocator's (Boreland) mandatory in the case was his brother-in-law, General Campbell, who was his wife's brother. The latter, his lordship said, had been sustained as a ground for the declinature of a judge in the case of Ommaney, to which he referred the Court.

The Lord President said he was of opinion the declinature of Lord Kinloch ought to be sustained. As the latter reason assigned by his lordship was clearly a good ground for his declining—on the authority of the case of Ommaney—it was unnecessary to decide whether the former alone would have been sufficient.

All the other Judges concurred.

The Glebe Sugar Refining Company v. Lusk.—*May 17th.*

Damages—Slander.

This was an action of damages at the instance of the above company, which carries on business at Greenock, and Provost Grieve, and others, the partners thereof, as individuals. The defender, Mr. Lusk, wholesale grocer and sugar-broker in Greenock, was charged with having, in the course of conversation in the Reading-room of Greenock, on the evening of the 14th November, the day of the last municipal election, characterised the proceedings of the Glebe Sugar Company in the matter of Ker Street as "most infamous." Mr Lusk explains on record what was the Ker Street business which gave rise to the observation. He says that in 1862, when the glebe was for sale, the authorities were thinking of buying it in order to extend Ker Street into East Clyde Street, so as to provide an improved access to Albert Harbour; but Messrs M'Kirdy & Steele, having learned that this was their only object, entered into an agreement with the Greenock Harbour and Police Trustees, whereby they were to be allowed to purchase the property on condition of conveying to the town enough to make the street proposed. The glebe was accordingly bought by M'Kirdy & Steele, and steps were taken in implement of the arrangement to form the new street; but when, in 1865, the property passed from M'Kirdy & Steele to the Glebe Company, they refused to implement the arrangement with the town, on the ground that being singular successors, and a formal disposition having never been executed in favour of the town, they were not bound by it. The result was that the Glebe Company, having claimed the *solum* of the new street, got £20,000 from the Greenock and Ayrshire Railway Company for the ground they required for their undertaking—the purchase from M'Kirdy & Steele having only cost them a few months previously about £3000. It seems that the Glebe Company is composed of Provost Grieve and others who took an active part in carrying through the arrangement with M'Kirdy & Steele, under which the town was to have got access to the Albert Harbour; and the subject having imparted a lively interest to the last municipal election, Mr Lusk says that he disapproved of the conduct of the defenders in repudiating obligations which they themselves, as magistrates, had imposed on their predecessors, or the owners of the premises in question; but he pleads that the remark in question was justified, or at least did not exceed the limits of fair comment on the conduct of public men.

The case having come before this Division for the adjustment of issues, the pursuers intimated that they did not ask damages as individuals for the wrong done to them individually, but only as a company. The Court then, on the motion of the defenders, dismissed the action so far as it was laid at the instance of the pursuers as individuals, and adjusted an issue for the trial of the cause, in which the question was put, Whether the slander was of and concerning the company, and represented that the company had been guilty of dishonourable and dishonest conduct?

Laing *v.* Nixon.—*May* 18.

Damages—Relevancy.

The pursuer in this action was John Laing, manufacturer in Hawick, and the defender William Nixon, sole partner of the firm of John Nixon & Sons, hosiery yarn spinners at Lynnwood, near Hawick. The pursuer has been in the habit of making large purchases of yarn from Nixon & Son, for a number of years previous to 1864, at prices stated in the price-lists issued by the firm. The pursuer now alleged that these price-lists were false and fraudulent, having been prepared and issued by the defender as showing the genuine and true prices at which he was selling his goods, while he well knew and concealed from the pursuer that they were false, and calculated to mislead the pursuer and others. The pursuer further alleged that the defender had been in the practice of granting abatements, and selling hosiery yarns to various of his customers, rivals of the pursuer in trade, at prices much lower than those in his price-lists, in consequence of which these parties were enabled to undersell the pursuer, who was thus forced to curtail, and subsequently to abandon his business. The pursuer claimed damages to the amount of £10,000, and proposed an issue, whether he had been induced to purchase yarns from the defender, at the prices specified in the defender's price-lists, by false and fraudulent representation on the part of the defender, that these were the fixed prices charged to all customers, to the pursuer's loss, injury, and damage.

The defender objected to the issue, and also to the relevancy of the action.

The Lord Ordinary (Barcaple) reported the cause. His Lordship indicated an opinion that the ground of action, as put in the proposed issue, was not relevant. It was not said that the pursuer had paid too high a price for the yarns; it followed that a verdict for the pursuer would not impart that the purchases were in themselves injurious to him, and yet the wrong for which damage was sought consisted in inducing him to make these purchases. If the contract was not hurtful, there was no damage done, and there could, therefore, be no reparation. Nor was this issue warranted by the case of the pursuer on record, which was but an alleged abatement given to other customers. But further, his lordship doubted whether this was a relevant case for an issue of a different kind. The essential element of damage here was the abatement to other customers, which was a wrong only on the footing of breach of contract, which was not in the present case. The fact that the other purchasers undersold the pursuer appeared likewise to be a material part of the pursuer's case; but if they had proposed to value large profits rather than undersell the pursuer, the pursuer would have suffered no loss for the abatements. The damage suffered by the pursuer was thus only consequential, and would not sustain the action.

A new issue was lodged for the pursuer, whether the pursuer made the purchases by false and fraudulent representations on the part of the defender, that the prices in the price-list were the fixed prices charged to all customers; and whether the defender granted abatements to certain parties in consequence of which they were enabled to undersell the pursuer; but the Court sustained the objections by the defender to the relevancy of the action, and dismissed the case.

Paterson *v.* Somers.—*May* 19.

Defamation—Damages—Expenses.

The pursuer in this case, which was an action of damages for defamation at the instance of Dr. Paterson, against the proprietor of the Glasgow *Morning Journal*, moved the Court to apply the verdict, and for expenses. The defender contended that the verdict, which was for one farthing of damages, was not one which ought to carry expenses, especially as the defender had in his defence disclaimed all intention of making any imputation against Dr. Paterson's moral character. The Court, however, held that there was nothing to take the case out of the general rule, that such a verdict as this carries expenses. On the contrary, some things occurred in the evidence—especially in the evidence of the writer of that particular article—which made it very clear that the pursuer was entitled to go to a jury with this case. The Court applied the verdict with expenses.

SECOND DIVISION.

Ritchie's Trustees v. Craig's Trustees.—*May* 15.

Legitim—Election—Homologation—Trustees.

The antenuptial marriage contract trustees of Mr and Mrs Ritchie brought this action of count and reckoning against the trustees of Mr Craig, Mrs Ritchie's father, to recover legitim alleged to have been due to Mrs Ritchie in her own right, and in right of her deceased brother. Mr Craig's settlement conferred an alimentary liferent of his whole estate on his widow, burdening the liferent with the education and maintenance of his children. The fee was given to the children, their shares not to vest till the mother's death. The trustees entered on office at Mr Craig's death in 1844, but, although appointed tutors and curators to the children, made up no inventories under the Act 1672. In 1859 Mrs Ritchie was married to Mr Ritchie, her mother being a party to the antenuptial contract, and conveying thereby an annuity of £250 to her daughter, Mr Ritchie and the children of the marriage, successively. Mrs Ritchie made over her whole property to her husband. She died in minority soon after her marriage. The defenders stated that they had accepted office both as trustees and as tutors and curators, and in the latter capacity had elected for the children to take the provision in the settlement as being more for their advantage than the legitim, which they averred amounted at the truster's death to £40 a-year to each child. The pursuers claimed £5000 as the amount of legitim for the two children. The defenders proposed issues of election, and of homologation by Mr and Mrs Ritchie of the settlement of her father. The pursuers contended that there were no relevant averments to entitle them to such issues.

The Lord Justice-Clerk said—The real question was, whether the defenders had stated any relevant defence. The settlement of Mr Craig gave a total liferent to his widow, and the fee to the children only if they survived their mother. The children were in pupillarity at their father's death, and had right to legitim independently of the provision in their father's settlement; and that claim would not have excluded their provision under the settlement, because it does not say that the contingent gifts of the settlement were in full of legitim. In that state of matters, it was doubtful whether any guardian could renounce legitim for children. The election might be necessary in certain circumstances; but there was no ground of any such necessity here. There was no case of urgency which required the trustees to make the election which it is said they did. Further, assuming the trustees had a power to elect, it was clear they did not do it. They did not accept, in terms of the Act of Parliament, by making up inventories and complying with other solemnities. Now, nothing having been done by the defenders to enter on their office, how could they make the election? A mere opinion existing in their minds that the election of the settlement provisions would be good for the children, could hardly be accepted as an equivalent to the discharge of the office of tutor in so delicate a matter as making an election. In regard to what occurred on Mrs Ritchie's marriage, it is said that in the marriage-contract Mrs Craig made a handsome provision, and that Mrs Ritchie and her husband could not take this without homologating the settlement of Mr Craig. That depended on whether they knew their legal rights. His Lordship's impression was that all parties were unaware of their legal rights; and in these circumstances it was impossible to hold the acceptance by the daughter of a free gift from the mother as a renunciation of them.

The other Judges concurred; and the defences were repelled, and the case remitted to the Lord Ordinary.

Gillespie v. Young.—*May* 18.

Damages—Revelancy—Consequential.

In this action Mrs Honyman Gillespie, the heiress of entail in possession of the estate of Torbanehill, with concurrence of her husband, sued Mr Young, and two firms of manufacturing chemists in which he was a partner, for £23,900 of damages. Torbanehill estate contains a seam of a valuable mineral substance commonly called the Torbanehill mineral. It is of great value from yielding a large quantity of paraffine oil by the process of destructive distillation. The defender obtained in 1850 a patent giving him the exclusive right to manufacture paraffine oil from bituminous coal. He advertised that this patent included the manufacture of oil from the pursuer's mineral, and threatened and instituted legal proceedings against several manufacturers who had purchased Torbanehill mineral for distillation into paraffine. The pursuers maintain that their mineral is a bituminous *shale* or schist, and not a coal, and therefore that the patent did not extend to it; and in 1860 they intimated to the defenders that their representations were unfounded, and that they would be held liable in damages if they persisted in them. The defenders continued to claim by advertisement and otherwise a monopoly of the right to manufacture the Torbanehill mineral, and began to issue licenses to other manufacturers, granting them the privilege of manufacturing it. The pursuers received a lordship from their mineral tenants of one-seventh of the actual output. They aver that the defenders diminished the marketable value of that portion of the pursuer's excavated mineral which came into their own hands as lordship from their tenants; partly in so far as persons were deterred altogether from purchasing it, and partly in so far as those who did purchase offered a smaller price than they would have given but for the proceedings complained of. The defenders are alleged to have caused this injury by falsely, fraudulently, and maliciously representing that their patent comprehended the manufacture of paraffine oil from the pursuer's mineral, so that it could not therefore be legally carried on without a licence from them, for which they charged a tax of so much per ton of the mineral manufactured, and it is alleged that they thus compelled the persons who purchased from the pursuer to pay that tax or licence, and thereby diminished the price which they could afford to give for the mineral, and deterred others from purchasing it at all, by inducing the belief that they would be liable in damages for infringement of the patent.

The Lord Ordinary (Barcaple) held that the acts complained of did not in law constitute a good ground for claiming reparation. The pursuer reclaimed; and the Court adhered, holding that the alleged representations of the defenders that their patent gave them the exclusive right to manufacture paraffine oil from the Torbanehill mineral, did not amount to a legal wrong entitling the pursuer to reparation. The question whether these representations were well or ill founded depended on whether the Torbanehill mineral was a *shale* or a *coal*: and as that was truly a matter of opinion dependent on scientific classification, and one on which there was great dispute, and not a matter of fact in the ordinary sense of the term, the averments of the pursuers, that the defenders' representations were false, fraudulent, and malicious, were therefore quite inappropriate to the case disclosed. It was a matter of notoriety that scientific men were divided in opinion as to what class the mineral in question belonged. The Court further held that the damage claimed was eminently consequential damage, and therefore not recoverable in law, and depended on calculations which were very intricate and speculative in their nature. The effect of the defenders' representations on the shale market, from which the damage was said to have resulted, were purely matters of opinion, and belonged to the domain of political economy rather than of law.

HOUSE OF LORDS.

Lord Lovat v. Fraser.—*April 26.*

(In the Court of Session July 7, 1859, 21 D. 1154.)

Entail—Executor—Relief of Entailer's Debts against Substitute Heirs—Expenses.

The respondent, Archibald Fraser, of Abertarff, as executor of the late Archibald Fraser of Lovat, raised an action against himself and the heirs-substitute of entail of the lands of Abertarff seeking to have it declared that the lands of Abertarff were liable for the debts of the late Archibald Fraser, Esq., of Lovat, and for the expenses of litigation incident to the ascertainment of such debts. Archibald Fraser, of Lovat, had executed a number of deeds relating to the disposition of his property, both heritable and moveable, and in particular of these lands, one of which was found (1 Bell's App. 105) to constitute a valid obligation on the pursuer to execute an entail of the said lands, directing the fetters against himself. Various litigations arose between the appellant, Lord Lovat, the first substitute in the said entail, and the respondent, who was the grandson of the executor of Archibald Fraser. The respondent, or such executor, having paid debts to the amount of £6186, raised this action to make the amount a burden on the estate; and further claimed to be relieved, out of the estate, of a sum of £2791, as the expenses of litigation incurred by him *bona fide*, and beneficially for the appellants, the heirs of entail, in contesting certain claims for debts due by the entailer.

Lord Ordinary Anderson, in 1856, and Lord Ordinary Handyside, in 1855, found that the sum of £6186 was a burden on the estate, and superseded pronouncing decree for the amount till a certain discharge should be put in process; and as to the sum of £2791, the expenses of litigation, they held that the respondent was not entitled to decree for that amount. Both parties reclaimed; and the First Division recalled the interlocutor as to the £2791, and ordered parties to substantiate their respective averments in regard to it. The respondent then put in process the pleadings in the actions in respect of which the expenses were incurred; and Lord Ordinary Kinloch, in 1858, found the respondent entitled to charge the entailed land with the expenses of the litigation. The First Division recalled Lord Kinloch's last interlocutor, and instead of allowing £2791, allowed only £331, which was the sum incurred in costs by respondent to his own agent, in the only case in which he had been successful in reducing to a larger extent than the costs of litigation the claim made against the entailer. The rest of the costs, having been incurred by the respondent to his opponent in the litigation, was not allowed. Both parties appealed; but the Appeal Committee, in 1864, ordered Lord Lovat's appeal to be amended by striking out the part relating to the sum of £6186; so that that part of the appeal was now held incompetent on the part of Lord Lovat.

The Lord Chancellor (Cranworth) was in favour of Lord Lovat and his heirs. The expenses incurred by the executor in resisting litigations against the estate could not be treated as debts due by the truster or settler when a testator charged his debts upon his estate. There was no authority for stating that costs incurred in litigations, which were unjustly commenced against that estate, could be recovered by the executor as a charge on that estate. The law was not different in Scotland from what it would be in England. If the costs were improperly caused, the executors must recover them against those who commenced the litigation, but he cannot treat them as debts incurred by the testator. The case could not be put higher than if the executor had made some unfounded demand against a third party, and wholly failed; in which case it could not be disputed that the testator's estate would not be liable for the costs. It follows that the interlocutors up to the date of 1857, when the Inner House recalled part of Lord Anderson's interlocutors, ought to be affirmed, and the other part and the subsequent interlocutors ought to be reversed. Seeing that both sides were to some extent wrong, there would be no costs of the appeal.

Lord Chelmsford's mind had fluctuated considerably; but, upon the whole, he came to the same conclusion. It was immaterial whether the executor acted prudently or not, beneficially to the estate or not, in defending the actions brought against him as such executor. The debts incurred by the testator, no doubt, formed a charge on the estate, and all that was incident to and inseparable from such debts. But the costs of defending actions could not in any view be brought within the category.

Lord Kingsdown said that a difference of opinion had existed in the Court below, and he was sorry to say that that difference existed also among their lordships. He thought that the costs properly incurred by the respondent in the litigations, which were forced upon him, ought to be allowed to him, and therefore formed properly a charge on the estate. In that view, he thought the interlocutor of the Inner House ought to be affirmed.

Partly reversed, without costs.

MAGISTRATES OF GLASGOW AND OTHERS *v.* PATON AND OTHERS—*March.*

(In the Court of Teinds, July 6, 1864, 2 Macph. 1307.)

Church—Parish—Disjunction and Erection—7 *and* 8 *Vict.*, *c.* 44.

A process of disjunction and erection, *quoad sacra*, of the Chapel of Ease of Partick, in the parish of Govan, was raised by the managers of the chapel, with concurrence of the minister, against the University of Glasgow, as patron and titular; the minister and kirk-session of Govan; and the Presbytery of Glasgow. The 7 and 8 Vict., c. 34, sec. 3, enacts, "That it shall not be a valid objection to the competency of any process which shall be brought for disjoining or dividing a parish or parishes, and erecting a new kirk or kirks, that the consent of the heritors of a major part of the valuation of the parish to be disjoined or divided had not been given previous to such process having been brought into Court; and it shall be lawful for the Lords of Council and Session, before whom any such process shall have been brought, to appoint special intimation thereof to be made in such form and manner as the said Lords of Council and Session shall direct, to such of the heritors of the valuation of the parish as shall not have already either given their consent, or judicially stated their dissent, and to sist proceedings in such process for a definite time, for the purpose of allowing such heritors to state judicially their consent or their dissent; and such of them as shall not, within a time to be fixed by the said Lords of Council and Session, and to be specified in such intimation as aforesaid, judicially state their dissent, shall, in computing the statutory proportion of consents, be reckoned as consenting heritors." The Court, on 17th February 1864, appointed intimation of the process to be made from the precentors' desks in Govan and Partick Churches, immediately after the blessing in the forenoon service on the Sunday; and intimation also to be made once in the *Edinburgh Gazette* and *North British Advertiser*—all which intimations were to be made at least ten days before the process should be again moved in Court. The intimations were duly made on the 19th, 20th, and 21st February. The process was again moved on the 2d March, when condescendence and answers were ordered to be lodged. The Magistrates of Glasgow, as heritors, afterwards moved for leave to lodge a minute of dissent, on the ground that they had not received proper intimation, in terms of the statute. The Court held that the objection was very critical, and refused the motion.

The Magistrates of Glasgow, appellants, contended that the statute 7 and 8 Vict., was in its nature calculated to interfere with the rights of heritors; and its conditions should be rigorously fulfilled. Under the Act of 1707, the consent of three-fourths of the heritors was absolutely necessary to the commencement of a process of disjunction and erection; and the late statute merely made this change, that the consent of a major part of the heritors is now sufficient. In both respects, there was no change made in the mode of ascertaining the consents. The Court was bound, in its interlocutor, to specify a definite time, within which these consents were to be given; and it was a fatal objection that no such time was specified in this intimation. The notice given was too vague to be deemed by any one a peremptory notice. At the utmost, it was only a preliminary notice. It did not specify any fixed period from which the ten days could be calculated. By any computation that could be made, the ten days' notice could not have expired before the afternoon of the 2d March; yet the Court met that day at 11 A.M., and a motion was made in the cause. The respondents maintained that the practice of the last twenty years had been followed. It was plain that the words "special intimation" did not mean personal service of the notice, but must mean a kind of intimation which would be applicable to the case of populous parishes; and a notice published in a paper of extensive circulation might well satisfy such a description. In such a case, the day of publication was the date of intimation. Again, the intimation from the precentor's desk after forenoon service on Sunday was a usual mode in Scotland of publishing affecting the parishes. It was expressly ordered by the Court to be done in respect of the notices given to heritors under the Augmentation of Stipends Act.

The House took time to consider.

The Lord Chancellor (Cranworth) said,—The only question was, whether the heritors had had such notice given them as the Act directed. His Lordship thought they had not, because no time was specified within which they were to express their dissent. It was said that the time could have been discovered by reference to the dates of the notice. But that was a strange way of complying with a statute which directed not only special intimation to be made, but that the Court should sist proceedings for a definite time to allow dissent. The definite time ought to have been specified by the Court, and not left to be inferred from a comparison of the dates of other documents, and by reference to extrinsic circumstances. The time was left uncertain altogether, and therefore the interlocutor appealed against was wrong.

Lord Chelmsford differed, holding that there had been substantial compliance with the statute. A wide discretion was left to the Court, and the course followed was that which had existed since the passing of the Act. The form might have been more precise, but there could have been no difficulty in counting ten days from the publications.

Lord Kingsdown concurred with the Lord Chancellor.

Reversed.

Farquharson *v.* Byres.

(Not reported in Court of Session.)

Road—Servitude—Decree Arbitral.

The appellant, Mr Farquharson of Whitehouse, raised an action against Mr Byros of Tonley, a conterminous proprietor, seeking to have it declared that the defender had no right of commonty, or servitude, over the pursuer's lands, but merely had a right to a certain road therein; and secondly, that the defender as proprietor of a farm called Holes, had no right to use this road, and should be interdicted from so using it. Mr Farquharson's lands lay on the north of the Burn of Cattie or Everton Burn, which ran in a north-westerly course. On the south of the burn the defender had two farms, Holes on the east, and Edindurno on the west. Between Edindurno and Whitehouse a road had been in existence, which was a continuation of a road from Holes to Edindurno, but which, the appellant alleged, the owner or tenant of Holes had no right to use; though it is conceded the tenant of Edindurno has a right to use it. The tenant of Holes had latterly insisted on using the disputed road for the purposes of his farm, and the action was raised to prevent this use. The former owners of Whitehouse and Tonley in 1763, agreed to refer to an arbiter all claims, questions, controversies, and disputes betwixt them, and especially their rights to a piece of disputable ground between the road in question and the burn along which it ran. The award was that the laird of Tonley, and his tenants of Edindurno were to have the right and title to the road which was along the north bank of the burn, reserving always liberty to the laird of Whitehouse to water cattle without interruption at the burn, notwithstanding the aforesaid road, which is to be common to both. The meaning of this finding was said by the pursuer (appellant) to be, that he is the proprietor of the solum of the road, but that the respondent was to have a servitude over it, but for the tenants of Edindurno only. Since the date of the decreet-arbitral, the use of the road had been confined to the tenants of Edindurno, though for a great part of the time Holes was in the hands of the same tenant as Edindurno, who had used the road indiscriminately for both farms. But the pursuer contended this was by sufferance, so far as Holes was concerned, and the undisputed use had not been for forty years, nor had it been used as of right. The Court of Session decided that the road was common property, and moreover, that there had been forty years' prescription, and so that the pursuer could not succeed in the declarator.

The Lord Chancellor (Cranworth) felt grieved that these two gentlemen should have thought fit to bring to their Lordship's House this dispute, as to so trifling a matter. There was no doubt that the decreet-arbitral, pronounced by Mr Gordon in 1763, was intended to declare the rights of the parties, and that decreet declared Alexander Achyndachy, and his tenants of Upper Edindurno, to have right and title to a road on the north side of the Burn of Cattie, from the farm of Upper Edindurno westward, reserving always liberty to the proprietors and tenants of Meitflecabie to water their cattle without interruption at the said burn, notwithstanding the aforesaid road, which is to be common to both. The question was whether the use of the road was intended to be confined to the tenants of Upper Edindurno. The question was one of considerable difficulty, but his lordship had come to the conclusion that the respondent was entitled to the use of the road, not only for the purposes of Upper Edindurno, but also for those of Holes. If the words referring to Upper Edindurno had been left out altogether, there would have been no doubt that the respondent, who now represented Auchyndachy, had the right to the road for both farms. The circumstance that the tenants of one farm only were mentioned, may be due to the fact that the road originated with that farm. But it did not necessarily follow that the use of the road was to be restricted to the farm, nor could such intention be presumed in the arbitrator. As regards the other points, his Lordship thought the respondent wrong in contending that there was a common property in the road, or that there had been acquiescence by the appellant. As to the point of forty years' prescription, perhaps that ground of the respondent's claim might be well founded; but the judgment now given was rested solely on the construction of the decreet-arbitral.

Lord Kingsdown said that, though this was a very doubtful case, yet on the whole, he thought the Inner House was right, and unless he were clearly of opinion that the Judges were wrong, he would not seek to disturb a unanimous judgment. The decreet-arbitral, though made by a lawyer, had been drawn without much precision. Yet there were no sufficient words to restrict the use of the road to the tenants of Edindurno; and therefore, the interlocutor ought to be affirmed.

Lord Chelmsford said he had the misfortune to differ from his two noble and learned friends, for he was of opinion the appellant was right in his contention. The true construction of the decreet-arbitral was, that this road was merely a servitude road, reserved for the use of Upper Edindurno, but for no other persons. There could be no pretence for saying there was a common property in the road, or that there was acquiescence on the part of the appellant. It was well established both in England and Scotland, that if there was a servitude road for the tenants of one farm, that road could not be used by the tenants of another farm, even though both farms belonged to the same person. Therefore, the interlocutor of the Lord Ordinary was right, and that of the Inner House wrong.

Affirmed.

CIRCUIT COURT OF JUSTICIARY.

GLASGOW, *May* 8.

Appeal.—NEWLANDS *v.* STEWART.

Competency of Appeal— Notice—Association—Small Debt Summons.

The sheriff's judgment in an action for £4 as the value of fittings removed at the expiry of a lease, by an association, from premises of which they were tenants, was dated 14th Sept. The association lodged an appeal for the next circuit which was held on 28th Sept. Objection sustained that the appeal was not competent in terms of the Act of Geo. II. (Heritable Jurisdictions Act), which provides that 15 days must elapse between the judgment and the next Circuit Court at which an appeal against it can be heard, and that period not having expired. The appeal was then brought before the Spring Circuit Court. Objection repelled that ten days notice of the appeal had not been given to the opposite party in terms of the 34th Section of the said Act, and *held*, per Lord Cowan, that the notice for the former Circuit although bad for that Circuit, was a good notice for the first Circuit Court at which the appeal could be competently heard. Also *held*, per Lord Cowan, that the Association, which was the Associated Carpenters and Joiners of Scotland, and was unincorportated, was sufficiently called by its secretary Newlands, and that there was no disconformity between the summons which was brought against him as secretary, and the account libelled, which bears to be incurred "by the Association, per D. N., secretary."—(*Somerville* v. *Rowbotham*, 24 D. 1187)

STIRLING, *April* 26.

LORD ADVOCATE *v.* FORSYTH AND OTHERS.

Five panels were indicted for rape. A special defence averred that the woman was of unchaste character, and that she had had connection with other men, on specified occasions within three or four months of the alleged crime. Question by prisoner's counsel, in cross-examining the woman upon whom the crime was said to have been committed, whether she had ever asked men into her house during the last six or seven years, disallowed by Lords Cowan and Jerviswoode.

GLASGOW, *May* 2.

LORD ADVOCATE *v.* M'ARTHUR AND CAMERON.

Night Poaching—Relevancy—Assault.

The panels were indicted under § 9 of 9 Geo. IV. c. 69, and for assault at common law. *Objected*, that there was no sufficient allegation under the statute that there were three persons together, and none that all the three persons had a purpose to destroy game. The libel charged the crime against the panels "both, or each, or one or other" of them, and proceeded—"in so far as you the said J. M'A. and D. C., did both, or each, or one or other of you, in company with A and B, or one or other of them, or in company with some other person or persons to the prosecutor unknown, to the number of three or more together, by night," enter upon certain fields for the purpose of taking or destroying game or rabbits. The relevancy of the common law charge of assault was also objected to in respect that the minor contained no reference to the section of the statute authorizing gamekeepers to apprehend. It was averred that the gamekeepers having found the panels in the field, and trying to apprehend them, were thereupon assaulted by them. This was no crime, any man being entitled *vi et armis* to defend the liberty of his person. *Held*, per Lord Cowan, that the words "to the number of three or more together," controlled the alternatives in the libel, and satisfied the requirements of the statute, that the purpose was sufficiently alleged as regarded the whole party, and that if it should appear that the gamekeepers had no statutory power to apprehend, the panels would have the benefit of that by the jury. Objections repelled.

ABERDEEN, APRIL 27.

Proof—LORD ADVOCATE *v.* SHERIFF AND MITCHELL.

Competency of Witness—Insanity—Lunatic Asylum.

Two attendants in Banff Lunatic Asylum were charged with assault. The Advocate-Depute called as a witness, one Macpherson designed as "now or lately a lunatic patient in the Banff-shire District Lunatic Asylum. Objected to the admissibility of the witness as being a fatuous person, and argued that the very fact of his being a patient in a lunatic asylum was proof of his insanity. He could be legally detained there only if he were insane. There was at all events a presumption that he was fatuous, and no proof of lucid intervals had been tendered to rebut that evidence. Stair. iv. 437; 2 Hume 340; Dickson § 1682. Lord Ardmillan gave no opinion on an objection neither supported nor resisted by any evidence. Incompetency as a witness was not produced by the mere fact that a person was a patient in a lunatic asylum. His lordship thought however that, before administering the oath to such a person, medical evidence should be taken as to his state of mind, that the Court might judge of the competency and propriety of examining him. Lord Neaves concurred in holding that the mere fact that a man is confined in a lunatic asylum is not conclusive evidence that he is insane. The objection was repelled; but the medical officer of the asylum was recalled and examined as to the witness's state of mind. It appeared that he was subject to epileptic fits; that in the intervals he was tolerably calm and collected, and could give a sensible account of what took place in his presence; but that he had had four or five attacks since the date of the assault. The Court having called attention to a passage in Hume ii. 340, according to which this supervening insanity would disqualify the witness, the Advocate-Depute intimated that he would not examine the witness.

DUNDEE, *April* 18.

L. ADV. *v.* MULVIE.

Theft—Previous Convictions in Ireland—Proof.

Previous convictions at Quarter Sessions in Ireland, proved by certificates under the hand of the Clerk of the Peace spoken to by Irish officers; by evidence of the Clerk of the Peace as to the formality and sufficiency of the certificates, and by authenticated extracts from indictments showing the nature of the charges on which the convictions followed spoken to by the Clerk of the Peace (the certificates in Irish form, bearing simply to be convictions for *felony*, and not showing the precise crime.)

L. ADV. *v.* WILKINSON.

Culpable Homicide by Engine Driver.

A Railway Engine Driver convicted under the direction of the Court, of culpable homicide, and culpable neglect of duty, which consisted in failure to obey a signal near a railway station, although it was proved that the signal had for a considerable period been habitually disregarded, with the knowledge of the superior officials of the railway. But in the circum stances he was sentenced only to 14 days imprisonment.

PERTH, *April* 28.

L. ADV. *v.* STIVEN.

Theft—Intoxication—Special Defence.

Panel was charged with theft, aggravated by previous conviction, in so far as in the Salutation Hotel, Perth, he did wickedly and feloniously steal and theftuously away take four silver or plated jugs, and a knife. It was proved that he became intoxicated in the Hotel on the day libelled, and that, after he left, the jugs and knife were missed. Panel left Perth with the train for Dundee, but got out at an intermediate station, apparently supposing that he had arrived at Dundee. He made a present of one of the jugs to a porter at this station, and went on to Dundee with the next train, leaving the three jugs and knife in the waiting-room. When apprehended and charged with theft, next day, he was astonished, and said he knew nothing of the matter. A woman who cohabited with him was examined for the defender, and deponed, that she was with him in the Hotel on the day libelled, and put the jugs and spoons in his pockets without his knowledge, for a trick, and with the view of showing him how dangerous it was to get drunk; that she did not intend to let him take away the articles, but that in consequence of a quarrel she left the Hotel, without letting him know of the trick. Lord Neaves in his charge said, that the question was whether theft had been committed. The mere carrying away of property did not constitute theft; there must be a taking *lucri causa.* It would be for the jury to say, considering the nature of the articles, the condition of the panel, and his subsequent conduct, whether there was a felonious taking; the evidence of the woman examined for the defence, was, his lordship thought, suspicious, and did not improve the case for the panel. The defence set up was special, and should have been intimated to the prosecutor in the usual way beforehand, so that neither the prosecutor nor the Court might be taken by surprise.

INVERNESS, *May* 2.

L. ADV. *v.* MURRAY.

Panel charged with rape on a Ann Jones, described as of "weak or imbecile intellect." Medical men examined for the crown, deponed, that the girl was not a perfect idiot, but very imbecile, knew the difference between truth and falsehood, could give an accurate statement, though not a complete or connected one; and they did not think she understood the nature and obligation of an oath. The Advocate-Depute tendered the girl as a witness, but she was objected to by the prisoner's counsel. Objection sustained. The mother of the girl alleged to have been ravished was examined. Being interrogated as to statements made by her daughter immediately after the crime was committed, the question was objected to. If the girl could not be believed on oath, much less credit was due to her statements made not on oath. *Macnamara*, Arkl. 521.—Lord Ardmillan had had occasion to consider the point carefully, and would depart from the case of Macnamara, so far as not to withhold from the jury the first statement she had made to the witnesses who saw her immediately after the alleged outrage. This was really part of the *res gestæ*, and might be proved just as the cry of a child, or the scream of an animal. He would not admit the details of a conversation immediately after the assault, or anything whatever at a little distance of time, *e.g.* next day.

ENGLISH CASES.

SEA SHORE (*Public rights of Navigation.*)—The bed of all navigable rivers where the tide flows and re-flows, and of all estuaries, is vested in the Crown, but subject to the right of navigation, which belongs by law to the subjects of the realm, and of which the right to anchor forms a part; and every grant made by the Crown of the bed or soil of an estuary or navigable river must be subject to such public right of navigation. If a payment be claimed by the owner of the soil of an estuary or navigable river as an anchorage due, facts must be shewn from which it can be inferred that such soil was originally within a port or harbour, or that some service or aid to navigation was rendered to the public in respect of which the grant was made. Such claim cannot be supported on the ground of its having been immemorially made and submitted to. *Gann* v. *the Company of Free Fishers of Whitstable* (House of Lords), 35 L. J., C.P. 29.

RAILWAY CLAUSES ACT (*Payment of Fare where Ticket not produced.*)—The 8 & 9 Vict. c. 20, s. 103, enacts that, if any person travel without having paid his fare, with intent to avoid payment thereof, or if any person having paid his fare for a certain distance, knowingly and wilfully proceed beyond such distance without previously paying the additional fare, and with intent to avoid payment thereof, he shall forfeit, &c. A bye-law was made by a company, under their special act and the 8 & 9 Vict. c. 20, in the terms following: "No passenger will be allowed to enter any carriage on the railway, or to travel on the railway, without having first paid his fare and obtained a ticket. . . . Each passenger on payment of his fare . . . will be furnished with a ticket, specifying the class of carriage and the distance for which, or places for travelling between which, the payment has been made, . . . which ticket such passenger is to shew whenever required by the guard in charge of the train, or other servant of the company, and which ticket such passenger is to deliver up before leaving the company's premises, upon demand, to the guard, or servant authorized to collect tickets. Any passenger not producing his ticket as aforesaid, or not delivering up his ticket as aforesaid, will be required to pay the fare from the place whence the train originally started, and in default of payment shall forfeit, &c." A passenger took at E. a return ticket from E. to S. and back. He travelled to S. and back to E; but instead of getting out at E, travelled, without a fresh ticket, to N. When he got out at N. he shewed his return ticket to E, and offered to pay the full local fare from E. to N. The company's officer demanded payment of the full fare from S. to N., which the passenger refused to pay. Held, that the passenger ought not to be convicted, under the above by-law, for not producing and delivering up a ticket to N., or for not paying his fare from S. to N., in the absence of any intention to defraud.—(*Dearden* v. *Townsend*, 35 L. J., Mag. Ca. 50; 1 Law Rep. Q.B. 10.)

HUSBAND AND WIFE.—The 22th section of 20 & 21 Vict. c. 85 (the Divorce Act), which provides that after a decree of judicial separation the wife "shall be considered a *feme sole* with respect to property of every description which she may acquire, or which may come to or devolve upon her," &c., applies to property to which a wife is entitled in reversion at the date of the decree, and which subsequently falls into possession. A wife having obtained a decree for judicial separation may avoid a mortgage made by her and her husband of a reversion in personality which falls in during the joint lives.—(*In re Insole*, 35 L. J. Ch. 177)

COMPANY. (*Lease Ultra Vires.*)—A company, established for the working and sale of porcelain clay, carried on business for several years without success; their resources having become nearly exhausted, and an entire reconstruction of their works and alteration in their mode of manufacture being found necessary, a resolution was passed for winding up. Before it was confirmed, a proposition was made, and finally accepted by a majority of more than two-thirds of the shareholders, for leasing their works upon terms apparently advantageous. The deed of settlement empowered the directors, with the sanction of two-thirds of the votes recorded at an extraordinary general meeting, to do any act which the whole body of shareholders, all consenting, could do. Upon a bill filed by a dissentient shareholder to set aside the lease as inconsistent with the purpose of the company, and as *ultra vires*—*Held*, that the lease was good, as being a lawful means of making the most of the assets of the company, and that it was not *ultra vires*.—*Featherstonhaugh* v. *the Lee Moor Porcelain Clay Co.*, 35 L. J., Ch. 84.

COMPANY (*Powers, Promoters.*)—A company is not bound by the contract of its promoters, where the thing contracted to be done is *ultra vires* of the company, and to that extent Lord Cottenham's doctrine, that a company is bound by the engagements of its promoters, must be taken to be overruled.—Doctrine of *Caled. and Dumb. Ry. Co.* v. *Mag. of Helensburgh*, 2 Macq. 391, followed by Kindersley, V. C. An agreement by promoters to pay a sum to a landowner, through whose estate their railway is to pass, for his support to the scheme, is *ultra vires* of the company when incorporated, and though adopted and acted on, will not be enforced against the company. It is not illegal for promoters to agree personally with a landowner, even (so long as there be no proof of corrupt influence on his vote) though he be a member of either House of Parliament, to pay him money for withdrawing his opposition to their bill or giving support to the scheme; but such payment is not an "expense incurred in obtaining the special act, or incident thereto," within the 65th section of the Companies' Clauses Act, and cannot so be upheld as a liability of the company.—*Earl of Shrewsbury* v. *N. Staffordshire Ry. Co.*, 35 L. J. Ch. 156.

COMPANY (*Contributory, Variation of Contract, Executor.*)—The directors of a company wrote to A, a shareholder, offering to allot him four reserved shares, and asking if he wished for any more, the price to be paid on or before 1st October. A wrote, agreeing to take the four shares, and applying for four more on the terms mentioned. The directors wrote that they had allotted him four shares, for which he had applied, in addition to the four previously accepted by him, and that the price must be paid on or before the 1st of October, or they would be forfeited. A did not pay for them, and before 1st October the company was ordered to be wound up,—*Held*, that A was a contributory in respect of the first four shares, the contract to take those shares being concluded by A's letter, but not in respect of the four additional shares, the contract as to these being left incomplete by the first two letters, and the third letter having introduced into the contract a new term, as to forfeiture, which A had not subsequently accepted. The deed of settlement of a company provided that the executors of a shareholder should either sell, or by executing the deed become proprietors in their own right of their testator's shares, and should not in the meantime receive the dividends; and also that no one person should hold less than five shares. The executors of D, a shareholder, were allowed by the directors to receive the dividends on D's shares for several years, and were not required to execute the deed of settlement. The directors, in pursuance of a resolution to allot certain reserved shares among the existing shareholders in proportion to their original shares, offered two reserved shares to the executors of D; and R, one of them, who held no shares in his own right, without consulting his co-executor, agreed to accept the two shares as executor of D. The company being wound up,—*Held*, that neither R in his own right, nor the executors as such, were contributories in respect of the two shares. In a similar case, both the executors having agreed to take two reserved shares "as executors," neither of them having previously any shares in his own right,—*Held*, that they were contributories as executors.—*In re Leeds Banking Co.*, 35 L. J., Ch. 75.

COPYRIGHT (*Alien Friend.*)—An alien friend is entitled to British copyright in a work composed by him, and first published in England during the time of his residence in any part of the British dominions; in this case in Canada. The word "author," in 5 & 6 Vict. c. 45, includes alien authors.—*Low* v. *Routledge*, 35 L. J., Ch. 114.

NUISANCE (*Increasing Pollution.*)—A brook, into which part of the sewage of Tunbridge Wells was discharged, flowed through the plaintiff's land, entering it 1½ miles from the town, and leaving it 4 miles from the town. The evidence showed that the water of the brook had been at some time (not clearly defined) fit to drink; that it was no longer so; that it was getting gradually worse, and that the deterioration was owing to the sewage,—*Held*, that the plaintiff was entitled to an injunction to restrain the defendants from allowing any sewage to flow into the brook so as injuriously to affect the water on the plaintiff's land, although the sewage there did not as yet amount to an absolute nuisance.—*Goldsmid* v. *the Tunbridge Wells Improvement Commissioners*, 35 L. J., Ch. 88.

STOPPAGE IN TRANSITU.—Where goods have been contracted to be sold, delivery by the vendors on board a ship ostensibly belonging to a firm of which the vendee is a member, and of which ship he is sole registered owner, is not a delivery of such goods to the vendee, so as to exclude the vendor's right of stoppage in transitu, if such ship is a general ship and takes up the goods in the course of one of its regular trips, even though the bills of lading, signed by the captain for such goods, should be made in favour of the vendee and his assigns, and one of such bills should be retained by the captain.—*Schotsman* v. *the Lancashire and Yorkshire Railway Company*, 35 L. J., Ch. 100.

SUCCESSION DUTY (*Testator domiciled abroad.*)—The operation of the Succession Duties Act, 16 & 17 Vict. c. 51, is confined to successions to which persons become entitled by the laws of this country. Therefore, where a testator, domiciled abroad, died, leaving pure personalty situate in England,—*Held*, per Cranworth, C., that no succession duty was payable in respect thereof.—*Wallace* v. *the Attorney-General*, 35 L. J., Ch. 124.

COMPANY (*Winding up.*)—An incorporated company was being wound up, under the Companies' Act, 1862; and a quarrying lease to the company (containing no provision against assigning) for a term, the chief part of which was unexpired, was assigned by the liquidator and the company to a stranger. On an application by the lessor, who objected to the assignment, the Lords Justices (reversing judgment of the Master of the Rolls) directed a claim to be entered against the company's estate for the whole amount of the future rent during the term.—*In re the Haytor Granite Co., ex parte Bell*, 35 L. J., Ch. 154.

INSURANCE ON PLATE-GLASS (*Notice of Loss.*)—The defendants insured the plate-glass in plaintiff's shop window "from loss or damage originating from any cause whatsoever, except fire, breakage during removal, alteration or repair of premises," and a condition of the policy was, that in case of damage notice be given "to the manager or to some known agent" of defendants. The plate-glass so insured was broken by a crowd assembled to witness a fire at a house adjoining plaintiff's, and who, having broken the glass, took away some of plaintiff's goods whilst he was engaged in removing his property to a place of safety. The fire never reached the glass or the shop front,—*Held*, that the proximate cause of the injury was the crowd, and that the damage did not originate either from "fire or breakage during removal" within the meaning of the exception in the policy. *Held*, also, that a notice of the loss to the local agent through whom the policy had been effected, though he had afterwards ceased to be the defendants' agent by reason of their transferring their business as insurers to another company, was a sufficient compliance with the policy.—*Marsden* v. *the City and County Assurance Co. (Lim.)*, 35 L. J., C. P.

LANDS CLAUSES CONSOLIDATION ACT, 1845.—Premises adjoining a railway, but untouched by it, were injured by vibration, noise, and smoke, caused by the running of trains after the railway had been completed. The premises sustained no structural injury,—*Held*, that the owner was not entitled to compensation from the company under the Lands Clauses or Railways Clauses Acts.—*Brand* v. *Hammersmith and City Railway Co.*, 35 L. J., Q. B. 53.

NUISANCE.—A difference is to be marked between an action for a nuisance on the ground that the alleged nuisance produces material injury to property, and an action for a nuisance on the ground that the alleged nuisance is productive of sensible personal discomfort. In certain cases persons living in society are required to submit to that amount of discomfort which may be necessary for the legitimate and free exercise of the trade of their neighbours, though they may not be required so to submit to circumstances the immediate result of which is sensible injury to the value of property. Therefore, where T. became proprietor of an estate, and shortly afterwards persons commenced smelting operations, which caused noxious vapours, whereby material injury was done to the trees and shrubs of T., it was held that, in an action brought by T. in respect of such injury, the Judge had rightly directed the jury to find for plaintiff if they were satisfied that real, sensible injury had been done to the enjoyment of his property, or the value of it, by the noxious vapours sent forth from defendants' works; and had also rightly directed the jury that the place where works were carried on so as to occasion an actionable injury to another was not, in the meaning of the law, a convenient place. *The St. Helens Smelting Co. (Lim.)* v. *Tipping* (House of Lords), 35 L. J., Q.B. 66.

PATENT.—A disclaimer cannot be used for converting a barren and unprofitable generality in a specification into a specific practical description, or to convert that which upon the description in the specification is not applicable to any one definite form into a description applicable to a specific and definite mode of proceeding. The object of the act authorizing disclaimers is, that where a specification containing a sufficient and good description of a useful invention is imperilled by the description having something annexed to it which is capable of being severed, leaving the original description good and sufficient, without the necessity of addition,—(except of such slight additions only as may be required to render intelligible that which remains),—the vicious excess may be lopped off. Therefore, where the specification of a patent for improvements in embossing and finishing woven fabrics, alleged the invention to consist in the use of rollers having any design grooved, fluted, engraved, milled, or otherwise indented upon them, and the disclaimer afterwards filed stated that the effect desired could only be produced by the use of a certain species of roller not particularly described in the specification (namely, a roller of hard metal or other suitable material having circular grooves around its surface), and all other rollers were disclaimed, such disclaimer was held to be bad. The description, "a roller of hard metal or other suitable material," was not too uncertain, on account of the use of the words "or other suitable material;" such words would mean any material equally sufficient for the purpose with hard metal—per *The Lord Chancellor, Westbury.* It is not every useful discovery that can be made the subject of a patent. It must be shewn that the discovery can be brought within a fair extension of the words "a new manufacture," per *Lord Cranworth. Ralston* v. *Smith* (House of Lords), 35 L. J., C.P., 49.

SHIPPING (*Conflict of Laws.*)—The rights of parties under a contract not expressly provided for thereby, but arising incidentally within the sphere of the relation created by it, are to be determined by that general law which the parties intended to govern the transaction, or rather by which they may justly be presumed to have bound themselves. *Primâ facie*, the law of the place where a contract is made is that which the parties intended, or must be presumed to have adopted, ought to prevail in the absence of circumstances indicating a different intention; but a contract of affreightment made between a charterer and owners of the ship, being persons of different nationalities, in a place where both of them were foreigners, to be performed partly there by the ship breaking ground in order to start for the port of lading, where both would also have been foreigners; partly at the latter port, by taking the cargo on board; and partly on board the ship at sea, subject there to the laws of the country of the ship; and partly by final delivery at the port of discharge, is to be construed by the law of the nation of the ship.—*Lloyd* v. *Ginbert* (in Exch. Cham.), 35 L. J., Q.B. 74.

CHARITY.—The court has jurisdiction to alter a scheme settled by it for the administration of a charity, and for the leasing of the charity estates, whenever lapse of time or change of circumstances makes an alteration desirable in the interests of the charity.—*Attorney-Gen.* v. *St. John's Hospital, Bath*, 35 L. J., Ch. 207.

CONTRIBUTORY.—B, the registered holder of 110 shares in a limited company, received a notice requiring payment of calls in arrear, and stating that on default his shares would be "forfeited without further notice," in pursuance of clauses in the articles of association, set out in the notice. B at the same time received notice of an extraordinary general meeting for considering as to winding up. Before the day named, B called and paid his arrears upon ten shares, explaining to the secretary that as to the remaining 100 shares he should submit to forfeiture. B attended the meeting, and was entered (without his knowledge) in the list of persons present, as the proprietor of 110 shares. The directors had previously passed a resolution that the shares of several defaulting shareholders should be forfeited, but no such resolution was passed as to B, and the directors had never intended his shares to be forfeited. Upon the winding up of the company, B applied to be struck off the list of contributories in respect of his 100 shares,—*Held*, per Wood, V. C., that the shares were not absolutely forfeited, but only liable to be forfeited at the option of the directors, and that the shareholder must be held as a contributory in respect of the full number of his shares.—*In re the East Kongsberg Mining Co. (Lim.); (Bigg's case)*, 35 L. J., Ch. 216; 1 Law Rep. Eq. 309.

COVENANT (*Running with the land: Acquiescence: Building scheme*).—A restrictive building covenant entered into by the grantee of one of several plots of ground with the grantor, his heirs and assigns, runs with the land in favour of subsequent assigns of other plots, and any such assign may alone sue the infringer. Acquiescence in a breach of covenant not attended with substantial damage, will not bar the right to restrain a subsequent breach so attended. The owner of building ground conveyed each plot, subject to a perpetual rentcharge; and the purchasers bound themselves, their heirs and assigns, by restrictive covenants entered into with the grantor, his heirs and assigns,—*Held*, that the plaintiff, owner of one plot, was entitled to maintain a suit for breach of covenant against the defendant, owner of another plot, who claimed under an original purchase-deed prior in date to plaintiff's, without making the owners parties. Also, that the grantee of the rentcharge on defendant's plot could not release the covenant. Where the owner of a house and garden was under covenant not to build on the garden,—*Held*, that throwing out a bow eight feet deep into the garden, was such an infringement of the covenant as the court would restrain, though not sufficient to maintain a suit for obstructing ancient lights.—*Western* v. *M'Dermot*, 35 L. J., Ch. 190.

SCOTCH SETTLEMENT (*English will: double portions*).—Testator by his will, executed in England and in the English form, gave legacies to the younger children of his deceased daughter. By a settlement of prior date made in the Scotch form upon his daughter's marriage, he had covenanted to pay to trustees a principal sum, to be divided, after the death of the parents, among the younger children of the marriage. The obligation was never satisfied in his lifetime, and no reference to it was contained in the will. The legacies were in excess of the portions which would have arisen from the settlement,—*Held*, that testator placed himself *in loco parentis*, and the will being construed according to English law, the legacies were to be taken in satisfaction of the provisions in the settlement.—*Campbell* v. *Campbell*, 35 L. J., Ch. 241; 1 Law Rep. Eq., 383.

COMPANIES ACT, 1862, Sec. 165.—The discretionary power conferred by the 165th Sec. of dealing summarily with delinquent directors and other officers of a company, applies only to cases in which the individual charged the alleged misfeasance is living, and cannot be exercised against his representatives if he is dead.—*In re the East of England Bank, ex parte Feltom's Executors*, 35 L. J., Ch. 196; 1 Law Rep. Eq. 219.

ADMINISTRATION BOND.—Scotch sureties to an administration bond allowed where there were no creditors, and the administrator was the only person interested in the estate of the deceased.—*In the Goods of Houston*, 35 L. J., Pr. and Matr. 41.

DISSOLUTION OF MARRIAGE (*Adultery: Collusion*).—If it be shewn that a husband has promised his wife to commit adultery in order that she may obtain a divorce, and that the wife follows a course the husband has indicated to watch him, that adultery takes place subject to that understanding, and that evidence is obtained accordingly, the court will hold that the parties are acting collusively, and will dismiss the petition.—*Todd* v. *Todd*, 35 L. J., Pr. and Matr., 34.

EVIDENCE OF MARRIAGE.—In a suit by a husband for dissolution of marriage, the only evidence of the marriage was that the petitioner and the respondent had, in May 1850, left England together for the purpose of being married at Gretna Green, that they shortly returned and stated that they had been married, and lived together for many years as man and wife,—*Held*, sufficient evidence of the marriage.—*Patrickson* v. *Patrickson*, 35 L. J., Pr and Matr., 48.

WILL (*Foreign, Change of Domicil, 24 and 25 Vict*).—Testator, being domiciled in Scotland, executed an ante-nuptial settlement, which he also intended should operate as his will. His marriage subsequently took place in Scotland. By the law of Scotland, such a document as a disposition of property at death is not revoked by the marriage of the contracting parties. Testator after his marriage became domiciled in England:—*Held*, that as the settlement was valid by the law of domicil as a testamentary disposition at the time of execution, as also subsequently to the marriage and at the moment when the testator left the country, it continued valid notwithstanding the change of domicil. *In the goods of Reid*, 35 L. J., Pr. and Matr. 43: 1 Law Rep., Pr. and Div. 74.

COMPANY (*Allotment of Shares*).—Where shares in a joint-stock company are applied for, they must be allotted by the directors within a reasonable time, otherwise the applicant may refuse to receive them, and may recover back the deposit paid on application. Where shares were applied for on the 8th of June and allotted on the 23d of November,—*Held*, not an allotment within a reasonable time.—*Ramsgate Victoria Hotel Co.* (*Lim.*) v. *Montefiore*, 35 L. J., Ex. 90: 1 Law Rep. Ex. 109.

Damages (*Breach of Contract, Consequential Damages*).—The declaration stated that, in consideration that plaintiff would bring his ship to defendants' dock at a certain time, defendants promised to dock her therein, and that plaintiff brought her to the dock at the time appointed, but that defendants refuse to admit her into the dock, by reason whereof she grounded outside the dock when the tide ebbed, and was damaged. Evidence was given that the dock-gate could not be opened because a chain had broken, and that plaintiff was informed of this immediately on the arrival of his ship opposite the dock. There was conflicting evidence as to the reason for the ship remaining in the river opposite to the dock-gate till she grounded. The jury were asked, first, whether there was a place of safety to which the ship could have been taken before the tide ebbed; and, secondly, whose fault it was that she was not taken there—the captain's or the pilot's. They returned no answer to the first question; and replied to the second, that neither the captain nor the pilot was to blame,—*Held*, by *Martin B.*, that the damages consequent upon the ship taking the ground were not too remote to be recovered by plaintiff. *Held*, by *Pollock, C.B.*, *Channell, B.*, and *Pigott, B.*, that without more assistance from the jury, the case was not ripe for the decision of the court. (*Hadley* v. *Baxendale*, 9 Ex. 341, discussed.)—*Wilson* v. *the Newport Dock Co.*, 35 L. J., Ex. 97.

Devise (*Words of Description, Easement*).—The devise by the owner of two adjoining houses of one of them, in the words "house, outhouse, and garden, as now in the occupation of T. A.," does not pass to the devisee a right to go to a pump in the yard of the adjoining house to get water, though the said T. A., there being no water supply on his premises, had been in the habit for some time previous to the making of the will of going to the pump, to the knowledge of the testatrix. (See *Ewart* v. *Cochrane*, 4 Macq., App. 117.)—*Polden* v. *Bastard*, (Ex. Cham.) 35 L. J., Q.B. 92; 1 Law Rep., Q.B. 156.

Marine Insurance (*Illegal Act of Master*).—A master of a vessel, though acting within the scope of his ordinary authority, who does an act in contravention of the laws of his country without the express knowledge or sanction of his owner, whether with or without a view to the owner's advantage, is guilty of an implied breach of orders. Therefore, where he has sailed on a voyage, within the 16 and 17 Vict. c. 107. ss. 170-2, with a portion of his cargo stowed on deck and without a certificate of clearance, and without the knowledge or authority of the owner, though with a view to the benefit of such owner, the illegality of the voyage does not affect the owner so as to prevent his recovering against an insurer for the loss of freight.—*Wilson* v. *Rankin*, (Ex. Ch.,) 35 L. J., Q.B. 87; 1 Law Rep., Q.B. 162.

Partnership (*Constitution, Annuity out of Business*).—Defendant's son having been elected a member at Lloyd's, on a representation made to the committee with defendant's sanction, that defendant would place £5,000 at the disposal of F (an underwriter), and would never let his son want further aid, if needed, the son entered into an arrangement with F, whereby the latter was to manage the underwriting business in his (the son's) name, and was to be paid a salary for doing so. The son, in consideration of defendant so guaranteeing him to the extent of £5,000, agreed to pay defendant an annuity of £500, which, on a given state of the profits, was to be increased to a yearly sum equal to one-fourth of the profits; but it was stipulated that defendant should not be considered as a partner in the said business. The son afterwards married, and by the marriage settlement all the monies and profits of the business were assigned to defendant and one D, upon certain trusts, the first being to pay the said annuity to defendant. The son kept no banking account, but paid such cheques as F gave him to defendant's bankers, on whom he was allowed to draw, until defendant put a stop to it,—*Held*, by the majority of the Court of Exchequer Chamber, reversing the judgment of the Court of Common Pleas, that, assuming the above arrangements to be real and not colourable, defendant was not liable as a partner.—*Bullen* v. *Sharp*, (Ex Ch.,) 35 L. J., C.P. 105; 1 Law Rep., C.B. 86.

FRIENDLY SOCIETIES.—The Friendly Societies Act (18 and 19 Vict. c. 63. s. 24) gives summary power to Justices to order an officer, a member of a friendly society, or his assignee, who by false representation or imposition may obtain possession of any monies, &c., of such society, or having the same in his possession, may withhold or misapply the same, &c., to deliver up such monies, &c., or repay the money applied improperly,—*Held*, that this section does not give the Justices power to order an assignee for the creditors of an officer of such society to repay out of his effects a sum equal to the balance of the society's monies in the hands of such officer at the time he made the assignment, such balance not consisting of specific monies, and the amount having come into the possession of the assignee solely in his representative character.—*The Minerva Lodge* v. *Gladstone; Ex parte O'Donnell*, 35 L. J., Mag. Ca. 99.

MARRIAGE (*Scotch Divorce—Legitimacy.*)—Buxton, an Englishman, married Elizabeth Hickson, an Englishwoman, in 1828, but was separated from her immediately after the marriage ceremony, and, being convicted of procuring the marriage by fraud and conspiracy, and sentenced to three years imprisonment, never lived with her afterwards. After vain attempts to procure an Act of Parliament declaring the marriage null, and subsequently to obtain a separation *a mensa et thoro*, an agreement was made between Buxton and his wife's friends, especially a Mr. John Shaw, who wished to marry her, in consequence of which Buxton, for a pecuniary consideration, went to Scotland, and resided there for forty days, in order to give the Scotch Court jurisdiction to entertain a suit against him by his wife for a divorce. The suit was instituted, and a decree of divorce, on the ground of adultery, was pronounced by the Scotch Court in 1846. Shortly afterwards, a marriage was solemnized in Scotland between Shaw, who was domiciled in Scotland, and practised as an advocate in Edinburgh, and Elizabeth Buxton, and three children of such marriage were born in Scotland during the life of Buxton: —*Held*, per Kindersley, V.C., that the Scotch divorce was null and void, and consequently the marriage with Shaw was invalid, and the children were illegitimate; that neither Shaw nor Elizabeth Buxton were justifiably ignorant of the subsistence of the prior marriage, notwithstanding the divorce, as an impediment to their marriage; and that even if either of them had been so ignorant (in which case their children would, according to an opinion of eminent Scotch advocates, have been legitimate according to the law of Scotland, notwithstanding the invalidity of the marriage), their children could not take under an English will, either real estate devised to the children lawfully begotten of Elizabeth, or personal estate bequeathed to her children. In an English instrument "children" will be construed, unless otherwise explained by the context, to mean children lawfully begotten.

The Vice-Chancellor observed:—Before the passing of the act establishing the Divorce Court, it was one of the incidents of an English marriage that it was indissoluble by the sentence of any Court whatever. The law of this country did not recognize the authority of any Court, domestic or foreign, to dissolve an English marriage for any cause or pretext whatever, and any judgment purporting to dissolve that marriage was treated as a mere nullity. This was decided in *Lolley's case*, which was much discussed, and though some suggestion is made as to *Lolley's case* being questioned in subsequent decisions, it appears to me that the law of *Lolley's case* has been asserted down to the present time as the law of marriage in this country.

Now, in decreeing a dissolution of the marriage with Buxton, the Court of Session took upon itself to disregard the quality of indissolubility, which the law of England attached to an English marriage, and dealt with the marriage with Buxton, not according to the law of England where it was solemnized, but according to the law of Scotland, in which country the suit for divorce was instituted; that is they dealt with it, not according to the *lex loci contractus*, but according to the *lex fori*. In so doing, the Scotch Court violated that very principle of international law now invoked by the Shaws as a reason for maintaining the validity of the marriage with Shaw. The sentence of divorce pronounced by the Court of Session must be treated by this Court and every English Court as a mere nullity, and as totally incompetent to dissolve the marriage with Buxton; and if that marriage remained undissolved, as unquestionably it did, the marriage with Shaw was not valid. If the validity of the marriage with Shaw were recognized by the Courts of this country, this consequence must necessarily follow, that an English Court of justice must hold that Elizabeth Hickson had two husbands simultaneously; Buxton was her husband by the law of England, and continued so, because the marriage could not be dissolved, and yet it is said that Shaw must be recognized as being at the same time her husband. The monstrous consequences are too obvious to require to be pointed out; whether such a state of things is possible by the law of any other civilized Christian Country, it is unnecessary to inquire; all I mean to say is, that it is impossible by the law of England. —*In re Wilson's Trusts*, 35 L. J., Ch. 243; 1 Law R. Eq. 247.

SHIPPING (*Collision—Liability for loss of life.*)—The liability of a shipowner in respect of loss of life to the seamen of a vessel run down by his ship, extends to, and is measured by £15, (and not £8,) per registered ton of such ship, affirming dec. of L. Romilly, M.R., *supra* p. 26.—(*Glaholm* v. *Barker*, 35 L. J., Ch. 259; 1 Law Rep. Ch. Ap. 223.)

VENDOR AND PURCHASER (*Contract for interest until completion*).—A contract for the purchase of land contained the usual clause that, if from any cause whatever, the purchase should not be completed by the day therein named, interest should be paid. There was a delay of upwards of ten years in consequence of the vendor having a difficulty in establishing his title; the interval was occupied by considerable litigation, undertaken with the knowledge and consent of the purchaser for the purpose of establishing the title. The purchaser had all along used the purchase-money in his trade:—*Held*, that no relief from the strict application of the clause as to interest could be given.—(*Williams* v. *Glenton*, 35 L. J., Ch. 284; 1 Law Rep. Ch. Ap. 200.)

CONTRIBUTORY (*Collusive forfeiture of shares.*)—Directors entered into an arrangement allowing a shareholder to retire. The arrangement was not within their powers:—*Held*, rev. decision of the *Master of the Rolls*, that though the transaction appeared in the share registry-book and in the minutes of the directors, and though twelve years had passed during which the shareholder was treated as having retired, yet his executrix was a contributory. It is no part of the duty of a shareholder to look into the management, nor will notice be imputed because he has not done so. *Spackman's case* followed. *Lord Belhaven's case* distinguished. All agreements with directors whereby a shareholder may, by payments or otherwise, be relieved from liability as a contributory are invalid.—(*In re Agriculturist Cattle Ins. Co., Stanhope's Case*, 35 L. J., Ch. 296, 1 Law R. Ch. Ap. 161.)

PRESUMPTION (*Age of child-bearing*)—A fund in court paid out and distributed upon the assumption that a spinster, aged fifty-three years and two months, would never have issue:—*Quære*, whether this age is not too low. *Haynes* v. *Haynes*, 35 L. J., Ch. 303.

LANDS CLAUSES CONSOLIDATION ACT (*Offer including costs*).—Upon a claim for compensation under section 68, the promoters offered a sum for compensation, such sum to include claimant's costs, and the jury gave a verdict for less than that sum:—*Held*, that claimant was not deprived of his right to costs under section 51, inasmuch as the offer was bad because it included costs. Such an offer to be valid must be for that which is the subject of compensation merely, unclogged with conditions. *Quære*—Whether a sum offered to a claimant under section 68, contemporaneously with service of the notice of the time and place of inquiry, but after the claimant has incurred the expense of attending at the nomination of the special jury, is a sum "previously offered" within section 51.—(*In re Balls* v. *Metrop. Board of Works*, 35 L. J., Q. B. 101; 1 Law R., Q. B. 337).

STOPPAGE IN TRANSITU.—A sold to B goods lying at X, one of defendants' stations; a portion were, by B's orders sent to Y, another of the defendants' stations, were there taken by him and paid for; B refused to take any more, but A sent the remainder to Y to him; B refused to take them and they were sent back to X; A also refused them, and they were again sent to Y, where they remained till B became bankrupt; A then directed defendants to keep them for him, and they did so. In an action of trover by B's assignee.—*Held*, that A had a right of stoppage *in transitu*, and that the defendants were therefore justified in detaining the goods for him.—(*Bolton* v. *the Lancashire and Yorkshire Rail. Co.*, 35 L. J., C.P. 137.)

MEASURE OF DAMAGES.—Plaintiff occupying premises under a lease from J. F, expiring 4th Dec., 1864, obtained from J. F. a reversionary lease for twenty-one years and twenty-one days, to commence from said 4th Dec., 1864, on payment of a premium. In Nov. 1863, J. F. died; and was found to have had no power to grant this reversionary lease. F. V. who was entitled to the premises, refused to ratify it, and plaintiff was obliged to accept a lease from F. V, to commence 28th Dec., 1863, for seven years only, at a greater rent. Plaintiff brought an action against the executor of J. F. on a covenant for quiet enjoyment contained in the void lease:—*Held*, that plaintiff was entitled to be indemnified for what he had lost by the breach of covenant, and that under the circumstances the difference between the value of the two leases might be used as a test of the amount of damages.—(*Lock* v. *Furze* (Ex. Ch.), 35 L. J., C.P. 141.)

PRINCIPAL AND SURETY.—The defendants gave a bond to the churchwardens of a parish in which, after reciting that S. had been appointed collector of the poor's rates of the said parish in March 1852, and that in March 1856 he had also been appointed collector of sewers and general rates under an Act, they became bound that S should pay to the churchwardens all sums collected by him in his said office of collector of all or some of these rates. In an action on said bond defendants pleaded that S's duties as collector were increased by certain statutes passed after the granting of said bond, under which S was appointed by said churchwardens collector of another rate; Plea held bad, collection of poor's rates being treated by the parties as a separate employment, and the plea did not show any alteration of S's condition as collector of poor's rates.—(*Bonar* v. *Macdonald*, 7 Bell's App. 379 explained. *Skillett* v. *Fletcher*, 35 L. J., C. P. 154; 1 Law R. C. B. 217.)

CARRIERS BY RAILWAY (*Packed Parcels.*)—Defendants, having a special act, containing an equality clause, in ordinary form, requiring them to take the same rates and tolls from all persons under the same or similar circumstances, were in the habit of charging a tonnage rate on packages weighing more than 1 cwt., and a higher rate on packages weighing less. When several parcels were delivered by the same person in one consignment, addressed to the same consignee, they were not weighed and charged for separately, but were weighed together, and a tonnage-rate charged for the whole consignment, if the gross weight exceeded 1 cwt. Plaintiffs, common carriers, trading under the name of "Pickford & Co.," were in the habit of collecting parcels in London and forwarding them to the country. Each parcel was addressed to the person to whom it was ultimately to be delivered; but it was labelled with the name of "Pickford & Co," and that of the station to which it was to be sent; and all the parcels for the same station were delivered in one consignment consigned to the plaintiffs at that station. Defendants refused to charge plaintiffs for the carriage of their parcels at a tonnage-rate upon the gross weight, and charged for each parcel separately according to its individual weight:—*Held*, that this created an inequality. *Held*, also, that the rule as to preferences or advantages to particular persons did not apply to arrangements made by a railway company with steam-boat owners for the conveyance of goods beyond the limits of their own line. (See *Napier* v. *G. and S. W. R. Co.*, 4 *Macph.* 87.)—*Baxendale* v. *South Western Ra. Co.*, 35 L. J., Ex. 108; 1 Law R. Ex. 137.

REVENUE.—(*Duties on Railway Fares—Parliamentary Trains.*) See *Great Western Ra. Co.* v. *Attorney-General* in H. of L., 35 L. J. Ex. 123; 1 Law Rep. App. 1

CONTRIBUTORY (*Executors.*)—Executors who accept reserved shares in a company allotted in respect of the testator's original shares, having no power to do so, are contributories in their individual capacity. Even if by the company's deed of settlement they had no right to hold shares in their own right, they are personally liable unless the contract be set aside. So held by L. Justices, rev. dec. of Kindersley, V. C. *In re Leeds Banking Co., Fearnside and Dean's Case.* 35 L. J., Ch. 307; 1 Law Rep. Ch. Ap. 231.

MINES AND MINERALS. A conveyance of lands in 1801, after reciting that the royalty was reserved to vendor, reserved to him "all mines and seams of coal, and other mines, metals, or minerals, as well opened as not opened, within and under" the lands, "with full liberty to search for, dig, bore, sink, win, work, lead, and carry away the same."—*Held*, per L. Justices, freestone included in the reservation, but that it could only be worked by underground diggings. *Mine* and *Quarry* distinguished.—*Bell* v. *Wilson*, 35 L. J., Ch. 337; 1 Law Rep., Ch. Ap. 303.

NUISANCE (*Prospective increase—sewage.*)—The Court will not generally interfere by injunction to prevent a nuisance, unless where the injury is proved to be serious and permanent. But, in estimating the injury, the Court has regard to all the consequences which may flow from the nuisance, not only to its present effect upon the comfort or convenience of the occupier, but also to any prospective increase of the nuisance and the probable deterioration in the value of the estate. Scientific conclusions from facts are to be regarded as secondary in importance to facts proved.—*Goldsmid* v. *Tunbridge Wells Commissioners*, 35 L. J., Ch. 88, 382.

COLLISION (*Evidence—admissions in the answer.*)—A steam vessel steering N.E. ½ N. and a schooner close hauled on the starboard tack and heading W. came into collision. The owners of the steam-vessel alleged that the schooner was seen three-quarters of a mile off on the starboard bow, but that she had no lights, and was mistaken for a vessel going the same way as the steam-vessel. All the crew of the schooner were drowned, and the evidence for plaintiff consisted of one witness as to the state of the schooner's lights some hours before the collision. The defendants called no witnesses:—*Held*, that plaintiffs were not bound to call witnesses from defendants' vessel; and that from the admissions the schooner was seen in ample time for the steam-vessel to have avoided her, and that, therefore, the steam-vessel was alone to blame.—*The Aleppo*, 35 L. J., Adm. 9.

CONTRACT (*Prostitution.*)—It is a good defence to an action for hire of a brougham for a term that defendant was a prostitute to the knowledge of plaintiff at the time of hiring; and it is not necessary to prove that it was supplied in the expectation that defendant would pay for it out of her earnings as a prostitute. —*Pearce* v. *Brookes*, 35 L. J., Exch. 134; 1 Law R., Ex. 213.

MARINE INSURANCE (*insurable interest.*)—The fact of a person's name appearing in a bill of lading as shipper and consignee is only *prima facie* evidence that he has an insurable interest in the goods. Plaintiff, a broker, sold on commission a cargo of goods, which were shipped under a bill of lading, deliverable to the order of plaintiff or his assigns, and he retained the possession of the bill of lading until the purchaser had accepted a bill for the amount of the goods. Plaintiff was not a factor, but a mere agent, who had not possession of the goods, or any lien for advances, commission or otherwise. The goods were lost; and in an action upon a policy of insurance effected by plaintiff, the jury found that there was no sale of the goods until after their loss; and it was ruled that plaintiff had an insurable interest, as the bill of lading made the goods deliverable to him or his assigns. *Held*, that such ruling was wrong, and that having, in fact, nothing to suffer and incurring no liability by the loss, he had no insurable interest.—*Seagrave* v. *Union Mar. Ins. Co.*, 35 L. J., C. P., 172.

COURT OF SESSION.

FIRST DIVISION.

PROUDFOOT *v.* LECHY.—*May* 22.

Jury Trial—Expenses.

The pursuer in this case brought an action of damages for wrongful dismissal from a situation in which he had a salary of £200 a-year—two years of his engagement being still to run at the date of his dismissal. The jury returned a verdict for the pursuer, with one farthing of damages. The pursuer moved the Court to apply the verdict, and for expenses.

The Court applied the verdict, but, in the circumstances of the case, found no expenses due to the pursuer.

Pet., HORNE FOR DISCHARGE.—*May* 22.

Sequestration—Discharge of Deceased Trustee.

This was a petition for the discharge of a trustee who died during the dependence of the sequestration. The Bankrupt Act makes no provision for such a case. The representatives of the deceased trustee applied by petition to the Inner House, who, *ex nobili officio*, entertained the petition, remitted to the Lord Ordinary to inquire into the circumstances, and on a report by his Lordship that the account of the trustees was correct, discharged the deceased trustee, and allowed the expense of the application to be charged against the sequestrated estate.

PATERSON *v.* THE PORTOBELLO TOWN HALL COY. (LIMITED.)—*May* 22.

Joint Stock Coy.—Lease—Reduction.

This is an action at the instance of Mr Paterson, the clerk to and representing the Magistrates of Portobello, as Commissioners of Police of the burgh of Portobello, against the Portobello Town Hall Company (Limited).

The action is brought to set aside, on a variety of grounds, a written lease granted by the defenders to the Commissioners of Police of Portobello, dated 10th and 12th February 1863. The defenders (who are incorporated under the Joint Stock Companies' Act, 1856), are proprietors of the building known as the Portobello Town Hall. A portion of the building was let by the defenders to the Commissioners of Police of Portobello for the accommodation of the police of the burgh, under a written lease (being that now sought to be reduced) for 15 years, as from Whitsunday 1863, at a yearly rent of £80, payable by moieties at Martinmas and Whitsunday. Under this lease the Commissioners of Police entered to the premises at Whitsunday 1863, and, after having been in possession for about six months, they raised various objections to the validity of the lease, declining to pay the first half-year's rent, payable at Martinmas 1863. A suspension of a charge for payment of this rent, afterwards brought by the Commissioners on precisely the same grounds as those on which the lease is now sought to be reduced, was refused by the Court, with expenses, affirming the judgment of the Lord Ordinary on the Bills (Lord Curriehill). After payment of the rent charged for, the present action was brought to reduce the lease, the

Commissioners, however, still keeping possession, which they held until about Whitsunday 1864, when they removed from the premises, which have, in consequence, ever since remained unoccupied. The leading grounds of reduction are those stated in the pursuer's first and second pleas, which are in these terms:—"1. The agreement between the Commissioners of Police of Portobello and the promoters of the Town Hall Company, for a lease of the premises in question, was illegal and contrary to law, and inept and ineffectual, in respect that at the time of said agreement the provost and bailies, and a majority of the Commissioners of Police, were promoters of the said Town Hall Company, and members of the provisional committee of said projected company. 2. The tack and duplicate tack called for are null and void and reducible, in respect that it was illegal in the Provost of Portobello and the other Commissioners of Police to enter into, or be parties to, such contract or agreement, while the Provost was chairman of, and he, and the other Commissioners of Police, or a majority of their number, or any of them, were directors of the Town Hall Company, or were interested as members of the provisional committee, or as promoters, or shareholders, or otherwise in the said undertaking."

The Lord Ordinary (Jerviswoode), appointed the pursuer to lodge issues for the trial of the case, being of opinion that it was inexpedient to dispose of the questions of law raised under the pursuer's first and second pleas, until the disputed matters of fact bearing upon the other grounds of reduction were ascertained.

The pursuer reclaimed, and asked the judgment of the Court upon the questions of law raised under his first and second pleas.

The Court adhered to the Lord Ordinary's interlocutor. As to the validity of the agreement mentioned in the first plea for the pursuer, they held there was no question before the Court, there being no conclusion in the summons for the reduction of that agreement. The only question was the one raised in the second plea. They were of opinion that the ground of nullity therein pleaded could not be sustained as an abstract rule of law, as the pursuer asked the Court to do. If all transactions between Commissioners of Police or other such bodies, and any company in which any of the Commissioners happened to be shareholders, were to be held to be null and void in respect of that fact, irrespective of whether the transactions were in themselves proper or improper, profitable or the reverse, the business of the country would come to a standstill. The present case, they were of opinion, differed in principle from the case of Blaikie Brothers *v.* the Aberdeen Railway Company, as decided in the House of Lords, on which the pursuer founded. In that case a contract between Blaikie Brothers and the Aberdeen Railway Company was held to be null, in respect Mr Thomas Blaikie, the managing partner of Blaikie Brothers (which consisted of himself and his two brothers), was at the time of the contract a director and chairman of the railway company. In that case the chairman, individually, had the principal interest, adverse to the company, in the contract made with them. In the present case the defenders were an incorporated company, having a separate person in law, with whom, and not with the partners individually, the lease in question was entered into.

Issues accordingly were ordered.

Wilson v. Wilson.—*May* 22.

Judicial Separation and Aliment—Adultery a Relevant Ground for Suing.

This is an action of separation and aliment at the instance of a wife against her husband. The pursuer avers that in consequence of bad treatment by her husband she left his house about ten years ago, and has since lived with her father, and that in August 1864 the defender committed adultery. The action was thus rested on two grounds—(1) Cruelty on the part of the defender, and (2) adultery. The Lord Ordinary (Ormidale) held that the cruelty averred was not sufficient to entitle the pursuer to judicial separation, but allowed a proof of the averment of adultery. A proof having been led, it was not disputed by the defender that his adultery was established, but he contended that judicial separation was not a competent remedy for adultery, the only remedy now known to the law being divorce *a vinculo;* and further, that the wife having absented herself from his house for ten years had thereby committed a breach of her conjugal duties, and was not entitled to sue for aliment. The pursuer, on the other hand, contended that adultery was a good ground in law for judicial separation, it having been the only remedy for adultery prior to the Reformation, and divorce *a vinculo* having merely been superadded after 1560 as an additional remedy. The pursuer further contended that she was entitled to decree for aliment, as by the defender's adultery she was debarred from returning to live with him, and entitled to remain separate. The Lord Ordinary held the adultery proved, and gave decree for separation and aliment in the pursuer's favour. The defender reclaimed; but, the Court, after argument, adhered to the Lord Ordinary's interlocutor with additional expenses.

Robert M'Kie v. White.

Parochial and Burgh Schoolmasters Act—Complaint—Competency of Review.

This was a petition and complaint under the Parochial and Burgh Schoolmasters (Scotland) Act, 1861, at the instance of the Rev. Robert Hill Whyte, clerk to the Presbytery of Lochmaben and county of Dumfries, and others, against Robert M'Kie, schoolmaster of the united parishes of Applegarth and Sibbaldbie, charging the said schoolmaster with immoral conduct unbecoming his situation, in respect, as said complainant alleged, he had committed ante-nuptial fornication. The respondent denied the charge, and pleaded that he and his wife were married persons for nine months at least prior to the date of the alleged offence, and he produced certain documents in support of his averments. The Sheriff-Substitute (Trotter) allowed a proof, and, after hearing parties thereon, repelled the defences, and found the charge of ante-nuptial fornication proven, and, in consequence, deprived the respondent of his situation of parochial schoolmaster. The respondent thereupon presented a note of suspension and interdict in the Bill Chamber, praying their Lordships to suspend the sentence of deprivation pronounced by the said Sheriff-Substitute. Answers having been lodged, the Lord Ordinary (Benholme) refused the note.

The schoolmaster reclaimed; and the Court adhered to the Lord Ordinary's interlocutor, on the ground that the offence charged was an immorality in the sense of the Act, and that whether the Sheriff-Substitute committed an error in admitting or rejecting evidence or not, there was no excess of jurisdiction to entitle them to review his judgment.

FERGUSON *v.* DUKE OF SUTHERLAND.—*May* 30.

Salmon Fishing—Interim Interdict.

This case originated in an application for interdict by Colonel Ferguson of Raith, Noran, and Culrain, against the Duke of Sutherland and his factor and others, asking to have the respondents prohibited from fishing for salmon in the Kyle of Oykell, *ex adverso*, of the estate of Culrain, and from molesting the complainer in his salmon fishings there. The Lord Ordinary granted interim interdict. The respondent asked to have the interdict recalled, mainly on the ground that he and his predecessors had possessed the fishings in dispute for a number of years, through, he alleged, his title to the Shin and Maikill fishings. The contention of the complainer on the other hand was that the respondent's possession of the fishings was to be attributed, not to his titles, but to a lease of the Kyle fishings, which he had had from the complainer. The Lord Ordinary (Mure) continued the interim interdict, and passed the note to try the question of title, and the Court adhered.

MAXWELL AND OTHERS *v.* PROVOST, MAGISTRATES, AND TOWN COUNCIL OF DUMFRIES.—*June* 1.

Burgh Customs—right to be interpreted by usage.

The burgh of Dumfries has right by virtue of certain charters confirmed by Act of Parliament, to exact certain customs and duties on articles of "merchandise" entering the burgh. The magistrates recently began to exact this custom on articles on which it had not formerly been charged, and also to raise its rate, and framed a new table intended to regulate its collection in future. A number of gentlemen of the county, on whose property this custom is chiefly levied, brought the present action to have it declared that the defenders had no right to levy custom, except in respect of such bestial or articles, and at such rates as should appear to have been charged for time immemorial.

The Lord Ordinary (Kinloch) held that the term "merchandise," as employed in the table of the burgh customs, comprehended all articles which were the subject of mercantile dealing, and were in use to be loaded, either on a horse or cart; but did not comprehend live animals, or the carcases of such as were dead. His lordship further found that the said term did not comprehend lime, coal, manure, either natural or artificial, trees or wood, drain tiles, stones, slates, hay, straw, agricultural implements, furniture, or machinery; that foals, calves, and lambs following their mothers were not chargeable; that swine were not chargeable, dead or alive; that no charge could be laid on carriers other than on the specified articles chargeable under the table; that herrings were chargeable under the head of fish, and clogs under the head of shoes; that horses were not chargeable when saddled or in harness: and that the defenders were not entitled to exact double rates on any particular day of the year more than on any other. His lordship further appointed the cause to be enrolled, in order that steps might be taken for having a table of bridge customs framed in conformity with the previous findings. The Lord Ordinary, in pronouncing the foregoing interlocutor, proceeded on the principle that no customs were chargeable by the defenders, except what had been sanctioned by immemorial usage.

The defenders having reclaimed, the Court to-day adhered to the Lord Ordinary's interlocutor.

ROUTLEDGE *v.* SOMERVILLE AND SONS.—*June* 5.

Action of Damages—Diligence to recover Documents.

In this case the pursuer sues the defenders, who are papermakers, for damages for breach of an alleged agreement to take all the esparto required for their business from him. Issues were adjusted, and a diligence granted to both parties. The defenders' diligence was for the purpose of recovering all books and papers showing the prices at which the pursuer was selling esparto to other parties. To-day the defenders asked for further diligence to recover all papers and correspondence in the possession of the pursuer tending to show the prices and dates at which he bought esparto in Spain. It was urged, *inter alia*, that this was necessary in order to ascertain the measure of the damage sustained by the pursuer, which must depend on the prices at which he bought and the profits which he lost by the defenders' breach of agreement. It was objected that to grant diligence in terms of the specification proposed would be to authorise an investigation into the whole history of the pursuer's business, at the instance and for the purpose of a rival in trade. The Court appeared to think that the time during which the pursuer had to keep his goods on hand in consequence of the loss of his sales to the defenders would supply the true measure of damages; and at all events that it was for the pursuer, not the defenders, to prove the amount of damages, and that it was at least premature for the defenders to take measures to check the estimates he was to lay before the jury. The diligence was therefore refused.

A. *v.* B.—*June* 6.

Outer House Procedure Act—Failure to lodge Issues.

In this case issues were appointed to be lodged by a certain day. The agent by mistake omitted to lodge them till the day after they were due. The Clerk to the Process received the issues, but refused to mark them. By the recent Act of Sederunt to regulate proceedings in the Outer House, it is enacted that all appointments for lodging or adjusting issues shall be held to be peremptory, and if the issues are not lodged by the time appointed, it shall be competent for the opposite party to take decree by default.

In this case the defender did not wish to take decree, and both parties concurred in asking the Lord Ordinary (Barcaple) to report the matter to the Court. His lordship did so to-day, and having stated that he was satisfied the failure to lodge the issues was accidental, the Court allowed them now to be received.

BREADALBANE'S TRUSTEES AND EXECUTORS *v.* CAMPBELL.—*June* 6.

Entail Improvements—Authority to Charge.

The late Marquis of Breadalbane executed certain improvements on his estates of the nature authorised by the Montgomery Act 10 George III.

c. 51, and obtained decree constituting the amount of his outlay under that Act at £25,000. He afterwards applied for and obtained authority under the Entail Amendment Act 11 and 12 Vict. c. 36, to charge the fee of the entailed estate with £20,000 of that sum, which he accordingly did by bond and disposition in security.

To-day, the Court held, affirming the judgment of the Lord Ordinary (Ormidale), (Lord Deas dissenting) that the proceedings of the late Marquis under the Entail Amendment Act, in regard to the £20,000, did not debar his executors from now proceeding against the next heir of entail, under the Montgomery Act, for the £5000 of balance of outlay.

Breadalbane's Trustees *v.* Campbell.—*June* 6.

Entail Improvements—Subscription of Accounts.

This is an action at the instance of the trustees and executors of the late Marquis of Breadalbane against Mr Campbell of Glenfalloch, as heir of entail at present in possession of the Breadalbane estates, concluding for payment of three-fourths of certain sums expended on improvements on the estates by the late Marquis, in terms of the Act 10 Geo. III., cap. 51. That statute requires that the proprietor of an entailed estate who lays out sums in improvements, "with an intent of being a creditor to the succeeding heir of entail," shall annually, during the making of such improvements, within four months after the term of Martinmas, lodge an account of the sums expended by him in such improvements "during twelve months preceding that term of Martinmas, *subscribed by him*, with the vouchers, &c." The accounts in question in this action, and which relate to improvements made in the course of the twelve months preceding Martinmas 1862, were never subscribed by the late Marquis of Breadalbane, who died on the 8th of November of that year, but were afterwards subscribed and lodged by the pursuers as his executors. The defender pleaded that he was not liable, as heir of entail in possession, for any of the outlay stated in these accounts, as they had not been signed by the Marquis.

The Lord Ordinary (Ormidale) sustained this plea, holding that it was imperative under the statute that the accounts should be subscribed by the heir of entail *himself*, who made the outlay on improvements.

To-day the Court unanimously recalled this interlocutor, and held that the subscription of the accounts by the executors of the Marquis was a sufficient compliance with the requirements of the statute. They did so on the grounds (1) that the statute contemplated the accounts of each year being made up to the term of Martinmas, and as the Marquis died on the 8th November, it was impossible that the accounts for that year could be signed by him; and if the signature of himself was held to be necessary, the result would be that his rights as creditor of the next heir of entail for that year's expenditure must be lost to his executors; (2) that a construction of the statute involving this result was at variance with its purpose, viz., the encouragement of heirs of entail to expend money in improving their estates; and (3) the object of the subscription appeared to be to authenticate the accuracy of the accounts, and the executors were the parties best qualified to do that.

COUTTS *v.* COUTTS.—*June* 8.

Aliment.

This is an action at the instance of Mrs Mary Paterson or Coutts, wife of John Coutts, Esq., advocate in Aberdeen, against her husband, concluding for aliment at the rate of £75 a-year. The pursuer and defender have not lived together since 1855. The pursuer says she left her husband in consequence of his cruelty to her. The defender denies this, and states that he has been all along willing to live in family with his wife, and he offers on record to receive her back. The summons does not conclude for judicial separation, but merely for aliment.

The Court dismissed the action as laid, on the ground that there being no judicial separation of the pursuer and defender asked for, and the latter being willing to receive his wife back into his family, it was incompetent to ordain him to pay aliment to her.

MACKENZIE *v.* THE INVERNESS AND ABERDEEN RAILWAY COMPANY.—*June* 9.

Lands Clauses Act—Heir of Entail—Submission—Decree Arbitral.

This is an action of reduction at the instance of Mr Mackenzie, of Seaforth, against the Inverness and Aberdeen Junction Railway Company. In 1861, a submission was entered into between the pursuer and his late mother on the one part, and the defenders on the other, whereby they referred to Mr Brown, of Linkwood, the amount of compensation to be paid by the defenders to the pursuers for the land belonging to them required for the formation of the Inverness and Ross-shire Railway. The Lands Clauses Consolidation Act provides, that when any question as to disputed compensation is referred to arbitration, and "the arbiter or their umpire shall for three months have failed to make their or his award, the question of such compensation shall be settled by the verdict of a jury." On 22d October 1862, Mr Brown pronounced his decree-arbitral, and the pursuer now seeks to have it reduced on the ground, *inter alia*—(1), that the submission had fallen before the decree-arbitral was pronounced, in respect it had not been issued in terms of the Act, within three months from the date of the submission; and (2), that the arbiter had exceeded his powers, as in awarding the compensation, he had not adhered to the rules applicable by the statute to the case of heirs of entail.

The Lord Ordinary (Ormidale) found that the decree-arbitral was invalid and ineffectual, and reduced the same accordingly.

The defenders having reclaimed, the Court unanimously adhered to the Lord Ordinary's interlocutor.

Their Lordships held that an heir of entail could only agree to dispose of part of the entailed estate to a railway company, on a strict compliance with the statutory requirements; that the submission entered into was purely a statutory submission; and, therefore, that the fact of the decree-arbitral not having been pronounced within three months of the date of the submission was fatal to it. They further held that the decree-arbitral was *ultra vires* of the arbiter, and informal, and reducible, in respect the arbiter awarded a slump sum as compensation to the pursuer and his mother, the late Mrs Stewart Mackenzie, who was then alive and in possession of the entailed estate, without separating and distinguishing how much was due to the pursuer, and how much to his mother, or how much was due in respect of the lands held under entail in which Mrs Mackenzie alone was interested, and in respect of that portion of the lands held in fee-simple, in which the pursuer alone was interested.

M.P., British Linen Bank *v.* Mackenzie, Muir, and Others.—*June* 15.

Donation—Proof.

This was a multiplepoinding at the instance of the British Linen Bank, to have it found to whom they ought to pay the sum contained in a deposit receipt for £100, which had been deposited with them by the late Mr Peter Ross.

The claimants were the representatives of the late Mr Ross and the present reclaimer Mrs Muir, who founds, upon certain circumstances which took place before his death, as giving her a right to the £100 in question.

Mrs Muir had made certain statements upon record, explaining how she had become possessed of the deposit receipt, viz., of her intimacy with the late Mr Ross, who had given her a promise of marriage, and that she came to his house to nurse him during his last illness, and that, believing himself to be on his death-bed, he had presented her with the deposit receipt before witnesses—after endorsation written on a receipt stamp—for the purpose of giving her authority to obtain the money for her own use.

She asked the Lord Ordinary in these circumstances to allow her a proof of the facts which she averred. Lord Kinloch, however, held that such a proof was inadmissible in a question of this kind, for the reason that donation could not be proved by parole testimony, and also that possession of the deposit receipt, although blank endorsed, was not a proof of property in it, and there were many cases which could be imagined where it would certainly not give rise to a presumption of property.

Mrs Muir reclaimed, and the Court recalled the Lord Ordinary's interlocutor, and allowed a proof before answer; and the Court now decided on the import of the proof.

The Court, while unanimously holding that it had been made out that Mr Ross had presented the deposit receipt to Mrs Muir for her own use, and that therefore the money belonged to her, did not negative the well-established rule that donation could not be proved by parole proof. The deposit receipt being in her possession, and blank endorsed, was evidence that the deceased had given her authority to receive the money from the bank, because the endorsation, which was simply a mandate to another to receive the money contained in the deposit receipt, proved that the deceased had intended to deal with the receipt in some way or other. The question was, with what intention had he given her the deposit receipt? and this could only be proved by facts and circumstances, or, in other words, by parole proof. The possession of a deposit receipt, blank endorsed, did not transfer the money. The further question was, *quo animo* was it transferred? and this might be competently proved by parole. In this case the Court had no difficulty in concluding that Mr Ross in endorsing and presenting the deposit receipt to Mrs Muir had intended her to have the money for her own use, as the witnesses spoke clearly to the fact of his saying that the deposit receipt was given Mrs Muir as a donation by reason of his good will and the gratitude which he owed to her. Mrs Muir was accordingly preferred to the fund *in medio*.

ROUTLEDGE *v.* SOMMERVILLE.—*June* 16.

Action of Damages—Diligence.

This was an action between two papermakers, in which the pursuer claimed damages in consequence of the defender's failure to take esparto fibre from the pursuer in terms of an agreement to that effect. The defender averred that it was a part of that agreement that the pursuer should communicate his method of using esparto fibre in making paper. The pursuer answered that he had imparted his method, and that the defender was actually using it. This the defender denied, and a counter issue was adjusted to try this question. The pursuer moved the Court for a diligence to allow him, his agent, and a man of skill to examine the defender's works, for the purpose of ascertaining whether he was using his (the pursuer's) method. This motion the defender resisted, chiefly on the ground of the prejudice he would sustain by the pursuer finding out his (the defender's) peculiar method of using esparto.

The Court granted the motion, looking specially to the averments on record, and to the fact that the defender had taken such a counter issue.

SIR W. C. CARMICHAEL, BART., *v.* SIR W. C. ANSTRUTHER, BART.—*June* 19.

Res judicata—Process

This was an action of declarator and payment, and was brought in order to enforce an obligation of relief from augmentations of stipend to the minister of Skirling, dated June 1724. The pursuer, *inter alia*, maintained that the Court had already pronounced a judgment so far back as 1821, which established his right to his present claim, and that the question was therefore *res judicata*. The Lord Ordinary (Kinloch) decerned in favour of the pursuer, and to-day the Court adhered. The circumstances of the case appear in the opinion of the Lord President, who said the objections by the defender to the regularity of the procedure in 1821 are numerous. It is said that there was not in that action any proper citation of the defender's predecessor in the entail, Sir J. A. Carmichael, who was then a pupil, nor of his tutors and curators, and that it did not appear that there was any execution of the summons against him or his tutors and curators. It does, in my opinion, sufficiently appear from the evidence, although this is not admitted by the defenders, that the summons was executed on John Ker, W.S., Edinburgh, their known agent on behalf of the pupil and his tutors and curators, and that he accepted thereof; but it is said that he had no right so to accept, and that his acceptance was therefore null. This constitutes the first objection. The next thing that appears in the action is a defence which bears to have been given in by the pupil and *tutor ad litem*, and it is objected that there is no evidence of such an appointment; that if it had been made, a notice of it must have appeared either on some of the papers in the process or in a separate paper, and would have appeared in the inventory of process; but the inventory, though apparently complete, contains no such notice; the inference therefore is, that it is a perfectly gratuitous statement that there ever was such an appointment: it is farther said, *esto*, there was a *tutor ad litem*, that would not make competent a process which was otherwise incompetent from want of service. Various answers are made to these objections, and besides maintaining the competency of the service on Ker, and the fact of the appointment of a *tutor ad litem*, it is said that the defence given in by the pupil and his *tutor ad litem* were merely dilatory defences, and that before anything else was done in the litigation, tutors dative were appointed, and that their appointment and interposition in this case was sufficient to obviate any previous irregularities of the kind stated, because it was quite in their power to waive any such objections, and it must be held that they did so. Without going into the merits of the formal objections, I am of opinion that the appointment of the tutors dative and their interposition, and proceeding with the litigation, which was a somewhat lengthy one, was sufficient to obviate these objections, even if otherwise valid, on which point I offer no opinion. But then there is a further objection, which amounts to this, that the tutors dative neglected their duty that they did not state a valid defence: in a question of this kind all that we have to look to is, whether the litigation was conducted fairly and with *bona fides*, and I can have no doubt that the present case was fairly and skilfully managed, and that there are no grounds for holding that the judgment is not now effectual. It will never destroy the effect of *res judicata* merely to say that former advisers omitted an argument which the ingenuity or better information of after counsellors have reared up. If this were admitted, there would probably never be *res judicata* in any case. I am, however, clearly of opinion that, had this plea of competent and omitted been otherwise sound, it is clearly no valid objection that the person against whom it is stated is an heir of entail. To hold any other view would amount to this, that there could never be any *res judicata* either for or against an heir of entail.

The other judges concurred.

CAMPBELL'S EXECUTORS *v.* CAMPBELL'S TRUSTEES.—*June* 19.

Jury Trial—Expenses—Counsel's Fees.

The question in this case related to the amount of expenses in a jury trial allowable as between party and party. The auditor reported the point for determination by the Court, whether the expense of three counsel ought to be allowed against the unsuccessful litigant, and there was a farther objection to the amount of the fees.

The Lord President, who delivered the opinion of the Court, said that it had long been the rule, with which the Court had no wish to interfere, that in a taxed account as between party and party not more than two counsel would be allowed to be charged against the adverse party, unless in exceptional cases. This did not appear to be an exceptional case. It was no doubt an important case for the pursuer, but not such as to justify the employment of three counsel. The parole evidence was not voluminous, and the documentary evidence, although important, could not have required much expiscation, for it had been for a long time under the consideration of parties. They were, therefore, of opinion that one senior and one junior counsel were the proper staff for conducting the trial, and they should therefore disallow the fees for one of the seniors. It did not matter which, as they were the same in amount, thirty, twenty, and ten guineas for the three days during which the trial lasted. Otherwise they saw no reason to interfere.

Pollock *v.* Meikle.—*June* 20.

Res judicata—Mode of Proof.

In this case the pursuer sought to have it declared that a piece of ground in Greenside Place, Edinburgh, which had been taken possession of by the defender, belonged to the pursuer. It appeared that the present pursuer had before raised a suspension and interdict against the defender for the purpose of preventing him from enclosing the piece of ground, as the pursuer then claimed the right of erecting an oven upon it. In that process it was apparently taken for granted that the ground belonged to the defender, and the Lord Ordinary there pronounced an interlocutor which gave effect, to some extent, to that view, and found that the piece of ground was within the defender's property. The defender contended that this decision operated as *res judicata* in the present action, and pleaded accordingly.

The Lord Ordinary (Ormidale) repelled the plea, and the defender reclaimed.

To-day the Court adhered chiefly on the ground that in the former case what the Lord Ordinary there dealt with was the question of possession, not property at all. There were no *termini habiles* in that case to enable his lordship to decide the question of property.

There was another question as to whether the proof should be led before a jury or by commission. The Court held that it was a case best suited for a proof by commission, and remitted to the Lord Ordinary to appoint it to be so taken.

SECOND DIVISION.

Wilsons *v.* Sneddons.—*May* 25.

Reparation—Culpa—Master and Servant—Underground Manager—New Trial.

The pursuers' husband and father, Andrew Wilson, a workman at the defender's coal-pit, was killed owing to the rope used for raising workmen from the coal-pit having broken, whereby he was precipitated to the bottom of the pit. The case was tried in February, when a verdict was returned for the pursuers, and the damages assessed at £175 for the widow, and £200 for the children. The defenders moved for a new trial, on the ground that the verdict was contrary to evidence. It appeared that the defender was in the habit of himself supplying the ropes; but that on the day before the accident, the rope at the pit having proved too short, the men at work, with the sanction of Gemmell, the defenders' underground manager, took a piece of rope which had been used by engineers employed in repairing machinery, and which was hanging near, and used it, instead of sending for the kind of rope usually provided. The next day the rope broke, whereby Wilson was killed. There was also a bill of exceptions, which it was found unnecessary to dispose of.

The Lord Justice-Clerk said—There were several matters of fact involved. The pursuer must prove that the death was caused by the breaking of the rope, and also that the breakage was owing to some insufficiency or defect in the rope; and further, that this defect was imputable to the fault of the defender. On the two first of these there can be no difficulty; the only question of nicety which arises is on the third. Now, assuming that there was fault on the defenders' part, such fault may be either personal fault on the part of the defenders, or the fault of some one for whom they were responsible. I am not prepared to say that there was not a case to go to the jury on the first question—*i.e.*, whether or not there was direct personal fault on the part of the defenders. The delicate part of the case arises under the second supposition. The pursuer maintains that there was fault on the part of Gemmell, who is described as an underground manager; but the defender's liability for his fault depends on the further question, whether that fault was committed by Gemmell acting in his representative capacity, or whether it consisted in his doing or omitting to do something which was not within the scope of the duty delegated to him. On the first supposition, the master would be liable; but the mere circumstance of Gemmell being underground manager, and in that capacity binding his master in things so delegated to him, will not extend the liability of the master to all his actions in whatever capacity, and under whatever circumstances, committed. It is on this point that I think the evidence defective on both sides; and it is necessary to clear up this both to enable the Judge to give the necessary directions to the jury, and to enable the jury to understand on what grounds they are to return their verdict. Here, as was to be expected, we have a general charge and a general verdict; and it is quite impossible to ascertain on what grounds the jury proceeded.

The other Judges concurred, and a new trial was accordingly granted, all questions as to expenses being reserved.

THE OFFICERS OF STATE *v.* ALEXANDER.—*May* 25.

Service of Heirs—Declarator—Reductions—Competency.

The defender in this action, which was brought in 1833, was Alexander Humphrey or Alexander, who claimed to be the Earl of Stirling, as the great-great-great-grandson of William, the first Earl, who died in 1640. He also claimed right under a charter granted to the first Earl by James VI. in 1621 to extensive possessions in Nova Scotia, including extensive heritable jurisdiction, the right of coining money, and the privilege of creating baronets of Nova Scotia. He obtained himself served heir in general and in special to the first Earl, and the present action was a reduction of these services. The defender was also tried on a charge of forging various documents in support of his claim; but he was acquitted, the jury finding that though they were forged, there was no proof that the defender was aware of it. Ultimately, both services were reduced, and it was thus held that the defender had not made out his claim. The case went to the House of Lords. In the summons of reduction there were, in addition to the reductory, also declaratory conclusions, which were insisted in by the pursuers against the son of the original defender, and on which the House of Lords considered it desirable to have the judgment of the Court before disposing of the appeal. The question now before the Court arose under the first plea-in-law for the defender, that "the summons, so far as it contains conclusions that the original defender, Alexander Humphreys or Alexander, was not the great-great-great-grandson of William, first Earl of Stirling, and that he was not lawful and nearest heir in general or in special of the said Earl, is incompetent;" and *separatim* "the Officers of State have no right to sue the action *quoad* these conclusions."

At advising the Lord Justice-Clerk said:—The Officers of State say that the charter of 1621 conferred privileges which it is impossible for any subject at the present day to enjoy; and, further, that these rights were, along with the territory of Nova Scotia, ceded to the French in 1632; and though restored in 1713 by the treaty of Utrecht, they were restored to the Crown, not to the Earls of Stirling. The Crown is clearly entitled to challenge any one who attempts to take up rights conferred by this charter. They might have done so in two ways; they might either have tried the validity of the charter, accepting the defender as a good contradictor, or they might say to the defender—You, in any case, have no right to this charter, because you are not the person you represent yourself to be. This is the course which they have adopted, and in which they have so far been successful, having reduced the original defender's services as heir to the Earl of Stirling. Now, all that is necessary for the reduction of a service is to show that the evidence produced by the claimant is insufficient. That is the only true and proper ground of reduction. Nothing has as yet been done to dispose of what are called declaratory conclusions, but we are now asked to give decree in terms of them. Four propositions are sought to be affirmed—(1), That the defender is not a great-great-great-grandson of the first Earl; (2), That he is not the Earl's lawful heir in general; (3), That he is not his lawful heir in special—*i.e.*, that he shall be found not to be entitled to make any such claims at any time hereafter; (4), That he has no right or title to the lands or territories in dispute. If we sustain the competency of these conclusions what will follow?—for the proof already taken is not applicable to these questions, however parties might afterwards be willing to adopt it. Assuming the case to go before a jury, what would be the issue, and what would be the position of parties? Is the Crown to stand pursuer in the issue and prove a negative, or is the defender to stand pursuer, and to prove first his propinquity, and then in respect thereof to prove that he is heir in special and also heir in general to the first Earl. This is a somewhat startling, and certainly would be a quite unprecedented form of procedure. Such proof cannot be led in the first instance in this Court, still less by a party who does not propose to have himself served as heir. It can only come under our notice as a court of review. Further, it is a clear principle that a person entitled *jure sanguinis* to take out an heritable succession to a party deceased can do so at any time, if he be not anticipated by some one else serving and prescribing on his service and *retour*. Such rights do not fall by mere lapse of time. Further, a person may make twenty attempts to prove his propinquity, and may fail nineteen times and still succeed in the twentieth. Nay, further, he may succeed on imperfect evidence, and his service may consequently be reduced, but still he may try again and be successful, for there is here no *res judicata*. Is there, then, any form of process by which a competitor who has not himself served, but thinks that he has a better case than the other, can prevent that other from ever serving himself? Here the only way that the one can put the other to silence is by getting himself served and retoured, and getting into possession; and even then his title may be challenged any time within twenty years. The pursuers stand in a weaker position than that of competing claimants. Assuming the charter under which the defender proposes to take up such extensive rights to be invalid, and that the Crown is not bound to try this question with a mere pretender, I should be prepared to support a declarator to that effect, but no further. Even if the Crown were claiming as *ultimus hæres*, a special declarator would be necessary; but they are making no such claim, and cannot possibly make it, because, according to their own statements, there are in existence heirs general of the grantee of the charter of 1621; but I do not rest my judgment on the question of title, but merely refer to it to show that the Crown is at least in no more favourable position than a competing claimant. What I go upon is the first branch of the first plea-in-law for the defender.

Lords Cowan and Neaves concurred.

Lord Benholme differed. The Crown had already reduced the defender's special and general services, and they had also reduced the precept and instruments of sasine, and they now wished to have certain declaratory conclusions affirmed, to the effect that the defender had no right or title such as he claimed. He was quite unable to see the incompetency of such proceeding. He did not understand how the Crown could be compelled to stop here, or why they should not be entitled to prove that the defender had no such rights as he claimed, and that because he was not the person he claimed to be. No doubt, they would thus have to prove a negative, and might find that very difficult, but this did not affect the merits of the case. It was said that successive services might be reduced, and new services again expede without any limit to their number. That was quite true, the reason being that in such reductions there were not as here declaratory conclusions. It was also said that this process was unprecedented. That was a very slender objection, and this was a most unprecedented case. If the crown had a title, there could be no doubt as to their interest in going on and establishing a perpetual immunity against the pretensions of the defender.

Macalister *v.* M'Clelland.—*May* 29.

Process—Bill Chamber.

A note of suspension of a decree of removal was passed on caution; before caution was found, but within the fourteen days allowed for finding it, the respondent died, and an application was accordingly made to sist the respondent's successor in his room. The Court on the Lord Ordinary reporting the case, were unanimously of opinion that the application was competent. An interlocutor passing a note of suspension on caution was an interlocutor subject to a suspensive condition. If the condition were not purified, the interlocutor fell with it, and the case still remained in the Bill Chamber.

Pickford & Co. *v.* Caledonian Railway Co.—*May* 31.

Contravention of the Railway and Canal Traffic Act, 17 *and* 18 *Vict.*, *c.* 31.

Circumstances in which a petition and complaint by a company of carriers averring that the Railway Company had given undue facilities to their rivals in business contrary to the provisions of the Act, was dismissed, the allegations so far as relevant not having been proved.

ANDERSON *v.* M'CALL & CO.—*June* 1.

Sale—Delivery Order—Usage of Trade—Bankruptcy—Constructive Delivery.

The pursuer, as trustee on the sequestrated estates of Andrew Jackson & Son, grain merchants, Glasgow, sued the defenders, corn factors, for the price of a quantity of grain sold to the defenders, and which the pursuer alleges was not so delivered to the defenders as to pass the property prior to the bankruptcy of Jackson & Co. The case was tried in March, before the Lord Justice-Clerk and a jury, who, under the direction of his Lordship, returned a special verdict, finding that the bankrupts from November 1860 and down to the date of their sequestration were owners of stores in James Watt Street, Glasgow; that Robert Angus, the foreman and storekeeper who managed the stores was paid by them in weekly wages; that this warehouse was used by the bankrupts partly for storing their own grain, and partly for storing the grain of other people, for which they charged warehouse duty; that in the books at the store, and also in the books kept at the bankrupts' counting-house, they were charged with warehouse rent for the grain which was their own property; that the bankrupts kept separate accounts for their business as storekeepers and as grain merchants, but carried the profit and loss arising from each business into the general profit and loss account of the firm; that there was a general understanding in the grain trade in Glasgow, that grain belonging to the owners of such a store as that kept by the bankrupts, when deposited in the store by the owners, might be effectually transferred by constructive delivery by means of a delivery order or transfer in the warehouse books in the same way as if the grain were in the hands of a third party; that prior to 10th March 1864, the grain mentioned in the issue was stored in the said store in name of the bankrupts, and was their property. The verdict finds that certain documents referred to the wheat in question, and *inter alia* an acceptance by the defenders of a bill drawn upon them by the bankrupts; that immediately thereafter the said wheat was entered on a separate page of the book kept by the said Robert Angus, under the name of the defenders, and as belonging to them; that the object of this was to give the defenders a security over the wheat in consideration of the above acceptance. The question of the validity of the security was left for the consideration of the Court. After the first deliverance in the sequestration the defenders, by delivery order addressed to Angus, and acted on by him, obtained possession of the wheat, and sold it in order to repay the money paid by them in retiring the said acceptance, and now offer to account for the balance, if any, due to the pursuer. The question in law left to be decided by the Court was, whether there had been an effectual delivery of the grain to the defenders prior to the first deliverance in the sequestration, or whether it had vested in the pursuer as trustee in the sequestration.

The Lord Justice-Clerk—The delivery order by the bankrupts was in absolute terms, and *ex facie* purported to be a delivery for sale. He therefore thought that no difficulty arose from the finding that the delivery was intended to be in security only, for the delivery to a warehouse keeper, and the entry in his books, put the possessor of the order in the same position as if his rights had been completed by a regular contract of sale. No doubt, the transaction was in reality a security; but it was unnecessary to say more on this point, as the defenders acknowledged the fact, and were prepared, after paying the amount advanced by them, to account for the balance. The real question turned on whether the warehouse keeper was not identical with the seller of the goods; for where a seller kept the goods in his possession, no entry in his books could operate delivery, and he thought that in this case it was quite clear that Angus was the mere servant of the bankrupts; but it was said that this case was affected by the usage of trade, and here they must attend very closely to what the jury had found that usage to be (reads *ut supra*). This was a very peculiar usage, and appeared to him to rest upon an understanding, which was a misunderstanding of the law, on an idea that the law was exactly the opposite of what it actually was. The usage itself did not appear to be a very general one. It only amounted to this, that in one particular locality, and in one particular branch of trade in that locality, the dealers were under a misapprehension as to the law, and acted upon that misapprehension; but however generally it had prevailed, it was the province of the Court to correct such misapprehensions. He therefore attached no importance to the finding of the jury as to the existence of this usage. The doctrine of our law that *traditionibus non nudis pactis transferuntur rerum dominia* was quite clear and well established. Whether constructive delivery was an exception to this rule or merely an illustration of it, it was not necessary to determine, because, to constitute effectively this kind of delivery, there must be three persons—vendor, vendee, and custodier; but if, as here, the vendor and custodier are identical, there can be no such delivery.

The other Judges concurred, and the verdict was entered for the pursuer.

Bell *v.* Black & Morrison.—*June* 5.

New Trial—Judicial Slander—Malice.

Circumstances in which a motion for a new trial in an action of damages for judicial slander, in which the jury had returned a verdict for the pursuer, was refused, on the ground that there had been some, though very slender evidence of malice to go before the jury. Observations by Inglis, J. C.

Murray *v.* Dickson.—*June* 7.

*Bankruptcy—Sheriff Court—Reduction—Competency—*19 *and* 20 *Vict.*, *c.* 91, *s.* 10.

The pursuer as trustee on a sequestrated estate, brought an action of reduction under the Act 1621, in the Sheriff Court of Kincardineshire, of an assignation of a lease granted by the bankrupt. The defender pleaded *inter alia* that such an action was incompetent in the Sheriff Court. The Sheriff-Substitute dismissed the action, but on appeal the Sheriff (Shand) reversed. The case was tried, and the assignation was reduced. The defender advocated, and again pleaded that the action was incompetent in the inferior Court. The 10th sec. of the Bankruptcy Act (1856), enacts that "all alienations of property by a party insolvent or notour bankrupt, which are voidable by statute or at common law, may be set aside either by way of action or exception." The 9th sec. of the Act of 1857 declares that the preceding enactment is to "be taken to apply to actions and exceptions in the ordinary Court of the Sheriff." The pursuer maintained that a plea by way of exception was always a plea in defence, and therefore, unless he could proceed by reduction, the statute conferred no benefit on him.

The Lord Justice-Clerk thought the matter hinged on the construction of the 10th sec. of the Act of 1856, because he did not think the 9th sec. of the Act of 1857 did, or intended to do, more than say that the Act of 1856 should apply to Sheriff Courts. Now, that was a remedial enactment. There must, therefore, have been an existing mischief and an intended remedy. The mischief was the expense and delay occasioned by the necessity of bringing actions of reduction to set aside certain alienations of property which were void by statute and common law. The remedy for this mischief would naturally be to declare reductions no longer necessary, and that was just the remedy provided by the statute. No doubt, a difficulty arose from the contention that the 10th clause permits a challenging in two ways only—that is, by way of action or exception, and did not permit it by way of reply, to the pursuer of an ordinary petitory action. But although in our old law language exception used to mean merely a defence, and a defence set up, not as an objection to relevancy, but to merits; yet it had now received a larger meaning, and the phrase *ope exceptionis* meant everything except by way of action, and included the reply. If this were so, the clause provided an adequate remedy, and it was not, therefore, necessary to attempt to construe it as introducing another remedy. The pursuer contended that a form of process was for the first time to be introduced into the Sheriff Courts, and the action so to be introduced was the very action which the clause was intended to do away with; the action, as being or professing to be an action of reduction, was therefore incompetent. The other Judges concurred. Advocate the cause and dismiss the action.

Crosbie *v.* Dickson.—*June* 8.

Conviction—Reduction—Jurisdiction—Review—Public-Houses Act, 16 *and* 17 *Vict.*, c. 67.

This was a reduction of a complaint, conviction, and sentence for a breach of certificate, under the Public-houses Act, at the instance of the Procurator-Fiscal. The certificate provided that the pursuer "do not keep open house, or permit or suffer any drinking on any part of the premises belonging thereto, or sell or give out therefrom any liquors, before eight o'clock in the morning, or after eleven o'clock at night of any day, with the exception of refreshment to travellers, or to persons requiring to lodge in the said house or premises." The statute (sec. 25), requires the particular place and time of the offence to be set forth; and also whether it was a first, second, or third offence. The complaint averred that the pursuer kept her house open, and the specific offence was said to have been committed "by permitting or suffering one or more persons to be therein who were neither lodgers nor persons requiring to be accommodated in the said house or hotel, all in breach of the regulations of said certificate; and such offence is the second offence."

The Court held that the Magistrate had jurisdiction only under the Forbes

Mackenzie Act, because the offence intended to be charged was a breach of that Act. The complaint said that the alleged offender kept her house open, which was a very different thing from "keeping open house;" and if the complaint had stopped there, there would have been no difficulty in holding it irrelevant, but, confounding together the second and third prohibitions, which were quite distinct, it went on to say that the specific way in which the offence was committed was "by permitting," &c. (as above). The mere suffering persons to be in the house did not imply either that drinking was permitted, or that liquor was sold. There was here plain disconformity with the terms of the certificate. The objection was therefore good, and it followed as a matter of course that there was no jurisdiction. It would be monstrous to hold that the pursuer, against whom no offence had been proved, had no means of wiping out the stain inflicted on her character. By the statute all review was excluded, but here the proceedings had not been conducted under the statute, and were therefore not protected by it. The same observation applied to the defender's contention that the action had not been brought within the statutory period.

MAXWELL WITHAM *v.* WHITE AND YOUNG.—*June* 12.

Landlord and Tenant—Additional Pactional Rent for Miscropping—Hypothec—Locus Pœnitentiæ.

A landlord and tenant agreed to conditions of lease by letters. Afterwards, a formal lease was signed by the parties on 22d May and 3d September 1862. The entry to the house, grass, and fallow, was at Whitsunday 1862, and to the land in crop at the separation of that year's crop. The conditions of lease, as well as the formal lease, stipulated *inter alia* that the *third* year of each rotation should be to be white crop, *sown out with at least two bushels of the best perennial rye-grass seeds*, and not less than six pounds of red clover, and two pounds of white clover to the acre; the *fourth* year to be a crop of rye-grass hay, or the land pastured; the *fifth* year, pasture. It was also provided that—"If the tenant should take upon himself to manage any of the lands let in any manner differently than above specified (except by allowance of the proprietors, by a writing under their hands), he should be bound to pay ten pounds of additional rent for each acre or part of an acre not so cropped, managed, or manured as above directed, and the same proportion for a smaller quantity, which additional rent shall not be considered penal, but pactional," for the year in which the deviation was made, and every year thereafter till the end of the lease. The year of Young's entry was the third year of the rotation in the field as to which the contravention was said to have taken place; and in this petition for hypothecation, which was advocated, it was alleged that, instead of sowing rye-grass seeds and clover seeds with the way-going white crop of the previous tenant on the field in question, Young, under the conditions of lease, and in virtue of the stipulations in the prior lease of the farm in favour of the outgoing tenant, and in accordance with the custom of the district, entered upon the farm after Candlemas and before Whitsunday 1862, and sowed out timothy grass seeds along with the said way-going crop; that the timothy grass seeds failed and gave no hay crop, and no pasture in the fourth and fifth years of the rotation. It was contended that Young had thus become liable for the additional pactional rent for the two years of his occupation, and that the crop of 1863, and the crop and stock of 1864 was subject to hypothec therefor.

The Lord Justice-Clerk was satisfied that Young had committed a legal wrong; but that was not the question. The only question was whether he had committed a contravention of the clause imposing additional rent. But his Lordship could not see his way to sustain the relevancy of the averments as to deviation. The case could not be brought under that clause. The question was whether by sowing timothy grass before his entry Young had taken upon himself to manage the lands in a different manner from that specified in the lease. The question of time was the important consideration. There was but one act. The *sowing* constituted the wrong, not as was contended, the *having* the wrong sort of grass on the ground. That was not a wrong, but only the consequence of the wrong previously committed. No doubt, Young had done that in anticipation of his entry under the lease, but it was impossible to say that there was any concluded contract. There were articles of set loosely agreed to by a letter, which might have become a good lease if followed by possession, but for anything that was seen Young might never have become tenant at all. Then did he enter on the ground in virtue of the previous tenant's lease? It was not said in consequence of what arrangement, or by permission of whom he entered. The important thing is that the act was done at a time when Young was not tenant, and was not in a position to take upon himself the management of the farm.

Lord Cowan concurred, and said this case might have raised the question, whether additional pactional rent was secured by the landlord's hypothec. Notwithstanding the decision in Robertson *v.* Clark, 4 D. 1317, the question deserved serious consideration. No doubt, the rent was exigible from Young as tenant; but if he had done something under an arrangement with the out-going tenant before his own entry, that could not fall under this clause or under the hypothec.

The other Judges concurred, and their Lordships dismissed the petition.

Bell *v.* Arthur.—*June* 16.

Process—Decree by Default—Reponing.

In a suspension of a decree in absence, the Lord Ordinary (Kinloch) pronounced this interlocutor:—"The Lord Ordinary having called the case repeatedly in the debate roll, and no appearance being made for the suspender, on the respondent's motion repels the reasons of suspension, finds the charge orderly proceeded with, and decerns; finds the suspender liable in expenses," &c. The suspender applied to be reponed, and offered to pay any expenses incurred by his failure to appear. The Court unanimously refused this application, the Lord Justice-Clerk remarking that he was not sorry that an opportunity had arisen for expressing the opinion of the Court on this point, that parties were not, as a matter of course, entitled to be reponed against a decree by default, even on payment of expenses; and that it was a matter for indulgence, and would not be granted unless special cause were shown. No such cause had been shown in this case.

Gardner *v.* Keddie—*June* 20.

Process—New Trial—Trial before Lord Ordinary—Remit.

A cause was tried before the Lord Ordinary and jury, and a verdict returned for pursuer. Thereafter the defender obtained a new trial, on the ground that the verdict was contrary to evidence. The Lord Ordinary having been moved to fix a day for a new trial, doubted whether the process was in the Outer House, no remit having been inserted in the interlocutor making the rule absolute. A note having been presented asking the Court to remit to the Lord Ordinary, Held that the cause was in the Outer House, and that the motion was incompetent.

M'Taggart *v.* M'Dowall—*June* 21.

Property—Boundary on Foreshore—Wrack and Ware.

The lateral boundary between properties on the shore of the open sea, or of a bay of which the sides are not substantially opposite and parallel, is not to be drawn across the foreshore according to the principle of *Campbell* v. *Brown*, 18th Nov. 1813, F.C., by dropping a perpendicular from the termination of the land-boundary on the *medium filum* of the firth or narrow sea. The proper method is to take a line representing the average line of the shore, drawn at such a distance seawards as to clear the sinuosities of the coast, and let fall on such a line a perpendicular from the end of the land boundary; or, which is the same thing, to raise a perpendicular from the end of the land boundary upon a line representing the average direction of the coast. It will depend on circumstances, and be a question of degree, whether in any particular case the one principle or the other is to be applied. The principle of this case is not necessarily to be applied to fishings and other rights further out at sea.

TEIND COURT.

The Minister of Tealing *v.* the Heritors.

The minister of Tealing asked an augmentation of three chalders. At last augmentation, in 1819, the stipend was modified at sixteen chalders, but understanding that twelve chalders would exhaust the free teind, the minister had only localled for that amount, and had drawn no more. It was stated that it had been discovered that certain lands, supposed to be held under a *decimæ inclusæ* title, were not really so, as the words *nunquam antea separatis* did not occur. Further, the teinds of a great proportion of the lands of the parish said to be valued were in fact unvalued. The minister was willing that the decree of augmentation should contain a reservation making it effectual only in the event of the existence of available teinds. An heritor opposed this application, on the ground that, even if the lands hitherto supposed to be exempt were not so, their teindable value would not be more than sufficient to make up the stipend to sixteen chalders, for which amount the minister had already obtained decree. All the other lands were valued, and had been so since 1637. They had nothing against the validity of this valuation but an unsupported statement.

The Court were of opinion that the application was premature. The minister had still a substantial interest in the locality of 1819, under which he only got twelve, though he held a decree for sixteen chalders. The proper course was to exhaust his rights under that decree, either by bringing a supplementary scheme or by a *pro forma* reduction of that locality.

COURT OF SESSION.

FIRST DIVISION.

Susp.—M'Kinnon *v.* Hamilton.—*June* 21.

Diligence—Poinding—Suspension.

This was a suspension of a poinding which had been executed by the respondent against the suspender. The poinding had proceeded on a charge given on a bill for £13 granted by M'Kinnon to Hamilton. The present suspension was brought on the ground—(1) That the poinding was excessive, being for an appraised value of upwards of five times the amount of the debt; (2) that no restriction was imposed upon the creditor as to the quantity of the effects which might be sold; and (3) that there was no precise time of sale fixed, inasmuch as the hour of sale was left to the creditor's discretion.

The Lord Ordinary (Mure) passed the note on consignation of £13, and £5 of expenses, and continued the interdict. Against this judgment Hamilton reclaimed, and contended that the poinding was not excessive, inasmuch as the poinder had to include the landlord's rent in the poinding; and also that it was not necessary or possible in such a case to introduce a restriction on the creditor in selling the poinded effects; and further, that it was not requisite, under 1 and 2 Vict., sec. 114, to fix precisely the hour of sale, such not being the practice in the Sheriff Court of Bute, where the poinding was issued, and ample notice of the hour of sale having been given to the debtor otherwise.

The Court, without hearing the suspender's counsel, adhered to the Lord Ordinary's interlocutor. Their Lordships were unanimously of opinion that the poinding, although it might have been executed in good faith, was excessive, and that such poindings might be made the instruments of inflicting great oppression.

The Lord President could not admit that a creditor in a poinding was entitled to poind to such an extent in order to protect himself from claims at the instance of the landlord.

Lord Deas thought that the argument rested on the landlord's claim told against the poinding creditor, since, had the latter poinded only for the amount of his debt, the landlord would not have had ground to interfere. The excessive amount poinded made it necessary for the landlord to protect his interest.

Foster *v.* Campbell and Others.—*June* 22.

Trust Deed—Construction.

This was an action of furthcoming against the defenders, Sir A. I. Campbell and others, who were arrestees, and against Lord Charles Pelham Pelham Clinton, common debtor. The pursuer had arrested certain rents of the estate of Congalton, in the hands of Sir A. I. Campbell and others. who were the trustees under the marriage settlement of Lord and Lady Charles P. P. Clinton. By that deed, and by a relative trust-disposition granted by her, Lady Clinton, then Miss Elizabeth Grant of Congalton, conveyed the estate of Congalton to these trustees for certain purposes therein specified. These trustees are thereby directed to pay the net revenues of the estate as to one moiety to the separate use of Lady Charles, but excluding all right of any kind on the part of her husband, and the other moiety to Lord Clinton (unless his rights therein should be forfeited), and to hold the fee or capital in the event (which has happened) of there being children of the marriage, for behoof of such children, till certain provisions in their favour shall have been vested. The purpose of the trust, which relates to the payment of the net revenue of the trust-estate, is in the following terms:—"The said trustees, and the survivors or survivor of them, and the executors and administrators of such survivor, do and shall, during the joint lives of the said Lord C. P. P. Clinton and Elizabeth Grant, while there shall be no child of the said intended marriage living, pay two equal third parts, and while there shall be any child of the said intended marriage living, one moiety or half part of the interest, dividends, or annual produce of the said trust-moneys, shares, stocks, funds, and securities, to the said Elizabeth Grant, for her sole and separate use, independently and exclusively of her said intended husband, and without being subject to his debts, control, interference, or engagement, but so that she shall have no power to sell, mortgage, or charge the same, or any part thereof, in the way of anticipation, and the receipts of the said Elizabeth Grant, and such receipts only, to be good and effectual discharges for the same; and do and shall pay the remaining one-third or one-half, as the case may be, of the said dividends, interest, and annual produce, to the said Lord C. P. P. Clinton for his own use, *till such time as he shall sell, mortgage, or charge the same, or some part thereof, or so to do, or become bankrupt or insolvent, or do or suffer any act or thing whereby the same or any part thereof, if hereby limited absolutely, would cease to be receivable by the said Lord C. P. P. Clinton for his own use.*" Founding on this clause the trustees maintained that the effect of the arrestments used by the pursuer, and also of certain other arrestments which had been used in their hands by other creditors of Lord Charles, was to cause the forfeiture and determination of all right on the part of Lord Charles Clinton to any part of the funds in their hands. The Lord Ordinary (Barcaple) repelled this plea, and the defenders reclaimed, and argued that on the decree of furthcoming being pronounced in this action, Lord Charles Clinton's right was forfeited, and, therefore, there would be no funds available to the pursuer.

The deeds having been executed in England, it was thought expedient to get the opinion of English counsel on their meaning, and a case having been prepared accordingly, Mr G. M. Giffard, Q.C., gave it as his opinion that the effect of the arrestments was only to *suspend* the right of Lord C. Clinton, not to make it *cease* altogether.

To-day the Court advised the case, and adhered substantially to the Lord Ordinary's interlocutor. The Court held that Lord Clinton's right had not ceased in consequence of the use of the arrestments. They did not make the rents payable to any one else. At present his right may be suspended, but it is not extinguished till the decree of furthcoming is pronounced, if then. The effect of that is not necessary to be considered now.

Dewar *v.* Pearson.—*June* 27.

Interim Execution pending Appeal.

This was a petition for interim execution pending appeal. The case originated in the Sheriff Court, and there the Sheriff had given decree for a sum of £367. An advocation of this judgment was brought, and the Court remitted *simpliciter* to the Sheriff. The present application is now presented for interim execution pending appeal. It appeared, however, that there might be some difficulties in the way of carrying out interim execution if granted, and the Court was of opinion that this being an appeal to the discretion of the Court—an application which the petitioner was not entitled to make at common law—there ought to be no obscurity in reference to what sum such interim execution was to apply to. The way in which it was to be extricated ought to be quite free from doubt, but that did not appear to be the case here. The granting of this petition would probably lead to further complication and litigation in the inferior Court. The petition was therefore refused, except as to the expenses of the advocation.

STEVEN *v.* M'DOWALL'S TRUSTEES.—*June* 27.

Copartnery—Fraud—Application of Verdict.

The pursuer, Mr Steven, was the nephew of the late Mr M'Dowall, ironfounder in Glasgow, with whom he had gone into partnership in the year 1850. The terms of the partnership were—that Steven was to get for the first two years one-fourth, and for the remaining years one-third of the profits, and in addition £100 a-year as salary. The pursuer contended that the business was practically conducted by him, with the exception of the cash department, which was managed by the late Mr M'Dowall. In the beginning of 1861, two brothers of the pursuer were taken into partnership with him, and at that time a balance-sheet, purporting to show the state of the former company's affairs, was prepared. This balance-sheet was adopted in the contract of copartnery of the new company as the basis of certain arrangements then made between the old and new firms. In the same year (1861) Mr M'Dowall died. Mr Steven now brought the present actions of reduction and count and reckoning, concluding that the balance-sheet and contract of copartnery, so far as related to the pursuer's share of the profits between the years 1850 and 1861, ought to be reduced and set aside as procured through the fraud of the late Mr M'Dowall, and that the defenders, who are Mr M'Dowall's trustees, ought to be ordained to count and reckon with him for his share of these profits. He grounded these actions on allegations that Mr M'Dowall had been guilty of fraud in inducing the pursuer to sign the balance-sheet and the contract of copartnery on the footing that these contained a true statement of the company's affairs. Instead of being a correct balance-sheet, however, the pursuer alleged that his share of the profits from 1850 to 1861, which he had never drawn, had been omitted, while during that time Mr M'Dowall was alleged to have drawn £30,000. It was for the pursuer's share of this sum that he sought to get the defenders ordained to count and reckon with him. The defenders deny that any fraud was committed by Mr M'Dowall, and assert that the pursuer had ample opportunity of satisfying himself as to the correctness of the balance-sheet. An issue was adjusted to try the question of fraud, and it having been tried, the jury unanimously found for the defenders, thereby negativing the charge of fraud.

To-day, the defenders moved the Court to apply the verdict and assoilzie them from the conclusions of the actions. The pursuer objected that, although the jury had found that his signature had not been adhibited to the balance-sheet and contract of copartnery through Mr M'Dowall's fraud, yet that the defenders were bound to count and reckon with him.

The Court was of opinion that the jury, having negatived fraud in the balance-sheet and contract of copartnery, these documents, which were signed by the parties and now stood unimpeached, must be taken as correct and as fixing the rights of parties. This was more especially the case, looking to the manner in which the balance-sheet had been referred to and acted on in the contract of copartnery of the second company. It would not do to allow the pursuer now to go into a count and reckoning in reference to the matters involved in that balance-sheet. The Court therefore applied the verdict, and assoilzied the defenders.

YOUNG *v.* HARDIE.—*June* 28.

Interdict—Circumstances in which refused.

This was a suspension and interdict, in which Mr. Young sought to have the Messrs. Hardie interdicted from using the railway which leads through the lands of Langmuir from the lands of Saddlersbrae to the lands of Corbethill, and from conveying over said railway any coals or other minerals raised on the lands of Braes of Yetts or Wester Gartclash. Mr. Young, it would appear, had, in the year 1858, let the minerals of Langmuir to the Messrs. Hardie, and had thereafter granted to them a missive, in which he agreed to allow them, on paying a certain sum for surface damage, to "make a road or roads, or railways, across or upon my property of Langmuir, and to maintain and use the same for a period of nineteen years, or any shorter period you may require them, for the purpose of conveying the minerals of the neighbouring properties, and any other purpose for which you may require such roads or railways." It would also appear that Messrs. Hardie, at the time of receiving this missive, were tenants of the minerals of Langmuir and Saddlersbrae, and they subsequently bought the properties of Braes of Yetts and West Gartclash, with minerals in them. The last two properties adjoined Saddlersbrae, but did not adjoin Langmuir. Messrs. Hardie had been in the habit of using the railway on Langmuir for conveying minerals from Saddlersbrae and Langmuir, but latterly they had given up working the minerals on both these properties. They have let the minerals on Braes of Yetts and Wester Gartclash to two parties who now use the railway in question, while the minerals on Saddlersbrae are worked by other parties than Messrs. Hardie, and the railway is used by these persons under an authority derived from Messrs. Hardie. In these circumstances the present interdict is brought on the grounds (1) that the right to use the railway across Langmuir is personal to Messrs. Hardie; and (2) that that right was limited to the minerals raised from Langmuir and Saddlersbrae.

The Lord Ordinary (Barcaple) refused the interdict, and to-day the Court adhered. It was the opinion of the Court, which was delivered by Lord Deas, that the right of using the railway was not personal, but was validly communicated by the Messrs. Hardie, and also that it was not restricted to the lands of Langmuir and Saddlersbrae, but extended to neighbouring properties, which included Braes of Yetts and Wester Gartclash. His Lordship, farther, was not satisfied that it was incompetent (as had been contended by Mr Young) to explain the meaning of the words "neighbouring properties," in the missive by parole evidence of what passed at the entering into of the missive. Surrounding facts and circumstances might throw great light on the meaning of these words.

ANTERMONY COAL COMPANY *v.* WINGATE AND CO.—*June* 30.

Copartnery—Title of individual Partner to Sue.

This was an action at the instance of the Antermony Coal Company and Austin & Co. and Walter Wingate, the individual partners thereof, against Walter Wingate & Co., and the said Walter Wingate and G. C. Bruce, the individual partners of that firm. It was raised for the price of articles said to have been sold by the pursuers to the defender. Walter Wingate has, it is alleged, not authorised this action, and has gone to Australia, and Bruce, among other defences, maintains that the action cannot be farther prosecuted unless Wingate's authority for carrying it on is produced, in respect the remaining pursuers consist only of a descriptive firm, and one partner thereof, who cannot sue, it is said, without the consent of the other partner. The remaining pursuers contend that the action, being instituted by the Antermony Coal Company and Austin & Co., the other partner of that company, the instance is good, and they are entitled to carry on the case, although Wingate's authority is not produced.

The Lord Ordinary (Barcaple) gave effect to the contention of the pursuer, and repelled the defenders' plea founded on the want of Wingate's authority.

To-day, the Court unanimously adhered, holding that the partners of a firm were each able to bind the company for a company debt. They had *præpositura* to take such steps as were necessary to enforce a company debt, and generally to wield the powers of the company for company purposes. In a case like the present it would amount to a denial of justice if the consent of the other partner were required, since as he was a defender, he never would consent. Here the purpose of the action was to recover a company debt, and the action was raised by the company and one of its partners. The instance was accordingly sufficient.

KEITH *v.* CASSELS.—*June* 30.

Application to Sheriff by Pauper receiving Relief for additional Relief—Incompetent.

In this case, Keith, who is a married woman, in destitute circumstances, having one child in infancy, and having been deserted by her husband, presented, on 31st May 1865, a petition to the Sheriff of Lanark against Cassels, who is the Inspector of the Poor of the parish of Lanark, craving parochial relief *ad interim* for herself and child. Cassels, in his answers to the petition, alleged that Keith had, from 15th March 1865, been on the roll of paupers of the parish of Lanark, and had regularly received parochial relief since that date. He pleaded that the application was incompetent, as the Board of Supervision were the proper parties to apply to. It would appear that during the month of March Keith had got relief at the rate of 4s. per month, during April at the rate of 5s. per month, and during May at the rate of 6s. per month. The last advance was on 22d May 1865, when the inspector gave her 1s., and told her that she would get no more till 8th June 1865, when her case would be considered at the meeting of the Board to be held then. On 31st May 1865 she presented her application to the Sheriff; and the Sheriff-Substitute of Lanark, before whom the case first came, in respect that she was at that date in the receipt of parochial relief, found that the question raised was one as to the *adequacy* of the relief afforded, and therefore held the application incompetent, since that matter belonged to the Board of Supervision, not the Sheriff. Against this judgment Keith appealed to the Sheriff, who reversed the decision of the Sheriff-Substitute, on the ground that the inspector's intimation to her, on 22d May, when he gave her 1s., that she was not to come back till 8th June, was a virtual refusal of relief, and not the awarding of inadequate relief. This judgment was advocated, and Lord Mure (Ordinary) recalled it, holding that the question raised related to the *adequacy* of the relief afforded, and fell, therefore, to be decided by the Board of Supervision. Keith reclaimed, and argued that the Sheriff was right in holding the inspector's intimation as a virtual refusal of relief; that the words "poor person" in sec. 74 of 8 and 9 Vict., cap. 83,—the section which requires complaints against the adequacy of relief to be presented to the Board of Supervision,—meant persons on the roll of permanent paupers, not casuals, and that Keith's true remedy was the one now sought, viz., application to the Sheriff under sec. 73 of that Act. By that section any poor person who shall be refused relief may apply to the Sheriff, who, if satisfied that the applicant has right to relief, shall direct the inspector to afford relief. Cassels argued that the words "poor person" in sec. 74 included casuals, and, therefore, that Keith had mistaken her remedy, which was an application to the Board of Supervision.

To-day the Court adhered to the Lord Ordinary's interlocutor, thereby holding that Keith's application to the Sheriff was incompetent. Their lordships were of opinion that a person, if he got relief, and then sought more, and was refused, that could not be held to be in the position of being refused relief. Farther, being merely on the roll of permanent paupers was not the test of right to apply to the Board of Supervision. The Lord President said he had considered it proper to inquire into the practice on this point, and he had learned from the secretary of that Board that the practice is, and has been since 1845, that any poor person who has received relief is held entitled to apply to the Board, whether on the roll or not.

DEMPSEY *v.* EDINBURGH AND GLASGOW RAILWAY CO.—*July* 5.

Special Jury—Application for Refused.

In this case the defenders moved for a special jury. The action was one of damages for injuries sustained in a railway accident. The defenders assigned no reason why the case should be tried by a special jury, but relied solely on the 24th clause of the statute 55 Geo. III. c. 42, which allows either party to move for a special jury. The question thus raised was, whether, in every case of this kind, either party was entitled, without cause shown, to a special jury. The Court, in respect no reason for granting a special jury had been stated, refused the motion.

ANDERSON (WARD'S TRUSTEE) *v.* THE GLASGOW AND SOUTH-WESTERN RAILWAY COMPANY.—*July* 5.

Agent and Client—Confidentiality.

Mr Ward is a railway contractor who had contracted to execute certain works for the Ayr and Dalmellington Railway Company. In the deed of contract it is provided that all disputes arising between the company and Mr Ward should be referred to Mr Wm. Johnstone, the engineer of the company. Certain disputes did arise, and were submitted to Mr Johnstone, but pending the reference, Mr Ward says he discovered that Mr Johnstone had negotiated, or helped to negotiate, the union of the Ayr and Dalmellington Company with the Glasgow and South-Western Company, and in so doing he had stated the liabilities of the Ayr and Dalmellington Company at a sum which necessarily assumed Mr Ward's claims to be unfounded. Mr Ward farther says that Mr Johnstone gave evidence before the House of Commons in reference to the amalgamation of these companies, in which he stated the liabilities of the Ayr and Dalmellington Company in a similar manner. Mr Ward then raised the present action, concluding that it should be declared that Mr Johnstone had by these proceedings disqualified himself from acting as arbiter under the contract, and from deciding the questions in dispute. The action is now insisted in by Mr Anderson, Mr Ward's trustee. A proof having been allowed to both parties before answer, the pursuer lodged a specification of certain documents which he sought, and under it he proposed to get the precognitions or notes of the evidence given by Mr Johnstone before the committee of the House of Commons. At an examination of havers in London the pursuer called for, from the agent for the promoters of the Amalgamation Bill, the precognitions or notes of the evidence to be given by Mr Johnstone. The agent declined to produce them on the ground that they were confidential, and came into his hands as briefs. The commissioner ordered them to be sealed up, and the pursuer moved the Lord Ordinary to open the sealed packet.

The Lord Ordinary refused the motion *in hoc statu.*

The pursuer reclaimed, but the Court to-day adhered, holding that the nature of the documents was not known, and that, as the pursuer had a proof as well as a diligence allowed, the haver might have been examined as a witness as to the nature of the documents. This was not done. In the whole circumstances the interlocutor of the Lord Ordinary appeared to be correct.

SOMMERVILLE *v.* MAGISTRATES OF LANARK.—*July* 7.

Reduction of Decree—Relevancy.

The Magistrates of Lanark had raised two actions in the Sheriff Court against Sommerville for payment of certain rents of a mill which they had let to him, and in these actions they had obtained decrees against him. Sommerville now brought the present action seeking to get these decrees reduced, on the ground that the Sheriff erroneously repelled certain pleas which ought to have been sustained, and also on the ground that a lease, which was the foundation of the magistrates' case, was unstamped. In the present action, besides several subordinate conclusions, he also claimed damages in respect—1. That the magistrates failed to keep, as they were bound to do, the mill in good repair; and 2. That they were liable for abstracted multures.

The pursuer alleged that the magistrates were, by the lease of the mill, bound to keep the mill in repair; and also, that he was "entitled to the multures of all grindable corn growing within the thirle conform to use and wont," wheat excepted, and that the magistrates were bound to furnish him with a list of all lands belonging to them or under their management, the corn of which was thirled to the mill in question.

The magistrates denied generally these allegations, and specially maintained that they were not liable for abstracted multures in respect of a clause in the lease which bore that they did "not warrant the multures to the tenant to any extent, and it is expressly declared that the tenant shall not be entitled to retain the rent upon the pretext of abstracted multures, or to compensation for such abstraction." They farther maintained that no illiquid claim of damage could be maintained against their demand for payment of the rent of the mill.

The Lord Ordinary (Ormidale) had found the action irrelevant, except as regards the claim of damage for non-repair of the mill, in reference to which he allowed the pursuer, before answer, to lodge an issue. The pursuer reclaimed, but the Court to-day unanimously adhered. Their Lordships were of opinion that there were no averments in the summons sufficient to sustain the conclusions for reduction of the Sheriff Court decrees; and in reference to the claims for multures and for lists of the lands within the thirle, they also held them to be unsupported by the necessary averments. No lands were specified as in the magistrates' own hands, and it did not appear that there anywhere existed an obligation to furnish the lists sought. Their Lordships were disposed, however, to allow an issue to be lodged before answer on the question of damages.

Urquhart *v.* Bonnar.—*July* 10.

Special Jury.

In this case, John Urquhart, shoemaker, Cupar, now deceased, was pursuer, and George Lindsay Bonnar, M.D., practising there, is defender. The pursuer sought to get an assignation of a policy of insurance, which he had executed in favour of the defender, reduced, on the ground that he was, when he signed it, under essential error as to its nature and effect, induced through the fraud and misrepresentation or undue concealment on the part of the defender. The case has been twice tried before a common jury, and both the verdicts, which were in favour of the pursuer, have been set aside by the Court as contrary to evidence. It is now set down to be tried at the ensuing sittings for the third time, and to-day the defender moved for a special jury, on the ground that there had already been on two occasions a miscarriage of justice. The pursuer answered that this was no reason why a special jury should be allowed, the purpose of which was to enlist class prejudices on behalf of the defender; that the granter of the assignation had been a shoemaker originally, a working man, that he should be tried by his peers, and that persons of that class were better fitted to judge of his state of mind than special jurors. The defender replied that, in fact, he, and not the pursuer, was on his trial—a charge of fraud being made against him—and he was entitled to be tried by his peers; that in one-third of the cases tried by common juries, the verdict was afterwards set aside by the Court, which proved that that was not the best tribunal.

The Court held that no sufficient reason had been shown for granting a special jury.

Lawson *v.* Ferguson.—*July* 10.

Breach of Promise of Marriage—Judicial Tender—Expenses.

This was an action of damages for breach of promise of marriage, raised by Jane Lawson, residing in Elder Street, Edinburgh, against James H. Ferguson, draper, Elder Street, Edinburgh. During the progress of the case, the defender offered £52 10s. in full of the pursuer's claims. This offer was not accepted, and the case went on. The jury by which the issue was tried found for the pursuer, assessing the damages at £50. On moving the Lord Ordinary (Kinloch) to apply the verdict, the defender sought expenses from the date of his offer of £52 10s., as the jury had found the pursuer entitled to less than that sum. The Lord Ordinary found expenses due to neither party, and against this judgment the defender reclaimed, and contended that the rule fixed by several decisions was to give expenses from the date of the tender. The principle on which this was done was, that after a tender of more than the jury gave, the pursuer must be held to have been litigating unjustifiably.

The Court, without calling on the pursuer's counsel, unanimously adhered to the Lord Ordinary's interlocutor. Their Lordships held that while it was true that where pecuniary compensation only was sought, a tender of more than the jury gives generally carries expenses from its date, on the other hand, it was equally true that in cases where character was in issue, a tender was not enough, and would not always carry expenses. The case was one in which character was to a certain extent involved. The defender, along with his tender, had lodged defences, denying the promise to marry and the engagement. Besides, no reason whatever had been stated why the engagement was broken off. These affected character. The decision in this case did not derogate from the rules already laid down in previous cases. It turned entirely on the special circumstances existing here. The Lord Ordinary, whose judgment was now under review, had tried the case, and looking to the whole aspect of it, had found neither party entitled to expenses. His Lordship was well acquainted with its features, which the Court were not, and, on the whole, it did not seem expedient to alter his Lordship's judgment.

Note for J. Carment in Petition Hepburn—for Authority.—*July* 10.

Tutor ad Litem—Powers and Liabilities.

A petition for authority to disentail had been presented by Hepburn, and in that application a *tutor ad litem* had been appointed to one of the succeeding heirs of entail who was a pupil. In the course of the correspondence between the petitioner and the *tutor ad litem* in regard to the amount of consideration money to be paid to the latter for a consent by him on behalf of his ward, it was stated by the petitioner that he had been advised by counsel that the entail was defective. In these circumstances the *tutor ad litem* now applied to the Court for instructions as to whether in fixing the sum, on payment of which he ought to grant a consent for the pupil to the disentail, the element of the alleged invalidity of the entail should be taken into consideration.

The Court were unanimously of opinion that they ought not to interfere with the tutor in the exercise of the discretion committed to him. Under the statute (11 and 12 Vict., cap 36, sect 31) his powers are very large, and his immunities are equally large. No one is entitled to demand the grounds on which he may form any opinion, provided he acts honestly and fairly in performing the duties of his office. In these circumstances the Court were not disposed to quit the ordinary course of procedure.

LATHAM v. EDINBURGH AND GLASGOW RAILWAY—JAMIESON v. IDEM.—*July* 11.

Process—Petition for Recall of Arrestments—Competency.

These actions were on the 17th instant dismissed as irrelevant. While they were under discussion in the Inner House, a petition was presented to the Lord Ordinary, before whom the case had depended, for recall of certain arrestments to the extent of about £12,000, which had been used by the pursuer on the dependence. This petition was not insisted in at the time, but the actions having been dismissed on the 17th instant, the cases were to-day in the Lord Ordinary's roll, and the defender moved for recall of the arrestments. The Lord Ordinary, however, took the objection that he had no power to deal with the application after a final judgment by the Inner House, and that if the petition were competent at all, it ought to have been presented to the Inner House. His lordship, therefore, brought the matter under the notice of the Court. The Lord Ordinary's powers to deal with such applications were contained in the Personal Diligence Act 1 and 2 Vict., cap. 113, sec. 30. By that section the Lord Ordinary, before whom any summons shall be enrolled as judge therein, or before whom any action has or shall be enrolled as judge therein, may recall or restrict arrestments on caution or without caution. But his lordship was disposed to think that this provision applied only to causes in dependence before him.

The defenders maintained that it applied to any cause at any stage, even if it were under appeal to the House of Lords. This application was competent when presented, and would be competent after the appeal to the House of Lords, which was said to be in preparation, was intimated. Was there an intermediate stage at which it became incompetent?

Their lordships were by no means satisfied that the case was in dependence before the Lord Ordinary. It was extremely doubtful if this motion was competent, and their Lordships ultimately advised the Lord Ordinary to pronounce an interlocutor refusing to recall the arrestments in respect of the judgment of the First Division dismissing the actions.

M.P.—KEITH'S TRUSTEE v. EARL OF KINTORE.—*July* 11.

Trust Deed—Vesting.

The Ladies Maria and Catherine Keith, directed by their joint settlement, their trustees "to hold the sum of £6000 of the trust means and estate hereby conveyed, for the purpose of paying over from the first term of Whitsunday or Martinmas, after the death of the longest liver of us, to the Lady Mary

Keith, during her life, the yearly interest which they may draw for the said sum of £6000; and at the first term of Whitsunday or Martinmas after the death of the said Lady Mary Keith, the said sum of £6000 shall be paid over by our said trustee to the Hon. Wm. Keith (their nephew), whom failing, to his children equally between them, share and share alike." The last of the testators died on 24th August 1851. Both ladies were predeceased by Wm. Keith in 1846, and admittedly no right vested in him. He left two children, Dora (Mrs Lockwood), who died in 1856, without issue, leaving Lady Mary Keith, the liferentrix, surviving. Mrs Lockwood had executed a settlement on her marriage, disposing of her share of the £6000, on the assumption of its vesting in her. The liferentrix died on 5th July 1864, survived by Adrian Keith Falconer, the only other child of Wm. Keith. There is no question as to his right to £3000, but a competition has arisen between him and Mrs Lockwood's marriage contract trustees for the other £3000, and the right to this sum depends on whether between the death of the last survivor of the testators and that of the liferentrix, the sum had vested in Mrs Lockwood, and was carried by her settlement. If it did not vest till the death of the liferentrix, the whole £6000 would go to Adrian.

The Lord Ordinary (Kinloch) found that the right did vest in Mrs Lockwood at the death of the last of the testators.

The Court to-day adhered, holding that the two children of Wm. Keith were conditional institutes. There was no intention to postpone the payment to the beneficiaries for any other purpose than to secure the annual revenue to the liferentrix.

PETITION—MORITZ HARRIS MOSES AND CHARLES BURRY *v.* J. G. GIFFORD.
July 12.

Sequestration—Circumstances in which recalled.

This was a petition at the instance of Mr Moses and Mr Burry for recal of the sequestration of the estates of John George Gifford, designing himself as "Clerk, residing at Innerleithen, in the county of Peebles." It appeared that when this petition was in the Outer House, the Lord Ordinary (Mure) granted the recal in respect of the non-appearance of Gifford, after intimation to him that if he failed to appear recal would be granted. Against this recal Gifford reclaimed, and contended that the motion to recal on his failure to appear was incompetent, and that as he did not get the intimation before referred to, he was entitled to get the judgment recalling the sequestration altered. Before deciding this question, the Court heard parties on the merits of the application for recal. It was alleged for Mr Moses and Mr Burry, who were two English creditors of the bankrupt, that the bankrupt was a clerk in holy orders, having been curate of the chapelry of Holdenhurst; that he had come to Scotland and lived at Innerleithen for a short time solely for the purpose of acquiring a domicile to enable him to get sequestration under the Scotch Bankrupt Act. That, being at the date of presenting his petition (1864) a clerk in holy orders, the designation therein given of "clerk, residing at Innerleithen," &c., was erroneous, and was intended to conceal his application for sequestration, and mislead his creditors as to his identity. That the bankrupt was domiciled in England, where his whole estate and effects were situated, and where he had creditors to the extent of £2590, while he had creditors in Scotland only to the extent of £10 15s. In these circumstances, the estate ought to be distributed in England, and the sequestration recalled in terms of 23 and 24 Vict., c. 33, sec. 2.

The bankrupt denied these allegations generally. The Court adhered to the Lord Ordinary's judgment, and their interlocutor bore that they did so after having heard parties on the merits.

The Lord President thought it was evident that the bankrupt had come to Scotland to take advantage of our bankrupt law. It appeared that he had been in France for some time, that thereafter he had come to England, and thence to Innerleithen, in consequence, he admitted, of his affairs being in an embarrassed state. He then presents his petition for sequestration, and in it designs himself in a way in which it would be almost impossible for his creditors to recognise him. He says now that he has no funds in England, and he does not say that he has any funds here. It appears that he is not himself here now, but he is said to be "travelling," probably with his means with him. In these circumstances, it is desirable that the estate of this gentleman, if he has any, should be distributed where the majority of his creditors reside—the only debts owing by him in Scotland being such as he might have contracted after a few days' residence in Innerleithen.

The other Judges concurred.

BLUE v. TRUSTEES OF WEST KILBRIDE FREE GARDENERS' SOCIETY.—*July* 12.

Action of Damages against a Society—Relevancy.

In this case the pursuer sought to get damages from the defenders, as trustees of the West Kilbride Free Gardeners' Society. The ground of action was, that he had been illegally expelled from the society, of which he had been a member since its institution in 1829. He had been placed, in the year 1861, on the roll of "alimentors" of the society, with a weekly allowance of 4s. But in June 1864 this allowance was stopped, and he was expelled from the society on the ground that it was proved to the satisfaction of a certain committee of the society, "that he was intoxicated on the 17th June 1864." This expulsion was grounded on Rule 18 of the society, which provides that, "if any person be found pursuing his ordinary employment or tippling or intoxicated, or out of his house after ten o'clock at night while on the sick list, for any of these or similar offences, he shall be suspended from all benefit until such time as the committee take his case into consideration, which they are hereby bound to do within eight days." The pursuer denied that he was intoxicated on the occasion referred to. He farther alleged that he had no opportunity of defending himself from this charge of being intoxicated, or of proving, as he could easily have done, that it was false. He appealed against the resolution expelling him, but his appeal was not entertained, nor was the matter submitted, as he contended it should have been, by the rules of the society, to arbitration. In these circumstances, he brought the present action for £200. In the pleas, he sought this sum as "damages," but it was not so described in the conclusions of the summons. The Lord Ordinary sustained the defenders' pleas, to the effect that the action was irrelevant, and that a society like this could not be found liable in damages.

To-day, the Court recalled the interlocutor of the Lord Ordinary. The Lord President held the contention of the defenders, that the act of expelling was not the act of the society, was ill-founded. They had themselves, in one part of the record, treated it as their act. But, besides, the society acted through its committee and office-bearers, and this was therefore the society's act. The objection that Blue had not taken the proper method of appealing was also untenable. The defenders here had never said what was the proper method of appealing, and the course followed by the pursuer seemed to be correct enough in the circumstances of the case. The other ground of defence, and that chiefly gone upon by the Lord Ordinary, was that the funds of this society could not be held liable in damages. Now, the society had taken the act as one done by themselves. The nature of this case, too, was such as to distinguish it from the cases of Findlater and Duncan, and Heriot's Hospital, 19th March 1846, 5 Bell's Appeals, p. 37. Here the funds were contributed by members for their own benefit, and the result of the expulsion is to enrich themselves. This was quite different from the state of matters in these cases. The society is the party liable to the demand. It is the case of a company managing its own affairs. In the cases referred to funds were managed under a statute and the bill of the donor respectively. In these circumstances these cases did not appear to apply, and therefore the judgment of the Lord Ordinary, which proceeded on these cases, should be altered. The other judges concurred.

SECOND DIVISION.

Lindsay *v.* Mackenzie and Faichney—*June* 11.

Poor—Settlement—Continuous Residence—Lunatic.

20 *and* 21 *Vict. c.* 71, § 77 *and* 78. 8 *and* 9 *Vict. c.* 83, § 76.

In July 1860, William Fraser was apprehended at Broadford, in the parish of Strath, where he followed his trade as a saddler—taken to Portree, brought before the Sheriff as a dangerous lunatic, and after a week's confinement, and further examination, dismissed. There being no sufficient proof of insanity, the expenses connected with this apprehension and subsequent confinement were paid by Faichney, as Inspector of Poor for Strath, and notice purporting to be given under the Poor-Law Amendment Act, was sent to Mackenzie, Inspector for Kiltearn, the parish of the pauper's birth settlement, by whom these expenses were repaid. The present action was at the instance of the Inspector of Poor for the parish of Row, where Fraser had become chargeable as a pauper lunatic, and was directed alternatively against the parishes of Strath and Kiltearn. It was not disputed that Fraser continued in the parish of Strath for five years from 1856 downwards, and that by such residence he acquired an industrial settlement, unless its continuity and effect were destroyed by what occurred in July 1860. The question in law was whether the payment made by the Inspector for Strath in connection with the confinement of Fraser constituted parochial relief in terms of the 76th section of the Poor-Law Amendment Act, so as to be an interruption to the acquisition of a settlement by Fraser in that parish. The Lord Ordinary (Jerviswoode) held that it did not, and the Court unanimously adhered.

The Lord-Justice Clerk said—For the expenses of all these proceedings the lunatic is liable himself, after him the person otherwise bound to support him, failing whom the parish of his settlement. I have grave doubts whether if such expenses were paid by the parish, this could, under any circumstances, be held to be a giving of parochial relief; but I am quite clear that it cannot be so held here. The principal expenses appear to have been incurred—(1) In removing Fraser from a place where he was in business for himself, and conveying him to another place, where he was lodged in jail; and (2) In proceedings before the Sheriff, which were undertaken with a view of committing him as a dangerous lunatic, and which failed. A very important question may arise, whether, in the case of there being some one liable, in the ordinary case, to pay for the lunatic, he would be so liable where the proceedings were so abortive as these seem to have been; but it is the merest fallacy to assume such liability in the present case. But then, besides the other expenses, there is a sum of 7s. for Fraser's maintenance in prison, and laid out by whom? By the Procurator-Fiscal, for the public interest. It appears to be as wild a statement as I ever heard, to call this a receipt of parochial relief in any intelligible way. Still further, it is a fallacy to assume that because the Parochial Board may be bound to relieve the inspector, that that necessarily reduces the lunatic to the condition of a pauper. The statute merely says that he shall be treated as a pauper lunatic, but it does not make him one—nay, it contains provisions in case it shall eventually turn out that the lunatic is not a pauper. My opinion as to the total misunderstanding under which parties appear to have laboured is further confirmed by the fact that the notice given to Kiltearn professed to be given under the Poor Law Act—an Act under which there was no more authority for giving it than at common law. It is the Lunacy Act, and it alone, which authorises such notices.

Campbell *v.* Leith Police Commissioners.—*June* 22.

Burgh—General Police and Improvement Act, 25 *and* 26 *Vic.*, *cap.* 101—*Commissioners—Private Street—Notices.*

The Police Commissioners of the Burgh of Leith having adopted the provisions of the General Police and Improvement Act (1862), resolved, under § 150, to have a certain street in the Burgh, as being a "private street" in the meaning of the Act, paved and causewayed, and they gave statutory notice of their intention, in terms of § 394, by posting up, in a conspicuous place at each end of the street, a written notice as thereby directed. A different kind of notice is required by § 397, and this they did not give. The present action was brought by a proprietor of houses on both sides of the street. He pleaded (1) The street was not a private street in the sense of the Act; (2) Notices of the operations complained of should have been given under § 397. The Court repelled both pleas. Looking to and contrasting the definition of a public and private street, as given in § 3, and taking into consideration that this place had been designed for a street of some kind or other, had not been sufficiently paved or flagged at the date of the adoption of the Act, and had not been "maintained as a public street," they had no doubt that it came within the definition of a private street, as given in the Act. That being so, it was unnecessary to determine whether it was so in any other sense. As to the alleged insufficiency of notice, they thought that, looking to the interpretation clause in § 3, in connection with § 103, it was impossible to hold that the operations complained of were such as "fall to be provided for by way of private improvement assessment;" and therefore notices did not require to be given in terms of § 397. Doubts were expressed whether notices under § 394 were requisite; but as these had been already given, it was unnecessary to decide the point.

BRAIDWOODS *v.* THE BONNINGTON SUGAR REFINING COY., &c.—*June* 23.

Reparation—Employer and Contractor—Master and Servant—Relevancy—Conjunct and Several Liability.

This was an action of damages at the instance of the widow and children of the late John Braidwood, engineer, who was killed by the fall of a sugar refinery, in the course of erection at Bonnington. The fall was alleged to have been caused either by the insufficiency of the foundations, arising from a defect in the specifications and plans, or from a want of proper superintendence of the work during its execution. The action was directed against the proprietors of the building, and also against Black, Barclay, & Co., with whom they had contracted for its erection. It was not disputed that the established rule in law was, that where the contract for and erection of a building such as the present was entrusted to persons reputedly competent and qualified, the employers were not liable for any damage occasioned by insufficiency or defect in its construction; but the pursuers maintained that there was a specialty in this case, the Company having admittedly employed an inspector of works to superintend the erection. They had not separated their interests from those of the contractors whom they had employed, and were therefore liable for any loss occasioned by want of proper superintendence on the part of this inspector. The Court held that there was no specialty in the case to prevent the application of the general rule that employers are not liable for the fault of properly qualified contractors. The employment of an inspector was gratuitous on the part of the Company. He was their servant, and to them alone he was responsible. To the deceased he owed no duty, and therefore could fail in none. No doubt, he might be personally responsible for his own delinquency, but he could not bind his masters. So far as they were concerned, there was therefore no relevant case. As against the contractors, the case was clearly relevant. The fact that the action had been directed against them conjunctly and severally with other defenders, with respect to whom the Court had found that there was no relevant case, in no way affected the relevancy of the action so far as they were concerned.

EVANS, ARNOTT & CO. *v.* DRYSDALE'S TRUSTEES.—*June* 26.

Process—Trial without Jury—Verdict—Reclaiming Note—Competency.

In a trial before a Lord Ordinary (Kinloch) without a jury, under 13 and 14 Vic. cap 36, his Lordship returned a special verdict, which involved a judgment of absolvitor. The pursuers put in a note for a re-hearing, in which his Lordship was simply asked to recall his findings. The Lord

Ordinary adhered to his former interlocutor, and the pursuers reclaimed. The Court unanimously refused the reclaiming note as incompetent, in respect that none of the findings in the verdict involved any question of law. The Court were further unanimously of opinion that where any point of law was thought to be involved in such a verdict, the proper course was that parties should raise that question before the Lord Ordinary, and ask for a reconsideration of it in their note for a rehearing. Lords Justice-Clerk and Cowan expressed opinions to the effect that it was unnecessary and inexpedient for a Lord Ordinary to append a note to his verdict.

Lord Benholme dissented. He thought that the object of adding notes —viz., to explain to parties the grounds on which the verdict proceeded— was a very proper one, and he should be sorry to say anything to discourage such a practice.

Suspn.—Edinburgh and Glasgow Railway Co. *v.* Hall.—*June* 29.

Poor—Assessment—Deductions—Property and Income-Tax.

This was a suspension of a poinding for alleged arrears of poor-rates. The point on which the case was now before the Court was, whether the property-tax is one of the taxes for which deduction is to be made under sec. 37 of the Poor-Law Amendment Act. The Court held unanimously (altering the interlocutor of Lord Kinloch) that no such deduction was to be made. The 37th sec. directs that the annual value of lands and heritages shall be taken, for the purposes of rating, to be "the rent at which, one year with another, such lands and heritages might in their actual state be reasonably expected to let from year to year, under deduction of the probable annual average cost of the repairs, insurance, and other expenses, if any, necessary to maintain such lands and heritages in their actual state, and all rates, taxes, and public charges, payable in respect of the same." The Lord Justice-Clerk thought the above mode of fixing the annual value was equitable in itself, and precisely the same as was every day adopted in fixing the value of an estate with a view to a sale. In that case you deducted not the land-tax merely, but also the poor-rates, prison assessment, and other well-known rates and taxes; but was it ever heard of that the income-tax payable by the proprietor was deducted? This was a tax upon the free income of every subject of her Majesty above a certain amount, at the rate of a certain per centage upon that free income, and if they considered the operation of that tax, especially with reference to rents of lands, the thing they were then dealing with, it could not properly be said to be a public charge payable in respect of lands or heritages. A landed proprietor was not directly charged with this tax upon his rents. The 7d. in the pound was paid by the tenant, and deducted by him from his rent. Further, it entirely depended on the landlord's free income whether, even indirectly, he paid this 7d. or anything at all. If the estate were burdened up to its full amount, it would be his creditors who would pay that tax. It would be a strange thing to say that a tax, thus paid by persons who had either no connection with the lands at all, as in the case of personal creditors, or whose connection was merely that of being secured over the lands, should be called a tax payable or a public charge payable in respect of the lands and heritages. This would be a misconstruction of the fair meaning of these words. The purely personal nature of the tax was still more apparent if it were compared with an ordinary public burden, such as the poor-rate. There a proprietor had to pay according to the full rateable value of a subject, though it might not yield him a shilling. For income-tax he was ultimately liable only for the value which he actually received and retained.

WYLLIE AND OTHERS *v.* WYLLIE AND HILL.—*June* 30.

Contract of Copartnery—Arbitration Clause—Title to Exclude.

A contract of copartnery contained a clause, agreeing to refer all matters of dispute to arbiters therein named. In an action of count reckoning and payment, at the instance of several of the partners against another partner, the defender, who had previously raised and been unsuccessful in an action of declarator, that the present pursuers were not his partners, now pleaded that they were not his partners, and that he intended to appeal the judgment to that effect, and, alternatively, that, if they were, the present action was excluded by the clause of arbitration. The Court held that, as the only question at present was as to exhibition of the firm's books, and an account of intromissions, and the only defence that the pursuers were not partners,—a defence already repelled by the Court, and upon which they did not intend to constitute the arbiters a court of appeal—the submission clause was not applicable, whatever its effect might be in other questions between the parties.

GREEN *v.* MARR—*July* 5.

Trademark—Process—Interim interdict.

In an action of damages, containing a conclusion for interdict, for alleged infringement of the pursuer's trademarks, in which issues had been adjusted, the pursuer applied to the Court for *interim* interdict pending the trial. The Court, without deciding the general question as to the competency of such an application, unanimously refused it, on the ground that no precedent had been adduced, and no special cause shown for allowing what was thus admittedly a novelty in practice. That the pursuer had not brought an action of suspension and interdict in the ordinary way, rather appeared to them to imply that he did not at the time consider himself entitled to the remedy which he now sought.

M'CLELLAND *v.* BAIRD'S TRUSTEES—*July* 6.

Compromise—Co-obligants—Conjunct and several Delinquency—Relevancy —Process—Jury Trial—Remit to Accountant.

This action, at the instance of James M'Clelland, jun., accountant in Glasgow, as liquidator of the Western Bank of Scotland, and as representing the partners of the bank, was originally raised against the deceased William Baird of Elie, ironmaster in Glasgow, and is now insisted in against his trustees. The summons concludes for £299,736, 7s. 6d., as loss and damage sustained by the pursuers, through gross neglect of duty on the part of William Baird, as an ordinary director of the bank, both individually and in conjunction with his co-directors.

On December 1, 1865, the Lord Ordinary (Kinloch) pronounced an interlocutor, against which both parties reclaimed. The substance of that interlocutor, as well as the pleas of parties, were stated by

The Lord Justice-Clerk. The first part of the Lord Ordinary's interlocutor repels the objection to the title to sue. No argument was addressed to us in support of that plea, and all that we can do is to adhere to that part of the interlocutor. The interlocutor next repels the defence founded on the compromise and discharge engaged in with the other directors. While we are clearly of opinion that this plea does not afford a good answer to the claims of the pursuers in this action, as stated in the summons and record, it is possible that the case may disclose itself hereafter in such a shape as to render it an available defence against the claim as so disclosed; and we should not wish to prejudice any question of this kind which may hereafter arise. We shall, therefore, vary the terms of the interlocutor, so as to save, if possible, any injustice being done in that way. The Lord Ordinary then finds the action relevantly laid in so far as founded on an allegation of gross neglect of duty on the part of William Baird and other directors of the Bank in office along with him, but not relevantly laid in so far as founded on an allegation of individual negligence on Mr Baird's part. Now, it is not surprising that the Lord Ordinary should have been led to deal with the question of relevancy in this way, because the pleas of the pursuers certainly suggest the idea that it is intended to make two separate and distinct cases, or one founded exclusively upon what is called joint negligence on the part of Mr Baird and the other directors; and the other upon the sole and individual negligence of Mr Baird himself, upon the assumption that everybody else did his duty. But the Court are satisfied that that is not the nature of the case which the pursuers intend to make; but that their only case is one of negligence on the part of Mr Baird, which, combined with negligence on the part of the other directors, produced the losses complained of; and, therefore, while we cannot approve of the manner in which the pleas-in-law have been stated for the pursuers, we think it would be unsafe to hold that the case meditated in the first plea is, as a separate case, irrelevant, and for this reason chiefly—negligence upon the part of Mr Baird, must in one, and a very proper, sense of the term be his individual negligence; and it may be very difficult to say that, in every omission or act which constitutes the negligence of Mr Baird, there is a conjunction of everybody else along with him that happened then to be in the direction. To that effect, therefore, we shall alter the interlocutor. The last thing which the Lord Ordinary does is to appoint the pursuers to lodge within six days an issue or issues. Now that is a very important step; and the question presents itself for consideration whether the case is ripe for such an order, or whether that is the best way in which to put the case in shape for trial. We are all very clearly of opinion that this is not in any proper sense an action of damages. The summons concludes for payment of the sum of £299,736, 7s. 6d., a very precise, definite, and liquid amount; and when we analyse this large sum, it becomes still more clear that it is not properly an action of damages. It consists of three parts. There is (1) £132,670, 3s. 2d., consisting of losses by advances made upon current accounts. The sum of (2) £151,574, 11s. 8d., consisting of discounts given during Mr Baird's term of office, and lost to the bank. And the sum of (2) £15,491, 12s. 8d., the amount of premiums of insurance paid upon policies of insurance on the lives of debtors to the bank, recklessly and imprudently, and against the ordinary rules of good banking. Further, each of these principal divisions is separated again into its component parts, and as regards the advances in the accounts current, in the discounts and in the premiums of insurance, there is a precise specification of the loss sustained on each individual account or transaction. The remedy sought is, that Mr Baird shall replace the funds belonging to the bank, lost by his default. That being the nature of the action, it is not one of the enumerated cases, and we are under no obligation immediately or necessarily to send it to a trial by jury. I am not giving any opinion that Mr Baird's alleged gross negligence is not a proper question to be tried by jury. The question at present is whether this case, as it stands, is to be sent for trial without any attempt to simplify the issue, and reduce the subject-matter into something like a form in which it can be handled, with a prospect of reasonable success, in the course of one trial. Every one of these alleged losses—I mean the losses upon each one of the current accounts—must form the subject of a separate inquiry and examination before the jury; and the attention of the Court, and the jury at the trial, would require to be directed and confined to the one account while it was under examination, just as much as if it formed the subject of a separate issue. Now, a trial conducted in such a manner as that, and involving such great variety and extent of inquiry, would be altogether unmanageable, and would almost certainly result in miscarriage. To avoid such risk, and to reduce the case into a manageable condition, we propose, in the meantime, to have an inquiry by an accountant; and we are further induced to take this course also in consequence of the defences, which raise questions of pure accounting, and which being solved, would reduce the dimensions of this case very considerably.

An interlocutor was accordingly pronounced in accordance with the above opinion, Mr Charles Pearson, C.A., being nominated the accountant.

A similar interlocutor was pronounced in the case of M'Clelland *v.* James Baird of Cambusdoon, which was substantially identical with the above case.

Afterwards (July 13) the defenders petitioned for leave to appeal, but after hearing parties, the petition was refused.

ADVN.—HEWAT *v.* HUNTER.—*July* 6.

Poor—Settlement—Residence—Interruption.

The question in this case was whether the settlement of a pauper was in in the parish of Kelton, Kirkcudbright, or in that of Tongland, in the same county. The pauper was born in Tongland, and in 1856 went to reside with his wife and family at Rhonehouse in Kelton. At Martinmas of the same year he went to serve in Buittle parish, and after residing there about a year, returned to Rhonehouse. In 1858, he went to service in the parish of Kirkgunzeon, where he was engaged till August of the same year. From this time till August 1862, he took occasional service in several parishes. During the five years from 1857 to 1862, the period during which the pauper was said to have acquired a residential settlement in Kelton, he was nearly half the time in other parishes; and from 1856 to 1864, when he became chargeable as a pauper, his wife and family resided at Rhonehouse. Held by the Sheriff-substitute that he had not acquired a residential settlement in Kelton parish, on the ground that his absence in other parishes, both by its nature and duration, broke the continuity of his residence there.

The Sheriff reversed. But the Court returned to the judgment of the Sheriff-Substitute.

The Lord Justice-Clerk observed that it was impossible to account for the frequent periods of absence so as to be able to say in any reasonable way that there had been *de facto* a continuous residence; and so there had not been such a residence as was required by the statute. If the idea had ever been entertained that a pauper could maintain the continuity of his residence by the residence of his wife and children, such an idea should be at once and authoritatively rejected. What the statute meant by residence, was personal residence, not the mere possession of a residence; and the only relaxation of this rule was that kind of absence which either accidentally or incidentally must necessarily occur from time to time in the life of every one; but that was not the case here. The pauper's repeated absences were for the most part occasioned by his entering into contracts of service which thus made his absence compulsory.*

MURRAY'S TRUSTEES *v.* CARPHIN AND OTHERS.—*July* 12.

Marriage Contract—Construction.

The dispositive clause in an ante-nuptial marriage contract conveyed the wife's property to trustees, the interest to be paid to her during her life, "declaring that the said property and sums, and the whole interest and income to arise therefrom, shall belong to" the wife. The *jus mariti* of the husband was excluded, and the wife's sole receipt declared sufficient. The contract further directed the trustees, on the death of the longest liver of the spouses, to hold the estate for behoof of the children. Held that the property was effectually vested in the trustees for the purposes of the trust, and pleas to the effect (1) that the above declaration attached to the dispositive clause implied a reserved right of property in the wife, and therefore rendered the funds liable for her debts; and (2) that the children had not a *jus crediti*, but only a *spes successionis*, in consequence of the postponement of the trust for their behoof, until after the death of the survivor of the marriage,—Repelled.

Advn.—MOIR *v.* REID.—*July* 13.

Poor—Aliment—Son-in-Law—Husband and Wife.

In this case the question whether a husband is under a legal obligation to aliment his wife's parents has for the first time been authoritatively settled by the Supreme Court. The Sheriff-Substitute (Watson) held that the husband was not liable, but the Sheriff reversed this judgment; and to-day the Court unanimously confirmed the Sheriff's judgment. The facts were not disputed, and the defender put in a minute to the effect that the case should be disposed of on the footing that he was able to discharge the obligation if it lay upon him. The question of law, therefore, was purely raised. The grounds of judgment were, that prior to the daughter's marriage, although the claim at her parents' instance to aliment was not prestable, yet it was an existing and binding claim, and though dormant, might at any time have emerged. Marriage transferred all the wife's

* See Beattie *v.* Leighton, 1863, 1 Macph. 434.

debts and obligations to her husband, whether constituted, prestable, future, or contingent, because the person of the wife was sunk in that of the husband, and being in a state of coverture, she had no legal *persona*. As the wife would have been liable in the claim if it had emerged previous to the marriage, the husband was now liable, as by the marriage the obligation was transferred to him. It was contended by the defender that he was not liable because not *lucratus* by the marriage, but the Court held that this did not in any way affect the principle. *Observed* by Lord Justice-Clerk—The obligation to aliment a bastard equally with the obligation to aliment a legitimate child, rested on the law of nature. It was not, as had been contended, an ordinary civil debt. This erroneous view arose from confusing two claims totally distinct,—the claim which a bastard had on its parents, with the claim which one parent had on the other, the latter being, of course, an ordinary debt enforceable by an ordinary action. If he were right in this, the case of Aitken (Hume, p. 217) was an authority directly in point, for there a husband was found liable for the aliment of his wife's natural children born to other men before her marriage. No opinion was expressed as to the husband's liability, assuming the wife to have been dead when the obligation emerged.

THE HOUSE OF LORDS.

Howden *v.* Fleeming.—*June* 12.

Entail—Irritant Clause—Contracting Debt.

(In the Court of Session as Hawarden *v.* Dunlop and Others, March 24, 1865, 3 Macph. 748.)

The irritant clause of a deed of entail was as follows :—"It is hereby expressly declared, that if it shall happen any of the heirs of tailzie above-mentioned to contravene the provisions and limitations above written, or any of them, as the same are above expressed; then, and in that case, all such acts and deeds of contravention are not only hereby declared to be void and null to all intents and purposes, sicklike as if the same had never been made, but also the heir so contravening shall *ipso facto* amit, lose, &c."

The appellant contended that this irritant clause was invalid, because the words "sicklike as if the same had never been made," could only apply to deeds, and not to acts done, such as incurring debts otherwise than by deeds; and so, the clause being too narrow, the whole entail fell to the ground. Other objections to the entail were stated, which were not discussed in the House of Lords. The Lord Ordinary (Kinloch) found that the entail was valid, and the Second Division adhered. The defender appealed.

The Lord Chancellor (Cranworth) said that it was true that deeds of entail had always been strictly construed, so as not to fetter the ordinary circulation of property more than was absolutely necessary, and if the Court could fairly construe the deed in such a way that the entail would be defeated, the Court would be rather more astute to do so, than to find a construction which would support the deed. This rule was contrary to that which was followed in reference to other deeds and instruments; and it might be said to be always contrary to the intention of the maker of the deed, for it must always be said that every maker of such a deed must have intended, whatever way he expressed himself, to make a good entail. Though it thus often happened that the intention of the makers of these deeds of entail was defeated, still the rule referred to had always been adopted and acted upon. But then it did not carry one so far as that the Court was to pretend to see difficulties in the construction of a deed, where there were really none, and, especially, where a person not previously acquainted with the technical rule now referred to could have no real difficulty in the construction of the deed. Now, applying these observations to the present case, it was said that the heirs of entail had not been duly prohibited from contracting debt; for the irritant clause, after duly declaring void "all acts and deeds of contravention," adds the words "sicklike as if the same had never been made." It is said, because the mere negative act of contracting debt is not spoken of as an act or deed which is made, therefore the clause was not intended to apply to the contraction of debt otherwise than by deed. To that argument two answers, which are perfectly satisfactory, may be made. First, that even if the phrase is necessarily capable only of that meaning, it was only an incautious expression, and that it was not intended to limit what went before. The second was that, if the word "made" can only apply to written deeds of contravention, then the expression must be read *reddendo singula singulis*; and it does not interfere with the other acts of commission, such as contracting debts not by deed.

Lord Chelmsford said the phrase was not explanatory, but merely emphatic; and if it had been intended to restrict the previous sentence, it would be necessary to strike the word "acts" out of that sentence altogether.

Lord Westbury concurred.

Affirmed with costs.

Morris *v.* Bickett.—*July* 13.

(In the Court of Session, May 20 1864, 2 Macph. 1082.)

Property—River—Alveus—Appeal—Competency.

The pursuers and defender were proprietors on opposite sides of the water of Kilmarnock. The defender, the wall of whose tenement was washed by the stream, projected an improvement of that tenement, and in order to get rid of an irregularity in the line of his wall, he entered into an agreement with the pursuers, by which he was allowed, in consideration of a sum of money, to advance his wall into the channel of the stream as far as a line laid down on the Ordnance Map. It appeared that the defender, in building his wall, advanced farther into the *alveus* than the line upon the plan. The pursuers presented a note of suspension and interdict, and afterwards brought an action of declarator; and the processes were conjoined. Various pleas were stated, and a proof was led. It was found (18th March 1864) that the defender in constructing his wall had not in fact complied with the terms of the agreement. Counsel were afterwards heard on various other defences, the principal contention for the defender being that the pursuer was not entitled to object to the defender's extension of his wall into his own side of the *alveus*, unless he could shew that he was actually prejudiced thereby. The Court of Session (2d Div.) held that, there being nothing more uncertain than the operation of water, the mere apprehension of a risk of injury, nay, the mere fact of a change made in the *alveus* of a stream by one proprietor, gives his neighbour, who has a common interest in the water, a right to interfere. An interlocutor was accordingly pronounced, finding that the erection in question was an illegal encroachment on the rights of the pursuers, and the Lords "found and declared, decerned and ordained, interdicted, prohibited, and discharged, in terms of the conclusions of the summons," and in the suspension and interdict, they made the interdict perpetual.

The defender appealed. An objection was stated to the competency of the appeal.

The Lord Chancellor (Chelmsford), on the question of the competency of the appeal, was of opinion that, although this was one of the enumerated causes under the 28th section of the Judicature Act, yet the pursuer, having reclaimed against the decision of the Lord Ordinary, was precluded from objecting to the competency of the appeal. He further held that the fact that the appellant had by his building exceeded the limit conceded to him by the respondent, was established by the evidence. Upon the question of law, his lordship thought that the views of the Second Division, in particular Lords Benholme and Neaves, appeared to be perfectly sound in principle, and to be supported by authority. His Lordship said—The proprietors upon the opposite banks of a river have a common interest in the stream; and although each has a property in the alveus from his own side to the *medium filum fluminis*, neither is entitled to use the alveus in such a manner as to interfere with the natural flow of the water. My noble and learned friend, the late Lord Chancellor, during the argument, put this question—"If a riparian proprietor has a right to build upon the stream, how far can this right be supposed to extend? Certainly (he added) not *ad medium filum*; for if so, the opposite proprietor must have a legal right to build to the same extent from his side." It seems to be clear that neither proprietor can have any right to abridge the width of the stream, or to interfere with its regular course; but anything done *in alveo*, which produces no sensible effect upon the stream, is allowable. It was asked by the counsel in argument, whether a proprietor on the banks of a river might not build a boat-house upon it? Undoubtedly this would be a perfectly fair use of his rights, provided he did not thereby obstruct the river or divert its course; but if the erection produced this effect, the answer would be that, essential as it might be to his full enjoyment of the use of the river, it could not be permitted. *A fortiori*, when the act done is the advancing solid buildings into the stream, not in any way for the use of it, but merely for the enlargement of the riparian proprietor's premises, it must be an infringement upon the right and interest of the proprietor of the opposite bank. The proprietors on the banks of a river are entitled to protect their property from the invasion of the water by building a bulwark, *ripæ muniendæ causa*; but even in this necessary defence of themselves, they are not at liberty so to conduct their operations as to do any actual injury to the property on the opposite side of the river. In this case, mere apprehension of danger will not be sufficient to found a complaint of the acts done by the opposite proprietor; because, being on the party's own ground, they were lawful in themselves, and only became unlawful in their consequences upon the principle of *sic utere tuo ut alienum non lædas*. But any operation extending into the stream itself is an interference with the common interest of the opposite riparian proprietor; and therefore the act being *prima facie* an encroachment, the *onus* seems properly to be cast upon the party doing it, to show that it is not an injurious obstruction.

Lord Cranworth concurred. He said, *inter alia*, the most that can be said in favour of the appellant's argument is, that the question of the probabilities of damage is a question of degree; and so if the building occupies only a very small portion of the alveus, the chance of damage is so little that it may be disregarded. But this is an argument to which your Lordships cannot listen. Lord Benholme says truly that what may be the result of any building *in alveo* no human being knows with certainty. The owners of the land on the banks are not bound to obtain or to be guided by the opinions of scientific persons as to what is likely to be the consequence of any obstruction set up in waters in which they all have a common interest. There is in this case—and in all such cases there ever must be—a conflict of evidence as to the probable result of what is done. The law does not impose on riparian proprietors the duty of scanning the accuracy or appreciating the weight of such testimony. They are allowed to say:—We have all a common interest in the unrestricted flow of the water, and we forbid any interference with it. This is a plain, intelligible rule, easily understood, and easily followed, and from which I think your Lordships ought not to allow any departure.

Lord Westbury concurred, and observed:—This case, as far as I know, will be the first decision establishing the important principle that a material encroachment upon the alveus of a running stream may be complained of by an adjacent or an *ex adverso* proprietor, without the necessity of proving either that damage has been sustained, or that it is likely to be sustained, from that cause. I have felt much difficulty upon it, because, undoubtedly, a proposition of that nature is somewhat at variance with the principles and rules established on the subject by the Civil Law. I am, however, convinced that the proposition is one that is founded in good sense, and ought to be established as matter of law. My Lords, when it is said that proprietors of the bank of a running stream are entitled to the bed of the stream as their property, *usque ad medium filum*, it does not follow that that property is capable of being used in the ordinary way in which so much land uncovered by water might be used, but it must be used in such a manner as not to affect the interest of riparian proprietors in the stream. Now, the interest of a riparian proprietor in the stream is not only to the extent of preventing its being diverted or diminished, but also to prevent the course being so interfered with or affected as to direct the current in any different way that might possibly be attended with damage at a future period. His Lordship illustrated the uncertainty of the action of water, and the risks arising from trivial alterations and continued—It is wise, therefore, in a matter of that description, to lay down the general rule that, even though immediate damage cannot be described—even though actual loss cannot be predicated—yet if an obstruction be made to the current of the stream, that obstruction is one which constitutes an injury in the sense that it is a matter which the Courts will take notice of as an encroachment which adjacent proprietors have a right to have removed. In this sense the maxim has been applied in the law of Scotland—that *melior est conditio prohibentis*—namely, that where you have an interest in preserving a certain state of things in common with others, and one of the persons who have that interest in common with you desires to alter it *melior est conditio prohibentis*—that is to say, you have a right to preserve the state of things unimpaired and unprejudiced in which you have that existing interest.

Affirmed with costs.

COURT OF SESSION.

FIRST DIVISION.

Parker and Co. *v.* Handyside, *et e contra.—July* 14.

Shipowners—Damage to Goods from Perils at Sea—Onus of Proof.

These were conjoined actions—the one raised by Handyside and others, owners of screw steamer United Kingdom, of Glasgow, for the freight of a quantity of pease shipped on board that ship; the other raised by Parker and Co. for damage caused to these pease by injuries they had sustained on board. The shipowners alleged that the damage to the pease had been caused by perils of the sea. The merchants allege that the damage to the pease was caused by improper stowage. The Sheriff-Substitute of Glasgow (Strathern) found that the burden of proving that the damage was due to perils of the sea lay on the shipowners, and that they had not proved that. He therefore decerned against them. The Sheriff altered to the extent of finding that the damage was due partly to perils of the sea and partly to improper stowage, and that, in these circumstances, the presumption was for equality, and, therefore, that damage fell to be borne by both parties equally. The merchants, Parker and Co., advocated, and the Court to-day unanimously recalled the interlocutor of the Sheriff. Their lordships held that the onus of proving that the damage to the pease was due to perils of the sea lay on the shipowners, and they had not discharged it, and therefore held that the Sheriff-Substitute was right.

Downie *v.* Downie's Trustees.—*June* 17.

Heritable and Moveable—Jus relictæ.

In this case the pursuer is the widow of the late T. W. Downie, and seeks to have it found that she is entitled to her *jus relictæ* out of two sums of money of £5000 and £14,000 respectively. The former of these sums is invested on a mortgage granted by the Glasgow Waterworks Company, and the latter on security in Australia. It was objected on behalf of the trustees under Mr. Downie's settlement that these sums were heritable, and, therefore, not subject to the payment of *jus relictæ*. For the pursuer it was argued that the sum of £5000 was moveable, because the mortgage granted by the Glasgow Waterworks Company was neither in form nor in substance a bond. There were no habile words of conveyance of heritage, and the mortgagee could not have completed his title as to a heritable security by any mode known to the law of Scotland. The mortgagee had none of the rights of a heritable creditor; he could only enforce payment by appointment of a judicial factor, not by selling or entering into possession of the security, and the mortgage was not taken to "heirs," but to "executors, administrators, and assigns." The pursuer also maintained that the sum of £14,000, invested in Australia, must be treated as moveable, because by the law of that country it is so regarded.

For the defenders it was argued that the £5000 was heritable, because the security granted by the Glasgow Waterworks Company was heritable. It was in substance a heritable bond. Besides, interest was to be paid upon it before the term of payment of the principal, which of itself was sufficient to fix its character as heritable. Moreover, the Act 1641, renewed by 1661, c. 32, enacts that all "contracts and obligations for sums of money containing clauses for payment of annual rent and profit" shall be holden to be moveable bonds, except as to the widow and sister. This shows that these were heritable but for that Act, which does not affect them in relation to the widow. The defenders farther contended that the sum of £14,000 was heritable because Mr. Downie was a domiciled Scotchman when he died; and by the law of Scotland it was heritable, from being lent out at interest on landed security.

The Lord Ordinary (Jerviswoode) found that the pursuer was not entitled to her *jus relictæ* out of the £5000, because it was heritable; but that she was entitled to her *jus relictæ* out of the £14,000, because it was moveable.

Both parties reclaimed, and counsel having been heard, and cases ordered and lodged, the Court unanimously adhered to the Lord Ordinary's interlocutor.

The Lord President said this was an action to determine whether the pursuer is entitled to participate in certain funds, out of which she claims the *jus relictæ*. These funds consisted of (1) a sum of £5000 invested on a mortgage granted by the Glasgow Waterworks Company, and (2) a sum of £14,000 secured on an estate in Australia. The Lord Ordinary had found, in regard to the sum of £5000, that it is heritable, and of course it follows that out of it the widow cannot claim *jus relictæ*. I think that the Lord Ordinary is right. The question is not whether this sum is heritable by reason of its being invested on this security. The law is that this money is in the predicament to which the statute applies. The statute applies to all contracts and obligations for payment of money containing clauses for payment of annual rent. Nice criticisms have been pronounced on terms of mortgage. It is said that it does not contain any obligation to repay, and that there are no words of conveyance; but the meaning of it is that it constitutes a loan under which the money was to be repaid. Its character is determined by the circumstance of its being a loan for a tract of time, and bearing interest before the arrival of the time of payment of principal. Here the time of payment of the principal is distant three years; and at the expiry of that time it is renewed for another distant time. It is, therefore, within the character of the contracts and obligations contemplated by the statute. The statute, which removes such obligations from the class of heritable to moveable, excepted the interest of the widow. The institutional writers quoted declare that these obligations are moveable, except as to widow and sister. This is not quite correct. They are moveable by force of statute, but the right of the widow is excepted. As to the £14,000, if it had been invested here it would have been heritable, and it must be kept in view that the testator was domiciled here. It was not invested here, however, but in Australia. The principle has been recognised that the character of the security is to be deduced from the law of the country in which it is placed. The right to participate belongs to the law of this country. By that law it is said, however, that the law which shall regulate the application of that right is the law of the country wherein the security is situated. Here, that is Australian law, under which this sum is regarded as moveable. I therefore agree with the Lord Ordinary on this point also, and I think the pursuer is entitled to her *jus relictæ* out of this sum.

The other judges concurred.

LATHAM v. EDINBURGH AND GLASGOW RAILWAY COMPANY.—*July* 18.

Action of Manager of Railway Company for Remuneration for extra services—Relevancy.

This was an action at the instance of Mr Latham the late manager of the Edinburgh and Glasgow Railway Company, against that company for £4500, which he claimed as remuneration for extra services, and under an alleged agreement made with the directors of that company, to remunerate him for these services. The defenders denied that extra services had been rendered beyond those which were covered by various augmentations of salary which Mr Latham had received, and they also denied the alleged agreement to remunerate.

At advising, to-day, after stating the nature of the case, the Lord President said—This is a claim of a peculiar kind. I do not remember of ever having seen one of the same kind before. It is the case of a person employed as a general manager claiming remuneration for extra services. The employment as general manager requires a great variety of duties to be performed. It implies, as we were told in answer to a question put from the Bench, the occupation of the whole time of the person employed. In the course of that employment, the pursuer's salary was several times raised, but on the other side it is said that this was for the increase of the proper duties of his office, not for extra services. Now, I think that the allegations in such a case of retrospective claim must contain a clear statement of the services performed, but we have no such statement here. Again, there is no specific contract averred; indeed, the averments in reference to this branch of the case rather point to a general understanding. The action is also based on the resolution of the directors in 1865, but that only comes to this, that the directors recommended that justice and liberality required that the pursuer should be compensated for the loss of his office. It was deprivation of office which they put as the ground of compensation; compensation is now claimed on the totally different ground of extra services. I am of opinion that without more specific averment, this action cannot be sustained. If we held this case relevant as stated, it would come to this, that every employé who had been civil, and had made himself generally useful, and not refused to do anything he was asked to do, could at the end of his engagement demand extra payment for services performed during the whole course of the engagement. I am of opinion that to ground such a claim these services must be very distinctly described, and the contract under which they were performed must be clearly set forth.

Lord Curriehill concurred.

Lord Deas concurred also. His lordship thought that the resolution of the directors, if carried out, might have been fair and equitable in the circumstances. He rather thought that the directors had in view, in arriving at that resolution, all the grounds of claim competent to the pursuer. This might be a debt of honour, but it was not enforceable according to law. The only issue which could have been granted was that proposed by the Dean of Faculty at the bar, Whether the pursuer performed extra services, and whether the defenders agreed to remunerate him therefor. But the averments do not lay a foundation sufficient to support such a case. To do so would require (1) a clear specification of the duties of the office; (2) a specification of the extra duties performed. Here the absence of specification of duties of office accounts for the absence of specification of extra duties. 3. A distinct specification of the agreement to give remuneration. His lordship concluded by regretting that no compensation could be given.

Lord Ardmillan concurred in expressing his regret that the pursuer's claim could not be supported. There was here no claim unless there was a debt at the date of the amalgamation. Nothing in the nature of a contract prior to amalgamation had been alleged. The attempt is made to present a case midway between a general claim of *quantum meruit* and a claim on contract. But a *quantum meruit* claim would require the services to be beyond the duties of general manager, and would require these to be very specifically averred. The kind and extent of duties should be set forth, but here there are no such averments. His lordship therefore concurred in holding that no averments sufficient to sustain the conclusions of the summons had been set forth.

The action was therefore dismissed.

A similar judgment was pronounced in the case at the instance of Mr Jamieson, the secretary of the company, who had raised a similar action on the same grounds.

BARTOLOMEO *v.* MORRISON AND MILNE, *et e contra.*—*July* 20.

Summons—Amendment of—Disallowed.

In January last, the schooner Scotia of Aberdeen, belonging to Morrison and Milne, merchants there, and the Italian barque Ghilino, of Genoa, belonging to Guiseppe Ghilino de Bartolomeo, came into collision at sea, and both vessels were injured. The owners of the Scotia brought an action of damages against Francesco Massa, the master of the Ghilino, as master, and as representing the owners. He was a foreigner, and jurisdiction was founded by arresting the Ghilino. He pleaded that he was not owner of the ship, and that the arrestment of it, therefore, not being his property, did not found jurisdiction against him. The owners of the Scotia then brought a supplementary action against Bartolomeo, the owner of the Ghilino, concluding that the summons should be remitted to and conjoined with the action against Massa, the master, and that, "the said cases being so conjoined," the defender should be decerned to make payment of £1000, being the damages claimed in the first action. Bartolomeo objected to the conjunction of this action with the one against Massa, on various grounds. To obviate these, and to enable the pursuer in the action against Bartolomeo to get decree in it against him, without its being conjoined with the other, they proposed to amend the summons by adding after the words above quoted, "or whether they shall be conjoined or not," and by deleting certain other words.

The Lord Ordinary (Kinloch) sustained this amendment, and thereafter closed the record and conjoined the action with a counter action of damages which has been raised by Bartolomeo, the owner of the Ghilino, against the owners ef the Scotia.

Against this interlocutor Bartolomeo reclaimed, and to-day the Court unanimously recalled it. Their Lordships held that the proposed minute of amendment could not be sustained, as it was in effect changing the action from a supplementary to a substantive action, and therefore altering its basis and character, which could not be done by way of amendment.

SECOND DIVISION.

Advn.—The Glasgow Gas-Light Coy. *v.* the Glasgow Working Men's Society.—*July* 11.

Process—Sheriff—Interlocutor—A. of S. 15th Feb. 1851.

A case was decided by a Sheriff-substitute after a proof had been led, and appealed. The interlocutor of the principal sheriff contained no findings in fact. In an advocation of his judgment, the Court held that the Act of Sederunt of 15th Feb. 1851 was still in force, and was not superseded by § 13 of the Sheriff Court Act. Under the A. of S. the Sheriff was still bound to specify distinctly the material facts which he found established by the proof. The case was therefore remitted back to him to pronounce such findings.

Levett *v.* the L. & N. W. Railway Co.—*July* 17.

Record—Relevancy—Amendment.

The pursuer alleged that he had engaged the services of two persons for a concert at Falkirk; that through the fault of the Railway Co. they had been conveyed to a different place, and the concert accordingly had to be put off. For this he now claimed damages.

The Court held that, as the contract for the breach of which damages were sought was not made with the pursuer, action could not be maintained by him, unless the record were found to contain—(1) a statement of loss incurred by the persons with whom it was made (2) a legal assignation to their claims. In both respects the record was deficient, and could not now, after the record was closed, be so amended as to introduce for the first time a good ground of action.

Williamson *v.* M'Lauchlan.—*July* 18.

Suspension—Charge—Extract-Decree.

In a suspension of a charge, the grounds of suspension were—(1) the charge is null, as not giving the date of the extract-decree; and (2) the extract is not a legal warrant to charge, in respect that it was issued before the time for appealing had expired. Both objections were repelled.

With regard to the first, the charge bore to proceed in virtue of an extract-decree, dated 15th January and 17th April 1866, and there was nothing, either in the Personal Diligence Act or in the annexed schedule, rendering it imperative that the charge upon an extract-decree should specify any other date. The other objection was equally groundless. It was not disputed that if the provisions of the Act of Sederunt of 10th July 1839 were still in force, the extract was not issued until after proper time had been allowed to appeal, forty-eight hours being the time there allowed; but it was maintained that this Act was no longer binding, because by 16 and 17 Vic., cap. 80, seven days were allowed to appeal; and by sec. 51 the provisions of the Act of Sederunt must be held to be repealed, in order to let in and give effect to the provisions of the Sheriff Court Act in the matter of appeal. The Court were unable so to read the Act, which they thought was intended to restrict rather than to extend the right of appeal.

Sir W. S. Maxwell *v.* Commissioners of Inland Revenue.—*July* 20.

Marriage Contract—Personal Obligation—Stamp—Competency—28 and 29 Vic. c. 96, sec. 2—Note of Appeal.

This was a special case, prepared by the Commissioners of Inland Revenue at the request of the appellant, in terms of 28 and 29 Vic., cap. 96, sec. 2. By ante-nuptial contract of marriage, the appellant, *inter alia*, bound himself, at the first term after his death, to pay to trustees for the child or children of the marriage, other than the heir, and the lawful issue of such as should predecease him, the following sums of money:—If one child, £15,000; if two children, £20,000; if three or more, £30,000; and he disponed his heritable estate in security of these provisions, which were declared to be in full of *legitim* and other claims. The question for the opinion of the Court was, whether this obligation was to be held as a bond for a *definite and certain sum of money?* and whether the marriage contract was liable to be assessed with the *ad valorem* stamp-duty in respect of it as such bond, in terms of the Acts 13 and 14 Vict., cap. 97, and annexed schedule; 55 George III., cap. 184, schedule part 1; and 17 and 18 Vict., cap. 83, sec. 16? This was the only question raised in the case. In argument, the Commissioners asked the Court to pronounce a deliverance as to the stamp required in respect of a clause in the contract whereby the wife conveyed her whole estate, heritable and movable, valued at £11,000, to her husband. The Commissioners had not given any judgment on this clause.

The Court refused to express any opinion on the latter point, as it was not competently before them. The objections resolved into two—(1) that this was not a personal bond within the meaning of the statute; and (2) at any rate was not a bond for the payment of a definite and certain sum of money. As far as the mere words and legal construction of the deed were concerned, there could be no doubt that it was an ordinary personal obligation. But it was said that it was not a personal bond within the meaning of the Stamp Act, because it was liable as succession within the meaning of the Succession-Duty Act. It might be so, but that would not affect their decision; for it was the Stamp Act alone with which they had to do, and they could not take into consideration the effect which their decision might have on the interpretation of other Acts. The first objection, therefore, failed. With regard to the second, they thought the words "definite" and "certain" meant the same thing, and were equivalent to the expression of "ascertained amount." The intention of the statute plainly was to reach every personal bond which might ultimately come to be an obligation for payment of a sum of money; and they were of opinion that the words were quite broad enough to reach the present case, which was an obligation to pay a sum of money, subject to a contingency.

The case came originally before the Court simply on the case prepared by the Commissioners, but the Court being of opinion that they were not in a position to adjudicate unless a note of appeal was lodged by the appellant, this was accordingly done.

Dunn Pattison *v.* Dunn's Trustees.—*July* 20.

Superiority—Dominium Utile—Consolidation—Succession.

The late William Dunn of Duntocher, by deed executed in 1830, conveyed his whole estate, heritable and movable, to his brother Alexander, providing—but without prejudice to Alexander's right to dispose of the said estate, either during his life or by settlement—that if Alexander died intestate, and without heirs of his body, the estate should devolve upon certain persons named. *Inter alia*, the testator's lands of Mountblow and Dalmuir, and the superiority of his lands of Boquharnan, were destined to the eldest lawful son of his niece, Mrs Park or Pattison.

In 1832, William Dunn purchased the *dominium utile* of the lands of Boquharnan, of which he already had the *dominium directum*. He died in 1849, and was succeeded by Alexander, who made up titles to the lands of Boquharnan, superiority and property, and thereafter resigned the property in his own hands, as superior *ad remanentiam*. The effect of this the pursuer, who claimed as the eldest son of Mrs Pattison, contended was to give him right to the property, as well as the superiority, of Boquharnan in the event, which happened, of Alexander Dunn dying without exercising his power of disposing of these lands.

The residuary legatees, on the other hand, who would take the lands as residue in the event of there being no consolidation, maintained that the manner in which Alexander completed his feudal title did not affect the destination of the property, and that the pursuer had acquired no right thereto.

The Court (Lord Benholme dissenting) held that Mr. Dunn Pattison had no right to the *dominium utile*, but only to the superiority.

Pet.—Scott.

Divorce—Process—Oath of Calumny.

In an action of divorce, which had not yet been called in Court, the pursuer had to proceed on a voyage which would occupy about a year. On his application, the Court, on the authority of the cases of A. B. *v.* C. D., 16 S., p. 1143, and Pott, 2 D., p. 248, granted a commission to take his oath *de calumnia* to lie *in retentis* until the case was duly called and enrolled, due notice being first given to the defender, and proof that such had been given produced before the commissioner.

HIGH COURT OF JUSTICIARY.

H. M. Advocate *v.* Garret and Edgar.—*June* 4.

3 *and* 4 *Vict.*, *c.* 74—*Theft of Oysters—Relevancy.*

Held by a full bench, that an indictment contained a relevant charge of the statutory crime of taking and carrying away oysters from an oyster fishery, the property of another person, where it was stated in the minor that the panels held a license from the proprietor to dredge for oysters, and that it was provided by the regulations relative to the said license (neither the license nor regulations being libelled in the minor, but only referred to as productions) that they should not be entitled to take any oysters under two-and-a-half inches in diameter, but that in contravention of these regulations, the panels had, knowingly and wilfully, taken three thousand or thereby of such undersized oysters.

(Before a Full Bench.)

S. and L.—QUARNS *v.* HART AND GEMMEL.—*June* 4.

Review—Sheriff's Charge to Jury—Previous Convictions.

This was a suspension of a conviction for reset of theft, on the ground that the Sheriff, in his charge to the jury, had said, on the authority of Hume, Com. c. iii., s. 3, that a previous conviction for the same crime was a strong circumstance against the complainer, and was legal evidence to be taken into consideration by them, as tending to show the complainer's guilt of the special crime charged, and as proof of his guilty knowledge of the article having been stolen; and that the complainer's character, as proved by the former conviction, was also a strong circumstance to be taken into consideration in judging of his guilty knowledge. It was further complained that the Sheriff refused to give a different direction at the request of the panel's agent, or to take any note of the objections stated by him, or to hear further argument, stating that it was incompetent and irregular to ask such directions in a criminal trial after the judge's charge.

Counsel for the complainer on the question of the competency of the suspension, referred to 2 Hume, 514. Act of Adjournal of 17 March 1827, in Alison's Practice 42, 9 Geo. IV., c. 29; Bell's Notes, 307; Beattie *v.* P.-F. of Dumfries; Wilson, Arkley's Rep., 80; M'Allan, 1 Sw., 118; Burns *v.* Hart, 2 Irv., 571, and other authorities. The Court refused the suspension.

The Lord President—There was no precedent for interference with the Sheriff in his charge to a jury. There was no record provided for by the law, or in practice kept, and there was no provision, as in the Civil Court, for exceptions being taken down for the purpose of review. It would be a novel proceeding to go into an inquiry and take information from bystanders or from jurymen as to the precise propositions laid down by the Sheriff. It appeared to his Lordship that the Act of Adjournal referred to gave no authority for taking down objections to the Sheriff's charge, that it referred only to objections stated in the course of the proceedings. But, moreover, this was not an objection to the admissibility, but to the application of evidence. The Court was not in a position to inquire at all into the proposition itself; but his Lordship was not prepared to hold that in all circumstances a previous conviction must be totally excluded from the consideration of the jury. There might be distinctions as between one conviction and a number of convictions, and between recent convictions and more distant convictions in point of time.

The Lord Justice-Clerk was precisely of the same opinion. The complaint was two-fold—1st, That the Sheriff gave a wrong direction; and 2d, That he refused to enter in the record the objection taken. As to the latter, where were we to find any obligation on the Sheriff to take such a note? The provisions of the Act of Adjournal clearly prove that no such record was intended to be kept. Previously the evidence was taken in the form of depositions *ad longum*, and the objections formed a necessary part of the record. And when the note of evidence was substituted, it was thought necessary very properly to provide for minuting objections taken in the course of the proceedings. This was simply because otherwise review as to such objections would have been impossible. It seems to follow by necessary implication that the Act of Adjournal contemplated that no *other* objection should be entertained. His lordship also agreed that the argument that previous convictions could not be founded on to any effect as proof of the charge could not receive effect.

Lord Cowan was not prepared to say that previous convictions may be founded on as evidence of guilty knowledge, and had never admitted such evidence. His Lordship concurred as to the incompetency.

Lord Deas was not prepared to dissent on the general question, but thought it enough to dispose of the case that, even if the suspension was competent, the complainer was bound to make a very distinct statement of what the bad law complained of was, and also to show very clearly that it was bad law. His lordship was not prepared to say this was bad law, though it was certainly a proposition that required to be stated very guardedly to a jury.

Lords Ardmillan, Neaves, and Jerviswoode, concurred with the Lord President and Lord Justice-Clerk.

SCOTT *v.* CUMMING—*July* 6 *and* 7.

11 *and* 12 *Vict., c.* 107—*Summary Procedure Act—Order in Council of* 11*th April* 1866 (*Cattle Plague.*)

The Act 11 and 12 Vict. c. 107, for preventing the spread of contagious diseases among sheep, extends to Scotland. Under this Act, and the relative Order of Council of 11th April 1866 (Cattle Plague), two licenses are required for the removal of sheep, when the place from which, and that to which they are taken, are in different counties, one from Local Authority of each county. It is the duty of the owner of the sheep, and not of the Local Authority, to obtain the certificate required by Sec. 47 of the Order in Council. The schedules of the Summary Procedure Act are not imperative, but are to be observed "as nearly as circumstances will admit," and a conviction in the form of Schedule K No. 4 is not bad, because it allows fourteen days for payment of the penalty.

HOUSE OF LORDS.

WHITE AND OTHERS *v.* EARL OF MORTON'S TRUSTEES.—*July* 13.

Appeal—Competency—Partial Abandonment of Action—Issue—Applying Verdict—Right of Way.

(In the Court of Session, June 28, 1859, Dec. 5, 1861, 24 D. 116; June 6, 1862, 24 D. 1054.)

In 1846 the appellants raised this action, concluding to have it declared that certain rights of way existed near Aberdour—in particular, a foot-road from the harbour of Aberdour along or near to the sea shore to Starley Burn and Burntisland. The summons and condescendence originally contained claims of certain other roads; but on the 4th March 1851, before the record was adjusted, the pursuers abandoned the cause so far as related to the other ways or footpaths—reserving their right to bring a new action as to these roads. Afterwards the record was closed. In July 1854 issues were readjusted to try the question as to two roads delineated on a plan:—"Whether for forty years or upwards, or from time immemorial, there existed a public right of way for foot passengers, leading by or near the broad red line as shown in the plan No. 424 of process, from or near," &c. Before trial, the defenders consented by a minute to judgment "in the same way as if a verdict had been found for the pursuers on the issues in this cause." Before judgment was given on this minute, the Earl of Morton presented a note asking the Court to remit to Mr Wylie to define the road and lay it off. The remit was made, and after Mr Wylie had reported, and some other procedure had taken place, the Court, 22d November 1856, found the pursuers entitled to a public footpath as marked on his plan. Lord Morton died, and the action was transferred against the present respondents. The Court refused a motion of the pursuers to have obstructions removed in 1861 on the ground that there were no obstructions. The pursuers next lodged a minute praying that the other conclusions of the the summons might be exhausted; but the Court, 21st May 1862, found that the minute formerly lodged, and abandoning some of the roads claimed, was incompetent as having been lodged before the record had been closed; whereas it ought to have been lodged after it was closed. A new minute in the same terms was then lodged, and the Court, 6th June 1862, found, "that in the present state of the process, the pursuers are not entitled to abandon in terms of the said minute: found, &c., in terms of the declaratory and prohibitory conclusions of the summons as regards the footpaths laid down on Mr Wylie's plan, &c.: *quoad ultra* assoilzied the defendant, and found the pursuers entitled to expenses, subject to modification, prior to July 19, 1861; and neither party entitled to expenses subsequently incurred; and decerned." The pursuers appealed against several of those interlocutors, and an objection was made to the competency of the appeal.

The appellants contended that their right to the footpath mentioned on the plan was established by the minute consenting to a verdict for the pursuers, and the Court below ought to have ordered all obstructions to be removed; that the Court had no right to refuse to give effect to the minute of abandonment, or to deprive the appellants of the expenses incurred since 1861; at all events the Court ought not to have assoilzied the defenders as regards the claims to the roads which had been abandoned.

The Lord Chancellor (Chelmsford)—So far as regarded four of the interlocutors the appeal was incompetent. The issue, as framed, described the footway claimed as by or near the red line shown on plan. When the defenders consented to a verdict for the pursuers on such an issue, no definite line of road was pointed out; and probably it would be difficult to say how such a verdict could have been applied at all. But at all events the duty of the Court was clearly confined to the applying of the verdict. Now, what the Court did was, to remit to a surveyor to chalk out a road—not the road which the public were accustomed to use, but a road which would be least inconvenient to the defender. This the Court clearly had no power to do, and the interlocutor so pronounced, as well as all those founded upon it, were *ultra vires*, and being taken out of the ordinary judicial course were not subject to appeal. But with regard to the last interlocutor, in which the Court assoilzied the defenders from the conclusions of the summons as to the abandoned roads, that interlocutor might be affirmed.

It might be thought to have gone too far, and to exclude the public in future; but there was great doubt if such would be the effect, for it would be competent in any future litigation about those roads to show under what circumstances the interlocutor had been pronounced.

Lord Cranworth concurred.

Lord Westbury concurred. From the moment the Court pronounced the interlocutor professing to give effect to the consent of the defender to a verdict for the pursuer, the cause was taken out of the usual course of judicial procedure. The issue was inartificially framed in the first instance, and the Court tried to supply the defect; but the way in which that was done was such that what followed derived its effect from the consent of parties, and not from any judicial authority. The interlocutors, therefore, which followed that departure from the beaten track, were incapable of being appealed, and the appeal was to that extent incompetent. As to the last interlocutor assoilzieing the defenders as to the claim to the roads abandoned, that was matter of practice, which was best left to the Court below; but the interlocutor would not be conclusive as to any future claim which might be made to these roads.

Appeal dismissed without costs.

TEIND COURT.

Minister of Dunbar *v.* The Heritors—*July* 4.

Augmentation—Communion Elements—Burgh Jurisdiction—Competency.

In 1618, a decreet of the Commissioners of Teinds, declared in respect of the consent of Mr John Atchison, Provost of Dunbar, that the town was and should be obliged, "so often as the communion shall happen to be celebrate thereanent, in all time coming, to furnish the elements to the celebration of the communion at the said kirk." In all the subsequent decreets in augmentations of the stipend of Dunbar parish, especially in those of 1767 and 1833, the said obligation was expressed, "according to use and wont." It was admitted that bread and wine had been always supplied by the Magistrates out of the common good. But it was resolved by the Magistrates and Council, on July 8th 1866, to send only the quantity actually required, and accordingly three dozen of wine, which cost £6 6s., were sent. The petitioner refused to accept this, as not being "the lawful quantity." His predecessor had obtained an augmentation in 1861, in which the decree contained this clause—"The communion element money being paid by the burgh of Dunbar." He now presented this petition in the process of augmentation, praying the Court to exhaust the conclusions of the summons by decerning against the Magistrates of the Burgh for "either the annual allowance of twenty loaves of bread and six dozen of wine," "or else a money payment of £15 a year in lieu and place thereof;" and to remit to the Lord Ordinary to give effect to such decerniture in the locality. The Court held the application incompetent in the Court of Teinds.

The Lord Justice-Clerk said it was admitted that there was no case in which the Court had awarded communion elements, except in the terms of a summons of augmentation (which has reference only to *teinds*), and never but out of teinds. That went very far to show the incompetency of this petition for an award of communion elements out of the common good of the burgh. Further, the summons concluded for communion elements out of teinds. The judgment of 16th January 1861 granted the augmentation of stipend, and assigned as a reason for making no award for communion elements the fact that they were otherwise provided for. The conclusions were therefore exhausted, partly by the augmentation and partly by the declaration that no decree for communion elements was necessary. What was now asked, moreover, was not decree against the heritors, the defenders in this case, but against the burgh. The obligation on the burgh was constituted by a sort of judicial agreement in 1618, and was founded on a contract; and it was probably to be interpreted by use and wont. It was therefore a civil obligation, which might be enforced in a civil action.

Lord Deas gave no opinion as to the general question of jurisdiction of this Court, but concurred in thinking that the petition was incompetent under the summons.

The other Judges concurred with the Lord Justice-Clerk.

ENGLISH CASES.

Marriage (*Mormon—Divorce*).—A minister of the Mormon church was married in Utah, by the high priest in accordance with the matrimonial law of the territory. He, having been sent on a mission abroad, whilst his wife remained in Utah, renounced Mormonism, and was excommunicated by the authorities of Utah, who also declared his marriage void, whereupon the respondent and the co-respondent intermarried. It was proved that polygamy is recognized and encouraged amongst the Mormons:—*Held*, that as the contract of a polygamous union does not carry with it those duties which it is the office of the marriage law in this country to assert and enforce, such unions are not within the reach of that law, and the parties to such unions are not entitled to its remedies. "If the relation existing between men and women in countries where polygamy prevails is not the relation which in Christendom we recognize and intend by the words *husband and wife*, but another and altogether different relation, the use of a common term to express these two separate relations will not make them one and the same." "The matrimonial law of this country is adapted to the Christian marriage, and is wholly inapplicable to polygamy. . . . If its provisions and remedies were applied to polygamous unions, the Court would be creating conjugal duties—not enforcing them—and furnishing remedies where there was no offence. For it wonld be quite unjust, and almost absurd, to visit a man who, among a polygamous community, had married two women, with a divorce from the first woman on the ground that, in our view of marriage, his conduct amounted to adultery coupled with bigamy." "The Court does not profess to decide on the rights of succession or legitimacy which it might be proper to award to the issue of polygamous unions, nor upon the rights or obligations in relation to third persons, which people living under the sanction of such unions may have created for themselves." (Comp. per Lord Brougham in *Warrender* v. *Warrender*, 2 S. and M'L., 200.)—*Hyde* v. *Hyde*, 35 L. J., Pr. and Matr., 57.

Principal and Agent.—An auctioneer sold goods on conditions requiring the purchaser to pay in full in cash to him before delivery. Before delivery the auctioneer got from the purchaser a bill in part payment, and agreed to take it as cash, and it was discounted for him at his banker's. Before the bill came to maturity, the vendor gave the purchaser notice not to pay to the auctioneer. The bill was paid at maturity. The auctioneer having failed to pay over the whole receipts of the sale, the vendor sued the purchaser.—*Held*, that the auctioneer had no authority to take payment by a bill, and that the vendor was therefore entitled to a verdict. *Semble*, per *Blackburn, J.*, that if the bill had come to maturity before the vendor revoked the authority of the auctioneer, the payment by bill would have been good.—*Williams* v. *Evans*, 35 L. J., Q. B. 111.

PRINCIPAL AND AGENT.—Defendant advanced money to a factor on a general account, as against goods to be subsequently delivered to and purchased by defendant. Goods were delivered, part being those of plaintiff, who had employed the factor to sell them for him on a *del credere* commission. Defendant knew which were plaintiff's goods, and that the factor sold them only as agent for plaintiff. On a settlement between the factor and defendant the accounts were balanced by the latter paying the factor the difference between the price of the goods and the amount of advance. *Held*, defendant could not treat any part of advance as a pre-payment of plaintiff's goods, and that such advance was not a good payment as against the plaintiff.—*Catterall* v. *Hindle*, 35 L. J., C. B. 161; 1 Law Rep., Q. B., 352.

LANDS CLAUSES CONSOLIDATION ACT.—A railway company is not liable to the costs of an inquiry, under sec. 94, as to whether land intersected by its works is of less value than the expense of making a communication between it,—the statute providing for costs only where the right of the company to take land is not in question.—*Cobb* v. *Mid-Wales Rail. Co.*, 35 L. J., Q. B. 117; 1 Law R., Q. B., 342.

TURNPIKE (*Yeomanry cavalry*)—The exemption of volunteers from toll contained in section 45 of the Volunteer Act, 26 & 27 Vict. c. 65, does not extend to members of the yeomanry cavalry, who are not exempt if they drive instead of riding to the place of meeting of their corps.—*Humphrey* v. *Bethel*, 35 L. J., Mag. Ca. 150.

COPYRIGHT (*Directory.*)—In making a map, compiling a directory, or similar work, a previous publication of the same kind may be used for correcting the new work, or as an aid in collecting information, but may not be merely copied and verified.—Per Wood, V.C.—*Kelly* v. *Morris*, 35 L. J. Ch. 423, 1 Law Rep. Eq. 697.

PATENT.—In a suit to restrain the infringement of a patent, the validity of which has been determined in a previous action at law against different defendants, the Court may rest upon the decision at law as establishing the sufficiency of the specification, but will give defendant the option of having an issue directed as to the novelty of the invention.—Per Lord Romilly, M.R., *Bovill* v. *Goodier*, 35 L. J. Ch. 432, 2 Law Rep. Eq. 195.

SETTLEMENT (*Vesting, Power of Appointment.*)—The rule, that none can take by implication upon the non-execution of a power of appointment who cannot take under an execution of the power, only applies where there are no means of ascertaining the persons intended to take other than the terms of the power. Therefore, where real estate was settled upon trust for the settlor for life, with remainder to his wife for life, and after the death of the survivor, upon trust for sale and division "amongst all and every the children of the settlor, lawfully begotten or to be begotten, in such shares or proportions, manner, and form, as should be directed by any will or codicil then already, or at any time thereafter to be, duly executed" by the settlor, with no gift over in default of appointment, and the settlor died without exercising the power,—*Held*, that the above rule did not apply; that all the children took vested estates, liable only to be divested by the execution of the power; and, therefore, that a child who died before the settlor took, in default of appointment, equally with those who survived.—Observations (per Kindersley, V.C.,) on *Woodcock* v. *Renneck*, 1 Phill. 27; and *Winn* v. *Fenwick*, 11 Beav. 1138.—*Lambert* v. *Thwaites*, 35 L. J. Ch. 406. 2 Law Rep., Eq. 151.

SOLICITOR (*Certificate.*)—A solicitor who has been duly admitted and enrolled, but who has neglected to take out his annual certificate in proper time, is nevertheless competent, while without a certificate, to bind a client ignorant of the want of the certificate as between such client and third parties.—*Sparling* v. *Brereton*, 35 L. J. Ch. 461. 2 Law Rep., Eq. 64.

WILL (*Construction.*)—Testator, by reference, gave the income of a certain fund to L. M., who was unmarried, for life, with a gift to her husband (if any) for his life; and upon the decease of the longer liver of L. M. and her husband, he directed his trustees to pay, assign, and transfer the capital to his four children, A, B, C, and D, who should be then living, "or to the issue of such of them as should be then dead, such issue taking their parent's share. "Issue," as used in the will, was clearly equivalent to "children":—*Held*, that upon the death of any one of the four, A, B, C, and D, whether before or after the determination of the life estates, his children then living took vested interests in the fund, and that his children then dead were wholly excluded.—*In re Merricks' Trusts*, 35 L. J. Ch. 418. 1 Law Rep., Eq. 551.

PROMISSORY NOTE (*Payee, Uncertainty.*)—Defendant gave to the trustees of a chapel a document as follows:—"On demand, I promise to pay to the trustees of, &c., or their treasurer for the time being, the sum of," &c.:—*Held*, in an action by the trustees, that there was no uncertainty as to the persons to whom the money was to be paid, so as to make the document bad as a promissory note.—*Holmes* v. *Jaques*, 35 L. J. Ch. 130.

CARRIERS BY RAILWAY (*Railways Clauses Consolidation Act*, 1845, *ss.* 87. 92.)—In the absence of a contract to deliver at a particular time, the duty of a common carrier is to deliver goods intrusted to him at a reasonable time, looking at all the circumstances of the case; and since his first duty is to carry safely, he is justified in incurring delay and delivering after the usual time when delay is necessary to secure the safe carriage. By virtue of an agreement under the provisions of the Railways Clauses Act, 1845, confirmed by private act, the M. Railway Company exercised running powers over the line of the G. N. Railway Company. Goods intrusted to the G. N. Company were, solely by the negligence of the M. Company, in the exercise of those powers, delayed in transit and delivered so late as to cause loss to the consignor,—*Held*, that since the powers of the M. Company were conferred on them by statute for the benefit of the public, the G. N. Company were not responsible for the negligence of the M. Company in the exercise of those powers, and that the G. N. Company having used all reasonable efforts to forward the goods, and having delivered them at a reasonable time, were not answerable to the consignor for the loss occasioned by the delay.—*Great Northern Rail. Co.*, v. *Taylor*, 35 L. J., C. P. 210. 1 Law Rep., C. B. 385.

BILL OF EXCHANGE (*Railway Company*)—A Railway Company, incorporated by a special Act of Parliament, containing the usual clauses, incorporating the general acts, cannot accept bills of exchange.—*Bateman* v. *The Mid-Wales Rail-*[illegible] 35 L. J. C. P., 204.

[illegible]R-PARTY (*Freight payable in advance: lien*)—M. chartered defendant's [illegible]ry coal to Alexandria, where it was to be delivered on freight being [illegible]e charter-party stipulated "the freight to be paid on unloading and [illegible]ry of the cargo less advances, in cash, at current rate of exchange; [illegible] the freight to be advanced by freighter's acceptance at three months [illegible]ills of lading; owner to insure the amount and deposit with charterer [illegible]nd to guarantee the same." M. gave his acceptance for half freight, [illegible]t for such freight, as per charter-party, was indorsed on the bill of [illegible] was signed by the captain and afterwards indorsed to plaintiff for [illegible]e arrival of the ship at Alexandria, M. having in the mean time [illegible]ent, the master refused to deliver the cargo to plaintiff unless [illegible]ight was paid or guaranteed, although M's acceptance was not then [illegible] guarantee was given by B. for plaintiff under protest, the cargo was [illegible]ed, and B. being afterwards compelled to pay the amount of guarantee on [illegible]e dishonour of M's acceptance, plaintiff repaid him,—*Held*, (affirming judgment of Court of Common Pleas, 34 L. J. C. P. 268.) that plaintiff was entitled to recover the half freight from defendant, as during the currency of M.'s acceptance defendant had no lien for it, and the refusal to deliver the cargo was therefore wrongful.—*Tamvaco* v. *Simpson*, (Ex. Ch.,) 35 L. J., C. P. 196. 2 Law Rep., C. B., 363.

COPYRIGHT OF DESIGNS—By the Copyright of Designs Act, 1858, section 5, the registration of any pattern or portion of article of manufacture to which a design is applied, instead or in lieu of a copy, drawing, &c., shall be as valid and effectual as if such copy, drawing, &c. had been furnished to the Registrar under the "Copyright of Designs Act,"—*Held*, (aff. judgm. of Court of Q. B. 33 L. J., Q. B., 329.) that a design formed by the combination of shaded and bordered stars on an ornamented chain surface might be registered under this section, by simply depositing with the Registrar a piece of woven cloth to which this combination had been applied; as the design, which must be taken to be the combination of ornaments on the cloth, was sufficiently disclosed. It is a question for the Court whether a design is sufficiently disclosed by a pattern or piece of cloth.—*M'Crea* v. *Holdsworth* (Ex. Ch.) 35 L. J., Q. B. 123. 1 Law Rep., Q. B. 264.

NEGLIGENCE (*Consequential damage.*)—Plaintiff's colliery was flooded by water, which escaped from defendants' reservoir through some old mine-shaft workings under the site of the reservoir, and through old coal workings under the land intervening between plaintiff's and defendant's land. There was no personal negligence on the part of defendants; but the people who were employed by them in the construction of the reservoir had not exercised reasonable skill and care (with reference to the shafts) to provide for the pressure which the reservoir was to bear,—*Held*, reversing the judgment of the Court of Exchequer, 34 L. J., Ex. 177, that defendants were liable for the damage sustained by plaintiff. *Per Curiam*:—"We think the true rule of law is that the person who, for his own purposes, brings on his land and collects and keeps there anything likely to do mischief if it escapes, must keep it at his peril, and that if he does not he is *primâ facie* answerable for all the damage which is the natural consequence of its escape. . . . . The person whose grass or corn is eaten down by the escaping cattle of his neighbour, or whose mine is flooded by the water from his neighbour's reservoir, or whose cellar is invaded by the filth of his neighbour's privy, or whose habitation is made unhealthy by the fumes and noisome vapours of his neighbour's alkali works, is damnified without any fault of his own; and it seems but reasonable and just that the neighbour who has brought something on his own property (which was not naturally there), harmless to others so long as it is confined to his own property, but which he knows will be mischievous if it gets on his neighbour's, should be obliged to make good the damage which ensues if he does not succeed in confining it to his own property.—*Fletcher* v. *Rylands*, (Ex. Ch.), 35 L. J., Ex. 154., 1 Law Rep., Ex. 265.

SUCCESSION DUTY ("*succession*": "*predecessor.*")—H, by will dated in 1851, left certain real estate to his wife C, for life, giving her a general power of appointment. He died in 1856. C. exercised her power of appointment in 1858, in favour of E, the wife of the testator's nephew:—*Held* (*dub. Martin, B.*), that E.'s interest in the annuity was a "succession" within the meaning of the Succession Duty Act, 1853, and that she took from C. as "predecessor," and was therefore liable to pay a duty of £10 per cent.—*The Attorney General* v. *Upton*, 35 L. J., Ex. 130, 1 Law Rep., Ex. 224.

JURY (*discharge of Jury without verdict no bar to subsequent trial: admissibility of evidence: Sunday.*)—A jury sworn and charged with a prisoner may be discharged without giving a verdict by the presiding Judge, if a "necessity," that is, a high degree of need, for such discharge is made evident to the mind of the Judge. He alone is to decide when the "necessity" for such discharge is made evident to his mind, and his decision is not subject to review by any legal tribunal. The statement upon the record by the Judge of the result of such a decision is sufficient to establish the lawfulness of the discharge. Such a discharge, even if it be an improper exercise of discretion, is not a legal bar to a subsequent trial of the prisoner for the same offence, either on the same or upon a fresh indictment. If two prisoners be jointly indicted, and one alone be given in charge to the jury, the other is an admissible witness (though neither acquitted nor convicted, and though a *nolle prosequi* is not entered) upon the trial of the prisoner with whom the jury are charged. A record showed that on the trial of W. and H., jointly indicted for murder, the jury, after five hours' deliberation, at five minutes before midnight on Saturday night, were discharged by the Judge without giving a verdict, and without the consent of the prisoner or of the prosecution, on the ground that he, the Judge, for certain reasons, which he stated, "decided that it was necessary to discharge the jury." W. was afterwards given in charge to another jury, and tried alone upon the same indictment, when a verdict of guilty was returned, and judgment of death recorded; H. being admitted as a witness against her without having been either acquitted or convicted on the indictment, and a *nolle prosequi* not having been entered,—*Held*, affirming the judgment of the Court below (35 L. J., Mag. Ca. 121, 1 Law Rep., Q. B. 264) on a writ of error, that there was no error on the record. *Held*, also, that the question of the admissibility of H. did not arise upon the record; but that if it had arisen, and if the question of her admissibility could have been inquired into, she was admissible. *Semble*, per *Pollock, C.B.* and *Martin, B.*, that a Judge has the power, in his discretion, to give refreshments to a jury either before or after they have retired to consider their verdict.—*Winsor* v. *The Queen*, Ex. Ch., 35 L. J., Mag. Ca. 161.

Evidence (*competency: deaf and dumb witness.*)—It is the duty of the Judge presiding at a trial to decide as to the competency of a witness; and if he has admitted a witness to give evidence, but upon proof of subsequent facts affecting the capacity of the witness and of observation of his subsequent demeanour, the Judge changes his opinion as to his competency, the Judge may stop the examination of the witness, strike his evidence out of the notes, and direct the jury to consider the case exclusively with reference to the evidence of the other witnesses. —35 L. J., Mag. Ca. 186., 1 Law Rep., C. L. 33.

Lands Clauses Consolidation Act.—Where a public company takes land held in undivided shares, each part owner, *bona fide* employing a separate solicitor, is entitled to his costs of obtaining his share of the purchase-money; but two or more of such part owners employing the same solicitor are, in the absence of special circumstances, not entitled to more than one set of costs.—*In re Nicholl's Trust Estates*, 35 L. J. Ch. 516.

Statute (*Municipal Corporation: Compulsory Powers*).—A public body intrusted by the legislature to construct a public work for the public advantage and with no profit to themselves, was authorised to take compulsorily more land than was required for the improvements specified in their Act, with power to dispose of superfluous lands:—*Held*, that they were entitled to take the whole of the lands scheduled in their Act, even though with the avowed object of re-selling a portion of such lands to a railway company; one of the implied purposes of their Act being to obtain money for the improvements. *Held*, also, that they were not incapacitated from taking the whole of the lands comprised in the schedule, although before they obtained their power to take land they had contracted conditionally upon their obtaining such power to sell the lands for a certain sum. In such a case the intention of the Legislature may be gathered from the clauses of the Act generally. The word "street" means a thoroughfare with houses on both sides, not merely a road or footway.—*Galloway* v. *the Mayor, &c., of London and the Metropolitan Rail. Co.*, and *the Mayor of London* v. *Galloway*, House of Lords, 35 L. J., Ch. 477. 1 Law Rep., H. L. 34.

Bills of Exchange (*Forgery—Acceptance for Honour*).—P. presented to S. in England a Spanish bill of exchange bearing to be drawn by C. of Lima, on S., payable to order of R., and endorsed by R. and P. S., having stopped payment, sent to the plaintiffs the bills and a letter telling them that no doubt defendant would intervene for the honour of C. Plaintiffs sent the bill and letter to defendant, who accepted for honour of C., and on the faith thereof plaintiffs discounted the bill. The signature of C. turned out to be a forgery. *Held*, that as the bill was discounted by plaintiffs on the faith of defendant's acceptance, they were entitled to recover against him. And if it had been necessary to decide the point, the Court were inclined to hold that the bill must be considered to have been accepted as a bill payable to bearer.—*Phillips and Another* v. *Im Thurn*, 35 L. J., C. P. 220. 1 L. J., C. P. 463.

WAGER (8 *and* 9 *Vict. c.* 109, *s.* 18).—An agreement between two persons, each of whom possesses a horse, to ride a race, the winner to have both horses, is void, being an agreement by way of wagering, within the meaning of 8 & 9 Vict. c. 109, s. 18, and not an agreement to contribute towards a prize to be awarded to the winner of a lawful game, within the meaning of the proviso in that section. —*Coombs* v. *Dibble*, 35 L. J., Ex. 167. 1 L. R., Ex. 248.

RAILWAY.—LANDS CLAUSES CONSOLIDATION ACT (*Surplus Land*).—By section 217 of 7 & 8 Vict. c. xcii. (a section in almost the same words as the Lands Clauses Act, section 127), it is provided that if the company do not sell within ten years the superfluous lands not required for the purposes of their Act, such lands remaining unsold at the expiration of such period shall vest in and become the property of the owners of the lands adjoining thereto *in proportion to the extent of their lands respectively adjoining the same.* The company was amalgamated with others; and the new company, after the ten years had expired, obtained an Extension Act, providing that "the respective periods by the several acts relating to the company limited for the sale of their superfluous lands should be extended for five years from the passing of the Act, and those several Acts should be read and construed as if that period had been fixed by each of those Acts for that purpose:"—*Held*, first, that the obligation to resell the surplus land applied to reversions or other partial interests in land acquired by the company; secondly, that the words of the section, extending the time for re-sale, could not defeat the vested rights which had arisen from the lapse of the time allowed for the re-sale. The Court of Q. B. having decided (v. ante vol. ix. p. 167) that the surplus land forfeited by the company must be apportioned among the adjoining owners according to a line drawn from the point where their boundaries met to the nearest point of the land actually used by the company: *Held*, by the Ex. Ch., that this was wrong, and that the land ought to be divided among the owners of the adjoining properties in proportion to the frontage of each, that is, the length of the line of contact of each property, if the line were made straight from the point of intersection of the boundaries on one side, to the point of intersection of the boundaries on the other.—*Moodie* v. *Corbett*, Ex. Ch. 35 L. J. Q. B. 161. 1 L. R. Q. B. 510.

MARINE INSURANCE.—Where a ship with cargo on board is sunk in deep water, so that the ship and cargo are in common danger of destruction, and there is nothing to rebut the inference that the most convenient mode of saving either, or both, is by raising the ship together with the cargo, the shipowner, in considering whether there is a constructive total loss of the ship, on the ground that the cost of raising it will exceed its value when saved, is bound to take into account the fact that the outlay will be diminished by his claim for general average on the cargo and freight, which will be secured to him by a lien on the cargo, if recovered.—*Kemp* v. *Halliday*, Ex. Ch. 35 L. J., Q. B. 156. 1 L. R. Q. B. 520.

NEGLIGENCE.—Defendant having placed a machine in a public market for exhibition, a child was injured by putting his fingers between the cogwheels while another child was turning the handle:—*Held*, defendant was not liable for negligence in leaving the machine unguarded where it was.—*Mangan* v. *Atterton*, 35 L. J., Ex. 161. 1 L. R., Ex. 239.

ATTAINDER—PEDIGREE.—The descendants of one child of an attainted person may trace a heritable descent to the descendants of another child of such attainted person, even though the marriage, of which such children were the issue, took place abroad after the attainder.—*Kynnaird* v. *Leslie*, 35 L. J., C. P. 226. 1 L. R. C. P. 389.

MASTER AND SERVANT.—Under 4 Geo. IV. c. 34, s. 3, a workman may be convicted a second time for persisting on his return from imprisonment in absenting himself from the service of his employer, as the contract is not rescinded by the mere imprisonment. And although the offender *bona fide* believes that a conviction dissolves his contract, and opinions of judges can be cited in support of such a belief, this is no lawful excuse, but only matter for the discretion of the magistrates in imposing punishment.—*Unwin* v. *Clarke*, 35 L. J., Mag. Ca. 193. 1 L. R. Q. B. 417.

COMPANIES' ACT, 1862.—In sec. 133 "contributories" includes fully paid-up shareholders, so that liquidators may make a call on shares not fully paid up in order to reimburse fully paid-up shareholders.—*In re Anglesea Colliery Co.* (Lim.), 35 L. J., Ch. 546. 1 L. R. Eq. 379.

PARTNERSHIP (*Dissolution*).—Partnership articles provided that the business should be carried on "for the common benefit of the partners, and risk of profit and loss in equal shares and proportion;" that plaintiff should devote the whole of his time to the business, and defendant only so much as he should think fit; that fresh capital might be brought in, which should carry preferential interest, and might be withdrawn on notice; and that the nett profits beyond equal specified sums should be left in the business, and be carried to the respective credit of the partners as additional capital, to bear interest before division of nett profits. Defendant had brought in cash as fresh capital, and profits had been carried to the capital account in the books. On dissolution, the realized assets, after paying debts, proved insufficient to make good to defendant the excess of his capital; and defendant claimed to take the whole of the realized assets, and, in addition, to hold plaintiff liable personally to him for any deficiency:—*Held*, that defendant was entitled to payment in priority of the cash brought in, but that the surplus should be divided rateably according to the shares of capital after such payment. —*Wood* v. *Scoles*, 35 L. J., Ch. 547. 1 L. R. Ch. Ap. 369.

WINDING UP (*Companies' Act*, 1862: "*Registered*" *and* "*Unregistered*").— The words "registered companies," in the Companies' Act 1862, apply to companies registered under the Act itself, and "unregistered companies" to companies registered before that Act; therefore, a company registered under the Act of 1844 was held an "unregistered company" under the Act of 1862, and capable of being wound up under that Act. Ordinarily, where a valid debt, both at law and in equity, is established against a company, it is not, under the Act of 1862, discretionary with the Court to say whether the company shall be wound up or not; but it is their duty to direct the winding up. Where, however, the sole creditor of a company, claiming under a judgment upon which execution had been issued, and a return of *nulla bona* made, but which judgment was of a suspicious character, and was alleged to have been obtained by fraud, applied to have the company wound up, *Held*, that the company ought to have an opportunity of impeaching the debt by filing a bill, as there was a doubt whether a valid debt existed; and the petition for winding up ordered to stand over for that purpose. —*Bowes* v. *Hope Mutual Life Assurance Company* (H. of L.), 35 L. J., Ch. 574.

WINDING UP (*Companies' Act*, 1862).—A company, formed and registered under any of the Acts mentioned in the 175th section of the Companies' Act, 1862, is, under the 176th section, to be treated as if it had been registered under that Act, and is, consequently, capable of being voluntarily wound up.—*In re the London India Rubber Co.* (*Lim.*), 35 L. J., Ch. 592. 1 L. R. Ch. Ap. 329.

WINDING UP (*Negotiation of Bills—Set off.*)—The official liquidator should not, as a rule, discount bills of exchange which come to his hands, but should retain them until maturity, though there may be exceptions to this rule. He should not, in any case, negotiate bills without the sanction of the Judge in chambers, after notice to any person who might be prejudiced by the negotiation of the bills. Where the holders of certain overdue bills of an insolvent company in course of being wound up, were also acceptors of bills not yet at maturity, in the hands of the official liquidator, the Master of the Rolls refused to allow them to set off the sum due to them by the company against the amount due by them to the company on their acceptances, but directed the official liquidator not to negotiate the bills.—*In re the Commercial Bank Corporation of India and the East*, 35 L. J., Ch. 617.

DAMAGES.—In order to entitle the owner of land to proceed in an action against a neighbour for excavating near his boundary, appreciable damage must have been caused thereby. "Where there is an actionable wrong, such, for instance, as a person stepping on another man's land, or a returning officer refusing a vote tendered to him, or an interference with the flow of water to which a man is entitled, it is not necessary to prove pecuniary damage. But where an adjoining owner of land does a lawful act of ownership on his land, which is no wrong of itself, it may become actionable if appreciable damage be caused to his neighbour. Thus, if a man has a drawing-room window, and his neighbour builds a chimney which pours its smoke into it, the question of damages arises, and the maintainability of the action depends on the annoyance caused, and circumstances under which it occurs. Again, if dancing causes a vibration in a neighbour's house, there is not necessarily a cause of action; but if it would probably bring down the house, he has no right to have a ball, and would be liable after notice for the fall of the house, because damage occurred. So the noises of trades, as of a coffee-mill or plate-rolling mill, only become actionable grievances because of the damage."—*Per Erle*, C. J. *Smith* v. *Thackerah*, 35 L. J., C. P. 276.

COMPANY (*Power of Directors to bind Company*).—Seven persons signed a memorandum of association of a company, which was duly registered. There never were any articles of association. Two of such persons (one professing to act as managing director, the other as chairman of the company) engaged plaintiff as foreman at the company's brick-works. In an action by plaintiff for his wages, —*Held*, that, in the absence of proof to the contrary, the company must be taken to have given authority to the two persons to engage plaintiff.—*Totterdell* v. *the Fareham Blue Brick and Tile Co.* (*Lim.*), 35 L. J., C. P. 278.

LIBEL (*Report of Proceedings in Bankruptcy*).—The examination of a prisoner in gaol by the Registrar in Bankruptcy under the 101st section of the Bankruptcy Act, 1861, is a public judicial proceeding; and a fair and correct report without comment of the examination is privileged, even though it may contain statements not relevant to the inquiry, which injuriously affect the character of a third person.—*Ryalls* v. *Leader*, 35 L. J. Ex. 185. 1 L. R. Ex. 296.

MARINE INSURANCE (*Seaworthiness of Lighters*).—On an insurance of goods on a voyage policy, until the same be safely landed at the port of discharge, "including all risks to and from the ship," there is no implied warranty that the lighter used at the end of the voyage to convey the goods from the ship to the shore shall be seaworthy for that purpose.—*Lane* v. *Nixon*, 35 L. J., C. P. 243. 1 L. R. C. P. 412.

MARINE INSURANCE (*Suing and Labouring Clause: Particular Average*).—Plaintiffs, whose vessel was chartered to bring a cargo of guano to the United Kingdom for certain freight, payable after arrival at the port of discharge, effected an insurance with defendants on the chartered freight by a policy containing the usual suing and labouring clause, and also the exception, "warranted free from particular average, also from jettison, unless the ship be stranded, sunk, or burnt." The ship was driven by weather to put into Rio, where she became a total loss, without being "stranded, sunk, or burnt." The cargo was safely landed at Rio, and, without notice of abandonment, was sent on in another vessel to the port of discharge, and plaintiffs afterwards received the chartered freight:—*Held*, that the expenses of conveying from Rio having been incurred to save the subject-matter of insurance from a loss, could be recovered under the suing and labouring clause, notwithstanding there had been no abandonment; since such clause is not limited to cases where the assured abandons. The right to recover such expenses under that clause was not excluded by the warranty against particular average, as there was danger of the total loss of freight by the loss of the ship by perils insured against, and the expenses were thus incurred for the benefit of the defendants. *Semble*—That evidence that by usage in the business of marine insurance, the term "particular average" does not include expenses of recovering or preserving the subject-matter of the insurance, would be admissible, since it would not contradict the express terms of the policy.—*Kidston* v. *Empire Marine Insur. Co.* (*Lim.*), 35 L. J., C. P. 250.

Principal and Agent.—Defendant authorised a broker at Liverpool to underwrite marine policies for him "not exceeding £100 by any one vessel" The broker underwrote a marine policy for £150. At Liverpool it is notorious that there is generally a limit fixed between principal and broker, though not disclosed to the public:—*Held*, that the agent had no authority to underwrite for £150, and that the contract being indivisible, the assured could recover nothing from defendant in respect of the policy.—*Baines* v. *Ewing*, 35 L. J., Ex. 194. 1 L. R. Ex. 320.

Succession Duty.—Testator devised real estate to trustees on trust out of the rents to pay interest on certain mortgage debts, and certain annuities, and to pay the surplus to a *cestui que trust* for life, with remainder over. Power was given by the will to the trustees to pay certain sums to agents or receivers for collecting the rents:—*Held*, that in estimating the value of the succession of the *cestui que trust* no allowance was to be made for these payments for collection.—*In re Elwes* (2 H. and N. 719, 28 L. J., Ex. 46) extended. *In re Earl Cowley*, 35 L. J., Ex. 177. 1 L. R. Ex. 288.

Lands Clauses Consolidation Act, 1845 *s.* 69.—An order for the application to building purposes of the purchase money of land taken under the act, will not be made except under special circumstances. A corporation was authorized by statute to borrow for erection of municipal offices on the security of rates. Land belonging to it having been taken by a railway company and the purchase money paid into court, a petition by the corporation for the payment out of court of this fund, to be applied in the erection of municipal offices, refused, *diss.* *Knight Bruce*, L. J.—*Ex parte* Corporation of Liverpool, 35 L. J. 655

Merchant Shipping Act, *s.* 510, 511, 514 (*Collision at Sea: Loss of Life of Seamen*).—The liability of a shipowner for loss of life to the seamen of a vessel run down by his ship is not limited to £30 for damages payable in each case of death; and this rule applies whether the Board of Trade do or do not institute proceedings in respect of such loss of life. Where the aggregate damage sustained by all the claimants exceeds the whole amount for which the shipowner is liable (viz., at the rate of £15 per registered ton of his ship) the fund must be distributed rateably in proportion to the damages sustained by the claimants respectively; but where the whole amount of damages is less than that for which the shipowner is liable, the amount of damages sustained by each is to be paid in full.—*Glaholm* v. *Barker*, 35 L. J., Ch. 657.

Specific Performance (*Railway: Damages*).—A railway company agreed with a landowner to make a bridge and other accommodation works; and the works being commenced in a manner at variance with the agreement, the landowner filed his bill for specific performance, and for an injunction to restrain the completion of the works in progress. The motion for the injunction was ordered to stand over until the hearing of the cause, upon the company's undertaking to deal with the works as the Court should direct. Before the hearing the works were completed, and the railway opened for public use,—*Held*, *per* L. Romilly, M.R., that although the plaintiff had sustained some damage, the Court, taking into consideration the interests of the public, must refuse him any relief except in damages.—*Raphael* v. *the Thames Valley Rail. Co.*, 35 L. J., Ch. 659.

Trust (*Forgery by Solicitor, constructive notice*).—The equitable doctrine of constructive notice as between solicitor and client is founded on the principle that the solicitor is "alter ego," and his knowledge is the client's knowledge. A solicitor, one of three trustees, executed an assignment of leaseholds, part of the trust estate, to a purchaser for value. The solicitor, who acted as such for all parties, had forged the necessary written consent of the *cestui que trust* to the sale, and the signatures of his two co-trustees to the assignment,—*Held*, *per* Kindersley, V. C., that the genuine execution of the assignment by the solicitor passed the legal estate in one-third of the property, but that no beneficial interest passed to the purchaser, on the ground of constructive notice,—the fraud of the solicitor not affecting the general rule.—*Boursot* v. *Savage*, 35 L. J., Ch. 627.

EVIDENCE (*Negligence, Ship*).—A ship, of which defendant was registered owner, was lying in a dock under the care of a shipkeeper, by whose negligence one of the hatchways was left open. Plaintiff, in lawfully passing over the ship, fell down this hatchway and was injured. In his action against the defendant, it was proved and found at the trial that the injury was caused by the negligence of the shipkeeper; but the only evidence to fix defendant was his being described in the register as "owner,"—*Held* (diss. Mellor, J.), that this was evidence to be left to the jury, and that it would have justified them in finding that defendant had employed the shipkeeper.—*Hibbs* v. *Ross*, 35 L. J., Q.B. 193.

LETTERS PATENT (*Rights of the Crown, Petition of Right*).—By letters patent the Crown granted to the suppliant special licence, power, sole privilege and authority to use, exercise, and vend a certain invention for improvements in the construction of ships, and to "enjoy the whole profit, benefit, commodity and advantage from time to time coming, growing, accruing and arising by reason of the said invention for and during the term of," &c. The letters purported to be granted upon the petition of the suppliant, and "of our special grace, certain knowledge and mere motion;" and they contained a command "to all and every person and persons, bodies politic and corporate, and all other our subjects whatsoever," that they should not use the invention without the consent, licence, and agreement of the suppliant, his executors, &c., on such pains and penalities as could be justly inflicted, and liability to damages. There was also a clause that the letters should be void if the suppliant, his executors, &c., should "not supply or cause to be supplied for our service all such articles of the said invention as he or they should be required to supply by the officers or commissioners of the department of our service for the use of which the same shall be required," &c. It was further provided, that the letters were to be construed in the most favourable and beneficial sense for the best advantage of the suppliant, his executors, &c. The Crown having made use of the invention, a petition of right was preferred by the inventor,—*Held*, first, that the Crown was not excluded from the use of the invention. Secondly, if the effect of the letters was to exclude the Crown, yet that a petition of right could not be maintained in respect of the infringement of the patent right.—*Feather* v. *the Queen*, 35 L. J., Q.B. 200.

RAILWAY AND CANAL TRAFFIC ACT.—The decisions on applications for injunction against undue preference, under 17 & 18 Vict. c. 31. s. 2, ought not to bind the Court in the manner that a precedent in law binds, and therefore *Garton* v. *the Bristol and Exeter Railway Company*, 6 C.B. N.S. 639, and *Baxendale* v. *the South-Western Railway Company*, 12 C.B. N.S. 758, are not always to be followed when the vans of a railway company are admitted into their goods station after the hour when it is closed against the public in general. So held by *Erle, C.J.* and *Montague Smith, J.*; but held by *Willes J.* and *Keating J.*, that those cases are binding and that they are right.—*In re Palmer* v. *the London and South-Western Rail. Co.*, 35 L. J., C.P. 289.

CONTRACT (*Res perit domino*).—Plaintiffs contracted with defendant to erect certain machinery in his buildings; when it was only partly erected, a fire broke out in the buildings and destroyed both the buildings and the machinery then erected,—*Held*, that plaintiffs were entitled to recover from defendant the price of the portion of the machinery so erected and destroyed.—*Appleby* v. *Meyers*, 35 L. J., C.P. 295.

DAMAGES (*Consequential*).—Defendant sold to plaintiff a cow, which he knew to be infected with a contagious disease, falsely representing that she was free from disease. Plaintiff, believing the representation, put the cow in a shed along with other cows: *Held*, that plaintiff was entitled to recover, in addition to the purchase money, the value of the other cows which he had lost by their becoming thus infected, such damage being the natural consequence of the plaintiff's acting on the defendant's representation.—*Mullett* v. *Mason*, 35 L. J., C.P. 299.

CUSTOMS.—It is an offence, under sec. 6. of the Customs Act, 22 & 23 Vict. c. 37, to cause to be imported goods of one denomination concealed in packages of goods of any other denomination, though the goods are not subject to any import duty. Sec. 6. imposes a penalty on any person who "shall cause to be imported goods of one denomination concealed in packages of goods of any other denomination," and sec. 8. enacts, that the word "importer" in any act relating to the Customs is "to apply to and include any owner or other person for the time being possessed of or beneficially interested in any goods imported,"—*Held*, that the words "cause to be imported" in sec. 6. are not to be interpreted according to the meaning "importer" in sec. 8, which includes many persons not coming within sec. 6,—*Budenberg v. Roberts*, 35 L. J., Mag. Ca. 235.

SHIPPING (*Bill of lading*).—A bill of lading of forty-seven casks of oil contained a memorandum in the margin, "not accountable for leakage." The casks were, at the desire of charterers, stowed in the same hold with rags and wool (part of the cargo), whereby they became heated and leaked:—*Held*, that the condition as to leakage was not limited to the ordinary quantity of leakage, and that such memorandum protected the shipowner as to all leakage, unless caused by his own negligence, and that ignorance that casks so packed would become heated and leak did not amount to negligence.—*Ohrloff* v. *Briscall; The Hélène*, 35 L. J., P. C., 63.

SHIPPING (*Stoppage in transitu*).—M. & D., Bordeaux, through their agent at Hull, sold sixty tons of linseed cake to S. & T. The cake was shipped, and a bill of lading, indorsed by M. & D., was delivered to S. & T. in exchange for their acceptance at three months. The bill of lading was afterwards re-delivered to the agent of M. & D. to hold as security against the acceptance. Subsequently T. fraudulently obtained it from the agent and indorsed and delivered it to the appellants, who received the same for valuable consideration and without notice of the fraud. Before the arrival of the goods at Hull, S. & T. became insolvent:—*Held*, that S. & T. acquired no new title to the goods by the fraud of T., but merely obtained the means of transferring their property in the goods, and that by the transfer to the appellants for valuable consideration and without notice of the fraud, the right of the vendors to stop the goods *in transitu* was gone. An ownership which is perfect at law, though voidable as to part (viz. possession), cannot be treated differently from an ownership voidable as a whole, but in the interim protected by the interposition of a *bona fide* purchaser for valuable consideration.—*Pease* v. *Gloahec; The Marie Joseph*, 35 L. J., P. C., 66.

(COMPANIES' ACT, 1862, *s.* 35).—Shares in a limited company were allotted before the memorandum and articles of association were in existence. These differed materially from the prospectus. Upon motion by the allottee, under the Act, Wood, V.C., ordered his name to be struck off the register; and the order was affirmed by the Lords Justices. The Court has, under the Act, s. 35, a discretionary jurisdiction to remove the names of members of companies from the register. Mere lapse of time will not amount to acquiescence, nor attempts to sell shares; but receiving dividends or otherwise acting as a partner would bind the allottee.—*Ex parte Stewart*, 35 L. J., Ch. 738.

COMPANIES' ACT, 1862—LIMITED LIABILITY (*Contributory—Set off*).—A shareholder in a limited liability company being also a creditor of the company to a larger amount than that remaining unpaid upon his shares, is not entitled to set off so much of his debt as is equal to the amount of calls which have been made upon, but not paid by him, and to receive a dividend for the balance; nor is he entitled to have the dividend calculated upon the entire debt, and to be paid the balance of dividend after deducting the amount of the call; but he must first pay the call, and he will then be entitled to a dividend *pari passu* with the other creditors who are not shareholders. Difference in this respect between a member of a company with limited liability, and a member of a company with unlimited liability.—*In re Overend, Gurney & Co. (Lim.), Ex parte Grissell*, 35 L. J., Ch. 752.

LEGACY (*vesting*).—A testator gave his residuary estate to trustees upon trusts for his widow for life, and after her decease for distribution among such of his five nephews as should be living at the time of her death, in equal shares; but if any of them should then be dead leaving issue, such issue to be entitled to their father's share. One of the nephews predeceased the widow, leaving one daughter, who died before the widow, and therefore before the period of distribution:—*Held*, that the gift to the issue of the deceased nephews was an original and not a substitutional gift; that the condition annexed to the contingent gift to the parents was not to be extended by implication to the gift to the issue, and that the daughter of the deceased nephew, though dying before the period of distribution, took a vested immediate interest in the share which her father would have taken if alive at the period of distribution, although the amount could not be ascertained until the death of the tenant for life. The words "such issue to be entitled to their father's share" to be read as "such child or children to be entitled to their father's share."—*Martin* v. *Holgate* (House of Lords), 35 L. J., Ch. 789.

BOUNDARIES (*Evidence, Parole*).—A grant of a mine was made to L. by deed, with map indorsed; the southern boundary being "a straight line drawn from J. V.'s house" to a certain boundstone; and the description of parcels concluded "which said premises are particularly delineated by the map on the back hereof." On this map the line was drawn from the north-east corner of J. V.'s house. L. brought trespass against R. for working through this southern boundary and taking plaintiff's ore. At the trial, parole evidence was admitted to shew that J. V.'s house was wrongly placed on map, and that if corrected the line would run to the south of J. V.'s house, and the whole question was left to the jury:—*Held* (*Lord Westbury* diss.), that, though it was properly a question of evidence for the jury to identify and determine the position of J. V.'s house, it was a question of construction for the Judge to decide what was the true meaning of the deed; that in so doing the Judge was bound to look at the map, and that he ought to have directed the jury that the true boundary line was that drawn from the north-east corner of J. V.'s house when identified and correctly placed.—*Lyle* v. *Richards* (House of Lords), 35 L. J., Q. B. 214.

SHIPPING (*Barratry and Perils of the Sea, Negligence*).—Plaintiff shipped goods on board the *Black Prince*, under a bill of lading, which contained the exceptions of "barratry" and "perils of the sea." The *Black Prince* was lost in a collision with the *Araxes*. In an action on the bill of lading, there was evidence at the trial that the collision arose from the *Black Prince* starboarding instead of porting her helm, as required by the rules laid down by the Merchant Shipping Act, 1854; and a collision occasioned by non-observance of such rules is, by section 299 of that act, to be deemed to have been occasioned "by the wilful default of the person in charge" of the offending ship. The Judge told the jury that if the collision was brought about by negligence of those on the *Black Prince*, the loss would not be a peril of the sea, and that for that purpose he could not distinguish between gross negligence and negligence; and he left it to the jury to say whether there was want of due care on the part of the *Araxes*, by which care the collision would have been avoided:—*Held*, that the contravention of the rules of the Merchant Shipping Act, 1854, by those in charge of the *Black Prince*, in starboarding instead of porting the helm, did not amount to barratry within the exception in the bill of lading. *Held*, also, that, the direction of the Judge was right, and that he did right in not directing the jury that the loss of the *Black Prince* was caused by perils of the sea, within the exception in the bill of lading.—*Grill* v. *the General Iron Screw Collier Co. (Lim.)*, 35 L. J., C. P. 321; 1 Law Rep., C. P. 600.

WILL.—B. G. devised freeholds, upon trust for the use of E. G., his nephew, for life, with remainders to the use of his first and other sons in tail male, with successive remainders over for life, and remainders to the first and other sons of the successive tenants for life in tail male; and he bequeathed his residuary personal estate, upon such trusts, &c., as were thereby declared concerning the devised freehold hereditaments, "or as near thereto as the rules of law and equity would permit; provided, nevertheless, that such residuary personal estate should not vest absolutely in any tenant in tail, unless such person should attain the age of twenty-one years:"—*Held*, aff. the decision of *Westbury C.*, (*Lord St. Leonards* diss.), that the proviso merely narrowed the class who would have taken under the previous words of gift, and did not extend such class to tenants in tail by descent; and therefore the personality vested only in tenants in tail by purchase, and the gift was not void for remoteness. *Held*, also, that the words "as near as the rules of law and equity will permit," would not by their own force have controlled the construction. *Christie* v. *Gosling* (H. of L.), 35 L. J. Ch. 667.

Illegal Contract ("*Stifling a Prosecution*").—W. B. discounted bills to which he had forged his father's signature. The holders of the forgeries working on the father's fears for the safety of his son, but without holding out any direct threat, and without any distinct promise not to prosecute, obtained from the father equitable security for the amount of the bills. *Held*, that the security was void, as having been obtained by improper pressure; also, that the arrangement was invalid, being an agreement to stifle a prosecution. *Williams* v. *Bayley* (H. of L.), 36 L. J. Ch. 717.

Booty.—The enactment as to booty that the Court "shall proceed as in cases of prize of war," refers only to procedure, and does not assimilate in all respects the distribution of booty to that of prize. Even if the property captured is not strictly booty, or is of unusually large value, the principles applicable to actual and joint capture are, nevertheless, to be followed. In considering claims to booty, the Court will not be influenced by opinions expressed by the civil and military authorities *ante litem motam*. The decisions in cases of prize and the usage in grants of booty should be regarded, but not implicitly adopted. The principles, though not all the rules applicable to prize, may be followed in the adjudication of booty. The conditions of warfare on land and at sea, are so different, that a wider application of the term "co-operation" must be allowed in matters of booty than in cases of prize; but some practical limits must be assigned to the term. The rule of sight at sea and the extent of communication on land distinguished. As all the ship's company are considered the actual captors of prize taken by any of its members, so the whole division of an army, if in the field, usually constitutes the actual captors of booty taken by any of its detachments. "Association" for purposes of booty must be military, and not political; and there must be some limits even to military association. Troops are not associated as joint captors, because they are carrying out parts of a political plan involving military operations, or because their commanders receive instructions from the same political authority. The association must be under the *immediate* command of the same commander. "Co-operation" which will give a title to booty must directly tend to produce the capture in question. What tends to produce the capture cannot be exhaustively defined. Generally, strict limits must be observed of time, place, and relation. Services rendered at a great distance from the place of capture, or acts done long before the capture was contemplated, even though they affect the whole scene of operations, do not constitute legal co-operation. The right of a Commander-in-Chief to share in booty taken by his army is, to a certain degree, analogous to the right of a flag-officer to prize taken by a ship on his station. A flag officer on his station, *de facto* in command there, is entitled to share in every prize taken by a vessel under his command. But no flag-officer commanding in a port of the United Kingdom shares in prize made by any ship sailing thence by order of the Admiralty. And no flag-officer shares in a prize taken by a vessel nominally under his command, but detached by paramount orders upon a special, independent command. To entitle the Commander-in-Chief to share in booty captured by his army, he must himself be in the field, though not necessarily with the division which makes the capture. Being in the field with any division, he is, as to booty, in the field with all. But if a portion of his troops have been placed under the *independent* command of another, the Commander-in-Chief, though actually in the field, does not share in booty taken by those troops. To invest a subordinate officer with an independent command within the normal sphere of the Commander-in-Chief is an extraordinary arrangement, and strict proof is necessary to rebut the contrary presumption. The right of the general and personal staff to booty depends on that of the Commander-in-Chief; but only such members of the personal staff are entitled as are actually in the field. Under the circumstances, costs of rejected claimants allowed, and, to prevent the necessity of taxation, an account of disbursements, and a *quantum meruit* recommended.—*The Banda and Kirwee Booty*, 35 L. J. Adin., 17.

Jurisdiction.—The Court of Admiralty has no original jurisdiction in matters of prize. That which it exercises is derived from a royal proclamation issued at the outbreak of each war, and a commission requiring the Lords of the Admiralty to give the necessary powers to the High Court of Admiralty. The Court's jurisdiction with respect to booty commenced with the passing of the 3 & 4 Vict. c. 65. s. 22.—*The Banda and Kirwee Booty*, 35 L. J. Adin., 17.

Shipping (*Bill of Lading—Lien for Freight.*)—By charter party the cargo was deliverable "on being paid freight as follows: The ship to have a lien on cargo for freight; £3 10s. per ton of 50 cubic feet to be paid to the captain or his agents on right and true delivery at the port of discharge." The charterer shipped a portion of the cargo under a bill of lading which stated freight to be payable as per charter party." *Held*, that the rate of freight alone and not the stipulation as to lien, was incorporated in the bill of lading, so that the shipowner had no lien as against a *bona fide* onerous indorsee for the whole freight, but only for that of the goods mentioned in such bill of Lading.—*Fry* v. *Chartered Mercantile Bank of India, London and China*, 35 L. J. C. P., 306.

COURT OF SESSION.

FIRST DIVISION.

M.P.—Ker's Trustees *v.* Ker and Others.—*Nov.* 7.

Trust.—Marriage Contract.

By trust disposition and deed of settlement, dated 23d Sept. 1839, Robert Ker, senior, of Argrennan, directed his trustees to hold his estate in trust, for the use and behoof of his eldest son, Robert, and the heirs of his body; whom failing, for the use and behoof of his second and other sons in succession. He further directed his trustees, upon his eldest son attaining majority, to convey to him the said estate; but declaring that, in case his eldest son should marry, or otherwise conduct himself so as not to merit the approbation of his said trustees, the provisions made in his favour should only belong to him in liferent for his liferent use allenarly. By a codicil, dated 26th January 1847, the testator directed his trustees not to make over the estate to his eldest son until he should attain the age of twenty-five years. The testator died in 1854. His eldest son attained his majority on 22d July 1857. On 21st September 1858, he married Miss E. H. R. Macalpin, an Irish lady with a considerable fortune. On this occasion two settlements were executed—one in the English form settling the lady's fortune on herself and her children, with a liferent to Mr Ker; the other in the Scotch form, by which the estate of Argrennan was settled by means of a trust on Mr Ker in liferent and his heirs in fee, and Mrs Ker was provided with an annuity of £400. The marriage was intimated to the trustees under his father's deed, and approved of by them, and a minute of approval entered in their sederunt book. On 18th June 1861, and within a few weeks of Mr Ker's attaining the age of twenty-five, these trustees, in virtue of a power in the settlement, restricted his interest under that deed to a liferent, and declared that the provisions therein contained should belong to him in liferent only, and to his heirs in fee. Questions having been raised as to the effect of this minute upon Mr Ker, jun.'s right of fee, it was decided by the Lord Ordinary (Kinloch), and adhered to by the First Division, and affirmed by the House of Lords, that Mr Ker, jun.'s right under his father's trust-settlement was only one of liferent. Mr Ker, jun., however, had in his ante-nuptial marriage contract conveyed to trustees his whole "right and interest, present and future," under his father's trust-settlement, for the purpose, *inter alia*, of paying to him during the subsistence of the marriage, and in the event of his surviving his wife, to him thereafter, during the remainder of his life, the free balance of the income of the trust estate. This provision was declared to be alimentary, and not disposable by him to his prejudice. The contract also provided an annuity of £400 a year to Mrs Ker, and certain sums to the children of the marriage. Nearly two years after this date, viz., 28th July 1860, Mr Ker, junior, executed a deed in which, on the narrative of a certain sum advanced to him by Mr Justice, he conveyed his whole rights under his father's trust-settlement and under his marriage contract to that gentleman. The question now raised is, whether the trustee under the marriage contract, or Mr Justice, in virtue of the last mentioned deed, is entitled to be preferred to the rents and profits of the estate of Mr Ker, senior. The marriage contract trustees contended that they were entitled to the rents and profits because, at the time of the marriage, it was understood that Mr Ker was to become owner of the fee of his father's estate, and the contract had been framed on that footing, while, by the act of his father's trustees, his right had been restricted to a liferent. The security, therefore, for Mrs Ker's jointure had failed, and they were entitled to accumulate the rents in order to provide for the jointure and the claims of the children. They also contended that the provisions in the marriage contract were alimentary, and that Mr Justice ought to claim from them, as they had the right to these funds in the first instance. The Lord Ordinary (Kinloch) repelled the pleas of the marriage contract trustees, and decided in favour of Mr Justice.

MACLACHLAN *v.* GARDINER.—*Nov. 7th.*

Motion for New Trial—Credibility of Witnesses Question for Jury.

This was an action at the instance of a widow claiming damages for the death of her husband, who was killed in a colliery belonging to the defender. The issue was whether the deceased was killed by being thrown out of a cage owing to the defective machinery for working said cage, through the fault of the defender. The case was tried before the Lord President and a jury, at the last spring sitting, and the jury found for the pursuer. Thereafter, the defender moved for a new trial, on the ground that the verdict was contrary to evidence.

Lord Deas said—The question was, whether the accident happened in consequence of one of the spokes of a wheel being broken or insufficiently secured. Four witnesses swear it was broken. If it was broken that would cause accident. Seven witnesses swear it was not broken. If it was not, then that was not the cause of the accident. The jury believed the four witnesses. It was a question of credibility, not to be determined by number. There was no more proper jury question than that the jury have decided. Even if I leant to the side on which there were seven witnesses, that is not a sufficient reason for upsetting a verdict. But I am not prepared to do so. Of them, two were interested. The means of knowledge which the seven possessed, were not greater than those possessed by the four; while it is very important that no cause of accident is proved if it did not happen through the broken spoke.

Lord Ardmillan agreed. His lordship thought a distinction was to be drawn between a case, in which, on an inference drawn from proved or admitted facts, the Court thought the jury wrong. That would be a strong case for granting a new trial: but where the matter is not one of inference, but of antagonistic evidence, he was not disposed to upset the verdict of a jury who saw the witnesses. Demeanour and mode of giving evidence are so important that it was not advisable readily to interfere in such cases.

The Lord President thought at the trial that the question was a nice one, and felt rather disposed to side with the minority, but in the circumstances, would not differ.

M.P.—Hill's Trustees *v.* Hills—*Nov.* 8*th.*

Trust—Residue—Vesting.

By trust disposition and settlement, the late David Hill conveyed his whole estates to certain trustees. The first purpose of the trust provided that, in respect, the main object of the trust was to form a clear capital trust fund of £6500, to be disposed of as directed by the deed, the truster's brother, Robert Hill, should provide funds to the trustees for paying all his lawful debts, death-bed and funeral expenses, and the expenses of the executry. The second purpose of the trust was, that the trustees should make over to the said Robert Hill, the lease of Hallyards for the whole remaining years thereof, and also the truster's whole crop and stocking, and moveable estate generally, at the sum of £3500, which he should be required to pay as soon after the truster's death as convenient, and this sum, with the sum of £3000, of which the truster was himself possessed, was to form the capital of £6500, to be disposed of in the following way:—The said Robert Hill was to have the whole interest of £6000 thereof, until the youngest son of the truster's brother, Dr Andrew Hill, should attain the age of twenty-one years, and on that event, the said sum was to be divided as directed in the deed.

The truster died on 16th November, 1860, and his brother, Robert Hill, died on 18th February, 1864. Dr Andrew Hill's youngest son, however, will not attain majority till 1878, and a question has accordingly arisen as to the right to the interest of the £6000 until that event.

The heirs *in mobilibus* of the truster, claim this interest as undisposed of residue. The persons to whom the £6000 is to go in 1878 claim it, and the representatives of Robert Hill claim it. The trustees, therefore, have brought the present multiplepoinding and exoneration in reference to said interest.

The Lord Ordinary (Jerviswoode) preferred Robert Hill's representatives, holding the bequest to him as remuneratory for the outlay he was to incur, in paying the truster's debts in the meantime. The other parties reclaimed, but the Court to-day adhered. Their lordships were of opinion that this was not undisposed of residue, or residue properly speaking at all. The bequest had vested by Robert Hill's survivance, and his representatives were entitled to it.

Wilson v. Merry and Cunningham.—*Nov.* 9.

Motion for new trial—Verdict set aside as contrary to evidence.

This case was discussed to-day on a motion for a new trial, on the ground of the verdict having been contrary to evidence; and on a bill of exceptions. It was an action of damages raised by the mother of the late Henry Wilson, miner, who had been accidentally killed while at work in the employment of the defenders, Messrs. Merry & Cunningham, coal and iron masters, Glasgow. The case had been tried before Lord Ormidale and a jury on the 5th and 6th days of April 1866, under the following issue :—

"It being admitted that the defenders are proprietors of the Haughhead Pit, near Hamilton, in the county of Lanark, whether, on or about the 25th day of November 1863, the deceased Henry Wilson, miner, Haughhead, the son of the pursuer, while engaged in the employment of the defenders, as a miner in said pit, was killed by an explosion of fire-damp, through the fault of the defenders, to the loss, injury, and damage of the pursuer ?

Damages laid at £400.

The jury found for the pursuer.

At advising the Court granted a new trial, holding that the verdict was contrary to evidence—especially to certain circumstances of real evidence which had been satisfactorily proved at the trial.

The Lord President said—I cannot say I am prepared to differ from the opinion at which your lordships have arrived. On the contrary, the reasons given for granting a new trial weigh very strongly with me. The case attempted to be made out for the pursuer is that there was no opening at the rise side of the scaffold at all. This may mean either that there was no opening *in* the scaffold, or that there was no opening at the ends. But assuming that it is meant there was no opening at the side of the scaffolding, then we have the pursuer's witnesses saying there was no opening; and we have the defender's witnesses saying there were openings. But, if the pursuer's witnesses be right, the construction of the scaffolding, if done purposely, was most absurd. Then, was it accidental? Two of the pursuer's witnesses called the attention of the defender's manager to the fact that there was no arrangement for ventilation by reason of the way in which the scaffold had been constructed, and he replied that it would do quite well. If the pursuer meant that the attention of the defender's manager was called to the fact that there was no hole in the scaffold, and received for answer that it would do quite well, the meaning of the defender's manager being that the holes at the sides of the scaffold were sufficient for the purpose, this would be quite intelligible. As to the size of the hole, either there is some mistake in the notes or in the arithmetic of the witnesses. Williamson, a scientific witness, is made to say that "4 feet by 6 would be about 20 feet of superficies of hole." How he makes 4 multiplied by 6 to be equal to 20 it is difficult to understand. Another scientific gentleman (John Neish) is made to say:—"One of the openings is 4 feet long, and from 9 to 5 inches in breadth. Other hole 6 feet in length and from 8 to 5 inches in breadth. These two holes 5 feet square of superficial area." But these holes would not make 5 feet square, but 5 square feet. Five feet square would be equal to 25 square feet. This is a very material point if we come to the question of a *quantum*. But I agree with your lordships that the case attempted on the part of the pursuer has not been made out. With regard to the exceptions, as these arose on the special facts of the case, and do not involve any abstract question of law, it is unnecessary to consider them. Directions must arise on the special facts of the case. At a new trial it may be proved that the fault was other than that of Neish, or a different fault altogether from that which has been attempted to be made out.

Verdict set aside as contrary to evidence, reserving all questions of expenses.

BROWN *v.* BROWNLEE.—*Nov.* 13.

Action of Damages—Relevancy.

This was an action of damages raised by James Brown, baker, East Calder, against George Brownlee, auctioneer, Mid-calder. The pursuer claimed £300 as damages from the defender for having wrongfully poinded certain turnips, potatoes, and corn belonging to him for a debt due by his father. The allegations of the pursuer were that he had bought these articles on 22d September 1865 from his father, according to inventory, and had paid for them at various times; that, nevertheless, the defender on 23d September 1865 attempted to poind, and ultimately did poind, these articles which the pursuer had not had time to remove; that thereafter a warrant of sale was obtained from the Sheriff, and the pursuer thereupon brought a suspension, in which the note was passed and interim interdict granted on caution.

The pursuer founded on the Mercantile Law Amendment Act, 19 and 20 Vict. cap. 60, sec. 1, which provides that, when goods are sold and not delivered to the purchaser, but allowed to remain in the custody of the seller, "it shall not be competent for any creditor of such seller, after the date of such sale, to attach such goods as belonging to the seller by any process of law," to the effect of preventing the purchaser from enforcing delivery of the same.

The Lord Ordinary (Barcaple) reported the case on issues, and the Court, to-day, dismissed the action, in respect there was no averment that the seller was ever asked to deliver or prevented from delivering, and that the steps taken to prevent the sale were, so far as they went, competently taken.

HEWAT *v.* FOULDS.—*Nov.* 14.

Bankruptcy Act § 104—*Petition under.*

In this case Mr Hewat petitioned the Lord Ordinary on the Bills, in terms of the 104th section of the Bankruptcy Act, to have certain funds taken out of the sequestration of Alex. Wm. Crichton, writer, Glasgow, in which Mr J. C. Foulds is trustee. The funds in question consisted of the sum in a policy of insurance on the life of Crichton, and other sums forming part of the sequestrated estate of Alexander Guthrie, house-agent, Glasgow. The petitioner prayed to have those sums taken out of the sequestration of Alex. Wm. Crichton's estate, as not forming a part of said sequestrated estate, but belonging to Guthrie, and held for behoof of his creditors, Reddie and Crichton, and for the said Reddie and Crichton's creditors, of whom the petitioner was one. The respondent pleaded, first, that the petitioner had no title as not "claiming right" in the sense of the 104th section of the statute; and, second, that the petition was incompetent, as not setting forth relevant averments. The Lord Ordinary on the Bills (Mure) repelled, *hoc statu*, these pleas.

The Court to-day did not decide the question of law whether such an application, under the statute, was competent at the instance of a creditor of a creditor of the bankrupt, but adhered to the Lord Ordinary's interlocutor, in respect it repelled these pleas as preliminary.

Sir Coutts Lindsay *v.* Robert Thomson.—*Nov.* 15.

Encroachment on Channel of Stream.—Form of Issue.

In this action, the pursuer asks that an embankment erected by the defender in the Mohay Burn, within high water mark, opposite the farm of Milton, belonging to the pursuer, should be removed. The pursuer alleges that the embankment has reduced the superficial area of the channel of the Mohay Burn, and so raised the surface of the water and increased the velocity of the stream, and obstructed the drainage of his lands.

The following issue was reported by the Lord Ordinary (Jerviswoode):—

"Whether, in or about the year 1864, the defender wrongfully constructed an embankment of about 1000 feet in length, or thereby, on the south side of the said river or burn, and within high water mark of ordinary spring tides *ex adverso* of the pursuer's lands of Milton, part of the said lands and estate of Leuchars, to the injury of the pursuer's lands or any part thereof?"

The defender maintained that the issue should set forth that the embankment complained of was constructed in the alveus of the stream, and also that the amount of damage sustained by the pursuer should be expressly set forth.

The Lord President—This is a question between proprietors on the banks of a tidal stream. In this case substantial damage must be proved. I think the pursuer has libelled damage sufficiently. We approve of the issue.

SECOND DIVISION.

Susp. Malcolm *v.* Dick—*Nov.* 8.

Title to sue—Executor.

William Dick, the present respondent, brought an action of count reckoning, and payment against the suspender for the balance alleged to be due by him upon his intromissions as trustee under a disposition *omnium bonorum*, granted by the late Robert Dick in the suspender's favour. In the summons, Dick designed himself as "eldest son and nearest and lawful heir of the deceased Robert Dick," and also "as executor, or otherwise representing him," but he produced no title to act in either capacity. In that action, he obtained in absence a decree for £250, and, having charged Malcolm to make payment, the present suspension was brought. The Court gave effect to the contention of the suspender, that the decree ought to be suspended in respect that it was obtained in an action which the respondent had not at the time produced any title to pursue. The fact that he had in the suspension produced a decree dative in his favour did not obviate the objection.

The North Western Bank (limited) *v.* Bjornstrom and Bergborns—*Nov.* 9.

Ship—Shipmaster—Bill—Liability of Owners.

This was an action for the amount of a bill for £800, and was brought under the following circumstances:—In 1863, the ship *Tahti* was chartered by Ogle & Co., of London, for a voyage to Calcutta and back. The charter-party contained this stipulation—"sufficient cash at current exchange, not exceeding £1000, to be advanced on account of freight for ship's disbursements at Calcutta." At Calcutta, John Ogle & Co., agents for the charterers, advanced £800 to the master, Bjornstrom, and took therefor his bill at three months, drawn on Ogle & Co., of London, the charterers. This bill, which came eventually by indorsations into the hands of the pursuers, though accepted by Ogle & Co., remained unpaid, owing to that firm's failure, and the present action was accordingly brought against the owners of the ship, the Messrs Bergborn, and also against the master.

The Lord Ordinary (Kinloch) assoilzied the master on the ground of no jurisdiction, he being a foreigner—and the owners, on the ground that the master had no right to draw such a bill. The pursuers reclaimed in so far the judgment affected the owners. The Court unanimously adhered. The defenders were not parties to the bill, and therefore could not be made responsible in this action as debtors in a proper bill debt, but the pursuers had no other position than that of ordinary indorsees, it was an entire mistake to suppose that by the indorsation they acquired an assignation to the disbursement-debt, said to be owing to the Calcutta house; but further, there was no relevant case, for as it was quite clear that the money was advanced by the charterer's agents in terms of the charter-party and in return for the cargo delivered, it was absurd to say that they were not bound to make this advance, and neither they nor their assignees, assuming them to be assignees, had any claim against the owners of the vessel.

Birrel *v.* the Heritors of Pettinain.

Reparation—Culpa—Relevancy.

The widow and children of the parish schoolmaster of Pettinain sued the defenders for damages, on the ground that, by reason of their culpable conduct in failing to provide a schoolhouse fit for human habitation, Mr Birrel had contracted a severe illness, which resulted in his death. The

Court dismissed the action on the grounds—(1.) That Mr Birrel's proper remedy was not to stay in the house, if uninhabitable, but to go elsewhere, and then bring his action against the heritors for the expense; and (2.) That the allegations of *culpa* against the defenders were insufficient. They amounted to breach of obligation, but not to *culpa* in the sense that by their neglect of duty they caused his death.

Broomfield's Curator v. Lumsden, *Nov.* 16.

Partnership—Liability of Curator Bonis.

On the death of her husband in 1856, a *curator bonis* was appointed by the Court to Mrs Broomfield, who was and is a lunatic. The principal part of her late husband's estate, who died intestate, consisted of shares in the Western Bank of Scotland, and the curator agreed with the executors to accept such number of these shares as were equivalent to the amount to which his ward was entitled in cash. These shares were accordingly transferred to him as *curator bonis*, he signed the transfer as such, and in that capacity he appeared in the bank's books and in the register of shareholders. The bank having failed, and calls amounting in all to £125 per share having been made on the curator as a partner of the bank, he pleaded that he was not personally liable, and could only be required to pay the sums charged for out of the funds belonging to his ward. Lord Kinloch, on the authority of Lumsden *v.* Buchanan, as decided in the House of Lords in 1865, repelled this plea. The curator reclaimed, and the Court to-day adhered. The opinion of the Court was delivered by

The Lord Justice-Clerk, who said—The defender was in February 1856 appointed *curator bonis* to Mrs Jane Fairbairn or Broomfield. Since that time he has continued in the exclusive management of her property. That property consisted in 1856 of one-third part of her late husband's estate. What the curator was then entitled to was payment in cash of that third from the husband's executor, whose duty it was to realise the estate so as to enable him to make such payment. What the curator actually did was this: he entered into an arrangement with the executor whereby he consented to take over seven shares of Western Bank stock. Whether or not this was a proper act of curatorial management is beside the present question, as to that I offer no opinion: it is sufficient that it was a voluntary act on the curator's part. He was entitled to receive payment in cash, and he preferred to take value in stock. Now, it is quite clear that he had no power to make his ward a partner of any trading company; and, in point of fact, he made no such attempt. The executor had these shares conveyed to him by confirmation, and had power to dispose of them without becoming a partner of the company; but a party taking these shares from him by the ordinary deed of transfer necessarily became a partner of the bank; and this is exactly what the curator did. That being so, it is in vain to appeal to books kept by officers of the company with a view to show that he was not looked on by them as a partner. The defender has clearly become a partner, and it is vain to allege that he is only a partner *qua curator bonis*, or with any other qualification. It is now well established that no one can become a partner in a company such as the present with limited liability, or can possess any privileges which are not held in common with the other shareholders.

INDEX TO DIGEST.

I. MATTERS IN COURT OF SESSION.

NO. II. NAMES OF SCOTCH CASES.

III. MATTERS OF ENGLISH CASES.

PUBLIC GENERAL STATUTES

RELATING TO SCOTLAND,

PASSED IN THE

TWENTY-NINTH AND THIRTIETH YEARS

OF THE REIGN OF HER MAJESTY

QUEEN VICTORIA.

Printed by Authority.

EDINBURGH:
T. & T. CLARK, LAW BOOKSELLERS, GEORGE STREET.
GLASGOW: SMITH AND SON. ABERDEEN: WYLLIE AND SON.
LONDON: STEVENS AND SONS.

MDCCCLXVI.

TURNBULL AND SPEARS, PRINTERS, GEORGE STREET, EDINBURGH

ANNO VICESIMO NONO

VICTORIÆ REGINÆ.

CAP. XVI.

An Act for facilitating the public Exhibition of Works of Art in certain Exhibitions. [30*th* April 1866.]

WHEREAS the Owners of Works of Art have shown great willingness to lend them for public Exhibition: And whereas it has been proposed to hold Exhibitions of National Portraits by Means of Loans, and to contribute Works of Art now in this country to the Universal Exhibition at *Paris* in One thousand eight hundred and sixty-seven: And whereas it is expedient to facilitate the Loan of such Works of Art to the above-mentioned Exhibitions: Be it enacted by the Queen's most Excellent Majesty, by and with the Advice and Consent of the Lords Spiritual and Temporal, and Commons, in this present Parliament assembled, and by the Authority of the same, as follows:

Power to Owners of Works of Art to lend them to public Exhibitions.

I. The Owner for the Time being of any Work of Art may, without incurring any Responsibility for any consequent Loss or Injury, lend such Work to the Lord President for the Time being of Her Majesty's most Honourable Privy Council, for any Period not exceeding Twelve Months, to be exhibited to the Public by him or by his Direction at the above-mentioned Exhibitions.

Due Precautions to be taken for Preservation of such Works.

II. It shall be the Duty of the Lord President to take due Precautions for the Preservation of all Works of Art lent to him in pursuance of this Act, but he shall not be personally liable for any Loss or Injury any Article may sustain.

Definition of "Owner for the Time being."

III. The Expression "Owner for the Time being" shall include Trustees of Museums and other Bodies of Persons, whether corporate or unincorporate, having in their Possession or under their Control Works of Art, on trust for any public Purpose, or for any Artistic or Scientific Society, or possessed thereof on behalf of themselves and their Successors; it shall also include any Tenant for Life or other Person beneficially entitled (otherwise than as Mortgagee) to the Possession or Enjoyment of Works of Art for Life or any other limited Period, and being of full Age.

Short Title. IV. This Act may be cited for all Purposes as "The Art Act, 1866."

CAP. XVII.

An Act to regulate the Inspection of Cattle Sheds, Cowhouses, and Byres within Burghs and populous Places in Scotland.

[30th April 1866.]

WHEREAS it is expedient to make more effectual Provision for regulating the Inspection of Cattle Sheds and Cowhouses and Byres within Burghs and populous Places in *Scotland*: Be it therefore enacted by the Queen's most Excellent Majesty, by and with the Advice and Consent of the Lords Spiritual and Temporal, and Commons, in this present Parliament assembled, and by the Authority of the same, as follows:

Short Title. I. This Act may be cited as "The Cattle Sheds in Burghs (*Scotland*) Act, 1866."

Interpretation of Terms. II. The Words "Cattle Sheds," "Cowhouses," and "Byres" shall mean and include every House, Building, Shed, Yard, or other enclosed Place or Premises in which Bulls, Cows, Heifers, Oxen, or Calves are kept or intended to be kept.

Except as otherwise provided in this Act, the Interpretation Section (No. 3) and the Jurisdiction of Magistrates Section (No. 408) of "The Police and Improvement (*Scotland*) Act, 1862," are hereby incorporated with and shall be taken so as to extend to this Act.

Inspection and licensing of Cattle Sheds in Burghs, Scotland. III. The Magistrates of Royal Burghs and also of Parliamentary Burghs in *Scotland* shall have Power to require, and shall require, all Cattle Sheds and Cowhouses and Byres within their Burghs to be inspected by an Officer appointed by them, and, if found to be suitable for such Purpose, to be licensed by them for the Period of One Year; and the Magistrates shall likewise have Power, from Time to Time, to make Rules and Regulations for the proper sanitary Condition of the same, and to fix and determine in each License the Number of Cattle which may be kept in each such Cattle Shed or Cowhouse or

Byre; and if any Person shall keep any Cattle within any Burgh without such Inspection and License, or shall violate any of the Conditions of such License, or of any of the Rules and Regulations made by the Magistrates, he shall, on Conviction before any Two of them, be subjected to a Penalty not exceeding Five Pounds for each such Offence, and a like Penalty for every Day after the Conviction for such Offence upon which such Offence is continued.

Inspection of Cattle Sheds in populous Places in Scotland.

IV. In the Case of Burghs (other than Royal and Parliamentary Burghs) and populous places in *Scotland* which have adopted the whole or Portions of "The Police and Improvement (*Scotland*) Act, 1862," or previously to the passing of the said Act of 1862 had adopted the whole or any Parts of "The Police of Towns (*Scotland*) Act, 1850," the Commissioners under the said Acts shall have Power to require, and shall require, all Cattle Sheds and Cowhouses and Byres within such Burghs or populous Places to be inspected by an Officer appointed by them, and, if found to be suitable for such Purpose, to be licensed by them for the Period of One Year; and the Commissioners shall likewise have Power, from Time to Time, to make Rules and Regulations for the proper sanitary Condition of the same, and to fix and determine in each Licence the Number of Cattle which may be kept in each such Cattle Shed or Cowhouse or Byre; and if any Person shall keep any Cattle within any Burgh or populous Place without such Inspection and Licence, or shall violate any of the Conditions of such Licence, or any of the Rules and Regulations made by the Commissioners, he shall, on Conviction before the Magistrates, be subjected to a Penalty not exceeding Five Pounds for each such Offence and a like Penalty for every Day after the Conviction for such Offence upon which such Offence is continued.

Licence for Cattle Sheds and Cowhouses may be suspended in addition to Penalty imposed.

V. The Magistrates before whom any Person is convicted of Nonobservance of any of the Regulations made by virtue of this Act may, as often as they shall see Cause, give Notice in Writing requiring the Owner or Occupier of such Cattle Shed, Cowhouse, or Byre to make such sanitary Improvements in the same as they shall direct, within a Period of One Month from the Date of such written Notice; and in any case of Noncompliance with or Disobedience to such Notice, may, in addition to the Penalty imposed on such Person under the Authority of this Act, suspend, for any Period not exceeding One Month, the Licence granted to such Person under this Act; and such Magistrates may, upon the Conviction of any Person for a Second or other subsequent like Offence, in addition to the Penalty imposed under the Authority of this Act, declare the Licence granted under this Act revoked; and whenever the Licence of any such Person is revoked as aforesaid, the Magistrates or the Commissioners may refuse to grant any Licence whatsoever to the Person whose Licence has been so revoked.

Licences to be renewed every Year.

VI. Every Licence granted under this Act shall continue in force for the Period of One Year from the granting thereof, except it shall be suspended or revoked under this Act; and no Fee or Reward shall be taken for any such Licence; and such Licence shall be required to be renewed once in every Year; and if any Person shall use any Cattle Shed, Cowhouse, or Byre in any Burgh or populous Place without a Licence, he shall be liable for each Offence to a Penalty not exceeding Five Pounds, of which Offence the Fact that Bulls, Cows, Heifers, Oxen, or Calves have been taken into such Place shall be deemed sufficient *primâ facie* Evidence.

Licences after 15th May 1867.

VII. From and after the Fifteenth Day of *May* One thousand eight hundred and sixty-seven, before any Licence for the Use of any Cattle Shed, Cowhouse, or Byre can be granted, Fourteen Days Notice of the Intention to apply for such Licence shall be given in Writing to the Magistrates or Commissioners.

Extent of Act.

VIII. This Act shall apply only to *Scotland*.

Commencement of Act.

IX. This Act (Clause Seven excepted) shall come into force on the Fifteenth Day of *May* One thousand eight hundred and sixty-six.

CAP. XXVIII.

An Act to enable the Public Works Loan Commissioners to make Advances towards the Erection of Dwellings for the Labouring Classes.—[18*th* May 1866.]

WHEREAS by 'The Labouring Classes Lodging Houses Act, 1851,' Powers were vested in certain Local Authorities for the Purpose of facilitating the Erection of Lodging Houses for the Labouring Classes: And whereas it is desirable that further Provision should be made for facilitating and encouraging the Erection of Dwellings for the Labouring Classes in populous Places: Be it enacted by the Queen's most Excellent Majesty, by and with the Advice and Consent of the Lords Spiritual and Temporal, and Commons, in this present Parliament assembled, and by the Authority of the same, as follows:

Short Title.

I. This Act may be cited as 'The Labouring Classes Dwelling Houses Act, 1866.'

II. This Act shall be deemed to be incorporated with and shall be taken as Part of 'The Labouring Classes Lodging Houses Act, 1851,' and the Two Acts shall be read and construed together as if they were One Act. Act incorporated with 14 & 15 Vict. c. 34.

III. All the Clauses, Powers, Authorities, Provisoes, Enactments, Directions, Regulations, Restrictions, Privileges, Priorities, Advantages, Penalties, and Forfeitures contained in and conferred and imposed by the Act of the Session of the Twenty-fourth and Twenty-fifth Years of Her Majesty's Reign, Chapter Eighty (Public Works and Harbours Act), and the Acts therein referred to, or any of them, so far as the same can be made applicable and are not varied by this Act, shall be taken to extend to this Act, and to everything to be done in pursuance of this Act, and as if the same were herein repeated and set forth. Application of 24 & 25 Vict. c. 80. to this Act.

IV. For the Purpose herein-after mentioned, the Public Works Loan Commissioners, as defined by the said Act of the Twenty-fourth and Twenty-fifth Years of Her Majesty, may out of the Funds for the Time being at their Disposal from Time to Time advance on Loan to any such Local or other Authority as herein-after mentioned, namely, Authorities and Persons to whom Loans may be made.

- Any Council, Board, or Commissioners authorized to carry into execution 'The Labouring Classes Lodging Houses Act, 1851;'
- Any Local or other Authority invested with Powers of Town or Local Government and Rating under any Public General or any Local Act, by whatever Name such Local or other Authority may be called;
- Any Local Authority acting under the 'Nuisances Removal Act, 1855,' or any Act or Acts amending the same; 18 & 19 Vict. c. 121.

or to any such Body or Proprietor as herein-after mentioned, namely,

- Any Railway Company, or Dock or Harbour Company, or any other Company, Society, or Association established for the Purposes of this Act or for trading or manufacturing Purposes;
- Any private Person entitled to any Land for an Estate in Fee Simple, or for any Term of Years absolute, whereof not less than Fifty Years shall for the Time being remain unexpired;

And any such local or other Authority, or any such Body or Proprietor, may from Time to Time borrow from the Public Works Loan Commissioners such Money as may be required for the Purpose of this Act, subject and according to the following Provisions:

1. Such Advance on Loan shall be made for the Purpose of assisting in the Purchase of Land and Buildings, or in the Erection, Alteration, and Adaptation of Buildings to be used as Dwellings for the Labouring Classes, and in providing all Conveniences which may be deemed proper in connexion with such Dwellings:
2. Any such Advance may be made whether the Local or other Authority or Body or Proprietor receiving the same has or has not Power to borrow on Mortgage or otherwise, independently of this Act; but nothing in this Act contained shall repeal or alter any Regulation, statutory or otherwise, whereby any Company may be restricted from borrowing until a definite Portion of Capital is subscribed for, taken, or paid up:
3. No sum shall be advanced without the Approval of the Commissioners of Her Majesty's Treasury of the borrowing thereof, signified by some Writing under the Hand of One of their Secretaries or Assistant Secretaries:
4. It shall be lawful for the said Commissioners of Her Majesty's Treasury to make such Rules and Regulations as they shall from Time to Time think proper with respect to Applications for Advances under this Act, and the Terms and Conditions upon which such Advances are to be made, and to issue such Instructions and Forms as they may think proper for the Guidance of and Observance by Persons applying for or receiving Loans, or executing Works, or rendering Accounts of Monies expended under this Act; or regarding the Class of Dwellings towards the providing of which such Loans may be made, and the Adaptation thereof to the Purposes intended, and as to the Mode of providing for their Maintenance, Repair, and Insurance:
5. The Period for the Repayment of the Sums advanced shall not exceed Forty Years:
6. The Repayment of the Money advanced, with Interest thereon at such Rate as shall be agreed upon, but not at a less Rate than Four Pounds *per Centum per Annum*, shall be secured as follows; namely, in the case of an Advance to any such Local or other Authority as aforesaid, either by a Mortgage solely of the Rates leviable by such Authority, or by such other Mortgage as herein-after mentioned, or by both; and in any other Case by a Mortgage

of the Estate or Interest of any such Local or other Authority, or of any such Body or Proprietor as aforesaid, in the Land or Dwellings for the Purposes of which the Advance is made; and in the Case of an Advance to a Company any Part of whose Capital remains uncalled up or unpaid, by a Mortgage also of all Capital so remaining uncalled up or unpaid; and any such Mortgage as aforesaid may be taken either alone or together with any other Security which may be agreed upon; but it shall not be incumbent on the Public Works Loan Commissioners to require any other Security:

7. No Money shall be advanced on Mortgage of any Land or Dwellings solely, unless the Estate therein proposed to be mortgaged shall be either an Estate in Fee Simple or an Estate for a Term of Years absolute, whereof not less than Fifty Years shall be unexpired at the Date of the Advance:

8. The Money advanced on the Security of a Mortgage of any Land or Dwellings solely shall not exceed One Moiety of the Value, to be ascertained to the Satisfaction of the Public Works Loan Commissioners, of the Estate or Interest in such Land or Dwellings proposed to be mortgaged; but Advances may be made by Instalments from Time to Time as the building of the Dwellings on the Land mortgaged progresses, so that the total Advance do not at any Time exceed the Amount aforesaid; and a Mortgage may be accordingly made to secure such Advances so to be made from Time to Time.

9. For the Purposes of this Act every such Local or other Authority or Body as aforesaid is hereby authorized to purchase, take, and hold Land, and if not already a Body Corporate shall, for the Purpose of holding such Land under this Act, and of suing and being sued in respect thereof, be nevertheless deemed a Body Corporate with perpetual Sucession.

Incorporation of 8 & 9 Vict. cc. 18. and 19. with this Act.

V. *The Lands Clauses Consolidation Act*, 1845, and *The Lands Clauses Consolidation* (Scotland) *Act*, 1845, and any Act amending the same, except the Clauses in the said Acts respectively with respect to the Purchase and taking of Lands otherwise than by Agreement, shall be incorporated with this Act, and for the Purposes of those Acts this Act shall be deemed the Special Act; and any such Local or other Authority or Body or Proprietor as aforesaid exercising the Powers of this Act shall be deemed the Promoters of the Undertaking.

Incorporation of 10 & 11 Vict. c. 16 with this Act.

VI. The Clauses of *The Commissioners Clauses Act*, 1847, with respect to the Mortgages to be executed by the Commissioners, except so far as the same may be inconsistent with the Provisions of the said Act of the Twenty-fourth and Twenty-fifth Years of Her Majesty, Chapter Eighty, or of any of the Acts therein recited, shall be incorporated with this Act; and in the Construction of this Act and of the said incorporated Clauses this Act shall be deemed the Special Act; and the Local or other Authority, or the Body or Proprietor, to whom the Loan is made, shall be deemed to be the Commissioners; but the said incorporated Clauses shall not, so far as they prescribe the Manner of executing Mortgages, or so far as they require a Register to be kept of Mortgages, or Transfers of Mortgages, apply to any Mortgage made under this Act by any Proprietor being a private Person; and all Mortgages executed by any Proprietor being a private Person shall be executed in the usual Manner.

Special Powers of Mortgagees.

VII. Every Mortgage under this Act shall confer on the Mortgagee thereunder for the Time being all the Rights, Powers, and Privileges conferred on Mortgagees by Part II. of the Act of the Session of the Twenty-third and Twenty-fourth Years of Her Majesty, Chapter One hundred and forty-five, intituled *An Act to give to Trustees, Mortgagees, and others certain Powers now commonly inserted in Settlements, Mortgages, and Wills;* and any such Mortgage may confer on the Mortgagee such further Powers of Sale and other Powers, and may also contain all such Covenants and Provisions, as may be agreed upon; and nothing contained in this Act or in any Clauses incorporated in the "Labouring Classes Lodging Houses Act, 1851," or in this Act, shall be deemed to limit or prevent the Enforcement of any Rights or Remedies which, at Law or in Equity or by Statute, may be otherwise incidental to any such Mortgage, either under the Acts relating to the Public Works Loan Commissioners, or otherwise.

Powers to Companies.

VIII. Any Railway Company, or Dock or Harbour Company, or any other Company, Society, or Association, established for trading or manufacturing Purposes in the course of whose Business or in the Discharge of whose Duties Persons of the Labouring Class are employed, may and are hereby (notwithstanding any Act of Parliament, or Charter, or any Rule of Law or Equity to the contrary,) authorized at any Time or from Time to Time to erect, either on their own Land or on any other Land (which they are hereby authorized to purchase and hold for the Purpose, and to pay for out of any Funds at their Disposal), Dwellings for the Accommodation of all or any of the Persons of the Labouring Class employed by them, and shall have all the like Powers of borrowing and other Powers which are herein-before conferred on any such Body or Proprietor as herein-before mentioned.

IX. All Rules and Regulations made by the Lords Commissioners of the Treasury under the Provisions of this Act shall be laid before Parliament. Rules to be laid before Parliament.

X. This Act shall not extend to *Ireland*. Extent of Act.

Cap. XXX.

An Act to amend the Harbours and Passing Tolls, &c., Act 1861. [18*th* May 1866.]

Be it enacted by the Queen's most Excellent Majesty, by and with the Advice and Consent of the Lords Spiritual and Temporal, and Commons, in this present Parliament assembled, and by the Authority of the same, as follows:—

I. Where under the Harbours and Passing Tolls, &c., Act, 1861, any Loan has been or is about to be made by the Public Works Loan Commissioners to a Harbour Authority having borrowing Powers under a Special Act by which the Extinguishment of any Debt of the Harbour Authority by means of annual Payments of a prescribed Amount or within a prescribed Time is required, and the Board of Trade, on the Application of the Harbour Authority, are satisfied that by virtue of the Provision made or about to be made for Repayment within a certain Time of any such Loan or Loans from the Public Works Loan Commissioners there will be extinguished an Amount of Debt of the Harbour Authority not less than that which would in the same Time be extinguished under the Provisions of the Special Act, and the Board of Trade thereupon certify in Writing to the effect that it is expedient that the Operation of the Provisions of the Special Act relative to the Extinguishment of Debt, or such of them as are referred to in the Certificate, should as from a Time therein specified, and subject to any Conditions therein expressed, be suspended during the Period or Periods for Repayment of such Loan or Loans to the Public Works Loan Commissioners, then and in every such Case the Operation of those Provisions shall be and the same is by Virtue of this Act and of the Certificate suspended accordingly. Power for Board of Trade to authorize Suspension of Sinking Fund, &c., under certain Harbour Acts. 24 & 25 Vict. c. 47.

II. Any Money borrowed from the Public Works Loan

Restriction on re-borrowing.

Commissioners to which any Certificate of the Board of Trade under this Act relates, when paid off, shall not be reborrowed.

Short Title.

III. This Act may be cited as the Harbour Loans Act, 1866.

CAP. L.

An Act to revive Section Sixty-nine of 'The Nuisances Removal (Scotland) *Act,* 1856,' *relating to Burials in Burghs.* [16*th* July 1866.]

19 & 20 Vict. c. 108, s. 69.

18 & 19 Vict. c. 68.

25 & 26 Vict. c. 101.

WHEREAS an Act was passed in the Session held in the Nineteenth and Twentieth Years of Her Majesty Queen *Victoria*, being the Nuisances Removal (*Scotland*) Act, 1856, Section Sixty-nine of which Act contains certain Provisions for the Amendment of the Act of the Eighteenth and Nineteenth of Her Majesty Queen *Victoria*, being the Burial Grounds (*Scotland*) Act, 1855, so as to make the last-mentioned Act available in Burghs comprehending Parts of more than One Parish:—And whereas by the General Police and Improvement (*Scotland*) Act, 1862, the said Section Sixty-nine of the Nuisances Removal (*Scotland*) Act, 1856, was inadvertently repealed: Be it therefore enacted by the Queen's most Excellent Majesty, by and with the Advice and Consent of the Lords Spiritual and Temporal, and Commons, in this present Parliament assembled, and by the Authority of the same, as follows:

So much of s. 1 of 25 & 26 Vict. c. 101, as repeals s. 69 of 19 & 20 Vict. c. 108 repealed, and the said s. 69 restored.

I. That the First Section of the said General Police and Improvement (*Scotland*) Act, 1862, be and the same is hereby repealed in so far, but in so far only, as the same repeals and affects Section Sixty-nine of the Nuisances Removal (*Scotland*) Act, 1856, above recited: And the said Section Sixty-nine is hereby re-enacted and restored, and declared to be in full Force and Effect.

All Proceedings under 18 & 19 Vict. c. 68, and in Terms of said 69th Section, to be valid.

II. All Proceedings adopted and taken or to be adopted and taken under or in Terms of the Act passed in the Eighteenth and Nineteenth Years of the Reign of Her Majesty Queen *Victoria*, being the Burial Grounds (*Scotland*) Act, 1855, and under and in Terms of the Sixty-ninth Section of the Nuisances Removal (*Scotland*) Act, 1856, or either of them, shall be equally valid and effectual as if the said Section Sixty-nine had never been repealed.

Short Title.

III. This Act may be cited as the Burial in Burghs (*Scotland*) Act, 1866.

Cap. LI.

An Act to amend the Acts relating to Lunacy in Scotland, *and to make further Provision for the Care and Treatment of Lunatics.* [16*th* July 1866.]

Whereas an Act was passed in the Twentieth and Twenty-first Year of the Reign of Her present Majesty, intituled *An Act for the Regulation of the Care and Treatment of Lunatics, and for the Provision, Maintenance, and Regulation of Lunatic Asylums,* in Scotland; and another Act was passed in the Twenty-first and Twenty-second Year of the Reign of Her present Majesty, intituled *An Act to amend an Act of the last Session for the Regulation of the Care and Treatment of Lunatics, and for the Provision, Maintenance, and Regulation of Lunatic Asylums, in* Scotland; and another Act was passed in the Twenty-fifth and Twenty-Sixth Year of the Reign of her present Majesty, intituled, *An Act to make farther Provision respecting Lunacy in* Scotland; and another Act was passed in the Twenty-seventh and Twenty-eighth Year of the Reign of Her present Majesty, intituled *An Act to continue the Deputy Commissioners in Lunacy in* Scotland, *and to make farther Provision for the Salaries of the Deputy Commissioners, Secretary, and Clerk of the General Board of Lunacy in* Scotland: And whereas it is expedient that the said Deputy Commissioners should be continued, that certain of the Provisions of the said Acts should be amended, and that farther Provision should be made for the Regulation of the Care and Treatment of Lunatics, and for the Regulation of Lunatic Asylums, in *Scotland:*

20 & 21 Vict. c. 71.
21 & 22 Vict. c. 89.
25 & 26 Vict. c. 54.
27 & 28 Vict. c. 59.

Be it enacted by the Queen's most Excellent Majesty, by and with the Advice and Consent of the Lords Spiritual and Temporal, and Commons, in this present Parliament assembled, and by the Authority of the same, as follows:

Short Title. I. This Act may be cited as 'The Lunacy (*Scotland*) Act, 1866.'

Construction of Act II. This Act shall be construed with the recited Acts as One Act, and this Act and the said recited Acts may be recited together as the Lunacy (*Scotland*) Acts.

Continuance of Deputy Commissioners. III. The Provisions of the Twentieth and Twenty-first *Victoria*, Chapter Seventy-one, first recited, and of the Twenty-seventh and Twenty-eighth *Victoria*, Chapter Fifty-nine, last recited, in regard to the Appointment and

Salary of Deputy Commissioners, shall be and are hereby continued until Parliament shall otherwise determine.

Medical Officers of Asylums may not grant Certificates.

IV. It shall not be lawful for the Medical Superintendent, ordinary Medical Attendant, or Assistant Medical Officer of any Asylum, to grant a Certificate of Insanity for the Reception of any Lunatic, not a Pauper Lunatic, into such Asylum, except the Certificate of Emergency authorized by Section Fourteen of the third-recited Act.

Orders and Medical Certificates may be amended.

V. Section Thirty-six of the first-recited Act is hereby repealed; and in lieu thereof be it enacted, That if after the Reception of any Lunatic into any Asylum or House it appears that any Order or Medical Certificate upon which he was received is in any respect incorrect or defective, such Order or Medical Certificate may be amended by the Person who has granted the same at any Time within Twenty-one Days after the Reception of such Lunatic: Provided nevertheless, that no such Amendment shall have any Force or Effect unless the same shall receive the Sanction of the Board, and, failing such Amendment, it shall be lawful for the Board to report such Failure to the Sheriff, who shall, if satisfied that the original Order or Medical Certificates are in any respect incorrect or defective, and of the Failure to amend them, recal such original Order.

Orders to remain in force although Patient absent from Asylum.

VI. In every Case in which any Lunatic or any Person who has entered an Asylum for Treatment under Authority of this Act is temporarily absent from the Asylum or House for his Reception into which the Order was given, or shall escape from such Asylum or House, or from the Care of the Officers thereof, such Order shall remain in force in the same Manner as if such Lunatic or Person as aforesaid were not absent or had not escaped: Provided always, that such Lunatic or Person as aforesaid shall return or be brought back to such Asylum or House within a Period not exceeding Twenty-eight Days from the Day on which he left or escaped from such Asylum or House, or within a Period of Three Months where such Lunatic or Person as aforesaid is accompanied by or remains under the Care of the Officers or Attendants of such Asylum or House.

Determination of Orders.

VII. The Powers conferred by the Sheriff's Order for the Reception and Detention of any Lunatic in any Asylum or House shall cease and determine with the Notice of Discharge of such Lunatic given by the Superintendent of such Asylum or House to the Board; and in no Case shall the Sheriff's Order remain in force longer than the First Day of *January* first occurring after the Expiry of Three Years from the Date on which it was granted, or than the First Day of *January* in each succeeding Year, unless the Superintendent or Medical Attendant of the Asylum or House in which the Lunatic is detained shall, on each of the said First Days of *January*, or within Fourteen clear Days immediately preceding, grant and transmit to the Board a Certificate, on Soul and Conscience, according to the Form of Schedule A hereunto annexed, that the Detention of the Lunatic is necessary and proper, either for his own Welfare or the Safety of the Public.

Discharge on Probation of Pauper Lunatics.

VIII. Every Pauper Lunatic who is discharged on Probation from any Asylum or House shall remain subject to Inspection by the Commissioners during the Period of Probation; and it shall not be lawful for the Parochial Board to take any such Pauper Lunatic off the Poor's Roll, or to alter the Conditions on which probationary Discharge was granted, without the Sanction of the Board, during the Period of Probation; and every Inspector of the Poor who shall infringe these Provisions shall be liable in a Penalty not exceeding Ten Pounds.

Discharge of Pauper Lunatics by Authority of Parochial Board.

IX. It shall be lawful for any Parochial Board, by a Minute at a duly constituted Meeting, to direct that any Pauper Lunatic (not being a Lunatic committed as a dangerous Lunatic under the Fifteenth Section of the third-recited Act) with whose Maintenance it is chargeable, and who is detained in any Asylum or House, shall be discharged or removed therefrom; and if a Copy of such Minute, certified to be a true Copy by the Chairman for the Time of such Parochial Board, be produced to and left with the Superintendent of such Asylum, he shall, within Seven Days from the Production of such Minute, discharge such Lunatic, or cause or suffer such Lunatic to be discharged: Provided always, that, on the written Representation of such Superintendent that such Lunatic is dangerous to himself or the Public, or in any other Way not a fit Person to be discharged, it shall be lawful for the Board, after making such Investigation as they shall think expedient, to prohibit the Discharge of any such Lunatic; and any Inspector of the Poor removing any Pauper Lunatic from an Asylum or House against the written Representation of the Superintendent of such Asylum or House, without the Sanction of the Board, shall be liable in a Penalty not exceeding Ten Pounds.

Inspector of Poor to intimate Removal of Pauper Lunatics.

X. Whenever any Pauper Lunatic has been removed from an Asylum or House by a Minute of the Parochial Board, the Inspector of the Poor shall, within Fourteen Days, intimate to the Board the Date of Removal, the Situation of the House to which he has been removed, the

Christian Name and Surname of the Occupier thereof, and the Amount and Nature of the Parochial Allowances made to such Pauper Lunatic, and that under a Penalty of Ten Pounds; and it shall not be lawful for the said Parochial Board to remove such Lunatic to any other House, or to make any Alteration in the Nature and Amount of the Parochial Allowances, without the same being communicated within Fourteen Days, by the Inspector of the Poor, to the Board, under a similar Penalty; and it shall be lawful for the Board, at any Time whenever they see fit, to order the Lunatic to be replaced in an Asylum, and it shall not be lawful for the Relatives of any Pauper Lunatic for whose Removal to an Asylum the Board have issued an Order to take him off the Poor's Roll without their Sanction; and every Inspector of the Poor who shall delay for more than Fourteen Days sending any Pauper Lunatic to an Asylum, after receiving the Order of the Board to do so, shall be liable in a Penalty not exceeding Ten Pounds.

Pauper Lunatics may be removed from Poor's Roll and intrusted to private Parties.

XI. It shall be lawful for any Parochial Board, by a Minute at a duly constituted Meeting, to remove from the Poors' Roll any Pauper Lunatic in any Asylum or House for whose Maintenance it is responsible, and to intrust the Disposal of such Lunatic to any Party who shall undertake to provide, in a Manner satisfactory to the Parochial Board, for his Care and Treatment; and on the Demand of such Party, and the Production and Delivery of a Copy of such Minute, certified to be a true Copy by the Chairman for the Time of such Parochial Board, the Superintendent of such Asylum or House shall permit the Removal of such Lunatic: Provided always, that in every Case in which such Superintendent is of opinion that such Removal will be injurious to such Lunatic, or a risk to the Public, it shall be lawful for such Superintendent to detain such Lunatic for a Period not exceeding Fourteen Days from the Production of such certified Copy of such Minute, and to report the Case to the Board, and on the Report of such Superintendent, or on any Grounds which the Board may deem satisfactory, it shall be lawful for the Board to authorize the continued Detention of such Lunatic in the Asylum or House, and the Parochial Board shall continue to be responsible to the Asylum or House for his Maintenance.

Provision as to dangerous Lunatics.

XII. If at the Time when the Discharge of a Lunatic, not being a Pauper, is desired, the Superintendent of the Asylum in which he is confined shall be of opinion that he is a dangerous Lunatic, and that his Liberation would be attended with Danger to himself or to the Public, such

Superintendent shall forthwith communicate the Fact to the Procurator Fiscal of the District, and shall in the meantime detain such Lunatic in the Asylum; and it shall be the Duty of the Procurator Fiscal, if he shall see Cause, to take such Proceedings with respect to such Lunatic as are prescribed by the third-recited Act with respect to dangerous Lunatics; and if the Procurator Fiscal shall not see Cause to take such Proceedings, he shall signify such his Determination to the Superintendent of the Asylum, and the Lunatic shall thereupon be discharged, provided he is otherwise entitled to Discharge.

As to Lunatics received into any private House.

XIII. Section Forty-one of the first-recited Act is hereby repealed; and in lieu thereof, No Person shall receive or keep any Person as a Lunatic for Gain, without the Order of the Sheriff or the Sanction of the Board; and any Person who shall receive into or keep in his House any such Person, or any Person alleged to be a Lunatic, shall, within Fourteen clear Days thereafter, make Application for such Order or Sanction; provided always, that when the Lunatic is a Pauper Lunatic such Application shall be made by the Inspector of the Poor, and it shall be lawful in such Case for the Sheriff to grant his Order on One Medical Certificate: And every such Lunatic shall be visited, as often as the Board shall regulate, by a Medical Person, who shall enter in a Book to be kept in such House the Date of each Visit, and the Condition of the mental and bodily Health of the Lunatic at each such Visit; and any Medical Person who shall make any such Entry without having visited the Patient within Seven Days of making such Entry, or who shall knowingly make any false Entry in such Book, shall be liable in a Penalty not exceeding Ten Pounds for each Offence: And it shall be in the Power of the Board to order such Inspection and Visitation of every such House from Time to Time as to them shall seem proper: And every Person detaining or aiding in detaining any such Lunatic, or any Person who on Inquiry is found to be a Lunatic, without the Order of the Sheriff or the Sanction of the Board, or after such Order or Sanction has been withdrawn, shall be liable in a Penalty not exceeding Twenty Pounds: Provided that the Enactments of this Section shall not apply to any Case where the Person so received and kept has been sent to such House for the Purpose of temporary Residence only not exceeding Six Months and under the Certificate of a Medical Person, which Certificate shall be in the Form of Schedule G, to the first-recited Act annexed.

Board may inspect Lunatics in private Houses.

XIV. Section Forty-three of the first-recited Act is hereby repealed; and in lieu thereof, If any Occupier or Inmate of any private House shall keep or detain therein, without the Order of the Sheriff or the Sanction of the Board, any Person as a Lunatic, although not for Gain, beyond the Period of One Year, and the Malady is such as to require compulsory Confinement to the House, or Restraint or Coercion of any Kind, such Occupier or Inmate shall intimate the Case to the Board, and shall state the Reasons which render it desirable that such Lunatic should remain under private Care; and if the Board shall have reason to believe or suspect that any Lunatic, or any Person treated as a Lunatic, whose Case has thus been intimated to them, or of whose Case no such Intimation shall have been made, has been subjected to compulsory Confinement to the House, or to Restraint or Coercion of any Kind, at any Time beyond a Year after the Commencement of the Malady, or has been subjected to harsh and cruel Treatment, it shall be lawful for the Board, with Consent of One of Her Majesty's Principal Secretaries of State, or of Her Majesty's Advocate for *Scotland*, to authorize and empower any One or more of the Members thereof to visit and inspect such Lunatic or Person detained as a Lunatic, and to make such Inquiry respecting his Treatment, as to such Member or Members may seem fit; and if on such Inquiry it shall appear that such Person is a Lunatic, and has been so for a Space exceeding a Year, and that compulsory Confinement to the House, or Restraint or Coercion of any Kind, has been resorted to, or that he has been subjected to harsh and cruel Treatment, and that the Circumstances are such as to render the Removal of such Lunatic to an Asylum necessary or expedient, it shall be lawful for the Board to apply to the Sheriff, under a Procedure similar to that followed in the Cases of dangerous Lunatics, and the Sheriff, on being satisfied that the Person is lunatic, and has been so for more than a Year, and is subjected to compulsory Confinement, or to Restraint or Coercion of any Kind, or to harsh and cruel Treatment, shall issue his Order for the Transmission of the Lunatic to an Asylum, and his Detention therein until such Time as the Board shall sanction his Discharge: And the Sheriff shall grant Decree for the Expenses of the Inquiry and Procedure, and also for the Maintenance of the Lunatic in the Asylum, against the Parties legally liable for the Maintenance of such Lunatic.

XV. The Sixth Section of the third-recited Act is hereby

repealed; and instead thereof it is enacted as follows: It shall be lawful for the Superintendent of any Asylum, with the previous Assent in Writing of One of the Commissioners, which Assent shall not be given without written Application by the Patient, to entertain and keep in such Asylum, as a Boarder, any Person who is desirous of submitting himself to Treatment, but whose mental Condition is not such as to render it legal to grant Certificates of Insanity in his Case: Provided always, that every such Boarder shall be produced to the Commissioners at each of their Visits to such Asylum, that no such Boarder shall be detained for more than Three Days after having given Notice of his Intention or Desire to leave such Asylum, unless on Certificates of Insanity and an Order by the Sheriff being obtained, in which Case neither of the Certificates shall be granted by any Medical Person connected with the Asylum, or having any immediate or pecuniary Interest in it, and that Notices of Admission, Discharge, and Death with respect to all such Boarders shall be made to the Board in the same Manner as in the Cases of Lunatics.

As to Persons entering Asylums voluntarily.

XVI. Every Letter written by a Patient in any Asylum or House, and addressed to the Board or their Secretary, or the Commissioners in Lunacy, or any of them, shall, unless special Instructions to the contrary have been given by such Commissioners, or any of them, be forwarded to its Address unopened; and every Letter from the Board or their Secretary, or such Commissioner or Commissioners, to any such Patient, when marked "Private" on the Cover, shall be delivered to him unopened; and every Person who shall intercept or detain or shall open any such Letter without the Authority of the Patient by whom it is written or to whom it is addressed, shall be liable in a Penalty not exceeding Ten Pounds: Provided that the Board shall transmit a Copy of such Letter to the Superintendent of such Asylum or House if it shall appear to the Board that the Contents of the Letter are of such a Nature that it is of importance that the Superintendent should be made acquainted therewith.

Letters to and from Patients to be private.

XVII. It shall be lawful for the Board to obtain from the Accountant of the Court of Session the Names of all Lunatics having Judicial Factors, and a Statement of their Funds, and of the Sums allowed for their Maintenance, and for the Board to make such Investigation, by Inspection or otherwise, as shall, in their Opinion, be necessary to ascertain in what Manner such Lunatics are treated and cared for; and in case of such Treatment and Care being

As to Lunatics having Judicial Factors.

deemed by them unsatisfactory, the Board may present a summary Application to the Court of Session, or in Time of Vacation to the Lord Ordinary officiating on the Bills, who may order such Inquiry and direct all such Steps to be taken for the improved Treatment and Care of such Lunatics as to the Court or the Lord Ordinary shall appear proper, and may direct the Expenses of such Application, and of the Procedure following thereon, to be paid by the Judicial Factor out of the Funds and Estate of such Lunatic under his Control, and it shall not be competent to bring under Review of the Court any Interlocutor pronounced by such Lord Ordinary upon any such Application with a view to Investigation and Inquiry merely, and which does not finally dispose thereof upon the Merits, but any Order pronounced by such Lord Ordinary upon the Merits may be reclaimed against by any Party having lawful Interest to reclaim to the Court, provided that a Reclaiming Note shall be lodged with an Inner House Clerk within Eight Days, after which the Order or Judgment of the Lord Ordinary, if not so reclaimed against, shall be final.

Powers of Board to extend to Lunatics detained, &c.

XVIII. The Powers granted to the Board by Section Nine of the first-recited Act shall be and are hereby extended to embrace Lunatics detained under the Sanction of the Board.

Liberation of Lunatics committed as dangerous Lunatics.

XIX. It shall be lawful for the Sheriff to authorize the Discharge of a Lunatic committed as a dangerous Lunatic from any Asylum, on Certificates being granted by Two Medical Persons, approved of by the Procurator Fiscal, that such Lunatic may be discharged without Risk of Injury to the Public or the Lunatic.

Penalties for Infringement of Rules made by Board.

XX. It shall be lawful for the Board to enforce the Rules and Regulations which they shall make from Time to Time in relation to the Books or Minutes to be kept or made in Asylums or Houses, and the Returns of Entries therefrom to be made to the Board by the Superintendents of such Asylums or Houses, by imposing a Penalty for each Infringement or Violation thereof, not exceeding Ten Pounds.

As to Recovery of Penalties.

XXI. All Penalties imposed by or under Authority of this or any of the said recited Acts shall be recoverable by the Board, without Prejudice to their Right to enforce specific Implement of the Matters in respect of which such Penalties shall have been incurred; and such Penalties may be sued for by the Secretary of the Board before the Sheriff or any Court having Jurisdiction, and that either in any Application to enforce such specific Implement, or separately on summary Complaint; and such Penalties, when recovered, shall be applied as Fees received for Licences are directed to be applied by the first-recited Act.

Fees to be paid for Admission of Lunatics to District Asylums.

XXII. For every Order granted by the Sheriff for the Admission of any Lunatic or Pauper Lunatic into any District Asylum there shall be paid, for the general Purposes of the said first-recited Act, the Fees authorized by the Thirty-first Section of the said Act for the Admission of a Patient into a Public Asylum.

Commissioner not to be personally responsible.

XXIII. The Exemption from Responsibility conferred on the Commissioners by Section Eight of the said first-recited Act shall extend to everything done *bonâ fide* in the Execution of this or any other of the said recited Acts, or in the Exercise of the Powers herein and therein contained.

Actions against Medical Persons in respect to Certificates under Lunacy Acts to be tried by the Lord Ordinary without a Jury.

XXIV. In any Action at Law which may be raised against any Medical Person in respect of any Certificate granted by him under the Provisions of this Act, or of any of the recited Acts, the Issue or Issues, after being adjusted, shall be tried, and the amount of Damages (if any) assessed by the Lord Ordinary before whom such Action depends, without a Jury; and the Proceedings at and consequent on the Trial of such Issue or Issues shall be regulated by the Provisions of the Act, &c., intituled *An Act to facilitate Procedure in the Court of Session in* Scotland, with respect to the Proceedings at and consequent on the Trial by the Lord Ordinary without a Jury of such Issues as may under the Provisions of that Act be so tried; and such Action at Law must be raised within Twelve Months from the Time when any Person who may allege that he has sustained any Injury in consequence of the granting of any such Medical Certificate shall have been liberated from the Asylum in which he may have been confined in consequence of such Certificate having been granted.

Power to Directors to grant Superannuations to Officers, &c.

XXV. The Directors of any chartered Asylum in *Scotland* may grant a Superannuation Allowance out of the Funds at their Disposal to any Officer or Matron of such Asylum who shall not be less than Fifty Years of Age, who shall have been an Officer or Matron of such Asylum for not less than Fifteen Years; and such Superannuation shall be for such Term, and on such Conditions, and of such Amount, not exceeding Two-Thirds of the Salary of such Officer or Matron, as the Directors shall think fit.

Powers to Directors of public Asylums to borrow Money.

XXVI. The Directors of any Public Asylum in whom the Property thereof is vested may borrow on the Security of such Property such Sums of Money as they may think necessary for administering such Asylums, or for maintaining or extending their Means of Accommodation.

Power to Parochial Boards to borrow Money.

XXVII. Any Parochial Board which has erected or may erect Buildings for the Treatment of such Pauper Lunatics as they are authorized to receive and detain under the Provisions of the said recited Acts may, by themselves or the Trustees in whom the Property of such Buildings may be vested, borrow such Sums of Money as they may think necessary for the Administration, Maintenance, Erection, or Extension of the same, on the Security of such Buildings and the Lands on which they are erected, and on the Security of the Rates and Assessments leviable by them: Provided, that all such Sums shall be repaid by annual Instalments of not less in any One Year than One Thirtieth Part of the Sum borrowed, exclusive of the Interest on the same.

SCHEDULE (A).

I hereby certify, on Soul and Conscience, that I have, within a Period not exceeding One Month preceding the Date of this Certificate, carefully reviewed and considered the Cases of the Patients whose Names are subjoined, and I am of opinion that their continued Detention in the Asylum is necessary and proper for their own Welfare [*or* for the Public Safety, *as the Case may be*].

Superintendent *or* Medical Attendant.

Dated at this
Day of 186 .

CAP. LIII.

An Act to amend certain Provisions of the Sheriff Court Houses (Scotland) *Act*, 1860. [30*th* July 1866.]

23 & 24 Vict. c. 79.

WHEREAS it is provided by the Eighteenth Section of "The Sheriff Court Houses (*Scotland*) Act, 1860," that in case any Court House or any part thereof, not being the Property of private Parties or of the Magistrates and Council of the Burgh in which it is situate, shall cease to be used as such in consequence of other accommodation having been provided under the said Act, the Commissioners of Supply may sell the same for such Price as they may obtain therefor and convey the same to the Purchaser; provided always, that when the Building so discontinued forms Part of any Building used for other Purposes, the First Offer of the same shall be made to the Parties having

Right to the other Parts of the Building, at such Price as may be agreed on, or in case of Disagreement as may be fixed by Valuators appointed by the Sheriff of the County; provided also, that the Price received shall be applied to the Purposes for which an Assessment is authorized by the said Act, and in diminution *pro tanto* of the Sum so to be levied: Be it enacted by the Queen's most Excellent Majesty, by and with the Advice and Consent of the Lords Spiritual and Temporal, and Commons, in this present Parliament assembled, and by the Authority of the same, as follows:

Application of Sum received for Sale of Court Houses ceasing to be used.

I. When any such Court House or Part thereof shall be sold, the Price received shall be applied in the first instance towards the total Cost of any new Court House which shall be erected under the Provisions of the said Act, and the Sums to be provided for by Assessment or by Contribution from the Commissioners of Her Majesty's Treasury towards the building of any such new Court House shall be calculated after deducting from the total Estimate the Price of any such Court House or Property which may have been sold.

CAP. LXII.

An Act to amend the Law relating to the Woods, Forests, and Land Revenues of the Crown.—[6th August 1866.]

Be it enacted by the Queen's most Excellent Majesty, by and with the Advice and Consent of the Lords Spiritual and Temporal, and Commons, in this present Parliament assembled, and by the Authority of the same, as follows:

Permanent Improvements.

Power to Treasury to direct Cost of Improvements to be charged to Capital and repaid out of Income.

I. Where at any Time after the passing of this Act any Operation, Work, Matter, or Thing, being within the Description of the Improvement of Land contained in Section Nine of the Act of the Session of the Twenty-seventh and Twenty-eighth Years of Her Majesty's Reign, Chapter One hundred and fourteen, (The Improvement of Land Act, 1864,) is effected or done in or with reference to any Part of the Possessions and Land Revenues of the Crown under the Management of the Commissioners of Her Majesty's Woods, Forests, and Land Revenues (hereafter in this Act referred to as the Commissioners of Woods), the Commissioners of Her Majesty's Treasury (hereafter in this Act referred to as the Commissioners of the Treasury) may, if they think fit, direct, with respect to any such Operation, Work,

Matter, or Thing, that the Costs, Charges, and Expenses of and connected with the same shall be charged as a Principal Sum to the Account of the Capital of the Lands Revenue of the Crown; but in every Case where such Direction is given the Principal Sum so charged shall be repaid out of the Income of the Land Revenue of the Crown in such Manner and within such Time as in each Case the Commissioners of the Treasury from Time to Time direct, so nevertheless that in every Case Provision be made for the complete Repayment of Principal out of Income as aforesaid within a Period not exceeding Thirty Years from the Time at which the Principal Sum becomes a Charge as aforesaid.

Mines.

Capitalisation of Moiety of net Produce of Mines.

II. From and after the passing of this Act One Moiety of the net annual Income of the Land Revenue of the Crown received by the Commissioners of Woods in respect of any Coal, Ironstone, or Mineral, Stone, Slate, Clay, Gravel, Sand, or Chalk, or of any Substance obtained by mining, quarrying, or excavating, shall be carried to the Account of the Capital of the Land Revenue of the Crown, and the Residue of the net Amount received from the Sources in this Section mentioned shall be carried to the Account of the Income of such Land Revenue.

For the Ascertainment of such net Income as aforesaid there shall be deducted from the gross Amount received such sum as the Commissioners of the Treasury from Time to Time think fit in respect of the Salary and Expenses of the Crown Mineral Inspector and Expenses of local Management, and for the Purposes aforesaid the Commissioners of Woods shall keep a separate Account (in such Form as the Commissioners of the Treasury from Time to Time direct) to be called "The Mines Account," which Account shall include all Receipts and Outgoings in respect of the Sources of Revenue in this Section mentioned, and which Account shall show the respective Amounts to be from Time to Time carried under this Section to the Capital and to the Income of the Land Revenue of the Crown.

Consideration for Mining Leases.

III. On granting a Lease of any Coal or other such Substance as in the last preceding Section mentioned, or any Authority or Licence for the working thereof, or any Licence for the making of an Under-lease, Assignment, or other Disposition of the Interest of any Person under any such Lease, Authority, or Licence, the Commissioners of Woods, or One of them, may, if they or he think fit, with the Approval of the Commissioners of the Treasury, receive or agree to receive (in addition to any Rent, Royalty, or Reservation) such Sum of Money as seems to them or him sufficient Consideration for such Lease, Authority, or Licence.

New Forest and Forest of Dean.

Repeal of Sect. 9. of 14 & 15 Vict. c. 76.

IV. From and after the passing of this Act Section Nine of the Act of the Session of the Fourteenth and Fifteenth Years of Her Majesty's Reign (Chapter Seventy-six), "to "extinguish the Right of the Crown to Deer in the *New* "*Forest*, and to give Compensation in lieu thereof, and for "other Purposes relating to the said Forest," shall be and the same is hereby repealed; but nothing herein shall affect any Licence for any of the Purposes in that Section mentioned granted before the passing of this Act.

Power to Commissioners of Woods, with Approval of Treasury, to grant Licenses to hunt, &c. over New Forest and Forest of Dean.

V. From and after the passing of this Act the Commissioners of Woods, or One of them, on behalf of Her Majesty, may from Time to Time, with the Approval of the Commissioners of Her Majesty's Treasury, grant Licences to any Person or Persons to hunt, hawk, fish, and fowl on and over all or any Parts or Part of the *New Forest* and *Forest of Dean* respectively the Soil and Freehold whereof are for the Time being vested in the Crown, subject and according to the Provisions for the Time being in force relative to Licences by the said Commissioners or either of them in exercise of any Powers by Law vested in them or him to grant Licences to hunt, hawk, fish, or fowl upon or over any Forest belonging to Her Majesty, and under the Management of the said Commissioners or either of them; provided always, that notwithstanding anything in this Act contained, no such Licence shall be deemed to be or construed to operate as or in the Nature of a Lease or Demise.

Epping Forest.

Transfer of Management of Forestal Rights in Epping Forest to Commissioners of Works.

VI. From and immediately after the Thirty-first Day of *December* One thousand eight hundred and sixty-six the Commissioners of Her Majesty's Works and Public Buildings for the Time being shall perform and exercise the Duties and Powers of Management, and all other Duties and Powers, which if this Act had not been passed would have been performed and exercised by the Commissioners of Woods of and in relation to the Forestal Rights and Interests of the Crown in, to, or over that Portion of *Waltham Forest* usually called *Epping Forest.*

Transfer to Board of Trade.

Transfer of Management of Foreshore to Board of Trade.

VII. From and immediately after the Thirty-first Day of *December* One thousand eight hundred and sixty-six all such Parts and Rights and Interests as then belong to Her Majesty in right of the Crown of and in the Shore and Bed of the Sea, and of every Channel, Creek, Bay, Estuary, and of every navigable River of the United Kingdom, as far up the same as the Tide flows (and which are hereinafter for

Brevity called the Foreshore), except as in this Act provided, shall, subject to the Provisions of this Act, and subject also to such public and other Rights as by Law exist in, over, or affecting the Foreshore or any Part thereof, be and the same are hereby transferred from the Management of the Commissioners of Woods to, and thenceforth the same shall be under the Management of, the Board of Trade.

Board of Trade to have same Powers as Commissioners of Woods.

VIII. The Board of Trade shall have and may exercise all the Powers and Authorities, Rights and Privileges, whatsoever with regard to the Foreshore which the Commissioners of Woods now have or are entitled to exercise with respect to the same.

Execution of Deeds, &c.

IX. All Deeds and Instruments made by the Board of Trade under this Act shall be executed and signed by One of the Secretaries or Assistant Secretaries of the Board of Trade; but nothing in this Act or in any such Deed or Instrument shall extend to charge personally the Officer of the Board of Trade executing or signing the same.

Application to Board of Trade of Parts of 10 G. 4 c. 50.

X. The following Provisions of the Act of the Tenth Year of the Reign of King *George* the Fourth (Chapter Fifty), "to consolidate and amend the Laws relating to the "Management and Improvement of His Majesty's Woods, "Forests, Parks, and Chases, of the Land Revenue of the "Crown within the Survey of the Exchequer in *England*, "and of the Land Revenue of the Crown in *Ireland*, and "for extending certain Provisions relating to the same to "the Isles of *Man* and *Alderney*," shall extend and apply, *mutatis mutandis*, to the Board of Trade, their Deeds, Acts, Proceedings, Officers, and Servants under this Act, as if those Provisions were here repeated, with the Substitution therein of the Board of Trade for the Commissioners of Woods, and of the Foreshore under the Management of the Board of Trade for the Possessions and Land Revenues of the Crown to which that Act relates, namely,—Sections Seventy-four, Seventy-seven, Eighty-one to Eighty-five, and Ninety to Ninety-four (all inclusive)—save that such Consent of any Authority or Inrolment of any Instrument as is in any Case required by any of those Sections shall not be requisite under this Act.

Application to Board of Trade of Sect. 5 of 16 & 17 Vict. c. 56.

XI. The Provisions of Section Five of the Act of the Session of the Sixteenth and Seventeenth Years of Her Majesty's Reign, (Chapter Fifty-six), "to facilitate the Re-"demption of certain Charges on the Hereditary Posses-"sions and Land Revenues of the Crown, and to make "other Provisions in regard to the Management of such "Hereditary Possessions and Land Revenues," as amended by this Act, shall extend and apply to the Board of Trade, their Deeds, Acts, Proceedings, Officers, and Servants, under this Act, as if that Section were here repeated, with the Substitution therein of the Board of Trade for the Commissioners of Woods,—save that such Consent of any Authority as is in any Case required by that Section shall not be requisite under this Act.

Monies received by Board of Trade under this Act to be paid into the Exchequer, and to form Part of Consolidated Fund.

XII. All Money which is received by the Board of Trade in consequence of the Exercise of any of the Powers or Authorities, Rights or Privileges, conferred on them by this Act, and which if this Act had not been passed would have been carried by the Commissioners of Woods as annual Income to the Consolidated Fund of the United Kingdom, in this Act called the Consolidated Fund, shall be paid by the Board of Trade into the Receipt of Her Majesty's Exchequer, and shall be carried to and form Part of the Consolidated Fund.

Monies received by Board of Trade, which would have been applied as Capital by Commissioners of Woods, to go towards Reduction of National Debt.

XIII. All money which is received by the Board of Trade in consequence of the Exercise of any of the Powers, Authorities, Rights, or Privileges last aforesaid, and which if this Act had not been passed would have been applied as Capital by the Commissioners of Woods, shall be applied towards the Reduction of the National Debt in such Manner as the Commissioners of the Treasury from Time to Time direct; and a Copy of every Minute or Warrant of the Commissioners of the Treasury directing any such Application shall be laid before both Houses of Parliament.

Compensation to Crown to be determined by Arbitration.

XIV. The Amount of the Compensation to be paid to the Land Revenue of the Crown for the Transfer effected by this Act of the Rights and Interests of the Crown in the Foreshore shall be determined by Two Arbitrators appointed, one by the Commissioners of the Treasury, and the other by the Commissioners of Woods, or, in case of the Disagreement of the Arbitrators, by an Umpire appointed by the Lord Chancellor of *Great Britain* before the Arbitrators enter on the Reference.

Mode in which Compensation to be made good.

XV. The Amount of the Compensation so determined shall be made good to the Capital of the Land Revenue of the Crown after the making of the Award of the Arbitrators or Umpire in either or both, or partly in one and partly in the others, of the following Modes, as the Commissioners of the Treasury from Time to Time direct; namely,

(1.) By the Release (within Six Months after the making of such Award) to the Land Revenue of the Crown of any Debt due therefrom to the Consolidated Fund, which Release shall be made by a Warrant of the Commissioners of the Treasury:

(2.) By the Transfer (within Six Months after the making of the Award) to the Consolidated Fund of the

Charge for any Pensions, Annuities, or other annual Payments payable out of the Land Revenue of the Crown, which shall be specified in a Warrant of the Commissioners of the Treasury, and on the issuing of such Warrant the same shall become and are hereby charged on the Consolidated Fund, and thereupon the Land Revenue of the Crown shall become and is hereby discharged therefrom (every such Warrant being inrolled in Her Majesty's Court of Exchequer at *Westminster*):

The Balance (if any) of the Amount of Compensation so determined (the Amount of which Balance shall be specified in a Warrant of the Commissioners of the Treasury shall be charged on the Consolidated Fund, and shall be payable thereout at such Periods and in such Proportions as the Commissioners of the Treasury from Time to Time by Warrant direct, but so nevertheless that the whole of such Balance (if any) shall be paid within the space of Ten Years after the making of the said Award. A Copy of every Warrant made in pursuance of the present Section shall be laid before both houses of Parliament.

Immediate Valuation of Crown Land taken for Public Offices.

XVI. With a view to the Determination of the Amount of the Debt now due from the Land Revenue of the Crown to the Consolidated Fund, the Arbitration directed by the Acts described in the First Schedule to this Act, for determining the Value of the Property thereby transferred (forming Part of the Possessions and Land Revenues of the Crown), shall be had forthwith after the passing of this Act.

Exception of Portions of Foreshore described in Second Schedule, &c.

XVII. Nothing in this Act shall apply to the Portions of the Foreshore described in the Second Schedule to this Act, or to any other particular Portions of the Foreshore with respect to which the Commissioners of Woods are by any Act specially empowered to make any Disposition or Arrangement of or concerning the Rights of the Crown therein; and every such Act shall continue to operate, and every Disposition or Arrangement made or to be made thereunder shall have the like Validity, Effect, and Consequences, as if this Act had not been passed.

Exception of Portions of Foreshore sold, &c.

XVIII. Nothing in this Act shall apply to any Portion of the Foreshore in relation to which any Instrument has been before the First Day of *January* One thousand eight hundred and sixty-seven made or executed by the Commissioners of Woods, or either of them, in the due Exercise of any Powers for the Time being by Law vested in them or him.

Exception of Portions of Foreshore where Money [illegible]d into [illegible]rt, &c.

XIX. Where before the First Day of *January* One thousand eight hundred and sixty-seven any Money has been paid under any Act into the Bank of *England* or any other Bank in relation to any Portion of the Foreshore, then such Money and Portion of the Foreshore shall continue and may be dealt with as if this Act had not been passed.

XX. Nothing in this Act shall apply to any Portion of the Foreshore in front of or immediately adjacent to any Lands whereof or whereto Her Majesty, or any Person or Body in trust for Her Majesty, is on the Thirty-first Day of *December* One thousand eight hundred and sixty-six seised or entitled in possession, reversion, or remainder, or which Lands on the same Day are the Property of any Department of Her Majesty's Government, or in the Possession of any such Department or of any Officers thereof; and every such Portion of the Foreshore shall continue vested, and be subject to the Exercise therein of the same Powers, Authorities, Rights, and Privileges, as if this Act had not passed; and nothing in this Act contained or to be done by virtue of this Act shall take away, restrict, or diminish any Power or Right by Law vested in the Crown to use the Foreshore for the Purposes of any Salmon Fishings which may belong to the Crown.

Exception of Portions of Foreshore fronting Crown Property.

XXI. Nothing in this Act shall apply to any Beds, Seams, or Veins of Coal or Stone or any Metallic or other Mineral Substances in or under the Foreshore, or to any Mines or Quarries thereof, and the same shall continue and be vested, held, and enjoyed as if this Act had not been passed.

Exception of Mines, &c., under Foreshore.

XXII. Subject to the Provisions of this Act, all Persons for the Time being entitled, in right of or under the Crown, to or to the Management of any Beds, Seams, Veins, Mines, or Quarries as aforesaid in or under the Foreshore, or in or under any Lands immediately adjacent thereto, and their respective Tenants, may take into possession, or use or pass through, over, or under, any Portion of the Foreshore under the Management of the Board of Trade in order to do all or any of the following Things; namely,

Power for Persons interested in Mines, &c. to enter on Foreshore, &c.

To make or sink any Pits, Shafts, Adits, Drifts, Levels, Drains, Watercourses, Pools, or Embankments;

To make, lay, place, use, and repair any Spoil Banks, Roads, Ways, Brooks, and Banks;

To make, erect, and repair any Lodges, Shafts, Steam and other Engines, Buildings, Works, and Machinery;

To do any such other Acts as are for the Time being necessary or convenient for working, searching for, digging, raising, carrying away, dressing, making merchantable the Coal, Stone, or other Substances aforesaid;

Giving to the Board of Trade at least Two Months previous Notice in Writing of the Intention to exercise the

Powers of this Section (stating the Nature, Extent, and Duration of the proposed Interference with the Foreshore), and doing as little Damage as may be in the Exercise of those Powers, and making full Compensation to all Persons interested for all Damage sustained by them by reason or in consequence of the Exercise of such Powers, the Amount and Application of such Compensation to be determined in manner provided by *The Lands Clauses Consolidation Act*, 1845, *The Lands Clauses Consolidation* (Scotland) *Act*, 1845, or *The Railways Act* (Ireland), 1851, and any Act amending those Acts respectively (as the Case requires), for Determination of the Amount and Application of Compensation for Lands taken or injuriously affected.

Protection of Structures on or near Foreshore.

XXIII. Nothing in the foregoing Provisions shall authorize any Person, and it shall not be lawful for any Person, to sink, drive, or make any Pit, Shaft, Adit, Drift, Level, Drain, Watercourse, Pool, or Embankment, so as to injure, weaken, or endanger, or be likely to injure, weaken, or endanger, any Pier or other Structure on or near the Foreshore.

Provision to be made for Safety of Tenants, &c.

XXIV. The Persons for the Time being exercising the Powers conferred by the foregoing Provisions, or any of them, shall make and maintain all Works and Conveniences necessary or proper for the Safety and Accommodation of the Public.

Act not to increase Power of the Crown over the Foreshore.

XXV. Nothing in this Act contained shall extend or increase or be construed to extend or increase the Powers or Authorities, Rights or Privileges, of the Crown over the Foreshore, or any Part thereof, but as between the Crown and all other Persons such Powers and Rights shall continue as the same existed before the passing of this Act.

Arbitrations.

Power for Arbitrators, &c., to summon Witnesses.

XXVI. Where any Matter in difference, whether being the Subject of a pending Suit in any Court or not, or any Issue in any such Suit, is referred to Arbitration under Section Ninety-four of the said Act of the Tenth Year of the Reign of King *George* the Fourth, or under Section Five of the said Act of the Session of the Sixteenth and Seventeenth Years of Her Majesty's Reign, or under such Sections or either of them as applied by this Act, the Arbitrators or Umpire may, on the Application of either Party, by Summons require any Person to attend before them or him to be examined as a witness, or to bring before them or him any Books, Papers, Maps, Plans, and Writings in his Possession or Control relating to the Subject of the Reference; and every Person so summoned shall be bound to obey the Summons on a reasonable Sum being paid or tendered to him for his Expenses.

XXVII. The Arbitrators or Umpire may administer an Oath or an Affirmation (where an Affirmation in lieu of an Oath would be admitted in a Court of Justice) to any Person examined, and may take the Affidavit or Declaration of any Person. Power to examine on Oath, &c.

XXVIII. If any Person on whom any such Summons is served (either personally or by Delivery at his last known or usual Place of Abode or Business) fails to obey the same without reasonable Excuse, or refuses to be sworn or make Affirmation, or to answer any lawful Question put to him, he shall be liable on summary Conviction to a Penalty not exceeding Ten Pounds, without Prejudice to any other Remedy against him. Penalty for Non-attendance, &c.

XXIX. If any Person on any such Examination on Oath or Affirmation or in any such Affidavit or Declaration wilfully gives false Evidence he shall be deemed guilty of Perjury. Penalty for giving false Evidence.

Claremont.

XXX. It shall be lawful for Her Majesty to retain and have the Use and Enjoyment, during Her Life or Pleasure, of the Mansion near *Esher* called *Claremont*, and its Fixtures and Furniture, with the Park, Pleasure Grounds, and Gardens thereto belonging (containing by Estimation Three hundred and thirty-two Acres or thereabouts), and certain Plantations and Lands (containing by Estimation One hundred and thirty-two Acres or thereabouts), with a a Spring of Water rising therein (from which the said Mansion is supplied with Water), and the Waste Lands Parcel of the Manors of *Esher* and *Milbourne* or *Waterville Esher*. Power to Her Majesty to retain Claremont House with Park, &c. for Her Life.

General Saving.

XXXI. Saving to all Persons, Bodies Politic or Corporate, and their respective Heirs, Executors, Administrators, Successors, and Assigns, (other than Her Majesty, Her Heirs and Successors, in right of the Crown,) all such Estates, Rights, Titles, Claims, and Demands whatsoever as they respectively have at the passing of this Act, or might or could have had if this Act had not been passed. Saving of Rights of private Persons, &c.

XXXII. This Act may be cited as *The Crown Lands Act*, 1866. Short Title.

The First Schedule.

Acts relating to Crown Land taken for Public Offices.

24 & 25 Vict. c. 88.	An Act to vest in the Commissioners of Her Majesty's Works and Public Buildings a Portion of Saint James's Park as a Site for Public Offices.
25 & 26 Vict. c. 74.	An Act to enable the Commissioners of Her Majesty's Works to acquire additional Lands for the Purposes of the Public Office Extension Act of 1859, by way of Exchange for Land already acquired but not wanted for the Purposes of the said Act.

The Second Schedule.

Portions of Foreshore excepted from Transfer to Board of Trade.

Portions of Foreshore.	Acts relating to those Portions of Foreshore.
Foreshore of Thames	The Thames Conservancy Act, 1857.
Foreshore of Tees	The Tees Conservancy Act, 1857.
Foreshore of County Palatine of Durham.	21 & 22 Vict. c. 45.—An Act to amend the Provisions of an Act of the Sixth Year of King William the Fourth, for separating the Palatinate Jurisdiction of the County Palatine of Durham from the Bishoprick of Durham, and to make further Provision with respect to the Jura Regalia of the said County.

CAP. LXIX.

An Act for the Amendment of the Law with respect to the Carriage and Deposit of Dangerous Goods.—6th August 1866.

Be it enacted by the Queen's Most Excellent Majesty, by and with the Advice and Consent of the Lords Spiritual and Temporal, and Commons, in this present Parliament assembled, and by the Authority of the same, as follows:

Nitro-Glycerine to be deemed dangerous.

I. The Goods or Article commonly known as Nitro-Glycerine or Glonoine Oil shall be deemed to be specially dangerous within the Meaning of this Act.

Other Goods may be declared so by Order in Council.

II. Her Majesty may from Time to Time, by Order in Council, declare that any Goods named in any such Order (other than Nitro-Glycerine or Glonoine Oil) are to be deemed specially dangerous within the Meaning of this Act; and may from Time to Time amend or repeal any such Order; and any Goods which are by any such Order declared to be specially dangerous shall, so long as such Order is in force, be deemed to be specially dangerous within the Meaning of this Act.

Such goods to be marked, and Notice to be given of their Character.

III. No Person shall deliver any Goods which are specially dangerous to any Warehouse Owner or Carrier, or send or carry or cause to be sent or carried any such Goods upon any Railway or in any Ship to or from any Part of the United Kingdom, or in any other public Conveyance, or deposit any such Goods in or on any Warehouse or Quay, unless the true name or Description of such Goods, with the Addition of the Words specially dangerous, is distinctly written, printed, or marked on the Outside of the Package, nor in the Case of Delivery to or Deposit with any Warehouse Owner or Carrier, without also giving Notice in Writing to him of the Name or Description of such Goods, and of their being specially dangerous. And any Person who commits a Breach of this Enactment shall be liable to a Penalty not exceeding Five hundred Pounds, or at the Discretion of the Court to Imprisonment, with or without Hard Labour, for any Term not exceeding Two Years.

Provision for Case of Absence of Knowledge of Nature of Goods.

IV. Provided always, as follows:

(1.) Any Person convicted of a Breach of the last foregoing Enactment shall not be liable to Imprisonment, or to a Penalty of more than Two hundred Pounds, if he shows to the Satisfaction of the Court and Jury before whom he is convicted that he did not know the Nature of the Goods to which the Indictment relates:

(2.) Any Person accused of having committed a Breach of the said Enactment shall not be liable to be convicted thereof if he shows to the Satisfaction of the Court and Jury before whom he is tried that he did not know the Nature of the Goods to which the Indictment relates, and that he could not, with reasonable diligence, have obtained such Knowledge.

As to Forfeiture of such Goods.

V. Where Goods are delivered, sent, carried, or deposited in contravention of the said Enactment the same shall be forfeited, and shall be disposed of in such Manner as the Commissioners of Her Majesty's Treasury or (in case of Importation) the Commissioners of Customs direct, whether any Person is liable to be convicted of a Breach of the said Enactment or not.

Warehouse Owners, &c., not bound to receive such Goods.

VI. No Warehouse Owner or Carrier shall be bound to receive or carry any Goods which are specially dangerous.

Interpretation of "Owner" and "Carrier."

VII. In construing this Act the Term Warehouse Owner shall include all Persons or Bodies of Persons owning or managing any Warehouse, Store, Quay, or other Premises in which Goods are deposited; and the Word Carrier shall include all Persons or Bodies of Persons carrying Goods or Passengers for Hire by Land or Water.

Application of 25 & 26 Vict. c. 66, to Nitro-Glycerine.

VIII. The Act of the Session of the Twenty-fifth and Twenty-sixth Years of Her Majesty's Reign, Chapter Sixty-six, "for the safe-keeping of Petroleum," is hereby extended and applied to Nitro-Glycerine, and that Act shall be read and have effect as if throughout its Provisions Nitro-Glycerine had been mentioned in addition to Petroleum; save that so much of the said Act as specifies the maximum Quantity of Petroleum to be kept as therein mentioned without a Licence shall not apply in the case of Nitro-Glycerine, and any Quantity whatever of Nitro-Glycerine shall be deemed to be subject to the Provisions of the said Act.

Application of the same Act to other Substances.

IX. The said Act of the Session of the Twenty-fifth and Twenty-sixth Years of Her Majesty's Reign is also hereby extended and applied to any Substance for the Time being declared by any Order in Council under this Act to be specially dangerous, and that Act shall be read and have Effect as if throughout its Provisions the Substance to which such Order in Council relates had been mentioned in addition to Petroleum; save that the Quantity of such Substance which it shall not be lawful to keep as in the said Act mentioned without a licence shall, instead of the Quantity specified in relation to Petroleum in the said Act, be such Quantity as is specified in that Behalf in relation to any such Substance in any such Order in Council.

X. This Act may be cited as The Carriage and Deposit of Dangerous Goods Act, 1866. Short Title.

Cap. LXXI.

An Act to facilitate the letting on Lease, feuing, or selling Glebe Lands in Scotland.—[6th August 1866.]

Whereas it is expedient that Power should be given to grant Leases or Feus of Glebe Lands, or Portions thereof, in *Scotland*, or to sell the same, in manner after mentioned: Be it therefore enacted by the Queen's most Excellent Majesty, by and with the Advice and Consent of the Lords Spritual and Temporal, and Commons, in this present Parliament assembled, and by the Authority of the same, as follows; *viz.*,

I. This Act may be cited as 'The Glebe Lands (*Scotland*) Act, 1866.' Short Title.

II. In this Act, unless there be something in the Subject or Context repugnant to such Construction,—The Word 'Minister' shall mean the Minister of any Parish in *Scotland* for the Time who shall be in possession of a Glebe: The Word 'Presbytery' shall mean the Presbytery within the Bounds of which such Parish is situated: The Word 'Heritor' shall mean the Proprietor of any Lands within such Parish to the Extent of at least One hundred Pounds of Real Rent from Land yearly appearing in the Valuation Roll of the County within which such Parish is situated: The Word 'Glebe' shall mean the Lands appropriated to the Minister as his Glebe, and any additional Lands settled in perpetuity on the Minister for the Time being, and enjoyed by him along with his Glebe: The Word 'Court' shall mean the Court of Session as Commissioners for the Plantation of Kirks and Valuation of Teinds. Interpretation of Terms.

III. A Minister may, with Consent and Approval of the Heritors and the Presbytery, grant a Lease or Leases of his Glebe, or any Part or Parts thereof, reserving for the Use of the Minister not less than Five Imperial Acres Power to grant Leases not exceeding Eleven Years.

nearest and most convenient to the Manse, which shall be marked out by the Heritors and the Presbytery, for any Term not exceeding Eleven Years, for such yearly Rent or Rents, and upon such Condition or Conditions, as shall be approved of by the Heritors and the Presbytery, but without any Foregift or Grassum, and under the special Condition, if the said reserved Five Acres be included in the said Lease, that such Lease, in so far as they are concerned, shall cease and determine at the First Term of *Martinmas* Six Months after the Death, Deprivation, Resignation, or Translation of the Minister of the Parish; such Consent and Approval of the Heritors and the Presbytery to be signified by a Certificate written on the Lease or Leases, and signed by the Clerk to the Heritors and by the Moderator and Clerk of such Presbytery; and the Rent or Rents payable under such Lease or Leases shall be paid and belong to the Minister.

Power to sell Servitudes or Right of Pasturage.

IV. A Minister may, with Consent of the Presbytery and Heritors, sell or dispose of, for such fixed annual Payment in Grain or in Money as may be agreed on, any Servitude or Right of Pasturage over any Lands, which Servitude or Right of Pasturage is possessed by him as Minister of the Parish: Provided always, that if the Proprietor of the Lands over which such Servitude or Right of Pasturage exists elect to purchase it absolutely, the Purchase Money shall be invested at the Sight of the Heritors and Presbytery on such Securities and in such Manner as the Court of Teinds shall direct, and the Interests and Proceeds only shall be paid to the Minister.

Application to Court to grant Feus.

V. Subject to the Provisions of this Act, the Minister may from Time to Time, with the Consent of the Presbytery and of the Heritors as herein-after provided, make Application to the Court by summary Petition for Authority to feu his Glebe, or any Part thereof, or to grant Building Leases thereon for any Term not exceeding Ninety-nine Years.

Consent of Presbytery to be obtained before Application made;

VI. Previous to making any such Application the Minister shall intimate his Intention so to do to the Presbytery by a Letter addressed to the Moderator, and shall transmit therewith a Copy of the proposed Application, which Intimation and Application shall be laid by the Moderator before the Presbytery at their First Meeting after receiving the same; and if the Presbytery are of opinion that it would be for the Interests of the Benefice that the Glebe should be feued or let on Building Leases, they shall signify their Consent to such Application, subject to such Conditions, if any, as they think necessary or advisable, by a Certificate to that Effect written on a Copy of the proposed Application, and signed by the Moderator and Clerk.

also Consent of Heritors.

VII. Upon such Certificate being granted the Minister shall call a Meeting of Heritors, such Meeting to be summoned by Intimation from the Pulpit in the usual Manner, and by Notices, with a Copy of the proposed Application enclosed therein, delivered or sent Post to each Heritor or his known Agent, at least Thirty Days previous to the Day on which such Meeting is to take place within the Parish, such Meeting to be held on a Day and at an Hour and at a Place to be specified in such Citation and Notices, and at such Meeting every Heritor may vote by Proxy or by Letter under his Hand.

Consent of Heritors how to be determined and proved

VIII. At that Meeting a Copy of the proposed Application to the Court shall be submitted to such Meeting; and if approved of by Two Thirds in Value of the Heritors of such Parish, the Clerk to the Heritors shall grant a Certificate to that Effect under his Hand to the Minister.

Particulars to be stated in Application.

IX. Every such Petition shall state the Date of the Petitioner's Induction to the Parish, the Amount of the Stipend and other Sources of Emolument attached to the Living, the Extent of the Parish, the Population according to the immediately preceding Census, the Nature and Extent of the Glebe, the Purpose of the proposed feuing or granting Building Leases, the expected Rate of Feu Duty or Rent, and the Grounds on which the Petitioner submits that Benefit will arise to the Minister and his Successors in Office by Authority to feu or lease being granted; and there shall be produced therewith the Certificate of the Presbytery and Heritors, and the Form of Feu Charter or Building Lease proposed to be adopted.

Intimation to be made of Application.

X. The Court shall appoint the Petition to be intimated in the Minute Book and on the Walls in common Form, and to be served upon all Proprietors of Lands and Heritages conterminous with the Lands proposed to be feued or leased for building; and shall also appoint Notice of the Petition to be inserted once in the *Edinburgh Gazette*, and once a Week for Three successive Weeks in such local Newspaper or Newspapers as the Court my think proper.

Power of any conterminous Proprietor to appear and object in Court.

XI. It shall be in the Power of any Proprietor of Lands or Heritages conterminous with the Lands proposed to be feued or leased for building to appear and object to the Application being granted, on the Ground of Injury to the Value or Amenity of his said Lands or Heritages, and it shall be in the Power of the Court, on considering such Objections, to give Effect thereto by refusing the Application in whole or in part.

Court may remit Petition for Inquiry into Facts.

XII. After Intimation and Advertisement aforesaid the Court, on considering the Petition, with or without Answers from any Party interested, may remit to such Person or Persons as they shall appoint to inquire into the Facts stated in the Petition, and to report his or their Opinion or Opinions thereon, and as to any Conditions or Restrictions subject to which the Prayer of the Petition should be granted.

Court may grant Authority, subject to certain Conditions.

XIII. The Court may, by Order or Interlocutor, and subject to any Conditions or Restrictions they may deem expedient, grant such Authority, and shall in such Order or Interlocutor fix the minimum Rate at which the Glebe or any Portion thereof shall be feued or leased for building, and shall authorize and empower the Petitioner and his Successors in Office at the Sight of the Heritors and the Presbytery, subject to the Provisions of this Act, to grant and dispose of the Glebe, or any Part or Parts thereof, in Feu Farm, Fee, and Heritage, for the highest Feu Duties, or in Building Leases for the highest Rent in Grain or in Money, that can be got for the same, not being less than the said Minimum, and that either by Public Auction or Private Contract.

Court may authorize Construction of Streets, &c.

XIV. The Court may also, on such Application, authorize the Minister to make and construct such Streets, Roads, Passages, Sewers, or Drains in and through the Glebe or any Part thereof as the Court on Inquiry may find reasonable or expedient, with the view of the more advantageous feuing or leasing thereof.

To whom Feu Duties, &c. to be made payable.

XV. The said Feu Duties and Rents, and the Interest of any Monies arising from any Sale or Sales in Fee Simple of any Part or Parts of the Glebe invested as hereinafter provided, shall be taken payable to the Minister and his Successors in Office serving the Cure of the Parish for the Time, in all Time thereafter, and be recoverable by him or them: Provided that on the Death of any Minister, his Widow, Heirs, or Executors shall have Right to and shall be entitled to receive and discharge the said Feu Duties and Rents in the same Manner and for the same Length of Time as is provided by the Thirteenth Act of the Third Session of the Second Parliament of *Charles* the Second, passed at *Edinburgh* the Twenty-third Day of *August* One thousand six hundred and seventy-two, intituled *Act for the Ann. due to the Executors of Bishops and Ministers*, with regard to the Stipend of the Parish as Ann.; and provided further, that in the event of any Circumstance causing a Vacancy to be prolonged beyond the Term during which such Widow, Heirs, or Executors have a Right to the said Feu Duties and Rents, it shall be lawful for the

Heritors of the Parish and Presbytery of the Bounds to uplift and to apply the said Feu Duties and Rents to the Provision of Spiritual Superintendence and the Supply of Religious Ordinances in the Parish during the Vacancy.

Further Provisions as to Feu Duties.

XVI. Subject to the Provisions of this Act, the Feu Duties which shall become payable under any Contracts, Dispositions, or Charters of Feu, or Writs by Progress, and the Rents under any Building Leases, to be granted in virtue of this Act, shall in all Time thereafter belong to the Minister, and shall be held and enjoyed by him in lieu and place of the natural Possession of such Glebe, or the Rents, Mails, Duties, and Profits of the same, and subject always to the Burden of Payment of Interest on the permanent Burden after referred to, so long as it subsists: Provided that after feuing out or letting on Building Lease or selling the said Subjects or any Part thereof, in virtue of this Act, it shall not be competent for the Minister or his Successors in Office, to make any demand upon the Heritors, for providing him in a Glebe or in any Portion of Land in lieu of the Glebe Land so feued, leased, or sold: Provided always, that nothing herein contained shall preclude or prejudice any Claim which the Minister may have to any additional Glebe that might have been competent to him if this Act had not passed.

Right of Pre-emption by Proprietors whose Lands are conterminous with the Glebe.

XVII. When the Court shall have made an Order or Interlocutor granting Authority to feu or let on Building Lease, and fixing the minimum Feu Duty or Rent, any Proprietor whose Lands are conterminous with the Glebe mentioned in such Order or Interlocutor, may, within Thirty Days of the Date of such Order or Interlocutor, intimate his Willingness to feu or lease or to purchase so much of the said Glebe at such a Rate of Feu Duty, or Rent, or Price as the Court may on a Consideration of the whole Circumstances of the Case, and after directing such Inquiry as they may consider necessary, determine; and if to feu or lease, undertaking to grant Security over the whole or such Part of his Estate, in addition to the said Glebe itself, as to the Court shall seem necessary for the regular and punctual Payment of the Feu Duty or Rent fixed by the Court; and on such Intimation, and after such Rate of Feu Duty and Security therefor, or Price, shall have been so fixed, the Court shall, in case of feuing or leasing, interpone its Authority to the Bond or other Writ in Security, and decern accordingly, and in case of Sale shall pronounce a Decree of Sale thereof in favour of such Heritor, on which he shall be entitled to obtain a Charter from the Crown for Payment of a Blench Duty of a Penny *Scots*, and interpone their Authority accordingly:

Provided always, that such Heritor shall not be entitled to obtain an Extract of the said Decree of Sale until the Price shall be consigned in One of the Chartered Banks in *Scotland* for Behoof of the Minister; and in every Case of such Sale the Price, after Deduction of all Expenses connected with the Application to the Court, shall be invested at Sight of the Heritors and Presbytery on such Securities and in such Manner as the Court of Teinds shall direct, and the Interests or Proceeds only shall be paid to the Minister: And it is provided further, that it shall be lawful for any Heir of Entail in *Scotland* to burden the Lands and Estate of which he or she is in possession as Heir of Entail lying contiguous to such Glebe for the Amount of such Price, or to give Security over the same for the annual Payment out of the clear yearly Rents and Profits of the said Lands and Estate, the Interest of such Sum calculated at Four and One Half *per Centum*, or the Amount of such annual Payment, not exceeding Three Pounds *per Centum* of such clear yearly Rents and Profits after deducting all prior Burdens and Provisions, as the same shall be ascertained by an Average of the Five Years immediately preceding the Date of Creation of such Burden or Security.

Provisions as to Cost of Application to Court.

XVIII. The Court, on the granting of any such Order or Interlocutor, or at any Time thereafter, on the summary Application of the Minister on whose Application the Interlocutor or Order was granted, or His Heirs, Executors, Administrators, or Assignees, shall inquire into and ascertain the Sums which shall have been paid as the Costs, Charges, and Expenses of applying for and obtaining such Order or Interlocutor and incidental thereto, and of making and constructing Streets, Roads, Passages, Sewers, or Drains in or through the Glebe or any Part thereof, and shall decern the Amount thereof a permanent Burden upon the Glebe; and the Interest thereof, until extinguished, as after provided or otherwise, shall form a First Charge on the whole Produce and Revenue of the said Glebe.

Casualties to be applied to Extinction of Costs, and Provision as to Payment of Costs.

XIX. As long as any such Burden shall remain unpaid the Casualties of Superiority which shall become payable under any Contracts, Dispositions, or Charters of Feu, or Writs by Progress for entering Heirs or Successors to be granted as aforesaid, as well as any Payments which may be received from the Grantees thereof in respect of the Construction of Roads, Sewers, or Drains, shall be invested, at the Sight of the Heritors and Presbytery, on such Securities and in such Manner as the Court of Teinds shall approve, as a Sinking Fund to meet the said Burden, and the Interest of the said Fund shall be paid to the Minister for the Time being; and as soon as the said Fund shall amount to a Sum sufficient to pay the said Burden, the same shall be paid off; and thereupon the Casualties of Superiority thereafter to become due shall form Part of the Income of the Minister for the Time being, and be payable to him.

XX. The Minister, with the Consent of the Heritors and the Presbytery, as certified by the Clerk to the Heritors and by the Moderator and Clerk of the Presbytery, shall grant, subscribe, and deliver to the Feuar or Feuars, Purchaser or Purchasers, Lessee or Lessees, all Contracts, Feu Charters, Dispositions in Feu, Writs of Confirmation, Resignation, Clare constat, or Acknowledgment, Dispositions, Conveyances, or other Deeds or Writs, containing all usual and necessary Clauses for feudally conveying and vesting the Subjects so feued, sold, or leased in the Parties taking the same on Feu or Building Lease, or purchasing the same, and the Heirs or singular Successors who shall thereafter acquire Right to the same; and the said Contracts and other Deeds or Writs so to be granted shall be deemed and held to be as legal and valid Titles of Property in Feu and Heritage, or Fee Simple, or Lease, (as the Case may be,) of the Properties so feued or conveyed to the several Persons in whose Favour respectively the same shall be granted, and their Heirs and Disponees, as if granted by a Proprietor or Superior with a completed feudal Title holding immediately of the Crown, and the Subjects so feued or conveyed or leased under the Authority of this Act shall be subject to Payment of Poor Rates, any Law or Custom to the contrary notwithstanding; and the said Contracts and other Deeds shall be recorded in the Books of the Heritors. Title, how to be granted.

XXI. In all and each of the said Contracts and other Deeds or Writs the full Value of the Ground thereby feued or leased shall be stipulated to be paid in perpetual annual Feu Duties, or Rents for the Endurance of such Building Leases, in Grain or in Money, payable half-yearly, without taking any Sum or Sums of Money, or other Matter or Thing whatsoever, by way of Fine, Foregift, or Grassum; and all Casualties of Superiority accruing on the Renewal of the Title to Heirs or singular Successors shall be taxed at a Duplicate of the annual Feu Duty; and all Feu Duties, Casualties, or Rents shall be properly and legally secured upon the Ground for which the same are payable, and on the Buildings that may be erected thereon, under the usual Penalties and Forfeitures according to the Law and Practice of *Scotland* in Feu Holdings. Full value to be stipulated to be paid without taking Money by way of Fine, &c.

Minister to enjoy same Privilege as other Superiors.

XXII. After any such Contracts and other Deeds or Writs shall have been executed, the Minister shall have and enjoy all the same Remedies for enforcing Payment of the said Feu Duties and Casualties of Superiority thereby stipulated and agreed to be paid, and generally all other Rights and Privileges, which by the Law and Practice of *Scotland* belong and are competent to other Superiors in Feu Holdings; and the Parties taking any Lands in feu under the Provisions of this Act, and their Heirs and Successors, shall have and enjoy all the Rights and Privileges which by the Law and Practice of *Scotland* belong and are competent to Vassals in Feu Holdings, in the same Manner and to the same Effect as if they held the said Lands of and under the Minister as a Superior holding immediately of the Crown.

Court to pass Acts of Sederunt.

XXIII. The Court shall pass such Acts of Sederunt as they may consider necessary to regulate the Form of Procedure to be adopted under this Act for effectually carrying out the Purposes thereof.

Saving existing Acts authorizing the feuing of Glebes.

XXIV. This Act shall not affect any Act of Parliament now in existence affecting the feuing of Glebes in *Scotland*, or anything done or contracted to be done thereunder.

CAP. LXXV.

An Act to amend and explain the Act of the Twenty-fifth and Twenty-sixth Years of Victoria, *Chapter Fifty-eight, relating to Parochial Buildings in* Scotland.—[*6th* August 1866.]

25 & 26 Vict. c. 58.

WHEREAS by the Act Twenty-fifth and Twenty-sixth *Victoria*, Chapter Fifty-eight, intituled *An Act to make further Provision with respect to the raising of money for erecting and improving Parochial Buildings in* Scotland, (in this Act hereafter referred to as the recited Act,) it is enacted, by Section First, "that the Expression 'Parochial Build-"ings,' in the said Act, shall mean and include Church, "Manse, Churchyard, Walls, Schoolhouse, and School-"master's House respectively;" and it is further enacted "by Section Second, that the Heritors of any Parish in "*Scotland* in which any new or additional Parochial Build-"ing is to be erected, or any existing Parochial Building is "to be improved or to be enlarged, may, at any meeting of "such Heritors, resolve that the Money required to defray "the Expense of Erection, Improvement, or Enlargement "of such Parochial Building shall be raised by annual

"Assessments extending over a Period of Ten Years;" and on the Adoption of such Resolution, such annual Assessments for the Period specified therein shall be imposed, levied, and recovered from the Heritors of such Parish, and with the Liabilities and Rights of Relief as therein provided; and by the Third Section it is enacted, that on the Adoption of such Resolution it shall be lawful for the Heritors of such Parish to borrow the Money required to defray the Expense of the Erection, Improvement, or Enlargement of such Parochial Buildings, and in Security of the Repayment of the Money so borrowed, and the Interest thereof, to charge and assign the said annual Assessments by a Bond and Assignation, to be signed in manner therein mentioned:

And whereas Doubts have arisen as to whether the Powers to borrow Money and grant Bond therefor under said recited Act apply to the Purchase or Acquisition of Parochial Buildings as defined in the Act, and it is expedient that such Doubts should be removed, and the recited Act amended as herein-after provided:

Be it therefore enacted by the Queen's most Excellent Majesty, by and with the Advice and Consent of the Lords Spiritual and Temporal, and Commons, in the present Parliament assembled, and by the Authority of the same, as follows: viz.,

Interpretation of the Expressions "Erection, Improvement, and Enlargement" in recited Act.

I. The Expressions "Erection, Improvement, and Enlargement," contained in the recited Act, shall extend and apply to the Purchase or Acquisition of Parochial Buildings for the Purposes of the said Act, and the Improvement and Enlargement thereof, and the Power to borrow Money required to defray the Expense of the Erection, Improvement, or Enlargement of such Parochial Buildings, and to grant Bond therefor, and the Interest thereof, repayable in Ten Years; and the Power to charge and assign the said annual Assessments, as contained in the recited Act, shall extend to and include the Price of Parochial Buildings already erected, purchased, or to be purchased for the purposes of the Act, and the ground attached thereto, and the Expense of improving and enlarging the same, including the purchase of any Feu or Ground Annual payable for such Ground or Buildings; and the Creditors in or Persons having Right to such Bond and Assignation shall have the same Rights and Remedies for Recovery of the Sums, Principal and Interest, due under such Bond and Assignation, as are conferred by the said recited Act.

This and recited Act incorporated.

II. This Act shall be deemed to be incorporated with the recited Act, and the recited Act shall be read and have Effect accordingly.

CAP. LXXVII.

An Act to amend the Act of the Seventh and Eighth Years of Victoria, *Chapter Forty-four, relating to the erection of new Parishes* quoad sacra *in* Scotland.

[*6th* August 1866.]

WHEREAS by the Act of the Seventh and Eighth Years of the reign of Her present Majesty, Chapter Forty-four, intituled *An Act to facilitate the disjoining or dividing of extensive or populous Parishes, and the erecting of new Parishes, in that part of the United Kingdom called* Scotland, Provision is made (by Section Eight) in the case of a Church built or acquired, or undertaken to be built or acquired, and endowed or undertaken to be endowed by any Person or Persons at his, her, or their Expense, for the Erection of such Church, and a District to be attached thereto *quoad sacra*, into a Church and Parish in connexion with the Church of *Scotland*: And whereas there are in *Scotland* United Parishes in which there are already Two or more Parish Churches maintained: And whereas in such United Parishes an Increase of Population or other Change of Circumstances may take place, rendering it expedient under the Provisions of the said Act to apply for Disjunction from such United Parishes, and Erection into a Parish *quoad sacra*, of a District thereof: And whereas by the said Act no Power is conferred upon the Heritors of such United Parishes to convey or make over any one of the Parish Churches of such United Parish to the Party or Parties who shall have endowed or undertaken to endow such Parish *quoad sacra*: And whereas it is reasonable and proper that such Power should be conferred: Be it therefore enacted by the Queen's most Excellent Majesty, by and with the Advice and Consent of the Lords Spiritual and Temporal, and Commons, in this present Parliament assembled, and by the Authority of the same, as follows, viz.:

7 & 8 Vict. c. 44.

Power to convey to Quoad sacra Parish Trustees within a United Parish One of the Parish Churches.

I. On an Application being made in Terms of the said Act of the Seventh and Eighth Years of Her present Majesty, Chapter Forty-four, to the Lords of Council and Session as Commissioners for Plantation of Kirks and Valuation of Teinds, it shall be lawful for the Heritors of any United Parish in *Scotland*, being Proprietors within such United Parish to the Extent of at least One hundred Pounds Sterling of Real Rent yearly from Land appearing on the Valuation Roll of the County, by a Majority in value of those present at a Meeting summoned by Intimation from the Pulpit in usual Manner for the Purpose, to authorize the Chairman at the Meeting to convey and make over, to the Party or Parties who shall have endowed or undertaken to endow as a Parish *quoad sacra* a District within such United Parish, the one of such Parish Churches most convenient to such District, as the Church of such Parish *quoad sacra* in all Time Coming, and the Chairman so authorized shall execute the Conveyance of such Church in favour of such Party or Parties, and the Conveyance of such Church by the Chairman of such Meeting of Heritors shall be a valid Title thereto in all Time coming.

II. This Act shall be deemed to be incorporated with the recited Act, and the recited Act shall be read and have Effect accordingly. This and recited Act incorporated.

Cap. LXXXV.

An Act to facilitate the Establishment, Improvement, and Maintenance of Oyster and Mussel Fisheries in Great Britain.—[6*th* August 1866.]

Be it enacted by the Queen's most Excellent Majesty, by and with the Advice and Consent of the Lords Spiritual and Temporal, and Commons, in this present Parliament assembled, and by the Authority of the same, as follows:

I. This Act may be cited as The Oyster and Mussel Fisheries Act, 1866. Short Title.

II. In this Act the Words "Oysters" and "Mussels" respectively include the Brood, Ware, Half-ware, Spat, and Spawn of Oysters and Mussels respectively. Interpretation of Terms.

III. An Order for the Establishment or Improvement, and for the Maintenance and Regulation, of an Oyster or Mussel Fishery on the Shore and Bed of the Sea, or of an Estuary or tidal River, above or below, or partly above and partly below, Low-water Mark (which Shore and Bed are in this Act referred to as the Sea Shore, may be made under this Act, on an Application by a Memorial in that Behalf presented to the Board of Trade by any Person, Persons, Company, or Body desirous of obtaining such an Order (which Person, Persons, Company, or Body are in this Act referred to as the Promoters). Power for Board of Trade on Memorial to make Order for Oyster Fishery.

IV. If on Consideration of the Memorial the Board of Trade think fit to proceed in the Case, the Promoters shall cause printed Copies of the Draft of the Order as proposed by them (with such Modifications, if any, as the Board of Trade require) to be circulated in such manner as the Publication of Draft Order and Notice to Owners of adjoining Lands, &c.

Board of Trade think sufficient and proper for giving Information to all Parties interested, and shall give Notice of the Application, in such Manner as the Board of Trade direct or approve, to the Owners or reputed Owners, Lessees or reputed Lessees, and Occupiers (if any) of the portion of the Sea Shore to which the proposed Order relates, and of the Lands adjoining thereto.

Objections and Representations respecting Order.

V. During One Month after the first Publication of the Draft Order the Board of Trade shall receive any Objections or Representations made to them in Writing respecting the proposed Order.

Inquiry into proposed Order by public Sittings.

VI. Where the Promoters seek to obtain a Several Oyster or Mussel Fishery, the Board of Trade shall, as soon as conveniently may be after the Expiration of the said Month, and in other Cases the Board of Trade, if they think fit, at any Time after the Expiration of that Month, may, appoint some fit Person to act as Inspector respecting the proposed Order.

The Inspector shall proceed to make an Inquiry concerning the Subject Matter of the proposed Order, and for that Purpose to hold a Sitting or Sittings in some convenient Place in the Neighbourhood of the Portion of the Sea Shore to which the proposed Order relates, and thereat to take and receive any Evidence and Information offered and hear and inquire into any Objections or Representations made respecting the proposed Order, with Power from Time to Time to adjourn any Sitting; and the Inspector may take Evidence on oath or otherwise, as he thinks expedient, and may administer an oath or take any Affidavit or Declaration for the Purpose of the Inquiry, and if any Person wilfully gives false Evidence in any Examination on Oath in any such Inquiry, or in an affidavit to be used in any such inquiry he shall be deemed guilty of Perjury.

Notice shall be published in such Manner as the Board of Trade direct of every such sitting (except an adjourned Sitting) Fourteen Days at least before the holding thereof.

Report of Inspector.

VII. The Inspector shall make a Report in Writing to the Board of Trade setting forth the result of the Inquiry, and stating whether in his opinion the proposed Order should be approved, with or without Alteration, and if with any, then with what alteration, and his Reasons for the same, and the Objections and Representations, if any, made on the Inquiry, and his Opinion thereon.

Settlement and making of Order.

VIII. As soon as conveniently may be after the Expiration of the said Month, or after the Receipt by the Board of Trade of the Report of the Inspector, if any, they shall proceed to consider the Objections or Representations that have been made respecting the proposed Order and the

Report of the Inspector, if any, and thereupon they shall either refuse the Application or settle and make an Order in such Form and containing such Provisions as they think expedient.

Publication of Order.

IX. Where the Board of Trade make an Order, the Promoters shall cause it to be published and circulated in such Manner as the Board of Trade think sufficient for giving Information to all Parties interested, and shall give Notice of it, in such Manner as the Board of Trade direct or approve, to the Owners or reputed Owners, Lessees or reputed Lessees, and Occupiers (if any) of the Portion of the Sea Shore to which the Order relates, and of the Lands adjoining thereto.

Expenses connected with Order.

X. All Expenses incurred by the Board of Trade in relation to any Memorial, or to any Order consequent thereon, shall be defrayed by the Promoters, and the Board of Trade shall, if they think fit, on or at any Time after the Presentation of the Memorial, require the promoters to pay to the Board of Trade such sum as the Board of Trade think requisite for or on account of those Expenses, or to give Security to the Satisfaction of the Board of Trade for the Payment of those expenses on Demand.

Confirmation of Order by Act of Parliament.

XI. An Order of the Board of Trade under this Act shall not of itself have any Operation, but the same shall have full Operation when and as confirmed by Act of Parliament, with such Modifications, if any, as to Parliament seem fit.

Reference of Order to Select Committee if opposed.

XII. If in the Progress through Parliament of a Bill confirming an Order a Petition is presented to either House of Parliament against the Order, the Bill, as far as it relates to the Order petitioned against, may be referred to a Select Committee, and the Petitioner shall be allowed to appear and oppose as in case of a Private Bill.

Amendment of Order.

XIII. The Board of Trade may from Time to Time make an Order for amending an Order that has been confirmed by Act of Parliament, and all the Provisions of this Act relative to an original Order shall apply also to an amending Order, *mutatis mutandis.*

Power for Grantees to remove Oysters, &c. from public to private Oyster Bed at all Seasons, without Prejudice to Provisions of 6 & 7 Vict. c. 79.

XIV. Subject and without Prejudice to the Provisions of the Act of the Session of the Sixth and Seventh Years of Her Majesty's Reign (Chapter Seventy-nine), "to carry "into effect the Convention between Her Majesty and the "King of the *French* concerning the Fisheries in the Sea "between the *British Islands* and *France*," and of any Act amending the same, and of any Order in Council lawfully made thereunder, and notwithstanding anything in or done under any other Act, the Persons, Company, or Body obtaining an Order under this Act (who are in this

Act referred to as the Grantees), and the Owners of any private Oyster Bed lawfully formed independently of this Act, and their respective Agents, Servants, and Workmen, may at any Season dredge for and take Oysters from any natural public Oyster Bed for the purpose of supplying or replenishing therewith any Oyster Bed made under the Order, or any such private Oyster Bed (as the Case may be), and may apply the Oysters so taken accordingly; but if any Person applies or uses, or any Persons, Company, or Body knowingly authorize or permit to be applied or used, otherwise than in manner authorized by this Section, any Oysters so taken, such Person, or such Persons, Company, or Body (as the Case may be), shall be liable to all the like Penalties and Consequences to which he or they would have been liable if this Section had not been inserted in this Act.

Effect of Grant of Several Oyster Fishery.

XV. Where an Order of the Board of Trade under this Act confers a Right of Several Oyster or Mussel Fishery, the Grantees under the Order shall have by virtue of the Order and of this Act, within the Limits of the Fishery, the exclusive Right of depositing, propagating, dredging, and fishing for, and taking Oysters or Mussels (as the Case may be), and in the Exercise of that Right may, within the Limits of the Fishery, proceed as follows, namely,—make and maintain Oyster Beds, and (notwithstanding anything in or done under any other Act) at any Season collect Oysters or Mussels (as the Case may be), and remove the same from Place to Place, and deposit the same as and where they think fit, and do all other Things which they think proper for obtaining, storing, and disposing of the Produce of their Fishery.

Property in Oysters within Several Fishery.

XVI. All Oysters or Mussels being in or on an Oyster or Mussel Bed within the Limits of any such Several Fishery shall be the absolute Property of the Grantees, and in all Courts of Law and Equity and elsewhere, and for all Purposes, civil, criminal, or other, shall be deemed to be in the actual Possession of the Grantees.

Property in Oysters removed from Several Fishery.

XVII. All Oysters or Mussels removed by any Person from an Oyster or Mussel Bed within the Limits of any such Several Fishery, and not either sold in Market overt or disposed of by or under the Authority of the Grantees, shall be the absolute Property of the Grantees, and in all Courts of Law and Equity and elsewhere, and for all Purposes, civil, criminal, or other, the absolute Right to the Possession thereof shall be deemed to be in the Grantees.

Protection of Several Fishery.

XVIII. It shall not be lawful for any Person other than the Grantees, their Agents, Servants and Workmen, within the Limits of any such Several Fishery, or in any Part of the Space within the same described in this Behalf in the Order, knowingly to do any of the following Things :—

To use any Implement of Fishing, except a Line and Hook or a Net adapted solely for catching floating Fish, and so used as not to disturb or injure in any Manner any Oyster or Mussel Bed, or Oysters or Mussels, or the Oyster or Mussel Fishery :

To dredge for any Ballast or other Substance except under a lawful Authority for improving the Navigation :

To deposit any Ballast, Rubbish, or other Substance :

To place any Implement, Apparatus, or Thing prejudicial or likely to be prejudicial to any Oyster or Mussel Bed, or Oysters or Mussels, or to the Oyster or Mussel Fishery, except for a lawful Purpose of Navigation or Anchorage :

To disturb or injure in any Manner, except as last aforesaid, any Oyster or Mussel Bed, or Oysters or Mussels, or the Oyster or Mussel Fishery :

And if any Person does any Act in contravention of this Section he shall on summary Conviction be liable to the following Penalty, namely,—to a Penalty not exceeding Two Pounds for the First Offence, and not exceeding Five Pounds for the Second Offence, and not exceeding Ten Pounds for the Third and every subsequent Offence ; and every such Person shall also be liable to make full Compensation to the Grantees for all Damage sustained by them by reason of his unlawful Act, and in default of Payment the same may be recovered from him by the Grantees by Proceedings in any Court of competent Jurisdiction, whether he has been prosecuted for or convicted of an Offence against this Section or not.

Limits of Fishery to be kept marked out.

XIX. Provided always, That nothing in the last foregoing Section shall make it unlawful for any Person to do any of the Things therein mentioned, if at the Time of his doing the same the Limits of the Several Fishery or of the Space within the same described in that Behalf in the Order are not sufficiently marked out in manner prescribed by or under the Order, or if Notice of those Limits has not been given to him in manner so prescribed.

Fishery to be within County.

XX. The Portion of the Sea Shore to which an Order of the Board of Trade under this Act relates (as far as it is not by Law within the Body of any County) shall for all Purposes of Jurisdiction be deemed to be within the Body of the adjoining County, or to be within the Body of each of the adjoining Counties, if more than One.

Limitation on Term of Several Fishery.

XXI. The Board of Trade shall not in any Case make an Order conferring a Right of Several Oyster or Mussel Fishery for a longer Period at once than Sixty Years.

Condition for Cesser of Several Fishery, if no adequate Benefit.

XXII. A Right of Several Oyster or Mussel Fishery conferred by an Order of the Board of Trade under this Act, or by any Special Act of the present Session, shall, notwithstanding anything in the Order or in any such Special Act, be determinable by a Certificate of the Board of Trade (which Certificate they are hereby empowered to make) certifying to the Effect that the Board of Trade are not satisfied that the Grantees under the Order, or the Company under the Special Act (as the Case may be), are properly cultivating the Oyster or Mussel Ground within the Limits of such Fishery; and on any such Certificate being made, the Right of Several Fishery by such Order or Special Act conferred shall, by virtue of this Act and of the Certificate, be absolutely determined, and all Provisions of this Act or of such Special Act shall cease to operate in relation to such Fishery as a Several Oyster or Mussel Fishery; and Section Thirty-eight of The *Roach River* Oyster Fishery Act, 1866, is hereby repealed.

29 & 30 Vict. c. cxlv.

For the Purposes of this Provision the Board of Trade may from Time to Time, with respect to any such Fishery, make such Inquiries and Examination by an Inspector or otherwise, and require from the Grantees or Company such Information, as the Board of Trade think necessary or proper, and the Grantees or Company shall afford all Facilities for such Inquiries and Examination, and give such Information, accordingly.

Consent with respect to Rights of the Crown or Duchies of Lancaster and Cornwall.

XXIII. Where any Portion of the Sea Shore proposed to be comprised in an Order of the Board of Trade under this Act belongs to Her Majesty, Her Heirs or Successors, in right of the Crown, but is not under the Management of the Board of Trade, or forms Part of the Possessions of the the Duchy of *Lancaster* or of the Duchy of *Cornwall*, the Board of Trade shall not make the Order without such Consent as herein-after mentioned; namely,—

In the first-mentioned Case of the Commissioners of Her Majesty's Woods, Forests, and Land Revenues, or One of them:

In the secondly-mentioned Case of the Chancellor of the Duchy of *Lancaster* in Writing under his Hand attested by the Clerk of the Council of the Duchy:

In the thirdly-mentioned Case of the Duke of *Cornwall*, or other the Persons for the Time being empowered to dispose for any Purpose of Lands of the Duchy of *Cornwall*.

Compensation to Landowners, &c.

XXIV. Where any Portion of the Sea Shore comprised in an Order of the Board of Trade under this Act does not belong to Her Majesty, Her Heirs or Successors, in right of the Crown, or form Part of the Possessions of the Duchy of *Lancaster* or of the Duchy of *Cornwall*, the Board of Trade shall incorporate in the Order "The Lands Clauses Consolidation Act, 1845," or "The Lands Clauses Consolidation (*Scotland*) Act, 1845," as the Case requires, and shall apply the Provisions thereof respectively to the Purchase or taking of such Portion of the Sea Shore.

Order not to be made affecting Local Act, &c. without Consent.

XXV. It shall be the duty of the Board of Trade not to make in any Case an Order that will take away or abridge any Right, Privilege, Power, Jurisdiction, or Authority given or reserved to any Body, Company, or Person by any Local or Special Act of Parliament, or by any Royal Charter or Letters Patent, without the Consent of such Body, Company, or Person ; but every Order, when confirmed by Act of Parliament, shall be full of Force and Effect, any Local or Special Act, Charter, Letters Patent, Custom, Licence, Permission, Instrument, or Thing notwithstanding.

Order and Copies of Acts to be kept for Sale.

XXVI. The Persons, Company, or Body obtaining an Order under this Act shall at all Times keep at some convenient Place, in the Neighbourhood of the Portion of the Sea Shore to which the Order relates, Copies of the Order with the Act confirming it, and of this Act, printed respectively by some of Her Majesty's Printers, and shall sell such Copies to all Persons desiring to buy them at a Price not exceeding Sixpence for One Copy of each of the Acts and of the Order together.

If any such Persons, Company, or Body fail to comply with this Provision they shall for every such offence be liable on summary Conviction to a Penalty not exceeding Five Pounds, and to a further Penalty not exceeding One Pound for every Day during which such Failure continues after the Day on which the First Penalty is incurred.

Annual Report of Board of Trade.

XXVII. There shall be annually laid before both Houses of Parliament a Report of the Board of Trade respecting the Applications to and Proceedings of the Board of Trade under this Act during each Year.

Act not to extend to Ireland.

XXVIII. Nothing in this Act shall extend to *Ireland*, or to any Oyster or Mussel Fishery on the Coast of *Ireland* or in any Estuary thereof, or in any way to prejudice or affect the Owner of any such Oyster or Mussel Fishery, or to authorise the taking of Oysters or Mussels from any natural public Oyster or Mussel Bed in *Ireland*, or any Estuary thereof, by the Grantees of any Oyster or Mussel Bed under this Act, or by the Owners of any Private Beds lawfully formed independently of this Act, or by any other Person or Persons whomsoever, nor shall this Act alter or repeal any Law, Rule, or Byelaw now or hereafter to be in force having relation to *Irish* Fisheries.

CAP. XC.

An Act to Amend the Law relating to the Public Health. [7*th* August 1866.]

WHEREAS it is expedient to amend the Law relating to Public Health: Be it enacted by the Queen's most Excellent Majesty, by and with the Advice and Consent of the Lords Spiritual and Temporal, and Commons, in this present Parliament assembled, and by the Authority of the same, as follows:

Short Title of Act.

I. This Act may be cited for all Purposes as the Sanitary Act, 1866.

PART I.

Amendment of the Sewage Utilization Act, 1865.

Definition of "Sewer Authority:" "Lord-Lieutenant in Council,"

II. "Sewer Authority" in this Act shall have the same Meaning as it has in The Sewage Utilization Act, 1865. The Words "Lord Lieutenant in Council" shall mean in this Act the Lord Lieutenant or any Chief Governor or Chief Governors in *Ireland* acting by and with the Consent of Her Majesty's Privy Council in *Ireland*.

This Part to be construed with 28 & 29 Vict. c. 75.

III. This Part of this Act shall be construed as One with the Sewage Utilization Act, 1865, and the expression, The Sewage Utilization Act, 1865, as used in this or any other Act of Parliament or other Document, shall mean the said Sewage Utilization Act, 1865, as amended by this Act.

Power to Sewer Authority to form Committee of its own Members and others.

IV. Any Sewer Authority may from Time to Time, at any Meeting specially convened for the Purpose, form One or more Committee or Committees consisting wholly of its own Members, or partly of its own Members and partly of such other Persons contributing to the Rate or Fund out of which the Expenses incurred by such Authority are paid, and qualified in such other Manner as the Sewer Authority may determine, and may delegate, with or without Conditions or Restrictions, to any Committee so formed, all or any Powers of such Sewer Authority, and may from Time to Time revoke, add to, or alter any Powers so given to a Committee.

A Committee may elect a Chairman of its Meetings. If no Chairman is elected, or if the Chairman elected is not present at the Time appointed for holding the same, the Members present shall choose One of their Number to be Chairman of such Meeting. A Committee may meet and adjourn as it thinks proper. The Quorum of a Committee shall consist of such Number of Members as may be prescribed by the Sewer Authority that appointed it, or, if no Number be prescribed, of Three Members. Every Question at a Meeting shall be determined by a Majority of Votes of the Members present, and voting on that Question; and in case of an equal Division of Votes the Chairman shall have a Second or Casting Vote.

The Proceedings of a Committee shall not be invalidated by any Vacancy or Vacancies amongst its Members.

A Sewer Authority may from Time to Time add to or diminish the Number of the Members or otherwise alter the Constitution of any Committee formed by it, or dissolve any Committee.

A Committee of the Sewer Authority shall be deemed to be the Agents of that Authority, and the Appointment of such Committee shall not relieve the Sewer Authority from any Obligation imposed on it by Act of Parliament or otherwise.

Formation of Special Drainage District.

V. Where the Sewer Authority of a District is a Vestry, Select Vestry, or other Body of Persons acting by virtue of any Act of Parliament, Prescription, Custom, or otherwise as or instead of a Vestry or Select Vestry, it may, by Resolution at any Meeting convened for the Purpose after Twenty-one clear Days Notice affixed to the Places where Parochial Notices are usually affixed in its District, form any Part of such District into a Special Drainage District for the Purposes of the Sewage Utilization Act, and thereupon such Special Drainage District shall, for the Purposes of the Sewerage Utilization Act, 1865, and the Powers therein conferred, be deemed to be a Parish in which a Rate is levied for the Maintenance of the Poor, and of which a Vestry is the Sewer Authority, subject, as respects any Meeting of the Inhabitants thereof in Vestry, to the Act of the Fifty-eighth Year of the Reign of King *George* the Third, Chapter Sixty-nine; and the Acts amending the same; and any Officer or Officers who may from Time to Time be appointed by the Sewer Authority of such Special Drainage District for the Purpose shall have within that District all the Powers of levying a Rate for the Purpose of defraying the Expense of carrying the said Sewage Utilization Act into effect that they would have if such District were such Parish as aforesaid, and such Rate were a Rate for the Relief of the Poor, and they were duly appointed Overseers of such Parish.

VI. Where the Sewer Authority of any Place has formed

Appeal against Constitution of Special Drainage District.

a Special Drainage District in pursuance of this Act, if any Number of the Inhabitants of such Place, not being less than Twenty, feel aggrieved by the Formation of such District, or desire any Modification in its Boundaries, they may, by Petition in Writing under their Hands, bring their Case under the Consideration of One of Her Majesty's Principal Secretaries of State, and the said Secretary of State may after due Investigation annul the Formation of the Special Drainage District or modify its Boundaries as he thinks just.

Evidence of Formation of Special Drainage District.

VII. A Copy of the Resolution of a Sewer Authority forming a Special Drainage District shall be published by affixing a Notice thereof to the Church Door of the Parish in which the District is situate, or of the adjoining Parish if there be no Church in the said Parish, and by advertising Notice thereof in some Newspaper published or circulating in the County in which such District is situate; and the Production of a Newspaper containing such Advertisement, or a Certificate under the Hand of the Clerk or other Officer performing the Duties of Clerk for the Time being of the Sewer Authority which passed the Resolution forming the District, shall be Evidence of the Formation of such District, and after the Expiration of Three Months from the Date of the Resolution forming the District such District shall be presumed to have been duly formed, and no Objection to the Formation thereof shall be entertained in any legal Proceedings whatever.

Power to drain into Sewers of Sewer Authority.

VIII. Any Owner or Occupier of Premises within the District of a Sewer Authority shall be entitled to cause his Drains to empty into the Sewers of that Authority on condition of his giving such Notice as may be required by that Authority of his intention so to do, and of complying with the Regulations of that Authority in respect of the Mode in which the Communications between such Drains and Sewers are to be made, and subject to the Control of any Person who may be appointed by the Sewer Authority to superintend the making of such Communications; but any Person causing any Drain to empty into any Sewer of a Sewer Authority without complying with the Provisions of this Section shall incur a Penalty not exceeding Twenty Pounds, and it shall be lawful for the Sewer Authority to close any Communication between a Drain and Sewer made in contravention of this Section, and to recover in a summary Manner from the Person so offending any Expenses incurred by them under this Section.

XI. Any Owner or Occupier of Premises beyond the

Limits of the District of a Sewer Authority may cause any Sewer or Drain from such Premises to communicate with any Sewer of the Sewer Authority upon such Terms and Conditions as may be agreed upon between such Owner or Occupier and such Sewer Authority, or in case of Dispute, may, at the Option of the Owner or Occupier, be settled by Two Justices or by Arbitration in manner provided by The Public Health Act, 1848, in respect of Matters by that Act authorized or directed to be settled by Arbitration.

Use of Sewers by Persons beyond District.

X. If a Dwelling House within the District of a Sewer Authority is without a Drain or without such Drain as is sufficient for effectual Drainage, the Sewer Authority may by Notice require the Owner of such House within a reasonable Time therein specified to make a sufficient Drain emptying into any Sewer which the Sewer Authority is entitled to use, and with which the Owner is entitled to make a Communication, so that such Sewer be not more than One hundred Feet from the Site of the House of such Owner; but if no such Means of Drainage are within that Distance then emptying into such covered Cesspool or other Place not being under any House, as the Sewer Authority directs; and if the Person on whom such Notice is served fails to comply with the same, the Sewer Authority may itself, at the Expiration of the Time specified in the Notice, do the Work required, and the Expenses incurred by it in so doing may be recovered from such Owner in a summary Manner.

As to the Drainage of Houses.

XI. A Sewer Authority within its District shall have the same Powers in relation to the Supply of Water that a Local Board has within its District, and the Provisions of the Sections hereinafter mentioned shall apply accordingly in the same Manner as if in such Provisions "Sewer Authority" were substituted for "Local Board of Health" or "Local Board," and the District in such Provisions mentioned were the District of the Sewer Authority and not the District of the Local Board; that is to say, the Sections numbered from Seventy-five to Eighty, both inclusive, of the Public Health Act, 1848, Sections Fifty-one, Fifty-two, and Fifty-three of The Local Government Act, 1858, Amendment Act, 1861.

Supply of Water to District of Sewer Authority.

The Sewer Authority may, if it think it expedient so to do, provide a Supply of Water for the Use of the Inhabitants of the District by

(1.) Digging Wells;
(2.) Making and maintaining Reservoirs;
(3.) Doing any other necessary Acts;

and they may themselves furnish the same, or contract

with any other Persons or Companies to furnish the same: Provided always, that no Land be purchased or taken under this Clause except by Agreement or in manner provided by The Local Government Act, 1858.

Expenses of Sewer Authority in supplying Water.

XII. Any Expenses incurred by a Sewer Authority in or about the Supply of Water to its District, and in carrying into effect the Provisions herein-before in that Behalf mentioned, shall be deemed to be Expenses incurred by that Authority in carrying into effect the Sewage Utilization Act, 1865, and be payable accordingly.

Wells, &c., belonging to any Place vested in Sewer Authority, &c. 23 & 24 Vict. c. 77, s. 7.

XIII. All Property in Wells, Fountains, and Pumps, and Powers in relation thereto, vested in the Nuisance Authority by the Seventh Section of the Act passed in the Session of the Twenty-third and Twenty-fourth Years of the Reign of Her present Majesty, Chapter Seventy-seven, shall vest in the Sewer Authority, where the Sewer Authority supplies Water to its District.

Part II.

Definition of "Nuisances Removal Acts."

Amends the "Nuisances Removal Acts" for England, 18 and 19 Vict. c. 121, and 23 and 24 Vict. c. 77, ss. 14-34.

Part III.

Miscellaneous.

In Cities, Boroughs, or Towns, Secretary of State, on Application of Nuisance Authority, may empower them to make Regulations as to Lodging houses.

XXXV. On Application to one of Her Majesty's Principal Secretaries of State by the Nuisance Authority of the City of *London*, or any District or Parish included within the Act for the better Local Government of the Metropolis, or of any Municipal Borough, or of any Place under The Local Government Act, 1858, or any Local Improvement Act, or of any City or Town containing, according to the Census for the Time being in force, a Population of not less than Five thousand Inhabitants, the Secretary of State may, as he may think fit, by Notice to be published in the *London Gazette*, declare the following Enactment to be in force in the District of such Nuisance Authority, and from and after the Publication of such Notice the Nuisance Authority shall be empowered to make Regulations for the following matters; that is to say,

1. For fixing the Number of Persons who may occupy a House or Part of a House which is let in Lodg-

ings or occupied by Members of more than One Family:

2. For the Registration of Houses thus let or occupied in Lodgings:
3. For the Inspection of such Houses, and the keeping the same in a cleanly and wholesome State:
4. For enforcing therein the Provision of Privy Accommodation and other Appliances and Means of Cleanliness in Proportion to the Number of Lodgings and Occupiers, and the Cleansing and Ventilation of the Common Passages and Staircases:
5. For the cleansing and lime-whiting at stated Times of such Premises:

The Nuisance Authority may provide for the Enforcement of the above Regulations by Penalties not exceeding Forty Shillings for any One Offence, with an additional Penalty not exceeding Twenty Shillings for every Day during which a Default in obeying such Regulations may continue: but such Regulations shall not be of any Validity unless and until they shall have been confirmed by the Secretary of State.

But this Section shall not apply to Common Lodging Houses within the Provisions of The Common Lodging Houses Act, 1851, or any Act amending the same.

XXXVI. Where Two Convictions against the Provisions of any Act relating to the overcrowding of a House, or the Occupation of a Cellar as a separate Dwelling Place, shall have taken place within the Period of Three Months, whether the Persons so convicted were or were not the same, it shall be lawful for any Two Justices to direct the closing of such Premises for such Time as they may deem necessary, and, in the case of Cellars occupied as aforesaid, to empower the Nuisance Authority to permanently close the same, in such manner as they may deem fit, at their own Cost.

Cases in which Two Convictions have occurred within Three Months.

XXXVII. The Sewer Authority, or in the Metropolis the Nuisance Authority, may provide for the Use of the Inhabitants within its District Hospitals or temporary Places for the Reception of the Sick.

Power to provide Hospitals.

Such Authority may itself build such Hospitals or Places of Reception, or make Contracts for the Use of any existing Hospital or Part of a Hospital, or for the temporary Use of any Place for the Reception of the Sick.

It may enter into any Agreement with any Person or Body of Persons having the Management of any Hospital for the Reception of the sick Inhabitants of its District, on Payment by the Sewer Authority of such annual or other sum as may be agreed upon.

The carrying into effect this Section shall in the case of a Sewer Authority be deemed to be One of the Purposes of the said Sewage Utilization Act, 1865, and all the Provisions of the said Act shall apply accordingly.

Two or more Authorities having respectively the Power to provide separate Hospitals may combine in providing a common Hospital, and all Expenses incurred by such Authorities in providing such Hospital shall be deemed to be Expenses incurred by them respectively in carrying into effect the Purposes of this Act.

Penalty on any Person, with infectious Disorder, exposing himself, or on any Person in charge of such Sufferer causing such Exposure.

XXXVIII. Any Person suffering from any dangerous infectious Disorder who wilfully exposes himself, without proper Precaution against spreading the said Disorder, in any Street, public Place, or public Conveyance, and any Person in charge of one so suffering who so exposes the Sufferer, and any Owner or Driver of a Public Conveyance who does not immediately provide for the Disinfection of his Conveyance after it has, with the Knowledge of such Owner or Driver, conveyed any such Sufferer, and any Person who without previous Disinfection gives, lends, sells, transmits, or exposes any Bedding, Clothing, Rags, or other Things, which have been exposed to infection from such Disorders, shall, on Conviction of such Offence before any Justice, be liable to a Penalty not exceeding Five Pounds: Provided that no Proceedings under this Section shall be taken against Persons transmitting with proper Precautions any such Bedding, Clothing, Rags, or other Things for the Purpose of having the same disinfected.

Penalty on Persons letting Houses in which infected Persons have been lodging.

XXXIX. If any Person knowingly lets any House, Room, or Part of a House in which any Person suffering from any dangerous infectious Disorder has been, to any other Person without having such House, Room, or Part of a House, and all Articles therein liable to retain Infection, disinfected to the Satisfaction of a qualified Medical Practitioner as testified by a Certificate given by him, such Person shall be liable to a Penalty not exceeding Twenty Pounds. For the Purposes of this Section the Keeper of an Inn shall be deemed to let Part of a House to any Person admitted as a Guest into such Inn.

Guardians, &c., of the Poor to be the Local Authorities for executing Diseases Prevention Act.

XL. Where in any Place Two or more Boards or Guardians or Local Authorities have Jurisdiction, the Privy Council may, by any Order made under The Diseases Prevention Act, 1855, authorise or require such Boards to act together for the Purposes of that Act, and may prescribe the Mode of such joint Action and of defraying the Costs thereof.

Evidence of Family

XLI. In any Proceedings under The Common Lodging Houses Act, 1851, if the Inmates of any House or Part of a House allege that they are Members of the same Family, the Burden of proving such Allegation shall lie on the Persons making it.

In case of over-crowded Houses.

XLII. The Sixty-seventh Section of The Public Health Act, 1848, relating to Cellar Dwellings, shall apply to every Place in *England* and *Ireland* where such Dwellings are not regulated by any other Act of Parliament, and in applying that Section to Places where it is not in force at the Time of the passing of this Act, the Expression "this Act" shall be construed to mean the "Sanitary Act, 1866," and not the said Public Health Act, 1848. In construing the said Sixty-seventh Section as applied by this Act Nuisance Authority shall be substituted for the Local Board.

Extension to the whole of England and Ireland of Sect. 67 of 11 & 12 Vict. c. 63.

XLIII. Local Boards acting in Execution of The Local Government Act, 1858, may adopt the Act to encourage the Establishment of public Baths and Wash-houses, and any Act amending the same, for Districts in which those Acts are not already in force, and when they have adopted the said Acts they shall have all the Powers, Duties, and Rights of Commissioners under the said Acts; and all Expenses incurred by any Local Board in carrying into execution the Acts referred to in this Section shall be defrayed out of the General District Rates, and all Receipts by them under the said Acts shall be carried to the District Fund Account.

Local Board in certain Cases may adopt Baths and Wash-houses Acts.

XLIV. When the District of a Burial Board is conterminous with the District of a Local Board of Health, the Burial Board may, by Resolution of the Vestry, and by Agreement of the Burial Board and Local Board, transfer to the Local Board all their Estate, Property, Rights, Powers, Duties, and Liabilities, and from and after such transfer the Local Board shall have all such Estate, Property, Rights, Powers, Duties, and Liabilities as if the Local Board had been appointed a Burial Board by Order in Council under the Fourth Section of the Act of the Session of the Twentieth and Twenty-first Years of the Reign of Her present Majesty, Chapter Eighty-one.

Power to Burial Boards in certain Cases to transfer their Powers to Local Board.

XLV. If any Person wilfully damages any Works or Property belonging to any Local Board, Sewer Authority, or Nuisance Authority, he shall be liable to a Penalty not exceeding Five Pounds.

Penalty for wilful Damage of Works.

XLVI. The following Bodies, that is to say, Local Boards, Sewer Authorities, and Nuisance Authorities, if not already incorporated, shall respectively be Bodies Corporate, designated by such Names as they may usually bear or adopt, with Power to sue and be sued in such Names, and to hold Lands for the Purposes of the several Acts conferring Powers on such Bodies respectively in

Incorporation of Sanitary Authorities.

their several Characters of Local Boards, Sewer Authorities, or Nuisance Authorities.

Extent of Authority to make Provisional Orders respecting Lands under Sect. 7 of 21 & 22 Vict. s. 98.

XLVII. The Authority conferred on One of Her Majesty's Principal Secretaries of State by Section Seventy-five of the Local Government Act, 1858, to empower by Provisional Order a Local Board to put in force, with reference to the Land referred to in such Order, the Powers of The Lands Clauses Consolidation Act, 1845, with respect to the Purchase and taking of Lands otherwise than by Agreement, shall extend and apply, and shall be deemed to have always extended and applied to every Case in which, by The Public Health Act, 1848, and The Local Government Act, 1858, or either of them, or any Act extending or amending those Acts, or either of them, a Local Board are authorised to purchase, provide, use, or take Lands or Premises for any of the Purposes of the said Acts, or either of them, or of any such Act as aforesaid; and Sections Seventy-three and Eighty-four of The Public Health Act, 1848, shall be construed as if the Words "by Agreement" therein respectively used had been expressly repealed by Section Seventy-five of The Local Government Act, 1858.

Appearance of Local Authorities in Legal Proceedings.

XLVIII. Any Local Board, Sewer Authority, or Nuisance Authority may appear before any Justice or Justices, or in any legal Proceeding, by its Clerk or by any Officer or Member authorized generally or in respect of any special Proceeding by Resolution of such Board or Authority, and such Person being so authorized shall be at liberty to institute and carry on any Proceeding which the Nuisance Authority is authorised to institute and carry on under the Nuisance Removal Acts or this Act.

Mode of Proceeding where Sewer Authority has made default in providing sufficient Sewers, &c.

XLIX. Where Complaint is made to One of Her Majesty's Principal Secretaries of State that a Sewer Authority or Local Board of Health has made default in providing its District with sufficient Sewers, or in the maintenance of existing Sewers, or in providing its District with a Supply of Water in Cases where Danger arises to the Health of the Inhabitants from the Insufficiency or Unwholesomeness of the existing Supply of Water, and a proper Supply can be got at a reasonable Cost, or that a Nuisance Authority has made default in enforcing the Provisions of the Nuisance Removal Acts, or that a Local Board has made default in enforcing the Provisions of the Local Government Act, the said Secretary of State, if satisfied after due Inquiry made by him that the Authority has been guilty of the alleged default, shall make an Order limiting a Time for the Performance of its Duty in the Matter of such Complaint; and if such Duty is not performed by the Time limited in the Order, the said Secretary of State shall appoint some Person to perform the same, and shall by Order direct that the Expenses of performing the same, together with a reasonable Remuneration to the Person appointed for superintending such Performance, and amounting to a sum specified in the Order, together with the Costs of the Proceedings, shall be paid by the Authority in Default; and any Order made for the Payment of such Costs and Expenses may be removed into the Court of Queen's Bench, and be enforced in the same Manner as if the same were an Order of such Court.

L. All Expenses incurred by a Sewers Authority or Local Board in giving a Supply of Water to Premises under the Provisions of the Seventy-sixth Section of The Public Health Act, 1848, or the Fifty-first Section of the Local Government Act, 1858, and recoverable from the Owners of the Premises supplied, may be recovered in a summary Manner. **Recovery of certain Expenses of Water Supply.**

LI. All Penalties imposed by the Act of the Sixth Year of King *George* the Fourth, Chapter Seventy-eight, intituled *An Act to repeal the several Laws relating to Quarantine, and to make other Provisions in lieu thereof*, may be reduced by the Justices or Court having Jurisdiction in respect of such Penalties to such sum as the Justices or Court think just. **Power to reduce Penalties imposed by 6 G. 4, c. 78.**

LII. Every Vessel having on board any Person affected with a dangerous or infectious disorder shall be deemed to be within the Provisions of the Act of the Sixth Year of King *George* the Fourth, Chapter Seventy-eight, and although such Vessel has not commenced her Voyage, or has come from or is bound for some Place in the United Kingdom; and the Lords and others of Her Majesty's Most Honourable Privy Council, or any Three or more of them (the Lord President of the Council or One of Her Majesty's Principal Secretaries of State being One), may, by Order or Orders to be by them from Time to Time made, make such Rules, Orders, and Regulations as to them shall seem fit, and every such Order shall be certified under the Hand of the Clerk in Ordinary of Her Majesty's Privy Council, and shall be published in the *London Gazette*, and such Publication shall be conclusive Evidence of such Order to all Intents and Purposes; and such Orders shall be binding and be carried into effect as soon as the same shall have been so published, or at such other Time as shall be fixed by such Orders, with a view to the Treatment of Persons affected with Cholera and epidemic, endemic, and contagious Disease, and preventing the Spread of Cholera **Description of Vessels within Provisions of 6 G. 4, c. 78.**

and such other Diseases as well on the Seas, Rivers, and Waters of the United Kingdom, and on the High Seas within Three Miles of the Coasts thereof, as on Land; and to declare and determine by what Nuisance Authority or Authorities such Orders, Rules, and Regulations shall be enforced and executed; and any Expenses incurred by such Nuisance Authority or Authorities shall be deemed to be Expenses incurred by it or them in carrying into effect the Nuisances Removal Acts.

Periodical Removal of Manure in Mews, &c.

LIII. Where Notice has been given by the Nuisance Authority, or their Officer or Officers, for the periodical Removal of Manure or other refuse Matter from Mews, Stables, or other Premises (whether such Notice shall be by public Announcement in the Locality or otherwise), and subsequent to such Notice the Person or Persons to whom the Manure or other refuse Matter belongs shall not so remove the same, or shall permit a further Accumulation, and shall not continue such periodical Removal at such Intervals as the Nuisance Authority, or their Officer or Officers, shall direct, he or they shall be liable, without further Notice, to a Penalty of Twenty Shillings *per* Day for every Day during which such Manure or other refuse Matter shall be permitted to accumulate, such Penalty to be recovered in a summary Manner: Provided always, that this Section shall not apply to any Place where the Board of Guardians or Overseers of the Poor are the Nuisance Authority.

Recovery of Penalties.

LIV. Penalties under this Act, and Expenses directed to be recovered in a summary Manner, may be recovered before Two Justices in manner directed by an Act passed in the Session holden in the Eleventh and Twelfth Years of the Reign of Her Majesty Queen *Victoria*, Chapter Forty-three, intituled *An Act to facilitate the Duties of Justices of the Peace out of Sessions within* England *and* Wales, *with respect to summary Convictions and Orders*, or any Act amending the same.

Powers of Act cumulative.

LV. All Powers given by this Act shall be deemed to be in addition to and not in derogation of any other Powers conferred on any Local Authority by Act of Parliament, Law, or Custom, and such Authority may exercise such other Powers in the same Manner as if this Act had not passed.

PART IV.

[Contains the modifications necessary for the Application of the Act to Ireland.]

Cap. CII.

An Act to continue various Expiring Acts.

[Continues *inter alia*, 4 & 5 Vict. c. 30 (Survey of Great Britain), and the amending Act 19 & 20 Vict. c. 61, till 31st Dec. 1867;

11 & 12 Vict. c. 107 (Sheep and Cattle Diseased), with the amending Acts 16 & 17 Vict. c. 62, and 29 Vict. c. 15, till 1st Aug. 1867, and the end of the then next session;

25 & 26 Vict. c. 97, Salmon Fisheries (Scotland) Act, with amending Acts 26 & 27 Vict. c. 50, and 27 & 28 Vict. c. 118, till 1st Jan. 1868, and end of the next Session, as to powers of Commissioners;

26 & 27 Vict. c. 105 (Promissory Notes) till 28th July 1867, and end of then next Session;

28 and 29 Vict. c. 46 (Militia Ballots Suspension), till 1st Oct. 1867.]

Cap. CVIII.

An Act to amend the Law relating to Securities issued by Railway Companies.—[10th August 1866.]

Be it enacted by the Queen's most Excellent Majesty, by and with the Advice and Consent of the Lords Spiritual and Temporal, and Commons, in this present Parliament assembled, and by the Authority of the same, as follows:

I. This Act may be cited as The Railway Companies Securities Act, 1866. **Short Title.**

II. In this Act— **Interpretation of Terms.**

The Term "Railway" includes a Tramway authorized by Act of Parliament incorporating The Companies Clauses Consolidation Act, 1845, but not any other Tramway:

The Term "Railway Company" includes every Company authorized by Act of Parliament to raise any Loan Capital for the Construction or Working of a Railway, or for any Purposes connected with the Conveyance by such Company of Traffic on a Railway, either alone or in conjunction with other Purposes:

The Term "Debenture Stock" includes Mortgage Preference Stock and Funded Debt, and any Stock or Shares representing Loan Capital of a Railway Company, by whatever Name called:

The Term "Act of Parliament" includes a Certificate of the Board of Trade made under The Railways Construction Facilities Act, 1864, or The Railway Companies Powers Act, 1864, or any other Act of Parliament.

27 & 28 Vict. c. 120, 121.

Company to have Registered Officer.

III. Every Railway Company shall, on or before the Fifteenth Day of *January* One thousand eight hundred and sixty-seven, register, and shall always thereafter keep registered, at the Office of the Registrar of Joint Stock Companies in *England*, the name of their Secretary, Accountant, Treasurer, or Chief Cashier for the Time being authorized by them to sign Instruments under this Act, or, if they think fit, the Names of Two or more such Officers of the Company so authorized (and the Officer so registered for the Time being, and any One of the Officers so registered, if more than One, is in this Act referred to as the Company's Registered Officer).

Half Years for Purposes of Act.

IV. Half Years shall, for the Purposes of this Act, be deemed to end on the Thirtieth Day of *June* and the Thirty-first Day of *December*; and the First Half Year to which this Act applies shall be that ending on the Thirty-first Day of *December* One thousand eight hundred and sixty-six: but the Board of Trade, on the Application of any Railway Company, may (by Writing under the Hand of One of their Secretaries or Assistant Secretaries, which shall be registered by the Railway Company at the Office of the said Registrar) appoint, with respect to that Company, other Days for the ending of Half Years (including the First).

Loan Capital Accounts to be made half-yearly.

V. Within Fourteen Days after the End of each Half Year every Railway Company shall make an Account of their Loan Capital authorized to be raised and actually raised up to the End of that Half Year, specifying the Particulars described in the First Schedule to this Act, Part I. (which Account for each Half Year is in this Act referred to as the Loan Capital Half-yearly Account).

Form of half-yearly Account.

VI. The Board of Trade may from Time to Time, by Notice published in the *London*, *Edinburgh*, and *Dublin* Gazettes, prescribe the Form in which the Loan Capital Half-yearly Account is to be made.

Account to be open to Shareholders, &c.

VII. The Loan Capital Half-yearly Account of each Company may be perused at all reasonable Times, without Payment, by any Shareholder, Stockholder, Mortgagee, Bond Creditor, or Holder of Debenture Stock of the Company, or any Person interested in any Mortgage, Bond, or Debenture Stock of the Company.

VIII. Within Twenty-one Days after the End of each Half Year every Railway Company shall deposit with the Registrar of Joint Stock Companies in *England* a Copy, certified and signed by the Company's Registered Officer as a true Copy, of their Loan Capital Half-yearly Account.

Deposit of Copy of Account with Registrar of Joint Stock Companies.

IX. A Railway Company may also, if they think fit, deposit with the Registrar of Joint Stock Companies in *Scotland*, or with the Assistant Registrar of Joint Stock Companies in *Ireland*, or with each, a like Copy of any Loan Capital Half-yearly Account of the Company.

Deposit in Scotland and Ireland.

X. It shall not be lawful for any Railway Company at any Time to borrow any Money on Mortgage or Bond, or to issue any Debenture Stock, under any Act of the present Session or passed after the End of the Half Year to which their then last registered Loan Capital Half-yearly Account relates, unless and until they have first deposited with the Registrar of Joint Stock Companies in *England* a Statement, certified and signed by the Company's Registered Officer as a true Statement, specifying the Particulars described in the First Schedule to this Act, Part II.

Prohibition against borrowing before Registration of Act giving the Borrowing Power.

The Board of Trade may from Time to Time, by Notice published in the *London*, *Edinburgh*, and *Dublin* Gazettes, prescribe the Form in which such Statement is to be made.

A Railway Company may also, if they think fit, deposit with the Registrar of Joint Stock Companies in *Scotland*, or with the Assistant Registrar of Joint Stock Companies in *Ireland*, or with each, a like Copy of any such Statement.

XI. If at any Time any Railway Company fail to register or keep registered as aforesaid the Name of their Secretary, Accountant, Treasurer, or Chief Cashier, or to deposit with the Registrar of Joint Stock Companies in *England*, within the Time required by this Act, such a Copy as aforesaid of any Loan Capital Half-yearly Account, or borrow any Money on Mortgage or Bond, or issue any Debenture Stock, without having first deposited with the Registrar of Joint Stock Companies in *England* such a Statement as they are by this Act required to deposit, in any Case where they are so required, then and in every such Case they shall be deemed guilty of an Offence against this Act, and shall for every such Offence be liable, on summary Conviction, to a Penalty not exceeding Twenty Pounds, and in case of a continuing Offence to a further Penalty not exceeding Five Pounds for every Day during which the same continues after the Day on which the first Penalty is incurred.

Penalty on Company failing to register, &c.

XII. Every Person may inspect the Documents kept by any Registrar or Assistant Registrar under this Act on

Power to inspect Documents on

Payment of a Fee.

paying a Fee of One Shilling for each Inspection as regards each Railway Company; and any Person may require a Copy or Extract of any of those Documents to be certified by the Registrar or Assistant Registrar on paying for such certified Copy or Extract a Fee of Sixpence, and a further Fee of Sixpence for every Two hundred Words or fractional Part of Two hundred Words after the First Two hundred Words.

Fees on Registration of Name of Officer, &c.

XIII. Every Railway Company on registering the Name or Names of any Officer or Officers, or depositing any Account or Statement, under this Act, shall pay the like Fee as is for the Time being payable under The Companies Act, 1862, on Registration of any Document other than a Memorandum of Association.

Declaration by Directors, &c. on Mortgage Deed, &c.

XIV. There shall be put (by Indorsement or otherwise) on every Mortgage Deed or Bond made or given after the Twenty first Day of *January* One thousand eight hundred and sixty-seven by a Railway Company for securing Money borrowed by the Company, and on every Certificate given after that Day by a Railway Company for any Sum of Debenture Stock issued by the Company, a Declaration in the Form given in the Second Schedule to this Act, or to the like Effect, with such Variations as Circumstances may require.

Every such Declaration shall be signed by Two Directors of the Company specially authorized and appointed by the Board of Directors to sign such Declarations, and by the Company's Registered Officer.

Penalty on Company, &c. if Declaration omitted.

XV. If after the Expiration of the Time specified in the last preceding Section any Railway Company deliver any such Mortgage Deed, Bond, or Certificate without such a Declaration being first put thereon and signed as aforesaid, they shall be deemed guilty of an Offence against this Act, and shall for every such Offence be liable, on summary Conviction, to a Penalty not exceeding Twenty Pounds; and if any Director or Officer of any Railway Company knowingly authorizes or permits the Delivery of any such Mortgage Deed, Bond, or Certificate without such a Declaration being first put thereon and signed as aforesaid, every such Person shall be deemed guilty of an Offence against this Act.

Penalty on Registered Officer.

XVI. If any Director or Registered Officer of a Company signs any Declaration, Account, or Statement under this Act knowing the same to be false in any Particular he shall be deemed guilty of an Offence against this Act.

Punishment for Offences against Act.

XVII. If any Director or Officer of a Railway Company is guilty of an Offence against this Act, he shall be liable, on Conviction thereof on Indictment, to Fine or Imprisonment, or on summary Conviction thereof to a Penalty not exceeding Ten Pounds.

Nothing to affect Liability of Company, &c.

XVIII. Nothing in this Act, or in any Account, Statement, or Declaration under it, shall affect in any Action or Suit any Question respecting any Loan, Debt, Liability, Mortgage, Bond, or Debenture Stock as between a Railway Company or any Director or Officer of a Railway Company on the one Side, and any Person or Class of Persons on the other Side.

Account &c. not to be Evidence for Company.

XIX. An Account, Statement, or Declaration under this Act shall not be admissible as Evidence in favour of a Railway Company of the Truth of any Matter therein stated.

SCHEDULES.

The First Schedule.

Part I.

Particulars to be specified in Loan Capital Half-yearly Account.

A. Every Half-yearly Account to show—

(1.) The Act or Acts of Parliament under the Powers of which the Company have contracted any Mortgage or Bond Debt existing at the End of the Half Year, or have issued any Debenture Stock then existing, or the Act or Acts of Parliament by or under which any Mortgage or Bond Debt or Debenture Stock of the Company then existing has been confirmed, and the Act or Acts of Parliament under which the Company have any subsisting Power to contract any Mortgage or Bond Debt, or to issue any Debenture Stock (either on Fulfilment of any Condition or otherwise):

(2.) The Amount or respective Amounts of Mortgage or Bond Debt or Debenture Stock thereby authorized or confirmed:

(3.) Whether or not by any such Act or Acts the obtaining of the Certificate of a Justice or Sheriff for any Purpose, or the obtaining of the Assent of a Meeting of the Company, has been made a Condition precedent to the

Exercise of the Power thereby conferred of borrowing on Mortgage or Bond, or of creating and issuing Debenture Stock:

(4.) The Date at which such Condition has been fulfilled:

(5.) The Amount or the aggregate Amount, under the Powers of such Act or Acts, actually borrowed up to the End of the Half Year on Mortgage or Bond (distinguishing them), and then being an existing Debt, and of Debenture Stock actually issued up to that Time and then existing:

(6.) The Amount or the aggregate Amount remaining to be borrowed.

B. The Second and every subsequent Half-yearly Account to show also—

(7.) The Items described in Paragraphs (2.) and (5.) of this Part of the present Schedule for Two consecutive Half Years, and the Increase or Decrease of any of those Items in the Second of those Half Years as compared with the First.

Part II.

Particulars to be specified in Statement as to new Borrowing Power.

(1.) The Act of Parliament conferring the Power to borrow on Mortgage or Bond or to issue Debenture Stock (either on Fulfilment of any Condition or otherwise):

(2.) The Amount of Mortgage or Bond Debt or Debenture Stock thereby authorized:

(3.) Whether or not by such Act the obtaining of the Certificate of a Justice or Sheriff for any Purpose, or the obtaining of the Assent of a Meeting of the Company, has been made a Condition precedent to the Exercise of the Power thereby conferred of borrowing on Mortgage or Bond, or of creating and issuing Debenture Stock:

(4.) The Date at which such Condition has been fulfilled.

The Second Schedule.

Declaration on Mortgage Deed, Bond, or Certificate of Debenture Stock.

The   Railway Company.

We, the undersigned, being Two of the Directors of the Company specially authorized and appointed for this Purpose, and I, the undersigned Registered Officer of the Company, do hereby declare (each for himself) that the within-written [*or as the Case may be*] Mortgage Deed [*or* Bond *or* Certificate] is issued under the Borrowing Powers of the Company as registered * on the Day of , and is † not in Excess of the Amount

Dated this Day of 18 .

________________ } Directors.
____

________________ [Secretary *or* Accountant, *or as the Case may be*, and Registered Officer.

*Note.—Where the Case so requires with reference to a Statement under the First Schedule, Part II., leave out from the * to the end of the Form and insert* :—on the Day of and the Day of , and is not in Excess of the Amounts there stated as remaining and authorised to be borrowed.

Where the Mortgage Deed, Bond, or Certificate is issued under a Power of Re-borrowing, or of issuing Debenture Stock in discharge of Mortgage or Bond Debt, leave out from the † to the End of the Form, and insert :—in substitution for a Mortgage Deed [*or* Bond] which has since been paid off.

Cap. CXII.

An Act to make Provision in regard to the Mode of taking Evidence in Civil Causes in the Court of Session in Scotland. [10th *August* 1866.]

Whereas the Practice of taking Proofs by Commission in Causes before the Court of Session in *Scotland* is productive of unnecessary Expense and of great Delay in the Administration of Justice:

Be it therefore enacted by the Queen's most Excellent Majesty, by and with the Advice and Consent of the Lords Spiritual and Temporal, and Commons, in this present Parliament assembled, and by the Authority of the same, as follows:

Evidence to be taken before the Lord Ordinary.

I. Except as hereinafter enacted, it shall not be competent in any Cause depending before the Court of Session to grant Commission to take Proof; but where in such Causes it is, according to the existing Practice, competent to take Proof by Commission, and where in such Causes Proof shall be allowed (which the Lord Ordinary is hereby authorized to allow without the Consent of both Parties, and without reporting to and obtaining the leave of the

Inner House), a Diet of Proof shall be appointed, which Diet may be fixed, in the Discretion of the Lord Ordinary, either during the Sitting of the Court or in Vacation, at which the Evidence shall be led before the Lord Ordinary, and he shall himself take and either write down with his own Hand the oral Evidence, in which Case it shall be read over to the Witness by the Judge in open Court, and shall be signed by the Witness, if he can write; or the Lord Ordinary shall record the Evidence by dictating it to a Clerk, in which Case it shall also be read over to and signed by the Witness; or the Lord Ordinary shall cause the Evidence to be taken down and recorded in Shorthand by a Writer skilled in Shorthand Writing, to whom the Oath De fideli administratione officii shall be administered; and the Lord Ordinary may, if he think fit, dictate to the Shorthand Writer the Evidence which he is to record; and the Shorthand Writer shall afterwards write out the Evidence so taken by him; and the extended Notes of such Shorthand Writer, certified by the presiding Judge to be correct, shall be the record of the oral Evidence in the Cause; and the Lord Ordinary shall himself take or dictate to his Clerk or Shorthand Writer a Note of the Documents adduced; and any Ruling of the Lord Ordinary in reference to the Admission or Rejection of Evidence may be recalled or altered by the Inner House on a Reclaiming Note against the final Interlocutor of the Lord Ordinary disposing of the Cause; and the Proof shall be taken continuously in like Manner as at Jury Trials in Civil Causes before the Court of Session in *Scotland*, but with Power to the Lord Ordinary to adjourn the Proof upon such Grounds as Causes set down for Jury Trial may according to the existing Law and Practice be adjourned or postponed, or on such other special Grounds as to him shall appear sufficient, and under such Conditions, if any, as he shall think proper.

In what Cases Proof may be taken by Commission.

II. Provided always, That it shall be competent to the Judges of either Division of the Court or to the Lord Ordinary to grant Commission to any Person competent to take and report in Writing the Depositions of Havers; and also upon special Cause shown, or with Consent of both Parties, to grant Commission to take the Evidence in any Cause in which Commission to take Evidence may, according to the existing Law and Practice be granted; and also to grant such Commission to take and report in Writing according to the existing Practice the Evidence of any Witness who is resident beyond the Jurisdiction of the Court, or who, by reason of Age, Infirmity, or Sickness, is unable to attend the Diet of Proof; provided that nothing herein contained shall affect the existing Practice in regard to granting Commission for the Examination of aged and infirm Witnesses to take their Evidence to lie *in retentis* before a Proof has been allowed.

III. Where Proof shall be ordered by One of the Divisions of the Court, such Proof shall be taken before any One of the Judges of the said Division, or of the Lords Ordinary, to whom the Court may think fit to remit, in one or other of the Modes above provided in Section First hereof, and his Rulings upon the Admissibility of Evidence in the course of taking such Proof shall be subject to Review by the Division of the Court in Discussion of the Report of the Proof; and when the Court shall alter any Finding of the Judge respecting Evidence, they shall, if they think the Justice of the Case requires it, remit to have such Evidence taken; and where a Reference to Oath is made and sustained either by the Lord Ordinary before whom the Cause depends, or by One of the Divisions of the Court, the Deposition shall be taken in one or other of the Modes above provided. **Disposal of Questions on Admission of Evidence.**

IV. If both Parties consent thereto, or if special Cause be shown, it shall be competent to the Lord Ordinary to take Proof in the Manner above provided in Section First hereof in any Cause which may be in Dependence before him, notwithstanding of the Provisions contained in the Act passed in the Sixth Year of the Reign of His Majesty King *George* the Fourth, Chapter One hundred and twenty, Section Twenty-eight, and the Provisions contained in the Act passed in the Thirteenth and Fourteenth Years of the Reign of Her present Majesty, Chapter Thirty-six, Section Forty-nine, and the Judgment to be pronounced by him upon such Proof shall be subject to Review in the like Manner as other judgments pronounced by him. **With Consent, Evidence in Causes now depending may be taken before the Lord Ordinary.**

V. The Court of Session are hereby authorized and empowered to make from Time to Time such Orders and Regulations as to Forms of Process by Acts of Sederunt as they may consider necessary for carrying into execution the Purposes of this Act. **Procedure to be regulated by Act of Sederunt.**

VI. Nothing in this Act contained shall be held to affect "The Conjugal Rights (*Scotland*) Amendment Act, 1861." **This Act not to affect 24 & 25 Vict. c. 86.**

VII. This Act may be cited for all Purposes as "The Evidence (*Scotland*) Act, 1866." **Short Title.**

Cap. CXVII.

An Act to consolidate and amend the Acts relating to Reformatory Schools in Great Britain. [10th *August* 1866.]

Be it enacted by the Queen's most Excellent Majesty, by and with the Advice and Consent of the Lords Spiritual and Temporal, and Commons, in this present Parliament assembled, and by the Authority of the same, as follows:

Preliminary.

Short Title. I. This Act may be cited as The Reformatory Schools Act, 1866.

Application of Act. II. This Act shall not extend to *Ireland*.

Definition of Terms. III. "Managers" shall include any Person or Persons having the Management or Control of any School to which this Act applies:

"Justice" shall apply to *England* only, and shall mean a Justice of the Peace having Jurisdiction in the Place where the Matter requiring the Cognizance of a Justice arises:

"Justices" shall apply to *England* only, and shall mean Two or more Justices in Petty Sessions, and shall include the Lord Mayor or an Alderman of the City of *London*, or a Police or Stipendiary Magistrate or other Justice having by Law authority to act alone for any Purpose with the Powers of Two Justices:

"Magistrate" shall apply to *Scotland* only, and shall include Sheriff, Sheriff-Substitute, Justice of the Peace of a County, Judge in a Police Court, and Provost or Bailie of a City or Burgh:

28 & 29 Vict. c. 126. 23 & 24 Vict. c. 105. "Prison Authority" shall in *England* mean the same Persons as are defined to be Prison Authorities by The Prisons Act, 1865, and in *Scotland* shall mean the Administrators of a Prison, as defined by The Prisons (*Scotland*) Administration Act, 1860:

"Visiting Justice" shall in *Scotland* mean the Administrators of a Prison, defined as aforesaid.

Certified Reformatory Schools.

Mode of certifying Reformatory Schools. IV. One of Her Majesty's Principal Secretaries of State, hereinafter referred to as the Secretary of State, may, upon the Application of the Managers of any Reformatory School for the better training of youthful Offenders, direct One of Her Majesty's Inspectors of Prisons, who shall be styled the Inspector of Reformatory Schools, to examine into the Condition and Regulations of the School, and to report to him thereon; and, if satisfied with such Report, the Secretary of State may, by Writing under his hand, certify that such School is fitted for the Reception of such youthful Offenders as may be sent there in pursuance of this Act, and the same shall be deemed a Certified Reformatory School.

No substantial Addition or Alteration shall be made to or in the Buildings of any Certified Reformatory School without the Approval in Writing of the Secretary of State.

Inspection of School.

V. Every Certified Reformatory School shall from Time to Time, and at least once in every Year, be visited by the Inspector of Reformatory Schools; and the Secretary of State, if dissatisfied with the Condition of such School as reported to him, may withdraw the Certificate, and may, by Notice under his Hand, addressed and sent to the Managers of such School, declare that the Certificate is withdrawn as from a Time specified in the Notice, being not less than Six Months after the Date of the Notice.

Power to appoint Assistant to Inspector.

VI. The Secretary of State may from Time to Time appoint a fit Person to assist the Inspector of Reformatory Schools; and every Person so appointed shall have such of the Powers and Duties of the Inspector as the Secretary of State from Time to Time prescribes, but shall act under the Direction of the Inspector.

Resignation of Certificate by Managers.

VII. The Managers of any Certified Reformatory School may, upon giving Six Months, and the Executors or Administrators of a deceased Manager (if only One) of any Certified Reformatory School may, upon giving One Month's previous Notice in Writing of their intention so to do, resign the Certificate given to such School; and accordingly, at the Expiration of Six Months or One Month (as the Case may be) from the Date of the Notice (unless before that Time the Notice is withdrawn), the Certificate shall be deemed to be resigned.

Liabilities of Managers.

VIII. The Managers of a Certified Reformatory School may decline to receive any youthful Offender proposed to be sent to them under this Act, but when they have once received him they shall be deemed to have undertaken to educate, clothe, lodge, and feed him during the whole Period for which he is liable to be detained in the School, or until the Withdrawal or Resignation of the Certificate takes effect, or until the Contribution out of Money provided by Parliament towards the Custody and Maintenance of the Offenders detained in the School is discontinued, whichever shall first happen.

Effect of Withdrawal of Certificate.

IX. Whenever the Certificate is withdrawn from or resigned by the Managers of a Reformatory School no youthful Offender shall be received into such School after the Date of the Receipt by the Managers of the School of the Notice of Withdrawal or after the Date of the Notice of Resignation (as the Case may be); but the Obligation of the Managers to educate, clothe, lodge, and feed any youthful Offenders in the School at the respective Dates aforesaid shall, excepting so far as the Secretary of State may otherwise direct, be deemed to continue until the Withdrawal or Resignation of the Certificate takes effect, or until the Contribution out of Money provided by Parliament towards the Custody and Maintenance of the Offenders detained in the School is discontinued, whichever shall first happen.

Disposal of Inmates on Withdrawal or Resignation of Certificate.

X. When the Withdrawal or Resignation of the Certificate of a Reformatory School takes effect, the youthful Offenders detained therein shall be, by the Order of the Secretary of State, either discharged or transferred to some other Certified Reformatory School.

Publication of the Grant or Withdrawal of Certificate.

XI. A Notice of the Grant of any Certificate to a Reformatory School, or of the Withdrawal or Resignation of such a Certificate, shall within One Month be advertised by Order of the Secretary of State, as to a School in *England* in the *London Gazette,* and as to a School in *Scotland* in the *Edinburgh Gazette.*

Power to make Rules, &c.

XII. The Managers of any Certified Reformatory School may from Time to Time make all necessary rules for the Management and Discipline of the School under their Charge, but such Rules shall not be contrary to the Provisions of this Act, and shall not be enforced until they have been submitted to and approved in Writing by the Secretary of State, and no Alteration shall be made without the Approval in Writing of the Secretary of State in any Rules so approved.

Officers to have Privileges, &c., of Constables.

XIII. Every Officer of a Certified Reformatory School authorized by the Managers of the School, in Writing under their Hands or the Hand of their Secretary, to take charge of any youthful Offender sentenced to Detention under this Act for the Purpose of conveying him to or from the School, or of bringing him back to the School in case of his Escape or Refusal to return, shall, for such Purpose, and while engaged in such Duty, have all such Powers, Authorities, Protection, and Privileges for the Purpose of the Execution of his Duty as a Reformatory Officer as any Constable duly appointed has within his Constablewick by Common Law, Statute, or Custom.

Commitment of Offenders to and their Status at a Certified Reformatory School.

XIV. Whenever any Offender who, in the Judgment of the Court, Justices, or Magistrate before whom he is charged, is under the Age of Sixteen Years, is convicted, on Indictment or in a summary Manner, of an Offence punishable with Penal Servitude or Imprisonment, and is sentenced to be imprisoned for the Term of Ten Days or a longer Term, the Court, Justices, or Magistrate may also sentence him to be sent, at the Expiration of his Period of Imprisonment, to a Certified Reformatory School, and to be there detained for a Period of not less than Two Years and not more than Five Years: Offenders under 16 Years of Age may be sent to Certified Reformatory Schools.

Provided always, that a youthful Offender under the Age of Ten Years shall not be so directed to be sent to a Reformatory School unless he has been previously charged with some Crime or Offence punishable with Penal Servitude or Imprisonment, or is sentenced in *England* by a Judge of Assize or Court of General or Quarter Sessions, or in *Scotland* by a Circuit Court of Justiciary or Sheriff.

The particular School to which the youthful Offender is to be sent may be named either at the Time of his Sentence being passed, or within Seven Days thereafter, by the Court, Justices, or Magistrate who sentenced him, or in default thereof at any Time before the Expiration of his Imprisonment by any Visiting Justice of the Prison to which he is committed.

In choosing a Certified Reformatory School, the Court, Justices, Magistrate, or Visiting Justice shall endeavour to ascertain the Religious Persuasion to which the youthful Offender belongs, and, so far as is possible, a Selection shall be made of a School conducted in accordance with the Religious Persuasion to which the youthful Offender appears to the Court, Justices, Magistrate, or Visiting Justice to belong, which Persuasion shall be specified by the Court, Justices, Magistrate, or Visiting Justice.

It shall be lawful, upon the Representation of the Parent, or in the Case of an Orphan then of the Guardian or nearest adult Relative, or of any Offender detained in any such School, for a Minister of the Religious Persuasion of such Offender, at certain fixed Hours of the Day, which shall be fixed by the Secretary of State for the Purpose, to visit such School for the Purpose of affording Religious Assistance to such Offender, and also for the Purpose of instructing such Offender in the Principles of his Religion.

XV. The Gaoler of every Prison having in his Custody any youthful Offender sentenced to be sent to a Reformatory Removal of Offender to certified Reformatory School.

School shall at the appointed Time deliver such Offender into the Custody of the Superintendent or other Person in charge of the School in which he is to be detained, together with the Warrant or other Document in pursuance of which the Offender was imprisoned and is sent to such School.

The Possession of the Warrant or other Document in pursuance of which a youthful Offender is sent to a Certified Reformatory School shall be a sufficient Authority for his Detention in such School.

Power to Parent, &c. to apply to remove Offender to a School conducted in accordance with Offender's Religious Persuasion.

XVI. The Parent, Step-parent, or Guardian, or if there be no Parent, Step-parent, or Guardian, then the Godparent or nearest adult Relative of any youthful Offender sent or about to be sent to a Certified Reformatory School which is not conducted in accordance with the Religious Persuasion to which the Offender belongs, may apply to the Court by whom such Offender was sentenced to be sent to a Reformatory School, or to the Visiting Justices of the Prison to which he was committed by that Court, or to the Justices or Magistrate by whom he was sentenced to be sent to a Reformatory School (or Justices or a Magistrate having the like Jurisdiction), to send or to remove such Offender to a Certified Reformatory School conducted in accordance with the Offender's Religious Persuasion, and the Court, Visiting Justices, Justices, or Magistrate (as the Case may be) shall, upon Proof of such Offender's Religious Persuasion, comply with the Request of the Applicant, provided,—

First, that the Application be made before the Offender has been sent to a Certified Reformatory School, or within Thirty Days after his Arrival at such a School;

Secondly, that the Applicant show to the Satisfaction of the Court, Visiting Justices, Justices, or Magistrate that the Managers of the School named by him are willing to receive the Offender.

Discharge or Removal by Order of Secretary of State.

XVII. The Secretary of State may at any Time order any Offender to be discharged from a Certified Reformatory School, or to be removed from one Certified Reformatory School to another, but so that the whole Period of Detention of the Offender in a Reformatory School shall not be increased by such Removal.

The Secretary of State may also at any Time, after having given Ten Days Notice to the Managers, order a youthful Offender under Sentence of Detention in a Reformatory or Industrial School established under any other Act of Parliament, the General Rules for the Government whereof have been approved by the Secretary of State, to be discharged from such School, or to be removed therefrom to any Certified Reformatory School, and in case of Removal the youthful Offender shall after such Removal be deemed to be subject in all respects to the Provisions of this Act, but so that the whole Period of Detention of the Offender under his Sentence shall not be increased by such Removal.

Placing Offenders out on Licence.

XVIII. The Managers of a Certified Reformatory School may, at any Time after the Expiration of Eighteen Months of the Period of Detention allotted to a youthful Offender, by Licence under their Hands, permit him to live with any trustworthy and respectable Person named in the Licence willing to receive and take charge of him.

Any Licence so granted shall not be in force for more than Three Months, but may at any Time before the Expiration of such Three Months be renewed for a further Period not exceeding Three Months, to commence from the Expiration of the previous Period of Three Months, and so from Time to Time until the youthful Offender's Period of Detention is expired.

Any such Licence may also be revoked by the Managers of the School, by Writing under their Hands, at any Time before the Expiration of such Period of Three Months, and thereupon the youthful Offender to whom the Licence related may be required by the Managers, by Writing under their Hands, to return to the School.

The Time during which a youthful Offender is absent from a Certified Reformatory School in pursuance of a Licence under this Section shall, except where such Licence has been forfeited by his Misconduct, be deemed to be Part of the Time of his Detention in the School, and at the Expiration of the Time fixed by his Licence he shall be taken back to the School.

Any youthful Offender escaping from the Person with whom he is placed in pursuance of this Section, or refusing to return to the School at the Expiration of the Time fixed by his Licence, or any Renewal thereof, or when required to do so on the Revocation of his Licence, shall be liable to the same Penalty as if he had escaped from the School itself.

Power to apprentice Offenders.

XIX. The Managers of a Certified Reformatory School may, at any Time after an Offender has been placed out on Licence as aforesaid, if he conducted himself well during his Absence from the School, bind him, with his own Consent, Apprentice to any Trade, Calling, or Service, notwithstanding that his Period of Detention has not expired; and every such Binding shall be valid and effectual to all Intents.

Offences in relation to Reformatory Schools.

Refusal to conform to Rules.

XX. If any Offender detained in a Certified Reformatory School wilfully neglects or wilfully refuses to conform to the Rules thereof, he shall, upon summary Conviction before a Justice or Magistrate having Jurisdiction in the Place or District where the School is situate, be imprisoned, with or without Hard Labour, for any Term not exceeding Three Months; and at the Expiration of the Term of his Imprisonment he shall, by and at the Expense of the Managers of the School, be brought back to the School from which he was taken, there to be detained during a Period equal to so much of his Period of Detention as remained unexpired at the Time of his being sent to Prison.

Escaping from School.

XXI. If any Offender sentenced to be detained in a Certified Reformatory School escapes therefrom, he may, at any Time before the Expiration of his Period of Detention, be apprehended without Warrant, and, if the Managers of the School think fit, but not otherwise, may (any other Act to the contrary notwithstanding) be then brought before a Justice or Magistrate having Jurisdiction in the Place or District where he is found, or in the Place or District where the School from which he escaped is situate; and he shall thereupon be liable, on summary Conviction before such a Justice or Magistrate, to be imprisoned, with or without Hard Labour, for any Term not exceeding Three Months; and at the Expiration of such Term he shall, by and at the Expense of the Managers of the School, be brought back to the School from which he escaped, there to be detained during a Period equal to so much of his Period of Detention as remained unexpired at the Time of his escaping.

Penalty on Persons inducing Offenders to escape from Certified Reformatory Schools.

XXII. Every person who commits any of the following Offences, (that is to say,)—

First, knowingly assists directly or indirectly an Offender detained in a Certified Reformatory School to escape from the School;

Second, directly or indirectly induces such an Offender to escape from the School;

Third, knowingly harbours, conceals, or prevents from returning to the School, or assists in harbouring, concealing, or preventing from returning to the School, any Offender who has escaped from a Certified Reformatory School,—

shall, on summary Conviction before Two Justices or a Magistrate, be liable to a Penalty not exceeding Twenty Pounds, or, at the Discretion of the Justices, to be imprisoned for a Term not exceeding Two Months, with or without Hard Labour.

Expenses of Reformatory Schools.

XXIII. The Expense of conveying to any Certified Reformatory School any youthful Offender who has been directed to be detained in such a School, and the Expense of proper Clothing for him requisite for his Admission to the School, shall be defrayed as a current Expense by the Prison Authority within whose District he has been last imprisoned. **Expenses of Conveyance and Clothing.**

XXIV. The Commissioners of Her Majesty's Treasury may contribute, out of Money provided by Parliament, such Sum as the Secretary of State may recommend towards the Expenses of the Custody and Maintenance of any Offender detained in a Certified Reformatory School, or in charge of the Expenses of any Removal of an Offender which has been ordered under the Provisions of this Act. **Contribution by Treasury.**

XXV. The Parent or Step-parent or other Person legally liable to maintain any youthful Offender detained in a Certified Reformatory School shall, if of sufficient Ability, contribute to his Support and Maintenance therein a Sum not exceeding Five Shillings *per* Week. **Order of Justices for Contribution to Maintenance of Offenders in School.**

On the Complaint of the Inspector of Reformatory Schools, or of any Agent of the Inspector, or of any Constable under the Directions of the Inspector (with which Directions the Constable is hereby required to comply), at any Time during the Continuance of the Offender in the School, any Justices or Magistrate having Jurisdiction at the Place where the Parent, Step-parent, or other Person liable as aforesaid resides, may, on Summons to the Parent or Step-parent or other Person liable as aforesaid, examine into his or her Ability, and may, if they or he think fit, make an Order or Decree on him or her for the Payment to the Inspector of Reformatory Schools, or to an Agent of the Inspector, of such weekly Sum, not exceeding Five Shillings *per* Week, as to them or him seems reasonable, during the whole or any Part of the Period for which the Offender is liable to be detained in the School.

Every such Order or Decree may specify the Time during which the Payment is to be made, or may be until further Order.

In *Scotland* any such Order or Decree shall be held to be and to have the Effect of an Order or Decree in each and every Week for Payment of the Sum ordered to be paid for such Week; and under the Warrant for Arrestment therein contained (which the Magistrate is hereby authorized to grant if he sees fit) it shall be lawful to arrest weekly, for Payment of such weekly Sum as aforesaid, the Wages of the Defender due and current, and such Arrestment shall attach not only to the Wages due and payable to the Defender at the Date thereof, but also to the Wages current for the Week or other Term or Period in which such Arrestment is executed, any Law or Statute notwithstanding.

Every such Payment shall go in relief of the Charges on Her Majesty's Treasury, and shall be accounted for as the Commissioners of Her Majesty's Treasury direct.

The Secretary of State may, in his Discretion, remit all or any Part of any Payment so ordered.

Variation of Order.

XXVI. Any Justices or Magistrate having Jurisdiction to make such Order or Decree may from Time to Time vary the same as Circumstances require, on the Application either of the Person on whom the Order or Decree is made, or of the Inspector of Reformatory Schools, or of any Agent of the Inspector, on Fourteen Days Notice being first given of such Application to the Inspector or Agent, or to such Person respectively.

Power of Prison Authority to contract with Managers of Schools.

XXVII. Any Prison Authority may contract with the Managers of any Certified Reformatory School for the Reception and Maintenance therein of Offenders whose Detention in a Certified Reformatory School is directed by a Court, or Justices, or a Magistrate, acting for or within the District of the contracting Prison Authority, in consideration of such Payments as may be from Time to Time agreed on.

Contribution to Establishment and Enlargement of Certified Reformatory Schools.

XXVIII. A Prison Authority in *England* may from Time to Time contribute such Sums of Money, and upon such Conditions as it may think fit, towards the Alteration, Enlargement, or rebuilding of a Certified Reformatory School,—or towards the Support of the Inmates of such a School,—or towards the Management of such a School,—or towards the Establishment or building of a School intended to be a Certified Reformatory School,—or towards the Purchase of any Land required for the Use of an existing Certified Reformatory School, or for the Site of any School intended to be a Certified Reformatory School; provided,—

First, that not less than Two Months previous Notice of the Intention of the Prison Authority to take into consideration the making of such Contribution, at a Time and Place to be mentioned in such Notice, be given by Advertisement in some One or more public Newspaper or Newspapers circulated within the District of the Prison Authority, and also in the manner in which Notices relating to Business to be transacted by that Authority are usually given:

Secondly, that where the Council of a Borough is the Prison Authority, the Order for the Contribution be made at a Special Meeting of the Council:

Thirdly, that where the Contribution is for Alteration, Enlargement, rebuilding, Establishment, or building of a School or intended School, or for Purchase of Land, the Approval of the Secretary of State be previously given for that Alteration, Enlargement, rebuilding, Establishment, building, or Purchase.

In *Scotland* a County Board may contribute to any Certified Reformatory School with the Consent and in the Manner provided by The Prisons (*Scotland*) Administration Act, 1860.

Mode of obtaining Sanction of Secretary of State.

XXIX. In order to obtain the Approval of the Secretary of State as aforesaid where required, the Managers of the School, or Promoters of the intended School, shall forward to the Secretary of State Particulars of the proposed Establishment or Purchase, and a Plan of the proposed Alteration, Enlargement, rebuilding, or building, drawn on such Scale, and accompanied by such Particulars and Estimate of Cost, as the Secretary of State thinks fit to require; and the Secretary of State may approve of the Plan and Particulars submitted to him, with or without Modification, or may disapprove of the same, and his Approval or Disapproval shall be certified by Writing under his Hand.

Expenses of Prison Authorities and County Boards how defrayed.

XXX. Expenses incurred by a Prison Authority in *England* in carrying into effect the Provisions of this Act shall be deemed Expenses incurred by that Authority in carrying into effect the Provisions of The Prisons Act, 1865, and shall be defrayed accordingly.

Expenses incurred by a County Board in *Scotland* in carrying into effect the Provisions of this Act shall be a Charge on the Assessment for current Expenses incurred by that Board in carrying into effect the Provisions of The Prisons (*Scotland*) Administration Act, 1860.

Houses of Refuge, &c., in Scotland.

Power for Local Reformatories in Scotland to receive Offenders.

XXXI. Where in any City, Town, or Place in *Scotland* there has been erected under Local Act of Parliament or otherwise any House of Refuge for youthful Offenders, or any Reformatory School or other similar Institution, the Commissioners, Directors, or Managers thereof may receive and maintain therein if willing so to do, all such young Persons as are sent thereto under this Act, and may pay such Portion of the Fund under their Control as they think proper for the Training, Maintenance, and Disposal of such young Persons: Provided that such House of Refuge, School, or Institution is certified as a Reformatory School under this Act, and the Rules thereof, and all Alterations thereof from Time to Time, are approved by the Secretary of State.

Conditional Pardons.

Power to Secretary of State to send Offenders to Reformatory Schools on conditional Pardon.

XXXII. Where before or after the passing of this Act a youthful Offender has been sentenced to Transportation, Penal Servitude, or Imprisonment, and has been pardoned by Her Majesty on condition of his placing himself under the Care of some Charitable Institution for the Reception and Reformation of youthful Offenders, the Secretary of State may direct him, if under the Age of Sixteen Years, to be sent to a Certified Reformatory School, the Managers of which consent to receive him for a Period of not less than Two Years and not more than Five Years; and thereupon such Offender shall be deemed to be subject to all the Provisions of this Act, as if he had been originally sentenced to Detention in a Certified Reformatory School.

Evidence.

Rules respecting Evidence under this Act.

XXXIII. The following Rules shall be enacted with respect to Evidence under this Act:

(1.) The Production of the *London* or *Edinburgh* Gazette containing a Notice of the Grant or Withdrawal of a Certificate by the Secretary of State to or from a Reformatory School, or of the Resignation of any such Certificate, shall be sufficient Evidence of the Fact of the Publication of such Notice, and also of the Fact of a Certificate having been duly granted to or withdrawn from the School named in the Notice, or resigned by the Managers thereof.

(2.) The Grant of a Certificate to a certified School may also be proved by the Production of the Certificate itself, or of a Copy of the same, purporting to be signed by the Inspector of Reformatory Schools.

(3.) The Production of the Warrant or other Document in pursuance of which a youthful Offender is directed to be sent to a Certified Reformatory School, with a Statement indorsed thereon or annexed thereto, purporting to be signed by the Superintendent or other Person in charge of the School, to the Effect that the Offender therein named was duly received into and is at the Date of the signing thereof detained in the School, or has been otherwise dealt with according to Law, shall in all Proceedings relating to such Offender be Evidence of the Identity of and of the due Conviction and Imprisonment of and subsequent Detention of the Offender named in the Warrant or other Document.

(4.) A Copy of the Rules of a Certified Reformatory

School, purporting to be signed by the Inspector of Reformatory Schools, shall be Evidence of such Rules in all legal Proceedings whatever.

(5.) A School to which any youthful Offender is directed to be sent in pursuance of this Act shall, until the contrary is proved, be deemed to be a Certified Reformatory School within the Meaning of this Act.

Legal Proceedings.

XXXIV. The following Acts, that is to say,—

In *England*, the Act of the Session of the Eleventh and Twelfth Years of Her present Majesty, Chapter Forty-three, intituled *An Act to facilitate the Performance of the Duties of Justices of the Peace out of Sessions, within* England *and* Wales, *with respect to summary Convictions and Orders*, and any Acts amending the same; Recovery of Penalties.

In *Scotland*, The Summary Procedure Act, 1864,—

shall apply to all Offences, Payments, and Orders in respect of which Jurisdiction is given to Justices or a Magistrate by this Act, on which are directed to be prosecuted, enforced, or made in a summary Manner or upon summary Conviction.

XXXV. Any Notice may be served on the Managers of a Certified Reformatory School by delivering the same personally to any One of them, or by sending it, by Post or otherwise, in a Letter addressed to them or any of them at the School, or at the usual or last known Place of Abode of any Manager, or of their Secretary. Service of Notice on Managers of Schools.

Forms.

XXXVI. No Summons, Notice or Order made for the Purpose of carrying into effect the Provisions of this Act shall be invalidated for Want of Form only; and the Forms in the Schedule to this Act annexed, or Forms to the like Effect, may be used in the Cases to which they refer, with such Variations as Circumstances require, and when used shall be deemed sufficient. Use of Forms in Schedule.

Repeal of Enactments.

XXXVII. There shall be repealed the Enactments herein-after mentioned, that is to say,— Enactments herein named repealed.

Section Eleven of the Act of the Session of the First and Second Years of Her present Majesty, Chapter Eighty-two, intituled *An Act for establishing a Prison for young Offenders*; Sect. 11 of 1 & 2 Vict. c. 82.

The Act of Session of the Seventeenth and Eighteenth Years of Her present Majesty, Chapter Eighty-six, intituled *An Act for the better Care and Reformation of youthful Offenders in* Great Britain; 17 & 18 Vict. c. 86.

The Act of the Session of the Eighteenth and Nineteenth 18 & 19 Vict. c. 87.

Years of Her present Majesty, Chapter Eighty-seven, intituled *An Act to amend the Act for the better Care and Reformation of Youthful Offenders, and the Act to render Reformatory and Industrial Schools in* Scotland *more available for the Benefit of Vagrant Children;*

19 & 20 Vict. c. 109. The Act of the Session of the Nineteenth and Twentieth Years of Her present Majesty, Chapter One hundred and nine, intituled *An Act to amend the Mode of committing Criminal and Vagrant Children to Reformatory and Industrial Schools;*

20 & 21 Vict. c. 55. The Act of the Session of the Twentieth and Twenty-first Years of Her present Majesty, Chapter Fifty-five, intituled *An Act to promote the Establishment and Extension of Reformatory Schools in* England:

Provided that such Repeal shall not affect—

1. Any Certificate given or anything duly done under any Act hereby repealed:
2. Any Penalty, Forfeiture, or other Punishment incurred under any Act hereby repealed, or any Remedy for recovering or enforcing the same.

Application of Act to existing Certified Schools.

XXXVIII. This Act shall apply to all Reformatory Schools certified under the Acts hereby repealed, or any of them, and to all Offenders sent to any Reformatory School under the Acts hereby repealed, or any of them, in the same Manner in all respects as if such Schools had been certified and such Offenders had been sent thereto under this Act, with this Qualification, that no youthful Offender shall be detained in any Reformatory School in pursuance of any Order made under the repealed Acts, or any of them, for a longer Period than he would have been liable to be detained therein if this Act had not been passed.

SCHEDULE.

FORMS.

(A.)

Conviction.

to wit. } BE it remembered, That on the Day of at in the said [*County*] of

A.B., under the Age of Sixteen Years, to wit, of the Age of [*Thirteen*] Years, is convicted before us, Two of Her Majesty's Justices of the Peace for the said [*County*], for that [*&c., state Offence in usual Manner*]; and we adjudge the said *A.B.* for his said Offence to be imprisoned in the [*Prison*] at in the said [*County*] [*and to be there kept to Hard Labour*] for the Space of

And that, in pursuance of The Reformatory Schools Act, 1866, we also sentence the said *A.B.* (whose Religious Persuasion appears to us to be) to be sent, at the Expiration of the Term of Imprisonment aforesaid, to Reformatory School at in the County of (the Managers whereof are willing to receive him) [*or* to some Certified Reformatory School to be hereafter, and before the Expiration of the Term of Imprisonment aforesaid, named in this Behalf], and to be there detained for the Period of commencing from and after the Day of [*the Date of the Expiration of the Sentence*].

Given under our Hands and Seals, the Day and Year first above mentioned, at in the [*County*] aforesaid.

J.S. (L.S.)
L.M. (L.S.)

(B.)

Order of Detention.

to wit. } To the Constable of , and to the Keeper of the [*Prison*] at in the said [*County*] of .

Whereas *A.B.*, late of [*Labourer*], under the Age of Sixteen Years, to wit, of the Age of [*Thirteen*] Years, was this Day duly convicted before the undersigned, Two of Her Majesty's Justices of the Peace in and for the said [*County*] of , for that [*&c., stating the Offence as in the Conviction*], and it was thereby adjudged that the said *A.B.*, for his said Offence, should be imprisoned in the [*Prison*] at in the said [*County*], [*and be there kept to Hard Labour*] for the Space of ; and in pursuance of The Reformatory Schools Act, 1866, the said *A.B.* (whose Religious Persuasion appeared to us to be) was thereby sentenced to be sent, at the Expiration of the Term of Imprisonment aforesaid, to the Reformatory School at in the County of (the Managers whereof are willing to receive him therein). [*or* to some Certified Reformatory School to be before the Expiration of the said Term named in that Behalf,] and to be there detained for the Period of commencing from and after the Day of [*the Date of the Expiration of the Sentence*]:

These are therefore to command you the said Constable of , to take the said *A.B.*, and him safely convey to the [*Prison*] at aforesaid, and there to deliver him to the Keeper thereof, together with this Precept: And we do hereby command you, the said Keeper of the said [*Prison*], to receive the said *A.B.* into your Custody in the said [*Prison*], there to imprison him [*and keep him to Hard Labour*] for the Space of : [And we further command you, the said Keeper, to send the said *A.B.* at the Expiration of his Term of Imprisonment aforesaid as and in the Manner directed by The Reformatory Schools Act, 1866, to the Reformatory School at aforesaid [*or* to the Reformatory School named by an Order indorsed hereon under the Hands and Seals of us, or under the Hand and Seal of One other of Her Majesty's Justices of the Peace for the said *County*, being a Visiting Justice of the said Prison], together with this Order :] And for so doing this shall be your sufficient Warrant.

Given under our Hands and Seals, this Day of in the Year of our Lord at in the [*County*] aforesaid.

J.S. (L.S.).
J.M. (L.S.)

(C.)

Nomination of School indorsed on the Order of Detention.

IN pursuance of The Reformatory Schools Act, 1866, I, the undersigned, One of Her Majesty's Justices of the Peace for the [*County*] of hereby name the Reformatory School at in the County of as the School to which the within-named *A.B.* (whose Religious Persuasion appears to me to be) is to be sent as within provided [*add where required* in lieu of the School within (*or* above) named].

Given under my Hand and Seal, this Day of at in the County of

E.F. (L.S.)

(D.)

Complaint for enforcing in England Contribution from Parent, &c.

(E.)

Summons to Parent, &c.

(F.)

Order on Parent, &c. in England to Contribute a Weekly Sum.

(G.)

Distress Warrant for Amount in arrear.

(H.)

Commitment in default of Distress.

(J.)

Order on Parent in Scotland, &c. for Contribution.

The Sheriff [*or as the Case may be*] having considered the Complaint of *E.F.*, the Inspector of Reformatory Schools, made under

The Reformatory Schools Act, 1866, and having heard Parties thereon [*or* in absence of *C.D.*, *designing him*, duly cited, but not appearing], pursuant to the said Act, decerns *C.D.* complained on, weekly and every Week from the Day of to pay to the said *E.F.*, or to his Agent from Time to Time authorized to receive the same, the Sum of Shillings for the Support and Maintenance of *A.B.*, Son [*or as the Case may be*] of the said *C.D.*, now detained in the Certified Reformatory School of under an Order by of Date until the said *A.B.* attains the Age of Years or is lawfully discharged from the said School, and grants Warrant of Arrestment to be executed by any Constable or Messenger at Arms.

Given under my Hand, this Day of at in the County aforesaid,

[*Magistrate's Signature.*]

CAP. CXVIII.

An Act to consolidate and amend the Acts relating to Industrial Schools in Great Britain.—[*10th August* 1866.]

BE it enacted by the Queen's most Excellent Majesty, by and with the Advice and Consent of the Lords Spiritual and Temporal, and Commons, in this present Parliament assembled, and by the Authority of the same, as follows:

Preliminary.

I. This Act may be cited as The Industrial Schools Act, 1866. Short Title.

II. This Act shall not extend to *Ireland*. Extent of Act.

III. The Acts described in the First Schedule to this Act are hereby repealed; but this Repeal shall not affect the past Operation of any such Act, or the Force or Operation of any Certificate, Order, Rule, or Sentence made or passed, or the Validity or Invalidity of anything done or suffered, or any Right, Title, Obligation, or Liability accrued, before the passing of this Act; nor shall this Act interfere with the Institution or Prosecution of any Proceeding in respect of any Offence committed against, or any Penalty or Forfeiture incurred under, any Act hereby repealed. Acts described in First Schedule repealed.

IV. In this Act— Interpretation of Terms.

The Term "Justice" applies to *England* only, and means a Justice of the Peace having Jurisdiction in the place where the Matter requiring the Cognizance of a Justice arises:

Enlargement, rebuilding, Establishment, or building of a School or intended School, or for Purchase of Land, the Approval of the Secretary of State be previously given for that Alteration, Enlargement, rebuilding, Establishment, building, or Purchase.

In *Scotland* a County Board may contribute to any Certified Industrial School with the Consent and in the Manner provided by The Prisons (*Scotland*) Administration Act, 1860, respecting Contributions to Reformatories.

Mode of obtaining Approval of Secretary of State

XIII. In order to obtain the Approval of the Secretary of State as aforesaid where required, the Managers of the School, or Promoters of the intended School, shall forward to the Secretary of State Particulars of the proposed Establishment or Purchase, and a Plan of the proposed Alteration, Enlargement, rebuilding or building, drawn on such Scale, and accompanied by such Particulars and Estimate of Cost, as the Secretary of State thinks fit to require; and the Secretary of State may approve of the Particulars and Plan submitted to him, with or without Modification, or may disapprove of the same, and his Approval or Disapproval shall be certified by Writing under his Hand.

Classes of Children to be detained in Certified Industrial Schools.

As to Children under 14 Years of Age found begging, &c.

XIV. Any Person may bring before Two Justices or a Magistrate any Child apparently under the Age of Fourteen Years that comes within any of the following Descriptions, namely,—

That is found begging or receiving Alms (whether actually or under the Pretext of selling or offering for Sale any Thing), or being in any Street or public Place for the Purpose of so begging or receiving Alms;

That is found wandering and not having any Home or settled Place of Abode, or proper Guardianship, or visible Means of Subsistence;

That is found destitute, either being an Orphan or having a surviving Parent who is undergoing Penal Servitude or Imprisonment;

That frequents the Company of reputed Thieves.

The Justices or Magistrate before whom a Child is brought as coming within One of those Descriptions, if satisfied on Inquiry of that Fact, and that it is expedient to deal with him under this Act, may order him to be sent to a Certified Industrial School.

As to Children under 12 Years of Age charged with Offences.

XV. Where a Child apparently under the Age of Twelve Years is charged before Two Justices or a Magistrate with an Offence punishable by Imprisonment or a less Punishment, but has not been in *England* convicted of Felony, or in *Scotland* of Theft, and the Child ought, in the Opinion of the Justices or Magistrate (regard being had to his Age and to the Circumstances of the Case), to be dealt with under this Act, the Justices or Magistrate may order him to be sent to a Certified Industrial School.

As to refractory Children under 14 Years of Age in Charge of Parent, &c.

XVI. Where the Parent or Step-parent or Guardian of a Child apparently under the Age of Fourteen Years represents to Two Justices or a Magistrate that he is unable to control the Child, and that he desires that the Child be sent to an Industrial School under this Act, the Justices or Magistrate, if satisfied on Inquiry that it is expedient to deal with the Child under this Act, may order him to be sent to a Certified Industrial School.

As to refractory Children under 14 Years of Age in Workhouses, Pauper Schools, &c.

XVII. Where the Guardians of the Poor of a Union or of a Parish wherein Relief is administered by a Board of Guardians, or the Board of Management of a District Pauper School, or the Parochial Board of a Parish or Combination, represent to Two Justices or a Magistrate that any Child apparently under the Age of Fourteen Years maintained in a Workhouse or Pauper School of a Union or Parish, or in a District Pauper School, or in the Poorshouse of a Parish or Combination, is refractory, or is the Child of Parents either of whom has been convicted of a Crime or Offence punishable with Penal Servitude or Imprisonment, and that it is desirable that he be sent to an Industrial School under this Act, the Justices or Magistrate may, if satisfied that it is expedient to deal with the Child under this Act, order him to be sent to a Certified Industrial School.

Order of Detention.

Form and Contents of Order sending Child to School.

XVIII. The Order of Justices or a Magistrate sending a Child to a School (in this Act referred to as the Order of Detention in a School) shall be in Writing signed by the Justices or Magistrate, and shall specify the Name of the School.

The School shall be some Certified Industrial School (whether situate within the Jurisdiction of the Justices or Magistrate making the Order or not) the Managers of which are willing to receive the Child; and the Reception of the Child by the Managers of the School shall be deemed to be an Undertaking by them to teach, train, clothe, lodge, and feed him during the whole Period for which he is liable to be detained in the School, or until the Withdrawal or Resignation of the Certificate of the School takes effect, or until the Contribution out of Money provided by Parliament towards the Custody and Maintenance of the Children detained in the School is discontinued, whichever shall first happen.

The School named in the Order shall be presumed to be a Certified Industrial School until the contrary is shown.

In determining on the School the Justices or Magistrate shall endeavour to ascertain the Religious Persuasion to which the Child belongs, and shall, if possible, select a School conducted in accordance with such Religious Persuasion, and the Order shall specify such Religious Persuasion.

The Order shall specify the Time for which the Child is to be detained in the School, being such Time as to the Justices or Magistrate seems proper for the teaching and training of the Child, but not in any Case extending beyond the Time when the Child will attain the Age of Sixteen Years.

Temporary Detention in Workhouse, &c.

XIX. Two Justices or a Magistrate, while Inquiry is being made respecting a Child or respecting a School to which he may be sent, may, by Order signed by them or him, order the Child to be taken to the Workhouse or Poorshouse of the Union, Parish, or Combination in which he is found or resident,—or where (in *Scotland*) there is no such Poorshouse, or the Poorshouse is at an inconvenient Distance, to such other Place, not being a Prison, as the Magistrate thinks fit, the Occupier whereof is willing to receive him,—and to be detained therein at the Cost of the Union, Parish, or Combination for any Time not exceeding Seven Days, or until an Order is sooner made for his Discharge or for his being sent to a Certified Industrial School; and the Guardians of the Poor for the Union or Parish, or the Keeper of the Poorshouse, or other Person to whom the Order is addressed, are and is hereby empowered and required to detain him accordingly.

Power to Parent, &c. to apply to remove Child to a School conducted in accordance with Child's Religious Persuasion.

XX. If the Parent, Step-parent, or Guardian, or if there be no Parent, Step-parent, or Guardian, then the Godparent or nearest adult Relative, of a Child sent or about to be sent to a Certified Industrial School which is not conducted in accordance with the Religious Persuasion to which the Child belongs, states to the Justices or Magistrate by whom the Order of Detention has been or is about to be made (or to Two Justices or a Magistrate having the like Jurisdiction) that he objects to the Child being sent to or detained in the School specified or about to be specified in the Order, and names another Certified Industrial School in *Great Britain* which is conducted in accordance with the Religious Persuasion to which the Child belongs, and signifies his Desire that the Child be sent thereto, then and in every such Case the Justices or Magistrate shall, upon Proof of such Child's Religious Persuasion, comply with the Request of the Applicant, provided,—

First, that the Application be made before the Child has

been sent to a Certified Industrial School, or within Thirty Days after his Arrival at such a School:

Secondly, that the Applicant Show to the Satisfaction of the Justices or Magistrate that the Managers of the School named by him are willing to receive the Child:

Provided always, with respect to *Scotland*, that if any Child who has become chargeable to any Parish, and who is under this Section sent from *Scotland* to a School out of *Scotland*, might have been removed from *Scotland* (under any Act for the Time being in force relating to the relief of the Poor in *Scotland*) at the Instance of the Inspector of the Poor of the Parish to which he has become chargeable, had he not been sent out of *Scotland* under this Section, then and in every such Case the Chargeability on such Parish for such Child shall cease on his being so sent out of *Scotland*.

Where Order to be for Detention in School of Parochial Board.

XXI. In *Scotland* where a Magistrate is about to make or has made an Order for sending a Child to a Certified Industrial School, and the Child is chargeable at the Time to any Parish, or has been so chargeable within Three Months then last past, and there is in that Parish a Certified Industrial School maintained by the Parochial Board thereof, and conducted in accordance with the Religious Persuasion to which the Child belongs, and the Inspector of the Poor of such Parish certifies to the Magistrate (or to a Magistrate having the like Jurisdiction) that he requires the Child to be sent to the Certified Industrial School in such Parish maintained by the Parochial Board thereof, and conducted in accordance with the Religious Persuasion to which the Child belongs, then and in every such Case the Magistrate shall direct the Child to be sent to the last-mentioned School accordingly, the Inspector of the Poor defraying the Expense of conveying the Child thither; provided that where the Order of Detention has been made, the Application of the Inspector to the Magistrate be made within Fourteen Days of the Day of the making of the Order.

Order to be Warrant for Conveyance and Detention.

XXII. The Order of Detention in a School shall be forwarded to the Managers of the School with the Child, and shall be a sufficient Warrant for the Conveyance of the Child thither, and his Detention there.

Expenses of Conveyance to School.

XXIII. The Expense of conveying to a Certified Industrial School a Child ordered to be sent there shall be defrayed by the Police Authorities by whom he is conveyed, and shall be deemed part of the current Expenses of those Police Authorities.

XXIV. An Instrument purporting to be an Order of

Evidence of Order of Detention. Detention in a School and to be signed by Two Justices or a Magistrate, or purporting to be a Copy of such an Order and to be certified as such a Copy by the Clerk to the Justices or Magistrate by whom the Order was made, shall be Evidence of the Order.

Management of School.

Religious Instruction in School. XXV. A Minister of the Religious Persuasion specified in the Order of Detention as that to which the Child appears to the Justices or Magistrate to belong may visit the Child at the School on such Days and at such Times as are from Time to Time fixed by Regulations made by the Secretary of State for the Purpose of instructing him in Religion.

Lodging Child out of School. XXVI. The Managers of a School may permit a Child sent there under this Act to lodge at the Dwelling of his Parent or of any trustworthy and respectable Person, so that the Managers teach, train, clothe, and feed the Child in the School as if he were lodging in the School itself, and so that they report to the Secretary of State, in such Manner as he thinks fit to require, every Instance in which they exercise a Discretion under this Section.

Licence for living out of School. XXVII. The Managers of a School may, at any Time after the Expiration of Eighteen Months of the Period of Detention allotted to a Child, by Licence under their Hands, permit him to live with any trustworthy and respectable Person named in the License, and willing to receive and take charge of him.

Any Licence so granted shall not be in force for more than Three Months, but may at any Time before the Expiration of those Three Months be renewed for a further Period not exceeding Three Months, to commence from the Expiration of the previous Period of Three Months, and so from Time to Time until the Period of the Child's Detention is expired.

Any such Licence may also be revoked at any Time by the Managers of the School by Writing under their Hands, and thereupon the Child to whom the Licence related may be required by them, by Writing under their Hands, to return to the School.

The Time during which a Child is absent from a School in pursuance of a Licence shall, except where such Licence has been forfeited by his Misconduct, be deemed to be Part of the Time of his Detention in the School, and at the Expiration of the Time allowed by the License he shall be taken back to the School.

A Child escaping from the Person with whom he is placed under a Licence, or refusing to return to the School on the Revocation of his Licence, or at the Expiration of the Time allowed thereby, shall be deemed to have escaped from the School.

Power to apprentice Child.

XXVIII. The Managers of a School may, at any Time after a Child has been placed out on Licence as aforesaid, if he conducted himself well during his Absence from the School, bind him, with his own Consent, Apprentice to any Trade, Calling, or Service, notwithstanding that his Period of Detention has not expired, and every such Binding shall be valid and effectual to all Intents.

Rules of School to be approved by Secretary of State.

XXIX. The Managers of a Certified Industrial School may from Time to Time make Rules for the Management and Discipline of the School, not being inconsistent with the Provisions of this Act; but those Rules shall not be enforced until they have been approved in Writing by the Secretary of State; and Rules so approved shall not be altered without the like approval.

A printed Copy of Rules purporting to be the Rules of a School so approved and to be signed by the Inspector of Industrial Schools shall be Evidence of the Rules of the School.

Evidence as to Reception in School, &c.

XXX. A Certificate purporting to be signed by One of the Managers of a Certified Industrial School or their Secretary, or by the Superintendent or other Person in charge of the School, to the Effect that the Child therein named was duly received into and is at the signing thereof detained in the School, or has been duly discharged or removed therefrom or otherwise disposed of according to Law, shall be Evidence of the Matters therein stated.

Liability to Removal not affected by Stay a School.

XXXI. The Time during which a Child is detained in a School under this Act shall for all Purposes be excluded in the Computation of Time mentioned in Section One of the Act of the Session of the Ninth and Tenth Years of Her Majesty's Reign (Chapter Sixty-six), "to amend the Laws relating to the Removal of the Poor," as amended by any other Act.

Offences at School, &c.

Refusal to conform to Rules.

XXXII. If a Child sent to a Certified Industrial School, and while liable to be detained there, being apparently above Ten Years of Age, and whether lodging in the School itself or not, wilfully neglects or wilfully refuses to conform to the Rules of the School, he shall be guilty of an Offence against this Act, and on summary Conviction thereof before Two Justices or a Magistrate shall be liable to be imprisoned, with or without Hard Labour, for any Term not less than Fourteen Days and not exceeding Three Months, and the Justices or Magistrate before whom he is convicted may direct him to be sent at the Expiration of the Term of his Imprisonment to a Certified Reforma-

Evidence of Order of Detention.

Detention in a School and to be signed by Two Justices or a Magistrate, or purporting to be a Copy of such an Order and to be certified as such a Copy by the Clerk to the Justices or Magistrate by whom the Order was made, shall be Evidence of the Order.

Management of School.

Religious Instruction in School.

XXV. A Minister of the Religious Persuasion specified in the Order of Detention as that to which the Child appears to the Justices or Magistrate to belong may visit the Child at the School on such Days and at such Times as are from Time to Time fixed by Regulations made by the Secretary of State for the Purpose of instructing him in Religion.

Lodging Child out of School.

XXVI. The Managers of a School may permit a Child sent there under this Act to lodge at the Dwelling of his Parent or of any trustworthy and respectable Person, so that the Managers teach, train, clothe, and feed the Child in the School as if he were lodging in the School itself, and so that they report to the Secretary of State, in such Manner as he thinks fit to require, every Instance in which they exercise a Discretion under this Section.

Licence for living out of School.

XXVII. The Managers of a School may, at any Time after the Expiration of Eighteen Months of the Period of Detention allotted to a Child, by Licence under their Hands, permit him to live with any trustworthy and respectable Person named in the License, and willing to receive and take charge of him.

Any Licence so granted shall not be in force for more than Three Months, but may at any Time before the Expiration of those Three Months be renewed for a further Period not exceeding Three Months, to commence from the Expiration of the previous Period of Three Months, and so from Time to Time until the Period of the Child's Detention is expired.

Any such Licence may also be revoked at any Time by the Managers of the School by Writing under their Hands, and thereupon the Child to whom the Licence related may be required by them, by Writing under their Hands, to return to the School.

The Time during which a Child is absent from a School in pursuance of a Licence shall, except where such Licence has been forfeited by his Misconduct, be deemed to be Part of the Time of his Detention in the School, and at the Expiration of the Time allowed by the License he shall be taken back to the School.

A Child escaping from the Person with whom he is placed under a Licence, or refusing to return to the School on the Revocation of his Licence, or at the Expiration of the Time allowed thereby, shall be deemed to have escaped from the School.

XXVIII. The Managers of a School may, at any Time after a Child has been placed out on Licence as aforesaid, if he conducted himself well during his Absence from the School, bind him, with his own Consent, Apprentice to any Trade, Calling, or Service, notwithstanding that his Period of Detention has not expired, and every such Binding shall be valid and effectual to all Intents. Power to apprentice Child.

XXIX. The Managers of a Certified Industrial School may from Time to Time make Rules for the Management and Discipline of the School, not being inconsistent with the Provisions of this Act; but those Rules shall not be enforced until they have been approved in Writing by the Secretary of State; and Rules so approved shall not be altered without the like approval. Rules of School to be approved by Secretary of State.

A printed Copy of Rules purporting to be the Rules of a School so approved and to be signed by the Inspector of Industrial Schools shall be Evidence of the Rules of the School.

XXX. A Certificate purporting to be signed by One of the Managers of a Certified Industrial School or their Secretary, or by the Superintendent or other Person in charge of the School, to the Effect that the Child therein named was duly received into and is at the signing thereof detained in the School, or has been duly discharged or removed therefrom or otherwise disposed of according to Law, shall be Evidence of the Matters therein stated. Evidence as to Reception in School, &c.

XXXI. The Time during which a Child is detained in a School under this Act shall for all Purposes be excluded in the Computation of Time mentioned in Section One of the Act of the Session of the Ninth and Tenth Years of Her Majesty's Reign (Chapter Sixty-six), "to amend the Laws relating to the Removal of the Poor," as amended by any other Act. Liability to Removal not affected by Stay a School.

Offences at School, &c.

XXXII. If a Child sent to a Certified Industrial School, and while liable to be detained there, being apparently above Ten Years of Age, and whether lodging in the School itself or not, wilfully neglects or wilfully refuses to conform to the Rules of the School, he shall be guilty of an Offence against this Act, and on summary Conviction thereof before Two Justices or a Magistrate shall be liable to be imprisoned, with or without Hard Labour, for any Term not less than Fourteen Days and not exceeding Three Months, and the Justices or Magistrate before whom he is convicted may direct him to be sent at the Expiration of the Term of his Imprisonment to a Certified Reforma- Refusal to conform to Rules.

29 & 30 Vict. c. 117.

tory School, and to be there detained subject and according to the Provisions of the Reformatory Schools Act, 1866.

Penalty on Child escaping from School.

XXXIII. If a Child sent to a Certified Industrial School, and while liable to be detained there, and whether lodging in the School itself or not, escapes from the School, or neglects to attend thereat, he shall be guilty of an Offence against this Act, and may at any Time before the Expiration of his Period of Detention be apprehended without Warrant, and may (any other Act to the contrary notwithstanding) be then brought before a Justice or Magistrate having Jurisdiction in the Place or District where he is found, or in the Place or District where the School from which he escaped is situate; and he shall thereupon be liable, on summary Conviction before such a Justice or Magistrate, to be, by and at the Expense of the Managers of the School, brought back to the same School, there to be detained during a period equal to so much of his Period of Detention as remained unexpired at the Time of his committing the Offence.

If the Child charged with such an Offence is apparently above Ten Years of Age, then, on his summary Conviction of the Offence before Two such Justices or such a Magistrate, he shall be liable, at the Discretion of the Justices or Magistrate, instead of being sent back to the same School, to be imprisoned with or without Hard Labour for any Term not less than Fourteen Days and not exceeding Three Months, and the Justices or Magistrate before whom he is convicted may direct him to be sent at the Expiration of the Term of his Imprisonment to a Certified Reformatory School, and to be there detained subject and according to the Provisions of The Reformatory Schools Act, 1866.

29 & 30 Vict. c. 117.

Penalty on Persons inducing Offenders to escape from Certified Industrial Schools.

XXXIV. If any Person does any of the following Things, (that is to say,)—

First, knowingly assists, directly or indirectly, a Child liable to be detained in a Certified Industrial School to escape from the School;

Second, directly or indirectly induces such a Child so to escape;

Third, knowingly harbours or conceals a Child who has so escaped, or prevents him from returning to School, or knowingly assists in so doing,—

Every such Person shall be guilty of an Offence against this Act, and shall, on summary Conviction thereof before Two Justices or a Magistrate, be liable to a Penalty not exceeding Twenty Pounds, or, at the Discretion of the Justices, to be imprisoned for any Term not exceeding Two Months, with or without Hard Labour.

Expenses of Children in Schools.

XXXV. The Commissioners of Her Majesty's Treasury may from Time to Time contribute, out of Money provided by Parliament, for the Purpose, such Sums as the Secretary of State from Time to Time thinks fit to recommend towards the Custody and Maintenance of Children detained in Certified Industrial Schools; provided that such Contributions shall not exceed Two Shillings *per* Head *per* Week for Children detained on the Application of their Parents, Step-parents, or Guardians. Power of Treason to contribute towards Custody, &c. of Children detained.

XXXVI. In *England* a Prison Authority may contract with the Managers of a Certified Industrial School for the Reception and Maintenance therein of such Children as are from Time to Time ordered by Justices to be sent there from the District of the Prison Authority. Power to Prison Authority to contract for Reception of Children in Schools.

XXXVII. The Guardians of the Poor of a Union or Parish, or the Board of Management of a District Pauper School, or the Parochial Board of a Parish or Combination, may from Time to Time, with the Consent in *England* of the Poor Law Board, and in *Scotland* of the Board of Supervision, contribute such Sums as they think fit towards the Maintenance of Children detained in a Certified Industrial School on their Application. Power to Guardians of Poor, &c. to contribute.

XXXVIII. In *Scotland* where a Child sent to a Certified Industrial School under this Act is at the Time of his being so sent, or within Three Months then last past has been, chargeable to any Parish, the Parochial Board and Inspector of the Poor of the Parish of the Settlement of such Child, if the Settlement of the Child is in any Parish in *Scotland*, shall, as long as he continues so chargeable, be liable to repay to the Commissioners of Her Majesty's Treasury all Expenses incurred in maintaining him at School under this Act to an Amount not exceeding Five Shillings *per* Week, and in default of Payment those Expenses may be recovered by the Inspector of Industrial Schools, or any Agent of the Inspector, in a summary Manner before a Magistrate having Jurisdiction in the Place where the Parish is situate. Recovery of Cost of Maintenance in Schools in Scotland when Parishes, &c. are liable.

Provided always, that nothing in this Act shall prevent any Parochial Board on whose Funds the Cost of Support of any such Child has become a Charge from adopting such Steps for the Recovery of any Sums which may have been paid by such Parochial Board for any such Child against the Parish of his Settlement, or for his Removal, as may be competent to them under any Act for the Time being in force relating to the Relief of the Poor in *Scotland*.

XXXIX. The Parent, Step-parent, or other Person for the Time being legally liable to maintain a Child detained Contribution by Parent.

in a Certified Industrial School shall, if of sufficient Ability, contribute to his Maintenance and Training therein a Sum not exceeding Five Shillings *per* Week.

Order for Enforcement of Contribution by Parent, &c.

XL. On the Complaint of the Inspector of Industrial Schools, or of any Agent of the Inspector, or of any Constable under the Directions of the Inspector (with which Directions every Constable is hereby required to comply), at any Time during the Detention of a Child in a Certified Industrial School, Two Justices or a Magistrate having Jurisdiction at the Place where the Parent, Step-parent, or other Person liable as aforesaid resides may, on Summons to the Parent, Step-parent, or other Person liable as aforesaid, examine into his Ability to maintain the Child, and may, if they or he think fit, make an Order or Decree on him for the Payment to the Inspector or his Agent of such weekly Sum, not exceeding Five Shillings *per* Week, as to them or him seems reasonable, during the whole or any Part of the Time for which the Child is liable to be detained in the School.

Every such Order or Decree may specify the Time during which the Payment is to be made, or may direct the Payment to be made until further Order.

In *Scotland* any such Order or Decree shall be held to be and to have the Effect of an Order or Decree in each and every Week for Payment of the Sum ordered or decreed to be paid for such Week; and under the Warrant for Arrestment therein contained (which the Magistrate is hereby authorized to grant if he sees fit), it shall be lawful to arrest weekly for Payment of such weekly Sum as aforesaid the Wages of the Defender due and current, and such Arrestment shall attach not only to the Wages due and payable to the Defender at the Date thereof, but also to the Wages current for the Week or other Term or Period in which such Arrestment is executed, any Law or Statute notwithstanding.

Every such Payment or a proper proportionate Part thereof shall go in relief of the Charges on Her Majesty's Treasury, and the same shall be accounted for as the Commissioners of Her Majesty's Treasury direct, and where the Amount of the Payment ordered in respect of any Child exceeds the Amount contributed by the Commissioners of Her Majesty's Treasury in respect of that Child, the Balance shall be accounted for and paid to the Managers of the School.

The Secretary of State may, in his Discretion, remit wholly or partially any Payment so ordered.

Two Justices or a Magistrate having Jurisdiction to make such an Order or Decree may from Time to Time vary any such Order or Decree as Circumstances require, on the Application either of the Person on whom such Order or Decree is made, or of the Inspector of Industrial Schools, or his Agent, on Fourteen Days' Notice being first given of such Application to the Inspector or Agent, or to such Person respectively.

Discharge, &c., of Children from School.

Detention to cease on Child attaining Sixteen.

XLI. A Person who has attained the Age of Sixteen Years shall not be detained in a Certified Industrial School except with his own Consent in Writing.

Transfer to another School by Secretary of State.

XLII. The Secretary of State may at any Time order a Child to be transferred from one Certified Industrial School to another, but so that the whole Period of his Detention be not thereby increased.

The Secretary of State may also at any Time order a Child being under Sentence of Detention in an Industrial School established under any other Act of Parliament, the General Rules for the Government whereof have been approved by the Secretary of State, to be transferred to a Certified Industrial School under this Act; and in that Case the Child shall after the Transfer be deemed to be subject in all respects to the Provisions of this Act, but so that the whole Period of his Detention be not by such Transfer increased.

The Commissioners of Her Majesty's Treasury may pay, out of Money provided by Parliament for the Purpose, such Sum as the Secretary of State thinks fit to recommend, in discharge of the Expenses of the Removal of any Child Transferred under the Provisions of this Act.

Disharge by Secretary of State.

XLIII. The Secretary of State may at any Time order any Child to be discharged from a Certified Industrial School or from any Industrial School established under any other Act of Parliament, the General Rules for the Government whereof have been approved by the Secretary of State, either absolutely or on such Condition as the Secretary of State approves, and the Child shall be discharged accordingly.

Withdrawal, &c., of Certificate of School.

Power for Secretary of State to withdraw Certificate.

XLIV. The Secretary of State, if dissatisfied with the Condition of a Certified Industrial School, may at any Time, by Notice under his Hand addressed to and served on the Managers thereof, declare that the Certificate of the School is withdrawn as from a Time specified in the Notice, not being less than Six Months after the Date thereof; and at that Time the Certificate shall be deemed to be withdrawn accordingly, and the School shall thereupon cease to be a Certified Industrial School.

Resignation of Cer-

XLV. The Managers or the Executors or Administrators

for a longer Period than he would have been liable to be detained if this Act had not been passed.

THE FIRST SCHEDULE.

Acts Repealed.

24 & 25 Vict. c. 113.	The Industrial Schools Act, 1861.
24 & 25 Vict. c. 132.	The Industrial Schools (Scotland) Act, 1861.
25 & 26 Vict. c. 10.	An Act for continuing for a further limited Time, and for extending the Operation of Orders made under the Industrial Schools Act, 1861, and The Industrial Schools (Scotland) Act, 1861.

THE SECOND SCHEDULE.

FORMS.

(A.)

Order sending Child to Industrial School.

to wit. } BE it remembered, That on the Day of in pursuance of The Industrial Schools Act, 1866, we, Two of Her Majesty's Justices of the Peace for the said [*County*] of , do order that *A.B.* of (whose Religious Persuasion appears to us to be), being a Child subject to the Provisions of Section of the said Act, be sent to the Certified Industrial School at , and that he be detained there during .

(Signed) *L.M.*
N.O.

(C.)

Complaint for enforcing in England Contribution from Parent, &c.

(D.)

Summons to Parent, &c.

(E.)

Order on Parent, &c. to Contribute a Weekly Sum.

(F.)

Distress Warrant for Amount in arrear.

(G.)

Commitment in default of Distress.

(H.)

Order in Scotland on Parent, for Payment towards Maintenance of Child.

The Sheriff [*or as the Case may be*] having considered the Complaint of *E.F.*, the Inspector of Industrial Schools, made under The Industrial Schools Act, 1866, and having heard Parties thereon [*or*, in absence of *C.D.*, *designing him*, duly cited, but not appearing], pursuant to the said Act, decerns *C.D.* complained on, weekly and every Week from the Day of to pay to the said *E.F.*, or to his Agent from Time to Time authorized to receive the same, the Sum of Shillings for the Maintenance and Training of *A.B.*, Son [*or as the Case may be*] of the said *C.D.*, now detained in the Certified Industrial School of under an Order by of Date until the said Child attains the Age of Sixteen Years or is lawfully discharged from the said School, and grants Warrant of Arrestment to be executed by any Constable or Messenger at Arms.

Given under my Hand this Day of at in the County aforesaid

[*Magistrate's Signature.*]

CAP. CXXI.

An Act for the Amendment of the Law relating to Treaties of Extradition, [10th *August* 1866.]

WHEREAS Difficulties have been experienced in carrying into execution Treaties for the Extradition of Persons accused of Crimes between Her Majesty and the Sovereigns or Governments of certain Foreign States: And whereas the Statutes now in force for this Purpose have been found insufficient: And whereas it is expedient to amend the same, and to give greater Facilities than at present exist under the aforesaid Statutes for the Admission in Evidence of judicial or official Documents or Copies of Documents:

Be it enacted by the Queen's most Excellent Majesty, by and with the Advice and Consent of the Lords Spiritual and Temporal, and Commons, in this present Parliament assembled, and by the Authority of the same, as follows:

I. That Warrants of Arrest and Copies of Depositions signed or taken by or before a Judge or competent Magistrate in any Foreign State with which Her Majesty may have entered into, or may hereafter enter into, any Treaty

Warrants of Arrest Copies of Depositions to be received in

Evidence if authenticated in manner specified by this Act.

for the Extradition of fugitive Offenders or Persons accused of Crimes, shall henceforth be received in Evidence if authenticated in the Manner following, that is to say, if the Warrant of Arrest purports to be signed by a Judge or other competent Magistrate of the Country in which the same shall have been issued, and if the Copies of Depositions purport to be certified under the Hand of such Judge or Magistrate to be true Copies of the original Depositions, and if the Signature of the Judge or Magistrate in each Case shall be authenticated in the Manner usual in the respective States or Countries by the proper Officer of the Department of the Minister of Justice, and sealed with the official Seal of such Minister; and all Courts of Justice and Magistrates in Her Majesty's Dominions shall take judicial Notice of such official Seal, and shall admit the Documents so authenticated by it to be received in Evidence without further Proof.

This Act to be construed with 8 & 9 Vict. c. 113, and 14 & 15 Vict. c. 99.

II. This Act shall be construed with an Act passed in the Eighth and Ninth Years of the Reign of Her Majesty, Chapter One hundred and thirteen, intituled *An Act to facilitate the Admission in Evidence of official and other Documents*, and also with an Act passed in the Fourteenth and Fifteenth Years of the Reign of Her Majesty, Chapter Ninety-nine, intituled *An Act to amend the Law of Evidence.*

Duration of Act.

III. The Duration of this Act shall be limited to the First Day of *September* One thousand eight hundred and sixty-seven.

LOCAL AND PERSONAL ACTS,

DECLARED PUBLIC, AFFECTING SCOTLAND.

18. An Act to authorise the *Paisley* Water Commissioners to make and maintain additional Reservoirs and other Works, and to give an increased Supply of Water; and for other Purposes.

28. An Act for more effectually maintaining and keeping in repair the Roads, Highways, and Bridges in the Counties of *Ross* and *Cromarty;* for making new Roads and Bridges in the said Counties; and for other Purposes.

30. An Act to enable the *Morayshire* Railway Company to raise Capital by creating new Shares or Stock; and for other Purposes.

39. An Act for Supplying with Water the Burgh of *Tain* and Places adjacent.

66. An Act to amend an Act for repressing Juvenile Delinquency in the City of *Glasgow.*

67. An Act for more effectually maintaining and keeping in repair the Roads, Highways, and Bridges in the County of *Banff;* for making new Roads in the said County; and for other Purposes.

85. An Act for the Improvement of the City of *Glasgow*, and the Construction of new, and widening, altering, and diverting of existing Streets in the said City; and for other Purposes.

102. An Act for the Construction of a Wet Dock at the Harbour of *Montrose;* and for other Purposes.

104. An Act for erecting and maintaining a new Court House, Town House, County and Town Hall, Police, and other County and Municipal Buildings and Offices for the County and City of *Aberdeen;* and for other Purposes.

108. An Act for sanctioning the Construction of certain Deviations of the authorized Lines of the *Crofthead and Kilmarnock Extension* Railway, and of the *Glasgow and South-western* (*Kilmarnock Direct*) Railway; and for other Purposes.

133. An Act to enable the *Dundee* Water Company to execute additional Works, and to raise a further Sum of Money; and for other Purposes.

146. An Act to enable the *Glasgow and South-western* Railway Company to make and maintain certain Railways in the County of *Ayr;* and for other Purposes.

156. An Act to consolidate and amend the Acts relating to the Port and Harbours of *Greenock;* to authorize the Construction of a new Harbour and Graving Dock and other Works; and for other Purposes.

167. An Act for authorizing the *Leven and East of Fife* Railway Company to make and maintain certain Branches in the Parishes

of *Markinch* and *Wemyss* in the County of *Fife*; and for other Purposes.

171. An Act to authorize the *North British* Railway Company to make a Railway between the Two several Points in their Main Line in the Parish of *South Leith*; and for other Purposes.

172. An Act to amalgamate the *Leadburn, Linton, and Dolphinton* Railway Company with the *North British* Railway Company.

173. An Act to authorize the *North British* Railway Company to make several Railways in the Counties of *Lanark, Dumbarton*, and *Stirling* in connexion with the late *Edinburgh and Glasgow* and *Monklands* Railways; and for other Purposes.

181. An Act for making a Diversion of Part of the *Sutherland* Railway; for relinquishing a Portion of the said Railway; and for other Purposes.

188. An Act for supplying with Water the Town of *Kilmarnock*, Suburbs thereof, and Places adjacent.

200. An Act for leasing the *Esk Valley* Railway to the *North British* Railway Company; and for other Purposes.

202. An Act for conferring additional Powers on the *Glasgow and Southwestern* Railway Company for the Construction of Railways and Works, and otherwise in relation to their Undertaking; and for other Purposes.

208. An Act for the Construction of a Wet Dock and Railways at the Harbour of *Ayr*; and for other Purposes.

219. An Act to authorize the *North British* Railway Company to make certain Railways in connexion with their System in the Counties of *Lanark, Linlithgow*, and *Stirling*, and a Deviation in the *Forth and Clyde* Canal; and for other Purposes.

241. An Act for supplying with Water the Town of *Bridge of Allan* and Places adjacent.

243. An Act to enable the *Solway Junction* Railway Company to raise further Capital; and for other Purposes.

246. An Act for enabling the *Caledonian* Railway Company to make Railways to the *Albert* Harbour at *Greenock*, and to *Gourock* in the County of *Renfrew*, with a Pier at *Gourock*, and to acquire the Undertaking of the *Gourock* Harbour Company; and for other Purposes.

256. An Act to authorize the Company of Proprietors of the *Forth and Clyde* Navigation to raise further Monies.

266. An Act to authorize the *North British* Railway Company to make several Railways and purchase Lands in various Counties; to extend the Times for Purchase of Land and Construction of Works with respect to Part of their Railway System across the *Frith of Forth*; to make certain Alterations in the Capital; to authorize Agreements with the Corporation of *Edinburgh* as to a Fruit and Vegetable Market at *Edinburgh*, and with the *Midland* Railway

Company as to a Goods Station at *Carlisle;* and for other Purposes.

273. An Act to regulate the Police and Statute Labour of the City of *Glasgow;* and for other Purposes.

277. An Act to authorize the Construction of Branch Railways from the *Devon Valley* Railway into the Mineral Districts of *Fife* and *Clackmannan;* and for other Purposes.

278. An Act to authorize the *Berwickshire* Railway Company to raise additional Capital; and for other Purposes.

285. An Act to authorize the *North British* Railway Company to make Railways near *Glasgow;* and for other Purposes.

288. An Act to provide for the Sale or Lease to the *Great North of Scotland* Railway Company of the Undertakings of various neighbouring Companies, or the Amalgamation of those Companies with the *Great North of Scotland* Railway Company; the authorize the Abandonment of the Extensions of the *Banff, Macduff, and Turriff Extension* Railway to *Macduff;* to Extend the Time for making the Extension of the *Banffshire* Railway to *Buckie;* and for other Purposes.

291. An Act to authorize the *North British* Railway Company to make certain Railways in connection with their System in the Counties of *Linlithgow, Stirling,* and *Edinburgh;* and for other Purposes.

292. An Act to authorize the Construction of a Railway between *Wick* and *Thurso* in the County of *Caithness,* to be called "The *Caithness* Railway."

308. An Act for the Transfer to a Public Trust of the Waterworks and Property of the Board of Police of the Town of *Greenock* and of the *Shaws Water* Joint Stock Company; and for other Purposes.

309. An Act for better supplying with Water the Town of *Greenock* and Suburbs thereof, and Districts and Places adjacent, by the Execution of aditional Works; and for other Purposes.

324. An Act for improving the Harbour and making a Dock and other Works at *Burntisland;* and for other Purposes.

325. An Act for enabling the *Caledonian* Railway Company to alter the Terminus of their Railway at *Edinburgh,* to enlarge and improve their Station there, and to erect a Hotel in connection therewith; and for other Purposes.

326. An Act to authorize the *Devon Valley* Railway Company to raise additional Share Capital, and to confirm an Agreement and make Provision for an Amalgamation with the *North British* Railway Company; and for other Purposes.

327. An Act to consolidate and amend the Acts relating to the Bridges over the River *Clyde* at *Glasgow;* to provide for the Union of the Trusts and the rebuilding of the *Hutchisontown Bridge;* and for other Purposes.

328. An Act to authorize the Commissioners of the *Glasgow* Corporation

Waterworks to construct Reservoirs and other Works, and to take Water from the River *Clyde;* to provide for the Removal of the Weir across the said River; and for other Purposes.

329. An Act for making a Railway from the *North British* Railway to *Newport;* and for other Purposes.

337. An Act for making and maintaining a Harbour in *Ardmore Bay* in the *Firth of Clyde.*

341. An Act for making a Railway from the *North British* Railway to *Bo'ness* and *Grangemouth*; and for other Purposes.

342. An Act for enabling the *Caledonian* Railway Company to make certain Branch Railways in the Counties of *Lanark* and *Midlothian;* and for other Purposes.

349. An Act for making a Railway from the *North British* (*Border Union*) Railway near *Longtown* to *Brampton;* and for other Purposes.

350. An Act for authorizing the Amalgamation of the *Scottish North-eastern* Railway Company with the *Caledonian* Railway Company; and for other Purposes.

355. An Act to enable the *North British* Railway Company to make Branch Railways at *Dundee;* and for other Purposes.

INDEX TO THE GENERAL ACTS,

29 ET 30 VICTORIÆ,

SHOWING WHETHER THEY RELATE TO THE WHOLE OR TO ANY PART OF THE UNITED KINGDOM.

WHEN THE ACT IS PRINTED IN THIS COLLECTION REFERENCE IS MADE TO THE PAGE.

Lightning Source UK Ltd.
Milton Keynes UK
UKHW011039051118
331793UK00019B/1097/P

9 781527 929357